Beverw
A Dutch Village on the Ame

MW01036581

Beverwijck

A Dutch Village on the American Frontier,
1652–1664

Janny Venema

2003
Verloren / Hilversum, The Netherlands
State University of New York Press / Albany NY

This publication was partly made possible by the financial support of:
the J.E. Jurriaense Stichting,
the Stichting Dr Hendrik Muller's Vaderlandsch Fonds,
the M.A.O.C. Gravin van Bylandt Stichting,
and the Friends of New Netherland.

Library of Congress Cataloging-in-Publication Data

Venema, Janny.
  Beverwijck : a Dutch village on the American frontier, 1652–1664 / Janny Venema.
    p. cm.
  Includes bibliographical references (p.) and index.
  ISBN 0-7914-6079-7 (alk. paper) — ISBN 0-7914-6080-0 (pbk. : alk. paper)
    1. Albany (N.Y.)–History–17th century. 2. Dutch Americans–New York (State)–
  Albany–History–17th century. 3. Albany (N.Y.)–Social conditions–17th century.
  4. Frontier and pioneer life–New York (State)–Albany. 5. Albany (N.Y.)–Ethnic
  relations. 6. Indians of North America–New York (State)–Albany–History–17th
  century. 7. United States–Civilization–Indian influences–Case studies. I. Title.

F129.A357V46 2003
974.7'4302—dc21   2003054445

Illustrations on the cover:
Jan Rotius (1624–1666),
Dinner of officers of the marksmen of Hoorn, 1652.
Courtesy of the Westfries Museum, Hoorn,
and
James Eights (1798–1882),
View of State Street from St. Peter's Church down hill to Dutch Church.
Water color on paper, circa 1850. Albany Institute of History & Art.
Bequest of Ledyard Cogswell, Jr.

Table of contents

Acknowledgments

Years ago, when the director of the New Netherland Project (NNP), Dr. Charles T. Gehring, asked me to prepare a plan of Beverwijck, I promised to attempt it. Using the nineteenth-century and early twentieth-century translations of Jonathan Pearson and Arnold F. van Laer (How much work and enthusiasm these scholars showed, at a time when hardly any translations, and no computers, were available!) only brought results similar to the efforts made by these earlier translators, and also left similar problems unresolved. Hoping to be able to present a clearer picture of Beverwijck, I decided to take a fresh look at the original source materials, and to place Beverwijck's inhabitants in the context of their own lives and that of their community.

Personnel of the Albany County Hall of Records immediately allowed me to take the approximately 1,370 pages of Albany's early notarial records to the NNP for transcription, and Robert Alexander at Albany's First Dutch Reformed Church was hospitable enough to let me transcribe the deacons' account books whenever I wished. Jan Folkerts then encouraged me to research these church records further. Once that was done (with much-appreciated support from Dr. Gerald Zahavi), professor dr. A.Th. van Deursen and dr. Henk Zantkuijl both encouraged me to conduct further research into this Dutch village on the American frontier. Finally, when prof. dr. Willem Frijhoff was willing not only to advise me, but also knew the right way to help me initiate this new phase of Beverwijck research, the first step of a surprising journey was taken.

Since then, the work has been an exciting voyage of discovery, on which I met many who contributed to the following story, and to whom I owe many thank-you's. Above all, I want to express my gratitude to both my advisor Willem Frijhoff, and my employer Charles Gehring, for always being there as steady beacons and mental home bases – the one in the Old World, the other in the New World.

Whatever topic I was exploring, Willem Frijhoff, with his own enthusiasm, knew to refer me to elucidating literature, thus guiding me through the Dutch seventeenth century – which made exploring Beverwijck a new, surprising, and rich adventure. Especially, I experienced as a great source of inspiration Willem's own knowledge and his fresh, clear, and illuminating views on both the old and the new seventeenth-century worlds.

Charly Gehring, with whom I have worked for some eighteen years at the New Netherland Project, has been my source on original materials. Not only did he always know exactly in which documents I could find the information I was seeking, but his knowledge and his own enthusiasm, endurance, and resourcefulness with the work of the New Netherland Project (*'negatief onderzoek is ook onder-*

zoek') have always provided a working example for me, as I struggled to work with the sometimes difficult to read source materials. To be advised and encouraged in so many ways by these two inspiring and animated scholars in two countries has given me a continuous sense of being very privileged, and their confidence and trust in me as a researcher have offered the greatest encouragement to write this dissertation.

I also want to express my gratitude to Henk Zantkuijl. This inspiring scholar on seventeenth-century architecture not only read parts of my text – but, to my great surprise, he even made more than thirty architectural drawings to accompany some of the information on Beverwijck's architecture – How can documents be made more accessible? Jaap Jacobs gave valuable comments on three chapters, while Hester Dibbits, Jan Folkerts, George Hamell, and William Starna gave valuable suggestions on early versions of various chapters, as well.

I also thank Jaap and Bix Schipper, Kees Schilt, Renate van de Weijer, Ingrid van der Vlis, Fred van Lieburg, Hilde van Wijngaarden, and Adriana van Zwieten, who were willing to share their own research with me. Some of these people I met at the seminars led by Willem Frijhoff, which I experienced as very inspiring and encouraging. Dennis Sullivan provided me with many books and articles in the early phase of the research, while Pat Barbanell, Shirley Dunn, Alexandra van Dongen, Paul Huey, Johan Kamermans, Els Kloek, Ruud Koopman, Henk Niemeijer, Margriet de Roever, Dorothée Sturkenboom and Leo Nelissen added their suggestions for literature to the list.

While personnel at all archives and libraries were very helpful, I want to mention especially Bill Gorman and Jim Folts at the New York State Archives, Jim Corsaro and Fred Bassett at the New York State Library, Robert Alexander at Albany's Dutch Reformed Church, Margriet de Roever, Harm Snel, and Jaap Verseput at the Gemeentearchief in Amsterdam, all of whom helped making the research a pleasant experience.

Then there were friends in both the Netherlands and the United States who, throughout the process, were willing to hear my stories about these special Beverwijckers (some of whom I met in a new way), as they came not only with their support and interest, but also with ideas and suggestions for my research. Marijke Diesemer, Andy Sanders, Jan Folkerts, Lucas Ligtenberg, Eileen Heaney, Jaap and Lida Schiltkamp, Cecile Wolke, and Rinze Boersma gave or loaned books to me that they thought would be useful. I cannot thank Arthur Fontijn enough for his great hospitality, nor Emily-Ann Langworthy, Jim Morske, Ger Piek, and Greta and Bill Wagle for their confidence and interest in my research.

That he manuscript is readable is thanks to David Ford, who edited the entire manuscript and corrected many stylistic and grammatical errors.

My special thanks are reserved for my parents and my brother Henk, who (voluntarily or involuntarily) listened to numerous stories and who, in addition, always opened their hearts and houses for me whenever I was in *patria* – complete with a room to study! I am grateful for Mam's and Henk's support and encouragement, even during my father's illness and after he passed away.

I hope that the end result of my work will not disappoint those who have supported me so much. The story is for people and about people. Many people like to learn about their childhood in order to understand themselves better as individuals; I hope that this dissertation will serve this purpose for Albany, and that it will fill part of the gap in understanding the city's 'baby years.' I hope that it will help to let these seventeenth-century men, women and children become part of the city once again – by being recognized and valued for what they did: Laying the foundations for present-day Albany.

Glossary

aam	Liquid measure equal to 37.98 gallons of oil, 40.512 gallons of wine; 4 *ankers*; 153.6 liters.
anker	Liquid measure equal to 10.128 gallons of wine; 38.4 liters.
backer	Baker.
Beverwijck	Name given by Stuyvesant in 1652 to the new West India Company community around Fort Orange; there is a city of the same name in the province of North Holland, just northwest of Amsterdam. Literally the name means 'beaver district.'
beaver	Used as a monetary standard, equal to 8 *guilders*.
bijeenwoninge	Literally, 'living together'; village or commonalty.
brouwer	Brewer.
burgher	A class of citizenship in the community; the *grote burgerrecht* (great burgher right) was purchased for *f*50, qualifying the holder to serve in administrative offices and on special commissions; the *kleine burgerrecht* (small burgher right) cost *f*20, and served as a license for traders and tradesmen to operate within the designated jurisdiction.
can	Liquid measure equal to 1 quart.
Carolus guilder	One and a half guilder.
castle	Indian castle: Dutch name for a larger Indian settlement, often fortified with a surrounding palisade, and located on a hill above the river.
classis	regional authority for the church; an assembly of representatives of various consistories. New Netherland churches fell under the classis of Amsterdam.
colony	Rensselaerswijck was usually called the 'colonie' (colony).
commissary	Translation for *commis*, position appointed by the council in Manhattan to oversee West India Company trading operations at posts such as Fort Orange, and to serve as the commander of the garrison.
court messenger	Person appointed by the magistrates to serve court papers on litigants.
cuyper	Cooper.
daelder	Equivalent of 1½ *guilders*.
dominee	Minister of the Reformed church.

dosijnties	A kind of woollen cloth or kersey.
drieling	Inferior pelt; two-thirds of an entire pelt.
ell	Linear measure equal to 27 inches.
Esopus	Algonquian Indian name meaning 'river.' It was an early Dutch settlement in the Hudson Valley, at the approximate location of present-day Kingston; renamed 'Wiltwijck' under Stuyvesant, and then 'Swanenburgh' during the Dutch restoration of 1673-74, after the flagship of the Dutch fleet that recaptured the colony.
factor	Trading agent.
farmer of the excise	Highest bidder for collecting excise taxes on strong drink; payment for this service accrued from whatever was collected beyond the high-bid amount.
fathom	Linear measure equal to 6 feet.
florin	Synonymous with the guilder; source of the Dutch monetary symbol *f*, referring to the mint in Florence that once produced hard currency for the Habsburg empire.
foot	Linear measure; Amsterdam measure (*voet*) equal to 11.143 inches; Rhineland, 12.36 inches. Twelve feet equals 1 rod.
Fort Orange	Fortress and fur trading post located on the west bank of the Hudson River in present-day Albany, N.Y.; named for the Dutch royal house of Orange/Nassau; the Dutch attached this name to forts throughout their trading empire, from Brazil to Indonesia.
freeman	Colonist with no service obligation, either to the patroonship or the West India Company.
Fuyck	Probably the earliest name for the settlement north of Fort Orange that eventually became Albany. It means 'hoopnet,' which describes the configuration made by the two diverging trails running from the north gate of the fort.
general	Petrus Stuyvesant, director general of New Netherland; although he had no official military rank or training, he was commander of Dutch forces in the Carribean, as well as governor of Curaçao and other islands held by the Dutch.
glaesemaecker	Glazier.
Greenebosch	Pine woods; misinterpreted by the English in several place names as 'Greenbush.'
guilder	Monetary unit of the Netherlands, consisting of 20 *stivers*.
heer	Lord; a title of high respect.
hogshead	*Okshooft*; equal to 6 *ankers*, or 60.768 gallons (of wine); 230.4 liters.
kanne	Can; equal to 19.2 liters of French wine; 1 quart.
kerckendener	Sexton.
kil	Stream or creek; in the Netherlands, it referred to an estu-

	ary, as in Sluiskil in Zeeland; no longer an active place-name morpheme in Dutch; (the word's Dutch origin is rarely recognized by Dutch visitors to New York).
kleermaecker	Tailor.
lademaecker	Gunstock maker.
laecken/laken	Cloth.
Lords XIX	The nineteen directors of the Dutch West India Company.
magistrate	Local official of the court with executive, legislative, and judicial authority; selected by the director general and council in Manhattan from a double list submitted by the local burghers.
Mahican(der)	Mahican; an Algonquin tribe living in the upper Hudson region, around Fort Orange.
Manhatans	Manhattan; Algonquin for 'hilly island.'
Maquaes	Mohawk; the easternmost of the five tribes of the Iroquoian confederacy.
meester	Title of respect for a *schoolmeester* (schoolmaster), or short for *heelmeester* (barber-surgeon).
metsclaer	Mason.
morgen	Area measure: Rhineland, 600 square *roeden* or 2.103 acres; Amsterdam *morgen*, 600 square *roeden* or 2.069 acres.
mudde	Dry measure: 4 *schepels* or 3.056 bushels of wheat.
mutsje	Liquid measure, equal to 0.15 liter or 2.15 oz.
New Netherland	Area claimed by the Dutch with as boundaries the Hudson River, Delaware Bay, and the Connecticut River (*Noort Rivier, Suyt Rivier, Versche Rivier*).
Noorman	Norseman or Norwegian.
Noort revier	North River, or Hudson River.
oom	Uncle; also used as a term of endearment, sometimes following upon a name (for example, '*Jan-oom*,' or '*Pieter-oom*').
ondertrouwboek	Book of intended marriages.
patent	*Grondbrief*; an officially recorded document stating ownership of a specific piece of land.
patria	Latin, 'fatherland'; the Dutch often used this term when referring to their homeland.
patroon	According to the 1629 'Freedoms and Exemptions,' an investor could negotiate for land within New Netherland to establish a patroonship as a perpetual fief, with the obligation to settle fifty colonists within four years.
pound Flemish	6 *guilders*.
Rensselaerswijck	Patroonship founded by Kiliaen van Rensselaer, comprising almost a million acres of land – approximately the present-day counties of Albany and Rensselaer.

Republic	Dutch Republic; the United Provinces. A union of seven sovereign provinces (Holland, Gelre, Overijssel, Utrecht, Zeeland, Groningen and Friesland) who at the Union of Utrecht in 1579 had decided to share a common defense against Spain, and the therefor required expenses, and to share religious peace.
roede	Rod; linear measure: an Amsterdam measure equal to 13 *voeten* or 3.68 meters (12.071 feet); Rhineland, 12 *voeten* or 3.77 meters (12.36 feet).
roemer	Drinking vessel.
rooymeester	Surveyor.
sachem	Principal leader among the Iroquois men, called '*sacke-maas*' or '*sackemacker*' by the Dutch.
schelling	6 *stivers*.
schepel	Dry measure equal to 0.764 bushel of wheat; 1.29 bushels of salt.
schout	Appointed law enforcement officer with the combined duties of a sheriff and prosecuting attorney.
sewant	Wampum in the English colonies; strung pieces of shell with a specific value according to color, with six white equaling one purple; as a monetary standard, it represented 'light money,' or 15 *stivers* to the *guilder*.
Shrovetide	Shrove Tuesday (*vastenavond*): Mardi Gras.
stiver	One-twentieth part of a *guilder*.
stuck van achten	Piece of eight, worth 2.4 *guilders* or 48 *stivers*.
tonne	Barrel; 41.54 gallons of beer, or 155.4 liters.
VOC	*Verenigde Oostindische Compagnie;* Dutch East India Company.
voorleser	Lay reader who conducts prayer services in the absence of a minister, or who assists the minister by reading portions of the service.
voorsanger	*Precentor.*
weert	Innkeeper.
WIC	*West Indische Compagnie;* Dutch West India Company.

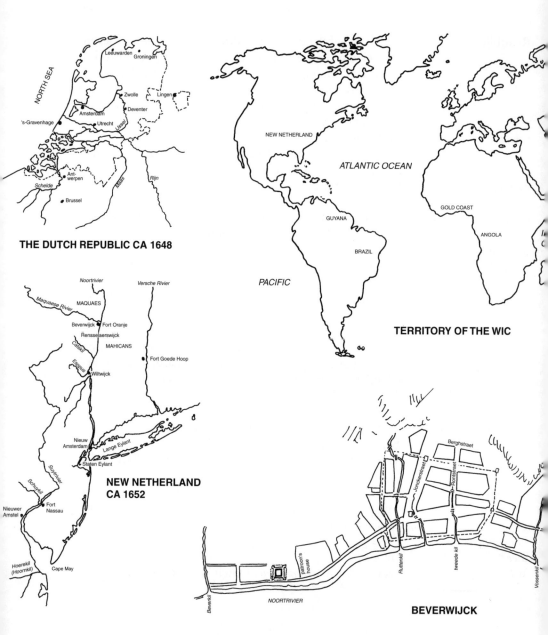

THE DUTCH REPUBLIC CA 1648

NORTH SEA

Leeuwarden · Groningen
· Zwolle · Lingen
Amsterdam · Deventer
's-Gravenhage · Utrecht
Antwerpen
· Brussel
Schelde · Maas · Rijn
IJssel

TERRITORY OF THE WIC

NEW NETHERLAND

ATLANTIC OCEAN

GUYANA

BRAZIL

PACIFIC

GOLD COAST

ANGOLA

NEW NETHERLAND CA 1652

Noortrivier · Versche Rivier
Maquaese River · MAQUAES
Beverwijck · Fort Oranje
Rensselaerswijck
Catskil · MAHICANS
Esopus · Fort Goede Hoop
Wiltwijck
Nieuw Amsterdam · Lange Eylant
Staten Eylant
Schuylkil · Suytrivier
Nieuwer Amstel · Fort Nassau
Hoerekil (Hoornkil) · Cape May

BEVERWIJCK

Berghstraet
Jonckerstraet
Fontestraet
patroon's house
Beverkil · NOORTRIVIER
Rutterkil
Tweede kil
Vossenkil

1. *Four maps: the Dutch Republic in 1648, territory of the West India Company, New Netherland, and Albany in 1698.*

Introduction

On September 26, 1636, the ship *Rensselaerswijck* departed from Amsterdam to sail to the upper Hudson area in New Netherland. After it arrived on April 7, 1637, some thirty-seven people started their work in the patroonship of Rensselaerswijck, hoping for a chance to improve their lives. One of them was Goosen Gerritsz van Schaick, who came from the province of Utrecht. He had contracted with patroon Kiliaen van Rensselaer for ƒ50 annually for the first three years, and for ƒ80 for the each of following three years. After the contract ended, he decided to stay. He married the daughter of a farmer who had come to the area earlier, in 1630, and who had been a magistrate. By 1650, some of his relatives would also come over. By 1664, Goosen would have eight children from two marriages. He owned at least five lots north of Fort Orange, land and two farms at the Esopus, and land and a farm at Half Moon. He was involved in various jobs, and would become one of the wealthiest and most honorable men in the community. He was a member of the court of Rensselaerswijck and the court of Beverwijck, while he also served as a deacon in the church.

It is unknown when Carsten Carstensz de Noorman had come to Holland, how much time he had spent there, and whether he had adjusted to Dutch culture at all. But in 1636, he would go to Rensselaerswijck aboard the same ship as Gerritsz. He did hard physical labor in the colony, and would also decide to stay. The documents are somewhat unclear about his residence: Carsten seems to have lived with various people. He did not build upon his 1652 or 1653 patent for a lot north of Fort Orange, which in 1655 would be given to someone else. Around 1658, he married and probably lived south of Fort Orange. By 1664 he would have three children. Although Carsten was Lutheran, he was well familiar with the Dutch Reformed Church, since he and his family regularly received alms from this church's deacons after 1658.[1]

Behold, in a nutshell, part of the lives of two men who, at the same time, left the Dutch Republic for New Netherland. Goosen was one of the Republic's nearly 1,850,000 inhabitants, while Carsten was one of many Norwegians who had come to Holland in the seventeenth century. They were both part of an expanding Dutch empire and of the growth of one of its two great trading companies, the West India Company (WIC).[2] Established in 1621, this company had a monopoly on trade and navigation to Africa south of the tropic of Cancer, and also on America and the islands in the Atlantic between the two meridians drawn over Cape Good Hope and the easternmost part of New Guinea. In the 1630s, it had some 100 ships at sea, and in 1641 it covered its largest territory.[3] In North America, the company claimed an area comprising the water systems of the Hudson, Delaware and Connecticut rivers, then known as the *Noort*, *Suydt* and *Varsche Rivier* – parts of the present-day states of New York, Connecticut, New Jersey, Delaware and Pennsylvania, a territory that named New Netherland and which had access to an extensive hinterland.

Somewhere between seven and eight thousand people settled in New Netherland before 1664.[4] At the upper Hudson, the West India Company built Fort Orange in 1624. Carsten and Goosen, after their arrival in the New World became part of the growth of the patroonship Rensselaerswijck, which had been established around Fort Orange in 1629, when the company allowed private investors to establish patroonships as a perpetual fief, with the obligation to settle fifty colonists within four years. After 1640, when the company gave up its monopoly of the fur trade, the two men would bear witness – not only that colonists in Rensselaerswijck were allowed to participate in the fur trade on half shares with the patroon, but also that, at the same time, many more traders came up the Hudson to find a quick fortune in the trade. By 1642, some 100 people had settled in the patroonship, and ten years later this number had more than doubled. By then, the colonists were busy building a *bijeenwoninge* (literally 'living together') around Fort Orange.[5] Carsten and Goosen subsequently would see how this center of the first spread-out settlement in 1652 became Beverwijck, a company village. Eight years later, this village would be inhabited by more than a thousand people and had acquired an urban appearance (see Appendix 1).

The two men continually had to adjust to their surroundings and the newly developing community, which was almost constantly moving. The friendship that developed between the Dutch and natives during the 1630s and '40s continuously brought Indians to the settlement; in the summer, they came by hundreds. Cold winters isolated the settlement for several months; but as soon as the river was navigable, usually sometime in March or April, European traders sailed up from Manhattan to do business at Fort Orange. New colonists then arrived, while others sometimes left at the end of their contracts.

In the process of adapting to the new environment and the continuous changes in their community, Carsten and Goosen also witnessed several changes in the domain's management. By 1641, a one-man directorship had been replaced by a triumvirate of three young men, who acted as commercial agent, *schout*, and secretary; together with a four-member council and two commissioners, these men meted out justice.[6] After Van Rensselaer's death in 1643, the guardians of his minor son and the second patroon, Johannes, put the domain's management in the hands of one man, Brant Aertsz van Slichtenhorst. Following their orders, immediately upon his arrival in 1648, this new director began the building of the above-mentioned – not on the river's east side, as Van Rensselaer had always ordered, but on the west side, around Fort Orange. By April 1652, more than fifty people had received lots there.[7] But then, Petrus Stuyvesant, the West India Company's director general for New Netherland, took the center out of the patroonship. Declaring it company grounds, he established a separate jurisdiction over the area within 3,000 feet around Fort Orange, which he named Beverwijck, and which he gave its own court.[8] A few weeks later, thirty-two, and possibly forty-two inhabitants, among them Goosen, received patents from the company for lots with a house or garden, mostly north of the fort, where Beverwijck's *bijeenwoninge* would be built. Some fifty people received patents in October 1653. In the following years, more patents would be distributed as more people came to Beverwijck, some of whom came from Brazil after the company lost that colony to the Portuguese in 1654.

After 1664, the two men still had to continue adjusting: Although the English, when they took over New Netherland, left most things the way they were, they still introduced some changes. When, in 1673, the Dutch reconquered New Netherland and renamed Albany 'Willemstad,' a new Dutch government again required some adjustment; subsequently, after November 1674, Carsten and Goosen would again have to get used to being subjects of the English king.[9]

As inhabitants of Rensselaerswijck and Beverwijck, Goosen and Carsten were an active part of this process of development and change. By doing their work in the settlement, perhaps in ways they knew from their home-places in Utrecht and Norway, while adjusting to changing circumstances as needed and participating in communal affairs, they helped shape a new community with specific Dutch features. After their contracts with the patroon had ended, they would both decide to stay in Rensselaerswijck – a decision that may have influenced the way they participated in building up the community. Goosen, by serving as a member of a court and consistory, helped make decisions that were important for the further development of the entire community; and by communicating with traders in patria, he also helped strengthen and stabilize the settlement's ties with the Republic. Although he was Norwegian and Lutheran, Carsten knew that, in need, he could go for help to the deaconry of the Dutch Reformed church. In some ways his dependency helped develop a way to apply the important Dutch institution of poor relief in the New World. Also, poorer inhabitants contributed toward laying the foundations of Beverwijck – and the future city of Albany.

Native Americans influenced the shaping of the village, as well; they frequently visited the settlement, while settlers often went into the surrounding woods to do business with them; their trails were important meeting places, and the fact that payments to Indians and among colonists were made in shell beads shows that the Dutch had adapted to a pre-existing social and cultural order. Dutch and Indians all tried to make a good deal, and in the meantime brokered in culture as well.[10]

The almost constant internal and external change, movement, and development to which Carsten and Goosen had to adjust was clearly visible in the *bijeenwoninge* itself, which within five years would expand from a settlement of some forty dwellings into a village of more than 120 houses, with a church and poorhouse in the middle.[11] These changes were visible in the appearance of bridges, street lines, defenses, development of lots into gardens, and the construction of dwellings, Indian houses, stables and other buildings. In this new community, where the outer appearance of the village may have changed almost daily, other parts of the community's culture were changing, too.

Problem defined

Culture in a border place is the central theme in this dissertation: culture in a situation of contact, in a situation where European and native civilizations met, and where borders were fluid and changed frequently; where, at the same time that Indians were visiting the village almost daily, strong communications were maintained with the Dutch Republic – which for most inhabitants was their country of origin, for many the country of destination, and for the entire community the frame of reference.

The central question, to which we will try to find an answer, is how a culture brought by the Europeans, in the beginning phase of this settlement, changed under influence of the physical environment and the native population. Focusing the study on Beverwijck limits the place studied to within 3,000 feet of the fort's perimeter – the area which, in April 1652, was carved out of the patroonship by Stuyvesant. The period only concerns the time that the settlement bore the name Beverwijck, from 1652 to 1664. We will try to find out what was different in 1664, compared to 1652, by asking such questions as: 'What was and remained Dutch?' 'What was new, or 'American?' and, 'Of which nature, direction, rhythm and intensity were the acculturation processes that took place?'

Culture has been defined in many ways. For my research, I found it most useful to consider a conception of culture of an anthropological, rather than an esthetic or moral, character – namely, that culture is shared by a group or society. Peter Burke's definition of culture as 'the system of shared meanings, attitudes and values, and the symbolic forms (performances, artifacts) in which they are expressed or embodied' emphasizes this group element.[12] We have to determine whether Beverwijck's inhabitants, by April 1652, constituted such a 'group.' Using Gerard Rooijakkers' pragmatic definition of popular culture, we will analyse the settlers' everyday culture or life-style, and search for 'the way these people shaped their daily life, and what was their general pattern of life in which everyone (rulers and subjects) shared, and which formed the basis of their society.'[13]

Who were the people who, by April 1652, made up Beverwijck's population? An important feature (similar to society in the northern Netherlands during the Dutch Republic) was its pluralistic character. This was already clear aboard the *Rensselaerswijck* in 1636-37: Goosen was one of five people aboard the ship who came from the province of Utrecht and Carsten was one of three Norwegians, while other passengers came from various other areas in the Republic and Europe. By 1652, more than 200 men, among whom many were farmhands and craftsmen from the countryside, had contracted to work in Rensselaerswijck, and several of them brought along their families.[14] Among them were at least ninety-nine from the Dutch Republic: Forty-one came from North and South Holland, thirty-one from Utrecht, fourteen from Gelderland, six from Brabant, and seven from other provinces. At least forty-seven colonists came from other countries, among them eleven Germans, seven Prussians, nine Scandinavians, seven Englishmen, and two men from the Southern Netherlands. There was even a man from Croatia, and at least two African slaves. Almost forty people had left after their contracts expired. Like Amsterdam, where over half of the population came from other regions and countries, the settlement at the frontier was inhabited by people with cultural 'baggage' from many different fatherlands.[15] These people, who arrived at different times between 1630 and 1652, did not share one typical Dutch culture.

But they did share other things. From the time of their arrival until April 1652, they had all been governed by the same patroon in the Republic; and although they had, during the first twenty years, lived scattered over some eighteen farms, their shared personal interests united them against the patroon. Church services where they met helped create a bond. The Dutch Reformed church prescribed and monitored the moral values and behavior of its members, and performed duties of a public church such as baptism and burial, thus knitting a society with certain common moral values. Among some inhabitants, family and provenance ties existed, as well as religious ties. In time, increasing neighbor-to-neighbor and work-related ties would develop, and several immigrants cooperated in various projects, such as a mill or a brewery. Their culture was greatly influenced by several factors they all had to deal with after their arrival in the New World. They all had to adjust: adjust to each other, to new physical surroundings, to the climate, to contact with natives, to continuously arriving newcomers. The introduction of slaves was perhaps one of the main indicators that the 'Dutch' community was becoming 'American.' A sizable group of Lutherans also had to adjust to the Dutch Reformed church, the only church allowed for worship. Perhaps the most important thing they shared was that, at some point, they had decided to leave their fatherland and go to Rensselaerswijck. Between 1630 and 1652, these shared experiences were added to the individual settlers' cultural baggage, and by 1652 they would create a certain level of cohesiveness.

People who had come at an early date clearly had advantages over the newcomers, as they had become very familiar with the patroon's management, the church, the physical surroundings, and contacts with each other and the natives. They had learned how to circumvent some of the patroon's rules; they knew which were the good locations for such projects as breweries, mills or farms; and, over the years, several early settlers had developed their own relations and trading systems with the natives.

During the late 1640s, Rensselaerswijck was a spread-out settlement with an open character, easy for natives to enter. But while in 1643 people lived scattered along the river, and were more or less part of the landscape, after 1648 they were in the process of changing this situation by establishing a *bijeenwoninge* around Fort Orange.[16] By April 1652, more than fifty people had lots on the river's west side. While it was ordered by the patroon, the inhabitants themselves may also have felt the need to live closer together near the fort, which could imply that they were increasingly prepared to share.[17] Living closer together not only offered people more safety, but also more stability and opportunities to communicate – to share more than they had before. The *bijeenwoninge* was a good foundation from which to work on a common future.

Although in the eyes of outsiders they may have appeared to be a cohesive group of Europeans, within this constantly growing group, individuals had to adapt themselves as much to each another as to their new surroundings. From the beginning, the settlers had developed a new culture – a new, local tradition of contact with each other, the government, the new land, and the demands of change. What culture the colonists shared, by 1652, was the product of continuous inter-

2. Fragment of the Rensselaerswijck map, 1632, perhaps drawn by Gillis van Schendel.

nal, as well as external, adjustment. This process did not come to a sudden halt when Petrus Stuyvesant brought the center of the patroonship into the West India Company's possession. When inhabitants received patents for lots and under certain conditions became landowners, in addition to focusing on their own property they had to adapt to rules prescribed by the company's directors in Amsterdam. The increase in new settlers during the 1650s brought along competition in trade and in work, and within a short time caused the village to acquire urban features within the 3,000-foot area around Fort Orange. During the 1650s and early 1660s, a predominantly agricultural, rural Rensselaerswijck culture would be transformed into a predominantly commercial, semi-urban Beverwijck culture.

Location near an abundant fur supply had been the main reason for the West India Company's establishment of Fort Orange in 1624; and when Van Rensselaer established his patroonship in 1629, he saw another benefit to the location: While Indians would continue to bring furs to the settlement, New Netherland could provide Brazil with wheat, and Brazil would then send its costly sugar to the fatherland. Rensselaerswijck would make New Netherland a great wheat supplier, filling an important place in the company's great Atlantic scheme.[18] It is my hypothesis that location played not only an essential role in the Atlantic setting, but also in laying out the village; it accelerated the development of the community, and provided individuals with particular opportunities.

Location and physical surroundings in 1652 played an important role in the design of the community. Similar to other colonies, location near navigable waters was of crucial importance, and the *Noortrivier* was the community's lifeline with

New Amsterdam, the Republic, and the rest of the European world.[19] Although frozen during the winter, the river's function as a major trading route was most important; in 1653, at least two sloops went from Manhattan to Beverwijck every Monday.[20] For a long time, the river had flooded the banks and islands during the spring, and thus creating fertile lands for agriculture, while the clay on its banks was good for baking bricks and tiles. While the river formed the eastern border of the *bijeenwoninge*, the hill formed an easy western boundary for the flat area at its foot within which it was built, and within which it was allowed to conduct trade. The first and third kills, more or less, marked the southern and northern boundaries of the *bijeenwoninge*. The presence of kills in the area was extremely important, as they allowed the building of saw and grist mills.

The great hinterland located toward the north and west provided the product that caused the Dutch to settle the area: beavers. By 1652, the existing economic sources were fully utilized: Almost since the first Dutch ships had sailed on the Hudson, Indians had seemed willing – and quickly became anxious – to buy European goods provided by the Dutch, and to pay for those goods with beavers. By 1652, the Maquaes had become the greatest trading partners, while Mahicans were willing to sell land. On some of this land they previously had grown corn, so that the colonists could in a relatively easy way develop farmland. By 1652, the patroonship had bought several large tracts; and when the West India Company allowed private settlers to buy land from the Indians, several men were eager to do this.[21]

Location also accelerated the community's development. Once it had been decided that the *bijeenwoninge* would be built north of the fort, on the river's west side, the basic functions of a Dutch settlement were systematically established in a short time. A burgher guard was established and the inhabitants obtained burgher rights. The court held weekly open sessions at the West India Company's warehouse in Fort Orange, and religious services continued to be held for several years in the patroon's house. A poorhouse and several taverns were located in permanent places in the *bijeenwoninge*, as well, so that their services would be within easier reach of the inhabitants. Bridges were built, roads laid out, and structures were built for protection. Certain areas were permanently designated for specific artisans's shops such as those of bakers, blacksmiths and gunstock makers. With the most important trades and services well represented, by 1664 Beverwijck would become an autonomous, semi-urban community with provisions for safety, poor relief, religion, education, and communal services. With the increase in population, houses were built closer together, making it easier to monitor the villagers' observance of court and church rules; as a result, Dutch laws and rules became more visible. While the building process stabilized and strengthened the community's Dutch character, it would simultaneously distinguish the settlement more sharply from its surroundings and the native inhabitants.

For individuals, a good location was important as well. When the area north of the fort became the settlement's center, people who received patents there were in the midst of important developments. Trails – which, since the first contacts be-

tween natives and settlers had been used by Indians carrying their furs to Fort Orange – were important meeting places; now they were converted into roads for
wagons and carts; and, consequently, they were among the first places that houses would be built. Those who lived along the trail leading into the woods – which
would soon be named *Jonckerstraet* (present-day State Street) – had the first
chance of meeting the Indians entering the village near present-day Pearl Street,
and thus had the best chances in the trade. To have a lot at a good location within
the *bijeenwoninge* provided an individual with particular opportunities. While
Goosen Gerritsz had several lots north of the fort in the *bijeenwoninge*, Carsten
de Noorman may have had one lot south of the fort. As the *bijeenwoninge*, unlike
the area south of the fort, became a center of all activities and development, location may very well have contributed to the fact that their circumstances were so
different from each other.

Historiography and definition

Beverwijck has drawn the attention of several historians and archaeologists.[22]
Donna Merwick described life in the Hudson Valley between 1630 and 1710. According to her, the inhabitants replicated and sustained a Holland-derived urban
mercantile culture, which she called *burgerlijk*, the organizing principle that controlled the use of space within communities, and which ordered economic activity. For example, when people thought of land, they would have seen trade routes
rather than land to use for farming, as trade was their main interest.[23]

When the English took over New Netherland and came to Beverwijck, they did
not, as Sung Bok Kim wrote, find a place with 'no more than two hundred inhabitants, all of whom had come there solely for the Indian trade'; but instead, as
Martha Dickinson Shattuck has shown, they found a village with more than a
thousand people.[24] Beverwijck was much further developed than Kim's 'one of
the congeries of the trading posts of New Netherland under a commercial direc-
torat.' There was, indeed, a community with good working trade systems, which
in addition was well provided with the necessary grain and dairy products by its
agricultural surroundings.[25] But, contrary to Thomas J. Condon's idea that there
were no firmly rooted institutions in Beverwijck, the study by Dennis Sullivan,
who examined Dutch punishment practices, has shown, like Shattuck's work, that
by 1664 Beverwijck's society was well ordered and regulated by a court after the
Dutch model, based on Roman-Dutch law.[26] My own research has shown that, by
that same year, the Dutch Reformed church had operated a well-functioning system of poor relief for more than twelve years.[27]

The English also found a community that maintained good relations with the
native population, especially the Mahicans and the Maquaes (Mohawks), the easternmost nation of the Iroquois. The works of Daniel Richter and José António
Brandão provide us with a deeper insight into Iroquois culture.[28] Richter, by con-
trasting Iroquois values and morals with those of the Dutch, illustrates some characteristics of Dutch colonial beliefs and behavior. Some of his work seems to be

echoed by Matthew Dennis, who explained the successful relationship between natives and settlers by the Dutch quest for profit, their tolerance, and their lack of curiosity.[29] Paul Huey, in his work associated with the excavation of Fort Orange, has provided information about various archaeological digs in Beverwijck, as well. And, in *The Evolution of the Onondaga Iroquois*, the archaeologist James Bradley pointed out appearances of acculturation between colonists and natives.[30] Jaap Jacobs recently published a synthesis of New Netherland, *Een zegenrijk gewest*, which is entirely based on primary sources, and in which Beverwijck has an important place. Jacobs demonstrates that although there were some differences between New Netherland and the fatherland, many features of New Netherland can only be understood by regarding the colony as an extension of the Dutch Republic.[31]

This dissertation is a study of the construction, structure, and operation of an urban community in a contact situation from the perspective of the fatherland. It is not my intent to present an institutional history of Beverwijck, as Shattuck and Sullivan did in their studies of the court; and when attention is paid to the decline of the trade, this is done mostly to focus on the influence it had on the way of life of every Beverwijcker – rather than to emphasize political history and the economic development of the community. References to other villages or towns in New England or New France, or within New Netherland, or to a specific location in the Republic are only general, as the focus of my research is not a comparison with such places. By applying the same principle as that used by Jacobs (i.e., to understand New Netherland as an extension of the Republic) to a small community, I hope to hear the voices of the individual inhabitants better. While Merwick emphasized urban merchants, I try also to look more closely at other people: the governed as well as governors; poor as well as wealthy; people from different regions and countries, as well as those from Holland; and – although they were not 'official' inhabitants, but were certainly very present in the village – the native Mahicans and Mohawks, along with the settlers. Colonial authorities indeed tried to copy and adopt the features of their political model, Holland; but they did this with the help of many people from elsewhere. While adjusting within the group of colonists, these people at the same time made many external adaptations. The combination resulted not so much in a generally unified Dutch culture, but rather in a culture that incorporated many Dutch or European features, along with external adjustments – a culture with a certain level of unity in diversity.[32] Although Albany's development after 1664 is not a focus of this book, I hope to provide a foundation for the studies of Albany after it was taken over by the English. The research material used provides background and context for many of the individuals studied by the Colonial Albany Social History Project, which is preparing a thorough analysis of Albany's population from 1664 through 1800.

Studying this small community immediately puts the spotlight on its members: individuals who all made choices in their lives, and who were all undergoing a process of adjustment to each other and to a new environment. What bound these individuals together the most was perhaps their decision to make New Netherland their new homeland. In his inspiring book, *Wegen van Evert Willemsz. Een Hollands weeskind op zoek naar zichzelf, 1607-1647*, Willem Frijhoff described how Evert Willemsz, who became a minister at Manhattan and called himself *Domine* Everhardus Bogardus, made this choice around 1638. Evert's 'mental horizon changed within a few years,' Frijhoff wrote elsewhere, 'and brought him in fact to an entirely new definition of his personal identity, both socially and with regard to his self perception.' No longer did he feel accountable to the West India Company in Amsterdam, but he felt his prime responsibility toward the local community. As a minister, he now used church rituals to shape a new communi-ty.[33] By creating a cross-section of Beverwijck's community, I hope to show a small piece of the lives of its inhabitants – many of whom, by choosing to stay in New Netherland, at some point went through a process similar to that of Evert Willemsz, although their responsibilities were quite different. By doing their work the way they knew how and, as the situation required, by communicating with their fellow villagers, by going to the court, church, poorhouse, school, or tavern, individuals such as Goosen and Carsten contributed to building one com-munity: Beverwijck.

Method and sources

Initially, I began to work on a description of the local Beverwijck community, as it appeared in the settlement pattern, after Charles Gehring requested a plan of the village. Faced with the lack of an original plan of Albany in the Dutch period like New York's Costello plan, but with a multitude of documents, some researchers in the past have made attempts to reconstruct it. Great effort has been put into this work by Jonathan Pearson, who translated four volumes of early records of Al-bany, containing contracts, leases, indentures of apprenticeships, mortgages, wills, and other notarial papers; but especially (and most important for this purpose), deeds, conveyances, and transfers of lots, houses and gardens situated in and around seventeenth-century Albany.[34] Based on translated confirmatory patents and his own translations, Pearson attempted in his 'Diagrams of the Home Lots of the Village of Beverwyck' to locate the village's house lots and gardens.[35] Un-fortunately these diagrams are not always correct, often due to mis-translation; in addition, they are incomplete. In the preface to these diagrams, Pearson stated that there were several gaps 'which no ingenuity of the compiler could fill, and several lots will be found so imperfectly described in the records, that he has to confess his inability to locate them.'[36] A scale model of the city in 1695, based on these di-agrams, was built between 1929 and 1955 by Paul Schrodt, and is now in the Al-bany Visitor Center.

The translator A.J.F. van Laer made a contribution toward the compilation of a map in 1926, when he traced the location of the early Dutch grants along the south side of State Street, more particularly between Green and South Pearl streets, which were distributed by director general Petrus Stuyvesant shortly after he laid out the boundaries of Beverwijck.[37] For Van Laer, more source materials had be-

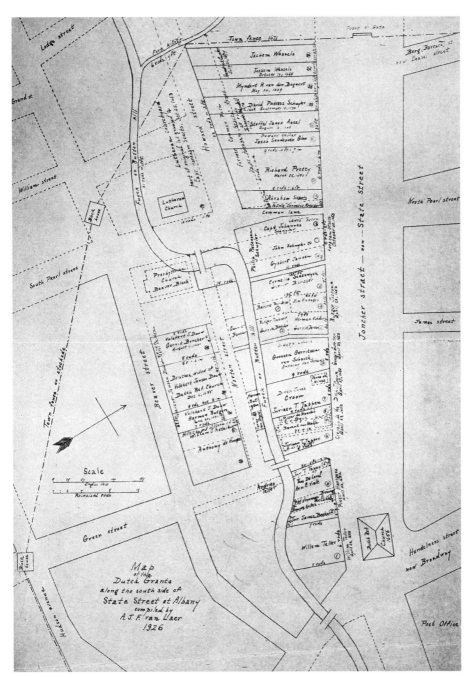

3. Dutch grants along the south side of State Street at Albany, compiled by A.J.F. van Laer, 1926 in the Dutch Settlers Society Year Book.

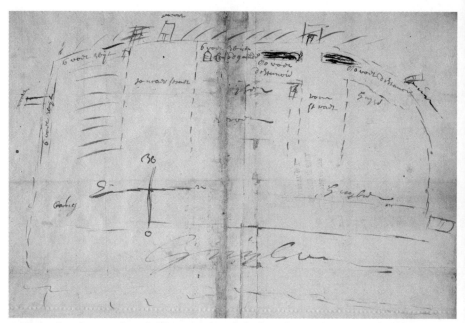

*4. The earliest known plan of Albany is a rough draft without a date. It was heretofore
reproduced as being of 1676 but likely it is a sketch of the design for the palisades built in
1659. 17x12³/₈ inches.*

come available, since by then he had revised volumes 2-4 of Pearson's translations
of the early records. He also had completed translations of the court minutes of
Rensselaerswijck and court minutes of Fort Orange, in addition to the Van Rensselaer Bowier Manuscripts.[38] Although Van Laer was not able to produce a plan of
the entire village of Beverwijck, he was convinced that the difficulties referred to
by Pearson 'were not insuperable and that from the available sources a map could
be constructed that would show the location and ownership of practically every
piece of property that is mentioned in the records prior to the Dongan Charter of
1686.'[39]

The thought of joining Pearson and Van Laer in their efforts to create a map of
Beverwijck, and to bring back to life this once-so-lively village, was encouraged
by a renewed interest in Albany's colonial history in the late 1990s. Archaeological excavations were being carried out at various sites in Albany; and to prepare
for these sites as well as possible, it was important to be aware of what could possibly be found, or perhaps damaged and made inaccessible forever. Efforts by the
city to promote histo-tourism in Albany also raised questions, again, about the intriguing early years of the city's existence. And while new school curricula asked
for more emphasis on local history, teachers found a lack of ready materials about
Albany's Dutch period. With so much information available from excavations,
various maps (albeit of later date) and, above all, Dutch-language texts, it seemed

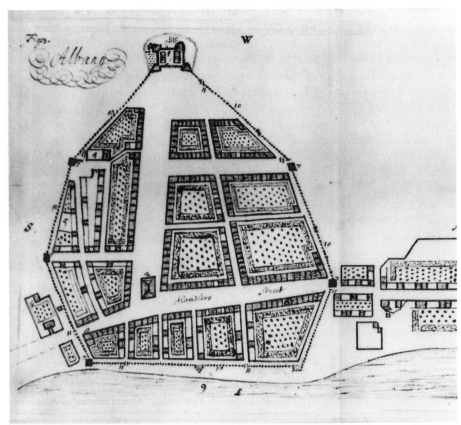

5 *'Albany,' in John Miller,* New York Considered and Improved.... *The so-called Miller plan.*

appropriate that the New Netherland Project should help provide those interested in Albany's history with a glimpse into the city's past.

For the evidence of my plan of Beverwijck, I drew some information from a sketch that Munsell had dated 1670 – but which, I believe, dates from about 1659, and served as a rough design for the construction of palisades around a part of the village.[40] The plan following thereupon, which is still in existence, was drawn from memory by the Rev. John Miller, chaplain of the garrison at New York, while he was a prisoner in France after having been captured by a French privateer on his way to England. It dates from 1695. The Miller plan shows the general appearance of the city as it then lay, enclosed in its stockade; but it is incorrect in several details. Norton Street, for example, is shown as running parallel to State instead of to Beaver Street, while South Pearl Street, which was then only a narrow lane, is placed too far to the west.[41]

Following thereupon, Colonel Wolfgang Wilhelm Römer, the King's chief engineer for the province of New York, who was sent to the Lords of Trade in 1698 by Governor Bellomont, drew the 'Plan de la Ville d'Albanie dans la

Province de la Nouvelle Yorck en Amerique.' A reproduction of it is found in the third series of *The Crown Collection of Photographs of American Maps*, selected by Archer Butler Hulbert.[42] In addition to the features of the Miller plan, this plan shows the hills and the various creeks; the location, size and remains of the old Dutch fort, and the gardens to the north and to the west of it, which are mentioned in early deeds. New maps of Albany would not be drawn until 1758, 1760, 1763, and 1770.[43] A plan drawn by Simon de Witt in 1794 shows, as did plans drawn by Römer and Robert Yates in 1770, the *Beverkil, Fuyckenkil,* and *Vossenkil,* and their origins. It also shows the area south of the fort, where by then a ferry house had been built. Neither Yates nor De Witt showed the streams, which, according to Römer's map, came down State Street and Maiden Lane.[44] To explain Beverwijck's construction and development, I have used Römer's map as the basis, as it shows more details and is more accurate than the Miller plan, while it is almost as close in time to the period studied, 1652-64.[45] Illustrations provided in order to explain location are based on Römer's map, as well.

As further evidence, I used written records, such as the land patents, property transfers, court minutes, and correspondence that were previously used by Pearson and Van Laer. In addition, I was able to use translations made by Van Laer after 1926, and by Charles Gehring after 1974.[46]

Work done by Pearson and Van Laer I gratefully included in my research, as far as justifiable. Since using data only from patents, land papers and conveyances appeared insufficient, I added further research about the village's inhabitants. Asking questions about Beverwijckers' history, work, family connections, religion, and activities in and out of the village – as well as their role, behavior, and place in the community, in general – led me to such 'new' sources as the deacons' account books in Albany's First Dutch Church, a court case instituted by Brant Aertsz van Slichtenhorst in 1656, which is stored in the Rijksarchief in Arnhem in the Netherlands, and documents in the Municipal Archives of Amsterdam.[47] Although I did not make a thorough comparison with one specific town in the Dutch Republic, general information about different places in the United Provinces provided a good amount of additional explanation. As a result of a research project in the Netherlands, *Cultuurgeschiedenis van de Republiek in de zeventiende eeuw*, several studies of towns in the Dutch Republic and in other Dutch colonies during the seventeenth century have recently been published.[48] The combination of source materials used for Beverwijck, these new publications, and other recent research about Dutch places in the Republic's Golden Age provide more insight and clarity into Beverwijck's community. In the end, asking questions of a more historical-anthropological and cultural-historical nature, combined with the information provided in the patents and property conveyances, did serve to bring me closer to individuals, and sometimes to their location in the village or in a specific neighborhood. At the same time, it made clear how important location was, for the individual inhabitants as well as for the development of the entire community. Space was as important as time.

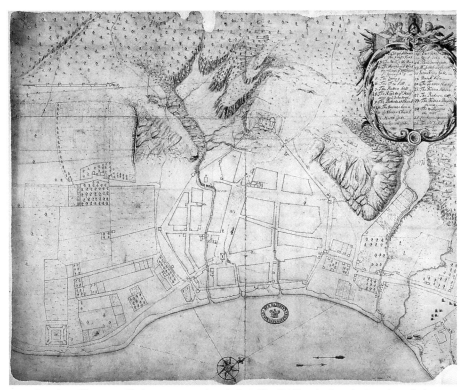

6. Colonel Wolfgang Wilhelm Römer, 'Plan de la Ville d'Albanie dans la Province de la Nouvelle Yorck en Amerique, 1698.' 22x17 inches.

Working with Beverwijck's written source materials has its own problems. Hardly any original patents on the early lots have survived, since there is a gap in the records of Dutch patents between 1652 and 1654, when most grants were made. Our knowledge about these grants must be derived from the Dutch deeds, property transfers, and confirmatory patents. In 1789, these confirmatory patents were translated into English, and these translations to-day can be found in the 'New York Colonial Patents Books, Albany, 1664-1690,' in the New York State Archives. Volumes 1 through 5 were used for this research. Unfortunately the original Dutch documents have not survived. The Dutch deeds and property conveyances were, as mentioned, first translated and published by Jonathan Pearson, and volumes 2 through 4 were revised by A.J.F. van Laer. I have transcribed the original documents from the first volume and, for my research, I have made use of this transcription. Currently this entire volume is being revised by Charles T. Gehring; it will appear in three volumes, entitled *Fort Orange Records 1650-1678*, of which the first volume was published in 2000. The question remains open, however, as to what extent these (so important) translated confirmatory patents can be relied on. While transcribing the original source materials for the deeds and property con-

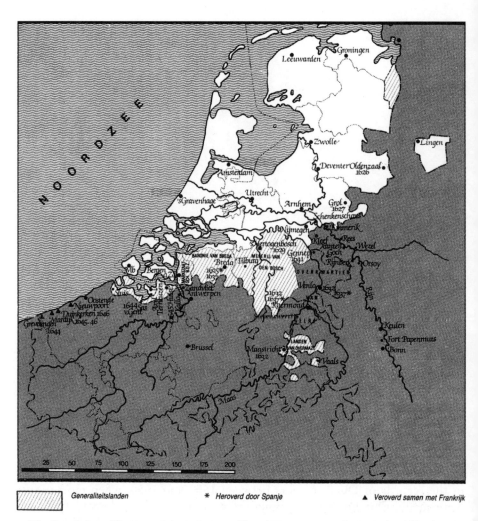

7. *The Dutch Republic in 1648, in S. Groenveld and H.L. Leeuwenberg,* De bruid in de schuit; de consolidatie van de Republiek *(Zutphen, 1985).*

veyances, I frequently found errors in the existing translations; it also repeatedly appeared that information provided by property conveyances did not correspond to information given in these patents.[49] While we are often left with questions about the correctness of a translation, it also appears, through conflicting descriptions of one lot, that the Dutch were inaccurate and unclear themselves when describing a location of a lot.[50] On rare occasions, the *Fort Orange Court Minutes* offer explanatory information, but these records also are incomplete – and they abruptly stop in the year 1660, leaving a four-year gap toward the end of the Dutch period. To describe the local community as it took shape in the settlement pattern, we often have to rely on incomplete and damaged evidence.

While archaeological excavations can never provide us with proof that the dwelling of a particular seventeenth-century inhabitant was on a specific lot, their findings sometimes confirm an assumption in a case of doubt. For example, the fact that parts of firearms were found at a certain location in Fort Orange strengthens the idea that the person who lived there was indeed Hendrick Andriesz – since, in Amsterdam, Andriesz had been listed as a gunstock maker.[51]

To find out how the Europeans' culture changed under the influence of the new physical surroundings and the native population during this beginning period of a settlement, I distinguished three components in my research: a general setting of the village, both physical and cultural; part of the lives of two important individual traders in Beverwijck; and three sub-groups: successful burghers, the poor, and those in-between.

In the first chapter, we will look at the way the village was founded and how it materially developed. The process of building will be observed, along with the way in which houses and streets were designed. In brief, how was the area within 3,000 feet of the fort's perimeter used in order to build a *bijeenwoninge*? Which buildings were built for communal services? What did inhabitants see when they walked out of their houses? What did visitors see? And how did inhabitants use the space on their own lots?

Subsequently, we will take a look at the community. Who were these Beverwijck-Dutch? Where had they come from and how did they communicate with each other? What were the institutions that made them into one community? How did these institutions work, while adjusting to their new environment and the native population?

The following chapter focuses on Beverwijck's trade. Which wares were traded, and when did this happen? Who were involved? Following Jan Baptist and Jeremias van Rensselaer, in their role as traders, provides us with an image of how small family-business firms operated in the transatlantic trade. It also gives an impression of the position of a wealthy trader in Beverwijck society and his life-style. The correspondence maintained by the Van Rensselaers lets us glance into the lives of others, especially of those burghers who were successful.

In the fourth chapter, the focus is on some of these burghers and the reasons for their success. How could men like Goosen Gerritsz climb the social ladder so rapidly and become part of the elite of the village? Who were these people and what were their backgrounds? And what did they do with the money they earned in the New World?

As in other communities, artisans kept the village going. The fifth chapter illustrates that, in Beverwijck, some trades were more lucrative than that they had been in the Republic. Smiths and gunstock makers, for example, had a large Indian clientele. Some breweries worked better than others, some bakers sold more bread than others, and some taverns attracted more customers than others. When we ask, 'Why?' it appears that accessibility to the main resources – location, in other words – often had much to do with it.

In a land of new opportunities there also were individuals like Carsten *de Noorman*, who were unable to survive on their own. What was their place in this new world? How did the community regard them? In the last chapter we will take a look at who these people were, why they needed support, and how they were helped in their needyness.

In the conclusion, we will examine this information from a broader perspective. How had Beverwijck's culture changed within its twelve years of existence? How Dutch, and how American, had Beverwijck been in 1652 – and why, and how, did this change by 1664?

I. Constructing a village: material planning

At midnight on every December 31st, at Albany's Empire State Plaza, a new year is heralded by a great display of fireworks. Hundreds of people gather to watch. Similarly, in the 1600s the exchange of the year did not go by quietly. Usually it was celebrated with much alcoholic drink and partying, and people making much noise by beating drums and shooting their muskets and firearms into the air. Authorities tried to control the festivities by prohibiting the sale of liquor and the shooting of guns on New Year's Eve and New Year's Day. In Rensselaerswijck, Abraham Stevensz *Croaet* was fined *f* 40 for shooting during the night in 1650.[1] At the changing of the year in 1651-52, West India Company soldiers at Fort Orange likely drank the customary New Year's drinks, and at some point purposely started to fire burning fuses onto the roof of the patroon's house, immediately to the north of the fort. The thatch caught fire, but was quickly extinguished by the patroon's director, Brant van Slichtenhorst and his son Gerrit, who lived in the house. The following day the 'festivities' continued. Soldiers suddenly grabbed Van Slichtenhorst's son by the hair, and simultaneously struck him on the forehead so that he fell down. In the presence of the newly appointed commissary of the fort, Johannes Dijckman, they not only beat Gerrit 'black and blue, but dragged him through the mud and mire, and treated him inhumanly as if he were a criminal.' They struck Van Slichtenhorst's two children with their guns and threatened to shoot them. Dijckman encouraged his soldiers in their evil work by calling out aloud, 'Beat him now and may the devil take him!'; and when he was told that the scandalous treatment of Van Slichtenhorst's children would be avenged, he ordered his gunner to load his pieces with [cannon ball], saying that they would fire through the director's house.[2]

The conflict expressed the existing tensions between patroonship and West India Company, which will be explained in this chapter. It indicated that here was an unbearable situation, which would ultimately result in the separation of the immediate area around the fort from the patroonship. First we will take a closer look at this conflict and its development. Subsequently, we will observe how Beverwijck, as the area around the fort was then named, further developed: Well over 200 Europeans had settled in the area before April 1652, and within eight years this number had quintupled. A community with so many people needed provisions and services; and despite the almost daily presence of large groups of Indians, especially in the summer, the minimal functions of a Dutch settlement were systematically established in a short time. When in 1664 the English took over New Netherland, they found in Beverwijck a full-fledged community with provisions for safety, poor relief, education, communal services, and religion.

Van Slichtenhorst, Rensselaerswijck, and the Indians

Van Slichtenhorst and Van Twiller's rule in Rensselaerswijck

In his function of *schout*, Van Slichtenhorst presided as chief officer over the court of Rensselaerswijck, acting as a public prosecutor and performing the duties of a modern sheriff and chief of police. As manager – the other part of his director's function – he held chief administrative office, and was required to collect the patroon's revenues from farms and mills, and issue licenses to trade, for which he had to render a strict account. He had to maintain friendly relations with the Indians, but was not to engage in the fur trade, or act as *commies* (agent). He had to make sure that people obeyed the ordinances, contracts and orders; and he was also charged with the advancement of religion according to the tenets of the Reformed church, including the sabbath observance, and prevention of fornication with Indian women. Further, he had to guard and defend the boundaries, privileges, rights, lands, jurisdiction, prerogatives and authority of the patroon.[3] He was assisted by a council of commissioners who represented the patroon, and who primarily had administrative duties. Two (later three) councilors, appointed by the commissioners, represented the colonists; their duties were mostly judicial; they were not in the patroon's service. Secretary Anthonie de Hooges was to assist the director in judicial matters and was to record in a book all instructions, commissions and executed contracts. The minister, *dominee* Johannes Megapolensis, advised in important matters.[4] While these people shared the responsibility for the development of Rensselaerswijck, the director's voice was the strongest.

As in previous years, it was of great importance that good relations with the West India Company were maintained. But the contacts between Van Slichtenhorst and Stuyvesant had been bad since the beginning. According to his instructions, upon arrival in New Amsterdam the 59-year old Van Slichtenhorst was immediately to address himself to the 22-years-younger director general of New Netherland, hand him a letter, and convey greetings and commendations of the patroon. He was to represent good correspondence and neighborship to Stuyvesant and the council, and offer to extend a helping hand to them on any occasion.[5] But, reportedly, Van Slichtenhorst first drank himself full, and then behaved 'as if he came there in order to have authority over Stuyvesant and as if he wanted to rule over him.'[6] That the two men at once had a disagreement about the method of payment for Van Slichtenhorst's journey, from the Virginias to Manhattan on a company ship, did not help to create a favorable first acquaintance.[7] Both men appeared to be strong and stubborn characters and, even after Van Slichtenhorst had gone to Rensselaerswijck, their relations did not improve. Rensselaerswijck's director would soon refuse to recognize the general day of prayer and fasting, which Stuyvesant had proclaimed for the first Wednesday in May, in honor of the Republic's peace with Spain in 1648. This clearly demonstrated his denial of Stuyvesant's authority inside the patroonship.[8] Especially the building of a community north of the fort – on the west side of the river, instead of on the east side – added to Stuyvesant's discontent. As soon as he stepped off the ship, the new director started issuing building permits in the area close to the fort, adding to the three houses that were already there.[9] In July, Stuyvesant ordered him not to build within the area of a cannon shot from the fort, since according to the company, the houses obstructed the fort. But Van Slichtenhorst continued, going so far as to offer people good deals for building there, and even prohibiting his colonists from using the patroon's wagons and horses to haul construction materials for the repairs to Fort Orange.[10] The fort had been severely damaged by flooding during the previous winter, and stone and timber were urgently needed for repairs, and also to build houses for some burghers inside its walls.[11] Van Slichtenhorst forbade the company laborers to quarry stone or to cut timber and firewood on the patroon's land without permission. At the same time, he caused more aggrevation with Stuyvesant by buying more land from the Indians at the *Paponicack kil* (Muitzes kill), Catskil and Claverack. By suggesting that the director general maintained correspondence with the English, Van Slichtenhorst more or less accused Stuyvesant of treason – which likely did not improve the relations between the two men, either.[12] To Stuyvesant, Van Slichtenhorst's attitude represented a usurpation of the company's authority and supreme jurisdiction in New Netherland. He reasoned that if such behavior were tolerated, then other 'colonies' such as Heemstede, Flushing, and Gravesend on Long Island could expect the same, which would deprive the company of timber needed for ships, churches, forts and other constructions; eventually, the company would have to beg the materials from its subjects, and pay for them at the highest price.[13] Stuyvesant did not want the company to be degraded in this manner. Thus, Stuyvesant and Van Slichtenhorst were flatly at odds with each other. Stuyvesant could not allow the company's authority to be eaten away, while Van Slichtenhorst considered the patroon's authority to be supreme in the area – which, he maintained, also included the ground upon which Fort Orange stood.[14]

That it was not only Van Slichtenhorst who was to blame for this bad relationship becomes apparent in a letter from the company's directors of the department of the Chamber of Amsterdam, to Stuyvesant at the beginning of 1650, in which they wrote that they clearly saw a threat in Wouter van Twiller, one of the patroon's guardians who, according to them, aimed to command the North River. 'He admits publicly that he does not intend to allow anyone to navigate the river for the purpose of trade,' they wrote, 'and says, he will resist anyone coming there or to Rensselaerswijck, maintaining besides, that Fort Orange is built upon the soil of Rensselaerswijck and that the Company has no right to let houses be built or private parties trade there.' They suspected Van Twiller of having 'once more the audacity to obstruct the navigation on the river by force,' and forbade his taking 600 lbs. of gunpowder and 600 lbs. of lead, on behalf of Rensselaerswijck, aboard his ship. They promised to send Stuyvesant some gunpowder and lead to use in defending the rights of the company.[15] The directors could not understand, they wrote in April 1650, how 'the colonists of Rentselaerswijck could take possession of *Beeren Eyland*, afterwards called Rentselaers Steyn [a small island at the most southern border of Rensselaerswijck], and go so far as to invest this place with the right of staple demanding from everyone, except the Company, a toll of five percent on his goods, and growing so impudent that they finally asserted Fort Orange was built on their territory, and they would not permit anybody to take his residence in the fort, even though the Company had given their consent, and engage in the fur trade.' They thought it astonishing that 'Van Twiller and his set' had dared to spread a report in the community 'that the Company owned no other soil in New Netherland than Manhattans Island, while it can be clearly proved that they have bought vast tracks of land on the South River, the Fresh River, Long Island and many other places in the neighborhood. These men are therefore grossly deceiving and try only to dispossess, if possible, the Company; but we hope to balk them.'[16]

Testimony by Nicolaes Blanche van Aken, in January 1651, suggests that Van Slichtenhorst was under much pressure. In 1649, Van Aken had sailed to Manhattan and Rensselaerswijck as a 'supercargo' (i.e., responsible for overseeing the cargo and keeping accurate accounts of all transactions) aboard the *St. Pieter*; and during his stay along the upper Hudson, he had spoken with Van Slichtenhorst on various occasions. Two years later, he testified that Van Slichtenhorst had complained to him that in the patroonship Wouter van Twiller sought 'to direct everything according to his will and intention, only in order to draw the whole trade to his private benefit.' To make sure his orders were followed, he had sent his brother Jan van Twiller who, under the pretense of representing the patroon, became a member of the council. Wouter van Twiller had ordered Van Slichtenhorst sharply, and under oath, not to send any information regarding Rensselaerswijck's situation to its co-directors, nor to maintain any correspondence with them.[17] Because he feared that Jan van Twiller (who boarded with him) could cause him problems, such as having his salary cut or other possible repercussions, Van Slichtenhorst had obeyed Van Twiller's orders; but he had asked Van Aken to tell his story to co-director Blommaert, so that Blommaert would know how poorly the general goods were being managed by private interests. Van Aken had also heard from Van Slichtenhorst and others that 'one Vastrick and consorts, at the order and in the name of Wouter van Twiller and Jan van Wely, as guardians representing the patroon,' publicly had forbidden all inhabitants 'to trade with any other trader, and not to buy any gold or sell any peltry as from and to him, Vastrick, as long as he had merchandise.' Gerrit Vastrick, a cousin of Van Twiller, had received a good amount of furs, which he had all traded in the name of the colony.[18] In 1650, after Jan van Twiller had gone back to the Republic, Vastrick was appointed to the council on Wouter van Twiller's order. Van Twiller's efforts to monopolize the trade were a great obstruction for all traders and inhabitants of the community.

Not only were the inhabitants unhappy with this trade policy, but Van Slichtenhorst also had trouble regarding rent payments. Accusing several farmers of cheating, he so harassed some of them with processes and other difficulties, according to Jan Baptist van Rensselaer, 'that it was unbearable.' Various persons had even inquired of Stuyvesant whether or not they could live under the authority of the West India Company, in order to have more freedom.[19]

With many inhabitants unhappy with the policy executed by Van Slichtenhorst, and with the West India Company feeling that it could not allow its authority to be undermined – which, at some point, could create a real defense problem – it is not surprising that Stuyvesant took drastic measures. He worried about threats from foreign enemies like the Swedes, English and French, as well as the Indians. By obstructing important defensive repairs to Fort Orange, by buying more lands from the Indians at Catskil – and even by more or less accusing Stuyvesant of treason – Van Slichtenhorst, a fellow countryman, continued to undermine Stuyvesant's authority and, little by little, kept knibbling away pieces of the company's authority.

The area at the upper Hudson was of great importance for the West India Company, as the region was the main supplier of furs in New Netherland; and good relations with the natives were a primary concern. Unlike in some other areas of New Netherland, war with the Indians had generally been avoided here.[20] In 1628, the Maquaes had ended their four-year war against the Mahicans by driving their enemies back to the east side of the river, thus gaining control of the area around Fort Orange. The European desire for furs had brought the Maquaes products that helped make them stronger, and which gave them more power – power they needed in their wars against other Indian nations, which they had been fighting for many years. Competition between Indian nations in order to obtain European goods, and between European nations to get furs, had in the 1630s and 1640s helped create a bond of friendship between the Maquaes and the Dutch, a bond in which both parties guaranteed each other access to the goods they wanted so much. A mutual dependance had resulted, along with a friendship that in later years they frequently would protect.[21]

By 1650, the natives' way of life in the upper Hudson had already been disturbed, as guns and flintlocks (*snaphaenen*) had replaced the bow-and-arrow in hunting and warfare, while a new focus on the beaver trade had changed the periods for hunting; metal objects had replaced stone, textiles were being worn along with leather skins, and for some Indians alcoholic beverages had become more important than water. In the course of thirty to forty years, a new generation of natives had become dependent on the newcomers for survival.[22] But along with the Europeans had come epidemics of smallpox, which now also raged in the New World; and by 1680, the oldest New Netherlanders would observe that there was 'not 1/10th part of the Indians there once were, not 1/20th or 1/30th; and that now the Europeans are 20 and 30 times as many.'[23]

After 1628, the Mahicans had sold land to the settlers on both sides of the river; by 1648, the patroonship would stretch from *Beeren Eyland* to *Unawat's Casteel* near the Cohoes Falls, with Fort Orange situated in the middle.[24] In 1648-49, Van Slichtenhorst bought more land from the Mahicans. His descriptions of these land transactions, reports on journeys to purchased lands, and specifications of the expenses made on these purchases show how the relationship between settlers and Mahicans developed.

Van Slichtenhorst and the Mahicans

Not five months after his arrival, Van Slichtenhorst bought the *Paponicack kil* (Muitzes kil).[25] The Mahican chief Schiwias, nicknamed *Aepjen* ('little monkey') by the Dutch, served as broker in the sale, and at the transfer all parties – sellers with their entourage, brokers, the 'gentlemen' (by whom Van Slichtenhorst likely meant interpreters, witnesses, and buyers), the minister, and the magistrates – were present. At some point the document, drawn up beforehand by the secretary, was signed by sellers, witnesses, perhaps an interpreter, secretary, and the director. The Dutch paid with two pieces of cloth, twenty-two ells of duffel, and two pounds of powder.[26] Having paid for the land and signed the document meant, for the Dutch, that everything was then settled. But the Indians had other expectations: The sale would be celebrated with many visits to, and entertainment in, the patroon's house. Not only before and during the transfer, but afterward as well, *Aepjen* and his group had spent several days in the patroon's house.' On seven or eight occasions, the Mahican chief had stayed there with seven or eight people, with each visit lasting five or six days. He always had some kind of errand, according to Van Slichtenhorst (involving the sale, for example, or the arrival of the sellers, or the price), and would then demand food, good beer, and two or three glasses of brandy a day for having brought this errand. At the sale itself, except for the women [*wijven*] and children, there were ten persons, all of whom stayed at the patroon's house for three or four days – and who were, along with 'the gentlemen,' *dominee* and magistrates, well entertained. *Aepjen* refused to part until 'they saw the barrels and brandy bottles empty,' and Van Slichtenhorst even had to go and get some more barrels of beer from Gysbert, *de weert* (the tavern keeper).[27] At the sales of Catskil and Claverack things proceeded in a similar way: Everything had to be eaten and drunk, and extra provisions were even fetched for presents on the Indians' return journey, so that 'the end would also be good.'[28] During the sale of Claverack, fifty Indians stayed in the patroon's house for three days. In the end, Van Slichtenhorst wrote, he had 'great trouble with all the Indian people, and great filthyness and stench of it, and everything at hand had been stolen, because one could not keep an eye on such a large crowd.'[29]

The colonists would soon find out that, even after the sale, ceremonial matters had not been concluded at all. If they wanted to claim the land theirs, they had to occupy it. When Van Slichtenhorst and Andries de Vos later went to inspect the water courses and the situation of the land, they felt compelled to again give presents and to entertain the Indians who were on the land – which, according to Van Slichtenhorst, ran up to a good sum.[30]

Van Slichtenhorst's accounts reveal the difference in the ideas about property and land use held by Europeans and natives. The Dutch applied their own concept of land ownership, in which they recognized the Indians as the native and rightful proprietors of the land. They approached the Indians in order to bargain with them about a possible exchange of land for payment and, when it seemed that they had reached an agreement, they prepared for the official ceremony of the sale. Official papers and purchase letters were prepared, witnesses and translators hired, the sellers invited, and the payment – often in the form of textiles, gunpowder, axes, and knives – was made ready. From their perspective, the Dutch did it all according to the rules.[31] While at the end, for the Dutch, a sale was final, and meant that they now possessed the land, the Indians were hardly familiar with this European idea of land ownership. They thought of land in terms of *usufruct*, whereby some form of social unit – a clan, for instance, or a family, or lineage – held a right to use the land undisturbed; and as long as they did so, others recognized this right. People could lay claim not on the land itself, but on the things that were on the land during the various seasons of the year.[32] If the new owners did not occupy the land, they did not use it – and the Indians thought they could remain there and live on the land. Thus, it should not be surprising that one piece of land was sold twice. Land purchased by the Dutch of Papsickene in 1637, for example, was not occupied by the Dutch – and in the 1660s, it was sold again by Papsickene's heirs. For the same reason, *Aepjen* and his family received goods in 1661 for land north of Bethlehem, which thirty years before had been included in the sale to Van Rensselaer.[33] To the Indians, the sale meant that they were allowing the Dutch to use the land, and along with that came the ceremonial exchange of gifts. Dutch concepts about the contents of the sale were unfamiliar to the Indians, while the interpretation, behavior and intentions of the Indians were largely unknown to the Dutch. But as both parties recognized enough of their own customs and rituals in the whole event, they felt confident that they had reached the point where everyone, buyers and sellers, could put their signature or mark on the contract paper to seal the occasion of the sale.[34]

Although it does not seem that Van Slichtenhorst understood the ways of life of the Indians, such as their matrilinear clan structure, their ceremonies, and their ideas on land use rather than land possession, he did learn something from these transactions. He warned that if the Dutch did not immediately occupy the land after the purchase, they would have to give presents every time they came there; and furthermore, the English were waiting for their chance to claim the land. Therefore he strongly suggested that the Dutch would not buy any more land from the Indians until there were enough settlers to populate the said land; otherwise, 'the daily costs will exceed the buying price itself!'[35]

Van Slichtenhorst and the Maquaes

These reports and land transactions reveal the complexity of dealing with different land policies. The Maquaes, who after 1628 remained in their own villages further to the west, had allowed those Mahicans who had not fled to use the land.[36] But although it was from the Mahicans that the Dutch bought land, the Maquaes were quick to say that the 'Christians possessed the land that they had conquered from the Mahicans by the sword.'[37] Later, starting with the selling of land at Schenectady in 1661, the Maquaes on occasion sold land that previously had been owned by the Mahicans, but which, after conquest, they considered to belong to them.[38]

It also seems clear that the Maquaes considered that the Dutch lived on their

8. *Marks and signatures of Mahican sellers and Dutch buyers under property transactions.*

land, when they obtained their annual tribute from the subjected nations situated about forty miles surrounding them and the patroonship. These nations were obligated to join the Maquaes in their war against the French Christians and Indians in Canada, 'with whom they have carried on a very cruel and inhuman war' between 1648 and 1651. The colony was situated in the middle, and the patroon's house was the meeting place of the field commanders; subjected nations were summoned to appear there. Indian passages took place from spring to fall, with one group arriving when the other left. The natives could or would not stay in Fort Orange, or in the three houses to the north of it, but the West India Company would send them, and their sick and wounded, to the patroon's house, where the front, middle, and rear house and the courtyard then filled with Indians. The chiefs were bold enough to take food and drink until it was finished. Once, according to Van Slichtenhorst, they killed two large hogs and ate them, leaving him only the heads. After being entertained for some days, the Indians even demanded corn, beans, peas, an axe, a breech-cloth, a pair of stockings, an awl, and other items. 'And if we were slow about it,' he stated, 'they claimed that they also had to fight for us Christians, and that we should supply them with every weapon: guns, powder, lead, and every other necessity, as the French do for their Indians.' They 'allowed the Christians to live there, because they should convenience them with everything, and otherwise the Christians might just as well cross the great water again.'[39] If the colonists did not do what the Maquaes wished, they threatened to kill the animals. Younger Indians (*loopwilden en kaephaenen*), especially, caused trouble in Rensselaerswijck; they walked around daily, saying: 'Give us bacon and meat; otherwise we will kill your cattle and hogs.'[40]

Tensions existed among the Indians as well as among the colonists, and special meetings were organized during a good part of August 1648 to address some of the issues. At the beginning of the month, eighteen sachems of three castles, along with their women and children, came and were given pieces of cloth, lead, and gunpowder to maintain the old friendships, and to ensure that their Indians would not kill any more horses, cattle, and hogs. Thereupon, Maquaes and other Iroquois from twenty-one castles, from as far as fifty or sixty miles, gathered and lodged for six days with their entourages in the patroon's house, according to Van Slichtenhorst. All Indians were called together, he wrote, and publicly – first in the house, and the following day on the hill – 'we called out for all of them that they should not kill any more cattle, horses and hogs of their brothers the Christians, and that they should maintain good peace and agreement with the Dutch.'[41]

After having suffered a big defeat at the 'great lake,' in which they lost some 500 or 600 people (most of their first two castles), the Maquaes began attacking the French again, and at various times brought them great damage. The Dutch paid large sums in ransom in order to keep some French captives alive. The settlers lived in fear because of all the great Indian meetings; and like the Maquaes, they feared a French attack, according to Van Slichtenhorst. The sachems of the first castle demanded, in the beginning of July 1649, that two Dutchmen come along to their castle with two horses to transport palisades. The Dutch were barely given time to think about it, as the Indians immediately threatened that, upon a negative response, they would kill the horses and cattle, take the two men with their horses by force, and kill the rest. The Maquaes were so afraid of a French attack that all male and female Indians left their land and houses at night and fled into the patroon's house. 'So that one can honestly say,' Van Slichtenhorst stated, 'that the first three years in the colony we have not been free of Indians for half a day.'[42]

Within five years, the friendship and brotherhood that had been established in 1643 seems to have grown into a relationship in which the Indians dominated the area.[43] The colonists may have caused some of the problems themselves, as many went into the woods to obtain furs, delivered notes, and sent brokers – all of which caused much mischief and discord. These activities should be stopped, the court judged, but that could only be done properly with the consent of 'those of Fort Orange.'[44] The Indians became so obtrusive that Rensselaerswijck's court and the commissary of the fort, under pressure, even granted permission to the Indian *Den Uyl* (the owl), or Stichtigeri, to erect a small house north of Fort Orange.[45] 'The insecurity of our lives and property oppresses us continually, living as we do under the unrestrained domination of inhuman people and cruel heathen,' Van Slichtenhorst reported, describing the colony's situation in September 1650, when rumors of a war with the Maquaes were circulating. Hope for a solution was placed in Arent van Curler, Gerrit Wencom, Cornelis Theunisz van Breuckelen, Thomas Chambers, and Volckert Hansz, who were willing to go with a gift to the Maquaes' territory, in order to renew the former alliance and bond of good friendship. When requested to do this, they also asked Jan Labatie, who lived in Fort Orange, and who was reasonably experienced in using the Maquaes' language. However, Labatie – who in the 1630s had frequently travelled into the Maquaes' territory – said that he would not accompany them for anything in the world, and that it did not make much difference to those in the fort whether it was war or peace.[46] No report of the journey seems to have survived, and it is not clear what happened. It is not listed in Van Slichtenhorst's court case as an expense, so perhaps they did not go. The feared war did not take place and, in November 1650, Rensselaerswijck's court gave its consent to Jan Labatie to buy the house from *Den Uyl* (who had become a great nuisance to the colony, as well as to the fort), on condition that a proper recognition to the patroon and co-directors of the colony be paid to the directors.[47] Van Slichtenhorst's accounts offer a unique insight into just how frequent and strong the native presence had become in the settlement – which, in the meantime, was growing steadily. In the following section, we will step back a few years and take a look at how Rensselaerswijck's center was planned.

Planning a center for Rensselaerswijck

Value of maps

Soon after he had bought land from the Indians, patroon Kiliaen van Rensselaer had a West India Company mapmaker draw a map of his domain. Maps offered power to individuals who possessed land elsewhere: With the help of a map, they could plan and lay out faraway areas, and make decisions about that land.[48] The new map allowed Van Rensselaer, from his house on the Keizersgracht in Amsterdam, to control an area located more than 3,000 miles away, as he could now plot out his colony. He was able to place names on his map, and to plan farms and mills at certain locations; he could indicate exactly where he wanted the colonists to live, and to create a center for the patroonship.

From the very beginning, he had planned to establish this center on the river's east side. He sent instructions and mapped-out plans to his agent in the domain, along with lengthy instructions. It was, for example, his 'definite intention that the church be put opposite Castle Island, north of the small grove and south of the farm of Gerrit de Reux, deceased, not far from the grove on a small hill near or on the bank on the east side of the river,' he stated in August 1639, in a letter to his agent Arent van Curler. 'Near the church ought to be built a dwelling for the minister and one for the sexton and this at the least expense,' he wrote, and he ordered Van Curler to inquire how much the carpenters would charge for these three buildings, with a palisade around the churchyard. 'I should also be pleased, and it would be advantageous to the people, if some of the mechanics and others would build their houses around the church, as for instance Reyer Stoffelsz Smith, who would be nearer to the farms there than anywhere else; also the wheelwright, the carpenter and such like, but as they are freemen, I can not command them.'[49]

By May 14, 1642, the patroon had worked out his plan further. Hendrick Albertsz would become ferryman and build his house near the *Beverskil*, in order to 'ferry the people from there to the church neighborhood and back, as the church, the house of the minister, that of the officer and further of all the mechanics must hereafter be built there, just as Abraham Staes and Evert Pels, beerbrewer, have agreed to settle there, for I do not in any way wish or consent that, with the exception of the farmers and tobacco planters who must have their houses near their farms or plantations, any people following other trades shall hereafter and on the expiration of their years of service settle anywhere but the church neighborhood, according to the accompanying order and plan, for if everyone lived where he saw fit they would be too far separated from one another and in case of sudden attack be in peril of their lives, as sad experience near the Manhatens has taught.'[50] A month later he would repeat the same instructions in a memorandum for *dominee* Megapolensis: The church neighborhood should be 'to the south of *De Laetsburgh*, placing the center thereof at the place on the river where inland the swamp is deepest and so may serve as defense in times of need, as Abraham Staes knows; and all houses must be located there as indicated on the accompanying small map.'[51]

Van Rensselaer never changed his mind about the location of the colony center; the last time he made mention of it was half a year before his death, when he wrote Van Curler that he had changed his mind about the church construction. He wanted a suitable building to be erected that could first be used for preaching, and later on be turned into a dwelling house. The location had to remain 'as directed and this dwelling must be placed with the others in proper order. Next to the house of *dominee* Megapolensis would not be unsuitable and later it could be used as a school.'[52]

The patroon may have been so persistent about this location because he wanted to avoid any possible problems with the West India Company. With the center of Rensselaerswijck at the opposite side of the river from Fort Orange, the members of the community would be less tempted to become involved in the fur trade; but in dangerous times, they would still have access to the safety of the fort. At the same time, they could provide the twenty-five men occupying the fort with grain, and other agricultural and necessary products, from their mills, farms, breweries and distilleries. Van Rensselaer estimated that his colony, in this way, could draw some ƒ2500 a year, and therewith pay the laborers' wages.[53] Since the very beginning of the colony, he had made great efforts to maintain a good relationship with the company, and this had proven to have a positive effect. Bastiaen Jansz Krol, commander of Fort Orange, had helped with the acquisition of the first two tracts of land from the Mahicans. During the years of anti-patroon policy from within the company's board, his nephew Wouter van Twiller, then director general of New Netherland, had assisted him in many ways – for instance, with buying cattle for him whenever possible and sending it up to Rensselaerswijck.[54] With Willem Kieft, who succeeded Van Twiller in 1638, the patroon had maintained correspondence and, to maintain a good relationship, presented him with some gifts.[55] Just how important this relationship was to Van Rensselaer he clearly expressed after being informed of an incident involving the lowering of the patroon's flag by Fort Orange officials. '... Believe me, Sir,' he wrote Kieft in May 1640, 'the success of my colony depends mainly on the good relations between your honor and myself and it is far from my purpose intentionally or knowlingly to hurt the Company in the least in their power or revenue. If my people speak any foolish words, it is by reason of their weakness and not of my orders.'[56]

Van Rensselaer was well aware of the West India Company's power and he did not wish to steal away its fur trade, but seriously intended to focus on agriculture.[57] After the company had given up its monopoly of the fur trade, in 1640, he was certainly interested in having a share in it, but only second to the company. To Arent van Curler he stated that he could not forbid the company, but only private individuals, the right to trade in his colony. 'Of substitution of private individuals for the Company there can be no question, for next to the Company, I come.'[58] Van Rensselaer needed good relations with the company for himself; when his farmers were disobedient to his orders, it was important that he could threathen them with interference by the militia commander of the West India Company, Hendrick van Dijck, who promised to help him suppress them.[59] The location of the patroon's trading house, at the edge of the moat around Fort Orange, may be proof of these good relations as well. No indications have yet been found as to exactly when it was built; but the trading house seems at least to have been there soon after the trade was opened up.[60] In 1640-41, Arent van Curler was able to have a house built for the patroon, just a little north of this trading house and the fort, which also suggests that patroonship and company were then maintaining positive relations. On various occasions, they actually seem to have cooperated – as in 1643, for example, when Van Curler, Jacob Jansz, and Jan Labatie of Fort Orange went together to visit the Maquaes.[61]

Some incidents indicate that, after 1644, contact between the West India Company and the patroonship turned downhill; and, especially after Van Slichtenhorst's arrival, relations changed dramatically.[62] New Netherland's new director general, Petrus Stuyvesant, arrived on May 11, 1647 in New Amsterdam; meanwhile, Jan van Wely and Wouter van Twiller (who had been recalled as New Netherland's director ten years earlier) as guardians of the young patroon, in November 1646 hired Brant van Slichtenhorst and changed the policy regarding the location of the patroonship's center.[63] After Van Slichtenhorst arrived, the building of a *bijeenwoninge* close to the fort would become a major disagreement between patroon and company. It seems clear that, by 1647, the guardians of the young patroon had changed Kiliaen van Rensselaer's original plan, and that they had instructed Van Slichtenhorst to establish the *bijeenwoninge* on the west side of the river, north of Fort Orange.

It is likely that Van Curler, who between 1645 and 1647 was in the fatherland, provided the guardians and Van Slichtenhorst with information during his stay. Being related (and, both he and Van Twiller were from Nijkerk and had experience in New Netherland), it is unthinkable that they would not have discussed the colony at large. Van Twiller had left New Netherland in 1638, while Van Curler had arrived in Rensselaerswijck at that time. Conditions had changed remarkably since then: The fur trade had opened up to everyone, and to the south a series of wars between the West India Company and the River Indians had produced a sense of insecurity among the colonists. Van Curler may have suggested building the center of the colony closer to the fort, instead of on the river's east side – an idea he may have shared with Cornelis Theunisz van Slijck, who, according to Kiliaen van Rensselaer in 1639, seems to have preferred that location. Perhaps more colonists felt this way.[64] Van Curler must have been well aware of the colonists' feelings; besides, he does not seem to have experienced bad relations between the inhabitants of the colony and those of the fort. Therefore, he would not have expected problems between the two. He may also have seen good possibilities in diverting the trade of those Indians who were then trading with French Indians to the patroon, as Kiliaen van Rensselaer already had considered doing in 1641.[65]

Often, Van Slichtenhorst is the individual blamed for changing the location of Rensselaerswijck's center to the west side of the river – a move that, in time, would cause great damage to the patroonship.[66] When we look at some of the correspondence, however, it becomes clear that Van Twiller and Van Wely had sent him to the New World with a brand-new design and map for the future *bijeenwoninge*, and that they had given him instructions to implement a plan that differed considerably from Kiliaen van Rensselaer's original ideas. On October 20, 1648, Van Slichtenhorst wrote to Stuyvesant and the council that 'he would have most cheerfully exhibited, and is still willing to show to his Honor and his councillors not only his commission and orders, but even the plan of the settlement itself.'[67] The patroon and co-directors may have been referring to the same plan, or perhaps a revised version, when they wrote to Van Slichtenhorst, in March 1651, that nobody should settle himself in the *bijeenwoninge* 'who has not previously accepted and subscribed, in the presence of the commissioners and secretary, the contract entered into with Andries Herpers [an influential inhabitant of the community] and others, and that the same *bijeenwoninge* shall be developed in accordance with the plan sent over therefor.'[68]

Unfortunately, no other correspondence, nor a copy of this map of the *bijeenwoninge*, have been found. So we are left with many questions. Who designed the plan – Van Twiller and Van Curler? And what were their purposes in erecting a center so close to the fort? Was their idea to establish a village? Or a town, perhaps, in the long run? Did they look at plans of other colonial settlements, and were they influenced by ideas about city designs of, for example, Simon Stevin's? Did they look at New Amsterdam's lay-out? What did the plan look like, and was it used in the later development of the village of Beverwijck? Only limited information of the planned lay-out of the *bijeenwoninge* has survived. Loss and fires have left their marks. An entry in the Rensselaerswijck court minutes may illustrate the difficulty of putting all information together: The planned location for a poor house had changed, but exactly at the place where the new location is written, the manuscript has been damaged by fire in such a way that the remainder of the page is unreadable.[69]

Building a bijeenwoninge

Immediately after his arrival Van Slichtenhorst, armed with a new map, started issuing building permits; and, by August, the *bijeenwoninge* had already expanded from three to eight houses.[70] On July 23, Stuyvesant warned that the buildings had weakened the fort, and he requested the patroonship to refrain from building within a cannon-shot from the fort.[71] Stuyvesant, who had spent several years on Curaçao, likely had the general rules and standards for a fort in mind.[72] Many Dutch forts were built with similar strategies. At Fort *de Goede Hoop* (Good Hope) at Cape Town, South Africa, for example, a building line was drawn all around the fort, and it was forbidden to erect structures within fifty rods of the fort because they blocked the view in the direct vicinity of the fort, and obstructed the field of the cannon. Only small gardens were allowed. Ron van Oers, who has studied Dutch town planning overseas during the East and West India Company eras, found that in nearly all Dutch settlements this open field of fire could be seen between the town and the fort. Often this space functioned as parade ground or a formal square, while it played a dominant role in the city plan.[73]

Van Slichtenhorst, however, protested against Stuyvesant's warning; the patroon's trading house, according to him, had stood undisturbed on the border of the moat of Fort Orange for several years, and that very ground (and all land around the fort) had for many years belonged to the patroon.[74] In August, Carel van Brugge, then commissary of Fort Orange, reported that Van Slichtenhorst had proceeded with the building of new houses; and on September 4, Stuyvesant ordered that the houses be pulled down. If Van Slichtenhorst were to offer opposition, additional men would be sent from Manhattan. The patroonship's director ordered the continuation of the building and, on September 14, publicly leased six more lots.[75] Four to six soldiers were then sent to the commissary, 'for the assistance and the better execution of his orders to demolish the house with the smallest loss to the owners.'[76] On October 20, Van Slichtenhorst protested that Carel van Brugge and Mr. Labatie, assisted by an armed soldier, had come unexpectedly into the patroon's house, declaring that some soldiers and sailors had been sent by Stuyvesant to demolish and pull down the house and building of Jan Thomasz and Rem Jansz, the smith, which house, according to him, was beyond a musket shot or 550 paces, and even out of sight of Fort Orange. Van Slichtenhorst thought it strange that, even though a hostile attack would come principally from the west, the patroon's woods to the west, southwest and northwest of the fort were not being meddled with; and he also found it odd that Stuyvesant had tolerated a number of streets full of buildings within thirty paces of the fort at Manhattan, and that he had not first applied a remedy there.[77] Van Slichtenhorst kept offering good deals for building in the *bijeenwoning*. The tailor Jan Verbeeck, for instance, could pay his debt to the patroon in five installments of *f*150 a year; and if he were to build on the west shore, he would for the first year be free from paying rent.[78] On October 31, Stuyvesant ordered Van Slichtenhorst to appear before him and the council on the first court day of April; and, in November, he authorized Van Brugge to maintain the West India Company's high jurisdiction and the use of the gardens and lands situated under the fort, unless he was ordered differently. Finally, Stuyvesant ordered the removal of the houses that were 'blinding and blockading the Company's fortress,' and which had been built within musket or small cannon shot range.[79] Stuyvesant's orders did not stop Van Slichtenhorst from pursuing his goal, however, and when Stuyvesant sent seven soldiers and five boatswains to tear down the houses, Van Slichtenhorst's son Gerrit, in the position of lieutenant, stood guard night and day and helped to prevent the demolition.[80] Van Slichtenhorst continued to distribute lots to construct the *bijeenwoninge* – promising Rutger Jacobsz in December 1649, for instance, that he would suffer no damage or loss for building on the first kill.[81]

Also matters of common interest were located within the *bijeenwoninge*. Religious services were now definitely held on the river's west side.[82] During Van Curler's administration, the patroon's storehouse (*packhuys*) had already been used for this purpose.[83] Between 1646 and 1648, Willem Fredericksz Bout had made a pulpit, a sounding board, a seat for the magistrates and one for the deacons, a window with two lights, a rail near the pulpit, with a corner seat, and nine benches. From a petition by Anthonie de Hooges in March 1648, we learn that the place where religious services were held had changed. He had to build a new house, he wrote, as the patroon's storehouse, which was assigned to him, had been changed into a church.[84] In the same year, Abraham Pietersz Vosburgh started to do some work on the patroon's house. In addition to major repairs and adjustments on the building itself, such as making two windows above in the church and a few doors underneath it, he made a table with two saw horses on which the Holy Communion was distributed. Evert Duykinck made new windows and repaired some old ones; he would be happy to make some stain glass windows as well, he wrote, and if Slichtenhorst so wished, he could just send off the coat of arms or the house marks (*wapens ofte marken*).[85] By 1649, the old storehouse seems to have been torn down and the services, from then on, were held in the rear part of the renovated patroon's house.[86] The church building on which, in 1650, a 'convenient staircase' was made, then, was probably the expensive house that Arent van Curler had built in 1640-41, and where he, and later Brant Aertsz van Slichtenhorst and the brothers van Rensselaer, lived.[87] (See illustration 42-44).

Attention was also paid to education. In 1648, Evert Nolden received permission to establish himself as a school master, and in September 1650 Arent van Curler and Goosen Gerritsz were appointed trustees of a fund for the building of a school.[88] It seems that teaching, as in many places in the fatherland, was done in the teacher's house, as nowhere it is mentioned that they succeeded in this building project. But since a community had a responsibility to support its more unfortunate settlers as well, a lot was designated for the poor in January 1651. Perhaps the settlers thought that, as long as there were not yet that many poor, teaching could be done in the poorhouse that would be built there.[89]

In January 1650, it was decided that attention should be paid to the maintenance of public roads, to reduce the inconvenience and danger to the inhabitants. A bridge with railings, and benches to sit on, needed to be built across the first kill in the *bijeenwoninge*. There also needed to be a bridge across the third kill, one with railings across the Beaver kill and, furthermore, a wagon bridge at the rear. Two years later, Steven Jansz was paid by Van Slichtenhorst for building a bridge in the *Fuyck* (the area defined by the eastern part of present-day State Street and Broadway) and one across the Beaver kill in 1651 and 1652.[90]

It is interesting that Van Slichtenhorst usually referred to the settlement as the *bijeenwoninge*, the 'living-together,' and not as *het dorp*, or 'the village.' If a name can be taken literally, the fact that, in August 1648, Nicolaes Coorn was granted permission to build a city tavern (*stadsherbergh*), at a place to be assigned, could indicate that the patroon was thinking in terms of a town, rather than a village. City taverns also existed in the fatherland and in other colonial town-like settlements: There was one in Manhattan, and both the fort at Colombo and the old town near this fort had one as well.[91] Like other city taverns, Coorn was not granted the exclusive right to operate a tap; at least four other people were allowed to serve liquor as well.[92] The intention may have been that the place would function in the community as a privileged and official meeting place that also would lodge important persons.

Company versus patroon: Escalation of the conflict

Van Slichtenhorst ignored Stuyvesant's order to appear before the council of New Netherland in April 1649; but when, in the spring of 1651, he was summoned again to Manhattan to explain his actions (he had torn down a posted West India Company ordinance concerning excise taxes), he went. Soon after his arrival in Manhattan he was thrown in jail; but in September he escaped, and was able to get a boat ride back.[93] During the rest of 1651 and the beginning of 1652, Van Slichtenhorst proceeded to grant new building lots within the disputed area around the fort.[94] In this tense situation, forty-five persons took the oath of loyalty to the patroon on the November 28, 1651.[95] Even when (as we saw earlier), at the turn of the year, it was so clear that the situation had become intolerable, Van Slichtenhorst kept defending the patroon's rights. On February 5, Fort Orange's new commissary, Johannes Dijckman, requested that some company ordinances be posted in Rensselaerswijck; but Van Slichtenhorst answered, 'In no way, as long as I have a drop of blood in my body, unless you show me first an authorization from their High Mightinesses or our honorable masters.'[96]

All this time, Stuyvesant had been directing his attention to a confrontation with the Swedish colony in the southern area of New Netherland at the Delaware River, and to negotiations of an eastern boundary with New England. But when, in 1652, the treaty of Hartfort had been concluded with New England, and Fort Casimir had been built on the Delaware to guard against further encroachments by the Swedes, he would turn his attention to Rensselaerswijck. On March 5, the council passed an ordinance proclaiming the West India Company's jurisdiction around the fort and ordering the erection of boundary posts.[97] When Van Slichtenhorst refused to publish the proclamation and tore it off the walls of the patroon's house and Gysbert Cornelisz' tavern, Dijckman responded by visiting the director with eight armed soldiers.[98] He hauled down the patroon's flag, rang the bell, and proclaimed the establishment of the court of Fort Orange and village of Beverwijck. Van Slichtenhorst was taken out of his house by the soldiers and, guarded by four soldiers, sent in the company sloop to Manhattan, where he spent the next sixteen months under detention (during which time his term of office would expire).[99]

On April 4, the directors of the Amsterdam Chamber of the West India Company had sent instructions to proceed against Van Slichtenhorst, in essence giving Stuyvesant a mandate to uphold the sovereignty of the fort, including the area within 3,000 feet of its perimeter. They had heard that the owners of Rensselaerswijck had agreed that Van Slichtenhorst would soon be replaced.[100] Jan Baptist van Rensselaer, the patroon's oldest brother, had been sent to check on the situation in the patroonship in 1651 and, while Van Slichtenhorst was in jail, he replaced him as director. A letter from May 8 stated that the patroon and co-directors had appointed him, and on July 24, 1652 Jan Baptist van Rensselaer took the oath.[101] In September 1652, Van Rensselaer reported that the company had taken the *bijeenwoninge*, Catskil and the flags. Dijckman, he wrote, with as many as forty men well provided with guns, had put three boundary markers at each side of the fort at 1,200 steps (or 600 paces), which included all of the *bijeenwoninge* and one small farm.[102] 'They have absolved the burghers from their oath to us, which they consider very suspicious, and took their oath and flag and made a court of justice in the fort where everyone should appear who has something to demand of those who live within the boundary posts, as according to them, nobody else as they has something to say there.'[103] The residents of the area within the 3,000-foot jurisdiction around the fort had been ordered to swear allegiance to the company, and were absolved from any obligations to the patroonship.[104] In one stroke, Rensselaerswijck had lost its major community, where most colonists had built houses and pursued their various trades.

When Van Slichtenhorst's civil arrest at New Amsterdam ended in July 1653, he returned to Rensselaerswijck, where he tried to collect his fines and close his accounts with Jan Baptist van Rensselaer and the commissioners.[105] They were not able to reach an agreement, and once he was back in the Republic he brought a court case against patroon Johannes van Rensselaer in order to receive payment for what he considered the patroon owed him. The case dragged on between 1656 and 1661; but when the patroon died in 1663, Van Slichtenhorst discontinued his action.[106] He would die in 1666, too soon to know of the West India Company's eventual recognition that the patroon was indeed the legal owner of the disputed land, on April 2, 1674. This recognition, however, added the clause that should the province again come under Dutch rule, the recognition would become invalid and the situation would revert to that of 1664.[107]

Although Van Slichtenhorst claimed in his court case that he had built a *bijeen-woning* of about a hundred houses before April 1652, I have been able to trace, in the available source materials, only fifty-two to fifty-four persons who received contracts for lots on the river's west side.[108] In twenty-two of these cases, it was specifically mentioned that their lots were located in the *bijeenwoning*. Another seventeen lots were definitely on the west side, eight of them were to the south of the fort, and eight or nine were between the fort and the first kill. Another thirteen were most likely also on the west side, somewhere between the second kill (along Broadway) in the direction of, and perhaps even north of, the third kill (see Appendix 2). The fact that Jan Baptist van Rensselaer wrote, in November 1652, that the *bijeenwoninge* had grown rapidly in a short time and that there were '38 houses standing and four or five were laying half finished,' suggests that Van Slichtenhorst had made quite an overstatement.[109] It seems unlikely that the West India Company would have ordered the soldiers to tear down fifty-seven houses, only to start rebuilding them elsewhere. Elsewhere, in his court case, Van Slichtenhorst would state that his son had helped prevent the demolition of the houses.[110]

While lots were also given out south of Fort Orange, the concentration of buildings where people lived together was north of it. Houses were planned along the two trails that shaped the area, which was frequently called the '*Fuyck*' by the inhabitants, a name that first appears in Rensselaerswijck's court minutes of September 1648.[111] Looking north over a coastal plain from the fort and the patroon's house, one could see a trail that, after crossing the first kill – also called the '*Fuyc-kenkil*' – split into a trail leading to the north along the river, and another trail that went more toward the west or northwest, parallel to the first kill, over the hill into the woods. The shape of the trails may have resembled that of a *fuyck*, which means 'hoopnet': The narrow part began just north of the fort and, where the trails split, the hoopnet started widening. The Maquaes had used these trails since the early trading days when they came to the settlement to trade their pelts; since 1628, they had stopped by during their journeys to other parts of their territory to collect tribute from the Mahicans. When they came from their settlements in the

Mohawk Valley, they would canoe with their furs until present-day Duanes-burgh. From there, they would continue their journey either with canoes on the Normanskill or on foot, as the high falls at Cohoes blocked further boat traffic down to Fort Orange. The trail leading up along the hill and into the woods was sometimes called the 'Maquaes *padt*' (Mohawk trail), and followed the route of present-day State Street as far as Schenectady. The trail northward went along the river where Broadway is now located. The first building lots were allocated along the river, at the mouths of the kills, along the sides of the *Fuyckenkil*, and between this kill and the Maquaes *padt*. By April 1652, several people had asked permis-sion to build between the two kills.[112]

With the loss of the *bijeenwoning*, according to Van Rensselaer, the patroon would suffer at least an annual damage of ƒ1500; most of the brewers were in the area now named 'Beeverswijck,' and they would no longer give the patroon 'a tun of money.' Several refused to pay a penny of the arrears they owed in rents for their lots, saying that Stuyvesant had ordered them to withhold payment.[113] Half a year after Stuyvesant's action, the loss of Rensselaerswijck's major community seemed to be an established fact. By then, Stuyvesant had distributed the first patents in the area among the inhabitants of Beverwijck.

Development of Beverwijck

Distributing patents

As Jan Baptist van Rensselaer had described, a lower court of justice (*kleine Banck van Justitie*) was erected in the fort, which went into effect on April 10.[114] The area around the fort no longer belonged to 'Van Rensselaer's wijck,' but had become 'Bever wijck,' emphasizing the central role of the beaver (and not Van Rensselaer) for all inhabitants. The new court immediately continued the building started by Van Slichtenhorst. On April 15, commissary Johannes Dijckman, Volckert Jansz, and Cornelis Theunisz van Westbroeck were appointed a committee to look after the surveying of lots and gardens, and Abraham Staets was requested to assist when possible.[115] The carpenters Dirck Jansz and Abraham Pietersz Vosburgh were chosen and appointed to make a proper survey for several persons who had applied for permission to build on some lots between the two kills.[116] Two days later they took the 'usual burgher oath' before the court, and April 23 at least thir-ty-two to forty-two persons received patents for lots for gardens and houses dis-tributed by Petrus Stuyvesant; twenty-six of those individuals had previously re-ceived lots from Van Slichtenhorst.[117] On October 22, 1653, the carpenter Harmen Bastiaensz also took the oath as surveyor (*rooymeester*, a term for a job, typical for an urban area), and three days later a second batch of patents for house- or garden lots was distributed among at least forty-nine, possibly sixty persons.[118] Of these, six to eight people had already received patents in 1652; and now they were given additional land, often to be used for a garden. Thus, by the end of 1653, seventy-four to possibly ninety-three individuals had received patents for lots,

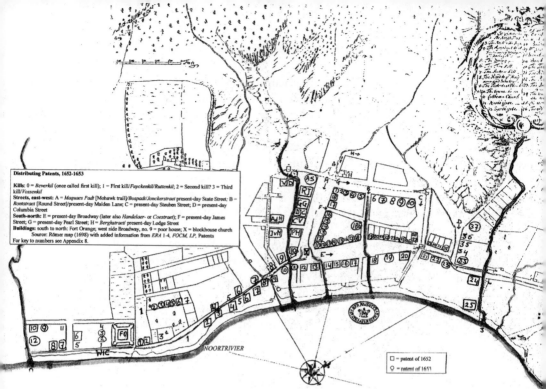

Distributing Patents, 1652-1653

Kills: 0 = *Beverkil* (once called first kill); 1 = First kill/*Fuyckenkil*/*Ruttenkil*; 2 = Second kill? 3 = Third kill/*Vossenkil*
Streets, east-west: A = *Maquaes Padt* [Mohawk trail]/*Bospadi*/*Jonckerstraet* present-day State Street; B = *Rontstraet* [Round Street]/present-day Maiden Lane; C = present-day Steuben Street; D = present-day Columbia Street
South-north: E = present-day Broadway (later also *Handelaer*- or *Coestraet*); F = present-day James Street; G = present-day Pearl Street; H = *Berghstraet*/ present-day Lodge Street
Buildings: south to north: Fort Orange; west side Broadway, no. 9 = poor house; X = blockhouse church
Source: Römer map (1698) with added information from *ERA 1-4, FOCM, LP, Patents*
For key to numbers see Appendix 8.

NOORTRIVIER

☐ = patent of 1652
○ = patent of 1653

9. *Distribution of 1652 and 1653 patents, filled in on Römer map.*

and at least forty-five of them had built or contracted for lots on the west side of the river prior to Stuyvesant's action. (See illustration 9 and 56). They were probably included in the 230 men able to bear arms, who were mentioned by Jan Baptist van Rensselaer in June 1653.[119] Also, during the following years various patents were distributed. In September 1654 there were daily calls for lots, and the court asked Stuyvesant and the council for places where new lots could be given out, as there were no more left.[120] Lots were never again distributed in such large numbers as in the years 1652 and 1653, but between 1654 and 1661 at least thirty-four, possibly fifty-six people were given additional lots.

TABLE 1.1: Number of people receiving patents[121]

	Certainly	Likely	Had earlier a patent
1652	32	42	
1653	49	60	6-8
1654	8	20	3
1655	4	8	4
1656	2	7	1
1657	2	2	1
1658	7	7	2
1659	5	6	3
1660	4	4	3
1661	2	2	1

For the colonists these must have been exciting days, especially during the first year. In November 1652, Jan Baptist van Rensselaer reported to the patroon that 'they already receive patents from the director and council at the Manhatans and their houses are worth now four or five hundred guilders. Now they think that they have a right to these lots.'[122] People received title deeds as proof of their ownership of a piece of land; and especially with the patroon's conditions (that one had to pay rent) having become a reality, this was a radical change.

It is difficult to trace back exactly how many lots were involved. Since very few original patents have survived, we have to use the series of translated confirmatory patents in Albany's patent books. Additional information is provided by court minutes, and by property conveyances in which reference is made to a patent. Sometimes it is impossible to discover whether a particular property was referred to in different documents at different times; while it seems that these manuscripts all concern different patents, in reality, they go back to the same source. It is not always clear, either, what kind of property the patent concerns. A patent is sometimes indicated as being for 'a lot,' for 'a house and lot,' for 'a lot and garden' or 'a house, lot and garden,' or 'a house and yard.' A patent for a 'lot' later often appears to have a house on it.

In Appendix 3, I have listed people who, according to the New York Colonial Patent Books, Albany 1664-1690, received a patent in Beverwijck. Wherever a destination is indicated, I have marked this. I have also included in the list information from the *Early Records of Albany* 1-4 (*ERA*), *Land Papers* (*LP*), and *Fort Orange Court Minutes* (*FOCM*), referring to a possible patent, or at least mentioning that a particular person was given a lot. According to the translated confirmatory patents (in the table printed with regular print), nineteen people received lots in 1652. Information drawn from property conveyances in the *ERA* add another twelve people, and the *FOCM* suggest that an additional ten people were given lots. An original patent for a lot for the poor is in Albany's First Dutch Reformed Church, so that over that year at least thirty-two, and possibly forty-two people seem to have received one or more patents. In 1653, fifty-five lots were distributed among thirty people, according to the patents; in the *ERA*, I counted another nineteen people who received lots; and according to the *FOCM*, eleven people may have received lots as well, making a total of forty-nine to possibly sixty, of whom six to eight had also received patents in 1652. Based on the combined information from the patent books, *ERA*, *LP*, and *FOCM*, thirty-four people received patents between 1654 and 1661, of whom half had already received one or more patents before. When we add all information found in the patents, *ERA*, *LP*, and *FOCM*, it appears that at least ninety-two and possibly as many as 111 people received a patent between 1652 and 1661.[123]

The patents show that of the lots distributed in 1652, at least fifteen had gardens on them, and fourteen were house lots. Twenty-two patents indicate only that they concerned a lot. Of at least seventy distributed lots in 1653, a good thirty-two had a garden and twenty-five a house. Of ten, it was only indicated that they were lots.

As Jan Baptist van Rensselaer wrote, people considered these lots their own.

But there were conditions. Adriaen Jansz van Leyden was summoned to the court, in February 1653, because he gave a lot away that had first been drawn by him, but afterwards was promised to someone else. The rule was that a person had no power to give away a lot, 'for if he did not wish to take possession of it, it reverted to the court.'[124] Similar to inhabitants of Manhattan, Beverwijck's inhabitants were obligated to build on the lots within a short time. In Manhattan, it was already necessary in 1648 to have an ordinance passed for the speedier erection of buildings, as the lots had been 'laid out too large and bigger than they could be built on by some inhabitants.'[125] Because other people desired to build and scarsely could find a spot on which a house could conveniently be built, the director general and council ordered 'all persons to erect proper buildings on their lots, or in default, they will dispose of suitable places to those who are inclined to build houses in this city New Amsterdam and to allow the present proprietors for them a reasonable indemnity at the discretion of the street surveyors.'[126]

In the West India Company's limited building space of Beverwijck, similar actions were necessary. If building was impossible, for instance, due to a lack of supplies, exceptions could be made; but, in general, people were made to follow the rules. In April and May of 1653, five persons were excused and granted an extension of time in which to fence in their gardens; but in December, eight people were fined because they had not 'built upon or fenced in their lots or gardens assigned and granted to them within the specified time.'[127] As in the town of Hoorn in North Holland, for example, the rule was that someone had to build upon a certain lot within a short period of time after the same lot had been granted, on pain of being deprived of them.[128] Marten *metselaer* (mason), for example, who in December 1652 had been granted a lot behind his house, did not build upon it within six weeks as required, and a year later was fined ƒ25 for still not having done so. At his request, it was resolved that his house and garden would be sold by the court, for the purpose of paying his joint creditors out of the proceeds of the sale.[129]

But the inhabitants did become owners of the lots, and they decided what happened on their property. The process of buying and selling lots had started at once, as Van Rensselaer indicated. One person, he wrote in November 1652, had sold a piece of his lot of about 100 square feet to someone else for ƒ500, who intended to put a brewery on it.[130] More people subdivided their lots and sold parts of them. Various property transfers were made that year, and this practice would only multiply over time. By 1657, dealing in real estate had become an important source of income for various people. Donna Merwick counted that, between 1655 and 1657, sixty-two property transfers took place.[131] Rutger Jacobsz, who in 1652 had received a patent, by 1664 had sold four parts of it, so that by then there were at least three or four houses on the original lot. The south side of present-day State Street was, in 1652, divided into patents of a length varying between eight and eleven rods and a width of five to eight rods, and distributed among seven people. By 1664, it had been subdivided and some fifteen owners had built at least twelve houses.

Laying out the village

It seems that the village construction designs started by Van Slichtenhorst were continued by the Beverwijck authorities. The surveyors Dirck Jansz, Abraham Pietersz Vosburgh and, later, Harmen Bastiaensz immediately went to work.[132] As surveyors, they had to measure out pieces of land, demarcate their boundaries with beacons or indicate to the owner where he should locate his beacon poles. In addition, they had to prepare diagrams and report the dimensions and extent of the lots. They were to keep a systematic register of properties for the West India Company. This documentation of trade and properties, the order of plots with designated streets and building lines, reveals what Van Oers described as 'the true nature of Dutch building practise: urban planning in a strict sense of the word. Centrally guided and painstakingly documented, but with respect for individual rights. It strongly suggests an open, visible and democratic way of working.'[133]

All three surveyors were carpenters, and surveying was probably not their usual work; they may not have had much knowledge of this kind of work, and actually may have learned it from having observed others. The work required that they be at least literate and have knowledge of some simple mathematical techniques. Even if they only had minimal education, they may have been aware of the principles taught at the engineering schools at, among others, Leiden, Franeker, or Amsterdam – principles that were widely accepted in the Republic. They may have been taught some of the practical applications that were spread through the institution. This school, which was founded in 1600, was an important step toward the institutionalized training of land surveyors and military engineers, as well as master carpenters and bricklayers.[134] A man like Vosburgh may have had some training, and at least had some mathematical knowledge, as he was involved in building bridges and houses, and also worked a saw mill.[135] He may not have been familiar with books such as those of Jan Pietersz Dou and Johan Sems, *Practice of Surveying* (*Practijck des Landmetens*, 1600) and *Of the Use of Geometric Instruments* (*Van het gebruyck der geometrijsche instrumenten*, 1600), in which the making of maps and measuring parcels of land, in order to determine the surface area, was emphasized. But undoubtedly he knew how to solve such problems as: 'Someone wants to build a bridge of which the arch will be a half round, of which the inner diameter CD is 12 feet; question: how many bricks does one need to make the same?' or: 'One wants to build a house as above; question: how many bricks does one need?' or counting boards, instead of bricks.[136]

Together, the committee and surveyors started the work in the northern part of the area within the 3,000-foot jurisdiction around the fort. Streets were staked off more or less conform to topographical circumstances. The river and the hills were the east and west boundaries for the early settlement, and the area between the kills and along the existing old Indian trails continued to be the first places to build upon. The lots bordering south and north of the first kill were quickly distributed. Also, on the north side of present-day State Street, house lots were given away in 1652, while along the east side of present-day Broadway various people who had asked 'to settle between the two kills' were granted this permission, and could start or continue their building process (see illustration 9 and 56). Unlike several other Dutch settlements such as New Amsterdam, Batavia (Jakarta), or Capetown, there was no one dominant direction of settlement, but two.[137] As in Rensselaerswijck, the first concentration of buildings was along State Street and the first kill, Broadway, and in the area in between – the area called *De Fuyck*. At more or less right angles to the two main roads, other roads were laid out in the course of time. Perpendicular to State Street were the present-day James and Pearl streets, and running to the west from Broadway were the present-day Maiden Lane, Steuben, and Columbia streets. This street pattern was the basis for further development and in 1749, when more streets had been laid out, the Swedish traveler Peter Kalm wrote that 'the long streets are almost parallel to the river, and the others intersect them at right angles. The street which goes between the two churches [State Street, then between the English and Dutch churches] is five times broader than the others...'[138]

Building along Broadway in a northern direction went as far as the area of the third kill. This kill was also referred to as *Vossenkil* (Fox kill), probably because Andries de Vos had his residence on it. The first kill north of the Fort, the *Fuyckenkil* (hoopnet kill), was later also called *Ruttenkil*, perhaps after Rutger Jacobsz, who had built a small water wheel on this kill behind his house. The naming of first and third kills leaves the open question: Which one was referred to as the 'second kill?' One would expect that it was either the stream that ran down State Street, or the stream running down Maiden Lane. But while the *Vossen* and *Fuycken* kills are well indicated on the 1770 Yates map and the 1794 De Witt map, these other streams are not. They only appear on the Römer map; but during Paul Huey's modern excavations on State Street, in 1972-73, not a sign of a stream bed was found.[139] Yet, in April 1650, Cornelis Theunisz van Westbroeck (Bos) had to give up one rod at the south side of his garden, which stretched as far as the second kill (Appendix 8, II, no. 17). The gardens, which were then allocated to Cornelis Theunisz, Pieter Bronck, Andries Herbertsz, Jan Thomasz, Hendrick Westerkamp, and Jan van Hoesem, were all located between the first and second kills. The patroon had planned 'a broad road to the river' between the old garden of Jan Thomasz and Andries Herbertsz.[140] The combined width of these gardens seems to fit between the first kill and the stream running down Maiden Lane. There is, however, also a chance that in the course of time the names changed and that the *Beverkil*, a creek south of Fort Orange where several individuals settled, and which was designated as the ferry place by Kiliaen van Rensselaer, was initially called the first kill, and the *Fuyckenkil* the second. After the settlement was concentrated north of the fort, the *Beverkil* became less important, while the *Fuyckenkil* became the center of the settlement – and perhaps then was named the 'first kill.' In this study, however, I adopt the basic assumption that the stream indicated on Römer's map as running down Maiden Lane was the second kill during the 1650s.

Magistrates, committees, and surveyors did follow certain town-planning principles, including rules prohibiting construction of alleys and houses that exceeded the specified building line (*rooilijn*), and there were clear instructions for the surveyors. Maps for the systematic inspection of buildings were probably used, and the surveyor made note of everything in his surveyor's book.[141] The problems involving the streetline that had occurred in 1647 at New Amsterdam provided the magistrates of Beverwijck with some good examples and guidelines. In an ordinance of July 1647, it was mentioned that people in New Amsterdam had extended their lots far beyond the survey line, and that they actually had set up hog pens and privies on the highways and streets. To resolve the problems, the ordinance warned the inhabitants of New Amsterdam not to proceed with the construction of any building on lots, or the enclosing of any gardens, without the prior knowledge of the appointed street surveyors.[142]

Also in Beverwijck, streetlines were staked out. In February 1653, Willem Fredericksz Bout was allowed to build a horsemill on his own lot in Beverwijck 'on condition that he would keep within the streetline,' and a month later Harmen Bastiaensz was fined ƒ50 for cutting down a street line post – which offense, according to the court, could result in 'serious consequences' in the future.[143] Patents and conveyances sometimes also refer to the layout of streets. When in August 1662, for example, Jan Labatie sold a lot to Jacob de Hinsse, reference was made to Labatie's patent of October 25, 1653, which stated that forty feet in breadth in front, toward the street, and twenty feet behind, should be 'taken off for the highway.' As at Manhattan, however, not everyone immediately obeyed the rules; the distribution of new lots, on the contrary, encouraged several individuals to obtain as much land as possible. Mistakes were made and rules violated, and the minutes of the newly established court offer an opportunity to gain insight into the policies followed for distributing and dividing the lots in the *bijeenwoninge*.

The distributed lots were, as mentioned, not always equal in size, which created problems. A good month after the court's establishment, its minutes mention that Hendrick van Driest had moved his clapboard fence to enlarge his garden. With the advice of Abraham Staets and Jan Labatie, who were appointed to 'make an inspection and take such measures as they saw fit,' this problem evidently was resolved, as the case does not appear in the minutes again.[144] Another case continued an already existing dispute among three neighboring bakers over the ownership of a certain lot close by the first kill, an area where several bakeries had been established. It indicates what a great change Stuyvesant's interference was for the members of the community. The court solved the bakers' problem by assigning the lot in dispute to a younger baker, while enabling the original, elderly inhabitant of the lot to live on the same lot for the rest of his life. The problem dated from the time that the *bijeenwoninge* had belonged to the patroonship and when, according to the third baker, who disputed the younger baker's ownership, 'no one had any ground of his own.'[145] Even people who became magistrates violated the rules. Sander Leendertsz, on his own authority, enclosed more land than was mentioned in his patent, saying that it was promised to him, and the court told Goosen Gerritsz that he 'must without delay move back the palisades enclosing his lot at the hill as far as the stakes that have been set by this court on the street line, besides the palisades.' The carpenter Stoffel Jansz, 'having set a post near his lot far outside of the line in the common road, to begin enclosing from that point,' did not get away with it either, and was likewise ordered to remove the said post.[146]

Very important to a surveyor's job was that he be a trustworthy and a responsible servant of the West India Company who would not, because of incapability or by deliberate fraud, cause the official record of patents to differ from the actual land holdings of the burghers.[147] But in the spring of 1654, Abraham Pietersz Vosburgh, disregarding the oath he had taken, was involved in several disputes among the inhabitants 'on account of faulty surveying and also on account of some gardens which without the knowledge of this court are being fenced in or have been granted away.'[148] He had, for instance, given Dirck Bensingh's garden, which formerly had been granted by the court to Jacob Jansz Schermerhoorn, to Andries de Vos. Twice he refused to hand in his surveyor's book, and he was told that at the third refusal he would be taken into custody. Of course, the case created tensions. 'That stake standing there is more trustworthy than you are, and if you do not survey according to those stakes standing there, you survey falsely,' Bensingh said while Vosburgh was at work. Vosburgh had no power to give away his garden, according to Bensingh, as the authority in the matter rested with the court. Vosburgh and Andries de Vos said that they would give the garden back to him if he would not make much fuss about it, and pay and reimburse them for the expenses incurred by them on it. But then it appeared that Vosburgh had misled the court on more occasions. He had given a garden lot to his brother-in-law, Lucas Pietersz, and to Cornelis Vos. The lot on which he dwelled himself he had, without the knowledge of the court, extended as well, and he also had added a piece to Anthonie de Hooges' garden lot. In July, the court fined Vosburgh 250 guilders and dismissed him from the office of surveyor. Andries de Vos could keep the garden he had enclosed, but the lot on which he resided and which he had, contrary to the order of this court, enlarged far beyond its proper limits, he had to reduce in size 'according to the pleasure of this court, without any objection,' while the whole extent of Lucas Pietersz's garden reverted to the court.[149] The carpenter Jan Roelofsz was chosen and appointed as a new surveyor, to work with Harmen Bastiaensz.[150] As of April 27, 1655, Vosburgh had not yet paid his fine and was given additional time to do so; but he was ordered to draw in the lines of his lot, which he had extended contrary to the orders and regulations, within 48 hours. Undoubtedly insults and perhaps even slanderous remarks had been thrown around during the whole affair; Vosburgh's wife Geertruy Pieters even had to appear before the court and declare that she had nothing to say about any of the members 'but what is honorable and of good repute.'[151] The committee distanced itself from the affair. Volckert Jansz Douw and other magistrates had shown Vosburgh the length and breadth of his lot, extending to certain stakes that were driven into the ground; but, Douw testified, Vosburgh had 'governed himself accordingly and he was not aware that any additional land was afterwards granted to the said Vosburgh. Also, as sworn surveyors ought to be trusted to make the survey that he has not verified the number of rods of the survey.'[152]

Distributing and dividing the land remained a sensitive issue, and the task of surveyor indeed was not always an easy one. In May 1655, Harmen Bastiaensz *rooymeester* requested that he be discharged from the office of surveyor, or properly be sustained therein, 'complaining among other things that Willem Teller has again moved out his palisades and that others had done likewise.' The court decided that he should be upheld in his capacity of surveyor and that Willem Teller would be notified to move back the palisades of his garden.[153]

Roads and bridges

A year later, the same Teller again caused problems. In the spring of 1656 he did not hesitate 'to close and fence off at both ends with boards and palisades a certain common or public road, alley, or footpath situated opposite from Abram Pietersz Vosburch, going to the river, whereby the same was made useless...' It was also found that he had enclosed within the fence of his garden 'about four and a half feet of ground of the aforesaid footpath or public road from the wagon road to the river and consequently lessened its width,' aside from the fact that he had 'encroached at least a foot or two along the public road outside of the old palisades and thereby narrowed the public wagon road.'[154] The variety of nouns used for the concept of 'road' (*wegh*) does not help to establish exact locations. Generally, roads were referred to as main road, highway, wagon road, or common or public road (*herewegh, wagenweg, gemeene weg*), and they were meant for traffic by horse and wagon. Present-day State Street, on the 1659 sketch named *Jonckaerstraet*, at one place was referred to as public woods road (*het gemeene bosch padt*). In several property transfers it was named the common way or road, the wagon way, or the broad or great street (*gemeene wegh, wagenwegh*, or *breede wegh*).[155] At certain times it may have been no more than a wide, muddy trail with a spring in the middle, which as a stream ran down to the river. By 1663, it seems to have been a relatively heavy travelled road, as in 1661 various inhabitants had moved out to present-day Schenectady. Many people went six or seven miles inland on this road, carrying goods and merchandises on wagons and horseback to Schenectady, in order to trade them with the Indians.'[156] Jeremias van Rensselaer in 1664 referred to this road as the Maquaes *padt* (trail).[157] A good eighty years later, it was described as being five times broader than the others, and serving as the marketplace. Maiden Lane was indicated as *Rontstraet*, on the 1659 sketch, while Broadway often was referred to as 'the street,' and later sometimes as *Handelaersstraet, Coestraet*, or *Brouwersstraet* (Merchants Street, Cow Street, or Brewers Street).[158]

Unlike at New Amsterdam, where at that time some streets were paved, nowhere in the Fort Orange records is there a reference to any street pavement.[159] It is first mentioned in a document from 1678, when inhabitants were ordered to 'clear their paved streets before these houses,' and in October 1679, when the sheriff was 'strictly enjoined to see to it that the streets and sidewalks [*stoepen*] are to be paved at the very earliest opportunity...'[160] Seventy years later, there still were various sand roads; Peter Kalm wrote that 'the streets are broad and some of them are paved.'[161] One wonders whether hogs, which in the 1650s were damaging the bastions of Fort Orange, would have damaged the streets as badly as they did at Manhattan, where hogs had to have rings through their noses to prevent them from rooting up the streets. The animals caused the roads and streets of the city to be unfit for driving upon in wagons and carts. In Albany, an ordinance like that did not come about until 1677.[162]

At a time that in the Republic behavior in the public space was more regulated, and having seen that at Manhattan people piled the streets with materials as wood, timbers, rubbish, filth, ashes, or dead animals, Beverwijck's magistrates wanted to keep the situation in their village under control.[163] In January 1653, for example, when baker Jochem Wesselsz piled his lumber in the public road, they were quick to warn him to remove it within twenty-four hours. In 1654, the street between the church and the fort must have been dirty, as in June the magistrates provisionally gave permission to those in the community who kept cattle to 'close the common road with gates so as to form a corral for the cattle, on condition of building a footstep on each side.'[164] This may have been the reason that the street later sometimes was called *Coestraet* (Cow Street). The practice of herding cattle from the church to the pastures may have been maintained for a long time, as in 1749 Albany's streets were described as being very dirty 'because the people leave the cattle in them during summer nights.'[165]

By the end of 1659, however, it seems that many people used the streets as they liked. Sleighs, carts and wagons could make use of the streets only with difficulty as burghers piled up their firewood there, greatly inconveniencing others. Golf-playing individuals damaged burghers's windows in the streets, and people had to watch out to avoid being injured by them. Regulation was needed, and the commissary and magistrates of Fort Orange prohibited the playing of golf along the streets, and ordained that none of the inhabitants would be allowed to let any firewood lie in the street for more than ten days, under penalty of confiscation of the wood and an additional fine of *f*25.[166] Apparently it was hard to change people's habits, and in 1670 people were ordered again to clear the streets in front of their houses of firewood, garbage, and manure within eight days.[167] It may have been the responsibility of a resident living at a particular frontage to keep a certain part of the road clean and accessible in order to protect people's shoes. Tjerck Claesz, in 1658, was allowed to lease his house if he would 'raise the ground behind his house and make a stoop in front of the house.'[168] Similar stoops may be shown in various drawings made by James Eights.

In 1651 and 1652, Steven Jansz had built several bridges across the kills, but in 1654 they were seriously damaged by heavy floods. This was a great inconvenience to the burghers, and Abraham Pietersz Vosburgh accepted the contract to repair immediately the bridge on the third kill.[169] It was not until September that he finished the work, and was paid *f*75 in partial payment for the two bridges.[170] A 1667 contract between Jeremias van Rensselaer and Jan Labatie for the building of a bridge suggests that these bridges looked fairly identical. As we noted above, the bridge in the *bijeenwoninge* over the *Fuyckenkil* had benches to sit on.[171] The bridge built by Jan Labatie across the kill, at Van Rensselaer's hill near *Broer* Cornelis, also had benches on both sides 'with leanings of 16 to 18 feet long.'[172]

Lots and fences

Thirty-two and possibly forty-two people received lots in 1652 (see appendix 3). Most of the first lots were located around the first kill and along Broadway, and were more or less rectangular in shape. From the first kill, they ran lengthwise north toward *Jonckerstraet* (State Street), and to the south toward the present-day Beaver Street, with their width bordering on the road or kill. From *Jonckerstraet* they also ran north toward *Rontstraet* (Round Street). From the river, the lots ran lengthwise from east to west, first mostly on the east, later also on the west side of Broadway. In general there was a regular pattern, although the village was not completely arranged in a grid. Lots were adjusted to the landscape, with the streets more or less parallel to the river and the hill, while the others ran parallel to the kills and connected river and hill. Other Dutch colonies showed a similar pattern. Remco Raben found that in Colombo (Ceylon/Sri Lanka)and Batavia (Jakarta), settlements were generally split up into rectangular blocks of houses of roughly the same dimensions, the blocks being intersected by straight parallel streets, showing a grid-like pattern.[173] Mauritsstad, located over against Recife in Brazil, had an orthogonal street pattern, with alternate streets ending on a bastion, while in Recife, two roads ran parallel to the coast and crossroads developed later.[174]

The lots were not equal in size; farther to the north, near the third kill, they were noticeably larger than the ones closer to the first kill. They also were not always of a regular shape, as the width or length of one side could be different from the opposite side. Rut Adriaensz was given a rectangular lot of four by five rods; but Frans Barentsz, for example, received a patent for a lot of six rods and five feet width at the west side, while at the east side it was five rods and six feet wide. The north side of his lot was nineteen rods, while it measured twenty-one rods on the south side. The unit of measurement was primarily the Rhineland rod, which had become standardized as equivalent to 12.36 feet (377.7 cm). Sometimes the Amsterdam rod was used, which equaled 12.071 feet to a rod. To measure quickly, one would count the number of steps he walked.[175] As a comparison, in Cape Town (South Africa) in the second half of the seventeenth century the division of lots was much more equal. Garden lots were ten rods wide, and uniformity also existed in the building lots, which were ten by five rods, while the streets were four rods wide.[176] Darret Rutman wrote that in Boston, in 1631-32, the half-acre house and yard lots in the center and an allotment in the town fields were not enough for one family.[177]

Walking around on the village's roads, one would have seen many fences, because a person who had received a lot for a house or garden was required to fence it in. These structures of posts and transverse boards clearly marked the area a person had at his disposal. The area within the fenced-in space was the private domain of the owner, and one could build a house, barns, sheds and other necessary buildings on the property, or lay out a garden or a bleach field. Fences provided protection against the hogs, chickens and other animals roaming through the village. At the same time, however, a fence marked the public domain; once it was built, an owner was no longer able secretly to take more ground or extend his lot. In November 1659, owners of private gardens at the riverside were ordered to build their fences closer to the water within eight days; they were to make them seven to eight feet high, to prevent access by the enemy from the riverside.[178]

The look of Beverwijck, as it slowly but surely filled with houses during its twelve years of existence, remains fairly unclear. Nothing of the buildings of the 1650s and 1660s is left, nor are there any paintings or drawings of the village. Even the kills are no longer visible, as they were covered in later times. Only by going onto the Hudson can one see where these (now underground) streams empty into the river. The street pattern has survived, but the steep drop of the hill disappeared after State Street was graded in the early nineteenth century.

Often, when looking for images of this time, one is referred to various sketches of the town of Albany made by James Eights, 'as it was in 1800, 1812 and 1814.'[179] Eights made watercolor duplicates of some of the views, and lithographs based on the originals were published later. His 'View of State Street from St. Peter's Church' does not show the stream running down State Street, which was drawn by Römer. This stream seems to have been fed from a spring halfway up *Joncker-straet*, and may have been covered sometime between 1698 and 1805. The painting does show, however, how steep the drop of the hill still was at present-day Lodge Street, then called *Berghstraet* (hill street). It also shows the coastal plain at the foot of the hill, where the earliest inhabitants of Beverwijck dwelled. By 1660 they had extended as far westward as Lodge Street.[180] Most likely, descriptions of 'a house at the hill' meant the houses located at the bottom of the hill in this watercolor. Many of the lots distributed in 1652, 1653 and the later 1650s were described as being located *aen het geberghte* or *aen de bergh*, which has frequently been translated as 'on the hill,' but which actually means 'at the hill.'[181]

The only known view of colonial Albany from an earlier date is a redrawing of an unlocated original, which shows the city as it appeared about 1720. A partially erased inscription in the lower left margin indicates that the work was copied from an original drawing of 1763. The original most likely was the work of William Burgis, who was in New Amsterdam from about 1717 to 1722 and who may have traveled to Albany to make a drawing similar to the one he made of New York City.[182] The copy of the view, however, does not provide us with much detailed information. The kills are missing or barely visible, while the buildings at *Jonckerstraet* seem incomplete. Although the houses seem small, very uniform and not detailed enough for the purposes of this study, they may reveal some truth about the size of Beverwijck's houses, before these were replaced by houses, similar to those depicted by Eights. (See illustration 11).

Houses

Not much clear information can be found on the size and arrangement of houses. What I did find on size I collected from the *ERA* and put in Appendix 4. Most house measurements are not clear; sometimes they appear as, 'as long as it is under its roof' (*in sijn kap ligt*), or 'in the back until the fence of...' I have excluded

10. James Eights (1798-1882), View of State Street from St. Peter's Church downhill to Dutch Church. *Water color on paper, circa 1850 (Albany Institute of History & Art, bequest of Ledyard Cogswell. jr.).*

descriptions like these from the table. Details about the structure and arrangement of the houses can be found occasionally in conveyances, a rare (superficial) type of building contract, or scattered throughout other source materials. In 1657, the village contained roughly 120 houses; the descriptions I collected date from the years between 1652 and 1683, and are limited to some twenty-four houses (see Appendix 4). Even these few descriptions provide us with only a few details per house, so that it is impossible to make generalizations about the architecture of Beverwijck's houses. Mostly, architecture was a product of the carpenters, who found good business there – and of whom I counted at least thirty, perhaps working at different times, throughout the period (see Appendix 6). They came from various areas in the Republic, sometimes even from other countries, and they may have known different building types and techniques. Their ideas and professional skills, combined with the wishes and demands of the person for whom they built the house and the available building materials, ultimately determined the appearance of early colonial architecture in the upper Hudson area.

The dimensions of the twenty-four houses suggest that Beverwijckers generally had small dwellings. They were not narrower than houses of common folk in the Netherlands in the seventeenth century, but they were less deep – the depth of houses in Haarlem, Gouda, Groningen and Dordrecht generally being three times the length of their frontage.[183] Regulations like those of the Republic, prescribing requirements that houses had to meet, do not survive – if they ever existed – and the limited number of descriptions does not allow for generalizations.[184] The

11. Unidentified artist after an original drawing probably by William Burgis, (ca. 1718-1721). Prospect of the City of Albany. *Ink and wash on paper, 1763 (Albany Institute of History & Art, gift of Mrs. Richard C. Rockwell).*

twenty-four houses varied in width between fifteen and thirty feet, and averaged about twenty to twenty-one feet (six or seven meters), which is similar to the width of houses in Recife (Brazil), and also similar to townhouses in seventeenth-century Holland.[185] Their length averaged about twenty-five feet, which in general was shorter than in New Amsterdam, where houses were about thirty feet or longer.[186]

Usually, the measures of a house were noted in Rhineland rods, Amsterdam rods, or wood feet; sometimes the length of a house was measured in boards, meaning that a board (or plank) equaled sixteen Rhineland 'feet.' In November 1651, Evert Jansz *kleermaecker* (tailor) obtained a lot in the *bijeenwoninge* on condition that he 'enter into a contract like other settlers and build a house at least two boards long'; and when Jan Verbeeck, in 1657, sold his house and lot to Claes Hendricksz, he promised to deliver a house of two planks length.[187] Verbeeck's house probably had been built sometime in 1649. In Beverwijck we can find several houses that did not meet the standard that may have been set in Rensselaerswijck. Pieter Bronck leased a house of one board length to Jacob Teunisz in 1659, and in 1658 Jan Harmensz sold a house that was eighteen feet long by eighteen feet wide (see also illustrations 12 and 13).[188] Houses in Fort Orange were not smaller: Evert Pels, in 1658, owned a house there of about thirty-nine or forty feet in length.[189]

Many houses could easily be enlarged by adding an *uytlaet*, or a 'side aisle.' Such additions indicate that these houses were built with a so-called H-frame or anchor beam construction, which made it simple to add an addition later. The added side aisle ran the full length of the building between the frame of the central part of the building and the low outer wall. This house type developed from the

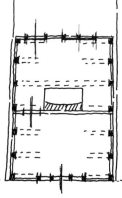

12. Henk Zantkuijl, house of Cornelis Vos, 1658. Usually measures were noted in Rhineland rods, feet and inches. De Vos's house is in front 18 feet and 4 inch wide, in the rear 18 feet. The side wall of both house and lot run aslant. The house is one foot narrower than the lot, so that there is drip space on both sides of 6″. It clearly shows an urban structure: a narrow, deep lot; the house adjusted to the lot. Henk Zantkuijl made this and the following reconstruction drawings of houses, based on the information of Appendix 4. The reconstructions (illustrations 12-21 and 24-26) are based on the following assumptions:
1. All houses have been drawn on the rooilijn, or on the building line, one step toward urban structure. As is visible on the New Amsterdam maps, the road is important.
2. The houses arbitrarily have been drawn in the right corner of the lot. This is an assumption: they could very well have been built in the left corner or in the middle. The New Amsterdam map shows that a location in the corner is favorite.
3. For the boundary line of the lot a 6-inch drip has been assumed. In situations that it did not occur, it was especially mentioned (for instance, with the old house of Cornelis Vos, illustration 24). A drip was not drawn in cases that the house was of a same width as the lot. It is possible that the lot was later divided, while the house was already there. In that case it is not strange that the house was the boundary.
4. The reconstructions are subjective, and based on knowledge of houses in New Netherland and houses in the Dutch Republic. Also knowledge of the woonhuys (dwelling) and experience in drawing reconstructions have influenced these reconstructions. Houses have been drawn as wooden houses with the well-known anchor beam construction and the much occuring arrangements, and wooden walls. They are all houses before 1660. Only when it was mentioned that a house was built of brick or of stone the drawing deviates from the original plan.

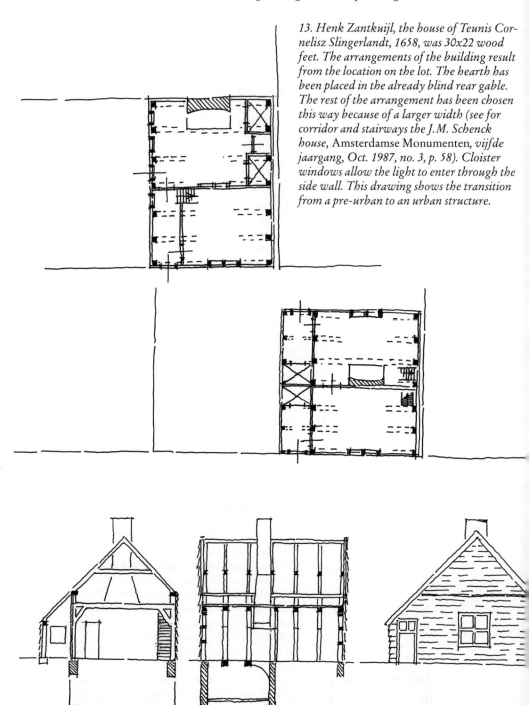

13. Henk Zantkuijl, the house of Teunis Cornelisz Slingerlandt, 1658, was 30x22 wood feet. The arrangements of the building result from the location on the lot. The hearth has been placed in the already blind rear gable. The rest of the arrangement has been chosen this way because of a larger width (see for corridor and stairways the J.M. Schenck house, Amsterdamse Monumenten, *vijfde jaargang, Oct. 1987, no. 3, p. 58). Cloister windows allow the light to enter through the side wall. This drawing shows the transition from a pre-urban to an urban structure.*

14. Henk Zantkuijl. The house of Jan van Hoesem, 1657, had a 5 ft. side aisle, a room, cellar, and attic; chosen is for a completely wooden house with a brick cellar. Brick cellars already appeared in 1659. They were often plastered. High water in 1660 caused the plaster wall of one cellar to fall down, which suggests that there were several brick cellars. Lot size 10x4 rods, which shows a pre-urban structure.

one- or three-aisled house, where people and animals lived under one roof. The frame consisted of a number of bents, each at a distance of about four to six feet from the other. Each bent was made up of two posts, a tie-beam, and two corbels or braces. These bents could be put together when lying down, and easily set up by three or four men. Originally, the side aisles often were the width of a cow or a horse; but later this was more in accordance with the width of a bedstead and other furnishings. A five-foot side aisle could provide space for a cellar, mezzanine room, some bedsteads or a small room.[190] Many houses in Beverwijck seem to have had this construction (see illustration 14 and 15). Tjerck Claesz, in 1660, sold a house of twenty feet long by thirty feet wide, including a side aisle, and Jacob *de brouwer* (the brewer) asked permission to build an addition to his house in 1652.[191] In 1660, the deaconry of Beverwijck's church paid ƒ33-18 to carpenter Willem Bout for the building of a side aisle on the already existing poorhouse.[192]

Usually the gable end of these houses was on the street side, although that was not always the case. Jurriaen Jansz Groenewout, for instance, in 1669 had a *dwarshuys* (literally transverse house), which had its gable end perpendicular to or

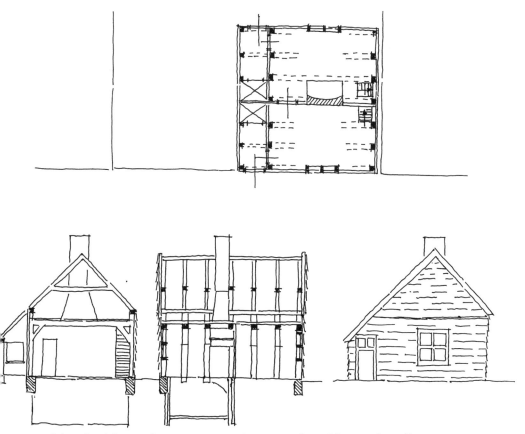

15. *Henk Zantkuijl, house of Jan van Hoesem. Same as 14, but with a wooden cellar. According to archaeological sources, wooden cellars appeared for many years.*

16. *Henk Zantkuijl, house of Ulderick Cleyn, 1658. Considering the measures of the house, this should be a* dwarshuis *(the roof timbers run parallel to the street). Chosen is for a narrow front house, corridor or small hall. The hearth is against the front wall. Chosen is for cloister windows because of the distance between the posts (See also Lucas van Alen House in* Amsterdamse Monumenten, *5de jaargang, no. 4, (Dec. 1987), p. 63-64). Shows a pre-urban structure on a lot of 4 x 8 rods.*

crosswise on the street[193] (see also illustration 16). Houses of this type did not, like the above-mentioned houses, have a so-called *osendrop*, the space that caught the water from the roof on the lot on which the house was built, usually varying from one foot to six inches. Instead, they had a drainage system on the street and the rear part of the lot.[194] In the Republic these *dwarshuizen* had dated back to the Middle Ages, and appeared more often in the provinces in the eastern part of the country, while in the province of Holland, houses usually had the gable end on the street

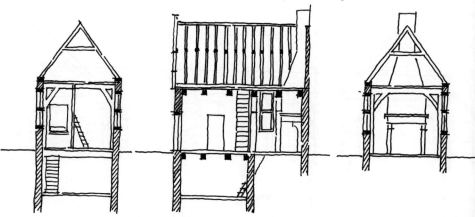

17. *Henk Zantkuijl, reconstruction of the house of Jacob Loockermans, 1659? Also a pre-urban structure. A small house on a 30 feet-wide lot. The small inner hearth here as kitchen. The small room is drawn as side room with in it a bedstead, as that could often be found in a side room. Brick walls with wooden skeleton. This version has a wooden cellar, as in Albany that was common until in the 18th century.*

side. A carpenter like Steven Jansz, who came from Nijkerk, may have brought along architectural customs from that part of the Republic.

In larger towns in Holland, lots were often narrow and long; and in the first part of the seventeenth century, the house was usually divided into a *voorhuys* (front house or entrance hall), with a direct connection to the street, and a *binnenhaard* (inner hearth) behind it, in which a fire could be kept. The *voorhuys* was used as work or business space. To use the *binnenhaard* efficiently, its space had to be lower than the *voorhuys*, and sometimes the floor level was lowered. This created enough room to make an *insteekkamer* or *opkamer* (mezzanine) above it, which also could be heated, and thus could serve as extra sleeping or living space. *Binnenhaard* and mezzanine received light through the higher *voorhuys*. In modest houses the *binnenhaard* functioned as living area and kitchen, while in more spacious houses these two functions were more likely separate. Often a kitchen was built in the back against the rear wall; light could still enter the *binnenhaard*, as this kitchen was only built over half the width of the house. By 1650, the *voorhuys* had often lost its business character because of the separation of a sideroom in houses without shop or workspace, and had become an entrance hall (see illustration 17 and 18).[195]

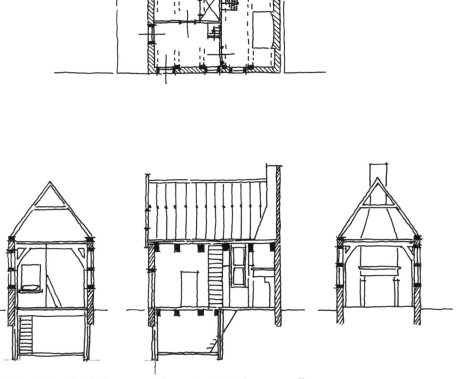

18. Henk Zantkuijl, the same as illustration 17 with a stone cellar.

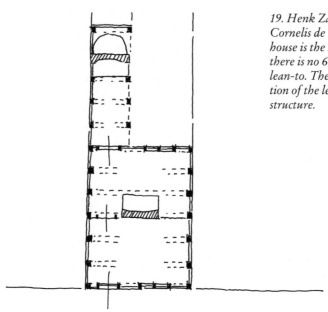

19. Henk Zantkuijl, house of Cornelis de Vos, 1661. Since the house is the same width as the lot, there is no 6″ drip. The oven is in the lean-to. The alley is in the continuation of the lean-to. An urban structure.

Beverwijck houses were mostly modest buildings, and many were probably like the houses of Jan van Hoesem or Jacob Loockermans, subdivided into a cellar, chamber and a garret. Stairways or ladders were used to go to the garret or cellar.[196] Hilletie Tyssingh, for example, rented the front part of her house, consisting of a cellar, *voorhuys* and loft, to Jan Harmensz; and in 1676, Elias van Ravensteyn rented the *voorhuys* from Hendrick Rooseboom. In this *voorhuys*, Van Ravensteyn would make two workbenches for gunstock making.[197] The *voorhuys* was the first space one would walk into from the street, and often people extended this space toward the outside by adding a lean-to (*afdackie*) or a counter (*toonbank*). Attics were usually used for storage of grain, and offered sleeping space. Thus living area, storage and work space were all under one roof. Like early houses near Manhattan, Beverwijck's early houses were of a more rural type; they could have windows and doors in the sidewalls, contrary to town houses, which only had those openings in the gable ends. Both houses, however, were similar in function, in that they each had a public part, an unheated front room where business was done.[198]

In order to get as much use out of their space as possible, many people, in addition to a side aisle, built an *afdackie*, or lean-to, against the house. These were open sheds, covered with a roof. Annetie Bogardus had a side aisle on the east, and a lean-to on the west side of her house. Cornelis Vos, in 1661, wanted to sell his house with a 'little *afdackje* on the east side of the house with the chimney and oven which thereto belongs'[199] (see illustration 19). Some used the lean-to for storage, while several people had an oven in it. The house sold by Jan Verbeeck to Claes Hendricksz had a kitchen of sixteen feet square attached to it, with a chimney and oven therein.[200] Perhaps because of the danger of fire, and to keep the heat out of the house in the summer, ovens are sometimes also mentioned as being separated from the house; for example, along with the great house, Rem Jansz would

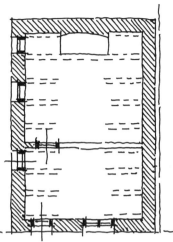

20. *Henk Zantkuijl. The house of Pieter Adriaensz Soogemackelijck, 1661, is 'fitly built up with stone on all sides.' Assumed is a lot of 4x10 rods, since otherwise it would be a decagon. The walls have been drawn 60 cm thick, because of the indication 'stone' (klipsteen). This, as a comparison with the houses that are built of stone. On a lot of 10x4 rods, this is a pre-urban structure.*

also receive a bleaching field with an oven.[201] In general, people seem to have kept on building fairly small dwellings. In July 1676, the commissaries of Albany ordered that 'all new buildings fronting the street shall be substantial dwelling houses, not less than two rooms deep and not less than 18 feet wide.'[202]

By 1664 in New Amsterdam, houses were mostly built of brick and had tiled roofs, while those on the outlying farmsteads were often made of stone. In contrast, houses in Boston, according to Colonel Cartwright (a royal commissioner sent from England in 1664), the houses by that time were 'generally wooden.'[203] Houses in Beverwijck were usually made of wood, like, for instance, Pieter Adriaensz's house, which was built sometime in 1653-54, or Pieter Bronck's log house.[204] That carpenter Thomas Chambers' nickname was 'Thomas Clapboard' may be an indication of his method of building with overlapping planks. But as was done in patria, people sometimes put brick on the inside of the clapboard walls, which, according to Henk Zantkuijl, created the possibility of plastering these walls and thus have brighter rooms. This may have been the case with the house of Jan Lambertsz, which in 1659 was 'built up all around with a half-brick wall.'[205] It is also possible that the 'half-brick' was put on the outside wall, to make the outside of the house look nicer. In 1661, Pieter Adriaensz sold his house in Beverwijck, which was 'fitly built up with stone on all sides.' This was probably done with a full-size brick, which would have been put on the outside[206] (see illustration 20 and 21).

In time, the looks of the house would become more important. When Thomas Jansz Mingael, in 1658, sold a house with 'the gable built up,' that could mean that the house was provided with a *topgevel* (gable end), or that it may have been built up with bricks on the outside. More people embellished their houses this way; Sander Leendertsz' house, in 1662, had a stone gable.[207] In 1676, it became a requirement that houses facing the street were to be 'built in front on the street of brick or quarry stone and covered with tiles, the commissaries intending and desiring that this order be strictly observed...'[208] In the next century, they would still do this. Peter Kalm, in 1749, wrote that the houses were 'very neat, and partly

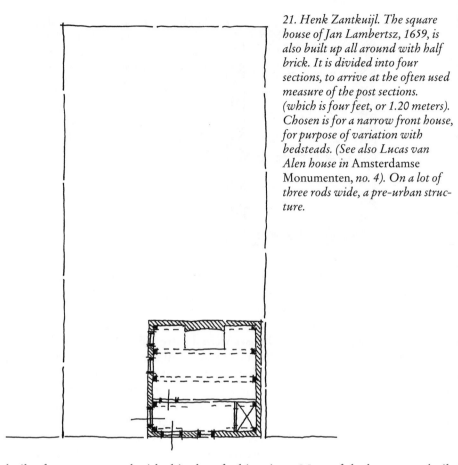

21. Henk Zantkuijl. The square house of Jan Lambertsz, 1659, is also built up all around with half brick. It is divided into four sections, to arrive at the often used measure of the post sections. (which is four feet, or 1.20 meters). Chosen is for a narrow front house, for purpose of variation with bedsteads. (See also Lucas van Alen house in Amsterdamse Monumenten, no. 4). On a lot of three rods wide, a pre-urban structure.

built of stones, covered with shingles of white pine... Most of the houses are built in the old Frankish way, with the gable end towards the street, except a few, which were recently built in a modern style.' These front gables often were the only brick walls, while all the other walls were made of boards. 'Houses built of both wood and brick have only the wall towards the street made of the latter, all the other sides being boards,' Kalm continued. 'This peculiar kind of ostentation would easily lead a traveller who passes through the town in haste believe that most of the houses are built of brick.'[209] The houses in the watercolor, 'Pearl Street near Maiden Lane in Albany as it appeared in 1805,' shows this feature.[210]

On January 18, 1655, Stuyvesant and the council had decreed that houses should no longer be roofed with straw or reed, and that chimneys should not be constructed of clapboards or wood.[211] Beverwijckers seem to have followed this order; Jan Baptist van Rensselaer, for example, in the spring of 1655 replaced the reed and straw that had covered the patroon's house with pantiles; and in February 1656, Willem Jurriaensz's straw roof was replaced by one of planks in order to prevent, as far as possible, all danger of fire.[212] In various conveyances, we find that chimneys indeed were made of brick; but, nevertheless, they often remained

22. James Eights (1798-1882), North Pearl Street west side from Maiden Lane North as it was in 1814. *Watercolor on paper, ca. 1850 (Albany Institute of History & Art, bequest of Ledyard Cogswell. jr.).*

the cause of fires, as orders in 1656 and 1658 for people to keep their chimneys clean reveal.[213]

It is not known whether people in the 1650s had porches like the ones described by Peter Kalm a hundred years later.[214] When Jeremias van Rensselaer wrote his brother about the appearance of the repaired patroon's house, he wrote that the cellar was level with the ground, and had a door with a window next to it; but he did not make any mention of a porch. He described the various types of windows, which provided the exclusive lighting source for a house, in more detail: one was a half-cross window (*bolcosijn*) of three lights, while some were cloister windows (*klooster cosijnen*). Gutters, rarely described in early documents, were an important means to catch the rainwater, and usually were hewn out of logs (see illustration 23; also of the patroon's house 49, 50; and of the poorhouse 64, 66).[215]

Houses may have been decorated or equipped in various ways. Some artisans, by bringing their work outdoors, invited potential customers almost into their front rooms. Evert Nolden used an extension table, and a cover over it, during the time he leased Femmetje Alberts' house.[216] People also attached signs to their houses. Cornelis Vos must have had a use for one when, proposing to sell the old house in which he lived, he wanted to keep the signboard. *Lange Maria* (Tall Mary) had a sign for her tavern, which probably had the tavern's name *De Vrouw Maria* (the woman Mary) on it.[217] These signs could display information about

23. Henk Zantkuijl, three types of windows: bolkozijn, kruiskozijn (cross window), and klooster-kozijn (cloister window).

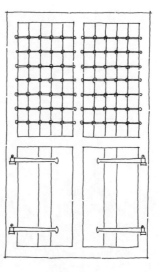

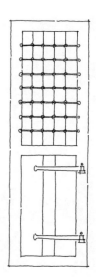

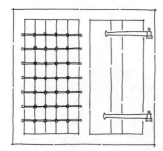

one's trade in many different ways. Jacob de Hinsse, for example, the local surgeon in the 1650s, may have had a sign on his dwelling on which a lancet and shaving knife were crowned by scissors, or the shaving knife and the scissors were crowned by the lancet. Such signs were fairly common for surgeons in the Netherlands. Sometimes the good Samaritan was depicted on it. Very early, a surgeon sometimes also placed a round, red-white-and-blue-striped pole with a yellow top before the door, or put it in one of his windows – which could have indicated that the master of the shop pulled teeth and healed broken legs (the white color), shaved beards (blue), and drew blood (red).[218]

In the course of twelve years, the number of houses steadily increased. As lots were subdivided more houses were built upon them, providing living space for a continually increasing number of inhabitants. While in the fall of 1652 there were about forty houses, there would be more than 120 in 1657. Some property conveyances illustrate how the area taken by the West India Company became more densely populated. A house sold by Rem Jansz in 1657, for example, was similar to a house sold by Pieter *de Maecker* in 1659 – exactly as wide as the lot (see illustration 24, 25). One of the houses sold by Cornelis de Vos was only four feet narrower than the lot on which it stood.[219] De Vos, when his old house was to be torn down, would have to provide a proper dripspace to the neighbors; and when Pieter Hartgers in 1658 sold a house built upon a part of the lot granted to him, he had to leave 'six inches free on both sides of the lot for drip' (illustration 24).[220] That houses stood fairly close together is also suggested by the condition Abraham Pietersz Vosburgh made when, in 1657, he proposed to sell a house and lot, probably located south of the first kill, namely that 'door and windows on the south side of the seller's house shall remain closed [*blint*].'[221]

By the time the English took over New Netherland, Beverwijck had become a village, and perhaps even resembled a small town. It had a densely populated center where houses, outbuildings, sheds, stables and small houses were cramped into

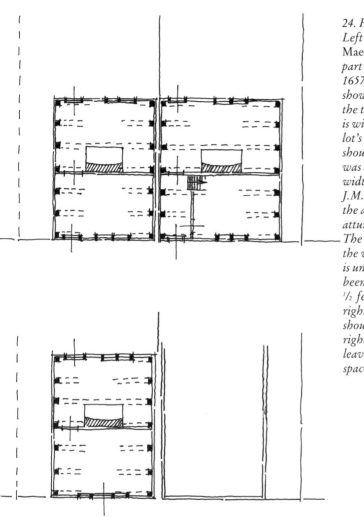

24. Henk Zantkuijl.
Left part is Pieter de
Maecker, 1659. Right
part Cornelis de Vos,
1657. The upper sketch
shows that, according to
the text, De Vos's house
is with one side on the
lot's boundary line. It
should have a 6˝ drip. It
was an old house. The
width is similar to the
J.M. Schenck house and
the arrangement
attuned to that house.
The drawing below:
the width of the left lot
is unknown and has
been assumed to be 25
¹/₂ feet (the lot on the
right). A new house
should leave on the
right side a drip of 6˝,
leaving a common drip
space of one foot.

the limited available space. To calculate the average density is difficult, as there is no exact number of houses given for an exact acreage. The 120 dwellings mentioned by the minister, in 1657, probably covered a larger area than the ground enclosed by the stockade in 1659, as this defense only surrounded a part of the *bij-eenwoninge*. But outside the palisades, to the north as well as to the south side, were dwellings as well.[222]

Other spaces and constructions on the lots

Besides side aisles and lean-tos, other spaces were created on the lots for storage and work. Barns, sheds, hayricks, hog sties, chicken pens, cow and horse stables – all were crammed into the limited space available[223] (illustration 26). Interesting is

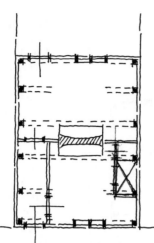

25. *Henk Zantkuijl, house of Gysbert Jansz, 1662. The house has the same width as the lot, so that there is no urban drop space. It seems that it concerns a town house or an urban lot, but because there is no drip side it is possible that it was a pre-urban house on a larger lot. With urbanization of the surroundings lots were divided; the measure of the house has become the measure of the lot. Because an urban situation developed the choice has been to draw a side room in the front house.*

the mention of little houses which seem to have been on the lots of various inhabitants. On the lots of Pieter Bronck and Annetje Bogardus, it was specifically noted that there was an Indian house (*wildenhuysje*).[224] It could be that the '*hansioos* little house in the rear wherein are a chimney and bake oven,' on the lot that David Schuyler had bought from Annetje Bogardus, was the same as the 'little Indian house' mentioned by Jonas and Pieter Bogardus, when they wanted to sell their mother's lot. The word '*hansioos*' is used elsewhere to describe jewelry, which suggests that it is an Indian word referring to the trade.[225]

Lots, on average, were not very large (and certainly not after they had been subdivided), and except for dwelling space they provided space for several other uses. It seems to have been fairly common for inhabitants to set aside a piece of their property for putting out their white linens to bleach, in order to keep them sparkling white. Annetje Bogardus had a bleach field behind her house and the minister may have had white shirts as well, especially after 1658, as Gysbert van Loenen then carted sod for 'mother for her bleach field at the poor house.'[226] Claes Hendricksz was allowed the use of a certain yard only to stack wood and for bleaching; and when Rem Jansz *smit* (smith) sold a house to Cornelis Theunisz, the sale included a bleaching field with a baking oven.[227]

Laundry may have been done at home by Pieter Bronck and Jan Bastiaensz van Gutsenhoven, as they had a well on their lot.[228] In 1657, Claes Hendricksz bought a lot, together with a well and a hog sty; and in 1666, Jeremias van Rensselaer paid someone three beavers for drilling his well.[229] Wells are not mentioned frequently in the records of the 1650s, but they probably were on many lots. When, in 1682, people who lived near the hill had thrown their manure into the streets, it was 'to the great detriment of the lower wells.'[230] That Carsten Fredericksz, in 1667, had a dry well on his property suggests that sometimes wells dried up.[231] Fredericksz then may have had to either drill a new well or, if it was impossible to find water on his lot, to share one with others. Jan Harmensz did that in 1658. He had a one-third interest in a well. While more people probably shared wells, there also were common wells, one of which Dirck Jansz Croon was the overseer in August

26. Henk Zantkuijl, reconstruction of the house of Symon Symonsz Groot. Nothing is known about the stable. Assumed is that the stable is of a normal size, and that it has a large side aisle for the horses. The middle part is for the wagons, straw, and hay. The dimensions of lot and house suggest a pre-urban structure.

1660.[232] People did their washing and laundry close to a well. In 1679, the well masters of two wells were ordered to 'see to it that no water is poured out near the wells, and that no rinsing is done there, in the space around the wells, which is to be paved.'[233] Some people seem to have shared their drainage as well. In 1654, Sander Leendertsz, Willem Fredericksz, Jan Machielsz, Jan Hendricxz and Herman Bastiaensz together dug a sewer and were ordered to build a bridge across it at the first opportunity, as 'otherwise it tends to obstruct the public road.'[234]

Gardens

Most people had a garden on the lot on which they lived, but separate garden lots were distributed as well. Along the river, between the fort and the village, a whole strip of gardens stretched along the river. They all were fenced in and of different sizes, but on average they were smaller than, for example, the regular garden lots of ten rods' width in Cape Town, measuring on average about five by seven rods.[235] The frequently flooding river left a strip of fertile soil, so that the gardens close to the river usually produced good crops. The river, on the other hand, also frequently caused problems. In 1654, the flooding washed away the West India Company's garden, of which scarsely a clabboard remained.[236] Adriaen van der Donck mentioned the numerous vegetables that were grown by the inhabitants, such as 'various kinds of salads, cabbages, parsnips, beets, endive, succory, finckel, sorrel, dill, spinage, radishes. Spanish radishes, parsley, chervil (or sweet cicely), cresses, onions, leeks, and besides what is commonly found in a kitchen garden.' In their herb gardens one could find 'rosemary, lavender, hyssop, thyme, sage, marjoram, balm, holy onions, wormwood, belury, chives, and clary; also pimpernel, dragon's blood, five-finger, tarragon, etc., together with laurel, artichokes, and asparagus, and various other things...'[237] Sometimes they also grew pumpkins, cucumbers or vegetables introduced to them by the Indians, such as corn and squash. Various people had cherry, apple or other fruit trees. Probably, as would be the case some hundred years later, women tended to the gardens.[238]

The ground around Fort Orange no longer belonged to the patroon. The inhabitants did not need to pay rent to him anymore, and had gained more freedom. They could buy property and sell it again. They were more or less free to build on it what they wanted. But now that the lots within the area taken by the West India Company had been distributed among the inhabitants, together they became more responsible for the development and maintenance of the area. In October 1653, the director general and the magistrates of Fort Orange and Beverwijck levied a general tax on the houses, lots, and private persons trading in the village. A finished dwelling should pay 15 guilders, and if leased, the tenant and owner should each pay half. A vacant lot or garden was taxed half as much, and a private person, not having any house or lot, one pound Flemish. The moneys collected by these taxes were to be used for such collective safety issues as the repair of the fort, the building of a guardhouse, or other works, such as necessary repairs to the bridges in Beverwijck.[239]

Constructions of general interest for the community

Corps de guarde

Fort Orange, of course, was the largest structure in the area of importance for the community; here, I only refer to the work of archaeologist Paul Huey, who has devoted an entire dissertation to this important fort.[240] But in the course of time, buildings of great importance for the community were built in the *bijeenwoninge* as well. According to the sketch, which probably was drawn in 1659, a corps de guarde was located close to the hill on the north side of *Jonckaerstraet*, where Pearl Street now crosses State Street (see illustration 4). Other than a reference to it in March 1655, in order to locate Jan Thomasz' lot number four, which was 'on the west side of the guard house,' the records don't mention this building.[241] Its strategic location at the place where the *Maquaes padt* entered the *bijeenwoninge* provided good supervision of people entering and leaving the village by the trail, which certainly was heavily travelled by fur-carrying Maquaes. The corps de guarde may have functioned as a first prison and screening room for people arrested at night, as was the case in the city of Amsterdam in Holland, which had four of these guard houses, or *kortegaards*. People who were caught there by the *schout*, his servants, or the rattlewatch during the night were first brought to a *kortegaard*, where the problem was taken care of by the captain of the guard. Sometimes the detainees were locked up until both parties could come to an agreement, or until the next day when they could be taken to another prison. It often happened, too, that detainees were released. Whether an individual got away with just a warning, or had to pay a fine or appear in court, or whether he was brought to another prison, seems to have depended on the nature of the offense he had committed.[242] It is not clear whether it was here that the deacons, in the summer of 1654, twice (for unknown reasons) provided 'the woman in the guard house' with bread, flour, and a chain.[243]

The blockhouse church

However strange it may sound, safety was one of the reasons for building a church. Living on the frontier, the settlers were frequently reminded of possible danger. Paying ransom to release prisoners who had been kidnapped by the Indians, and being confronted by those who had been captured, brought the Indian threat directly into people's daily lives. Repeatedly, settlers made donations toward activities having to do with the Indian threat. Events in other areas of New Netherland also influenced actions in the upper Hudson area. After the Peach war had begun at Manhattan in 1655 – leaving at least fifty colonists murdered, more than 100 (mostly women and children) captured, and 200 without their possessions – the consistory gave 200 guilders to the widows and orphans there. Three girls, the sisters Hendricks, were kidnapped that year by the Indians on Adriaen van der Donck's land (in present-day Westchester County). After they had been freed, two of the sisters, Saartje and Ytie, were housed in Beverwijck with Jan Koster van Aecken and Frans Barentsz Pastoor, while the deaconry paid for their board.[244] Money was also paid for the ransom of several Frenchmen – as fellow Christians, even though they were Catholic.[245] The sisters' experiences, or stories told by the two girls, may have brought the fear of warfare with the Indians closer to the community.

In the beginning of 1656, a blockhouse was built 'according to resolution, of [...] feet square and about a man's stature in height.' Four representatives of the community (*gemeensmannen*), however, desired to have it pulled down, and in its place they contracted for a house with trusses.[246] This blockhouse, according to Jan Baptist van Rensselaer, would by no means be able to save the farms, horses or cattle; it would only serve 'as defense of our body and limbs.'[247] The heavy wooden structure had canon mounted behind loopholes in the overhanging balconies, while its location in the middle of the intersection provided views of anyone approaching from the north, west, south, or the river. The building would be a place of refuge in case of an enemy attack.

At the same time, however, the blockhouse would be used as a church. During religious services women were seated on the ground floor while the men sat in the balcony, where they would be available immediately to man the canons should the need arise.[248] The West India Company had not considered creating an opportunity to keep religious services within Fort Orange, as had happened at New Amsterdam, or in Fort Oranje at Itamaracá (Brazil), which contained a chapel.[249] It took about four more years, after Beverwijck's court was established, for a decision to be made to build a church; and even then the building, a block house, would also function as a defense.

The changes made in 1648 to the patroon's house, of which the rear part was used as a church, and the convenient staircase that was ordered built on the outside of the church in January 1650, apparently provided churchgoers with enough convenience to keep this building in use for church services for another number of years.[250] Not much is known of this first 'church.' Perhaps the furniture made in 1645 or 1646 by Willem Fredericksz Bout was still used, while the improvements made in 1648 by Abraham Pietersz Vosburgh seem to have been sufficient, as well, to maintain services there for some time.[251] People who did not find a seat on one of the nine benches may have brought along their own chairs and found a place where they could hear *dominee* well, and also discuss the latest news with a neighbor. Women probably sat separately from the men. It may have been that, like some places in the Republic, the nine benches were placed against the walls and were occupied by the men, while the women would have had separate seats in the middle, perhaps their own chairs.[252]

Right from the start, following the separation of the *bijeenwoninge*, maintaining this 'church' did not happen without conflict. According to Jan Baptist van Rensselaer, the new court was 'not even ashamed to oppress God's church,' as commissary Dijckman prohibited the repairs to the patroon's house, in which Van Rensselaer and *schout* Gerrit Swart lived. He did not want to allow the enlargement of the church or the previous *packhuys*, which had become too small, Van Rensselaer wrote, because of 'the daily growth of God's blessing in his congregation.' In addition, the house was in great danger of fire due to the dilapidated chimney, which was leaking everywhere. When Van Rensselaer proposed to enlarge the same site by building a middle wall, Beverwijck's magistrates wanted to keep him from doing this; but he ordered the work to continue anyway[253] (see illustration 44). In October, Johannes Dijckman and some members of Beverwijck's court discussed how 'those of the colony, directly contrary to our instructions, intended to make improvements to their *logement*' (lodging). The court considered that Van Rensselaer and the *schout* thus far had occupied and resided in the house 'by sufferance'; and after mature deliberation, the matter was left to Stuyvesant's judgment.[254] Despite the bickering, services were still held in the rear

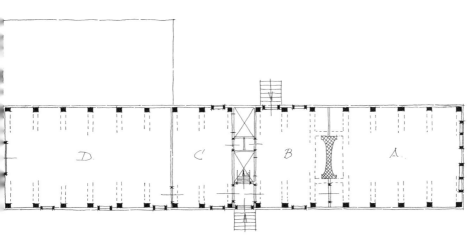

27. *Henk Zantkuijl, drawings of the patroon's house, which was used as a church for several years. Ground plan. Reconstruction of the situation before 1648. A = the front house or 'chamber' (meeting room); B = room in the middle house, kitchen, living room; C = room in the 'rear house'; D = ware house, or church with side aisle of 15 feet width. See also illustrations 28, 42-50.*

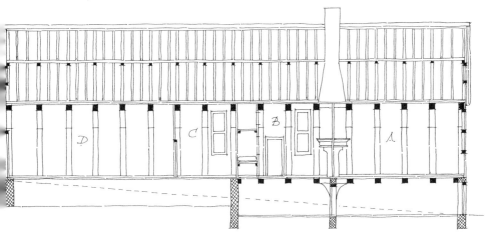

28. *Henk Zantkuijl, longitudinal section of the patroon's house. Reconstruction of the situation before 1648. A = front house or 'chamber'; B = room in the middle house; kitchen, living room; C = room in the 'rear house'; D = warehouse or church. See also illustrations 27, 42-50.*

part (*achterhuys*) of the patroon's house in November 1655.[255] Despite Kiliaen van Rensselaer's instructions, no church would be built in his colony for a good twenty-six years (see for various stages in the improvements to the patroon's house Zantkuijl's illustrations 42-50).

It was not unusual for the building of a church to take so much time. In Batavia (Indonesia), for example, financial difficulties, a fire, and a preference to build fortifications first had prevented services from being held in a good church for a long time; although the church consistory had been founded in 1621, a good city church would not built there until 1643.[256] But on April 18, 1656, Stoffel Jansz and Jan Roelofsz, 'in accordance with the specifications and by public bid,' contracted to build a blockhouse church in Beverwijck.[257] The court tried to find a new source of taxation to pay for it, and even asked the inhabitants of New Amsterdam for a liberal contribution, 'inasmuch as we gave for the church there.'[258] In February, the patroon subscribed in the amount of f1,000; f1,500 was appropriated from the fines imposed by the court of Fort Orange, and f1,000 to f1,200 and a bell were given on behalf of the West India Company.[259] On June 2, 1656, Rutger Jacobsz, one of the magistrates, laid the cornerstone of the building at the junction of present-day State Street and Broadway.

In general, colonial ecclesiastical architecture could not match its counterpart in the Netherlands. This was the case in Beverwijck and Rensselaerswijck, as well as in other Dutch colonies such as Batavia (Indonesia) or Colombo (Ceylon/Sri Lanka). Buildings were made to be functional, and adjectives describing the beauty of a particular structure in the upper Hudson area were rare. The West India Company, due to a lack of money and perhaps the subordinate position of the church, never commissioned the construction of an impressive church. In contrast to Spanish or French colonies, for example, churches and municipal buildings in the Dutch colonies remained modest in appearance and scale. The two architectural exceptions were the beautiful palaces in Brazil, *Slot Boa Vista* and *Huis Vrijburgh* in Mauritsstad, which were not financed by the company, but largely by the governor of Brazil himself, Johan Maurits van Nassau Siegen.[260]

The blockhouse church was not a monumental building, but according to *dominee* Schaets it was a pretty little church (*mooy kerckien*) that had been built in the heart of the community.[261] The structure, which was built of heavy wooden timbers in a square configuration, was erected squarely in the middle of the intersection of the two roads, so that the large weather vane in the form of a rooster could be seen from all directions.[262] This location gave it a central place in the community, while, even though it was still a small community, it may have created a certain sense of space.

For the interior of the church, Reynier Wisselpenninck was contracted in the fall of 1657 to build a baptistry, which together with the choir, was finished in the following spring. In May, the floors were laid and a window was provided in the choir.[263] The choir may have been the place where the sexton set the tables and two benches ready for the Holy Communion. By 1664, the church owned a table cloth and four napkins for this special service, which was held four times a year. A silver beaker, an earthen pitcher with a silver lid, and a pewter pitcher were used to pour and share the wine, symbolizing the blood of Christ.[264] The church interior itself may have been fairly simple. Starting in May 1660, the whole building was cleaned once a year: The walls were whitewashed and the floors scrubbed, and in 1667 there was a chandelier that needed to be scoured annually, as well. Stained glass windows with the coat of arms of Jan Baptist van Rensselaer and several magistrates of Beverwijck adorned the church, and likely there was a board to announce which psalms would be sung during a particular service. A pulpit present-

29. In 1715 a stone church replaced the existing block house church of 1656. By constructing the new church around the outside of the old wooden structure regular services could be continued, and only had to be interrupted once during the construction. In October 1715 services were suspended for two Sundays, when the old blockhouse church was disassembled and removed (Albany Institute of History & Art).

ed by the Amsterdam *classis* 'to inspire the congregation with more ardent zeal' arrived in 1657. Cornelis *Kystemaecker* (furniture maker) did some work on it in 1659, and perhaps provided it with the hourglass that is still attached to it.[265] The old pulpit, which was made by Willem Fredericksz Bout in 1645 or 1646, may have found a suitable place in the new church at the foot of the new pulpit, where the reader or precentor may have used it as a lectern – as it was not as high and elevated as the minister's place, but yet at a good location to be heard and seen.

Women sat downstairs in the new blockhouse church, and the men upstairs. It is unclear where the two benches, made in 1659, or the chair for the consistory were placed. Perhaps the nine old benches and the magistrates' bench were brought over from the old church. Nor is it clear whether these were closed benches, meaning that they had a small door at the side, whether there were any other benches or arranged seats in church, or whether people would bring their own chairs and place them wherever they preferred.[266] Many churches in the Republic had an open space in the center, where people could walk around. The fact that, in 1665, the inventory of a needy woman, *Trijntie Jans,* included a church stool suggests that, also in Beverwijck, people attending the service could bring their own chairs to church and place them wherever they liked. In Europe, folding chairs of more or less distinguished design had been used for this purpose since the Middle Ages. Some people may have preferred to stand during the service, thereby showing respect; at the same time, standing made it easier to switch places during the sometimes lenghthy services.[267]

Before July 1658, the churchyard had been in the *bijeenwoninge* as well; from just north of the fort, it seems to have been moved to a place south of the lot of Teunis Spitsbergen.[268] On the Miller map of 1695, the churchyard is shown between Hudson and Beaver streets. Not all burghers were buried here; Jeremias van Rensselaer, for example, was buried in the patroon's garden, which was close to the first churchyard; and Philip Pietersz Schuyler, who died in March 1683/4, was buried in the church. In 1694, *dominee* Gideon Schaets was buried there as well; it is unknown whether other people in the seventeenth century had their resting place in the church.[269]

The poorhouse

For several years, the authorities considered the patroon's house sufficient to serve as a house for worship and divine service. It is interesting that, instead of immediately building a new church in 1652, they first paid attention to another function of the church as a public institution: charity. That the arrangement of social care was one of the first concerns in a young, far-from-wealthy community may be interpreted as a urban reflex, typical of Holland, where care is constitutive for the community. The plans already initiated by the court of Rensselaerswijck were continued by the West India Company. Among the patents distributed in April 1652 was a patent to the deacons of the church for a lot, eleven rods in length and five rods in width, to 'enter upon, cultivate and employ and use the same for the need of the poor, without us, the grantors retaining any right, title or interest therein, but desisting from everything, from now and forever for the behalf of the poor.'[270] Likely it was on the same place as where, at the time, it had been planned by the patroon. To provide for the poor seems to have been part of a general policy of the Republic, which was followed by the company; in 1653, the deaconry of New Amsterdam erected a house for the poor as well.[271]

Between 1652 and 1654, millers, carpenters, masons and other artisans were paid for providing and carting boards, lath, stone and other building materials to the poorhouse. During 1653, payments were made for bricks, windows and work on the poorhouse; and in November 1653, Jacob Jansz van Noortstrant paid boarding money to the poorhouse, which suggests that the building was ready by then.[272] In June 1656, Peet Jelle was paid for laying up brick on the poorhouse, so that these walls later could be plastered, making the rooms brighter[273] (see illustrations 62-68). Although none of the sources mentions its location, the poor farm built in 1657 may have been on a different lot, since it was fenced in as well. The deacons may have followed the example of the board of overseers of the poor for Manhattan, who in 1655 had bought 'for the behalf and best of the poor a certain bouwery.'[274] In 1658, a bleach field was laid out on the poorhouse lot, and in the summer of 1660 the house was enlarged with a side aisle and a lean-to. In April 1669, there was a garden on the lot.[275] (See illustration 68)

In June 1657, *dominee* Schaets wrote that he had been able to live in the poorhouse, since there were not that many poor as yet. Unless people called the poorhouse *dominees huys* (*Dominee's* house), it seems that the situation had changed by June 1660, when the deaconry started paying artisans for work on a minister's house, suggesting that Schaets may have moved elsewhere and that the building was being used for the distribution of alms.[276] Although there is no mention of it in the records, it could very well be that the poorhouse also functioned as a community building for some time. People who came from afar may have met there after church, the consistory may have had its meetings there, the deacons may have paid bills for the deliveries of various kinds of alms, and other activities may have taken place such as the stringing of shell beads, called *sewant*, distribution of alms, and perhaps teaching.

A school

Dominee Schaets originally was a teacher, and his instructions did include teaching. There is, however, no evidence that he taught in the poor house; perhaps he instructed catechism there, although that probably happened in the church. Concerning the regular teaching, the only actual reference to a school building is the one already mentioned in 1650, when Arent van Curler and Goosen Gerritsz were appointed as a committee to oversee the building of a school. That anything came of this is unlikely, as the sources mention no specific school building. Gideon Schaets, if he taught at all in Beverwijck, probably did this in the poorhouse, when he lived there. In the Republic children were sometimes taught in a former monastery, but in many places there were no specific school buildings. Adriaen van Ilpendam, and Ludovicus Cobes for a short period, like most school masters in patria, probably taught in their own dwellings. In Manhattan, schoolmasters kept school in rented houses. A new school had not yet been built there in 1650, and it would not be until 1652 that the place 'where the Nine Men usually meet' was mentioned as a central place where school was kept.[277] Mention of an actual school building in Beverwijck would not occur until far into the eighteenth century.

Mills

Mills were of great importance to the community. Unlike Virginians, who used the mortar-and-pestle well into the eighteenth century, northern settlers ground their grain in mills – and without mills, a community had no flour for bread and other daily food. In the New England town of Springfield, the loss of a gristmill in 1675 left some inhabitants 'on the brink of despair, with talk about abandoning the town rampant.'[278] Sawmills were just as important, as they provided boards to build houses and other necessary structures. No wonder Kiliaen van Rensselaer was excited when he first heard that the mills in his colony actually worked.

Since Pieter Cornelisz had reported, in 1638, that the first sawmill in the patroonship was in operation, several other mills had been constructed. In 1640, the first gristmill was entirely finished, and it was reported that it ground excellent meal.[279] From 1648 until 1654, the mills at the fifth kill were leased by Rutger Jacobsz and Pieter Cornelisz's former helper ('boy'), Barent Pietersz Coeymans. In February 1654, Jacob Jansz Gardenier, nicknamed Flodder, obtained the lease of these two mills for eight years.[280] This gristmill was so important for the community that in 1653, despite their mutual animosity, the West India Company helped the patroon build a redoubt at the fifth kill, in order to protect the mill against a possible English attack.[281] But most of the time this gristmill was out of order, or was 'too inconvenient for the inhabitants on account of the sailing back and forth, which regularly was made more difficult because of the breaking of the ice, or winter time, or high water.' By 1646, Pieter Cornelisz already had contracted with Anthonie de Hooges to build a horse-powered mill in Greenbush.[282] This mill was rented by Flodder in 1647, and by Evert Pels from May 1649 until 1658.[283] At the Normans kill were two sawmills that, between 1652 and 1672, were rented by Albert Andriesz *de Noorman*. The mill east of the Hudson, to the south of the Poestenkill and Thomas Chambers's farm, was leased for six years in 1656 by Abraham Pietersz Vosburgh and Hans Jansz van Rotterdam. From February 1653 to 1654, Flodder rented a sawmill at Bethlehem, which had been taken over by Eldert Gerbertsz.

Although the various mills in the colony supplied the village with their products, the presence of a gristmill in the *bijeenwoninge* would make the village less dependent on the patroonship, and was considered of great importance for the community's interest. When, at the beginning of 1653, Willem Fredericksz Bout asked for permission to erect a horse-powered mill for the convenience of the burghers, he was granted permission to do so on his own lot if he would keep within the street line. Regarding his request for exclusive privileges, however, Bout was referred to the colonial government at Manhattan.[284] A year later, the court mentioned that they would like to see him and Rutger Jacobsz build a proper horse-powered mill on a lot that had been taken by Sander Leendertsz 'for the use and convenience of the burghers here, the said place being all the more suitable therefor because it is close to the kill and the river, so that it is convenient to convey the grain to and from it by water.' (Appendix 8, I, no. 9). Thus far, the court had not been able to find a more suitable location for 'this necessary structure.'[285] It seems that Bout had his horse-mill later, not on this particular spot, but somewhat more to the north, on a lot that he had bought from Cornelisz Theunisz (Appendix 8, II, no. 18). In November 1660, he and Arent van Curler promised to deliver a horse-mill on his lot in proper running order, with two good draft horses to be used in the mill for three years. Reyer Cornelisz leased it for that time. Two years later, Van Curler sold his half of the mill in Beverwijck to Bout for *f*900 in good beavers, and Bout sold the mill, house, horse-mill with the stones, and the lot and garden on the same day to Jeremias van Rensselaer, in exchange for a house and outbuildings on the other side of the river.[286] In the *Fuyckenkil*, Rutger Jacobsz was granted permission in 1656 to make or suspend a waterwheel for a small mill behind his dwelling house.[287] In April 1659, Pieter Bronck and Harmen Bastiaensz requested permission to build a sawmill on the *Beverkil*. The request was granted by the court, on condition that Abraham Vosburgh have the first choice of location, as he was the first applicant.[288]

Some sawmill owners possessed a yacht to deliver the boards for the villagers at the shoreline in Beverwijck. Grain was transported to the village by boat, frequently by canoe, and it was stored in people's attics. The attics in the patroon's house and the poorhouse, and sometimes even the attic in the church, were also used for storing grain.[289] Perhaps Van Slichtenhorst and his committee had a special delivery and loading place in mind when they stipulated that there should be a broad road to the river between the gardens of Andries Herbertsz and Jan Thomasz.[290] (Appendix 8, II, no. 14, 15). In view of the fact that several bakers had had their lots just south of it since 1650, next to the first kill, it seems reasonable to assume that flour from the mills was brought here by boat. After 1652, the continuing concentration of bakers in one area probably encouraged the creation of a central place for unloading grain and flour, as did the presence of two breweries near the second kill, and the building of another brewery on the lot between the river and one of the bakers. Of the five breweries north of Fort Orange, three were between the river and present-day North Broadway, with two more to the west along the *Fuyckenkil* (see illustration 56). A broad road connecting Broadway with the river certainly would have made it easier to transport flour and grain to the various bakers and breweries by cart or wagon. That there were at least three men in the village, who at times were called *de karman* (cartman), suggests that there certainly was work for them to do.[291]

Beverwijck did not have a weighing house – unlike Manhattan, which established such a facility in the spring of 1654.[292] In November 1656, Jacob Jansz van Noortstrant, originally a cooper, was appointed as wager of the casks. In 1660, when so many different sizes of casks were in circulation that there was great confusion among the burghers, Van Noortstrant again applied for the position.[293] His appointment in 1668, as sealer of weights and measures, lends credence to the idea that Van Noortstrant may have gone to people in years past to inspect the size, not just of the casks, but of the measures and weights as well.[294]

Brick and tile yards

In addition to the presence of saw mills, the existence of brick and tile yards was important for the construction of the village, as well.[295] There was good clay along the river in Rensselaerswijck; Van Rensselaer had sent over Cornelis Lambertsz *steenbacker* (brickmaker), who baked both tiles and bricks around 1630, perhaps a little south of the first kill.[296] It seems that, by 1634, Lambertsz had left the colony. In 1642, someone else may have been running the brickyard, as boys were needed to help with the making of brick and tile; but a year later, the patroon would write that he was in urgent need of a brickmaker. When he heard that there were brick-makers among the English at the Fresh River, he intended to contract them.[297] According to Hendrick Jansz Westerkamp in 1652, a brick yard may have been in operation 'a little south of the first kill, which belonged to the company and where they had a small house.' Nothing else is known about this brick yard. In January, 1652 Reyer Elbertsz, who in 1651 had leased some land between the third and fourth kills, asked for permission to burn brick. He was granted permission to try it, and if he were successful a formal order on the subject would be made; the site would then be shown to him.[298] In October 1653, Elbertsz obtained a patent for a larger lot than he had leased before; his land now extended not only to the north of the kill, but also included land to the south of it.[299] In her effort to locate the various brick and tile yards in Beverwijck, Pat Barbanell concluded that it is not possible to pinpoint the exact location of Elbertsz's brickyard; but she suggested that it may have been south of the kill.[300] Elbertsz was running the kiln at least until January 1660, when Jeremias van Rensselaer paid him for various kinds of bricks.[301]

North of the *Vossenkil*, Johan de Hulter established another brick kiln and a tile yard. De Hulter had sailed over in 1653; also aboard the ship was 'one extraordinary... [Steinbacker], ...who may have been the same person as Jan Andriesz de Graef, who was a brickmaker in the colony around that time.'[302] After De Hulter's death, his widow Johanna de Laet sold some of his property, including the tile and brick kilns. Pieter Meesz Vrooman bought the tile kiln for ƒ3,717 in 1657, and sold it two years later to Andries Herbertsz, who had been the surety for Vrooman when he had purchased the kiln.[303] In June 1659, Herbertsz delivered 4,000 pan tiles for the renovation of Jeremias van Rensselaer's house, at ƒ50 a thousand. A certain Jan Schoone may have worked the kiln at that time; in August 1660, this man was paid for having fired-up 3,000 pan tiles and ridge tiles. Gerrit van Slichtenhorst bought Herbertsz's kiln for ƒ1,900 in November 1662, on condition that a certain Kees Pot would work for one more year according to his contract with Andries Herbertsz.[304] After an ice flow caused serious damage to the kiln in 1666, Van Slichtenhorst apparently sold the kiln to Pieter Bont Quackenbos.[305]

The baking of bricks in De Hulter's brickyard was done by Pieter Jacobsz Borsboom. In 1657, Johanna de Hulter sold the brickyard for ƒ1,100 to Adriaen Jansz van Ilpendam; but it seems unlikely that the schoolteacher would have done the work himself.[306] Pieter Bont, who in later years would buy the tile kiln, seems to have been responsible for the work; in May 1657, Bont started a court case against Pieter Jacobsz Borsboom, whom he wanted to fulfill his contract with De Hulter, but Borsboom was released from his contract.[307] In addition to Bont, Andries Herbertsz may have done work in the brickyard as well, as he was paid several times by Jeremias van Rensselaer for bricks.[308] In 1668, Van Ilpendam sold the brickyard to Pieter Quackenbos.[309]

Barbanell did not mention another brickyard in Rensselaerswijck that seems to have been run, possibly for only a short time, by Ysbrant Eldersz, who on occasion was nicknamed the '*steenbacker*,' and who lived in Rensselaerswijck.[310] Jeremias van Rensselaer paid him several times for shaping stone (*steen vormen*), stone, and hard bricks at ƒ10 a thousand – the same price as the one asked by Reyer Elbertsz for his 'good bricks.' [311] Eldersz's brick-making operation does not seem to have been very successful, as in 1659 and 1660 he needed financial support of the deaconry on three occasions, while thereafter he became a steady recipient of alms until 1669.[312]

The brickyards produced a variety of bricks. In addition to 'good' bricks at ƒ10 a thousand, Reyer Elbertsz also delivered also bricks at ƒ8 a thousand, and ƒ6 a thousand, as well as 'very good' bricks at ƒ6 for 500, to Jeremias van Rensselaer in 1660.[313] Andries Herbertsz and Pieter Bont were paid several times for hard bricks (*moppen*) and regular bricks, and Jan Bryn was paid ƒ18 in beavers for 2,210 red bricks.[314]

After January 18, 1656, it certainly seems that there was plenty of work to do for people involved in brick and tile making. An ordinance on that date stipulated that chimneys were no longer to be made of wood or clapboards, and that roofs could no longer be covered with straw or reed.[315] By that time, several people also were having their walls bricked up, as described earlier in this chapter. Brick makers were even busy producing bricks for other areas in New Netherland: On various occasions, 'Fort Orange bricks' were transported to the South River, where they were used for the construction of chimneys and for brickwork at Fort Altena.[316]

Indian accommodations

Relations between the Indians and the Dutch around Fort Orange had been easier than at Manhattan. For the Indians, friendship with the settlers meant a choice of European trade goods and good deals, while for the Dutch it ensured a steady supply of beavers. Great efforts, then, were made on both sides to maintain good relations. Although Van Slichtenhorst stated that, between 1648 and 1651, not half a day could pass without Indians visiting, no documents reveal that the patroon's house hosted so many Indians during the years that it was occupied by the Van Rensselaers. Jan Baptist's letters detail various uses of the house, but mention no meetings with Indians. In general, relations seem to have been so positive between Indians and settlers – to the extent that, should the English bother the settlers, the Dutch could count on being able to 'use the might of the Mahicans and Maquaesen as lawful means of defense.'[317] Some meetings between Indians and Beverwijck's magistrates were held in the fort, but they seem to have taken place with a smaller number of representatives than in prior years.[318] When we read through the Fort Orange court minutes, Indians are first mentioned in an entry for March 4, 1653, almost a year after the establishment of the court. The issue before the court reveals that bakers counted on a steady presence of Indian buyers; but it is not clear how many natives were expected.[319] In November 1655, commissary Den Deckere wrote that 300 Maquaes had arrived, proposing to go fight the French Indians. It is not clear how long these Indians stayed, but this suggests that they continued to come in great numbers.[320]

Probably the natives stayed at private homes in the *bijeenwoninge*, which was allowed. In May 1654, for example, a party of drunken Indians was found at Jan van Hoesem's house. Willem Bout, who had provided them with good beer, was fined ƒ25; but Van Hoesem, who hosted the group, was not bothered.[321] The Indians may have stayed in the small bark house that Volkje, Van Hoesem's wife, had erected on their lot in 1652, and which the couple may have used to accommodate the Indians.[322] Van Hoesem's house was not the only place where these gatherings took place. Other settlers also had special houses to accommodate the Indians. Rem Jansz *smit*, Sander Leendertsz, Dirck Jansz Croon, Abraham Staets, and Theunis Cornelisz all had 'little houses' on their lots, the use of which is not explained. Sometimes they were specifically named 'Indian house' or 'little Indian house' (*wilden huysje*), and in one case *hansioos huysje*, which was probably used for the Indian trade.[323]

At least until 1655-56, it was probably common for Indians to be lodged in dwellings of individual Beverwijckers or in structures built by the inhabitants on their lots, and most likely this happened later as well. When problems with the Indians broke out at Manhattan in October 1655, Petrus Stuyvesant ordered that, for the following month, 'No Indian, coming to any place, village or hut, shall be allowed to remain there overnight, except in a special place, to be fixed for that purpose according to the localities of the village.'[324] Jan Thomasz, who had been building a shed to accommodate the Indians in 1657, was told to tear it down within three months, and was prohibited from using it during that time.[325] Apparently, private burghers were no longer allowed to build any structures for Indians on their lots. This prohibition, however, seems to have been followed only temporarily in Beverwijck. In February 1658, Jan de Wever was accused of serving beer to two Indians who lodged at his tavern, but no legal action was taken against De Wever for hosting them.[326] That the prohibition was not strictly applied in Beverwijck was also indicated when Maria Becker rented the house and lot of Catrijna Jochims in 1661. Maria was allowed to erect a small house on the lot and use it for her convenience, while she could also retain the use of a little house that was already there.[327] It seems that Thomasz was the only person warned by the court.

In August 1665, nearly 400 Oneidas and Maquaes stayed for more than a week in the *Fuyck*, waiting for a group of Onondagas, but no mention is made of their accommodations.[328] The natives caused no problems and, according to Jeremias van Rensselaer, behaved very well.[329] The English commander, Captain Richard Nicolls, must have been referring to Stuyvesant's order when he wrote, in January 1665-66, that he was 'surprised to hear that you do not persist in your own resolution and order, duly issued and founded on good reasons, to wit, that all Indians are to lodge in the houses erected by you for that purpose, but that on the contrary some parties, twenty, thirty, or forty strong, have been admitted to lodge in the houses of private citizens. What reason you may have for this I do not know, but it seems to me that you would do better to accustom the Indians to it that, no matter how small the party may be, they may lodge nowhere but in the houses built for that purpose at the expense of the inhabitants.'[330] The issue remained hard to resolve, and the officer was frequently misled in the continuing general confusion regarding the lodging of the Indians. In May 1672, the magistrates expressly forbade anyone from lodging any Indians, 'whether in large or small groups, directly or indirectly, except some old sachems, the consent to which remains subject to the consideration of their honors aforesaid.'[331] This order seems to have been followed, since on August 13 of that year some burghers presented a petition, 'praying a favorable answer to their request to build a shed on the plain for the savages for the profit of the entire village, as they derive no profit from those who come and go.' The court would examine 'whether it is most convenient to build such a shed on the plain or near the river.'[332]

Palisades

Beverwijckers may not have been afraid to lodge Indians in their houses or on their lots; but when war broke out between Dutch and Indians at the Esopus, in September 1659, the threat was felt stronger than ever before. After three Beverwijck inhabitants – Abraham Pietersz Vosburgh, Harmen Jacobsz Bamboes, and Jacob Jansz Stol – were killed there at the beginning of November, the commissary and former and current magistrates met in the house of Dirck Jansz Croon 'to plan a much-needed defense of this village of Beverwijck against attacks by the Indians in these dangerous times, and to have this defense built as speedily as possible with the materials at hand.' It was decided that the defense would be 'made of posts and planks, of eight boards high, with seven bastions to protect the curtains, which [fence] shall surround the greater part of the village of Beverwijck, the length of its circumference being 250 rods [83 meters].' Françoys Boon, Dirck Jansz Croon, Captain Abraham Staets, and Adriaen Gerritsz were appointed as overseers of the work, and they immediately summoned the wood cutters Carsten *de Noorman* and Harmen Bastiaensz to furnish as many posts as needed for the said work.[333] On November 24, it was reported that the work progressed daily. In order to prevent access by the enemy from the river side, everyone who owned property there was ordered to 'set back the fence of his respective garden to the line already laid down, and make the said fence of posts and planks from 7 to 8 feet high.'[334] In July 1660, Stuyvesant issued an ordinance for a one-time tax of 3 guilders for each chimney, in order to pay for 'the heavy expense they have undergone in putting up a plank fence against a sudden incursion of Barbarians, and other outlays made for the repair of bridges, etc. whereby the public treasury is very much exhausted...'[335] An undated small sketch or rough draft, which Joel Munsell has dated 1670, seems to have been meant as a rough design for the construction of these palisades.[336] (See illustration 4). The sketch indicates that there was an 80-foot distance for two blocks of houses, just south of Pearl Street. Two streets are named, *joncaerstraet*(present-day State Street) and *rontstraet* (now Maiden Lane). According to Munsell, this 'rounds passage' was kept open for patrol in times of threatened attack by the Indians or the French.[337] Present-day Broadway, which runs perpendicular to these two streets, is not named in the sketch, but houses are shown on its east and west sides. A bridge is shown where the street crossed the *Fuyckenkil*.

The decision to build a defense was a clear sign that, fifteen years after *dominee* Megapolensis wrote about how much the inhabitants trusted the natives, this faith had disappeared.[338] Instead of counting on the Indians' help in the case of a possible enemy attack, the settlers now feared them – and felt the need to protect themselves, not only against the English, but also against the natives, whom they once had trusted. The palisades probably strengthened the Europeans' feeling that they now had a home base, in which they were protected and safely separated from their sometimes dangerous surroundings; and in their anxiety and fear of a common enemy, the settlers were perhaps more joined together than before. For the Indians, the palisades may have marked an artificial divide between the settlers' area and their own. The defense, with its gates, openly demonstrated the distrust. Yet, Governor Nicolls's remark, in 1665, that great parties of Indians were lodged in the houses of private citizens, seems to suggest that the palisades would eventually not be a barrier to accommodating Indians in the village. In order to trade, and to give the Indians a fair chance to choose the goods for which they would sell their beavers, natives were allowed to trade their beavers where they pleased, which suggests that the Indians could freely wander from house to house in the village. When Stuyvesant was at Beverwijck in 1660, during a great crisis in the trade, he and the court were 'unable to discover any better expedient than to renew and maintain the ordinances heretofore enacted on that subject,' which implied that Indians should be allowed to go unhindered where they pleased in order to trade their peltries.[339]

The palisades may have created a sense of security for those who lived within the enclosed space; but at the same time, this barrier may have changed people's perspective, as well: Their view of the river and the hill was now blocked by a fence that was higher than a person. To reach the woods, the river, or a garden outside the fence, one now had to go through a gate. The 250-rod structure around part of the *bijeenwoninge* interrupted the views of the inhabitants' surroundings, and one wonders whether it also changed their attitudes. They may have felt safer; but would it have diminished their fears of the Indians? Children, women who had their gardens near the house, and perhaps the elderly probably spent less time outside the area that was now protected by palisades. Women who had their gardens outside of the palisades, in the area along the river, may have felt less at ease while working in them. Palisades protected the community; but the defense may have locked the inhabitants in, as well, while alienating them from their environment, in ways that both diminished and increased the settlers' fear of Indians. In the event of a surprise attack, those living outside the palisades would have had to flee toward the village center for safety, leaving their property and belongings behind. The palisades must have changed life remarkably for settlers both inside and outside the *bijeenwoninge*. There seem to have been fewer Indians in the village for some time; between the end of November 1659 and the end of December 1660, the court minutes do not report any cases of selling alcohol or baked goods to natives, or the presence of drunken or abusive Indians in the village. However, that may not have been a result of the erection of the palisades. The Indians were occupied with the Esopus war and did not visit Beverwijck; as a result, the trade was so low in 1660 that hardly any burghers had beavers.[340]

Aside from creating a sense of security, the palisades may have had another effect on inhabitants of the *bijeenwoninge*. Before they were built, the village had been more or less inclusive of its surroundings; and although its spatial and functional layout may have been peculiar in the landscape, the village may not have looked typically European, either. Within the enclosed area, the palisades may have brought European features together: lined-up streets crossing each other at more or less right angles, kills with bridges and sheetpiling, fenced-in lots, 'Dutch' houses (many probably provided with signs), and a centrally located church. The palisades may have emphasized these features, thereby strengthening the feeling of 'Dutchness' or 'Europeanness' among the inhabitants – as opposed to what was, for many settlers, the undefined world from which the Indians came. Without the palisades, the open village was part of the landscape, as the Indian and European worlds repeatedly merged and separated. The barrier separating these two worlds was built in 1659.

The palisades confirmed that Beverwijck was increasingly becoming a place with its own identity – for some, perhaps, a true 'Dutch' home base. The community, with its continuously arriving new settlers, was now separated from the natives. Instead of adapting to their surroundings, the inhabitants, despite the great differences among themselves, may have gained a stronger feeling of solidarity against a common threat from those surroundings; the palisades may have stimulated a certain sense of togetherness, a feeling of not being native – of being, perhaps, Dutch or European. In their consideration of whether or not to declare war on the Esopus Indians, Stuyvesant and the members of the council clearly expressed their feelings of distrust, and the sense that the two peoples were opposites. In their request to West India Company directors for more troops, they referred to sentiments that existed among the people in the Dutch Republic: The injuries, affronts and massacres committed by the 'cruel barbarians' (*wreede barbaren*) in the Esopus were, to some members of the council, 'too horrible and unbearable for an honor and freedom loving country, which through God's blessing had wrested out of the Spanish tiranny and Inquisition.' To pay as much ransom as was asked for individuals captured by the Indians was 'ignominious and unbearable.'[341] When they spoke of the 'suffered affronts and the restoration of the almost defunct Batavian reputation (as an Indian nowadays feels himself worth as much as two Dutchmen),' they expressed sentiments also described by Hugo de Groot in his *Treatise of the Antiquity of the Batavian, now Hollandish Republic* (*Tractaet van de oudtheyt van de Batavische, nu Hollantsche Republique* ('s-Gravenhage, 1610), and by Petrus Scriverius in his 1650 revision of the history of the counts of Holland, *Principes Hollandiae, et Westfrisiae*. According to Scriverius, the counts of Holland and their province were the natural successors of the Batavian people. Historians in other parts of the Dutch Republic, such as Gelre or Nijmegen, saw their fellow countymen and townsmen in such a role, and it seems that New Netherland officials added to the provincial character this myth had acquired by extending it to the New World.[342] However, these sentiments were not expressed by the commissary of Fort Orange, Johannes La Montagne, or Jeremias van Rensselaer. Perhaps these men felt less distance from the Indians than did the settlers at Manhattan. Maybe they lived more on a frontier, and felt more closely connected with the Indians.

The palisades may have had another effect. Except for permitting more control over Indian traffic, the new barriers also made it easier to supervise people's comings and goings. In May 1660, the court prohibited settlers from going any further than the hill, 'as far as the houses stand, to inquire where the Indians wish to go, and likewise to the strand, where the Indians arrive.' If they acted to the contrary, settlers would be fined *f*300 and suspended from their business for two months.[343] Subsequently, the sending of brokers into the woods to attract or entice Indians was prohibited. Violators of the new orders could easily be spotted from the new city fence.[344]

The early sketch shows that there was a 6-foot distance between the houses and the palisades along present-day Pearl Street, while at the north side of *Jonckerstraet* (State Street), just within the palisades, was a corps de guarde. The gates in the defense seem fairly narrow and, from the seven bastions, it was possible to oversee the streets – so that, in general, people who came into the *bijeenwoninge* via the Maquaes trail or any other entry point, or who were merely in any street, could easily be noticed. Some inhabitants of the community may very well have considered the palisades to be a limitation of their freedom, now that they could not so easily go unnoticed outside the village center, while Indians were allowed to come into the village to trade and visit with whomever they pleased. The villagers may have had to organize new tactics in order to get the best deal in the trade. The location of one's dwelling next to a gate may have become more important than before, as it was now more difficult for people to see the Indians approaching. Unless others met the Indians at the boundary post, people living next to the gate were the first to see them. But while the court may have been able to exercise more supervision on who came and went, in reality this control may not have amounted to much. It seems that people could pretty much go in and out of the village as they pleased. For example, when Jan Harmsz was asked, in June 1660, whether 'in coming out of the woods, he did not enter by one of the two gates from the hill,' he answered that he had come 'through the gate near *Lange Maria*'s,' which likely was the gate at the north side of present-day Broadway.[345]

That people tried to meet Indians before they entered the settlement remained a problem. In August 1662, posts were set up on the hill within sight of Fort Orange and the village of Beverwijck, and placed wherever necessary.[346] Anyone 'found either on foot or on horseback outside those limits to allure any Indians or to entice them by presents either personally or through runners,' the ordinance warned, 'would be fined 20 pounds Flemish.'[347] For various people, the area around the post then became a zone on which they focused their hopes, and many 'graceless and idle loafers' remained 'loitering near and about the erected post, entire days from morning until night, even on the Lord's Sabbath and day of rest in wait for the Indians without any other calling, passing the time in an unprofitable, yea an ungodly, manner, drinking, card playing, and other such like disorders.' These 'runners and enticers of the Indians' laid hands on the natives to frighten and obstruct them.[348]

For several seventeenth-century Albanians, waiting at the post for Indians coming from the west had become a way to take a chance on luck and speculation.

The defense separated the worlds of settlers and Indians, but the west remained an area of attraction for the colonists – an area from where good fortune came, an area of which many had high expectations. For some time the founding of Schenectady, in 1661, provided a way to circumvent the rules. By 1663, many individuals had started to use the road to this new settlement for illegal trade. Despite the prohibition on trade with the Indians at Schenectady, settlers carried goods and merchandise on wagons and horseback six or seven miles inland in order to barter with the Indians. There was the danger 'that the goods would be attacked and set upon the way, whereof some instances have already occurred, viz.: in attacking of wagons, firing some shots at them, yea, attempting to stop women on their way thither, and other additional insolences, already committed by the Barbarians, both in the settlement itself, and on the road'; but several people took the risk anyway.[349] But this journey would become increasingly dangerous; and by the summer of 1664, few people dared to travel the Maquaes trail anymore, as the Maquaes had 'infested' it.[350]

The palisades may have functioned, for the settlers, similarly to the walls around a European city, and thus may have have signaled a change from a 'village' to a 'town' identity. Walls are typical town features, and it seems that many inhabitants felt that their community resembled a town more than a village. They frequently spoke of the palisades as the *stadtsheyninge* (city or town fence), and in 1655, bakers already had requested the urban privilege of establishing a guild. As we will see more clearly in chapter 5, by the time the palisades were built, the enclosed area could count on workers representing the most important trades: smiths, shoemakers, tailors, carpenters, coopers, bakers, brewers – trades found in any semi-urban center; as in many towns in the Republic, several of these trades (bakers and smiths, for instance) were concentrated in particular areas.

Conclusion

The area within 3,000 feet of Fort Orange, once owned by the patroon, became the possession of many in 1652. The twelve years that the community went under the name 'Beverwijck' were years of constant change. The building process, begun during Van Slichtenhorst's directorship, continued rapidly. In developing the village, Beverwijck's court and the special committee to oversee the surveying of lots and gardens followed, more or less, the concepts already developed for a patroonship center in the early 1650s. By adjusting wherever necessary, the settlers were able to bring European concepts into the American landscape. They built bridges across the creeks, sheet-piled those creeks when the banks threatened to cave in, used old Indian trails to develop roads, and began building a village with European features in the American wilderness.

Almost continuously during the 1650s carpenters, masons, glaziers, and blacksmiths worked to create the new village. Sworn surveyors laid out streets as much as possible at right angles; house and garden lots were staked off, and had to be built upon and fenced in within a limited time. As empty lots were developed, parts of them were designated as bleaching fields or were occupied by sheds, stables, storage spaces for wood, and other structures. Along with such 'new' crops as squashes, corn and pumpkins, settlers' gardens produced vegetables and crops similar to those in the Republic. Houses and other structures were built, rebuilt, extended or in other ways changed; many houses were built with their gabled ends on the street side. Thus was a center constructed north of the fort with taverns, shops and breweries. While some artisans' shops were scattered through the few streets, others, as in urban areas in the fatherland, were concentrated in special areas. Community structures such as a church and poorhouse were built in the center of the *bijeenwoninge*, while mills, brick and tile yards, and the fort were located to the north and south; the court was held in the West India Company's trading house within Fort Orange. As the number of inhabitants increased, houses were built closer together – which, together with the protection of a surrounding 'wall,' gave the settlement a more urban character. Within twelve years, the community's most important activities had moved from Fort Orange to the *bijeenwoninge*. The area north of the fort had been fully developed in a European manner.

The outer appearance of the village was in part Dutch; but at the same time, it had developed out of relations with the Indians and the English. While the community was inclusive of its surroundings and was open to Indians in the early 1650s, living at the frontier would increasingly be experienced as dangerous. As the population increased, a blockhouse was built in 1656 at the center of the village, where people could flee for their lives in the case of threats from outside. In 1659, increased fear of enemy attacks spurred the community to build a town fence around a large part of the *bijeenwoninge*; if necessary, the settlers could separate one civilization from another.

Overall, when they took over New Netherland, the English found in the upper Hudson area an organized community of well over a thousand inhabitants who occupied closely built Dutch-type dwellings, a great part of which were located within an area protected by palisades. Within this urban-looking community, various features and structures provided the inhabitants with the minimal functions of a Dutch settlement: public safety, religion, education, poor relief, and communal services. People worshipped in a specified building, and could receive an education in the schoolmaster's house. During periods of scarcity, they could collect gifts of charity in a building especially erected for the benefit of the poor; and if they thought an injustice had been done to them, they could go to the court house in Fort Orange. In the next chapter, we look at some of the institutions that occupied these structures, and which shaped Beverwijck socially and culturally – thereby strengthening the change in Beverwijck's appearance from that of a rural settlement into an increasingly urban community.

II. Beverwijck:
creating an orderly village

Sworn surveyors laid out streets in a European fashion; a church was built in the center; various artisans of one trade concentrated in certain areas; the inhabitants contributed to defense works; and a town fence was built to protect the community – all of these facts encourage the thought that the designers and builders of the *bijeenwoninge* may have had something greater in mind than just a village. We can only wonder what Beverwijck's true nature was meant to be.

Considering the international mix of people which populated the settlement year-round, it is not hard to draw a parallel with Amsterdam, where around 1650 more than half the population had not been born in the city itself.[1] When the river became navigable again in the beginning of spring, traders from the Republic, New Amsterdam, and even some from New England, would arrive in Beverwijck with their duffels, wine, shirts, kettles, tools, and other trading goods – and joined the inhabitants. The hundreds of Indians who came from the inland, ready to trade their pelts for European trading goods, added to the population; and the *bijeenwoninge*, filled with so many souls, likely breathed a cosmopolitan atmosphere. The inhabitants gladly saw the visitors arrive, as it meant the beginning of a season in which they hoped to do the most important business of the entire year. In addition to the regular spring and summer activities of maintaining gardens or harvesting and processing crops, everyone was in some way involved in the trade. Many rented out a dwelling or a room; bakers, brewers, tavern and innkeepers, and even the notary did most of their work and made their best earnings between May and November, with the peak usually being between June and August. The trading season was an active time, in which everyone tried to make his best deals. The latest news, fashions, ideas, and instructions poured in from Europe; auctions were organized in the local inns, and people's visits to taverns occasionally exceeded church attendance. While snow and ice in winter would isolate the community from New Amsterdam and *patria*, leaving the year-round inhabitants to each other, the trading season was an urban-like period – a time of business and new initiatives, a period of activity and change.

Except for analyzing Beverwijck's society, in this chapter we will also take a look at the institutions of church and government that ruled Beverwijck. While the Dutch presence in the upper Hudson had slowly grown after 1629, it would gain momentum during the 1650s. The creation of a *bijeenwoninge* may have emphasized the organizational and binding aspect of the community and given these institutions a clear and more recognizable place, so that a more structured community arose. Before 1652, religion had already provided the structure for much of the time and values in peoples' lives; now that most people were concentrated in the *bijeenwoninge*, religion became more present and visible, for example, in organized churchgoing and charity. While the church guarded and promoted moral values through its ecclesiastical discipline, the court, under the West India Company's supervision, developed laws and rules, and established institutions such as the burgher guard and the orphan masters. With church and court overseeing morality and public order, it was possible to work toward a place were order, union, and harmony prevailed.

Beverwijck's identity, however, was not determined by Dutch rules and customs alone; relations with the outside world greatly influenced the settlement's development, as well. Good contacts with the Indians were necessary for the trade, which required meetings and maintaining contacts at all times, even to the extent of helping the natives protect themselves against other Europeans in New France. New England settlers, who clearly were interested in extending their borders westward, demanded attention as well. And in the course of time, Beverwijckers found themselves even looking for protection against an increasing number of fellow countrymen from New Amsterdam – who threatened their livelihood when they came up-river to try their luck in the Indian trade.

Throughout its twelve-year existence, Beverwijck's community was in constant motion and development; while the departure of some inhabitants and the arrival of new settlers constantly caused internal change, Indian, French, and English policies influenced its development as well. Laws and ordinances were written and rewritten, as moral values and ways of life were adjusted. Church and state were constructive and stabilizing institutions, greatly determining the development of a common way of life – as much 'Dutch' as possible – and the social dynamics of this frontier village.

By the end of the Dutch period, Beverwijck had more than a thousand inhabitants. Many, if not all, came with hopes of profit from the trade; and in addition, they worked hard to organize a well-functioning society similar to towns in Holland.[2] The institutions they established and used – which resembled those in *patria*, and stipulated the terms of life in the community for the greater part of the century – had a long-lasting influence and distinguished Beverwijck from any other colonial settlement in North America.[3]

We can wonder whether the inhabitants of Beverwijck, through their burghership and participation in a burgher guard, felt themselves to be town dwellers, rather than inhabitants of a village. The idea that the directors had a town in mind when they established the court of Fort Orange, rather than a village, seems to be reinforced by the fact that these institutions had been established in the early years.

Beverwijck's society

A mix of people

Apart from the features of landscape and design described in the previous chapter, people in the streets also contributed to Beverwijck's particular look and identity.

It would not have been difficult to distinguish the Indians, whose speech and dress were different. In the summer, around nine o'clock on a Sunday morning probably would have presented a lively picture, as the settlers moved toward the church in their Sunday outfits. Residents of the *bijeenwoninge* would have come on foot, while others who had farther to travel may have come by carts, wagons, perhaps on horseback, and some even by boat or canoe. Some women may have worn a headdress with their cloth skirt and bodice, a psalm book chained to their waist. Men may have worn their best gray or black hats, and shirts with lace collars, jerkins, knee pants, stockings with bands and ribbons and Spanish leather shoes. There were Germans, Scandinavians, French, Flemish, Walloons, African slaves, and a Croatian – people from Scotland, Vienna, and various provinces of the Dutch Republic – and one would have expected their dress to reveal something of their place of origin. Clothing was a mark of social identity and many settlers, even though several had lived for some time in the Dutch Republic before they went to the New World, probably had brought along their original clothes. In the New World, additions to clothing were limited to those items available through the supplies brought by the ships. Tailors brought along their own traditions and fashions, so that after some time clothing may not have betrayed much of the settlers' backgrounds. The differences between them probably were a more internal matter.

Although not linked together as loosely as the populations of old and New Amsterdam, as much as a quarter of Beverwijck's population may have been of non-Dutch origin.[4] And, although government and church rules in New Netherland were established in the province of Holland, only a few of the 'Dutch' settlers in the upper Hudson area had their roots in that province. Most came from the countryside and the small towns of the inner provinces, especially the area of the *Veluwe* in the province of Gelre. After the Eighty Years War, provincial and local identity in *patria* was still very strong. Each province had its own character, and many distinctions existed between the different areas. For the people of one province, another province's inhabitants could be as foreign as people from another nation. The wealthy scholar and West India Company director Johannes de Laet, for example, who was active as a geographer and publicist in Leiden, called the inhabitants of Gelre 'militant.' Hollanders, he thought, were candid, diligent, and thrifty, while inhabitants of Utrecht were ingenious and friendly.[5] Whatever the truth of these generalizations, each colonist undoubtedly brought memories, traditions, and customs from his or her own place of origin.

The inhabitants' diversity was not only influenced by their origins. Between 1630 and 1644, immigration to Rensselaerswijck had been dominated by young single men; but by the 1650s, and especially after 1657, more women and families came to New Netherland and Beverwijck, although men would always remain the majority. But in the 1650s and 1660s, women occupied their own separate place in society – which, as in the fatherland, was in the household – where they were masters of the private space, and where they guarded the domesticity of the home.[6] Although under guardianship of her husband, a woman could own property and, jointly with her husband, she owned their common property, which at their marriage had been brought together. Within the marriage women were partners, actively participating in work, and being equally responsible for debts. The husband had autonomous control over their property; but a wife, if she thought he was mismanaging her estate, could appeal to the court to have her husband removed as administrator. A woman had rights and the capacity to act; and in some cases in *patria*, women were even guild members. Some towns, including Amsterdam, explicitly accepted women as merchants, and this tradition existed as well in Beverwijck.[7]

There also were people with different religious beliefs in Beverwijck. In general the Dutch Reformed church, as a public church, was a binding factor that brought the people together for religious services at least once a week, and usually more often. When *dominee* Schaets walked off the ship that had brought him to Rensselaerswijck in the summer of 1652, he found about 130 church members. By 1660, this number had increased to 200. But not all inhabitants joined the church. Many people felt sympathy for the reformed religion, but did not want to make the confession necessary to be recognized as full member of the church, and commit themselves to participate in the Holy Communion; they were called *liefhebbers* (sympathizers, or 'amateurs') of the reformed religion. Notwithstanding the distance some had to travel, sometimes between 300 and 400 people would come to church, according to the minister in June 1657. 'And if they all would have been *liefhebbers*, there could be as many as 600 people in church,' he wrote, 'except for the traders who visited the place during the summer.'[8]

Then there were some seventy to eighty Lutheran families, often of German and Scandinavian origin, who made their residence in Beverwijck and its surroundings. In 1649, they already had requested, together with other Lutherans in New Netherland, a minister and the right to practice their religion publicly. In the larger cities in the Republic, Lutherans were allowed to worship in private houses on the condition that they not criticize the Dutch Reformed church. Although their freedom remained limited in space and time, the Lutherans' meeting place in Amsterdam – although unrecognizable from the outside – had been consecrated as a fully fledged church in 1633.[9] Practical tolerance toward the Lutherans may have been less in Beverwijck than in towns in Holland, as such decisions were made not by the local magistracy, but the colonial government a good distance away in Manhattan where the director general, an autocratic Calvinist, had much influence. The New Netherland Lutherans' 1649 requests were refused and, in 1653, they would turn again in vain to the Lutheran Consistory and the States General.[10] But similar to *patria*, local authorities sometimes connived with other religions if that was better for a peaceful coexistence; in 1652, 1653, and 1655 the Lutheran Volckert Jansz Douw, who had signed the 1653 Lutheran petition, was even member of Beverwijck's court.[11] Fort Orange's court records don't mention Lutherans until February 1, 1656, when an ordinance was issued against having separate divine worship.[12] Tjerck Claesz was fined *f*6 on that day for having performed a worship service in the company of the Lutherans. A week later Hendrick Jansz *de koeherder* (the cowherd) was fined *f*25 for holding a separate worship service at the house of Willem Jurriaensz with fifteen other people.[13] In

March 1656, the court informed Stuyvesant that they had posted a special placard against the congregation of certain persons of the Lutheran sect; but this action does not seem to have had much effect.[14] Douw, who was present at almost all court sessions during his term, would retire as magistrate on the usual date of the first of May.[15]

Local civil authorities at times clearly tolerated Lutherans, who surely were considered valued community members. The Lutherans were the largest group of non-Calvinists and the greatest worry of Beverwijck's minister. In October 1657, it was said that a hundred beaver skins were collected at Fort Orange for their minister, Joannes Ernestus Gutwasser, who had come to New Netherland that summer. Soon after his arrival, Stuyvesant and the council ordered that the Lutheran minister not be admitted into New Amsterdam or elsewhere in New Netherland, and that he should return to the fatherland. When Gutwasser thereupon went into hiding, various Lutherans tried to support him, but there was a lack of unity; and, if some of the Fort Orange pelts had not helped to cover the expense, the minister could hardly have been supported. The beaver skins (with a value of ƒ800) collected at Fort Orange were considered 'the surest pay in this country,' according to the ministers Megapolensis and Drisius at Manhattan.[16] After two years, Gutwasser would go back to his Amsterdam consistory where, in July 1659, he reported how he had been driven from his congregation and forced to depart because of the severe persecution by the director general and council.[17] But the problem had not left with Gutwasser's departure, and in September 1660 *dominee* Schaets would write to the Amsterdam Classis that the Lutherans were again collecting subscriptions for the salary of a Lutheran minister. He probably understood the low degree of orthodoxy in his congregation when he described his fear that, if a Lutheran minister were to come, it would create a great schism in the congregation, which 'is now at peace, especially because there are several [Lutherans] who are gradually being led to us. Some of them are on the point of becoming members, who were at home of different opinions.'[18] Beverwijck's court did not consider being Lutheran a serious crime, however, and in the spring of 1659 Douw was again nominated for magistrate; but the colonial government did not select him.[19] Not until after 1664, under English rule, would the Lutherans be allowed to have their own church and minister. For many people in the village, the church was a social place that strengthened communal feelings between all villagers; and whether one was Dutch Reformed or Lutheran does not seem to have been totally decisive in determining an individual's place on the social ladder.

The Lutherans seem to have been the Dutch Reformed minister's main concern. He did not have to deal with Quakers and Independents, who were in English towns on Long Island, or with Jews. And although no less than sixty-two Catholic meeting places had been observed in Amsterdam in 1656, according to the *Vertoogh van Paepsche Stoutigheit alhier binnen Amsterdam*, Catholics do not seem to have been a threat to Beverwijck's church either.[20] Only a few Catholics lived in the village, and there is no indication that they joined together for worship. The Jesuit Father Joseph Poncet, during his stay at Fort Orange in

September 1653 met a young man who wanted to make his confession. He had been captured by the Iroquois and ransomed by the Dutch, whom he served as an interpreter. There was also a Brussels merchant – 'a good Catholic,' Poncet wrote – whose confession he heard upon his departure.[21] A person with the nickname '*de Paus*' may have been another Catholic living in the village.[22] In 1657, Simon Le Moyne visited Fort Orange and New Amsterdam, undoubtedly to strengthen both the German and French 'papists,' as Johannes Megapolensis explained.[23]

To a lesser degree than New Amsterdam's population, Beverwijck's inhabitants were a mix of different origins, sexes, and beliefs – and this variety provided grounds for an unstable society. Conflicts of interest could easily set people against each other; conversely, negotion, adjustment, or some connivance could also put them into agreement again. The tolerance required to coexist with such a mixture of people was easily broken when an individual felt that his or her honor had been called into question. Honor – meaning someone's reputation, his or her 'good name' in the eyes of others – was an important principle of the public order in seventeenth-century society. Dishonorable behavior could cause someone to loose his honor; and much of a person's activity was oriented around the showing, maintaining, or repairing of honor, as it justified the sense of pride one could claim on social rank. An individual had to be honorable, for instance, to perform a government job. One's honor depended on his or her public behavior, on what others noticed and saw, and was person-specific. Losing one's honor could have important consequences for public life; in practice, it meant that he could loose his burgher rights. A sentence and the execution of punishment could greatly humiliate a person in public, sometimes even visibly. Loss of honor could mean the loss of one's circle of friends – his or her 'social capital' – which could have great economic consequences.[24]

Through its ecclesiastical discipline, the Dutch Reformed church helped people guard their honor, and warned them when it considered them to have exceeded the moral boundaries the church had set. Before a person was anonymously exposed, the church would offer an individual many chances to better his or her life, and only as a last resort would the 'sinner' and his or her wrong-doing be made public – and the person would be suspended from participating in the Holy Communion. People considered this punishment to be very serious; often, merely the threat of excommunication was sufficiently persuasive to correct one's way of life.[25]

Tempers of Beverwijckers were most often raised over money issues, and most cases brought into the court concerned debt and damaged reputations – both matters of honor. The expression used most by men and women in a disagreement was 'thief,' or words that inferred economic irresponsibility such as 'scoundrel,' 'bloodhound,' 'rascal,' 'extortioner,' or 'roving bandit.'[26] A counter-slander against the accusation of being a thief was often 'whore,' when the opposing party was a woman. Merely telling a man that his wife was a 'whore' served to defame not only the wife, but the husband as well. Sexual misbehavior easily could damage a person's honor, especially a woman's, and a person so 'damaged' considered it necessary to protect his or her honor by beginning a counter-offensive at the court, or in the presence of witnesses in the neighborhood. Honor brought with it various regulations and codes. As head of the family, a man was responsible for the family's honor, and thus for the behavior of his wife and children. Except for marital life, however, it also touched all other aspects of public life, such as work, social life and social functions. As honor had to do with public, visible acts that could confirm or damage one's honor, a man always had to keep up his reputation, control himself, earn a living for himself and his family, and manage his finances. Being unemployed, going bankrupt, having committed theft or assault, or having sexually misbehaved were matters that could cause one loose his or her honor. Church members who had behaved dishonorably first had to show remorse to the church for their faults before they could try to gain back their honor elsewhere.

Honor was closely related to one's social position. In the Dutch Republic, independent and autonomous work, in general, was considered more honorable than day labor, and 'head' labor was more honorable than hand work. Not having to work was more honorable than working, but it was important that one had earned his free time with honest work. At the end of someone's life, it was important to recognize the person's honor by providing him or her with an honorable funeral attended by family members, neighbors, co-workers, and others who could testify to the deceased's good name and reputation – that is, who could testify to his honor.[27]

Honor was an important principle of the public order in society, as well. Beverwijckers may have been people of different origins; but at some point they adopted and assimilated cultural rules, mostly following the example of the province of Holland, which had been defined and were now operating in the New World. They committed themselves to share one social system with the same cultural values. Although to a lesser degree than New Amsterdam, Beverwijck was a melting pot that absorbed, and at some point transformed, the different cultures of all its inhabitants.[28]

Burghership

The concept of honor provided one with the possibility of occupying a positive position in the surrounding world, as well as a reason to maintain and improve his or her position. Honor gave a person a claim to pride, rank and class, as Frijhoff and Spies wrote, and to stand up straight in the world.[29] Another concept – burghership – gave a person the capacity to exist and make a living in the community. In the Dutch Republic, burghership was the basic organizing principle of a community. While in the countryside the right to vote was always connected with land ownership, burghership was connected with the individual; ownership was not decisive, although possessing a house and lot were good guarantees for one's burghership.[30] The *burgerij* had its origins in the Middle Ages when a group of socially equal people formed the *schutterij*, a sort of citizen's militia, in order to guarantee quiet, order, and safety in their town. This organization brought along certain rights such as the exclusive exercise of some trades and a certain amount of legal security, while it also created a number of obligations such as performing military services and paying taxes.[31] The concepts of '*burger*' and '*burgerij*' had developed over centuries, and by the 1600s had become one of the sustaining forces of urban society. Local space was the frame of reference for all people in a village or town, Frijhoff and Spies wrote; and the well-being of a town was the product of active burghers' concrete care for their own interests in a town commonwealth, which was provided with adequate political institutions. When one was a burgher, one could participate in the town's life: One could become a member of a guild in order to perform a trade; during illness, one could claim charity or the care of an orphanage; and one could, if he or she was a member of the Reformed religion, hold a political or town government function.[32]

Together with the concept of honor, colonists took their idea of burghership along to the New World; however, the explicit regulation of burgher rights in New Netherland did not occur until 1657.[33] In the upper Hudson, people thought in terms of burghership. In November 1651, for example, Van Slichtenhorst had already used the word '*burger*' in Rensselaerswijck when, in the heat of the battle with Stuyvesant, he had forty-five inhabitants of the colony take the '*burgerlijke* oath of allegiance' to the patroon. This may have had the same text as the oath Steven Jansz *timmerman* had taken, in July 1649, when he swore to be faithful to the patroon and co-directors, subjecting himself to the court of the colony and promising 'to demean himself as a good and faithful inhabitant or burgher, without exciting any opposition, tumult or noise; but on the contrary, as a loyal inhabitant, to maintain and support offensively and defensively, against everyone the right and jurisdiction of the colony.'[34] Taking the oath brought with it obligations and some privileges. As in the fatherland, one became part of the community by taking the oath, and thus received certain rights and assumed certain responsibilities. Jan Michielsz and Jan Verbeeck, for example, were protected from competitors when, in April 1648, they were allowed to take up the tailor's trade 'to the exclusion of all others.' Their privileged position did not exist long, however, since in October of that same year Evert Jansz, also a tailor, was granted permission to go to Rensselaerswijck and support himself by exercising this trade, as well.[35]

In April 1652, the inhabitants of the *bijeenwoninge* were excused from their oath to the patroon and, in Jan Baptist van Rensselaer's words, were taken 'under oath and banner' by the West India Company. From the beginning, the inhabitants of Beverwijck were called 'burghers'; they had to take a new oath that made them members of the community.[36] The same tailor Jan Verbeeck, for example, became an inhabitant of Beverwijck and on April 17, 1652 took the 'usual burgher oath.'[37]

In New Amsterdam, burgher right was not regulated until 1657; and for the upper Hudson area, no regulations at all have been found. It is, however, clear that people in Beverwijck expected benefits from having taken the oath, such as the prerogative of exercising a trade. In March 1655, in response to the charge that 'some bakers who are freemen bake without having taken the oath,' the court of Beverwijck decided to issue further resolutions on the subject, 'as elsewhere no one is allowed to exercise a trade who has not taken the burgher oath.'[38] The ordinance, which was passed by the director general and council of New Netherland on January 30, 1657, established the criteria for and rights of burghers of New Amsterdam; it distinguished between 'small' and 'great' burgher right as it existed in the city of Amsterdam, where this system had been introduced in 1652.[39] Small burgher right could be bought for *f*20, and allowed a person to open a shop or exercise a trade. 'Small burghers' were obligated to contribute direct taxes and take part in the guard. Such right was granted to everyone who had kept fire and light in the city for longer than one year and six weeks, or to all persons born in the city, anyone married to a burgher or burgher's daughter born in the city, and to anyone who wanted to trade or exercise a trade in the city and was willing to pay the *f*20 fee. Great burgher right was required to occupy positions in city government, and could be bought for *f*50. Advantages for 'great burghers' were partial freedom from the obligation to take part of the guard, and immunity from arrest by any lower benches of justice in New Netherland. Great burghership was automatically granted to members of the colonial government and to mayors, magistrates, ministers, and officers of the burgher guard with the rank of *vaendrigh (ensign)* and higher. For others, such right was available from the mayors for *f*50. Great burghership was declared heriditary in male lines.[40] A decision by the director general and council, in the spring of 1664, indicates that the same principle was followed in Beverwijck.[41]

The immediate cause of the regulation of burgher right at New Amsterdam were the so-called Scottish traders. They were not inhabitants of New Netherland, but came in the trading season and often passed Manhattan to continue on their way directly to Beverwijck. 'Scottish' traders could compete well, at low cost with lower prices than those traders who lived in New Netherland, since they did not contribute the usual taxes or help protect the community against the English and Indians by participating in the burgher guard. People in New Amsterdam considered these outsiders to be a source of irritation, and saw their demands answered by the regulation of burgher right.[42] But in 1664, Beverwijck also felt New Amsterdam's competition, and in turn wished to be protected against the 'burghers of Manhattan and their wives' who spoiled the trade for them, to the disadvantage of the inhabitants, 'whom they took the bread out of their mouths, while they had to bring up all the costs of the community and stand guard.' More than forty-five inhabitants, some wealthy and some struggling to survive, petitioned for protection; but the decision did not turn out as favorably as they had hoped. The beaver and fur trades should not be stopped for anyone, the director general and council judged, as it was 'the stimulus and the source of the possession and population of New Netherland.' But the director general and council consented that the trade with Christians be restricted to those who had kept fire and light in Beverwijck for more than one year and six weeks, or 'have hereafter purchased the burgher right at a moderate price.'[43] Burghership was the basis of one's public identity; it meant that one could be an active member of society and participate in town affairs, including government and administration of justice. Burghership gave a person the right to exist in a town.[44]

The burgher guard

One consequence of being a burgher was that one was obligated to participate in the guard. In Dutch towns, with some exceptions, all able-bodied men had to be members of the burgher guard. The main purpose of this institution was to protect the town and its inhabitants against enemies from the outside, and to guard public order and safety within the town. They did this, among others, by making the rounds and standing guard, and as such it had a preventive effect.[45] Before 1652, the inhabitants of the patroonship were already organized in some way to protect the settlement. In their oath to the patroon, they agreed that they would 'as a loyal inhabitant, [to] maintain and support offensively and defensively, against everyone the right and jurisdiction of the colony.'[46] In Beverwijck, as in New Amsterdam, there may have been some rules. One of the four rules regulating the burgher guard in New Amsterdam in 1643 illustrates how they tried to maintain some of the atmosphere of brothership that so marked the *schutterijen*, and later the burgher guards, in the Dutch Republic: One should not swear, nor speak ill of others in the guard.[47]

Scattered through the documents we can find pieces of information about Beverwijck's burgher guard. In 1653, Jan Baptist van Rensselaer wrote that 230 able-bodied men lived in Beverwijck and Rensselaerswijck combined.[48] Inhabitants of Rensselaerswijck had their own corporal's guard; in 1660, Jeremias van Rensselaer supplied them with powder.[49] It seems safe to assume, however, that at least half of them, or two-third of the 230, men would have served in Beverwijck's burgher guard. A non-dated ordinance 'on the burgher guard at the fortress Orangie village Beverwijck' provides sixteen rules for organizing this burgher guard.[50] These instructions probably date from sometime between the establishment of the court and the summer of 1653.[51] The ordinance stipulated that, as in *patria*, all burghers and inhabitants were obligated to appear in the evening at the ringing of the bell at the corpus de guarde at their respective corporalships with their full hand and side-arms, and provided with at the least ten shots' worth of powder in their cartridge boxes (*maeten ofte patroontassen*). Not appearing or arriving late was, except in case of illness, fined. The lower officers were required to obey without contradicting those higher ranked. In marching, they were either standing, or while marching, not allowed to step out of their row, without being so commanded. While doing the rounds (*ommetrecken*), no one was allowed to load his gun or to shoot at the banner, or at any windows, gables, coats of arms, or protruding signs. It was important to remember the password and to keep it secret. Appearing drunk at the guard was forbidden, as was drinking until drunk, or fighting. No one was allowed to molest the sentry, and anyone who fell asleep while on guard duty was fined. In doing the rounds, officers and cadets had to try, as much as possible, to prevent trouble and, after the ringing of the bell, to prohibit all tapping, drinking, drunkenness, or other noise. In case of necessity, all or half of the corporalship would have to stay as long as the captain, lieutenant, ensign or sergeant ordered, and also to continue the guard during the day. Those who would be absent for a longer time, because of a trip to Manhattan or elsewhere, would pay a fine of 14 stivers, and announce their departure beforehand.

Unfortunately there is no master roll of the several companies of the burgher guard. In New Amsterdam's burgher guard, thirty-two commissioned and non-commissioned officers and fifty-five marksmen were appointed in 1653, for a total of eighty-seven men. One captain, one lieutenant, and one ensign headed the whole company, which was sub-divided into four corporalships, each of which had one sergeant, one corporal, one lance corporal, four sergeants, four cadets, and twelve to sixteen marksmen.[52] At that time, New Amsterdam may have had between 800 and 1,000 inhabitants. In 1656, the city had 120 houses (like Beverwijck in 1657), and an estimated population of 1,000.[53]

As in Dutch cities, magistrates who retired at the end of each year were exempt and relieved from attending the usual burgher watch for one year after the expiration of their term of office. In November 1656, this resolution was communicated to and accepted by the military council, a body consisting of officers that frequently consulted with the magistrates.[54] It is not surprising that Abraham Staets – who frequently was a magistrate and a member of the church consistory – was captain of the guard: In the Dutch Republic, this position was often filled by someone with political influence. In Dutch towns, the captain was often appointed by the marksmen and the town board for two or three years. It was something of an honorary office that conferred an air of bravery and status.[55] The same applied more or less to the position of lieutenant, who usually was appointed for two or three years as well. Tavern owner Hendrick Jochemsz filled this position in 1655.[56] Lambert van Valckenburgh was sergeant in 1656-57, and had command over a part of the company; he was the one who carried the halbert (a battle-axe with a long handle).[57] In 1653, carpenter Dirck Bensingh and baker Jochem Wesselsz were responsible, as corporals, for the organization of the night watch, including recruitment of new marksmen and the finances of the corporalship. In the Dutch Republic, corporals were usually appointed for two years. While in the Republic their position was lower than that of sergeant, in Beverwijck it seemed the other way around. Lambert van Valckenburgh, who was at Fort Orange in 1649, was sergeant in 1657, but needed help from the deacons' poor fund on various occasions between 1660 and 1665; but Wesselsz, who was a corporal, fared fairly well. Except for Staets, none of these men were ever magistrates or members of the Reformed consistory in Beverwijck.[58] Schoolmaster Adriaen Jansz van Ilpendam was the burgher guard's clerk in 1653, and carpenter Dirck Jansz, as *vaandrig*, had the duty to carry and maintain the banner, the symbol of the marksmen's company. In the Netherlands, the *vaandrig* often was unmarried, and an aura of romance surrounded him, with his beautiful and trendy clothes. He often was wealthy and capable, and parties of the guard would often end up at his house. If Dirck Jansz was the same person as the trader Dirck Jansz Croon, he may have fit some of this description. When he lived in Beverwijck, he was one of the important traders, capable of breaking at least two women's hearts.[59]

An atmosphere of brotherhood marked the Dutch *schutterijen*, or burgher guards. They had once symbolized the heroic Dutch citizenry: As loyal protectors of the privileges and prosperity of their town, they took care of its order and safety.[60] They had a prospering social life, which ideally included brotherly and

30. Jan Rotius (1624-1666), Dinner of officers of the schutterij *(citizen's militia)* of Hoorn, 1652.

harmonious contact. One of the rules of the burgher guard in Alkmaar, for example, was that no member of the guard could speak viciously to, or swear at, another guard-brother, 'as it is not pleasing to the Lord and people.'[61] In addition to a political and military obligation, membership in the burgher guard also created opportunities for men to be away from work and family. It was a form of gendered sociability that often created ties between men, some of which were stronger than the solidarity of family, neighborhoods or guilds. Numerous paintings of the dinners and festivities of the *schutterijen* testify to this social atmosphere. In Holland and Zeeland alone, at least 134 of these *schutterstukken* remain today.[62]

'Not swearing' and 'not speaking ill of others at the guard' are not included in what remains of the rules of Beverwijck's burgher guard, but these proscriptions may have been taken into consideration anyway. Only on two occasions between 1652 and 1660, the Fort Orange Court Minutes record a dispute at the burgher guard ending in a fight.[63] One tradition was kept at least one year. In 1655, tavern keeper Hendrick Jochemsz, who was lieutenant of the burgher guard, was allowed to have the guard 'shoot the parrot,' on the condition that he kept good order and took care that no accidents occurred or resulted.[64] In the Netherlands, this event, also called *koningschieten*, was part of an annual festival that was held on May Day or Pentecost. During three days of feasting, local marksmen would attempt to shoot the figure of a parrot from the top of a pole. The winner would be

proclaimed 'king of the marksmen' until bested. Everywhere in the Dutch Republic this was considered a great event. In Alkmaar, the king of the marksmen
did not have to pay excises in 1650, and for a year he was a member of the council
of war. In Amsterdam, the winner was given a traditional marksman's chain and a
scepter. When, in 1645, that city's mayor was first to shoot the parrot off the pole
for the third time in a row, the famous poet Joost van den Vondel even wrote a victory hymn.[65]

In August 1659, at the request of the burghers that they be relieved of night-
watch duty, the court issued instructions for a 'rattlewatch,' for which Lambert
van Valckenburgh and Pieter Winnen were appointed. The two men were to appear at the burghers' guardhouse after the ringing of the nine o'clock bell, and at
ten o'clock they would begin to make their rounds together, giving notice of their
presence in the streets of the village of Beverwijck by sounding their rattle and
calling out the hour at every hour of the night, until four o'clock in the morning.
They had to pay special attention to fire and upon the first sign of smoke, unusual light or other danger signs, to warn the people by knocking at their houses. If
they saw any likelihood of fire, they were to sound the alarm by rattling and calling, and then by running to the church (to which they had a key) and ringing the
bell. If they found thieves breaking into any houses or gardens, they were supposed try to prevent the crime to the best of their ability, arrest the thieves, and
bring them into the fort. And if they were not strong enough to do so, they had to
call for help to the burghers in the vicinity, who were duty-bound to lend a helping hand, as part of tending to the common welfare. In case of resistance, the rattlewatch was authorized to use force; and they were not liable for any accident
that might result from such opposing force, if it was used in the rightful performance of their official duties. Van Valckenburgh and Winnen were appointed on
the condition that, together, they were to receive 1,100 guilders in *sewant* and 100
guilders beavers worth for the term of one year.[66] When in 1659 Evert *de backer*
was ordered to pay three guilders for the rattlewatch, it seems to indicate that, as
in New Amsterdam, each householder contributed to pay for this service. Women
whose husbands were away from home, widows, preachers, and individuals who
were in someone's service may have been excluded.[67] Despite the fact that it was
performed by men who were not professional policemen and only had limited authority, Beverwijck's court minutes reveal no problems with the rattlewatch.

Community feelings

The records reveal nothing of the social aspect of Beverwijck's burgher guard. We
don't know whether it created the sense of comradery, friendship and brotherhood among its members, as it did in so many places in the fatherland. No great
burgher guard meals are recorded. It is not even known whether the event of
'shooting the parrot' was successful, who became king of the marksmen, and
whether it was ever repeated. In fact, not much is known about feelings of community in Beverwijck in general. Here and there, the records reveal something
about communal events; but well-organized social clubs, as they existed in the

Dutch Republic, had not yet been founded. Sometimes sleigh races were held on the ice in winter, and throughout the year people got together to celebrate and drink in the taverns, to play *trick-track*, (backgammon) cards, or a game of billiards on the *trocktaefel* (pool table).[68] For some inhabitants, *Vastenavond (Shrove Tuesday, or Mardi Gras)* was an occasion to dress up and party together, and entertain themselves as a group by games such as 'pulling the goose.' On January 26, 1654 some people dressed 'in strange clothes, some men in women's clothes, and walked publicly along the street, having fool's masks before their faces and more scandalous and unseemingly things.'[69] In *patria*, the walking along the streets was often done in combination with drinking and dancing, while important people were sometimes ridiculed.[70] In Beverwijck, these activities probably took a similar course, and the partiers were forbidden from continuing on pain of a *f*25 fine. Abraham *Crabaat* (Croation), who also had walked along the street in woman's clothes, on Shrove Tuesday in 1654, declared that he did not know that he was doing wrong; he was fined *f*6 and told not to repeat the offense on pain of being punished arbitrarily as an example to others. The court reasoned that 'not only many improprieties thereby take place, but the farm and other servants not only cease from their service and by that means lose time, but fights, blows, blasphemy, oaths and other irregularities happen.' Thereafter, *Shrovetide* seems to have been celebrated more within the houses.[71] During this celebration, physical violence often occurred in fights or in ritualistic, sadistic games with animals, such as 'pulling the goose.' In this game, horseback riders attempted to carry away a greased goose suspended from a pole by grabbing its neck, all of which was accompanied by heavy drinking. In the fatherland this game was prohibited by the church, but in various places it was tolerated and connived at. In contrast with the colonial government's prohibition, Beverwijck's court winked at the game, as well, when some in Beverwijck played the game in February 1655.[72]

No reference to people celebrating Saint Nicolas (*Sinterklaas*) in Beverwijck has been found until March 5, 1675, when Maria van Rensselaer paid *f*2-10 to baker Wouter Albertsz vanden Uythoff for some *Sinterklaasgoet*.[73] In Amsterdam, where Saint Nicolas had been a patron of the city and its old church (*Oude Kerk*) for a long time, this holiday was celebrated by everyone, high and low, rich and poor, young and old, within the homes: and every year, the church councils (consistories) protested about it, and used excuses to suppress the festivities by complaining about the stands in the streets where 'popish' candy was openly sold. These stands, they said, were the cause of parents telling their children that they had received this all from Saint Nicolas, thus indoctrinating the children with old 'popish superstitions' and 'fables.'[74] Such protests never actually referred to Catholics, but were more a means to suppress and fight the celebration. The absence of the celebration in the records does not mean that it was not celebrated. Such common customs were taken along overseas, and often they are not mentioned in the records. They are part of the unspoken activities of daily life. In Beverwijck, people basically followed a Dutch way of life, as that was what they were familiar with; and these celebrations were part of it, even though they are not mentioned in the source materials. Instead of assuming that the lack of information indicates that no attention was paid in Beverwijck to this popular children's feast, we could also assume that the fact that it is not mentioned anywhere indicates that these celebrations took place in a way similar to the ways of the fatherland. And that an important inhabitant of the colony would openly buy this candy after the English takeover suggests that it was celebrated. It could also indicate that, in 1675, Maria van Rensselaer, as well as the baker, were well aware of the consequences of having become English, and that *Sinterklaas* by then was on its way to becoming an ethnic celebration.[75] Social events likely were spontaneously and individually organized, for example, people visiting their neighbors; such events did not reach the written records.

Ties between people did exist. Even in the New World community, several inhabitants would be related, and frequently they lived near each other. Three sisters of Scottish origin, for example, lived near the *Ruttenkil* (Appendix 8, I, no. 9; II, no. 8, 10). The documents reveal nothing about their communications, but it is hard to imagine that they would not have helped each other out in practical matters of the household, childrearing, and perhaps the trade as well, and that they did not socialize and share happiness and sadness. Volckert Jansz, for example, helped his brother-in-law and neighbor, Rutger Jacobsz, when he had financial problems.[76] (Appendix 8, XI, VJD, RJ). The relationship between the surgeon Jacob de Hinsse and his apprentice Cornelis van Dijck was very good, as well, when Van Dijck finished his apprenticeship. In 1671, seven weeks after the death of his wife, De Hinsse married Van Dijck's sister Ryckie Hendricks, who was the widow of gunstock maker and trader Jan Dareth.[77] As in the fatherland, kinship ties held people together, creating some stability in a time when there was no social security. Family members helped each other out, for instance, in personal or financial matters. Seventeenth century people needed a collective strategy of survival, and much effort was invested to maintain the friendship – for example in the form of services and favors, gifts and obligations. As early settlers married and raised families, the kinship ties became more recognizable in Beverwijck. Although the basis usually was a broad family group that could stretch to distantly related family members, neighbors, work relations and people with whom one associated in church could belong to this friends group, as well. Together, they contributed to a sense of solidarity, and helped each other in times of depression. These friendships existed between people with common interests, who helped each other through practical, concrete aid and moral support.[78]

Neighbors in Beverwijck cooperated on certain undertakings as well. Five men jointly dug a sewer, for example, and several people shared a common well, for which they had appointed an overseer.[79] In 1655, a neighborhood undertook joint action to help out one man in their area and to protect themselves. Two men petitioned the court about the danger of fire to the straw roof of their needy neighbor, Willem Jurriaensz (Appendix 8, II, no. 12). The court subsequently requested them and other neighbors to help out, whereupon some ten men contributed in the form of boards, timbers, nails and money. Herewith, they replaced the fire-prone roof with one covered with planks, and in return received a share of ownership of Willem's house.[80] It seems that such collective undertakings were spontaneous, and probably they happened frequently. We know about those mentioned in the court records because some additional action had to be taken. The sewer inconvenienced the inhabitants, for example, and the sewer makers were asked to build a bridge across it. The records don't mention specific neighborhoods (*gebuurten*) as they existed in Dutch towns, whose residents voluntarily arranged their rights and obligations, and who's aim was that neighbors would dwell and live in peace and harmony together. It is likely that certain things were organized, like the sharing of a well or a sewer and, as in the fatherland, people may very well have organized neighborhood boards and neighborhood dinners, and probably also attended a neighbor's funeral; these things may have been part of normal life, but don't appear in the records.[81]

In the workplace, it was not unusual for people to cooperate on certain undertakings. The neighbors Goosen Gerritsz and Rutger Jacobsz, for example, together ran a brewery for several years. Others joined forces and capital as well, and invested in a brewery, a mill, or a farm in an outlying area, such as Halfmoon, Catskil or the Esopus. Although it is not specifically mentioned in the sources, the fact that several people with the same trade, such as bakers, or blacksmiths and gunstock makers, lived next to each other suggests cooperation, as well. Guilds, as they existed in Dutch towns, were not established in Beverwijck. As we will see in the chapter five, a request in 1655 for permission to form a bakers' guild was 'for certain reasons' not considered advisable by the court.[82]

People did follow certain communal customs in the world of work. Commissary La Montagne, for example, felt obliged to maintain the custom of spending a barrel of good beer among the builders when the old company house was torn down. On the occasion of laying the first stone for a new building, the masons and carpenters were provided with brandy, wine, or beer; and when the roof of a house in Beverwijck was covered with tiles, the owner of the building, as at Manhattan, treated the workers to 'tile beer' (*pannenbier*). When a house was totally finished, the custom was that the owner would treat all workers to a certain meal or dinner called *de kroegh*.[83] There also may have been customs like these among other tradesmen, but no social clubs are mentioned in the records. At that time, there was probably too little tradition and cohesion in the local community. Social life, in the first place, seems to have been spontaneous and followed certain customs.

Most inhabitants participated in some kind of community event; only African slaves are never mentioned in this context.

Forced labor: Slaves

Only a few Africans were in the upper Hudson area in 1652. We only know of a certain Jan *de neger*, who in 1646 was induced to serve as hangman for one special execution – a dishonorable job no Dutchman wanted to perform. In the late 1640s there was commissary Carel van Bruggen's negro Pieter, who was probably in service to the West India Company, and in the spring of 1652 one private inhabitant owned a female negro.[84]

Since its founding, the West India Company had been involved with slaves, and in 1628 some female Angolese negro slaves were in New Amsterdam.[85] When patroonships were established, the company promised to supply the patroons with as many blacks as possible, but no records confirm that the company indeed brought them to Rensselaerswijck.[86] The 1637 conquest of São Jorge da Mina, or Elmina, on the West African coast of Guinea was the beginning of the company's organized slave trade. Slavery was sometimes justified by clergymen if the slaves retained certain rights, and especially the right to humane treatment. Slaves would have more opportunities to come to the 'right' religion, one minister reasoned, and seven years after conversion they could regain their freedoms and live as free Christians.[87] Although most of the company's slaves were brought to Brazil, some ended up in New Netherland, where there may have been about a hundred by 1639. Once Curaçao began to develop as a transit station in 1645, slave imports into New Netherland became more regular. In 1646, the first slave ship arrived directly from the coast of Guinea; and, in 1647, the company promised to send more slaves, so that they could be employed advantageously in agriculture.[88] Most of these slaves were owned by the company; but in the spring of 1652, some private traders were allowed to sail to the African coast and fetch as many negroes at the coast of Angola as they needed; a paper form was now made to enhance the trade.[89] This was the first step toward providing slaves for sale to the colonists of New Netherland. Especially after the loss of Brazil in 1654, New Netherland became a more important slave market for the company and for private traders. Between 1660 and 1664, at least 400 slaves were delivered at New Amsterdam.[90]

The first clear proof of private slave ownership in the upper Hudson dates from March 1652, when Sander Leendertsz's negress was sued for slander and theft.[91] The next indication is not until 1657, when Jeremias van Rensselaer bought a negro named Andries for his brother Jan Baptist. Catharina Roelofs, who had grown up in Rensselaerswijck, was the seller. She was the widow of Lucas Roodenburg, a former vice director of Curaçao, which by 1654 had become the main slave depot for the entire Caribbean.[92] It seems that 'the tall and quick fellow' worked so well that, although slavery was not allowed in the Dutch Republic, after he had returned to *patria* Jan Baptist requested that Andries be sent over in order to take care of his horse. However, Jeremias could not spare his worker and, in any case, thought the negro would be too proud to serve his brother in a free country.[93]

Prices for slaves depended on their sex, age, and condition, and rose over the years. At an auction in New Amsterdam in 1664, prices for a male negro varied between ƒ315 and ƒ615, while female negroes went for between ƒ260 and ƒ335; a female was sold with her child for ƒ360.[94] In 1659, Jeremias van Rensselaer paid his brother quite a bit more than Wouter van Twiller had paid to Samuel Ax in 1636, when he bought three slaves from Ax for ƒ40 apiece.[95] Jan Baptist received fifty beavers for the slave, with the explanation that Andries was not worth much more, 'for that sort of negroes is too treacherous, although he is among the best.' Negroes who had been in the West Indies for twelve or thirteen years, and who had lived continuously with Dutch people for a year or two, had been sold at public sale for 300 or 350 guilders, according to Jeremias, and 'they were a better sort of negroes.'[96] Probably, he was referring to a public sale of three negroes and one negress that had been held in Beverwijck a good month earlier, and where Abraham Staets had bought one negro for ƒ350.[97] This public sale was the first and only recorded slave auction in Beverwijck. Other such sales are known to have taken place in New Amsterdam. In 1661, for example, the ship *De Nieu Nederlantsen Indiaen* arrived from Curaçao with forty old and young negroes and negresses. Thirty-six of them would be sold at a public sale to the highest bidder. Payment could be made with beavers, or with meat, bacon, wheat or peas of equivalent value (in beavers); the reasoning for this method of payment was that if cash beavers or tobacco at beaver's price were demanded, no burgher or farmer would be able to buy a slave.[98]

In 1664, Van Rensselaer bought another slave for ƒ400 from Stuyvesant, who probably was the largest private owner of slaves in New Netherland: He had forty slaves employed in farm labor and domestic work in 1660.[99] At Stuyvesant's urging, Van Rensselaer also bought the negress with whom the negro had a relationship for ƒ350, which may indicate that slaves were free to choose a marriage partner. She was 'a [good] sound wench,' Jeremias wrote, and he would try to start raising [damaged document] with her.[100] He would let the *schout* employ the male negro when he needed him, which suggests that this slave did similar work as the company negro in commissary La Montagne's service. This man kept the fire in the guard house, functioned as a messenger, and on occasion helped to guard prisoners.[101] By that time, more company negroes had come to Fort Orange, and most likely they had to do work similar to that of negroes at New Amsterdam; when repairs on the fort were made, they may have helped carry stone and other building materials.[102] More private individuals in the upper Hudson area bought slaves as well, sometimes employing them on their farms.[103]

Only in Van Rensselaer's correspondence we can find a small reference to these slaves' way of life, and to how they were regarded in Beverwijck's society. Andries, it seems, was expected to do chores around the house, take care of the horse, and do such errands as fetching wine.[104] According to Van Rensselaer, it was 'bad enough to get him to do anything for anybody' if he did not expressly order him to do so, so that at times he had to punish him. When he wrote to his brother that, in any event, people cared about his protest 'as much as if my negro had said it,' that may indicate that he did not feel much respect for Andries as a human being; he seems to have been content with Andries' work and presence, since Andries was still running errands for him at Anthony Jansz' tavern in 1667.[105] However, Jeremias would send back to New Amsterdam a negro he had bought in about 1660: The man was a burden, for he 'could do no more work than a child and ate as much as three men.' Immediately after the purchase, Van Rensselaer had already noted that 'he was even more refractory and a useless, dirty beast.'[106]

One wonders why Van Rensselaer had bought this slave. It seems that he did not need one, but rather that it was a symbol of wealth: Individuals such as La Montagne, Sander Leendertsz, Goosen Gerritsz, Abraham Staets, and probably others had slaves, and by that time having a negro may have become a status symbol. The West India Company had several slaves in its service at Fort Orange and

New Amsterdam; therefore, Jeremias may have thought that possession of slaves would maintain the patroonship's prestige.[107]

Possibly some freed negroes were also in the area, as there were at Manhattan. The two negroes who died as the result of an explosion in the fort, in 1652 or 1653, 'were there trading.'[108] Arent van Curler's widow appears to have freed some of her negroes; one of them, Bastiaen Pietersz, was 'residing with Juffrouw Curlers' in 1669, and Pietersz himself stated that he was a servant of the widow (and not a slave). If Bastiaen is the same individual as Bassie *de neger*, he was buried by the Dutch Reformed church in 1671, indicating that he attended church.[109]

Forced work had found its way to the upper Hudson. By 1664, the documents show at least four (and probably more) private slave owners in the community.[110] By the end of the 1670s, even the minister had two slaves, who may have served in his household and on his travels to other congregations. Gerrit Bancker, Sweer Theunisz, Theunis Spitsenbergh, Abraham Staets, and Jacob Jansz Flodder used slaves on their farms.[111] Tom Burke has estimated that, by 1714, unfree blacks accounted for 29.7 percent of Rensselaerswijck's population alone, while in Albany this number was 9.9 percent.[112]

Whether they were free or slaves, the status of negroes was low; nowhere is there mention of blacks having been burghers or of their participation in the burgher guard. But this does not mean that they had no legal rights. Negroes had the right to own property, to work for wages, to sue or be sued, and to give testimony in court; and they were protected from abuse by their masters or others.[113] That no African went to Beverwijck's court between 1652 and 1660 to sue a European settler may indicate either that they had no complaints about their treatment, or that there were hardly any blacks. It could also mean that, unlike other inhabitants of Beverwijck, negroes did not understand that the civil rights of men and women were protected under the law, as in the Dutch Republic, and that they could make themselves heard by Beverwijck's court whenever they felt that their rights had been violated.

Stabilizing factors in a new society: The state

The court

The local court of Fort Orange was the place to which the inhabitants of Beverwijck could turn – where they directed their petitions and concerns.[114] Typical of colonial development, the legal concerns of Beverwijckers were often personal, and the court's judgments affected their lives. If necessary, inhabitants expected the court to represent their interests before the provincial council.

On Monday, April 15, 1652, Beverwijck's inferior bench of justice (*kleine banck van justitie*) met for the first time. The opening line of the first minutes, 'In the name of the Lord, Amen,' is an indication of the context in which the court was to operate. These words suggest that the magistrates had opened the session with a prayer, perhaps in a similar way as the magistrates of the new municipal court of

New Amsterdam, at their first court session almost a year later.[115] These men thanked God that it had pleased Him to make the members of the court of New Amsterdam the 'rulers of the people in this place,' and they prayed that God would give them the grace to use the power He had granted them for the general benefit of the authorities of the church, the protection of the good, and the punishment of the bad.[116] Although state and religion were separated, a religious philosophy provided the context in which the court reached its decisions.

Beverwijck's court was patterned after the inferior courts in the Netherlands (also called the court of *schout en schepenen*) and consisted of a *schout* appointed by the director general and council with West India Company approval, and six *schepenen* or magistrates, including one extraordinary magistrate who also was appointed by the director general and council. When the English took over New Netherland in 1664, sixteen of these inferior courts were operating in the colony.[117] In contrast to the fatherland, however, these towns had no representation in the colonial government, which consisted of a director general and a two-man council appointed in the Dutch Republic. New Netherland's government was strongly centralized, and the colonial council alone determined the scope of the local courts' jurisdiction.[118] The institution of the *Lantdagh*, where representatives of various villages and localities in New Netherland had gathered since March 1649, and which was meant to advise the director general and council, may have had some influence; but it never had any administrative or judicial power. After Stuyvvesant declared its 1653 meeting invalid – it had been organized without being called together by director general and council – the *Lantdagh* would not be called together again until 1663.[119] Although, within the usual legislation, everyone in the Netherlands had the right of appeal from the town to the provincial and hence to the supreme court, in New Netherland no appeal was allowed beyond the colonial council.[120] As the primary duty of the director general and his council was to protect the company's interests above all, they were afraid that if a town had too much power, it easily could lessen the company's authority.[121]

The procedures the court had to follow in maintaining peace and justice in society were prescribed by the director general and council through detailed procedural laws and customs. As Shattuck has described in her dissertation about Beverwijck's court and community, these regulations were stipulated in numerous laws and ordinances, thereby organizing the lives of the inhabitants. There were regulations and certificates for collecting the excise tax; regulations and forms governed the auctioning of buildings, land and crops, as well as the follow-up sale agreements. There were certificates attesting to the good name of a wrongfully slandered person, and rules to be followed by tavern keepers, tapsters, brewers, and bakers. The duties for secretaries, clerks, and notaries were thoroughly explained – from the keeping registers to giving receipts.[122] Sometimes the smallest details were considered: Sixteen articles in an ordinance regulated the duties and fees for court messengers.[123] The colonial government's influence was considerable at the local level: They could, for example, determine which towns received charters, and the extent of a town's authority. Courts could make local ordinances for surveying, fencing and the like, but had to submit these to the council for ap-

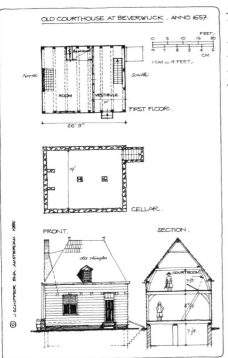

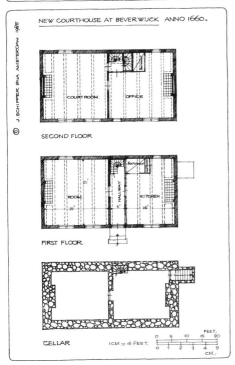

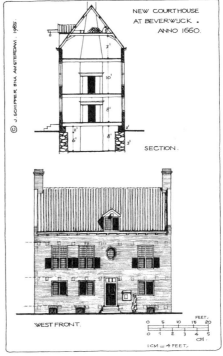

31. *Jaap Schipper B.N.A., Amsterdam, 1985. Three drawings of the old court house anno 1657 and the new court house anno 1660. Based on descriptions by Johannes La Montagne (NYSA, NYCM 9, pp.228-230. See also FOCM, xxvi).*

proval; and a town had no control at all over the appointment of a *schout*.[124] The council also handled criminal cases and capital punishment, based on evidence submitted by the local court. Altogether, Shattuck concludes, Beverwijck was a firmly regulated society.[125]

As in *patria*, government represented the burghers; but women, people not living in Beverwijck, and anyone who was not a member (or at least a *liefhebber*) of the Reformed religion could not be a member of the court. Initially the inhabitants of Beverwijck submitted a list of names to the colonial government, which then choose the magistrates from this group. Thereafter, according to the custom of the fatherland, the council choose the magistrates from a double-roster of nominees submitted annually by the incumbent magistrates, and which was sent to the director general and council for selection. As in the fatherland, these nominees were not men trained in the law; rather, they were drawn from the inhabitants. They belonged to the wealthiest and most honorable, prominent, moderate and peaceable burghers of the community; in other places, words like 'the most capable, honest and most qualified' were added, as well. A new magistrate had to live in the village; actually, he had to have lived there for seven years.[126] Jan Labatie, who served on the first court, had to quit the position of magistrate when he moved to Rensselaerswijck.[127] Qualified individuals were obligated to do this, and were expected to put aside their own occupations if called to public service. Possession and authority had been ordained by God, who had also chosen regents to govern.[128] In 1648, for example, Goosen Gerritsz considered himself incompetent to serve on Rensselaerswijck's court; he declared that he was not bound to serve in the patroon's court since he owned no house and lot, while he also was not yet on a free basis with the patroon. But Gerritsz' reasons for declining employment in the capacity of magistrate were found to be of insufficient weight; therefore, he was 'kindly requested to voluntarily accept the vacant office; otherwise, though very reluctantly,' the court would find itself 'forced to resort to other means.'[129] Although for some it may have meant a sacrifice, serving as magistrate was not only considered a duty, but also meant the recognition of one's status in society. The office brought along prestige and rewards as well; for instance, one's family coat of arms would be painted on stained glass and incorporated into the church windows.[130] Magistrates also had the right to appoint certain offices like rattle-watches or beer carriers, and thus were able to create a network of influence and protection, sometimes by making friends or family members the beneficiaries of their patronage.

Of the six magistrates, two retired every year. The term of office was two years, and a year off the bench was required before a magistrate could be asked to serve again.[131] Of the men who dominated the court between 1652 and 1664, several had come from the province of Holland; but other magistrates had their origins in the provinces of Utrecht, Gelderland, or Brabant. Some were even from outside the Dutch Republic, from the areas of Schleswig-Holstein, Denmark, East-Friesland, France, and Scotland.[132] Several had come to Rensselaerswijck as a farmer, farm-hand, shoemaker, carpenter, surgeon, or performer of some other trade under contract to Kiliaen van Rensselaer. Upon completion of their contracts with the patroon, they usually became free men who invested in real estate, or in such undertakings as a farm, brewery, mill, or a ship. Their education went as far as learning how to read and write, and in Beverwijck they saw a chance to become large fur traders, merchants, shipowners, or brewers.

The vice director of Fort Orange and Beverwijck was commissary of the fort, in which position he remained in charge of the fort, the fort's stores and the trade. But in addition, he sat as president of the newly established court, sharing an equal vote with the magistrates, while the vote of the majority bound the court's decision. He also held the office of *schout*, which was similar to a law enforcement officer and prosecuting officer. When in this function he prosecuted a case, he stepped down from the bench and could not vote, although he did make recommendations for the court's decisions. When this happened, or when he was away, one of the five magistrates served as president. As *schout*, he prepared court sessions and sentences, in which capacity he was responsible for convening the court, demanding justice of the magistrates, collecting the votes for each case, and executing the commands of the magistrates after the judgment was rendered – meaning that he had to oversee the execution of all public punishments.[133] He probably had access to books similar to those sent by the patroon to *schout* Planck in 1634 – for instance, Joost Damhouder's *Practijcq Crimineel*, which dealt with criminal procedures, *Ars Notariatus*, concerning notarial procedures, and a *Maniere van Procederen*, which was probably Paul Merula's civil procedure of the courts of Holland, Zeeland and West Friesland.[134] He must have been familiar with Grotius's *Inleydinge tot de Hollandsche rechts-geleertheyt* (Introduction to the Jurisprudence of Holland; 1631) as well, which had been brought over by Brant van Slichtenhorst; this work was the primary source on Roman-Dutch law, as it clearly and concisely systematized the existing collections of laws, and was written in Dutch (instead of Latin).[135] Various laws and ordinances reflect the use of these books.[136] The *schout* had a powerful position: He had to make sure that the area stayed clear of riffraff and offenders of the law, and in judicial processes he was the one who requested the punishment, and who interrogated. Doubtlessly, he was a central figure when issues such as small insults, scolding, or frays were settled out-of-court. Before individuals were arrested, the *schout* and bystanders may have first tried to appease the disputing parties. For his services, he was 'to receive a third part [of all fines] for his seizure.'[137]

We gain a more detailed picture of the duties of a *schout* by reading the instructions for Gerrit Swart, who was hired in April 1652 for the colony of Rensselaerswijck. Among other things, he was expected to take care that public worship was maintained, that the Sabbath was observed, and that colonists did not mingle with the Indians. The conduct of all criminal suits – their institution, execution, description, and final prosecution – was to be in his name, although he should not commence any suit except by order of the commissaries. He had to make sure that all placards, ordinances, resolutions, contracts and commands of the patroon and co-directors were observed; finally, the *schout* was not allowed to receive any gifts from anybody. His annual salary was ƒ400, plus a third of all fines above ƒ10.[138] In Rensselaerswijck the *schout* was appointed by the patroon, and in Beverwijck by

the director general and council under instructions from the West India Company directors. He could serve for an unlimited period of time. Swart was *schout* for
eighteen years; he was first appointed in Rensselaerswijck in 1652, where he
served until 1665, when the patroonship's court was incorporated into the court
of Albany, Rensselaerswijck and Schenectady. There, he continued in this function until 1670, when he was replaced by Captain Sylvester Salisbury, who was
then commander of Fort Albany.[139]

The *schout* was the full extent of law enforcement in the Beverwijck community, for all practical purposes. Certainly during the trading season, he was busy
enough to request an assistant from the court to help him carry out his duties by
keeping the village clear of riffraff. In December 1652, Johannes Dijckman was
given a deputy in the person of Evert Brantsz from Amersfoort, a soldier who had
just retired from West India Company service. His appointment only lasted until
the following May. In the first three months of 1657, the position of deputy *schout*
seems to have been filled by Jan Daniel, who on occasion caught people drinking
in a tavern during the church service.[140] In the same year, the colonial government
promised that Poulus Symonsz would replace Jan Daniel; but Symonsz, not content with the salary, did not show up.[141] In February 1658, we find the position
filled by Hans Vos, the former court messenger of Rensselaerswijck, who held the
job until he was caught selling alcohol to the Indians during the following trading
season.[142] In the beginning of that year, Jacob Theunisz *de Looper* was hired to
serve as *schout bij nacht*, a deputy-level position whose basic duties involved com-
munity-wide surveillance during the night. He was assaulted by Pieter Ryverdingh and Adriaen Jansz van Leyden as he tried to arrest them for selling alcohol
to the Indians.[143] The *schout* was often asssisted by a company negro, who worked
as a jailer or tended the fire in the guardhouse. In 1656, Johannes de Deckere had
help of one negro and some soldiers, and La Montagne had two servants and a negro.[144] They may also have had help from other company negroes who were in
Fort Orange.[145] It seems that after the West India Company became involved in
the slave trade, company officials were eager to use negroes as a workforce. At the
time, Kiliaen van Rensselaer also considered providing a negro for schout Adriaen
van der Donck's assistance in Rensselaerswijck, and his son Jeremias bought a negro in 1664, whom he meant to make available for the *schout*'s service in the
colony.[146]

For several years the vice director, in addition to his functions as commissary,
schout and president of the court, also served in the capacity of court secretary,
which required him to record the minutes of all court transactions. Ordinances of
1638 and 1640 stipulated that contracts, promissory notes, and rental or sale
agreements only were valid if they were recorded by the court secretary.[147] In
1646, and again in 1649, it was ordained that affidavits, contracts, testaments,
agreements and other important documents not written by the secretary or other
duly authorized person were invalid, as 'grave mistakes occur in the writing and
drawing up of evidence of the truth by private individuals, who are neither bound
by oath nor called by authority thereto, whereby many things are written to the
advantage of those who have the papers drawn up.'[148] In January 1658, an ordi-

nance regulated the instruction and fees for secretaries, notaries, and clerks. It described in detail the duties and fees of notaries and other officers: They were to take an oath to submit to the ordinance, and to keep a register of their official transactions. They were not allowed to take money in advance or gifts for services, or agree on payment for future services; but they could receive their fee before or after the suit, upon rendering proper accounts and specifications. They had to sign and seal every instrument executed by them, whereby they were allowed six stivers as the legal fee. When required, they were bound to give a receipt for fees, when paid. The ordinance also defined the types of work and the fees to be charged for them, such as fees for petitions, registrations, summonses, answers, copying, deduction, petitions directed to the director general and council, contracts, inventories, and interrogatories. They could demand and receive various fees, depending on the length of the piece. The ordinance even went into such detail as to describe the number of lines on a page (25 to 30) and the number of characters in a line (30-36). The poor and indigent, 'who asked such as an alms, they were to serve gratis and *pro Deo.*'[149]

The first records of Fort Orange's court were kept by vice director Johannes Dijckman. Complaints from his superiors that they were no longer able to read his notes came in 1655, at the same time as he seemed incapable of maintaining his work. During the following year his successor, Johannes de Deckere, often kept the minutes himself as well; but vice director Johannes La Montagne brought along Johannes Provoost as secretary, who served during all of La Montagne's tenure.

Rensselaerswijck's secretary, Dirck van Schelluyne, simultaneously worked as a notary public in Beverwijck between 1660 and 1665. The coming to Beverwijck of a public notary marked an important change since, from then on, official documents did not always have to be signed by a member of the court; this work was organized this way in the eastern provinces of the Netherlands – for example, in Gelre and Overijssel, the place of origin of Kiliaen van Rensselaer. Van Schelluyne's appointment could indicate that Beverwijck's system had become more in accordance with that of the province of Holland. He had been notary in The Hague before coming to New Netherland and was not appointed by the West India Company, but was commissioned by the States General in April 1650 to exercise the profession of notary at Manhattan and throughout New Netherland. His commission was part of the States General's answer to a Remonstrance that had been presented to them by some delegates of the commonalty of New Netherland, in support of their grievances against director general Petrus Stuyvesant. When Van Schelluyne first arrived, he immediately took an active part in the opposition to Stuyvesant; as a result, he became an object of persecution by the director general, who in 1651 prohibited Van Schelluyne from practicing his profession. Another intervention by the States General restored Van Schelluyne to his function; but only when New Amsterdam obtained a city government would affairs begin to take a more favorable turn for him.[150]

The services of a Dutch notary public were similar to those of a modern-day family attorney, in that they were required in connection with the drawing up of all formal legal contracts, except insofar as the acknowledgment of such contracts was also permitted or especially reserved to the secretaries and magistrates of the local courts. To the latter belonged the formal transfers and mortgages of real estate and documents involving the administration of an oath. Aside from these, practically all legal papers, including contracts for the sale of real estate and depositions in the form of affirmations, indentures of service, assignments, leases, wills, marriage settlements and inventories of estates, which might afterwards be sworn to before the proper officer, had to be executed before a notary and witnessed by two trustworthy males over 24 years of age.[151] The originals of such documents were kept by the notary, who was prohibited from giving anyone access to his records or to issue copies or extracts therefrom to any but the interested parties. The originals and the first copies, containing the date as well as the genuine, notarized signatures of the parties were held as authentic by all courts.[152]

The court messenger issued citations to those summoned to appear before the court. To show that he was on official business when he appeared at burghers's homes, the court messenger usually carried an official staff, as was the custom in towns and outlying districts of Holland. Shortly after Beverwijck's court was founded, Pieter Ryverdingh, the first court messenger, was allowed to charge 6 stivers for each citation, 12 stivers for each attachment, and 4 stivers for presenting a petition.[153] Sixteen articles in an ordinance of April 23, 1658 further regulated the duties and fees for court messengers in detail. The ordinance described, for instance, how to handle summonses both with the defendants and before the court, and how to collect debts and attach property.[154] When Pieter Ryverdingh made known his intention to return to the Dutch Republic in 1656, Ludovicus Cobus successfully applied for his job as court messenger to the director general and council of New Netherland, 'as he was not able to perform any trade, because in his youth he always had studied.' Cobus was working as court messenger by February 27, 1657.[155]

The jurisdiction of the court of Fort Orange covered a large area; until 1661, it extended beyond the village to the Catskill and Esopus region, about sixty miles downriver. Other small communities that had been settled along the Hudson River also fell under the court of Fort Orange: Coxsackie to the south, Claverack and Kinderhook on the east side of the river, and Schenectady, eighteen miles to the west along the Mohawk River. Most of the profits in New Netherland could be made in this area, which was the major source of the fur trade. At a distance of 150 miles from Manhattan, however, it was impossible for the colonial government to survey and intervene continuously. Traffic upriver was difficult between November and April; the often frozen river isolated the area for a good part of the year. Therefore, it was very important to appoint capable men at Fort Orange who would ensure that its community was stable and productive.

The three vice directors who headed the court between 1652 and 1664 had an important job that combined the roles commissary, president of the court, *schout* and, until 1656, secretary. The post required literate persons who were trusted by the directors and provincial government. All three vice directors came from outside the community, and were known to the directors of the West India Compa-

ny's Amsterdam chamber. Dijckman and De Deckere were appointed at the suggestion of the company directors; and when Stuyvesant appointed La Montagne,
the directors in Amsterdam had no objections.

Johannes Dijckman served as vice director from April 1652 until June 1655. Before coming upriver in 1651 to be the commissary of Fort Orange, he had worked
as a bookkeeper for the West India Company at Manhattan. During his journey to
New Netherland on the ship *De Waterhondt*, it had been noted that Dijckman
misbehaved on board in 'drunkenness and disorder,' behavior that he seems to
have continued in Beverwijck.[156] When Dijckman became incapacitated in June
1655, the company directors suggested replacing him with Johannes de Deckere,
who had worked as a public notary in Schiedam and had good connections with
the Amsterdam chamber. De Deckere arrived in New Netherland in April 1655,
and was appointed by the council as provisional director in July; the directors had
given instructions that he should be given the first vacant office in New Netherland. A year later, De Deckere refused the post of commissary, and in August 1656
Johannes La Montagne offered to go to Fort Orange.[157] La Montagne, a Huguenot, had been a *doctor medicinae* in Manhattan when Kieft appointed him to his
council in 1638, in which position he served until he came to Fort Orange in the
fall of 1656. La Montagne's instructions reveal how much responsibility was involved in the position of vice director: He was to make sure that good order was
maintained at Fort Orange and Beverwijck regarding all matters of trade, police,
justice and militia, as well as military personel, 'boat people,' free persons, high
and low officers whatever their state or rank, whether or not they were already
there or the director general and council sent them later. As vice director, he had
to help conduct and command over those places, maintain everything in good order for the service and well-being of the company, and administer both civil and
military law and justice.[158]

On March 5, 1652, the director general and council officially ordered the commissary of Fort Orange no longer to permit the erection of any building either to
the west or northwest of the fort, nor to erect boundary posts.[159] It is very well
possible that Beverwijck was given a charter after this; but if it ever had one, the
document no longer exists. Thus, it is difficult to say how restrictive the charter
may have been.[160] According to Martha Shattuck, the colonial council displayed
considerable trust in the ability of the court. In general, the court carried out the
overall policies laid down by Stuyvesant and the council, who were aware that
contacts with Indians on a frequent basis were necessary; therefore, negotiations
and conferences with the Indians were handled by the local magistrates. Imple-
mentation of Indian diplomacy, then, was handled judiciously and successfully by
the men on the scene. Further, Shattuck points out, Stuyvesant also granted the
court of Fort Orange the right to enact its own ordinances against the smuggling
of liquor and illegal trading practices; and although the first surveyors had been
approved by Stuyvesant in 1652, Jan Roelofsz was 'chosen and appointed' by the
local court in 1654, indicating that the court had received authority over its local
appointments.[161] Beverwijck's court may have had broader powers than other inferior courts, Shattuck suggests. They set aside thorny problems for Stuyvesant's

visits, or sent emissaries and letters to the council requesting decisions; but the local magistrates usually got their way. The court was careful not to overstep its authority; it deferred to Stuyvesant and the council for advice and consent, and regularly kept the director general apprised of the community's problems, successes
and needs. This diplomacy paid off in increased authority and flexibility.[162] An
important sign of the colonial government's trust was also displayed in 1657,
when the court appointed Jan Verbeeck and Evert Jansz Wendel as orphan masters
who were to report directly to the court of Fort Orange and Beverwijck.[163]

Orphan Masters

Until 1657, the church usually took care of orphans,[164] while the *schout* was called
'protector of the orphans.' In January of that year, the court appointed former
consistory members Jan Verbeeck and Evert Jansz Wendel as curators of the estate
of the surviving children of Jacob Luyersz, deceased. A month later the court,
'having considered the need of orphan masters in this place and experienced the
faithfulness of Jan Verbeeck and Evert Wendels, have for the service and best interest of the country appointed them orphan masters, to take charge of all estates,
which [otherwise] would remain uncared for through the death of the husband or
wife.'[165] In 1655, forty colonists had died and a hundred had been taken captive by
the Indians in the Peach war in New Amsterdam, leaving many widows and orphans to the care of the church. The need was so great that Beverwijck's church
sent ƒ200 to help out.[166] At the request of New Amsterdam's burgomasters,
Stuyvesant allowed the city to establish an orphan chamber in 1655, as there had
been in Amsterdam.[167] In the fatherland, the institution of orphan masters had existed at least since 1355. As Beverwijck did not have a separate orphan chamber,
Wendel and Verbeeck were to report directly to the court of Fort Orange. On
February 27, 1657 they declared in court, for example, that they had seen the bad
management of Christoffel Davidsz in administering the estate left undivided between himself and his children, the heirs of Cornelia de Vos, his deceased wife.
They proposed that Andries de Vos, the mother's father, and Arent Andriesz,
their mother's brother, should become curators of the estate of the minor children.
The court granted them authority as lawful curators of the estate and guardians of
the children with power 'to do therein and in all that is connected therewith as
they jointly shall see fit for the benefit of the said estate and children.'[168]

In the Dutch Republic, it was the law that all persons under the age of twenty-
five as well as individuals above that age who, on account of mental or other disability, were deemed incompetent to manage their own affairs (for example, single
women, widows, or insane people), were provided with a guardian. The rule was
that, as soon as a parent had died, the orphan masters were informed, who then
immediately made a description of the estate and appointed guardians.[169]
Guardians often emerged from family circles, and were designated by will or appointed by the orphan masters. They were in charge of the education and maintenance of the minor, as well as of the administration of his estate, and were at all
times under the direction and control of the orphan masters. If a conflict arose,

parties could turn to the civil court, which acted as a supreme guardian. The guardian first had to make an inventory and appraise the property of the deceased, which could also be done by a notary in the presence of the relatives and guardians. Then an agreement was made with the survivor as to the portion that each child was to receive and how a division should proceed. After the agreement had been recorded by a notary, the guardians reported back to the orphan masters for their approval or for further disposal of the estate. The agreement specified the procedure of the division. The 'Orphan Chamber' ordinance required a surviving parent to exhibit the orphan's property, which was called 'making proof' (*aen de wees sijn goet bewijsen*, shortened to *bewijs doen*).[170] If one of the parents had died, the *usufruct* of the orphan's goods (*wezengoed*) was left to the surviving parent. A child's portion was determined from the inventory and, after the movable and immovable property was divided, the child's share was brought to the orphan chamber. All furniture and goods allotted to the orphan, such as household effects, clothes, jewels, and ornaments, were to be sold at public auction in the presence of the children and the nearest relatives, unless the guardians, in agreement with the orphan masters, thought otherwise. Turning goods into cash that could be invested, or making something unproductive productive, was the thought behind the public sale. Since the money often was used to pay for the upbringing of the children, it was not unusual for the child's share to be used up before he or she had reached majority.[171]

To continue the example of the estate of Christoffel Davidsz and the late Cornelia de Vos, their inventory was made in the presence of Davidsz himself, Jan Verbeeck and Evert Wendel at the request of guardian Andries de Vos (and in the absence of fellow guardian Arent Andriesz) and Johannes La Montagne, as officer at Fort Orange and Beverwijck – who had the goods, which consisted mostly of clothing and bedding, locked and sealed in a great chest.[172]

There was a way for widows or widowers to circumvent this procedure. In 1664, for example, Goosen Gerritsz agreed with the orphan masters regarding the buying out (*uitkoop*) of his daughter Geertie Goosens' interest in her mother's estate and inheritance. Gerritsz promised to:

> ... deliver to Geertie, in full satisfaction of her said maternal inheritance and of her just portion, the house and lot which she now occupies, ... together with all the linen and woolen clothes of her said mother, as they are together at present, to be appraised by impartial persons; also a bed and one cow... On the other hand said Goossen Gerritsz shall remain in full possession of the estate, all debts and credits to be his loss and profit, without any prejudice to the rights of the three younger children, the said house and lot, linen and woolen clothes to be received and delivered to this end by and to said Geertie Goossens.[173]

Thus, a surviving spouse could retain the estate and buy out the interest of the child by placing a monetary value on the orphan's share.[174] When the child was a minor, the parent could deposit the buy-out sum with the orphan chamber, which then had the responsibility of obtaining interest on the orphan's portion. The orphan masters exercised control over the management by the guardians and, as stated above, in case of conflicts the parties could turn to the court, which functioned as super-guardian.

At New Amsterdam, by order of the orphan chamber, no one was allowed to marry for a second time without having reached an agreement with the guardians about the settlement of the children's inheritance.[175] This rule was also applied in Beverwijck; in 1663, for example, when Mijndert Fredericksz (widower of Catharyna Burger) intended to remarry, he signed a statement that out of his estate, 'to wit, from the estate left by Cataryna Burger, deceased, be reserved the sum of eight hundred guilders payable in beavers, for the children left by her.' The new couple also had to bring up the six- and three-year-old boys 'in the fear of the Lord, and teach them how to read and write in the schools, to maintain them in food and clothing till their majority or married state, without diminishing their maternal estate.'[176]

Both the poor and the rich shared the obligation to report to the orphan masters, since every orphan needed to have a guardian. The orphan chambers thus offered more security for the poor than for the more well-to-do inhabitants, who were capable of providing security themselves.[177] Wealthier people sometimes made wills in which they included rules for the management of the estate. Sometimes, by an 'act of seclusion,' they excluded the orphan masters. Jan Fransz van Hoesem and his wife Volckie Jurriaens did that in 1665, 'not being willing that they shall meddle therewith,' and in their place they appointed the survivor of either of them as guardian.[178] The notary, instead of the orphan masters, then became the responsible party. Other people, such as Jeremias van Rensselaer and his wife Maria, and Goosen Gerritsz and Annetje Lievens, also excluded the orphan masters.[179] David Narrett has pointed out that excluding the orphan chamber showed a testator's desire to benefit a widowed spouse. According to Narrett, it also could have expressed a 'popular distrust of judicial authority'; but, in all likelihood, the main objective was to keep possessions within the family.[180]

Medical care

The right to appoint orphan masters shows the trust of the director general and council in Beverwijck's court. It is not known how medical care was handled by the West India Company in Beverwijck, or whether the local surgeon was even appointed by the company. On the first of February, 1642, Kiliaen van Rensselaer had 'at the good recommendations of his master Johan Dircsz Brim, surgeon at Amsterdam' hired the 24-year-old Abraham Staets from Amsterdam for the duration of six years to perform the office of surgeon, to the exclusion of all others. The contract does not provide a detailed job description, but general information regarding medical training and activities in *patria* may shed some light on his activities in the colony. In August 1635, Staets had finished his apprenticeship with Jan Eckius, after which he probably worked with Brim for a number of years.[181] While a surgeon often also kept a barbershop, there were differences in schooling for the two trades. In general, a barber was examined about blood-letting, and a surgeon about important elements of surgery; however, applicants were not admitted to take the test if they had not served a surgeon for five years. As an apprentice, Staets' work probably had consisted mostly of shaving the regular customers and learning surgical procedures, such as treating sores and abscesses, pulling teeth, taking care of fractures, and healing internal diseases.[182] Like other apprentices, Staets had probably first taken the tests to prove that he was able to make bandages, to prepare a *cauterium potentiale* and apply it at the correct place, to make lancets, and to dissect part of a corpse. Once that test had been successfully completed, he may have been questioned about veins and nerves. After answering the test questions satisfactorily, the apprentice received a signed and sealed letter – and he was allowed to open a barber-and-surgeon's shop. The inventory of Gysbert van Imborch, a surgeon at Esopus, gives some idea of what instruments surgeons may have had available in performing their trade: There were, for example, copper and white earthenware basins used for shaving, three pairs of copper scales with the balances, a barber's case with instruments, a penknife, a small glass with juniper oil, and a small glass with yellow medicine.[183]

On July 11, 1648, Staets canceled his contract with the patroon, and does not appear in the records as a surgeon after that date; thus, it is unclear whether or not he subsequently did any surgeon's work. Between 1654 and 1671, Jacob de Hinsse, usually referred to as *Meester* Jacob, acted as surgeon; in the records he appears as *barbier, chirurgijn* and once as 'doctor,' a title used by people for both a surgeon and a *doctor medicinae*.[184] The status of the latter title, however, was certainly higher than that of an artisan surgeon. There was only one *doctor medicinae* in Beverwijck, Johannes La Montagne, whose academic education placed him far above the other inhabitants. The only reference to his medical career found in the court minutes of Fort Orange is an entry in August 1653 that refers to his work at Manhattan.[185]

It is not clear where De Hinsse came from, or where he received his training. Although a 1650 document in the Bontemantel Collection lists surgeons as West India Company servants, there is no information with respect to whether he was hired by the company or received a company salary.[186] On this list, surgeons are sometimes mentioned as belonging to the second tier of servants, following in the hierarchy the first tier – which consisted of ministers, the director, and vice director of New Netherland, among others. A surgeon's salary, according to this list, ran around *f*25 per month, which was *f*5 less than that for school teachers, who also belonged to this group.[187]

As a surgeon, De Hinsse contributed to maintaining good order in the village. In case of an incident, he was to report it immediately to the *schout* (tavern and inn keepers also had to do this); and whenever he dressed a wound, he had to inquire of the patient who had wounded him. If he failed to do so, the surgeon had to pay the fine imposed for making the wound.[188] The court minutes list two instances when De Hinsse made such a report. In October 1656, Jurriaen *Glaesemaecker* cut and wounded Cornelis Pietersz Hoogenboom on his right arm; but De Hinsse's report reveals that the wound was not dangerous.[189] In August 1660, he reported that Philip Hendricksz had cut Gerrit Visbeeck in the arm with his cutlass, as a result of which the last three fingers were lame; and Visbeeck had some symptoms that could cause his death.[190]

People seem to have had confidence in De Hinsse, including the Indians. In August 1660, Jeremias van Rensselaer paid him not only for 'another year of barber's work for himself, but also ƒ40 for surgeon's fees of *Aepje*, a Mahican sachem.'[191] His work may often have involved the letting of blood, giving a lotion for scurvy or shaving a beard; but on several occasions De Hinsse had to find solutions for more complicated injuries or diseases. After 1663, for example, he repeatedly treated Van Rensselaer's wife, Maria van Cortlandt, in an apparently competent manner for what later appeared to have been septic arthritis accompanied by osteomyelitis of the femur, which may have entered Maria's hip from a secondary infection of a smallpox lesion.[192] Nothing in the records indicates that people did not trust De Hinsse or relied on other means – unlike the situation in New Amsterdam, where on one occasion surgeon Kierstede's medicine failed to work immediately, and friends of the wounded Hendrick *de sewantrijger* (stringer) gave him a small pint of buck's blood to drink. Hendrick died the next day with a fever.[193]

In 1662, De Hinsse was joined in the surgeon's work by his apprentice, Cornelis van Dijck. Van Dijck's contract of June 14, 1661 states that he 'had served De Hinsse honestly and faithfully for four successive years, ending the tenth of this month June, having performed service in the art of surgery and what appertains thereto as well as otherwise, well and faithfully to the satisfaction of the subscriber and trained himself and duly and honestly served out his apprenticeship...'[194] In 1665, continuing the tradition of surgeon's education in Albany, the 13-year-old Gisbert Schuyler was apprenticed to Van Dijck, who was himself but 23 years of age. For three consecutive years, Philip Schuyler promised to pay Van Dijck 100 guilders annually for his son, while the arrangement is unknown for the fourth year. In the evening the boy was to go to school – without neglecting his master's service, but at his father's expense.[195]

In Beverwijck, we find no complaints concerning the position of *chirurgijn* (surgeon). But in New Amsterdam, Hans Kierstede and Jacob Huges – who considered shaving to be part of their job – asked in 1652 for the exclusive right to shave, as they were being disadvantaged by unqualified persons. Stuyvesant and the council answered that shaving did not really belong to surgery, but was only an 'appendix.' They could not forbid others from doing this work, as these individuals did not charge and did not keep open shop. As a response to their other complaint that some inexperienced professional barbers had made large errors, they forbade ship barbers from treating anybody on land without the knowledge and consent of the requesters and doctor La Montagne (who, probably in his capacity as a medical expert and supervisor, at that time was a member of the council).[196]

In 1656, the village had a midwife as well. Trijntie Melcherts would not be officially appointed as Albany's midwife until May 27, 1670; but the order mentions that she had already done this work for the past fourteen years, 'in good reputation not refusing her assistance but on ye contrary affording her best to ye poorer sorte of people out of Christian charity as well as ye richer sorte for reward & there being severall other less skilfull women who upon occasion will pretend to be midwives where they can gaine by it but refuse their help to ye poore...' In 1676 she was joined by Trijntie Jansen, who also swore that she would 'never refuse, but always be willing to render her services to rich and poor alike and fear no one.'[197] Trijntie may, like New Amsterdam midwife Hillegond Joris, have earned about ƒ100 a year from her work.[198]

While people knew that the law protected their rights, they also were well aware that to find some structure, focus and guidance they could go to church, which gathered the inhabitants together and provided them with a sense of morality and values.

Stabilizing factors in a new society: The church

Church and state

Besides government, the Reformed church was a great stabilizing factor in Beverwijck. The Calvinist or Dutch Reformed church had much influence, which was in accordance with the Calvinist view: According to Calvin, the church prescribed the spiritual life of the community. It taught the state the order established by God, while it was the state's duty to maintain this order by making sure that people would obey God's commandments and prohibitions.

In the lives of seventeenth-century Europeans, the institutions of church and government worked together as an organic unit. The thirteenth article of the *Union of Utrecht* (1579) guaranteed individual freedom of conscience in the Dutch Republic. Under this basic principle of tolerance, no one could be persecuted on account of his or her private beliefs. This pluralism differed from place to place: In the northern provinces of Friesland, Groningen and Drenthe, for example, some 85 percent of the population was Protestant, while in the province of South-Holland this percentage was no higher than 30 percent.[199] By lowering its demands for the confession of faith in the course of the seventeenth century, the church – which had once been a church for people with a calling – became a church for many.[200] In Beverwijck, there were 130 church members in 1652.[201] Many individuals may not have been willing to subject themselves to the moral censure, the ecclesiastical discipline and the confession of faith; but they were sympathetic to the Calvinist doctrine, and were called *liefhebbers* of the Reformed religion. Schaets pointed out that, in 1657, the Beverwijck church had some 160 members, but 300 to 400 people attended the services; and if all the *liefhebbers* had attended, this number would have risen to around 600.

In the Dutch Republic, a majority of church membership was female.[202] In Batavia, two-thirds of the members were women in 1674; at Manhattan 54.5 percent of the members were women until 1660, while 53.5 percent of the newly admitted members between 1660 and 1664 were women.[203] While no lists or consistory meeting reports have been found for Beverwijck, it is not known whether there was such a division here; it is probably good to keep in mind, too, that more men than women came to the colony between 1657 and 1664.[204] Apart from the women, the leading people in the village, including most of the magistrates, were among the church members. For example, Jeremias van Rensselaer joined the church after becoming director of Rensselaerswijck, which was expected of him. His mother, Anna, thought this was necessary and fitting, in light of the high position Jeremias occupied in the community.[205] Anna may have been influenced by religious movements within the Reformed church that were searching for a deeper experience of faith, and which found expression in the 'Further Reformation' (*Nadere Reformatie*). Answers were sought to problems such as the perceived moral decay of the nation. Were not the loss of Brazil, floods, the war with England, and the appearance comets all expressions of God's wrath? Teachings of Petrus Wittewrongel, Theodorus à Brakel, and others encouraged prayer, the reading of the Bible and the singing of psalms at home with family members and servants.[206] A booklet meant for practicing catechism at home, the 'Short Understanding of the Christian Doctrine' (*Korte Begrijp der Christelijcke leere*), published by Borstius in 1659, soon found its way to the colony.[207] Anna van Rensselaer reflected some of these thoughts in a letter to her son, in which she wondered whether or not Jeremias' 'bad luck' in some affairs had been a result of his not being a member of the church – in other words, he had not served God. About a year later, Jeremias van Rensselaer would express his excitement about learning the psalms and participating in the Holy Communion.[208]

By 1660, the number of church members had increased to 200.[209] If we accept Shattuck's estimate for a population size of 1,050 in 1660, that would mean that about 40 percent of the adult inhabitants belonged to the group of people who participated in communion, and who subjected themselves to ecclesiastical discipline. But except for being a community of believers, the church had always been a public institution as well, and as such it served the whole community. A life without the church playing that role was simply unthinkable, as it had been that way for centuries. After the Eighty-Year War against Spain, the Reformed church had taken over the role of publicly recognised church in the Republic – which meant that, besides providing for its own followers, the church also had to provide for the needs of a broader public. In a Christian state, certain religious provisions had to be available to everyone. Church services, for instance, had to be public and always accessible to all. The church also was obligated to baptize every child brought to church for baptism; and if a baptized man and woman asked to be married, the church had to perform their wedding. In addition, the church was required to perform church services for days of thanksgiving and days of prayer, as proclaimed by the secular authorities.

The civil authorities recognized the Reformed church as a public church; they administered its possessions and paid the salaries of the ministers, whose appointments they could influence as a result. In principle, only church members, or sometimes *liefhebbers des geloofs* (sympathizers of the belief), could occupy government jobs. Likewise, school teachers had to be members of the church; they were required to teach children the Reformed catechism and psalms, which had to be public and accessible to all. In practice, however, all of these provisons were dependent on local situations, which throughout the Dutch Republic varied re-

markably. One of the most specific ways to illustrate the church's public character was the publication in 1637 of a new translation of the Bible, the so-called
statenbijbel, which by the end of the century would become a generally accepted
Protestant Bible.[210] In January 1651, a Grand Assembly (*Grote Vergadering*)
clearly arranged the position of the churches. The 'true Christian Reformed' religion would continue as the only public religion, and would be maintained by the
civil authorities; other Protestant denominations were to be tolerated where they
already existed, but would not be allowed to expand; prohibition of Catholicism
would be maintained and strictly executed; religious services at the houses of foreign ambassadors were not to be held in Dutch and were not to be attended by
outsiders; in the *Meierij van Den Bosch* in Brabant and other areas under control
of the central authority, religious reform of the civil service would be enforced.[211]
But it was also clear that this church had been created by the state during the long
struggle for independence; and as a result, it would always be dependant on the
state. When a conflict arose between religious and political interests, the magistrates would set aside the demands of the church. Thus, in reality, the state was superior to the church.[212]

We should keep this background in mind when looking at people's daily lives in
Beverwijck. As in the Dutch Republic, the Calvinist or Dutch Reformed church
had much influence, which was in accordance with the Calvinist view: Its role of
instructing government in how to organize the state according to God's order, in
theory, gave the minister a place beside the director. The minister could point the
director toward his duties, while the director should do everything required to
help the minister perform his tasks in the congregation and to convert the 'heathens.' Minister and director were each autonomous on their own terrain; but
morally, they had power and obligations in each others fields.[213] Although the
minister's place should have been alongside the director, in the end it was the West
India Company that wielded the power. But the interrelationship between church
and state was omnipresent. There was cooperation in many ways: Often the
church stipulated the rules in social and cultural areas, while the government
helped to ensure that people complied with them.[214]

The church in New Netherland was strongly connected with the West India
Company, of which most directors and shareholders were strict Calvinists. In
New Netherland, the company exercised the same authority in religious matters
as the civil power exercised within the United Provinces. Being so strongly connected with the Reformed church, the company prohibited all public worship in
New Netherland other than Calvinist forms, although freedom of conscience was
allowed.[215] The company's Chamber of Amsterdam, which bore most of the expenses for New Netherland, had assumed the administration of the province. In
the establishment of preachers, the Amsterdam consistory had been in charge until 1636, after which the *Classis* of Amsterdam, which had regional power, became
the superior ecclesiastical authority over New Netherland, directing and supervising its colonial church. When the company directors wished to employ someone as a preacher in a certain place, the *classis* would select and propose the individual after examining him – which it did only after reading the attestations of his

previous employers, teachers, or other reliable persons. Responsibility for contents rested with the *classis*, while the company was the employer; in Rensselaerswijck, this role was filled by the patroon.[216] Church servants, ministers, comforters of the sick, and schoolmasters thus were appointed by the directors of the company's Chamber of Amsterdam (in Rensselaerswijck, by the patroon) and commissioned by the *Classis* of Amsterdam, but inducted by some colonial officer. In reality, they were appointed in New Netherland by the director general and council.[217] As in *patria*, most of Beverwijck's magistrates were members of this church, which facilitated cooperation between church and court. Commissary Johannes La Montagne was a church elder in 1660-62, while Jeremias van Rensselaer served as a deacon of the consistory from 1667 to 1669, and again as an elder in 1673.

When the government protects the church, it seems that the church would also be supportive and obliging toward the magistrates. For example, in many Dutch towns it was customary for the minister, on the Sunday before the election of new magistrates, to provide an explanation in church about the tasks of the government and the obligations of the burghers toward the civil authorities. In reality, this did not have much effect; but the main idea behind these sermons was to create respect for their government among the inhabitants.[218] The pulpit normally was the place for public announcements after religious service (the so-called *kerkespraak*). *Dominee* Schaets seems to have expected that, as well. In January 1654, he announced that whoever had any charges to bring against Brant van Slichtenhorst, who had returned to Rensselaerswijck after his imprisonment, had to do so at once at the court of Rensselaerswijck. Dijckman and the court protested that the church was not intended for the administration of justice, and sharply reprimanded Schaets. After this encounter with the Beverwijck court and Petrus Stuyvesant, who visited the village a good month later, and who perhaps spoke with him, there is hardly any other information about Schaets's relationship with the civil authorities until in 1663, when he took no action in the case of his daughter Anneke, who was pregnant by Arent van Curler.[219]

In attempting to understand inhabitants of the seventeenth-century, we should keep in mind that, for these people, the institutions of church and state were both placed directly under God's authority, where they formed a unit; on a certain level, they were interwoven. Although church and state each had formal authority only in its own field, their moral authority (and also their duty) extended onto each other's terrain. Perhaps this was visible in the stained glass windows in Beverwijck's new church, which displayed the coats of arms of various magistrates' families, and in the special seats from which magistrates could attend the services. But after the peace of Münster in 1648, which concluded the Eighty-Years War, it was clear that the two institutions were no longer equal powers. The Grand Assembly of the States General, in 1651, recognized the Reformed religion and promised to maintain it as the basis of her existence. When it came down to it, the civil authorities were above the ecclesiastical – which, in Beverwijck, meant that the West India Company held the highest authority.

A public church

As a public institution, the church was required to provide for the needs of a broad public. Church services had to be public and always accessible to all. The church was obligated to perform baptisms, marriages, or funerals for all inhabitants who wished them – which implies, conversely, that sacraments performed in the public church did not point inexorably to membership in that Reformed church. As a public institution, the church prescribed the arrangement of much of the time and activities of the community's inhabitants, and secular authorities made sure that these rules were complied with. Every Sunday, and on all other holidays and days of prayer or thanksgiving proclaimed by the colonial government, people were expected to go to church. In Holland, a regular Sunday morning service, preceded by the ringing of the church bell, usually lasted an hour and a half to two hours; the sermon, which usually was about the birth of Christ, sinfulness, and salvation, was limited to one hour. In the afternoon catechism session the children, guided by a teacher, were to recite questions and answers in the presence of the whole congregation. This service lasted about two hours. Both services were opened and closed by the singing of psalms, and during the services deacons collected gifts of charity by passing around a collection bag.[220] Services in Beverwijck may not have lasted as long; on a Sunday morning, people were usually in church between nine and ten o'clock.[221] On holidays there were two services, as well, and on other church days such as Ascension and Good Friday there was one service. Sometimes there would be penitential sermons on Friday evenings, during which sinners were admonished to atone for their sins. Before the Holy communion sermon, the confession of faith was usually offered in a trial sermon.

The government supported the church by encouraging inhabitants to attend services, while the church, in return, held services on the days of prayer and thanksgiving proclaimed by the government. When Brant van Slichtenhorst refused to do this in April 1648, he thereby openly denied the authority of the colonial government in Rensselaerswijck.[222] Usually held on Wednesdays, these special days of observance were sometimes proclaimed in order to placate divine wrath caused by the sins of people, to avert the threat of an Indian war or a pestilential disease, to preserve the purity of the Calvinist faith endangered by the growth of dissent, or to express gratitude for peace – for example, the peace of Münster in 1648, or peace with the Indians or the English.[223] In March 1653, Stuyvesant and the council ordered that the first Wednesday of each month was to be a day of fasting and prayer.[224] While, in *patria*, these special days often were observed more strictly than regular Sundays, court minutes don't reveal whether that was the case in Beverwijck, as well; deacons' accounts seem to suggest the contrary, as the yield of collections on these days was much smaller than for regular Sunday services.[225] People could be very occupied by activities organized by the church. A count of the different church services in 1657 reveals that a person could have attended an average of five to six services a month in that year alone, including nine in March (which had four Wednesday services and one on a Friday) and two in August.[226]

32. *When the blockhouse church was ready in 1656, a temporary pulpit was first erected for the use of the minister. The settlers then subscribed 25 beavers to purchase a more splendid one in Holland. The Chamber of Amsterdam added f75, for 'the beavers were greatly damaged' and 'with a view to inspire the congregation with more ardent zeal' presented them in the course of the next year with a bell 'to adorn their newly constructed little church.' In the year 2003 this pulpit is still in use in Albany's present-day First Dutch Reformed Church. Attached to the pulpit was an hour glass. Photograph R. S. Alexander.*

Calvinist religion, with the support of the government, decided what people could or could not do on a Sunday. As early as 1641, ordinances proclaimed by the director and council stipulated that no liquor was to be sold or consumed during the religious services on Sundays.[227] These 'morality' stipulations paralleled the struggle in *patria* to honor the Sabbath.[228] As in Manhattan and in the fatherland, people in Beverwijck frequently violated the ordinance. In December 1655, Hendrick Jochemsz and Herman Bamboes were both fined for entertaining company in their taverns on Sunday before and after noon; and in March 1656, Claes Jansz, Frans Pietersz, and Poulus Lambertsz were fined for drinking in Bamboes's tavern on a Sunday.[229] In October 1656, a 1648 ordinance regarding Sunday observance was renewed. 'Any ordinary labor, such as plowing, sowing, mowing, building, woodsawing, smithing, bleaching, hunting, fishing, or any other work, which may be a lawful occupation,' was prohibited on Sundays, as was 'any lower or unlawful exercise and amusement, drunkenness, frequenting taverns or tippling houses, dancing, playing ball, cards, tricktrack, tennis, *balslaen* or ninepins, going on pleasure parties in a boat, cart or wagon before, between or during divine service...' In particular, tavern keepers or tapsters were not to entertain any clubs, or provide any brandy, wine, beer or strong liquor to any person before or during the sermons on pain of a ƒ6 or ƒ3 fine to be paid by every person found drinking during that time.[230] These regulations also concerned the days of prayer or thanksgiving proclaimed by the government. Deputy *schout* Jan Daniel, in March 1657, accused nine men of playing ice hockey on the day of prayer, and demanded the fine indicated in the ordinance.[231] The court minutes make no mention of people who were fined for working on the Sabbath. Perhaps there was connivance, as in the fatherland, where individuals were allowed to perform work that truly could not be delayed. The idea was that people should not work slavishly or solely for temporary profit.[232] Such accommodations were more aspects of a changing civilization – the arrangement of one's personal life, family, school, congregation, and public morals – than of Christianization. The magistrates themselves, for example, did not hesitate to call a Sunday meeting in 1654, when they considered it necessary.[233]

After September 1663, people were required to obey the ordinances during the whole Sabbath, from sunrise to sunset. Director and council not only renewed the old ordinance, but also prohibited gaming, boating, riding in carts and wagons, fishing, fowling, running and roving in search of nuts and strawberries, and trading with Indians or any such activities, as well as the unrestrained and excessive playing, shouting and screaming of children in the streets and highways.[234]

Religion influenced every aspect of life; and it is in that context that all community functions such as the administration of justice, education, and charity should be understood. Religious holidays marked the main events of the year. Easter, Pentecost, and Christmas were all celebrated for two days, with two church services offered on both days. At Christmas and Easter, one of the two days often included the celebration of communion, which was held four times a year. New Year's day, Ascension day, and Good Friday were church days as well. Although they are not mentioned in the deacons' account books, private events such as baptisms, weddings, and funerals also were church affairs. Baptismal ceremonies generally concerned infant baptism. An infant would be baptized, irrespective of the parents' denomination, so long as they were Christians. Usually the infant would be baptized, in the presence of the father and witnesses, on one of the first Sundays after its birth. The fact that fathers were asked to educate their children in the Dutch Reformed religion may have moved a Lutheran father to ask a friend of the Reformed persuasion to assume his place in church for that moment. After the minister had baptized the child with water in the name of the 'Father, the Son, and the Holy Spirit,' a spoken thanksgiving and prayer were offered. The service was followed by a baptismal meal and party at the parents' home. Adults could also be baptized, but only those who had not been baptized before – and only after they had signed the Reformed Confession of Faith.[235]

As a public church, the Reformed religion also was responsible for enabling people to marry legally. Marriage banns had to be read publicly three times before an official wedding could take place, which probably often occurred during a regular Sunday service. The Beverwijck deacons' account books mention no weddings until October 1671; the weddings then took place on weekdays, and money for each ceremony was collected in church over two days.[236] The public character of the church also brought with it the duty to bury the dead, irrespective of the religious background of the deceased. Usually, the church took care that the death of a person was announced in public, that the church bells were rung, and that a grave was dug. A pall could be rented from the deaconry to drape over the coffin during the funeral. The minister usually would speak briefly at the graveside during a sober funeral ceremony prior to burial. It was important to give an individual an honorable funeral attended by neighbors, relatives, and fellow artisans and workers who bore witness to the deceased's honor. This was considered so important that even the poorest inhabitants tried to avoid a burial provided through charity ('pro Deo'), turning first to family, friends, or neighbors for help with this service. In the town of Zwolle in the fatherland, it was even considered a neighbor's duty to attend a funeral and drink together, and to help carry the coffin.[237] It is unlikely that funeral orations and abundant meals accompanied funerals in Beverwijck, as the church tried to prevent these activities.[238] In later years, the deaconry would sometimes take care of funeral expenses for the poor. The funeral of Ryseck Swart, *schout* Swart's widow, for whom the deacons had provided care for three years in return for her possessions, was an exception for which they paid the large sum of $f220$ in 1700 – which included payment for the undertaker's work, the coffin, good beer, rum, madera, sugar and spices, sugar cookies, tobacco, and pipes.[239]

The documents don't provide us with an abundance of examples of the rituals of baptism, marriage, or funerals, and such information mostly appears in fragments scattered throughout the records. But these ecclesiastical celebrations and customs, which had been an important part of people's lives in the Dutch Republic for a long time, were undoubtedly brought along to the New World. That these events are not mentioned in the source materials does not mean that they did not occur; rather, as normal aspects of life, they simply took place – and unless something unusual happened, it was not considered necessary to record them in official documents. The same could be said for certain other deeply imbedded traditional or pre-Reformation holidays that sometimes were celebrated as well, but which were suppressed as 'popish superstitions.' Although prohibited by the Calvinist church, such observances were tolerated and connived at in many parts of the Dutch Republic. Stuyvesant and the council prohibited *Shrovetide* in New Netherland, for example, as a 'detestable pagan and popish feast'; but in Beverwijck, some inhabitants celebrated this holiday in 1654 and 1655, nevertheless.[240]

The church then, was an important force in Beverwijck's community. As a public institution it formed the axis of social life in the seventeenth century and contributed greatly toward making Beverwijck society more stable. The church building occupied a solid place in the community where all inhabitants – even Lutherans – came regularly. People could prepare for the church service, dress up, leave work behind them, and exchange thoughts about various issues once they arrived at church. In church they would find a place from which they could hear the *dominee* well, and where they could share thoughts with a neighbor. Women usually sat separate from men, and may have found time to discuss matters regarding the household, childrearing, and other issues. For the women, more than for their husbands – who were more connected with the outside world through their work – the weekly church visit may have been more of an outing, a possibility for greater contact with the world outside their homes. Especially in the afternoons, when children also attended, a church service may in some ways have been quite a family affair. After the service or between the two Sunday services, people may have visited with each other, dressed on their Sunday best, or perhaps went to one of the nearby inns, with Hendrick Jochemsz' inn being the closest. Whatever the churchgoers did, the church stimulated communal feelings and was a binding factor for the whole community. To be a member of the church – and, especially, to participate four times a year in the Holy Communion service in order to share the bread symbolizing the body of Jesus, and to drink from the beaker of red wine symbolizing His blood – created and enhanced the kind of solidarity and respectability desired by many inhabitants. To belong to this group was so important that in 1660, according to *dominee* Schaets, even some Lutherans were at the verge of taking the step of becoming Reformed church members.[241] Being a member of the church council (or consistory) was even more respectable. The place of the elders and deacons was clearly marked by a special consistory seat; newcomers could recognize them immediately. Their special status was also a sign that these people did well economically; it provided good opportunities for a position in the local government. At the same time, the church was the place where people who were unable to survive on their own could find support, and where they could turn to in case of need.

The church was the place of culture and development. After it had more or less combined the inhabitants' habits and customs into one common culture for the whole community, the church would maintain this Dutch culture even after the English had taken over, creating strong solidarity among the settlers of 'Dutch' origin. The preservation of the Dutch language in church was the clearest sign of this. Until the 1790s, at least one Sunday service would be performed in Dutch, while the deacons kept their account books in Dutch, as well. And even then, people protested against the disappearance of the Dutch language in church. As late as the fall of 1846, a new group of immigrants would find that the majority of elderly church members understood Dutch fairly well, 'although it was not used in church services anymore.'[242]

The minister

In 1648, *dominee* Megapolensis welcomed the end of his contract with the patroon and his return to the Dutch Republic, but the *Classis* of Amsterdam and the patroon were not happy to see him leave. He had served them very well, and it was unclear how he could be replaced. When they finally agreed to approve his discharge in April 1649, they asked him to 'establish some fixed order, that some form of worship may be kept up, with the reading of God's word, the singing of psalms, the reading of some edifying sermons, etc., so that the church do not at once become demoralized and the good work begun there and advanced by your diligence, decline.'[243] The search for a new minister then could begin: the search for a man who would preach the word of God, administer the sacraments of baptism and communion, attend to the needs of the congregation and, together with the elders, exercise ecclesiastical discipline; and who would ensure that church affairs were handled with honesty and maintained in good order.[244] For many people in *patria*, the minister was the personification of culture; and to meet their expectations, the minister definitely had to possess the unusual gifts of godliness, humility, modesty, good intellect, and tact, as well as gifts of eloquence.[245] Furthermore, it was important that he be articulate. A weak voice, for example, was a problem; well-known ministers had voices like trumpets. Besides being eloquent, a minister was supposed to make appropriate gestures, preach from memory, use simple and clear language, and not make his sermon too long. As ambassador of Christ, a good minister had the gift to bring God's word across to the people; but in addition, he had to study hard in preparing his sermons, as critical members of the congregation had great expectations of them.[246] A typical seventeenth-century sermon was a plea in which various texts were linked together; it required a profound knowledge of the Bible.[247] The calling of a minister afforded him a level of respect that far exceeded the respect acquired by birth or income. For the sake of the church and to avoid irritating non-members of the church, he was also expected to lead a pious life, be amiable and intimate in his contacts with people, and friendly in conversation. In addition to performing the various sermons and administering the sacraments, the minister was expected to consecrate marriages, comfort the dying and their families, speak at the graveside during funerals, make regular house visits in the company of church elders, and preside over council meetings. His good name was not only important to himself, but also for the community as a whole.[248]

The 'fixed order' that the *classis* requested from Megapolensis would come in a way the church had not intended. Around the time Megapolensis left Rensselaerswijck, *dominee* Wilhelmus Grasmeer, who had married Megapolensis's daughter Hillegont, had fled trouble with his wife and his parish of Graftdijck in North-Holland. Megapolensis, however, remained in Manhattan, where he accepted the minister's position. At that time, the *classis* had censored Grasmeer for abandoning his church. Grasmeer was accused of domestic quarreling, abandonment of his wife, drunkenness and other great faults that were reaffirmed by the Synod of North Holland.[249] Grasmeer refused to defend himself against their charges and, with the knowledge that his father-in-law's former pulpit lay vacant, fled to Rensselaerswijck – where he would be preaching in November 1650. Despite warnings sent to New Netherland, Grasmeer was welcomed in the colony with open arms. The inhabitants may have assumed that his testimonials negated the warning that they had received from Amsterdam. They were so impressed by Grasmeer's preaching that they agreed to pay his salary themselves, a commitment which the patroon had been unable to persuade them to accept in the past. The new minister was assisted by Anthonie de Hooges, who was paid for reading (*voorleeserschap*) from August 1, 1650 until May 11, 1652.[250] But in November 1651, after filling the pulpit in the colony for more than a year, Grasmeer – under pressure from the *classis* and at the request of his mother, who had sailed over to persuade her son to return to Amsterdam and clear his name – decided to face the church's discipline. By the spring of that year he had reconciled with his *classis* and the synod, and would accept a legitimate call to another church in North Holland. Although he had served the colonists without official sanction, it appears that Grasmeer's ministry served a constructive purpose for both the church and the community, by providing continuity for the young congregation at a critical juncture in its history.[251]

Meanwhile, the Amsterdam *classis* had been looking for a successor to Megapolensis. There were a few applicants, of whom Johan Oly from Hoorn was rejected because he had caused a scandal there, and his recommendations were very meager.[252] Johannes Episcopius, a very able student at Franeker, was excused from filling the pastorate of Rensselaerswijck in April 1652, at his own request, 'in view of the dubious condition of affairs between England and this country' (i.e., the war).[253] In May, the church leaders found another candidate in 44-year-old Gideon Schaets, a school master at Beesd, who desired to become a minister. Since 1647, he had held preaching exercises for the *Classis* of Buren; and in 1649, following his preparatory exams, he was admitted as a 'proponent.' In June 1649, Schaets asked to go to the East Indies as a comforter of the sick, but was directed to 'seek to push his desires in the synod.'[254] He was approved by the *classis* in 1652, and expressed his wish to go to Rensselaerswijck. His peremptory exam so pleased the Assembly in Holland that it was resolved to proceed to his examination, the result of which was sufficiently satisfactory. Accordingly, Schaets was ordained, after which he signed the *acts of the formulae of concord in the faith*.[255]

School teachers who became ministers the way Schaets had were called *Duytsche clerken*. Unlike theology students at the Dutch universities, Schaets had not followed an academic course of study in Reformed theology; so he may not have had a good knowledge of classical languages. Schaets may only have been able to speak Dutch, also called *Nederduyts, Duytsch*, or *Diets* – hence the name *Nederduytse clerici*, which was corrupted into *Duytse Clercken*.[256] His predecessor Megapolensis had been a very learned man, hardly lower in status than Johannes La Montagne, who would later come to Beverwijck as vice director, and who had an education as *doctor medicinae*. Schaets's lesser education as clerical leader may have placed him in a less elevated status, above the rest of the people, than his predecessor or the secular leader La Montagne. If the difference between the two leaders of the community was great, that was only coincidental – not fundamental. The patroon had hired Schaets for three years, at ƒ800 annually, to perform religious services, to 'use all Christian zeal there to educate the heathen as well as the heathen children in the Christian religion, to practice catechism and teach the Holy Scriptures among the people and to exercise the office of schoolmaster for old and young.' He would be reimbursed in the event that he boarded and took care of any 'heathen' children.[257] Schaets's salary was increased to ƒ1,000 in 1653, and to ƒ1,300 in 1655. The second renewal of the contract with the patroon came to an end in the fall of 1657; in October of that year, Stuyvesant wrote the directors of the West India Company that, at the request of the congregation, he had appointed Schaets at ƒ100 per month.[258] Until about 1670, the patroon would contribute half of the *dominee*'s salary.[259] Although he was described in

1658 as a man of feeble health, Schaets served the community for about forty years as a minister, pointing his congregation to the 'right' path at least twice a week, and frequently more often.[260] In 1683, he would be joined by Godefridus Dellius; and, in 1688, Schaets would preach only once in a two-week period. By 1690, he would not preach anymore at all and only administered the sacraments. After that year, he no longer signed the deacon's account book.[261] Undoubtedly, through his sermons and his function as president of the consistory, Schaets had great influence on the morals and values of the community during his ministership; and he left an important mark on the lives of the church and its members.

Strikingly – and in great contrast to the era of Megapolensis as well as his successor, Godefridus Dellius – native Americans are absent from the information uncovered about *dominee* Schaets; if he was actively involved in converting Indians, the records don't show it. Although his contract with the patroon mentioned that he should also educate Indian children, and that he even might board them, Schaets's name is never mentioned in a context that includes Indians. Was hope converting the Indians abandoned? In New Amsterdam, Megapolensis took an Indian into his house and taught him for two years; but, in 1657, he acknowledged that the experiment had failed badly. The Indian, according to Megapolensis and Drisius, 'took to drinking brandy, he pawned the Bible, and turned into a regular beast, doing more harm than good among the Indians.'[262] It is hard to imagine that a minister in the upper Hudson settlement would not have put any effort into dealing with the Indians, converting them or, as his contract stipulated, teaching some Indian children. Yet the only times the documents suggest that Schaets even thought about Indians were the occasions when the deaconry ransomed various prisoners from the Indians; at least then, the natives must have been discussed by the consistory. That Schaets is not mentioned at all in reports of the French Jesuits Radisson and Poncet, who stayed in the community in 1653, seems strange as well. When Radisson actually mentioned that there was a 'minister that was a Jesuit' who had given him a great offer in October 1653, he most likely was referring to Megapolensis, who had been a catholic in his early years.[263] Unfortunately, no baptismal records or consistory minutes from the 1650s have been found. Today, we can only assume that it was Schaets who baptized Illetie, the daughter of an Indian woman and Cornelis Theunisz van Slijck, and we can only wonder whether he baptized any other children of Indian mothers and Dutch fathers. A woman named Illetie appears in a report made by Jasper Danckaerts and Petrus Sluyter, two Labadists who traveled to New York in 1679-80, in search of land to settle a religious colony.[264] Like other Maquaes children, Illetie had grown up among the Maquaes, with her mother and siblings, before going to the Christians. In the Dutch community, she told Danckaerts, she had lived for a long time with a woman who taught her the Dutch language, and reading and writing. When Illetie had begun to understand the language and what was expressed in the New Testament, she learned more and more about the religion; finally, she had made her profession of faith and was baptized.[265] The fact that the woman who brought up Illetie would later be described as a sharp female trader, whose second husband may have been a 'papist,' erases any possibility that it might have been Schaets's wife who had boarded the girl during her early years among the Christians. It is interesting that Illetie did not mention having gone to church or to school; instead, she told the visiting Labadist that she had learned reading and writing from this 'truly worldly woman.'[266] It seems that the girl had been partially brought up in Rensselaerswijck or Beverwijck. Her brother had been born in 1640, and Illetie herself died in February 1707.[267] In 1660, the *classis* wrote that children of negroes or Indians should only be baptized if the parents had become Christians; as long as the parents remained 'heathen,' their children were not allowed to be baptized. No adult person could be baptized without having previously made the confession of faith. Therefore, adult negros and Indians had to be educated and make their confession of faith before they could be baptized.[268]

That the West India Company hired Schaets in 1657, at the request of the community, suggests that he was liked by the people; but it does not mean that Schaets had the respect of every inhabitant. In February of that year, the *dominee* filed a complaint in court, charging that Cornelis Theunisz Bos had slandered him and injured him in his reputation and calling, by claiming that he had seen the minister drunk at times. Bos's wife Marretie had even argued:

> Those who are willing to feast and gorge themselves with the Domine are his friends and because I do not want to do it, I am a child of the devil. If I only could sit in church with a book before me like the hypocritical devils, I would be a child of God; but because I refuse to do it, I am a child of the devil; but let me be a child of the devil.[269]

In 1663, Schaets's reputation suffered remarkable damage due to the behavior of one of his children, and his own reaction thereupon. His worries about bringing up his children in a place where 'they learn nothing but rudeness instead of useful things' (*niet veel anders als wilts in stede van goede oeffeninge*) seem to have become a painful reality when his daughter Anneke was, for a long time, accused of whoring and adultery with the respectable, but married, Arent van Curler.[270] At first, the minister had denied the accusations 'with harsh, scolding, threatening, yes, almost swearing words'; but then, when a child was born out of the relationship, he would defend it, 'under cover of God's Holy Word and the sad falls of holy men in the same, such as Loth's incest, David's adultery, and similar examples.' According to vice director La Montagne, many people stopped going to catechism or religious services as a result; and (although the collection yields seem not to confirm this statement) they even avoided participating in the Holy Communion ritual. Most likely, Schaets baptised his grandson himself; it was rumored that the child, when presented for baptism, had been 'draped with black mourning clothes and several black ribbons and bows.'[271] Because a minister's name in some ways represented the congregation as a whole, this episode must have been an enormous humiliation for Schaets, with his entire congregation gossiping.[272] If consistory minutes had been kept, and if those documents had survived, we might have known how the problems surrounding this issue were resolved.[273] The minister's daughter had lost her honor – one of the most important values in the life of a seventeenth-century person – and, as head of the family, Schaets would have been held responsible for his daughter's behavior. The fact that many people skipped catechism and church services, and even the core ritual of Holy Communion, suggests that Schaets continued his service in a regular way, including the administering of communion, despite the shame his daughter had put on the family.

Schaets was certainly not appreciated by everyone. In 1680 the Labadist Jasper Danckaertsz, when he visited the area described him as a 'poor, old, ignorant person' who was 'not of good life.' [274] But altogether, Schaets through his sermons and his presidency of the consistory must have had considerable influence on the development of the community. Despite his own problems, he still was a personification of culture, and a representative of God, and more or less prescribed spiritual and moral life in the settlement.

The consistory

In his behavior and attitude regarding his daughter's love affair, Schaets had to deal with the members of the church council or consistory. Johannes Megapolensis, soon after his arrival in Rensselaerswijck, established a consistory according to the way Calvin, in his doctrine, had prescribed; likewise, Michaëlius had done this at Manhattan in 1628. The church was organized along the principles of the Dutch Reformed church in the Republic; through its organization, the church tried to preserve the purity of the doctrine, and kept an eye on church members' conduct in life. In the 1650s, a consistory – which consisted of a minister (who was president) and usually three elders and three deacons – represented the church's authority in Beverwijck. They reported to the regional authority, the *Classis* of Amsterdam, which was the assembly of representatives of various consistories. Above the *classis* were the provincial and national synods.[275] While a minister was the permanent president of the consistory, the elders and deacons were chosen for three years; every year, two members were replaced by cooptation. In important matters such as the calling of a new minister, or suspension of members from the Holy Communion, a former consistory member could take up his previous duties, as well.[276]

Members of the consistory were expected to be compassionate and active church members, as they had great responsibilities. They also were expected to lead irreproachable lives and be sound in the faith. While no clear instructions remain for the elders or deacons of Beverwijck's church, probably their tasks were similar to those of consistory members in other congregations in the Dutch Republic – where, for example, elders assisted the minister by distributing the bread and wine among church members during the Holy Communion ritual, and made sure that non-members did not participate. Sometimes they would advise the *dominee* in the choice of Biblical books for his sermons; elders made sure that sermons were held at the regular time, and that baptism and marriage services were performed. They also visited sick people who were unable to attend church service and needed to be comforted. In addition, since one of their most important tasks was to exercise ecclesiastical discipline, the elders saw to it that the minister and deacons remained true to their calling.

Not too long before the Holy Communion service, consistory members usually visited church members at home, together with *dominee*. During those visits they were expected to look for possible 'sins'; if they found any sins, the elders would reprimand the members in question; serious cases would be passed along to the full consistory. In a particularly grave case, if the sinner showed no remorse, he or she could be suspended from participating in the Holy Communion – which, for church members, was a very solemn occasion. In his sermons and discipline, the minister paid attention to the undesirable behavior of all members.[277] Thus, the consistory guarded morality in the congregation by exercising the ecclesiastical discipline. All forms of irritating behavior were censured – drunkenness, marital quarrels, adultery, bankruptcy – and church members guilty of these errors were put on the spot. By keeping an eye on the moral quality of public life, and by paying attention to such matters as the observance of the Sunday's rest, or dancing and other entertainment, the consistory and minister greatly contributed to the generalization of middle-class behavior.[278]

When the minister and elders found that people had 'sinned,' they could apply several stages of censure. First, a few members of the consistory could talk with the accused, and admonish him or her. If this conversation did not solve the problem, the individual had to appear before the entire consistory. If the accused person showed genuine repentance, there would be a reconciliation and he or she would be received back 'in grace.' But if such was not the case, the consistory could provisionally withhold the rite of Holy Communion from the 'sinner'; while this action would be announced from the pulpit, the member's identity was kept secret at that point. The 'sinner's' name would be announced to the congregation if the individual persisted in his or her sin – and church members would be asked to admonish the accused, and pray for him or her. Once the censure had gone to this stage, the accused would have to confess his or her sin openly in order to be readmitted to the communion ritual. In severe cases, a long probationary period could be imposed. A final step could be taken if there clearly was no repentance after this point: It would then be announced that the church planned to cut off the offending member from the congregation. This was the worst punishment the church could impose. In Delft, for example, the whole congregation in one case was told not to communicate with the 'sinner' at all, unless it was strictly necessary, so that he would repent in shame.[279] In New Netherland, a harrowing case took place in 1635, when New Amsterdam's *dominee* Bogardus excommunicated the colony's highest judicial servant, its *fiscael* (public prosecutor) Lubbert Dinclagen.[280] For 'sinners,' reconciliation could be a humiliating experience. When the sin had been small, a confession before the consistory would sometimes suffice, perhaps along with a confession to one's nextdoor neighbors. The 'confession under covered name' – or the announcement of the sin in absence of the unnamed 'sinner' – was more difficult, since in a small community people usually could guess the name of the accused. It also must have been difficult for the accused church member to listen as his or her sin was publicly announced from the pulpit – and then to be required to confirm it aloud. In a small place like Beverwijck, inspection of the observance of the prohibition was easy; and among the group of church members, the social and psychological burden of even a temporary exclusion from the Holy Communion must have been heavy.

After his arrival, Schaets had been obliged to suspend several people from the 'Lord's table' 'on account of their inconsistent walk.' The people were reckless, he wrote, and many stayed away from communion for the smallest reason, while most of the time the taverns were full.[281] The lack of consistory minutes from these years makes it impossible to know the reasons behind Schaets's measures, or with what sort of problems he and the elders had to cope.

A few court cases reveal some of the consistory's activities. In 1655, for example, the consistory asked the court to examine Claes Ripsz, the father of a child recently born, who wanted to wait before marrying the mother until he had heard from his own father, whose approval he may have wanted for the marriage. When Claes refused to marry the woman, with whom he still slept under one cover as man and wife, he was put in irons; barely a month later, after Claes showed remorse, prayed for forgiveness and confessed his guilt, he was granted forgiveness.[282]

The court's approval was also requested for a case of both ecclesiastical and political nature: It concerned a memorial, in which the consistory had stated that the marriage of Michiel Anthonisz and Femmetje Alberts was annulled. The memorial had been drawn up after Grietge Jacobs, the wife of Anthonisz, came to Beverwijck. Anthonisz had been away from the Dutch Republic for nine years, and for five successive years had not heard a word or sign from Grietge until a neighbor told him that she had died. However, it appears to have been his mother who was buried, instead. When the court was asked for advice, the magistrates approved the memorial and declared the first marriage – that between Anthonisz and Grietge Jacobs – to be valid, while Femmetje was given a letter of freedom.[283] As mentioned above, in 1663 the consistory shouldered a heavy burden in dealing with the *dominee* himself and his family; undoubtedly the consistory – especially Abraham Staets, Cornelis van Nes, and Adriaen Gerritsz, who then were elders – had long discussions with Schaets.[284] Even Stuyvesant and La Montagne corresponded about the matter.

Besides the three elders, Beverwijck's consistory usually included three deacons, who were given the task to take care of the poor and the sick in the community. They encouraged people to donate to the poor and collected the gifts. After consulting with the whole consistory, the deacons would distribute the collected money or aid in the form of food, clothing, or other necessities to those in need of help. This work required literate individuals who were able to keep accounts and who had some financial skills, as they had to oversee the budget, grant loans, and negotiate with suppliers of food, clothing, and other supplies to be distributed among the needy. Until February 1657, the deacons also took take care of widows and orphans, together with the *schout*, who was called the protector of the right of orphans.[285] Thereafter, Evert Jansz Wendel and Jan Verbeeck, who had been members of the consistory in the previous year, would be appointed orphan masters and be required to report to Fort Orange's court.

Deacons and elders were obligated to attend all consistory meetings; even more so than for the magistracy, when someone was asked to serve as elder or deacon in the consistory, he could not refuse the responsibility – as it was 'a service of

God.'[286] When, in January 1656, Frans Barentsz Pastoor was allowed to be relieved of his duties as deacon and his job of taking up the monthly collection ordered by Stuyvesant, because the work caused him 'great discomfort, loss, and inconvenience,' the court ordered and requested Evert Wendel to take up the collection – and Wendel then became a deacon.[287] Elders were usually considered of higher prestige than deacons; except for commissary La Montagne, who served only as elder, consistory members in Beverwijck seem to have performed both functions. In general, a man would be deacon for a term of three years, and then serve as elder in a later term. The respectability gained by holding a position in the consistory may have made up for the time the work demanded. Various brewers, tailors, a gunstock maker, the surgeon, the commissary of the fort, and the director of the colony – all would put their signatures in the deacons' account book at the end of the year, showing that they had served as consistory members. As in several places in the fatherland, we can find many of these men serving as magistrates as well, which does not seem to have caused any problems; on the contrary, their overlapping roles contributed to good correspondence between church and court.[288] A young community like Beverwijck may not yet have had enough 'wealthy, honorable, prominent, moderate and peaceful' burghers at its disposal to fill all the available positions of both state and church. The secular authorities, on the other hand, may also have decided that control of the public church – as 'carrying element' of the Dutch Republic – could not be left to the 'little man' without political responsibility.[289]

Other church functions

Certain other jobs were connected with the church. In June 1657, Schaets wrote that he himself had to fill the positions of reader (*voorleser*) and precentor (*voorsanger*), as 'there was none yet.' Anthonie de Hooges had been credited with ƒ56 in salary as reader from August 1, 1650 until May 11, 1652, and again during two months and one week in 1653; but he died in October 1655.[290] In May 1660, Pieter Claerbout was given an annual contract for the position of precentor at the church, which paid him a hundred *daelders* a year. In August, 1661 he is also referred to as reader, while after the sexton's death in 1663 he also did various other jobs at the church. Jeremias van Rensselaer in 1664 paid him, for instance, for taking care of the church and keeping the pulpit clean. He is often referred to as *Pieteroom, Meester* Pieter, or, as he also took care of burials, uncle Pieter, the gravedigger.[291] His jobs as reader and precentor were important. The reading he did was limited to reading from the Bible without any interpretation.[292] Thus, his lectern may have stood at the foot of the *dominee*'s pulpit, at a lower level than the minister's place. It is easy to imagine that Claerbout had a good-sounding voice, as the work of reader and precentor required strong voice volume and experience. The singing of psalms was the only part of the service in which the churchgoers could actively participate, and most likely they could have used good guidance. Datheen's rhymed version of the psalms was used, as it was probably as popular in the colony as in *patria*, where it remained in use for more than 200 years – and where, in some strict Reformed congregations, it is still used today. The texts were simple and known to most people, while the melodies were popular. Van Deursen calls these real folksongs, written with tone and contents for the common man.[293] Without an organ or any other instrument to accompany the singing, the lead of the precentor most likely had great influence over the collective voice of the 300 to 400 people attending the service. Constantijn Huygens once wrote that he had heard singing at a church in the Dutch Republic that sounded as if 'there was more crying and shouting than human singing.'[294] Claerbout's work seems to have been appreciated, since in January 1662 he was given ƒ25 with the approval of the consistory.[295]

Pieter Jacobsz *kerckendener* was probably hired for his job as sexton when the new building was ready; in November 1657, he was paid ƒ125 for a year's service. Until his death in May 1663, he was paid about ƒ36 for three months' salary as sexton. A sexton usually had a central position in the church environment. He kept the keys to the church, dusted and kept the church clean, and made everything ready for the services (e.g., put Bibles in place and hung the numbers of the various psalms to be sung). In winter, without a heating system, it may hardly have been possible to sit for so long in the cold church. Although it is not mentioned in the accounts, Jacobsz may, like sextons in *patria*, have prepared a fire in order to provide the churchgoers with glowing coals for their foot stoves.[296] Four times a year – at Christmas and Easter, one Sunday in June or July, and one in September or October – Jacobsz would prepare the table for the Holy Communion ritual. He also maintained the pall that was rented out by the deacons for funerals and, in addition, he dug the graves and took care of funerals. In January 1659, Jeremias van Rensselaer paid him five beavers for watchman service at the church. The sexton's tolling over the dead at a funeral, and tolling the bells before church services to make sure everything happened on time, caused some people to dub him 'Pieter Jacobsz *klockluyder*.'[297] After Jacobsz's death, Pieter Claerbout took over some of his work.[298]

The Dutch Reformed church was the basis for other cultural and social institutions in Beverwijck, such as education and charity. The youth were to be shaped into good Christians and church members; and, as education was a means to maintain and extend ideas and culture, the church made a great effort to create opportunities to accomplish these goals.

Education

By law, parents had to take care of a child until he or she turned 25; in addition to providing shelter, clothing, and food, they were required to ensure that their child learned a trade.[299] Parents certainly were aware of the value of education; in their wills, they often instructed the survivor to make sure the children were trained in reading and writing. No manuscripts revealing more about school and learning in Beverwijck have been found; but the settlers may had attitudes similar to those prevalent in Nieuw Amstel on the South River (Newcastle in Delaware). Evert Pietersz, who taught there, wrote in August 1657 that people in that part of New

33. Pieter de Bloot, Service in a protestant village church.

Netherland certainly were enthusiastic about learning: 'As soon as winter begins and they can no longer work the soil, old and young will come to school and learn to read, write (and cipher)...'[300]

In the Netherlands and in New Netherland, girls as well as boys could attend primary school, and private schoolmasters taught for a fee.[201] When Pietersz became a school teacher at New Amsterdam in 1661, he was allowed to ask 30 stivers of each child, above his annual salary, for a quarter-year of teaching the child the spelling and reading of the alphabet. For teaching a child to read and write, which demanded paper, ink, and a quill in addition to the intensive guidance of the teacher, he could ask 50 stivers. And for teaching reading, writing, and cyphering, he could charge 60 stivers.[302] Those who attended school in the evening and 'between times' he could, accordingly, charge a reasonable fee. The poor and destitute, who desired education 'for God's will,' he was expected to teach for free. He was allowed to take half a quarter-year's school money from those who came to his school before the first of December; after the half quarter-year, he was not to demand or receive any more money for that quarter.

The most important part of education was religion. The church was to be a cat-
echizing church, and in order to teach the religion some level of literacy was necessary; in order to maintain and extend its ideas and culture, the church was almost required to offer good schools. Thus, it was expected that the church should
exercise control over the schools. Teaching catechism became the task of the
schoolmaster, while the ideal was that free education should be provided for the
poor so that they, too, could learn the catechism. Children were to be taught the
fundamentals of the 'true' religion and be filled with true devotion, not only by
the church and their parents, but also at school. All teachers, according to the Synod of Dordt in 1618-19, were required to sign the Forms of Unity (*Formulieren
van Enigheid*) or a similar document, in which they promised to teach nothing
that would conflict with the 'true' Reformed doctrine.[303] Catechism was usually
prepared by the teacher and discussed by the minister in the Sunday afternoon
service. Teachers were supposed to take their students to church and supervise
them to make sure the children paid good attention until the very end of the service. The children were expected to know the answers to various catechism questions; this must have been difficult for them, as the same catechism was used by
adults, and one could not have expected a child to understand it. An abstract of
these questions was included in the 'small' catechism, which was meant as preparation for participating in the Holy Communion ritual for the first time.

School books found at Esopus in September 1665, in the inventory of schoolmaster and surgeon Gysbert van Imborgh, give some idea of what was being
taught.[304] The inventory lists a great number of school books, among which were
those used to teach reading and writing, such as the 110 'ABC books.' In the
Dutch Republic, reading was taught first. The youngest children (three to six
years old) had to learn the letters of the alphabet, the prayers, and the 'little questions,' which were simple questions about the Bible and catechism. An 'ABC
board,' or small ABC boards, could have been used, and the 'ABC booklets.' The
booklet started with some letters of the alphabet, followed by syllables such as
'ba-be-bi-bo-bu.' Once the children knew their letters (both gothic and Roman),
they could start spelling, beginning with syllables. This was followed by religious
texts that were printed on the rest of the pages, such as 'Our Father' (*Onze Vader*), the Confession of Faith, the Ten Commandments, and some Dutch (*Nederduytse*) prayers. Working through the whole ABC booklet, a child would learn
spelling. More advanced students then continued with more spelling, reading,
grammar, and difficult words in the 'Arts of Letters' (*Letterconsten*), the 'Steps of
Youth' (*Trappen der jeught*), 'General Circulars' (*Gemeene Sende brieven*) and,
when they were more advanced, 'David's History' (*De Historie van David*). Due
to irregular school attendance, this stage was often reached only after many years.
But a student would not be considered ready to write before he or she could correctly read a sentence. Writing required skillful and controlled handling of the
quill, which demanded intensive guidance by the teacher. Since many parents took
their children out of school at this age, both in New Netherland and in the Dutch
Republic, many people could read but were unable to write.[305]

The church supervised all teaching materials; the government helped out by prohibiting all education without lawful permission, and by banning school books that were inconsistent with Reformed doctrine. Van Imborgh's inventory included various introductions to the Christian religion: a hundred catechisms; twenty *Corte Begrijpen*; and edifying literature for more or less advanced readers, such as eighty-three histories of Tobias and eight histories of David, three *Uytterste Willen* and seven *Uyren des Doots*. There were also some thirty copies of *Heerlijcke bewysen van des menschen ellende*, twenty-three *Historiën van Joseph*, eight *Evangelie-ende epistel-boecken*, and one copy of the *Korte Manier van Megapolensis*, probably his printed catechism booklet, which was printed around 1651, but of which no copies have been found.[306] The forty-eight issues of *Kort Begryp* by Jacob Borstius, mentioned in Van Imborgh's inventory, indicate that newer teaching methods soon found their way to New Netherland. This helpful booklet, meant for practicing catechism at home, was first published in 1659 and would remain the text most used by Calvinist youth in the Netherlands for 150 years. It contained very simple questions that could even be learned and studied by children who were not yet able to read. The first seventy-one questions were about the Christian religion, followed by 158 questions about the Bible, of which 133 concerned the 'Old Testament' – for example, '*Who created you? God. How many gods exist? One God.*'[307]

By 1664, some concern had emerged about the religious education of the growing number of children in New Netherland. On March 17, 1664, an ordinance was passed for the 'better and more careful instruction of youth in the principles of the Christian religion.' It was thought 'highly necessary and most important that the youth from childhood up be instructed not only in reading, writing and arithmetic, but especially and chiefly in the principles and fundamentals of the Reformed religion.' Schoolmasters were ordered to appear in church with their students on Wednesdays, before the commencement of the sermon; after the service they were expected to examine their students, in the presence of the ministers and elders, on what they remembered of the Christian commandments and catechism, in order to determine what progress they had made; afterward, the children would be given the day off for 'a decent recreation.'[308]

The importance of education to parents in New Netherland is also reflected in apprenticeship contracts. Ron Howard has pointed out the importance of apprenticeships for occupational schooling.[309] In New Netherland as well as the Dutch Republic, apprenticeship was perceived as a vital economic and educational institution. Jeremias van Rensselaer, for instance, when he read that his 18-year-old brother Richard had changed his apprenticeship from a lady shopkeeper to a merchant in Amsterdam, wrote to him that he 'must take care to learn something, for it is high time for you to learn; and by changing in this way from one person to another, one cannot acquire any business method.'[310] Later, Maria van Rensselaer would make sure her son Kiliaen had a good apprenticeship. As in the fatherland, apprenticeship contracts frequently required that the child learn how to read and write.[311] In many cases, however, we can only wonder whether that really happened. Apprentices often had to work long hours and, as Frijhoff suggests, they must have had an iron discipline to attend classes after work. Therefore, rudi-

mentary reading may well have been the extent of a child's training if he or she
were sent out to work or apprenticed at an early age, which was fairly common in
the Netherlands.[312] Howard found that, unlike New England, where children
were usually bound-out at the age of puberty to another family, occupational
training in New Netherland almost always took place within the family setting.[313]
Parents often trained their own children, or else apprenticed them out to relatives
or friends, or to acquaintances in various trades or professions. But this was not
always the case; and a master, by taking on an apprentice, more or less took over
the task of the parents, especially when the apprentice came to live with him. He
then became responsible for the apprentice's religious and moral education. But
along with parental authority, the master did not always assume the parents' care,
love, and affection for the child; this arrangement could, and frequently did, lead
to severe and unscrupulous exploitation of a child.[314] Usually, children were apprenticed because of occupational advantage or economical necessity. The advantages of these apprenticeships were valuable, not only for the trade that was
learned, but for the personal contacts that were made as well, which could be vi-
tally important in converting occupational skills into a successful livelihood.[315]

No correspondence or any other document survives to provide us with information about the work of a teacher in Beverwijck; but instructions for Evert
Pietersz, who accepted the New Amsterdam schoolmaster's office in 1661, provide us with a practical look into his school – and teaching in Beverwijck's school
was most likely done in a similar way. Pietersz had to make sure that the children
came to school at the usual hour, in the morning at eight o'clock and in the afternoon at one o'clock. He had to maintain good discipline over the students and
teach them the Christian prayers, the Ten Commandments, baptism, the Holy
Communion rite, and the answers from the catechism, which was taught every
Sunday afternoon in church. Before the end of the school day, he would have the
students sing some verses of a psalm.[316] Regarding the treatment of children, people may have had varying ideas. In 1591, North Holland school teacher Dirck
Adriaensz Valcoogh, in his 'Rule of Dutch Schoolmasters' (*Regel der Duytsche
schoolmeesters*), had already emphasized the need to handle young children tact-
fully and with sweet words when they first came to school; at the same time, however, he complained that parents let their children run and play, instead of making
them learn the catechism in depth.[317] Not to punish children for something they
had done was considered sinful, and to beat children was considered good for
them; but apparently, in Rensselaerswijck, there were limits.[318] When, in November 1651, school teacher Evert Nolden lost control and struck Adriaen Dircksz in
the face with a pair of tongs, thereby 'completely smashing his nose and mortally
wounding him (*doodelijck gewondt*), without any reason for it,' the director of
the colony demanded arbitrary punishment and a fine of *f*300, or that Nolden be
put to hard labor. It is not known what Nolden's actual punishment was, but the
sources do not show him as a school teacher again.[319] This may have been the reason that Adriaen Jansz van Ilpendam came from New Amsterdam to teach in the
upper Hudson area.

It is not totally certain which persons were involved in teaching the children and adults in Beverwijck. *Dominee* Gideon Schaets had previously been a school-master, and his contract mentioned that besides the minister's duties he should 'exercise catechism and the education of the Holy Scriptures among the people and perform [or: fulfill, exercise] the schoolmastership there for old and young.' The original reads: '*Oock aldaer te oeffenen de Cathegisatien ende onderrichtinge der heylige schriftuer onder den volcke ende het schoolmeesterschap mede aldaer waernemen voor oude ende jonge.*' O'Callaghan translated this as 'pay attention to the office of schoolmaster for old and young'; but Schaets was not credited with teaching, and there are no documents suggesting that he performed this function.[320] But would he, contrary to his contract, really not have taught? He certainly had experience, and he was probably familiar with the different books. In some places in the Dutch Republic (e.g., in the classis of Dordrecht), a minister was sometimes a teacher as well, and in that function taught catechism. In this way, the *classis* could keep a firm grip on education.[321]

In Beverwijck, however, there were other possibilities. Before Schaets's arrival in the New World, Evert Nolden had performed the job of schoolmaster for a few years in Rensselaerswijck; soon after Nolden's dismissal in November 1651, Van Ilpendam had come up from New Amsterdam to fill the post. In the same month, the court of Rensselaerswijck granted Van Ilpendam 50 guilders toward the payment of his house rent, and about half a month later he was reported as being schoolmaster at Fort Orange and Rensselaerswijck.[322] If Schaets taught in 1652 or 1653, he probably was a teacher in service of the church, while Van Ilpendam may have been a private schoolmaster. But whether two schoolmasters were needed remains an open question. In the Dutch Republic, one teacher could sometimes have as many as sixty to a hundred students in one class; and with no more than 650 inhabitants, the number of children would not have been so high as to require two teachers. While there are no indications that Schaets actually did teach, the instructions laid out in his contract should be kept in mind. If he taught and maintained the ministry simultaneously, he would have been extremely busy; perhaps his role was limited to teaching small children reading, based on religious content. In that case, it is possible that the private schoolmaster may have taught older children and adults.

But Van Ilpendam had the exclusive right to keep day and evening school in February 1655. He seems to have taught at least until September 1660, when he brought suits against two of his patrons for unpaid tuition. In one case he demanded $10\frac{1}{2}$ beavers and 12 stivers on account of school charges and, in the other case, two beavers (f16) for one year's school fees. If the latter case did not include instruction in calculus, the school charges were, as we saw, higher than in *patria*.[323] When Ludovicus Cobus also was granted permission to keep day and evening school in November 1655, one would have thought that there was some demand for teachers in the rapidly growing community; but most likely teaching did not provide a sufficient source of income for Cobus, as he successfully applied for the office of court messenger about nine months later.[324] Some entries in the deacons' account books raise the question whether there may have been a woman who taught. Between June 1658 and April 1661, the accounts frequently mention a *ma-*

tres. Her presence may have meant that she did what a *matres* would have done in *patria* – that is, she took care of children until they were about six years old, ready to attend elementary school, if both parents worked and were unable to care for the children themselves. But the accounts only show that she was paid for stringing sewant, while no teaching is mentioned.[325] Neither does it seem that Anthonie de Hooges, Pieter Claerbout or, later, Hendrick Rooseboom (Claerbout's successor as precentor) ever taught as precentor or reader, as precentors sometimes did in *patria*.[326] There is no evidence that Jan Juriaensz Becker taught school at Beverwijck before the surrender of the province to the English in 1664. A license granted to him by Governor Lovelace in May 1670 states that he had 'a graunt to keep ye Dutch school at Albany for ye teaching of youth to read and to wryte,' whereas Jacob Joosten was to teach the younger children.[327] Keeping open the option that more people may have been involved in teaching, it seems plausible to assume that only one man actually performed the work of a teacher. In 1656, when New Amsterdam's community had about 120 houses and about a thousand inhabitants, and its youth were 'quite numerous,' Harmanus van Hoboken seems to have been the only schoolmaster there; this would suggest that in Beverwijck, which had about 120 houses in 1657 and a good 1,000 inhabitants in 1660, Van Ilpendam may have been the only one teaching.[328]

Charity

Another basic institution of which the church for a large part took care was charity.[329] A world without the poor was unthinkable for a seventeenth-century person, and the deacons took care of the organization. According to Calvin, God had given the supervision of earthly goods to the wealthy in order to distribute it among the poor. Giving was not considered a virtue in the first place, but a religious obligation of every person able to do so. Calvin had instituted the deaconry in order to supervise the distribution of material goods by receiving and distributing the goods. Between the deacons he had distinguished between those who managed the alms, and those who took care of the poor and sick.[330] In accordance with Calvin's ideas, the deacons of Beverwijck's church urged wealthier inhabitants to donate generously for the poor; and they gathered gifts of charity through collections in church, 'poor boxes' placed at strategic locations, or donations, and distributed the goods among the poor. It was a duty of the rich to give alms, according to Calvinist doctrine, and the voluntary contributions of Beverwijck's inhabitants were almost always used to help the poor.

Secular authorities cooperated in the care of the community's needy. Various ordinances were written with the benefit of the poor in mind. In June 1651, for instance, the poor were allowed to 'lay in small beer free of excise, with the right to retail the same at a reasonable advance by the small measure.'[331] The poor were also exempt from a fee for weighing; furthermore, by ordinance all secretaries, notaries and clerks were 'bound to serve the poor and indigent who ask such as an alms, gratis and pro Deo.'[332] In Beverwijck, the poor and indigent were, as in New Amsterdam, exempt from the fees for going to school.[333] Of fines imposed in court sentencing, a portion was destined for the benefit of the poor. Among the patents distributed in April 1652 was one for the deacons for a lot to be used for the benefit of the poor. And in 1661, when the director general and council at New Amsterdam passed the first law for support of the poor in New Amsterdam and the rest of New Netherland, in which it was stated that every place should collect money for its own poor, the measure did not bring much change in Beverwijck, where the deacons had been collecting money for the poor since the early 1640s and the poorhouse had been in working order since the early 1650s.[334]

Their strategy for distributing such resources meant that the deacons tried to use a minimal amount of funds to ensure the highest possible level of poor relief. According to this 'efficiency' principle, people only received help if they could not survive on their own income. Before they could receive assistance, they had to first use up their own possessions and, if possible, they were required to work, for which the deacons often provided possibilities themselves. Not only can one recognize Calvin's work ethic here, but also some ideas of the Spanish humanist Juan Luis Vives. According to Vives, who lived in Flanders, poor relief should mean not only that the poor were given some money, but should also elevate public morality; this could be achieved by looking for every alms recipient's own capabilities, providing education, building orphanages, and finding suitable work for everyone. The poor, according to Vives, were innocent victims of the accumulation of property; they had fallen into such deep misery that their material decline brought about moral decline. By working, they could earn the respect of other people; at the same time, they could give something back for the help they received. Thus, working was also a way for people to retain their honor.[335] At the same time, it was easy for the consistory to keep some control over their members' behavior. Through their ecclesiastical discipline, they knew that they were only supporting the 'decent' poor. In Amsterdam, people who had been suspended from participating in the Holy Communion due to their behavior were automatically removed from the poor list during the time of their censure.[336] Whether this also happened in Beverwijck is not known.

By trying to keep the costs of charity low and, if possible, even prevent poverty, it was of great advantage for nearly everyone to have access to a piece of land where vegetables and other crops could be grown. This way, people could keep a cow, hog, or some chickens for meat and dairy products. The deacons provided another way to cut costs, and even prevent poor relief by offering the possibility of borrowing money at a 10 percent interest rate. Although this percentage was considerably higher than in the fatherland, where it often was 5 percent or lower for a long term loan, it created the opportunity to buy land, or start a new business in a period of setbacks, or to offer some breathing space after an unproductive year.

That the deacons contributed to the medical well-being of the poor certainly was in accordance with the 'efficiency' principle, as well. Repeatedly, the deaconry paid for surgeon's fees and, in November 1664, they contracted with surgeon Cornelis van Dijck on an annual basis to serve and cure the poor. If necessary, the deacons would provide the sick, or women in childbirth, with beer, wine, or brandy to sooth the pain. They also made sure that patients, the elderly and orphans were cared for by paying various poor individuals for boarding them.

In two ways, the deacons tried to fight poverty. As in Amsterdam and many places in the countryside of the Dutch Republic, they boarded people out for payment, and they supported people who lived on their own. Sometimes they paid for one's house rent, or gave the needy person money for housing or other necessities. They also often provided the poor with food, clothing, blankets and firewood. On occasion they paid school money, while sometimes they paid for someone's coffin, and for brandy and beer at the funeral. The help they provided was always given with the idea in mind that it should be 'efficient.' The sooner an ill person recovered, the sooner he could go back to work; likewise, if a child received an education, he would later be more able to work and not become a burden to the deaconry.

A new environment: Contacts with Indians

Beavers and sewant as currency

While church and state determined Beverwijck's Dutch identity, the environment added characteristics as well. Beverwijck thus became a village different from any village in the Republic or any other colony; it became a Dutch village on the North-American frontier. The reason that Dutch and Indian cultures met was the Europeans' desire for beaver pelts that were provided by the Indians, who brought them from the interior to Fort Orange. Due to the lack of precious metals and the financial problems of the West India Company, it was not possible to make coins in New Netherland or to import silver money from the fatherland; thus, other means of payment were used for the trade.[337] Beavers, in addition to being a commodity, then became the means of payment – and as such, the settlers used pelts in real estate and business transactions, for house rents, and wages. In 1656, the company stipulated that the price of one 'merchantable' (*leverbaer*, of a predetermined quality) beaver pelt should be ƒ6; but the exchange rate shifted occasionally, as in November 1657, when the value of a pelt was changed to ƒ8. In general, this remained the value for the inhabitants throughout the Dutch period.[338] At a time when the value of a beaver pelt in Amsterdam was no more than ƒ6, the company ordered that the value for its employees should be reduced to ƒ7 in 1662, and to ƒ6 in 1663, so that they would receive their pay in some degree equivalent of Holland money.[339]

The other currency used was *sewant*, which were small, relatively scarce cylindrical or barrel-shaped white beads made from a seashell found along the Atlantic coast, the knobbed or chanelled whelk (*busicon carica* or *busicon canalculatum*). Since the turn of the seventeenth century, people on Long Island Sound had also made black beads from the purple spot of the quahog, or hardshell clam.[340] Early on, the Dutch had discovered that shell beads held great symbolic value for the In-

34. Engraving of a beaver in the files of the Holland Society of New York. Courtesy of the Holland Society of New York.

dians and were highly desired objects. They were used in many rituals, especially those of condolence. These shells were found in large quantities along the shores of Long Island Sound; since the 1620s, the Dutch had controlled the supply of these beads.[341] Their experience with the use of *cowrie* shells as currency in the Niger delta of West Africa, in the late sixteenth century, had taught the Dutch that specific kinds of shells possessed substantial commercial value; in order to obtain furs, they began offering these beads to the Indians in exchange for their furs.[342] The Indians accepted this exchange, thereby adding commercial value to the beads' ritual value. Thus, native Americans began to participate in the capitalistic market exchange. Originally, *sewant* – as the Dutch called the beads, using their Algonquian name – consisted of loose beads of various sizes and shapes; but 'true' *sewant* consisted of small tubular beads that had been finely drilled for stringing. The archaeologist James Bradley has described *sewant* as a cross-cultural product of European-Indian contact.[343] In the early 1640s, the Dutch introduced standard techniques to native manufacturers, after which the Dutch sold European goods in exchange for *sewant* to the Algonquians in southern New England and on the north shore of Long Island, who produced the beads. The Dutch then exchanged the beads with the Iroquois and Mahicans for beaver pelts; subsequently, they would send the furs to the Dutch Republic in exchange for new trade goods. Through this trade triangle, an enormous quantity of these beads went to the Five Nations. Daniel Richter has estimated that as many as 3 million beads of *sewant* may have come into circulation in Iroquoia, which made possible the creation of the ceremonial *sewant* belts composed of thousands of beads.[344]

Initially, the Dutch exchanged both loose and strung beads; but in May 1650, fraud and depreciation would compel the colonial government to mandate that only strung *sewant* be used as currency. Strings of uniform length were to com-

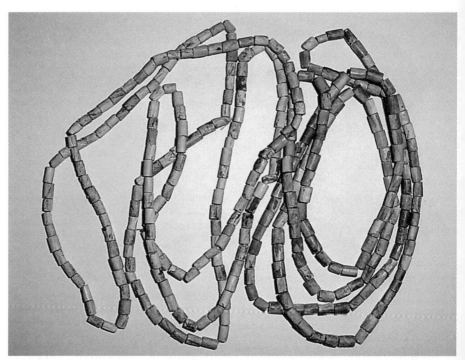

35. Restrung white and purple (faded), archaeological sewant beads, c. 1650. Sewant beads like these were used by Beverwijck's inhabitants to trade with the Indians and among themselves.

pensate for differences in the size of individual beads, while the beads themselves were to be examined for quality.[345] Using *sewant* 'as merchandise, to buy, barter, sell and rebarter it at wholesale, according to the value and quality thereof,' the colonists used it among themselves as currency for everyday expenses, and sometimes for wages.[346] Unlike the price of beaver pelts, which had a market value in Europe, the price of *sewant* was established by ordinance. Called 'light' money, it was worth 15 stivers to the guilder. In 'heavy' or coin money, the guilder equaled 20 stivers. *Sewant* was a more volatile currency than the beaver pelts, and was subject to inflation. In 1650, the rate of exchange for good *sewant* rose from four white beads per stiver to six, while the black beads (which usually had double the value) rose from two to three beads per stiver.[347] After New England minted America's first metal coinage in 1652, the pine tree shilling, an abundance of *sewant* of varying quality flowed into New Netherland, which resulted in a period of inflated costs in the Dutch colony throughout the 1650s and early 1660s.[348] By 1657, the value of *sewant* had decreased so much that one beaver pelt was worth 10 to 12 guilders in *sewant*.[349] A year later, when the beaver trade had begun to decline (but there still was a surplus of *sewant*), one pelt was worth ƒ15 in sewant, and its rate had fallen to eight/four beads per stiver.[350] Due to the 'increasing dearness of wares and even of the more necessary articles such as beer and bread,' an ordinance then placed a limit of *f*24 on payments in *sewant*, and also set the prices for brewers, tapsters and bakers. In 1662, however, when a beaver pelt was worth only *f*6 in Amsterdam, the value of *sewant* in New Netherland even declined to *f*20-24 per pelt, while the exchange rate was reduced from sixteen to twenty-four white beads per stiver.[351] That may have been the peak, since the English used an exchange rate of eight white or four black beads per stiver in their Articles of Agreement with Albany/Beverwijck in October 1664.[352]

After 1657, the effects of inflationary conditions and the dwindling fur trade on Beverwijck's economy would be well noticed. Martha Shattuck has found that there was an increase in debt litigation as creditors tried to force payments, so that their own accounts would not be jeopardized.[353] Although, after 1655, payments were also sometimes made in tobacco, grain or boards, *sewant* remained the most commonly used means of payment throughout the Dutch period.

Meetings and the exchange of gifts

Although *sewant* was used as a means of payment, its ceremonial use was maintained in the official meetings between delegations of settlers and natives. For the Indians, reciprocal gift exchanges sealed relationships, while creating and maintaining unity and reciprocity between kin. Instead of buying and selling items, economic exchanges among Indians took the form of gift giving. Upon a person's death, members of another kin group would conduct funeral rituals, provide feasts, and bestow gifts in order to ease the mourners' way back to normal life. The beads had great symbolical value. The whiteness of the shell beads added more to their value; white was associated with light, and light was mind, knowledge and the 'greatest being.' The positive quality of light colors found their greatest expression in the presentation of white wampum or *sewant* belts, which conveyed a semantic context of peace, as well as a desire for understanding and sociability for the oral message that accompanied it. While white connoted the cognitive aspect of life, black represented the non-cognitive and asocial aspects of life. The presentation of a black wampum belt conveyed a semantic context of death, mourning, and asociability.[354]

To maintain their friendship, Indians frequently gave the Dutch *sewant* belts or strings and beaver pelts, for which they received gifts in return.[355] Thus, *sewant* was used in its dual capacity: as ceremonial offerings in diplomatic transactions in which the Dutch participated, and in exchange for furs. By the middle of the seventeenth century, according to James Bradley, *sewant* had become an 'acculturative product, a blending of traditional native and novel European conceptions. It was precisely for this reason that it worked so successfully.'[356]

The contracts and negotiations between Indian *sachems* and Dutch officials differed remarkably from those between officials in the Dutch Republic, and may have had more in common with native rituals. In 1679-80, Jasper Danckaerts described how contracts between Indians were concluded with *sewant* strings or belts, which he called 'counters':

een Mahakuaes Indiaen, met hun Steden en woningen

36. *A Mohawk (Maquaes) Indian and two types of Indian villages in the background. Picture from the pamphlet by Johannes Megapolensis jr.,* Een kort ontwerp vande Mahakvase Indianen [A short Account of the Mohawk Indians] *(Alkmaar z.j. [1644]).*

They hold one in their hand as long as that point is being discussed, and when that article is being decided upon and the entire gathering on both sides is satisfied with it, then the counter is marked, or they make it understandable and then put it away. When they come to another article, they take another counter and do as with the other until the whole contract has been concluded. Then they add up their counters representing so many articles and the specific meaning which each signifies. As they can neither read nor write, they are gifted with a powerful memory; and as it is done so solemnly, they consider it absolutely unbreakable... Then all children who have the ability to understand and to remember it are called together; they are told by their fathers, *sachems* or chiefs how they entered into such a contract with these parties. Then the markers are counted out to them, showing that the contract consists in so many articles and explaining the significance given to the markers and the story of how it was done. Thus they acquire understanding of each article in particular. Then these children are commanded to remember this treaty and to plant each article in particular in their memory, and they and their children [are commanded] to preserve it faithfully so that they may not become treaty breakers, which is an abomination to them. Then all these shells or counters are bound together with a string in such a manner, signifying such a treaty or contract with such and such a nation. After they have been bound together, the bundle is put in a bag and hung up in the house of the *sachem* or chief where it is carefully preserved.[357]

A French observer once expressed his admiration for the protocol of Iroquois council: '... their restraint in never interrupting a speaker, their patience of a reasoned argument, their coolness in reply, their prodigious memories, and their historical sense, supported by wampum belts.'[358] While the Dutch partially adjusted to the Indians' ways, they also found solutions for making negotiations easier and less time-consuming. Van der Donck described how the Dutch and Indians maintained contacts and how they handled several proposals:

> When making a request to one of them or generally, one sends an offering to the respective person or locality. The offering is hung up, the request is put, and those to whom it is addressed examine and deliberate the proposition seriously. If they take the offering, the request as made is accepted and consented to; but if it remains where it hangs for over three days, the matter is held in abeyance and the petitioner has to alter the conditions or augment the offering, or both.[359]

That they did not always organize meetings may have had to do with the generally different ways of speaking and behavior of the two cultures. Danckaerts described Indian speech, like everything the Indians did, as 'intense and pregnant with meaning.' Coarse and common people among the Dutch despised it – while the Indians, for their part, hated the settlers' 'precipitancy of comprehension and judgment, the excited chattering, often without knowing what is being said, the haste and rashness to do something, whereby a mess is often made of someone's good intentions.'[360] Nevertheless, the Dutch and Indians did organize official meetings from time to time for important occasions. Just as they recalled the origins of the Great League of Peace and Power at their own League councils, Iroquois leaders often may have repeated the history of the friendship between Indians and colonists at their meetings with the Dutch. For example, the Dutch did this in September 1659, in response to proposals made earlier by the Maquaes, by referring to the contract of 1643, saying that their sixteen-year-old friendship and brotherhood treaty had never been broken.[361]

In the course of the 1650s, Indians and settlers met several times to negotiate various issues. In November 1655, for example, some Maquaes *sachems* proposed that the Dutch remain neutral in the war they intended to renew against the French. The natives also made other proposals based on their principles of reciprocity and kinship: They complained that they were not being entertained as well by the Dutch as they entertained their Dutch visitors, and that the Dutch did not repair their guns (which, together with gunpowder, had become a regular trade item in the 1640s) except for payment. Altogether, they did not consider the Dutch behavior very brotherly. Following each proposal, the Indians gave a belt of *sewant*; gifts and words for them were inseparable, and words without gifts did not mean much to them. The Dutch gave gifts in return – although they were not keen on it, since the Indians, according to Van der Donck, tended to demand too much in return, and appropriated what the other party did not give of his own accord.[362] Along with their answer to the first proposal, the Dutch gave fifteen bars of lead; and upon their answering the last proposals, they laid down twenty-five pounds of powder – which, according to commissary De Deckere, who reported on the meeting, the Maquaes received 'with their usual barbarian applaus.' De Deckere, who had been appointed commissary of Fort Orange only five months earlier, does not seem to have gained a high opinion of the Indians. While he did not reveal what the Indians' 'other trifles of the like kind' were, his characterization may have been an expression not only of his opinion, but also his level of understanding of (and his willingness to understand) the basis for the Indians' complaints.[363]

Reading such a description, one could question the Dutch attitude toward Indian propositions, as it suggests that De Deckere firmly believed the Dutch to be superior to the natives. Dutch self-image, in general, was very positive; their high self-esteem had only increased during their struggle for independence from Spain – and with the Dutch victory in 1648, it may even have seemed justified. Works of contemporary authors praised the Dutch patriotic virtues of 'the spirit of freedom and candor, simplicity and austerity, courage and intelligence, love of peace and true piety.' These virtues were said to have originated with the Batavians, a free people who had unified because they chose to join voluntarily, and who strove for freedom and equality.[364] This Batavian myth, Frijhoff and Spies have pointed out, was a symbolic story, a patriotic metaphor from which had emerged the Dutch spirit of freedom that was used to justify their rebellion against Spain.[365] The fact that immigrants and foreign visitors also considered the Dutch Republic more or less as 'a miracle of God and the diligence of the Dutch themselves' contributed to this positive self image. Others also praised the Dutch Republic, and especially Holland, for its freedom and economic prosperity, and regarded the Dutch government as taking on the role of 'God's bulwark' in a hostile environment; they even considered the physical existence of the country, which had been conquered from both sea and enemy, to be a miracle.[366]

Against this backdrop, it may not be so surprising that De Deckere, who had not spent much time in New Netherland, felt superior to the Indians in the North American wilderness. According to Adriaen van der Donck, who had lived in Rensselaerswijck in the early 1640s, naming the natives '*wilden*' had not happened with forethought; but he thought the name was quite appropriate, in any case. The Indians had little or no religion; and with respect to marriage and the recognition of landed property, they deviated so far from general European laws that they appeared to act almost at will. He thought that the natives indeed were 'quite wild and strangers to the Christian religion.'[367] Not all colonists may have shared De Deckere's opinion in 1655; someone like Jeremias van Rensselaer, who stayed longer in the colony, certainly showed respect for the Indians in his correspondence.[368]

Meetings between the Indians and the Dutch were planned in advance. *Sewant* donated by the Indian *sachems* was provided by their followers, in whose name it was presented, which signified that the kin agreed with what their *sachems* said. Usually, the *sachems* would distribute in the community gifts received in return, such as belts and strings of *sewant*, which in turn would raise their prestige. Thus, gifts given by them to the Dutch represented, more or less, assurances that promises were likely to be carried out. Gifts symbolized that the speaker represented his kin and followers. As a leader he spoke their words, and he distributed gifts from and to them; as such, he was a provider and distributor of economic re-sources.[369]

Sometimes the Dutch also planned in advance who would bring which presents to these meetings. In July 1654, the magistrates planned to send a Dutch delegation to the Maquaes in order to renew the old alliance, and also to discuss prices of merchandise and the killing of cattle by the Indians. Some of the 'most favorably disposed of the citizens' were asked to contribute presents, which they did in the form of *sewant*, kettles, axes, and gunpowder. It was arranged that the presents which the Indians would give, 'as they are accustomed to do,' would be divided among the settlers in proportion to the amount they had contributed.[370] In particular, the gift of gunpowder indicates the importance of the trade in ammunition, and how far the officials were willing to go in order to maintain the trade. In almost all meetings and land transactions between Maquaes and Dutch officials, kettles, axes, gunpowder and lead were among the Dutch exchange gifts.[371] The Indians frequently gave strings of *sewant* and beaver pelts.[372] By the 1650s, however, the Dutchmen's gifts of copper kettles, iron tools, cloth and arms had assumed large proportions, and almost imperceptibly would replace earthen pots, stone implements, and animal skins. The generation of natives who knew how to survive without these European tools had passed away. A new generation of Indians had grown up with European goods, and had been left without much knowledge of the traditional techniques, for example, of making pottery. For their very survival, this new generation of Indians had become largely dependent on commerce with the Dutch.[373]

Communication: Maintaining an iron chain

In addition to trading issues, the growing Dutch community had to face other problems with the natives. Between 1653 and 1657, Dutch officials and Indian *sachems* of various tribes frequently met to discuss such issues as maintenance of friendship, Dutch neutrality or help in the Maquaes's war with the French, the killing of the settlers' livestock by the Indians, help from the Dutch to protect the Indians' castles, or the sale and free repair of firearms. Especially after 1658, when the trade declined, the Indians repeatedly added complaints to their list, among which were insolent treatment by the Dutch and the sale of brandy.

Meetings in 1659 and 1660 would express great differences in the interpretation of their old friendship, which had been established in 1643 when Arent van Curler, Jan Labatie, and Jacob Jansz van Amsterdam had made a trip on horseback to three castles in the Maquaes country.[374] This delegation had been given a symbolic greeting at the wood's edge: At this ritual threshold, persons who wished to enter the Maquaes community were made 'fit' through various rites of physical, spiritual and social transformation before they could proceed. The purpose of these rituals, according to George Hamell, was to create or reaffirm kinship and kinship responsibilities.[375] The Dutchmen may have given some of their presents at that time, as usually the purposes of this ritual greeting were confirmed by the reciprocal exchange of gifts, often *sewant*. After this journey, it seems that the Indians became regular guests in Fort Orange and the patroonship. An account written by *dominee* Megapolensis reveals interesting details about the relations between Maquaes and colonists, and suggests that by 1644 it had grown and established itself more or less as a friendship, and that the Dutch trusted their neighbors. During visits, the Indians did them 'every act of friendship'; the colonists were not afraid of the natives, walked with them into the woods and met with them, sometimes at a distance of an hour or two from any houses; they did not think more about it than if they had been meeting with a Christian. 'They sleep by us too,' the minister wrote, 'in our chambers before our beds. I have had eight at once lying and sleeping upon the floor near my bed.'[376] By 1648, the patroon's house had become a rendez vous for Maquaes war commanders and, according to Brant van Slichtenhorst, *sachems* of the Maquaes castles, following their old custom, would come and stay in the patroon's house.[377]

A proposition issued by a 1659 meeting in the first Maquaes castle named Kaghnuwage, noted that it had been sixteen years since the first treaty of friendship and brotherhood had been made between the Indians and all Dutch settlers, 'which we then joined together with an iron chain, and which until now has not been broken by us or our brothers, and we have no fear that it will be broken by either side; ... [we] shall all be and remain as if we had lain under one heart.'[378] By entering into their contract of friendship and brotherhood, both sides had committed themselves to treating each other as brothers. But to be adopted into an Iroquois kinship relationship entailed rights and obligations to share; the Maquaes called it 'not brotherly,' for example, that the Dutch were only prepared to repair guns for payment. Maintaining a relationship with an Iroquois woman would also bring a Dutchman into the world of their kin; but the Dutchmen do not seem to have taken this much into consideration. One of the Maquaes' complaints was that Dutchmen should donate one or two suits of clothes to the relatives of the deceased, if their Maquaes mate had died and left children.[379] This suggests that, in general, these partners maintained limited or no contact. Not only were the Maquaes unhappy with the Dutch, but other Iroquois also came with similar grievances about not receiving gifts in return, being abused by the Dutch, being unable to trade freely, and having to pay for lead and gunpowder.[380] But to the extent that the conferences between the Dutch and Indians made clear that more problems arose during the 1650s, at the same time they are a sign that these issues could be negotiated. The Dutch were well aware that their very survival depended on the maintenance of the natives' friendship, while the Maquaes had become too dependent on European trade goods to give up the relationship of friendship and brotherhood with the providers of those goods. The iron chain, Francis Jennings has pointed out, seems to have functioned as a two-way affair in which arms were provided to the Maquaes, rebellious tribes in New Netherland were repressed, damage was inflicted on New France, and the delivery of furs to Fort Orange ensured.[381] That Beverwijck never was attacked by Indians was, according to Jennings, a result of its open market and the frequent renewal of their alliance at various meetings.

The Dutch delegations that went to these meetings usually included members

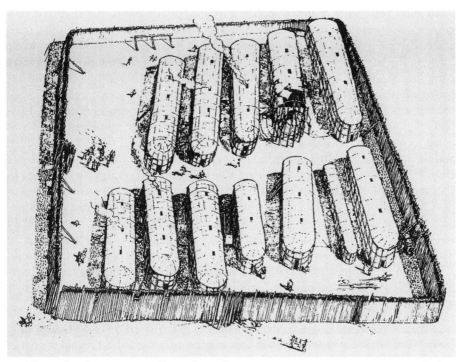

37. The Mohawk (Maquaes) village of Caughnawaga 1666-93. In 1659 a meeting took place at this castle, where the first treaty of friendship and brothership was remembered. It was then likely located elsewhere.

of the settlement's two civil courts, sometimes accompanied by former court members and 'some burgher people,' usually important traders.[382] As the matters needing discussion became more complicated, and involved important concerns with respect to the safety and survival of the community, a simple trade jargon was no longer sufficient. In 1660, the colonial government – in order to ensure the highest level of communication in important matters such as peace and war – hired Claes Jansz Ruyter (who was able to understand and speak the Indian language well) as an interpreter in West India Company service for *f*400 per year.[383]

In the upper Hudson community, several men had some mastery of Indian languages and occasionally served as interpreters at meetings. *Dominee* Megapolensis may have written, in 1644, that some Dutch were only able to use a kind of jargon sufficient to carry on trade; but in the course of time, this would change. Of Jan Thomasz, who had come to the colony in 1644 and frequently served as translator, it was said in 1656 that he was 'well acquainted with the Mahican language' when he examined the Mahican Macheck Sipoeti in court.[384] Seven years later, he translated a letter from the governor of Nova Scotia about Indian problems in the north into the Maquaes tongue for the chief Saheda.[385] The differentiation in the two cases, Lois Feister has point out in her study on communication, indicates that Thomasz was using more than a simple trade jargon alone.[386]

To enter into trade dealings and understand conversations that involved religion or government with only limited mastery of the language, for example, indicates a certain level of contact on a positive basis. Establishing relationships, while learning the basics of the language and other methods of communication, involve complicated, intensive, and long-lasting processes; this should be taken into account when analyzing relationships between people of different cultures. Since the Indians were unfamiliar, for example, with the abstract concepts of the Christian religion, they had no words with which to explain these ideas; and in order to come to some understanding, one had to analyze words and phrases thoroughly, and their translation often needed to be revised before a definite meaning became clear.[387] The fact that both peoples were able to accept and respect (or chose *not* to accept or respect) each other's ideas indicates a significant amount of communication. To say that the Dutch kept as much distance as possible from the natives denies all these early processes, and seems to contradict the source material.[388] In 1644, the learned scholar Megapolensis was busy compiling a vocabulary, as he was undoubtedly well aware of the difficulties and misunderstandings that could arise when preaching abstract concepts in a language he had not mastered.[389] Settlers in New France encountered similar problems. The Jesuit Father Garnier would later describe how difficult it was to convert the Hurons:

> ... The difficulties are far greater than one thinks ... The conversion of the Indians takes time. The first six or seven years will appear sterile to some; and if I should say ten or twelve, I would possibly be not far from the truth.[390]

Seen in this light, it seems somewhat unfounded to portray the learned Megapolensis – who had been in Rensselaerswijck less than two years when he wrote his friends, probably without the intent of publishing his writing – as a person who 'dabbled in the Mohawk language and displayed his superficial knowledge of Iroquois culture.'[391] It likewise seems premature to 'question his ability as an ethnographer' based on a lack of facility in the language.[392]

Adriaen van der Donck described the relationship between the two peoples as one of much interaction as well; it was true, he wrote, that at first sight the Indians appeared 'somewhat strange to our people, because color, speech and dress are so different, but for those who associate with them frequently the strangeness soon passes.'[393] Over the years, several people would acquire knowledge of some Indian languages. The Huguenot Jan Labatie, in 1650, was said to be reasonably experienced in the use of the Maquaes language; Abraham Staets, Rut Jacobsz, Arent Andriesz, Jan Dareth, Thomas Chambers, Jacob Loockermans, Jacob Jansz Stoll, Aernout Cornelisz Viele, and Gerrit van Slichtenhorst also served as *taelsmannen* (interpreters) on occasion.[394] Several of these men had lived in the colony since the 1640s, long enough to have become well acquainted with some Indians. Considering the frequency with which Indians visited the settlement around Fort Orange, it should not be surprising to find translators in the 1660s who had spent much of their childhood in the colony. Sara Roelofs Kierstede, for example, a daughter of Roelof and Anneke Jansz, had lived in Rensselaerswijck on De Laetsburch (obliquely across the river from Fort Orange) between her fourth and seventh years, an age at which children are most susceptible to learning other languages without effort; she may have learned their language while playing with Indian children. In May 1664, Sara would serve as translator for Stuyvesant in peace negotiations with the Esopus Indians, an Algonquian tribe.[395]

In daily life, the function of an interpreter was probably not needed. Little more than simple trade jargon was required to do business, and it is likely that signs, gestures, sounds, and facial expressions remained an important part of daily communication. In August 1658, when Hendrick Martensz offered his services to the court to intercede with the governor of Canada on behalf of the Maquaes, '... [it] pleased the savages very much and they expressed their joy by all kinds of gestures.'[396] For the Dutch, it may not have been so unusual to be flexible in their communication. As the settlers' places of origin varied remarkably, their use of language may sometimes have been limited to a superficial level, even among the settlers themselves. While groups of people with the same origin may have spoken their own native language, they were perfectly able to make themselves understood in the community. Jochem Wesselsz, a baker who from Jeveren, in Oost (East) Friesland, could well negotiate with Pieter Pietersz, a West India Company negro, when they stood talking on the strand. While the baker may have been best at speaking in German or Frisian, and Pietersz may have preferred to speak Portuguese, together they were perfectly able to discuss, perhaps in simplified Dutch, how they would divide the gunpowder that Pietersz would take from the company for Wesselsz.[397]

Indian-Dutch relationships

The Indians' business visits also had a social element. The records mention instances of Indians visiting with colonists often enough for us to assume that this was done frequently.[398] Court minutes often mention these visits in the context of cases in which the Dutch broke the law by giving or selling alcoholic beverages to the Indians. By the 1650s, the Dutch were well aware that natives did not share their custom of collective drinking as a ritual of social cohesion. On the contrary, Indians who had become familiar with alcoholic beverages often lost their all-important virtue of self-control; for them, drinking was not an act that reinforced the group; rather, it isolated individuals from their own group.[399] Although the Dutch knew that Indians frequently lost their tempers as a result of drinking, or became violent and destructive, there always seemed to be individual settlers who acted contrary to the law, notwithstanding the frequently renewed ordinances prohibiting the provision of alcoholic beverages to Indians. In June 1654, for example, Elmerhuysen Kleyn and Gerrit Slichtenhorst had provided an Indian with brandy, after which the native picked up a mallet and forcibly banged open the door of a settler's house, so that the door sprang out of its hinges. He then seriously molested the family and committed many outrages.[400] In another case, at the end of the 1656 trading season, an intoxicated Maquaes Indian had come into Andries Herbertsz *constapel*'s house and, after committing many acts of violence, left some personal items behind. When he came back to get his belongings the next day, he claimed that the wine that had made him drunk was fetched from Barent Pietersz *molenaer* by three Indian women.[401] That similar offenses also happened during the winter suggests that some Indians visited the village year-round.[402]

Just how dangerous were the effects of alcohol on Indians, as well as the reactions of Dutchmen, had become evident in the Esopus, where events took a bad turn. In September 1659, some Indians had been rewarded with a bottle of brandy for helping Thomas Chambers with the harvest. When the natives retired and collectively became drunk, Jacob Jansz Stoll gathered five Dutchmen who began shooting at the Indians, killing one in his sleep. The following day, Indians killed thirteen men, layed siege to the fortified village, killed livestock, and burned the outlying buildings. This series of events led to a war, for which peace would not be negotiated until July 1660.[403]

Although such incidents in Beverwijck remained limited to violence directed at people's houses, and at times the killing of livestock, the Maquaes' request in 1659 not to sell them any more brandy clearly indicates the extent of this illegal trade and the effect it had on them: Anticipating war with the French, the natives said that if they drank themselves to intoxication, they would not be able to fight.[404] The offense of providing Indians with alcoholic drink was considered dangerous, and therefore was brought to Beverwijck's court and sometimes to the colonial council. But numerous meetings between Dutch and Indians also must have taken place without problems. The Indian who had become violent at Andries Herbertsz's house was not afraid to come back the next day and talk with Herbertsz. The tavernkeeper Jan Martensz, when he denied supplying two Indians with brandy or beer, suggested that socializing did not necessarily have to be accompanied by drinking alcohol: The natives had just been lodging at his house and sat by the fire. Accommodating the Indians was not the charge in this case, but providing them with alcohol.[405] Some individuals developed long-lasting friendships over the years. For example, Volckert Jansz Douw, who had come to Rensselaerswijck in 1642, received land in 1665 from the Mahican Indian Wattawit, who presented it as 'a token of his friendship and in satisfaction of an old debt for maize.'[406]

There were also Dutchmen who had relationships with Indian women. In 1644, Megapolensis had already noted that Dutchmen were keen to run after Maquaes women, who were 'exceedingly addicted to whoring,' and who would 'lie with a man for the value of one two, or three schillings'; this does not seem to have changed much by the 1650s.[407] The Maquaes' proposal in September 1659, that a Dutchman should give one or two suits of clothes to the relatives of his deceased Maquaes mate, indicates that in most cases these sexual encounters did not bring the two cultures closer together.[408] Jacob van Leeuwen, a trader who visited New Netherland in the 1650s, certainly did not feel any ties with the kin of a 'certain Indian woman of beautiful figure.' After they had sexual intercourse in the attic of the court house during church time, he gave her a necklace of blue and red beads that she was wearing when they came down the staircase, and which she often wore later. Back in Amsterdam, Van Leeuwen would be reminded of the affair when his pregnant wife demanded testimony about the adultery; but the Indian woman probably never heard from him again.[409]

Although there were some good relationships, and although Indians and colonists greatly influenced each other's lives, their worlds remained separate.[410] This should come as no surprise; and that the Dutch did not regard the natives as part of colonial society was not so strange, either. The Dutch had entered a world in which Indian culture had existed for centuries, a world in which people had their own values, morals and standards – their own culture. The Indians had their own interests, and worked for the benefit of, and out of, their own society – and, as such, they came to the Dutch as trading partners and as visitors. Sometimes they did work for the settlers. In 1659, for instance, eight Indians helped Thomas Chambers bring in the harvest, and Indians served as couriers on various occasions, especially during the winter months, when contact with Manhattan was almost impossible via the river. In 1689, the deacons hired an Indian to clear the church's pasture. But the natives were paid for their work.[411] At some point, they went home – to their own Indian community, where they lived according to their own rules of kinship, rituals, values – and where they had their own culture. There was no need for them to change their life-style and culture into a culture that they did not consider of higher quality than their own. They could visit the village whenever they wanted; and around 1650, if Van Slichtenhorst is to be believed, not half a day went by when the settlement was free of Indians. In the 1650s, Indians were often present in the village, as well – and not just during the summer months. To many Dutch, it may sometimes have looked as a massive invasion when natives would arrive in great numbers; but they were all there as individuals, as well, perhaps visiting with old friends among the settlers like Douw. They could try to obtain the trade goods they were interested in, and to use them for their own purposes – in their own way, fitting them into their own culture. Indians maintained their role as trading partners with the Dutch; but they remained in their own separate world.

Yet for some people it was different. They became part of both worlds, as their worlds sometimes merged. Only a few settlers are known to have had sexual relations with Indian women; it is unclear how exactly these partners communicated in daily life. Arent van Curler, for example, who is said to have been known for his good relations with the Maquaes and Mahicans, had a daughter with a Maquaes woman. Like other Maquaes children, the girl grew up among the Indians with her mother, and belonged to her mother's kin.[412] The records do not reveal how much contact Van Curler had with his daughter; but there probably was some contact, as people in the village were well aware of her existence and, in 1676 (nine years after Van Curler's death), knew exactly where she lived.[413] Van Curler's relationship with the mother may have provided entrée to her kin, which in turn may have enabled him to benefit greatly from the situation; he may have gained commercial profit and political power as the Indians reciprocated by accepting him. It is easy to imagine him providing the natives with arms, while they in turn benefited Van Curler in the trade or helped him gain access to land at Schenectady, for example. He was so respected by the Indians that, following his death, they made his name '*Corlaer*' into a title by which they addressed later governors of New York. Unfortunately, the documents reveal nothing else about Van Curler's daughter; we may assume that she continued to live in her own clan among the Maquaes. We know more about the children of his neighbor, Cornelis Theunisz van Slyck, and a Maquaes woman. The report of the Labadist Jasper Danckaerts on his meeting with Van Slyck's daughter, Illetie, sheds an interesting light on the effect of some of these personal bonds between natives and colonists in the 1650s. Like most other children born of these relationships, Illetie probably grew up with her mother, who had remained among the Maquaes. Danckaerts wrote:

> ... Her mother would never listen to anything about the Christians, or it was against her heart, from an inward, unfounded hate... Sometimes she went with her mother among the Christians to trade and make purchases, or the Christians came among them, and thus it was that the Christians took a fancy to the girl, discovering in her more resemblance to the Christians than the Indians, but understand, more like the Dutch, and that she was not as wild as the other children. They therefore wished to take the girl and bring her up, which the mother would not hear to, and as this request was made repeatedly, she said she would rather kill her. The little daughter herself had no disposition at first to go; and the mother did nothing more than express continually her detestation and abhorrence of the Christians.

But the daughter would begin to mistrust her mother's views after this happened several times:

> ... she never went among them without being well treated, and obtaining something for her. She therefore began to hearken to them; but particularly she felt a great inclination and love in her heart towards those Christians who spoke to her about God, and of Christ Jesus and the Christian religion. Her mother observed it, and began to hate her and not treat her as well as she had done before. Her brothers and sisters despised her, and did her all the wrong they could; but the more they abused her and maltreated her, the more she felt something growing in her that attracted and impelled her towards the Christians and their doctrine, until her mother and the others could endure her no longer while she could no longer live with the Indians. They ceased not seeking to wrong her, and compelled her to leave them, as she did, and went to those who had so long solicited her. They gave her the name of Eltie or Illetie. She lived a long time with a woman with whom we conversed afterwards, who taught her to read and write and do various handiwork, in which she advanced so greatly that everybody was astonished.

Illetie then lived with different families; after she had learned the Dutch language and the contents ('what was expressed in') of the New Testament, she made her confession and was baptized. But she also clearly saw the Christians' faults. Danckaerts's journal continues:

> 'How many times,' said she, 'have I grieved over these Christians, not daring to speak out my heart to any one, for when I sometimes would rebuke them a little for their evil lives, drunkenness, and foul and godless language, they would immediately say: 'Well, how is this, there is a sow converted. Run bos, to the brewer's, and bring some swill for a converted sow,' words which went through my heart, made me sorrowful and closed my mouth.'

Illetie had a brother, Danckaerts wrote, 'also a half-breed, who had made profession of Christianity, and had been baptized.' She also had a nephew, a full-blooded Maquaes named Wouter,

> … who she had taught as well as she could, among others, how he must pray. He had betaken himself entirely to the Christians and dressed like them. He also suffered a lot from the other Indians and his friends.[414]

The story told by Illetie and written down by Danckaerts indicates that Illetie, as well as her brother and nephew, were not accepted by the Indians when they showed sympathy to the Dutch; and the Dutch, for their part, ridiculed Illetie when she criticized their way of life. In both worlds she experienced hard times, periods of not being fully accepted due to her connections with the two peoples. What we don't know, however, is her character, and what she chose to remember after a good thirty years. Her story provides us with a glance into her life between the two worlds; but her life is viewed through two windows – her own, and that of the Labadist Danckaerts, who had his own critique of the way of life of the Calvinist settlers.

We can only wonder what the story of other children of Maquaes mothers and Dutch fathers may have been like; but unfortunately, those stories have not been written down. Perhaps *Smits* Jan's tale was different. Best known as 'the Flemish bastard,' he was described as 'a savage who is much beloved by the Maquaes.'[415] Under the name Canaqueese, he carried a letter from the court of Fort Orange to Canada in 1653 to help facilitate a peace agreement between the French and Maquaes; and ten years later he volunteered to serve as an interpreter during the Esopus Indian troubles. In July 1666, he and several Maquaes leaders peacefully turned back a French army headed for the Maquaes country. When peace came a year later, he and others were left behind as hostages at Quebec, where he became Catholic.[416]

Van Curler's daughter, Illetie and her brother, Canaqueese, and others who remain unknown, were the children of people who lived at the frontier, and through whom cultures came into contact. While Van Curler's daughter apparently stayed with the Maquaes; Illetie was familiar with both cultures and elected to become a Christian. The worlds of Illetie, her brother Ackes, and Canaqueese were part of two cultures – both of which had their own agendas. They repeatedly made use of their background and not only assisted as interpreters, but also did much more than that – by acting simultaneously as cultural brokers between the two cultures.[417]

Morality and values were insecure in a time when so much was changing. A new community was in the process of being constructed, a community with Dutch values, Dutch traditions, life-styles, religion – all of which had been brought into a strange wilderness and would be adjusted to this new environment. In the process, people of two cultures met and interacted, often without understanding the background and the depth of each other's culture. The development of the Dutch village and their interaction with settlers would lead the centuries-old Indian communities into a process of great change, as well. Just as the Dutch community was a melting pot, the Maquaes had become one as well. This process had already started with the arrival of the French, and the Dutch presence in the Hudson area intensified it. Disease brought over by the Europeans had drastically diminished the native population; in 1689, it would be said that not even 10 percent of the Indians remained.[418] In 1633, for example, the Maquaes population alone fell from about 10,000 in the pre-epidemic period, to approximately 4,500 following the initial small pox epidemic.[419] Such losses required the replacement of people in their nation, which they did by conducting 'requickening' ceremonies in which the deceased's name, social role and duties were transferred to a successor. Survivors were then assured that the social functions and spiritual potency embodied in the departed's name had not disappeared, and that the community would endure. People of high status were usually 'replaced' from within the lineage, clan or village; but, at some point lower on the social scale, an external source of surrogates inevitably became necessary. Warriors took their captives from battles and warfare back to their villages, where often these captives would later be adopted to replace the deceased person and strengthen the family.[420] José Brandão has found that, after 1600, the Iroquois' need to replace their populations decimated by warfare and disease led to intensified and new wars to capture people. The practice of adopting captives enabled them to retain a large enough population to remain a powerful political force well into the eighteenth century.[421]

At the same time, Iroquois life was changing dramatically due to their growing dependence on European trading goods, and the availability of firearms after 1640.[422] Where the new community of Beverwijck was being constructed out of 'baggage' from the old world and adjustments to a new one, ancient Indian communities had entered a process through which, slowly but surely, they would be destroyed – as the foundations of their communities were gradually hollowed out and not renewed.

Conclusion

With so much intercultural contact with the Indians and the population being, albeit in another sense than New Amsterdam, a 'melting pot' of people, Beverwijck's society provided a good basis for unrest and instability. Nevertheless, when the English took over New Netherland in 1664, they found in Beverwijck a fairly organized society. First of all, there were ties within society – ties between relatives and neighbors, and between people who joined their work force on such undertakings as a farm, brewery or a mill. It is also clear that Beverwijck's inhabitants, through their burghership, considered themselves to be burghers of a town; like the residents of Dutch towns, they participated in the guard, contributed in taxes, and felt entitled to some kind of protection when people from the outside threatened their livelihood. This attitude was clearly expressed by bakers, who asked for protection against competition from people who only baked during the trading season, and by many people who petitioned to be protected against Scottish traders and merchants from New Amsterdam.

There was a good deal of stability in Beverwijck's community because people knew that they could turn to the court if they felt their rights had been violated, when they liked to change their circumstances, or when they felt an injustice had been done to them. They knew that if they were able to bring in the required written proof, the court would try to come up with an honest resolution to their problem; if necessary, they could appeal to the colonial government. Consideration was also given to those who were not capable to stand up for themselves. The rights of orphans were protected, especially after 1657, when orphan masters were appointed. By maintaining order and justice, and making sure that people followed the law as much as possible, the court helped create an orderly and regulated society.

By exercising ecclesiastical discipline, the church guarded the moral level of society. The minister and elders made house visits to nearly half of the population (40 percent), during which they pointed out the 'right' way to 'true' Calvinist values by admonishing people to live correctly, by which they meant according to standards set by the Reformed church. But the church was also a public institution and church services were open to everyone. Whether or not they shared the Reformed beliefs, anyone could come to each service and count on such public services as baptisms, marriages and burials. Individuals who were not able to survive on their own were provided with charity, whether they were church members or not. The church established certain regulations that concerned all inhabitants, and which were supported and overseen by the civil authorities. By encouraging education, it spread the ideas of Calvinism. Most people were aware of the importance of education for their children and the opportunities for learning the community offered; they made sure their children at least learned how to read, and often how to write. By practicing ecclesiastical discipline, and by providing church services, education and charity, the church greatly contributed to the cultural and social values and needs of the community. As a result, the church influenced the lives of many, and contributed to the establishment of a civil culture in Beverwijck.

But Beverwijck was not a typical Dutch village. Its unique identity did not result solely from the importation of Dutch institutions, customs and values into a new world; in addition, it was a product of accommodation and confrontation with new surroundings and new neighbors, whose situation also was in flux, and which shed new light on cultural elements imported from Europe. In the midst of Indian surroundings, a continuous stream of new settlers, merchandise and ideas repeatedly refreshed the Dutch character of the community. Beverwijckers, despite their contacts with Indians, English, and Frenchmen, held onto their own culture, and established and strengthened their 'Dutchness.' They were guided by Dutch values, rules, and laws that were continuously reinforced by the newly arriving settlers, who, like Johannes de Deckere, may have brought a fresh dose of 'Dutchness' - and, at the same time, a great unfamiliarity with the Indians. The concentration of people and institutions in one place, the *bijeenwoninge*, emphasized this 'Dutchness,' and its stabilization as a well-ordered community made this even stronger. Within some thirty years, people of different backgrounds, sexes, and religions had all come together in Beverwijck, where they started to share a culture modeled on towns in the province of Holland. Establishment of the institutions of state and church helped create guidelines, structure, stability, and sometimes even some harmony and unity in a community some of whose the members had carried to the New World their own images and memories from regions and countries other than Holland. To see that a certain degree of union (concord, or *eendracht*), so highly esteemed in Holland, had been established in Beverwijck, we only need to look at the court, of which several members almost always came from regions outside Holland, and sometimes even from other countries.[423]

By 1664, Beverwijck had become a community with its own identity. As a community, it asked for protection, not only against people from other nations, but against another New Netherland community as well. They knew that, as a community, they had to defend their own ground, their own businesses and their own livelihood. That they were only partially granted this protection illustrates that the colonial government understood their need; but it was not willing to grant Beverwijck's burghers the privilege of the Indian trade – they still put the interests of the colony above those of one local community. In the first years after the English takeover, things did not change very much. The various institutions established between 1652 and 1664 were maintained, and they functioned as they had before. Not until 1674, after the second surrender of New Netherland, would the Duke's Laws be extended to the whole colony, bringing changes in the Dutch system.

In the late 1650s and 1660s, more inhabitants started buying land from the Indians. New Netherland had provided the settlers with a better life than they could have expected in the fatherland, and some individuals even became prosperous. They were not planning to go back to Europe; instead, they invested their earnings in various undertakings in the New World, such as a mill, a brewery, or a ship. But they were all interested in buying land and starting a farm. Since the West India Company supervised land possession and took a critical approach to the patroon's domain, it allowed more private individuals to buy land from the Indians. This company policy, which encouraged farmers to leave Rensselaerswijck in great numbers, could eventually drive the patroonship to the brink of total ruin. As their patroonship declined, trade would become increasingly important to the Van Rensselaers.

III. The Van Rensselaers as commercial entrepreneurs

Beverwijck had become a village with strong urban features where the lives of inhabitants were centered around the fur trade. Several Dutch trading companies invested in trade with Beverwijck, driven by the thought of realizing as much profit home as they could. The place of trading companies in Dutch society was significant: Annually, some 400 to 500 ships were being built, and by 1650 the Republic had a merchant fleet of as many as 2,000 seaworthy ships. It is no surprise that trade and navigation were considered important for the entire country.[1] Johan de Witt, the son of a regents' family, who became Pensionary of Holland in 1653, called navigation and commerce the 'soul of the state,' and declared that 'the pious merchants had above all the general welfare of the people in mind, and that they held the well-being of the people for their law.' G. Groenhuis has stated that the general thought in *patria* was that merchants brought prosperity to the fatherland – and prosperity and well-being were signs of God's blessing. Their prosperity was considered of interest for the entire country, as wealthy traders were thought to generate the well-being of the entire country. In time of war, one of the greatest fears was that the prosperous traders would leave the country. The interests of leading merchants were inextricably bound up with the welfare of the whole nation.[2]

The Van Rensselaers, often together with some other family firms, continued to trade with New Netherland throughout the 1650s and '60s; they had put a great part of their family fortune into New Netherland, and were most interested in receiving as much as possible back from their patroonship and trade with the upper Hudson area. It clearly had been Kiliaen van Rensselaer's purpose to have his sons continue his work, collecting profits of the patroonship. 'They are still too young to send thither,' he wrote in March 1643, 'but I hope this can be done by and by.'[3] When the patroon died seven months later, he left nine living children. From his first marriage with Hillegond Bijlaer, only one eighteen-year-old son, Johannes, was still alive. With Anna van Wely, Kiliaen had four daughters and four more sons: Jan Baptist, the oldest boy, was fourteen, followed by Maria at age twelve and the eleven-year-old Jeremias. Hillegond was ten in 1643, and Eleonora eight. The youngest children were Nicolaes at age seven, Susanna at age five, and Richard who was only four.[4] According to Van Laer, the boys (possibly with the exception of Johannes) followed a business education, which usually involved a seven-year apprenticeship with a merchant.[5] Anna van Rensselaer's brother, Jan van Wely, and Wouter van Twiller (Kiliaen's nephew) became their guardians, and in that position took responsibility for the patroonship and the New Netherland trade.[6] When relations between Rensselaerswijck and the West India Company had sunk to a low point, it was not twenty-five-year-old Johannes (who had succeeded his father as patroon) who went over to Rensselaerswijck in 1651 to inspect, but twenty-two-year-old Jan Baptist. In July 1652 he became director of the domain. In addition to administering the patroonship, Jan Baptist continued, together with Jeremias (who joined him in 1654) the trade that their father had started by re-establishing their overseas trade network. During the 1650s and '60s, in cooperation with their relatives, the brothers further developed the system through which they would become one of the major trading companies that continued to trade with New Netherland even after the English assumed power in 1664.

The Van Rensselaer brothers' roles as representatives of the patroon and major traders gave them a special place in the community. They still were the largest landowners, lived in the largest house, and were the wealthiest men in the area. Their way of life followed old Dutch customs, which may have differed little from those of important traders in the fatherland. The family's regular correspondence allows us to glean an understanding not only of their trade, private lives, and lifestyle, but also to learn more about other traders, for whom the Van Rensselaers's way of life may very well have served as an example.

In this chapter, we will take a look at the way the New Netherland trade was organized in Amsterdam, New Amsterdam, and Beverwijck; we will also take a closer look at how it determined the rhythm and character of Beverwijck's growing community, in general. During late spring, all summer, and early autumn, the trade greatly determined the inhabitants' activities, which had everything to do with the Indians and their catch of furs. Items traded for furs required regulation; but rules governing the overall trading process became more and more necessary as the number inhabitants increased, while the beaver supply decreased. That trade was performed by women, as well as men, becomes clear when we consider the role played by women in the work process. After taking a look at the general situation of the trade in the village, we will focus on the Van Rensselaers: What were their merchants' activities? How did they organize their business? How did success become visible, and why? How did a successful merchant live in Beverwijck?

Trade in the upper Hudson

The trading season

The springtime arrival of traders from the fatherland and New Amsterdam must have been a welcome event in Beverwijck, which during the winter months usually was isolated from the rest of New Netherland, the only contact being an occasional visit from an Indian who delivered messages between Beverwijck and New Amsterdam.[7] But once the river opened again, sometime in April, traders from New Amsterdam and Holland would sail upriver with their merchandise. At least twice a week ships would arrive from Manhattan.[8] The inhabitants must have been happy to see their friends and business partners again after having been separated for some months. Sometimes the arrival may have coincided with the celebration of Pentecost and, if they took place, the burgher guard's 'shooting of the parrot' festivities. But whether that was the case or not, the traders' arrival was undoubtedly celebrated with as much enthusiasm as their departure. Pieter Symonsz Michielsz van Oostsanen, for example, referred to the 'last farewell' he had with the friends in Evert Wendel's room, an occasion 'the friends' probably celebrated with a few drinks, as may have been the custom in Beverwijck.[9] The alcoholic drink consumed could amount to quite a goodly quantity; after Jan Baptist van Rensselaer's departure for the fatherland in September 1658, about thirty friends drank to his health and safe voyage, consuming about a half-*aam* of wine[10] (a half-*aam* is 76.8 liters, or 20.26 gallons). The visiting traders from New Amsterdam, the fatherland, and occasionally New England would greatly augment the population during these months – which, in addition to the acquisition of merchandise, also created extra business for the inhabitants.

The period when the traders were in the village was important, as many business deals were negotiated then. Beverwijck traders who had ordered duffels, blankets, wine, anise, and other merchandise received it, often promising payment in beavers during or after the trading season, or mortgaging some personal property (often their house and lot) to settle the debt. Plans for an upcoming trading season would be made and new provisions negotiated. Letters were written to confirm the receipts of goods, to comment on their condition, and to order new merchandise. Sometimes these negotiations were conducted in a trader's home, sometimes at one of Beverwijck's taverns. Much planning was done during these the weeks, and negotiations were generally accompanied by 'lustily drinking to one another.'[11] Auctions, especially, were held in this season, adding to the bustle and filling the taverns with bidders and visitors. Some people would come just to join-in on the activity, while others would bid seriously on the items being auctioned. Tavern keepers did well by so much activity, as business was always accompanied and sealed by the parties' drinking beer or wine.[12]

Traders from *patria* prearranged where they would stay: in an inn, or with someone in the village. Pieter Symonsz Michielsz intended to repeat his previous visits to Beverwijck in 1664; in December 1663, he asked Evert Wendel to reserve his room for him, as he planned to arrive in the spring.[13] Traders from New Amsterdam like Poulus Leendertsz van der Grift, Nicolaes de Meyer, and Asser Levy regularly came to Beverwijck at that time of year, as well, in order to manage their business, often staying with relatives or friends. Undoubtedly, Johannes van Brugh, after he had married Catharina Roelofs (a daughter of Anneke Jans's first marriage, to Roelof Jansz van Masterland), stayed with his mother-in-law or with Pieter Hartgers, his brother-in-law. When Hartgers moved back to *patria* in 1660, Van Brugh took over a lot with a garden from him.[14] The New England trader John Willett, who was in Beverwijck in 1663, perhaps stayed with the Teller family.[15] Some people from New Amsterdam owned houses in Beverwijck, which they occupied in the trading season. In 1662, for example, Cornelis Steenwijck had a house and lot between the first kill and *Jonckerstraet*.[16]

The settlers at the upper Hudson looked forward to the arrival of these traders. It enabled them to buy merchandise, for which they usually committed themselves to pay in beavers during or after the trading season, often somewhere in the middle of July. They risked investing in pelts, often pledging their house and lot as security, since for many consecutive years the yield in beavers had been rich. It was a time in which people's hopes were high in expectation of the coming trading season. Of thirty-six shipments made between June 20 and September 27, 1657, four were the Van Rensselaer's; in addition to Van Rensselaer's beavers, some 37.940 pelts were sent from Fort Orange to New Amsterdam.[17] In general, all went well until 1658, when no Indians came with furs. That year, Cornelis Vos was not the only one who could not pay for the merchandise he had bought. In September, he mortgaged his house and lot to pay his ƒ624 debt to Barent van Marle, a New Amsterdam trader. The following years did not bring much relief; and in July 1661, Vos – who by then was also indebted to others – sold the house to Van Marle for ƒ1,020.[18] Many Beverwijckers had to make similar arrangements, and increasing numbers of New Amsterdam traders obtained property in this way, or had some other type of investment in Beverwijck.[19]

Although the Indians visited the village throughout the year, the trade generally took place during the summer months.[20] Indian men spent one or two months far away from home during their early winter hunting season. After each hunter returned with some forty to eighty beavers and some other skins, women scraped and processed the skins during the late winter and early spring. Men subsequently brought the pelts to the Dutch settlement somewhere between May and November.[21] Most of the Indians usually arrived somewhere around the middle of June or July. From the interior, they came to the place where Schenectady would later be founded, some twenty miles west of Beverwijck. From there, carrying packs of furs on their backs, they went on foot through the woods, entering Beverwijck via the *bospadt* or *Maquaes padt*; the natives may also may have canoed down the Norman's Kill in order to arrive at the river bank near Beverwijck. The Indians' arrival meant the beginning of the fur trade. It was a competitive period in the village: Where would the Indian guests stay? How many furs would they bring? Whose merchandise would they like best in exchange for their furs? They often slept with the inhabitants in their houses, or perhaps in some of the little Indian, or hansioos, houses on people's property.[22] The rule was that, within the village, natives could go from house to house in order to find the best bargain in goods in exchange for their furs. Exactly how many traders and Indians visited Beverwijck during these months is unknown; Indians may have come in the hundreds, men as well as women. In 1665, there were four hundred Indians, and in 1667 a thousand were expected.[23]

Sometime in August or September, traders would send most of their peltries to Manhattan, New Netherland's staple port, where the goods had to be declared at the West India Company's custom house before they could be shipped to Holland. The fur trading season at Manhattan would begin after ships from other parts of New Netherland had arrived with their furs. Depending on the supply of beavers and expectations of how many pelts still might come in, the Manhattan traders would move back to New Amsterdam about that time; several Beverwijck traders would also go to Manhattan to do the required work there to get their furs and other colonial wares ready in time for shipment to the fatherland. Some Beverwijck traders stayed with relatives or friends, as there were many family ties between the two communities. Others owned property in New Amsterdam themselves, where they spent some time.[24] Although there was still plenty of opportunity during the fall to travel back and forth between New Amsterdam and Beverwijck, the departure of the traders meant the end of the trading season. It was a first indication that the village would be isolated again; in December, people would just be waiting for the north wind to begin to blow sharply, causing the river to close for some time. They would have to get through the winter with those wares they had acquired over the previous season, as new supplies of merchandise would not arrive until the following spring.

The extent to which Beverwijckers were involved in a trade with the English colonies is unclear. Charlotte Wilcoxen has pointed out that the trade between New Netherland and English settlements at Plymouth, Massachussetts Bay, Connecticut, and Rhode Island was of a volume hitherto grossly underestimated; one reason for this inaccuracy was that such trade was often contraband in nature.[25] Not until the fall of 1669 would Jeremias van Rensselaer report on trading with New England; he then made a trip to Boston, during which he sold three lasts of wheat for 17 stivers Holland net per *schepel*:

> One can not get anything like that here. We have chartered a sloop to make another voyage thither in the spring with some grain and to exchange that for some goods which can be sold here for beavers.[26]

It does not appear that Beverwijckers frequently went into New England. In 1659, Van Rensselaer was still unfamiliar with New England's countryside; in May of that year, he went to Milford, where he had bought a horse and traveled as far as New Haven in order to see something of the country.[27] But there certainly were some contacts. For example, when the servants Pieter Pietersz Lassen and Willem Symonsz ran away in September 1659, their master, Volckert Jansz Douw certainly knew to appoint Paulus Schrick, a merchant from Hartford who was in Beverwijck during the trading season, to inquire after the runaways in New England or elsewhere.[28] Hartford, on the *Versche Rivier* (Connecticut River), also was the place to which Pieter Jansz, *lademaecker* (gunstock maker) at Beverwijck, and Jan Bembo had intended to flee; but the governor of Hartford sent news that they had been murdered on the way.[29] In 1663, the blacksmith and principal trader Jan Koster van Aecken sold a hundred beavers to John Willett, a free trader who formerly lived in New England, but was then at Fort Orange. Willett, who also did business with other principal Beverwijck traders, then owed Van Aecken 304 pieces of eight at 48 stivers apiece.[30] Manhattan traders maintained a tobacco trade with Virginia and Maryland in which Cornelis Steenwijck, who also owned property in Beverwijck, and Govert Loockermans, who was already trading there in the late 1640s, were especially involved.[31] The renewal in 1656 of an ordinance against importing and selling contraband articles of war clearly mentions that much ammunition came from other places than the fatherland, especially Virginia. It is unlikely that Beverwijck traders, who had many connections with Manhattan traders, were not involved in this trade as well.[32] Information regarding this trade is sporadic and needs further research.

Trade items

Traders brought many wares over to New Netherland. As long as the fur trade went well, it was not hard to find buyers for various glassware, tools, farm equipment, kitchen and housewares, shoes, shirts, or regular clothes made of good quality cloth. Often the goods were sold at auctions, where Beverwijckers could bid on various items listed for sale. Textiles like ribbon, silk, lace or fine braid, as well as other products, most likely found their way to local tailors and other inhabitants of the villages, as well as to the Indians.[33]

The Indians brought great business to the local artisans. While the locally produced baker's goods and smith's products were high on the Indians' 'want list,' shoemakers probably had extra work as well, because the Indians often liked the European shoes better than their own footwear.[34] Inhabitants could often make good deals in trading the items obtained from the traders from *patria* or Manhattan. Cloth and duffel, the heavy woolen cloth from Kampen and Leiden, were popular and frequently worn by the Indians as a wrap. Black and dark colors, and later whites, were special favorites; bright colors like red could easily be seen when traveling in the woods, and so were not much in demand.[35] Blankets, stockings (especially the waterproof *faroese* stockings), shoes, shirts, beads, tobacco pipes, kettles, spoons, knives, adzes, axes, and awls were frequently traded in exchange for beaver, otter, deer, bear, and sometimes fox skins brought by the Indians.[36] Archaeological excavations not only confirm this great variety of trade goods, but they also reveal that both quantity and variety increased over the years. Small tools, lead cloth seals from Amsterdam, glass beads, pipes, mirrors, files, scissors, 'cootie combs,' and iron mouth harps have been found at several archaeological sites.[37]

Some items traded with Indians created great danger. Alcoholic drink had a negative influence on the Indians. Despite notices posted stating that it was illegal to sell alcohol to natives and that violators would incur a 50-guilder fine, Poulus Jansz, Kit Davidsz, Jacob Simonsz Clomp, and Hans Vos were all caught, at one time or another, selling alcoholic beverages to the Indians – sometimes taking their canoes, rowboats, or other vessels as far as Catskil and the Esopus to make the sale.[38] For tavern keepers it was especially hard, when the fur trade dwindled, not to try their luck in this business; alcoholic drink was often wanted by the natives, who could not resist buying it, despite the danger.[39] Egbertje Egberts and Dirckie Harms, Maria Goosens, and Susanna Jansen were only a few of these violators.[40] The sale of alcohol to Indians always remained illegal, as it created the danger of disturbing the balance between the two peoples.

Trade in firearms and gunpowder was illegal as well; but, unlike the trade in alcoholic drink, these items in time would become official staple commodities of the fur trade; knives, axes, hatchets, adzes, kettles, gunpowder, lead, guns, muskets, and firelock guns quickly became major items of exchange in diplomatic transac-

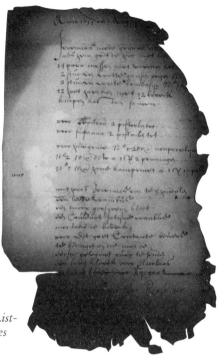

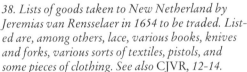

38. *Lists of goods taken to New Netherland by Jeremias van Rensselaer in 1654 to be traded. Listed are, among others, lace, various books, knives and forks, various sorts of textiles, pistols, and some pieces of clothing. See also* CJVR, *12-14.*

tions between the two peoples, and served as payments for land, as well.[41] In a short time, the trade in ammunition and firearms had increased rapidly: While guns were unknown to the Indians in 1624, fifteen years later this situation had changed dramatically. The Iroquois, and probably the Mahicans as well, were by then well provided with guns, gunpowder, and lead through an active arms trade – which in 1639 led to publication of the first ordinance prohibiting this trade. This first ordinance called for the death penalty for those who disobeyed it;[42] but the penalties were quickly lowered, and by 1648 several people would be caught in a large-scale smuggling case.[43] Despite Stuyvesant's initial efforts to enforce the prohibitions, the trade continued; and, in the spring of 1648, traders at Rensselaerswijck petitioned for permission to trade some arms and ammunition – before the Indians murdered them in retaliation for withholding the arms.[44] The West India Company directors had, in the meantime, advised Stuyvesant to supply the tribes very sparingly with guns and ammunition, through company officials rather than private traders – revealing that this trade had by then reached a stage where it could no longer be forbidden without danger of war. In 1650, the directors again suggested providing the Indians with gunpowder sparingly. The lure of tremendous profits induced traders consistently to defy the law: while it was suggested that guns be sold for 6 guilders, pistols for 4 guilders, and a pound of powder for 6 stivers, everyone was well aware that the Indians would 'readily purchase guns in the spring at 120 guilders, and a pound of powder for 10 or 12 guilders.[45]

An ordinance of April 1652 regarding the illegal trade in gunpowder, lead, and guns does not seem to have been very strictly enforced; in June 1653, the directors at Amsterdam observed:

> ... that you have been obliged, at the written request of those of Fort Orange and of the colony of Rensselaerswijck, to connive somewhat in regard to the edict enacted about contraband goods. You ought to deal herein with a sparing hand, and take good care that through this winking no more ammunition be sold than each one had need of for protection of his house and for obtaining the necessaries of life, so that this cruel and barbarous nation may not be able, at any time, to turn and employ their weapons against ourselves there.[46]

In February 1654, Stuyvesant and the council were informed of 'the scarcity of powder and lead among the Maquaas nation and of the incessant demands, which they consequently make on the inhabitants of Fort Orange, the village of Beverwijck, and the people of the Colony.' They argued that denying the Maquaas, who were now 'our good friends,' armaments at Fort Orange would only drive them to the English. If the Indians were to obtain the ammunition from them, the whole fur trade, along with the Maquaas' friendship, would soon be diverted away from New Netherland, which would bring more and greater misfortune to this dangerous situation. Therefore, it was considered proper and necessary to accommodate the tribe with a moderate trade in ammunition, which was to be sold to them through the magistrate Rutger Jacobsz – but 'as sparingly and secretly as possible.'[47] In August 1654, some Maquaes and Senecas, according to longstanding custom, made a present to the court. The court thought it proper to present them with, among others things, twenty-five pounds of powder. Abraham Staets was therefore requested to 'let them have the same from the company's powder, which is in his custody, provided that he shall be discharged from the obligation to account for it to the General and hereafter communicate to his honor the contents of the present.'[48] When the Maquaes complained, in 1659, that they had not received enough gunpowder and that they had been required to pay the smiths for repairs to their guns, the Dutch response illustrates how the arms traffic was by then no longer subject to regulation: The special emissaries who went to the Indian Castle Kaghnuwage took with them, as gifts, seventy-five pounds of gunpowder, one hundred pounds of lead, fifteen axes and two beavers' worth of knives.[49] The sale of armaments to the Iroquois had not been curtailed by Stuyvesant's efforts in 1648 to prohibit it; and a decade later most official Indian presents contained quantities of gunpowder and lead. By 1664, gunpowder had become the staple commodity of the fur trade, and merchants had a 'well stocked public powder house to draw on' during the trading season. One merchant at Fort Orange, according to the company directors in Amsterdam, had a full 600 pounds of gunpowder on hand; according to this merchant, his supply was very small compared with that of other traders.[50] This was possible because of the great trade in firearms that was carried on, not just between the colony and the fatherland, which at that time was one of the greatest arms exporters in Europe, but with other places as well, especially Virginia.[51]

We know about trading practices because individuals were caught in illegal trading and called before the court. The cases reveal that not only wealthy traders, but people in all social strata, were active in the Indian trade – women as well as men, and the poor just as much as the wealthy. The wife of the minister or a surgeon, a carpenter, and a needy beer carrier – they all tried to seize their opportunities in the trading season.[52]

After 1657, however, the situation for trading would change dramatically. While an oversupply of *sewant* in the early 1650s had already caused inflation, the decline of the beaver trade caused a rapid worsening of the situation. Beginning in 1658, there were summers when hardly any Indians showed up in the village, as they were preoccupied with other affairs such as war with the French and the Esopus wars. The natives' involvement in wars also threatened the safety of the Maquaes' trading route to Beverwijck.[53] At the same time, Beverwijck's population grew rapidly during the 1650s, increasing the number of people who wanted to share in a decreasing number of furs. Combined with low beaver prices in *patria*, it would not be long before the community was seriously divided over the very reason for its existence – the trade – notwithstanding the many regulations that tried to organize it.

Trading regulations

Although three to four thousand furs had come from Fort Orange by the fall of 1643, neither Van Rensselaer's *commis* Arent van Curler, nor the West India Company, had any trade that year.[54] By going into the woods to intercept the Indians before they had reached the fort or the patroon's house, private traders had seized the opportunity to 'steal' away the business with Indians. No better analysis has been made of the development of the trade in the upper Hudson between 1639 and 1660 than Martha Shattuck's study of Beverwijck's court and community, and which this paragraph follows.[55] In clear wording, Shattuck describes how Van Rensselaer's 1642 ordinance prohibiting inhabitants from lodging 'foreign residents and private traders without previous consent' did not work. Neither did his attempt to forestall traders from sailing into his domain by developing Rensselaers Steyn on *Beeren eylandt* as a staple market and control center of Rensselaerswijck's trade have any effect on the private traders; They conducted trade with the Indians anyway.[56] To prevent this, in 1642 the company and the court of Rensselaerswijck had issued a joint ordinance that set a maximum price of nine handfuls of *sewant* and outlawed 'running in the woods.' That the ordinance had little effect becomes clear in Van Curler's letter, when he mentions that neither the company nor he had shared in the great trade of 1643. In a 1645 ordinance, the commissary of Fort Orange and the court of Rensselaerswijck prescribed some stricter rules and attempted to make the trade and sales promotion indoor activities, by prohibiting settlers from meeting and bartering with Indians outside their houses.[57] But with great profits within reach, such ordinances did not work very well; it would take strict, severe measures to bring the trade under control. In 1649, Van Slichtenhorst warned three men who had licenses to carry on lawful trade, and forbade them to carry on illegitimate trade,

> ... as is daily done by you in running into the woods to meet the savages who come with beavers and in promising them presents of stockings, hatchets and other goods if they will come to your houses to trade; and after having thus traded with them giving them a little note to tell other savages where you dwell and such presents as will induce them to come to you to trade.

After the traders failed to observe the order, their licenses were revoked a month later.[58]

Beverwijck's court inherited the problem of how to conduct the trade, and various renewals of the ordinance indicate that illegal trading continued. In 1652, the director general and council of New Netherland stipulated that the Dutch were not allowed to go into Indian territory to trade without a special permit.[59] In 1654, the colonists were forbidden from going into the woods and using either Christian or Indian brokers; the Indians would be able to go from house to house and to find competitive prices for their furs. This ordinance was renewed each year.[60] In 1655, the director general and council gave Beverwijck's court permission to make an ordinance regarding the trade itself, without having to obtain their approval.[61] While the ordinance then produced is not in the records, it most likely prohibited going into the woods to trade and limited the use of Indian brokers – 'limited' in that it prohibited sending Indians as brokers into the woods to entice other Indians to go to the same place to do business, a stipulation that was also renewed in the following years.[62] The ordinance immediately sparked a protest from one village inhabitant, Jurriaen Jansz, who more or less accused the magistrates of 'trying to reserve the entire trade to themselves.' At about the same time another Beverwijcker, Gerrit Bancker, who had used an Indian broker to bring other Indians to trade at his house, was fined ƒ300 and suspended from the trade for one year.[63]

The use of Indian brokers was expensive, and excluded many inhabitants from the trade; if it was not too obvious, illegal trading probably took place and was winked at. But after the disastrous trading season of 1658, Cornelis Theunisz Bos, Jacob Thijsz, Leendert Philipsz, and Claes Jacobsz presented a petition in June 1659, also in the name of others, 'praying that they be permitted to do their best in regard to the question of trade to promote the interest of their households.' The court then allowed the use of Indian brokers for that year only, with the provision that they were not to be sent into the woods with presents, and with the special injunction that no Dutch brokers were to be employed. Several trading abuses were noted in the court minutes during the following year, indicating that those who were able to give presents to Indians in order to obtain beavers did so anyway.[64] Cornelis Theunisz Bos caused great problems when he openly showed his disregard for the law and rejected the magistrates' authority. A month after he had presented the petition, he was accused of having defamed the court by saying that 'if Philip Pietersz and Pieter Hartgers, who were caught, were not punished first [for going into the woods], that he wiped his ass on the ordinance.' He did not 'give a damn for the magistrates,' he stated, and he would 'go into the woods to prove it, and they are a lot of perjurers if they do not punish the others.'[65] According to Stuyvesant, in September 1659 everybody in the community was complaining against his neighbor 'because of the decline of the trade, which grows worse from year to year.'[66]

Great conflict indeed existed about the way the trade should be conducted. La Montagne, in his report of the state of affairs at Beverwijck, painted a clear picture in 1660, when he described how, on May 25, a petition,

> ... [a petition] by the principal traders of this place was handed in against the *placat* issued by Director General and Council and since republished annually, that only Indian brokers should be admitted to carry on trade. After the bench had taken it into consideration, it was ordered to call the whole community into the fort, to learn their opinion on this matter. They assembled on Wednesday and having been heard individually they expressed a different opinion, *viz* that it would be better, to give the enormous amount of brokerage, which went now yearly into the pockets of the Indian brokers – about fifty thousand guilders – to Dutchmen. As this opinion went directly against the request of the petitioners, the latter, increased to twenty-five altogether, presented Wednesday a second petition, repeating their former demands. Friday the other, small traders, also presented a petition signed by fifty-four persons and now they began to scold and call each other bad names and threats were uttered: Saturday the Court was convened to deliberate how to settle this matter, in which the parties were so bitter and hostile against each other: the Court could not come to any conclusion and on that account was adjourned over till Monday, when the Court, having assembled, decided to deny the petitions of either party and ordered that in accordance with the *placat* neither Dutch nor Indian brokers should be employed during the trading under a penalty of 300 guilders and suspension from their pursuits for the time of two months. Since that time I have been obliged to go into the woods with soldiers to prevent mishaps and to see that the ordinances are observed. It comes very hard upon me, as I have no deputy sheriff, and it has gone so far, that I must frequently remain overnight in the woods...[67]

A month later, when it proved impossible to maintain this ordinance, the court allowed Indian as well as Christian brokers, 'protesting meanwhile their innocence of all misschief that may result therefrom, the more so as some of the petitioners said they would do it anyway, whether it was permitted or not.'[68]

By 'mischief,' the court meant the increasing violence of Dutch people toward the Indians. On September 6, 1659, the Maquaes came to the fort with a long list of propositions that included complaints about insolence and injuries to the Indians by beating and throwing stones; one of their requests was that the Dutch cease their viciousness and not beat them, as they had done in the past. October 19, two Maquaes *sachems* made some propositions at another joint court session in Fort Orange; they also complained about the way the Indians were treated by the Dutch, saying that the Dutch had abused them and called their nations 'dogs and scoundrels.'[69] As competition between the growing number of inhabitants and traders increased, the abuse had intensified. The following trading season would start out badly. On June 26, 1660, the Maquaes came to Fort Orange again and said that when the Dutch were in the woods to fetch Indians, they had beaten them severely with fists and had driven them out of the woods. They requested that no Dutchmen with horses, or otherwise, be allowed to roam in the woods to fetch Indians with beavers, because they mistreated them greatly. Sometimes ten or twelve men at once would surround an Indian and drag him along, saying 'Come with me, so-and-so has no goods,' thus undercutting one another – which they feared would end badly. The Dutch had kicked, beaten and assaulted them: and if the abuse were not prevented, the natives would 'go away and not be seen by us anymore.' The court, fearing war and the loss of trade, prohibited the inhabitants from roaming in the woods as brokers to attract Indians with beavers, on penalty of a ƒ300 fine and suspension from the trade for that year.[70] But the measure did not work. On July 15, La Montagne prosecuted nine individuals for brokering in the woods, among them a sitting and a former magistrate. Two other men, one of whom was another sitting magistrate, defaulted.[71] The problem would become so great that Stuyvesant came upriver; but on July 22, he and the court were unable to resolve the matter any differently than to repeat what had already been stated in previous ordinances: No one was allowed to send any Christians or Indians into the woods as brokers, either with or without presents, to fetch or entice any Indians; no one was allowed to take any beavers from the Indians, whether in the woods, outside or within the settlements, houses or places, or to carry pelts for the Indians on horses, carts, or on their backs; no one was allowed to take away or lock up peltries of the Indians against their will, much less impede, prevent, or hinder the Indians from going with their peltries anywhere they pleased; and it was again prohibited to sell alcoholic beverages to the Indians.[72]

These events concerned business and dealings with the outside world. The manuscripts usually describe public spaces, which commonly were the domain of men, which may create the impression that only men were involved in trade. But men often represented their families to the outside world, and wives probably influenced their decisions.

The role of women

A woman's domain was the household, a private space where she took care of the household and raised the children.[73] Running a household was no small task. Cooking and baking were year-round chores, and did not end with preparing food for dinner, lunch, or breakfast, which in itself demanded various skills and techniques. Building and regulating a cooking fire was necessary throughout the year, and could be quite complex if more than one dish were being prepared simultaneously. Especially in the summer, it may not have been pleasant to maintain the fire and carry the copper and iron kettles, pots, and other kitchenware. The planting of a garden in the spring was part of food preparation, as well, and was followed by the need to tend it through the summer, and to ensure that any remaining vegetables and herbs were processed (as were fruits of the orchards) so that they could be used during the long winter months. A wife may also have been busy feeding chickens, hogs, or cows during the year, as well as processing milk, collecting eggs, and helping with the slaughter of an animal – the meat from which she would subsequently process, usually in the 'slaughter month' of November. Scouring, sweeping, and polishing were regular activities required to keep the house clean and fit to live in, and contributed to making the house a place agreeable to welcome outsiders; chores related to the appearance of inhabitants included the washing, ironing, repairing, knitting, or sewing of clothing. By creating situations to share food and drink, a wife most likely set the stage for good conversation, not only with guests, but also among family members.

Usually a woman's work was accompanied by the raising and educating of children. Many women gave birth about every other year and raised several children – sometimes large families – which bound them to alternating cycles of pregnancy and lactation. Neighboring women, and sometimes relatives, would be there to assist in childbirth. Undoubtedly, women had their own network through which they assisted each other in childbirth, helped when there was illness, visited with each other, and cooperated with chores such as processing garden produce, watching the children, and sharing each other's tools.

As a man's work was often done at home, it is not surprising that women participated and that business matters were discussed. As a matter of fact, travelers to the Dutch Republic, especially Holland, described the women there not only as beautiful and virtuous, and as good housewives with their own authority in the household, but also as active in the trade and autonomous in society.[74] Although some of these attributes may have been uncommon in the upper Hudson, others – and certainly women's activity in trade – were found there. Goods for the Indian trade may have been at their disposal in the small, or *hansjoos*, houses some women used (and where the Indians would visit in order to make their bargains), or in their homes. In particular, in the front room of the house was the place where the artisan performed his regular trade and where business was done. The wife and other family members often were physically present, and undoubtedly ran an errand or took an order at times, or were involved in the business in some other way. When, for some reason, wives had to represent their husbands in a public place, they clearly showed that they were fully aware of the situation; this rarely caused a problem, and demonstrates that business was certainly discussed between marriage partners. Wives undoubtedly influenced their husbands in making decisions, and also served as business partners.

Notarial papers illustrate women's involvement; there is no evidence that men considered this unusual, or that they did not trust their wives. That was not so strange, since by joining their possessions and raising their children, women had just as much interest in a successful business as their spouses. In all court cases between 1652 and 1660, Martha Shattuck found only one exception to the custom of men giving their wives the right to act independently, and trusting their ability to represent them in court and in business transactions. Shattuck also found that, of eighty-four women appearing in court between 1652 and 1660, sixty-six were married and fifteen clearly were acting for absent husbands. Others were acting on their own behalf.[75] So it was not rare for a woman to appear in court as a representative, to make sure that debts were paid, or the family's good name was not damaged. Economics concerned the whole family; it was a matter in which wives were involved and active, and which was discussed between the marriage partners. When a man's name appears in the records, we should not forget that, beforehand, long conversations may have allowed the wife to influence her spouse's important decisions.

Wives often played an important role in business by being actively involved in their husband's work, and in the Indian trade. Even when they were considered among the most successful inhabitants of Beverwijck, we should not forget that most of these women originally had not belonged to the wealthiest population group in the fatherland, where it was common and necessary for wives to work in order for a family to make ends meet.[76]

In the fatherland, many women worked. In a seafaring nation like the Dutch Republic, where in 1630 some 46,000 men were at sea (more than 15 percent of all men in Holland), women were frequently called upon to arrange matters during the absence of their husbands. Not infrequently they lost their spouses, and then took on responsibility for the household and the family's place in the public domain. A quarter of Dutch households were headed by women.[77] Not only did women replace their husbands or act for them, but they also frequently worked on their own. Undoubtedly, Jeremias van Rensselaer was not the only person in the village who paid a female washer to do laundry, and another woman to clean the house; he also was not the only one to have a maid; surgeon Jacob de Hinsse, for example, contracted overseas for a maid with an orphanage in Amsterdam.[78] As in *patria*, a woman could run a tavern independently. This was something a single woman could easily do: It did not require an education or a large space, and the earnings could keep a person from having to ask for poor relief.[79] It is what Maria Goosens did; before her separation in 1655, Maria and her husband had a tavern jointly; afterward, she ran a tavern on her own with the support of Goosen Gerritsz (whose relationship to her is unclear) at another location; according to the articles of separation in 1663, Maria also was responsible for bringing up their children.[80] Maria Dijckman, after her husband became incapacitated, was more or less responsible for the family's income, as well. For a few years she ran a successful tavern; but after 1666, her family became dependent on help from the deacons' poor fund.[81] The deacons' account books list several women who took care of elderly or ill people, who cleaned the church, or who worked as wet nurses. The deacons' notes only concern poor people, but also not-so-poor women would have performed these jobs.[82]

When a husband died, a woman often remarried; but if she did not, a woman could still maintain her own authority, especially in trade, as many town charters in the Dutch Republic recognized the independent status of female traders (*koopvrouwen*).[83] Quite a few women appeared as members of guilds, especially in retail trade, second-hand sales, and the textile industry. In Beverwijck, it certainly was not uncommon either for women to be involved in trading. Keeping a small store did not require much education and capital, and various women in Beverwijck could be found behind the counter. In the 1660s, Jeremias van Rensselaer bought clothing, various textiles, buttons and liquor, at Elisabeth Bancker's shop; and nails, raisins, prunes, rice, a horse cover, scissors, and shirts at Mary Loockermans.[84] Undoubtedly, wives of bakers and tavern keepers frequently worked behind the counter as well. As a matter of fact, men counted on their wives' contributions, as *dominee* Schaets suggested when he mentioned that without his wife's trade, his family would have been 'still more miserable.'[85]

At first sight it may seem that researching Beverwijck's successful traders brings us in contact with a world of men; they determined where the money in the village was to be earned, and how much. But it soon becomes clear that women actively participated in the trading business, as well. Abraham Staets's wife, Catrijn Jochems, rented-out property; and in 1658, when she was bidding at an auction of Bastiaen de Winter's goods, she certainly was no exception in the village; Immetie *de backster*, *Dolle Griet*, Geertge Bouts, Dorothee (Volckert Jansz Douw's wife), and even the minister's wife bought goods at auctions. And in 1659, a woman was auctioning goods. This was not unusual; in the fatherland, women often bought second-hand clothes, furniture, or household goods at auctions in order to sell those later again. The work of assessing these goods was typically a women's job, performed by a sworn *priseerster*.[86]

It is clear that women were quite capable of taking care of business. One of the first female settlers, Anneke Jans, was able to get involved in the fur trade after the death of her second husband, Everhardus Bogardus.[87] Sander Leendertsz's wife Cathalina was an active female trader as well, and was even accused of illegal trading. She may have resembled, or perhaps even was the woman referred to by Jasper Danckaerts in 1680, when he spoke of 'a truly worldly woman, proud and conceited, and sharp in trading with wild people, as well as the tame ones... ' The trading, according to Danckaerts, was not without fraud, and the woman he described was not free of it. She traveled across the country to carry on trading, and eventually became 'one of the Dutch female traders, who understand their business so well.'[88] Lysbeth van Eps (also known as Elisabeth Banckers) was, like her mother Marietje Damen, so well aware of business that her mother and her husband Gerrit Bancker entrusted her with arranging important financial matters with Abel de Wolff in Amsterdam.[89]

Marriage in the Dutch Republic, perhaps more so than in the rest of Europe, was based on partnership and mutual duties and responsibilities.[90] In a marriage, not only was the work force of both husband and wife joined together, but also networks of friends and properties, thus creating its own basis for the husband, wife, and their children. Marriage could and often did contribute much to the success of a business. Philip Schuyler knew this well when he married Margaretha van Slichtenhorst, the daughter of Rensselaerswijck's director at the time. The marriage brought Schuyler into Van Rensselaer's trading network, of which he repeatedly made use. Wives could add important relations to the husband's network of friends, which could benefit the whole family. Family ties usually meant that there were people on whom one could count in times of distress; Volckert Jansz, for example, helped out his brother-in-law Rutger Jacobsz by offering him help when debts needed to be paid. Family would usually provide support when important decisions like the purchase of a house or land were made; Sander Leendertsz provided surety for his brother-in-law Thomas Poulusz, when Poulusz bought a house; and when the wife of his other brother-in-law Willem Teller died, he became partially responsible for the upbringing and inheritance of Teller's children by his appointment as their guardian.[91]

Sometimes women brought in considerable property; by pooling their capital, husband and wife expanded their business potential. Dutch inheritance laws prescribed the equal division of an estate among all children of a marriage.[92] No wonder, then, that in 1660 Philip Pietersz Schuyler was just as interested as Gerrit van Slichtenhorst in claiming his wife's share of the estate that would be left by his father-in-law.[93] Widows of wealthy men were especially good catches for a man, as they could bring in many resources; the success of their business sometimes greatly increased their possibilities.

Married people usually made a joint will, appointing the survivor as the 'sole and universal heir.' Children then inherited equally in a half-share of the deceased parent's estate. Minor children received their share at marriage or majority, while the interest of the capital invested for the minor children was for the use of the survivor. In 1650, after the death of her first husband Dirck Evertsz van Eps, a shoemaker in Amsterdam, Marietje Damen married the gunstockmaker Hendrick Andriesz van Doesburch, and went with him to the upper Hudson, where she became a well-to-do merchant and real estate speculator with investments in the East and West India companies.[94] Andriesz died before 1664 and, on his sickbed, 'expressly desired that the estate left behind should remain with her, for the reason that most of it came from her side.'[95] When Marietje married Cornelis van Nes in March 1664, she had property from two previous marriages.

Dutch society used a patriarchal system and, while unmarried women could gain some legal capacity when they reached majority at the age of 25, women who married were put under the guardianship of their husbands; in essence, a man could do whatever he wanted with family possessions.[96] Unlike an English wife, however, a Dutch wife could own property, and after marriage she had joint ownership with her husband of the communal property; if, according to a wife, the husband had mismanaged her estate, she could appeal to the court to have him removed as administrator.[97] There was another option for a woman to remain entitled to her possessions and secure her children's inheritance: She could marry with a prenuptial agreement. This was sometimes preferred by a woman who was marrying for the second time and who had inherited the entire estate of her first husband; this is exactly what Marietje Damen did when she married for the third time.[98]

Women made sure that there was a solid and stable homestead for their husbands and children. That a woman's place was more in the house, and a man's place was more oriented toward the outside world, does not mean that they lived in totally separate worlds, and that women had no voice in making decisions related to the outside world. The two worlds were connected and made each other's existence possible. A strong and healthy homestead, then, was in many cases the place where successful traders made important decisions for their families. The normal marriage contract gave both husband and wife joint ownership of their possessions and made them both equally responsible, and in general people considered it normal for wives to be informed of their husbands' businesses, considering that they created the home base for that business. Focusing on one family, the Van Rensselaers, will illustrate how important the role of a woman in a trader's family could be.

The Van Rensselaers and the trade

Maintaining the trade in Amsterdam

In 1643, Kiliaen van Rensselaer left not only a patroonship with settlers in the New World, but also the trading system he had built up with New Netherland. Particularly after the trade opened up, Kiliaen van Rensselaer had intended to become a major trader, second only to the West India Company.[99] Like most merchants in the Dutch Republic, he worked in a small business firm together with relatives and reliable business partners. In July 1643, he and his brothers-in-law Johannes and Thomas van Wely had established a trading company for one year; together, they would buy, arm, and equip the ship the *Wapen van Rensselaerswijck*. Half of the costs related to the ship, purchase, equipage, provisions, and monthly allowances would come from Van Rensselaer's account, while his mother-in-law, the widow van Wely, would be responsible for eight-tenths of the other half. For the cargo, ƒ11,000 had to be paid in advance, while contracted people and goods sent to the patroonship would be credited to Van Rensselaer's account.[100]

After Van Rensselaer's death, Johannes van Wely and Wouter van Twiller, uncles and guardians of Van Rensselaer's children, continued the trade, following the pattern of financial arrangements he had established. In 1647, they sent the *Prins Willem* to the colony with Van Twiller's cousin Gerrit Vastrick as 'supercargo' and Cornelis Coenraetsz van Kampen as skipper. They completed that journey, and repeated it in January 1649.[101] The supercargo they sent along aboard the ship was to administer and trade loaded cargo, 'always seeking the owner's greatest advantage and profit.'[102] Like other firms, they also sent agents (*factors*) who remained in the colony, where they would prepare a return cargo before the ships arrived.[103] By living in the area, these agents were often well informed about the local situation, market conditions, and prices. They built up relationships with the Indians and the colonists, establishing their trust so that they could count on these people to sell them colonial products and buy their trade goods. The agents were solid overseas connections.[104] When Jan Baptist went to Rensselaerswijck in 1651, he probably sailed on the *Gelderse Blom*, which was now chartered and on which Cornelis Coenraetsz was skipper, again with the same conditions as the previous trip.[105] The *Gelderse Blom* seems to have made a voyage to New Netherland once a year until it was sold in 1657; Wouter van Twiller's widow Maria Momma and her brother Guilliam then hired a larger ship, the *Sint Jan Baptist*.[106]

At the time of Van Rensselaer's death, his children were still minors.[107] In addition to the regular education they received at the Latin school, his sons, like other boys in the Dutch Republic, may have had an opportunity to learn about navigation, as well as arithmetic at the French school and 'double' (or 'Italian') book-keeping to enable them to convert from one kind of weight to the other, for ex-ample, or from one sort of money to another.[108] Merchants' sons were often ap-prenticed to a friendly merchant in Holland or another country, in order to gain some experience after their theoretical schooling. Moreover, after their education, they frequently used the new calculus and bookkeeping records that were then re-placing older methods, namely use of the abacus or drawing board. For example, the second volume of *Cijfferinge* (Arithmetic) by Willem Bartjens, published in 1637, was written specifically for traders. Over the next two centuries, it would be repeatedly reissued.[109] It is unknown exactly where the Van Rensselaers gained their business experience; like other traders (especially the sons who later took over their fathers' businesses), they probably learned much about the trade at home, and their uncles Van Twiller and Van Wely most likely contributed to their training.

From them, the brothers undoubtedly learned about the various trading insti-tutions that had been established in Amsterdam, and which guaranteed a good series of business and financial transactions. The Exchange (*Wisselbank*), the first public bank in Europe outside of Italy, had been founded in 1609 with the pur-pose of providing fast, efficient, and reliable exchange facilities to prevent un-scrupulous money changers from dictating the course of exchange rates every-where. On workdays, the Exchange was open for business for at least six hours a day. It was a civic institution, not privately owned; its accounts and deposits re-mained secret, and were controlled by the *burgomasters*. For merchants it meant, among other things, that they had immediate access to rapid money changing, prompt settlement of bills, and low bank charges.[110] It paid out bills of exchange, and would become a clearing house for world trade where debts were continu-ously settled and capital transferred.[111] At the Amsterdam bourse (*Amsterdamse Beurs*), completed in 1611, traders could easily buy and sell a great variety of products; throughout the seventeenth century, between 400 and 600 different kinds of goods from various countries were traded there. The press ensured that information on prices and news that influenced prices, such as war and other threats, was always available. Starting in 1613, price lists, which had been pub-lished irregularly since 1583, appeared twice a week. They listed not only prices of goods, but also the exchange rates and sea insurance premiums. For the mer-chant, the bourse meant that he could count on a quick sale, immediate payment, and good opportunities to reinvest the proceeds. If the prices were not profitable, it was also possible to borrow money to store goods in warehouses until better opportunities arose.

The Amsterdam Loan Bank (*Bank van Lening*, 1614) made it easy to secure loans, especially bottomry loans with the ship pledged as security, in order to fi-nance voyages to distant destinations. Usually these loans carried high rates of in-terest to be paid upon the return of the vessel against which the loan was issued – or, if the ship were lost, not at all. The city of Amsterdam's support for the insur-ance of trading goods for international trade, by its establishment of a chamber of insurance and damage (*Kamer van Assurantie en Averij*, 1598/1612), meant that

39. Emanuel de Witte (1615/1617-1691/1692), The Amsterdam bourse, 1653.

the Dutch mercantile fleet was more able to withstand the risks of war, piracy, and other damage. Opportunities to spread the risk by dividing ownership of a ship into a great number of shares that could be traded (*partenrederij*), and to pawn a ship and its cargo in order to raise capital for its equipment and voyage (*bodeme-rij*), also helped make it possible for people with less capital to enter the trade. The standard form of bottomry bonds permitted a merchant to borrow a substantial sum of money from willing lenders by offering the keel, or 'bottom,' of a ship he owned as collateral.[112] Bottomry loans were a form of credit that, when combined with insurance, enabled businessmen of modest means to risk their vessels and cargoes in remote parts of the globe.[113] In 1617, a bourse specializing in wheat, the *Korenbeurs*, was founded. Jonathan Israel has described how these institutions helped bolster Dutch world-trade primacy:

The Dutch entrepôt as a whole furnished goods more efficiently and cheaply than any rival, ... and Amsterdam provided an unrivalled array of mechanisms for settling bills and balances, financing trade, and investing in commodities expected or already stockpiled. But along with that came the perennially low interest rates at which one could borrow. In Holland merchants could borrow at 2.5, 3, or 4 percent, whereas in England rates were double and in France or Germany higher still. The merchant elite of Holland and Zeeland had at their disposal financial institutions and resources, and a degree of specialization in financial, brokerage, and insurance techniques, such as none of their rivals possessed, and which together afforded an immense and continuous advantage in the international arena.[114]

The Exchange and the Amsterdam Loan Bank, in particular, enabled small traders to participate. In 1650, it was possible to borrow money at a 5 percent interest rate, and in later years the percentage was often even lower. The public trusted the Amsterdam market because the government supported these institutions.[115] Sons of merchants like Kiliaen van Rensselaer were most likely educated by these institutions; and once Jan Baptist and Jeremias were twenty-two years of age, they were ready to start working in the family business – and to go to New Netherland to manage the affairs of Rensselaerswijck.

While her oldest sons were in New Netherland, their mother Anna van Rensselaer and sometimes brother Richard, when he became older, contributed much to maintaining the trade for the Van Rensselaers in Amsterdam.[116] This was not an easy task, as much needed to be done before a ship could sail; the chartering, outfitting, freighting, equipping, and insuring of a ship to go to the New World involved negotiations with different people. Together with her brother Jan van Wely and Wouter van Twiller's widow, Maria Momma, and her brother Guilliaem Momma, Anna arranged for various shipments of goods to the patroonship: goods to be used in the trade with the Indians, provisions to be traded with the colonists, and items for the personal use of her sons. These preparations took much organization. In Amsterdam, arrangements had to be made to acquire goods for the trade, to transport them to the ship's location, and subsequently to load them into the ship. Family members hoped to make a good profit by sending such goods as lace, braid, pistols, silverware, buttons, hat clasps, linen, second-hand suits, duffels, blankets, glasses, distilled liquors and candles; even the servant girl Talckien invested all the money she had – and, hoping that they would be traded well in the colony, bought ƒ30-worth of silver spoons and a pair of silk stockings for ƒ10.[117]

A ship needed to be hired; that was usually done for a certain sum per month, often with six, seven, or eight months guaranteed; but a voyage could last much longer, depending on weather and winds. In 1637, the sixty-ton ship *Rensselaerswijck*, for example, was able to depart directly from Amsterdam, sail to the island of Texel, just to the north of the province of Holland, and from there depart for the New World. If, however, the journey to the New World was made on a ship too large to sail directly from Amsterdam, arrangements had to be made for the goods to be loaded onto a flat-bottom boat or a lighter craft; this vessel would transport the goods to Texel, where they were transferred to the larger ship. This part of the journey alone could last several days. When the winds were favorable,

Den Dubbelen Arent een Weftindis Vaerder,

40. The West Indiaman Dubbelen Arent.

the trip to the New World could be made in six to eight weeks; but usually – and most certainly if the weather did not cooperate, or there were unexpected delays – it took considerably longer.[118] The *Rensselaerswijck* was away from Amsterdam for more than a year in 1637. It took five months to sail from Amsterdam to Rensselaerswijck, and the return journey to Holland lasted almost three months.[119] It was not unusual for the journey to last a long time. In 1641, it took *the Coninck David* about four months to sail from Texel to Manhattan.[120]

Anna also had to consider insurance. After her son Jeremias had left for New Netherland on the *Gelderse Blom* in September 1654 with trade goods for his relatives, she heard a rumor that many 'Turks' (Algerian pirates) were upon the ocean; after seeking advice, she insured his goods for ƒ400 and his life for ƒ1,000.[121] Trade with New Netherland was risky. All kinds of things could happen: War could break out, prices could develop in an unexpected way, a ship could be attacked by pirates, and other disasters could happen at sea. For example, when *the Prinses* was shipwrecked in 1647, as many as 16,000 pelts were lost.[122] As noted above, Amsterdam's support of insurance for international trade gave the Dutch mercantile fleet a distinct advantage over its competitors when risking war, piracy, and other damage on the high seas.[123] According to Dennis Maika, insurance and interest rates on bottomry loans (generally referred to as '*agios*') were usually high. For an average round trip voyage of eight months, *agios* would range from 3 to 4.5 percent per month, or at least 24 percent for an average voyage.[124] Many traders tried either to take the risk, or to diminish it by dividing their merchandise over various ships. Anna learned her lesson after *De Otter* was shipwrecked in the fall of 1656. If she had foreseen such a loss, she later wrote, she would have insured the beavers for 200 or 300 guilders. It was too late for that shipment; but the event did help her decide to take out ƒ1,000 or ƒ2,000 for insurance from her account when ships were expected and, if there was less, to pay a half-percent discount.[125]

When the ships returned with peltries, tobacco, and other colonial products, there was much work to be done as well, as the goods needed to be traded again in Amsterdam. The beaver pelts were usually sent on to Russia for treatment. The Russians had developed a process by which they combed out the undercoat hairs of the pelt – the wool used in felt making. The long 'guard' hairs remained undisturbed, and the skin processed in this way was considered attractive as trimming for garments. Thus, the Russians sent American beaver for pelting and trimming, along with their own furs, back to western Europe. In 1657, the market for beaver pelts in Amsterdam was very poor; merchantable pelts were sold for only 6 guilders, as 'more beavers arrive than can be sold in Muscovy.'[126] The pelts that Anna tried to sell in May 1658 were so small that she could get no more than ƒ4.18 per whole beaver; she complained, 'Then I must also pay on each beaver 5 stivers for freight, convoy duties, average, and I know not what else.' In addition, she had to let the tobacco that Jan Baptist had sent go 'for 5 stivers a pound, and after the tobacco had been weighed and the tarra had been deducted and allowance had been made for the stems, according to custom, there remained 643 lbs. net, so that the sum amounted to ƒ160, of which I paid ƒ66 for expenses, leaving me a total of ƒ94. Isn't that a fine income for the household?' Disappointed, she wrote: 'Verily, I say, if no other wind blows from New Netherland, it will look pretty bad.'[127]

It is likely that Anna van Rensselaer had plenty of opportunities to get advice for her trading activities. Sometimes her sons asked other businessmen to help her. When Jeremias sent her two cases with beavers in October 1656, he arranged for Nicolas Bevelot (a New Netherland trader who had returned to Holland with the *Vergulde Beer*) to advise his mother about the selling price.[128] Anna's friends would have been well aware of the ways of the trade. All of them probably knew how to deal with transferable securities, such as shares in companies and public promissory notes (*overheidsobligaties*), or how to negotiate marine insurances, arrange cargoes, and get information about foreign exchanges. The friends likely kept track of the commodity price lists to which they may have subscribed. Perhaps they would meet in one of the many taverns in the business district, where they could lounge for hours at the time discussing what they had read – contemplating trends, the latest news, and doing the best deals.[129] Both Anna's father Jan van Wely, one of Amsterdam's most successful jewelers, and her husband Kiliaen van Rensselaer were involved in business, and would have witnessed the establishment of the Exchange, bourse, Amsterdam Loan Bank, and other institutions that would make Amsterdam the most advanced business center of Europe. Anna had lived in a business environment all her life; even her house on the Keizersgracht was close to the business district.[130]

Anna was involved in the trade until her sons were able to take over the business; and when Jan Baptist returned in the fall of 1658, his mother would be relieved of her work. By taking care of business in Amsterdam, and bridging the period of her eldest son's absence, Anna did what many other merchant's widows had done.[131] She had been looking forward to Jan Baptist's return for more than a year; after 1658, Anna's letters reveal no further involvement with the trade.[132]

Jan Baptist van Rensselaer came home with the confidence that it was possible to conduct a profitable trade between Amsterdam and New Netherland; in the years that followed, he would continue the fur and provisioning trade with the colony, in which he would remain involved until his death in 1678. He maintained the arrangement set up by his father, who in 1636 had concluded a charter agreement with Gerard de Forest under which they both shared equally in the cost of building, rigging, and outfitting the 60-ton ship *Rensselaerswijck*, which would make a voyage to New Netherland. By selling shares of the vessel on the Exchange, the two men sought to profit. A one-tenth share, for example, was sold for ƒ1,200 to the Amsterdam furriers, the brothers Varlet. Other shares, constituting nearly 50 percent of the ship's total insured value, would be sold before she sailed to the colony.[133] These financial arrangements, according to Oliver Rink, established a pattern that would be followed by all Amsterdam merchant firms trading with New Netherland. They encouraged cooperation and contacts between the major suppliers of New Netherland. Rink found, in Amsterdam's notarial records, that Kiliaen van Rensselaer held sufficient shares in the voyages of various ships to be named as an owner; his portion of the operating capital of at least two large ships entitled him to be designated as a 'principal freighter' (*hoofdbevrachter*); and he also had small investments in other ships. He likely participated in voyages organized by the merchants Verbrugge and De Wolff.[134]

Jan Baptist van Rensselaer, upon his return, followed his father's strategy and immediately participated in some voyages in 1659.[135] In December 1660, he arranged to send Pieter Hartgers – a longtime upper Hudson resident, and one of the area's most influential inhabitants – three pieces of red duffel and five pieces of blue duffel on the *Kock*; and in the spring, he sent twenty-two pieces of duffel on the *Bever* or another ship; Hartgers was to take on the duffel at the rate of 3³/₄ ells to one beaver.[136] Between 1661 and 1664, Jan Baptist, in partnership with his uncles and brothers, chartered and outfitted at least another six ships. He also cooperated with other Amsterdam merchants. With Abel de Wolff and Gerrit Zuyck, he pooled capital to purchase ships, hire crews, and obtain trade goods. In each of these investments he had a substantial stake, for which he was designated a part-owner or principal freighter.[137]

Chartering a ship was expensive. In April 1661, Jan Baptist cooperated with

Gerrit Jansz Cuyper, who by marriage was related to the De Wolffs, whose company also traded with New Netherland; together, they hired the *St. Jan Baptista* for six months at 625 *carolus* guilders a month. The ship carried trading goods such as wine and brandy to the colony. At Manhattan, the ship would be unloaded for inspection, loaded again with colonial products, and sail back to Amsterdam. To protect the *St. Jan Baptista* against any dangers at sea, such as Dunkirk pirates, the ship was armed with eight *gotelingen* (light cast-iron cannons on a ship), and 150 pounds of gunpowder.[138] As charterers, Van Rensselaer and Cuyper paid nearly all expenses for the crew and captain. They had to take care of a crew, skipper and victualers themselves and pay their wages; the lessor of the ship, Jan Roelofsz van Edam, would sail along himself, at no cost, to oversee the cargo. It was important to load the ship within a specified time, so that it could sail in the shortest time possible. Charterers took on great risks: They were responsible for the replacement of lost or damaged equipment, arranged for marine insurance to cover the value of the ship, and paid for the required dock labor at each port of call – which included labor at Amsterdam, sometimes at Texel, at Manhattan, and at Fort Orange or any other port in New Netherland.[139]

In 1662, it would become clear that trade did not depend on supply alone. At a moment when people in the upper Hudson were expecting a good beaver trade, Robert Vastrick would write that the price of beaver pelts was down again in Amsterdam, from about 7 guilders in 1659, to *f*6-*f*6¼. A cousin of Wouter van Twiller, Vastrick was one of the friends with whom Jan Baptist had formed a company in 1661 to engage in the shipping business to New Netherland. He wrote: 'As little merchandise is being sent over, we shall this year for our company send only one ship, for this year there is no prospect of making any profit, as in Mascoven [Muscovy] the situation is very bad.' It was not until 1664, that beaver prices would rise again – to *f*7¾.[140]

In addition to the risks, there was the disadvantage that considerable amounts of money could be tied up for an extended period; a trader involved in overseas trade sometimes had to wait a long time before being paid for his merchandise. For example, following the path of sixteen hogsheads of *haenties* wine, brandy, duffels, and blanketing sent by Jan Baptist van Rensselaer and Pieter Hartgers in April 1663 on *De Bonte Koey*, it appears that Jeremias was unable to make the last payment for these goods until July 1668.[141]

Only few private traders could maintain a trade with so many risks. Oliver Rink, in his study of the economic and social history of Dutch New York, found that adequately capitalized, long-term trade relationships and cooperation between traders were required to assume the risk of transatlantic trade. The Van Rensselaers worked together with their relatives and other business partners such as Cuyper, the De Wolffs, and Van Hoornbeeck to withstand the periodic losses caused by shipwrecks and other disasters.[142] Only experienced firms, according to Rink, could afford to cut profit margins in order to undersell rivals, monopolize shipping, and buy out would-be competitors. In addition to the Van Rensselaers, the most important other merchant firms that played a significant role in New Netherland's commercial life were the companies of Gillis and Seth Verbrugge,

Dirck and Abel de Wolff, and Gillis van Hoornbeeck and Associates.[143]

By 1664, business in Amsterdam was starting to look more promising, and at least eleven ships would sail for New Netherland before August.[144] Jan Baptist van Rensselaer and Arent Jansz Moesman each had a sixteenth-part ownership in the *Gekruyste Hart*; and in the freighting, Moesman had a quarter-interest and Jan Baptist three-sixteenths. The vessel sailed around mid-January; upon its arrival at Manhattan in April, Stephanus van Cortlandt, the son of Olof Stevensz, would report that the ship had arrived with thirty *ankers* of distilled liquor from Jan Baptist, to be traded for tobacco.[145]

This was the last ship they would send to New Netherland; the *Gekruyste Hart* brought back wheat, furs, and lumber. After the English conquered New Netherland in September 1664, and renamed it New York, Jan Baptist van Rensselaer would try to diversify his trade. Carel H. Janssen found that Jan Baptist and Abel de Wolff together, with the consent of the West India Company, fitted out ships at Enkhuizen to trade merchandise on the *Grein* and the Ivory Coast for grain and elephant tusks between 1666 and 1671; but Jan Baptist would remain involved in the commercial affairs of New York and Rensselaerswijck.[146] In 1667, he invested in the *Eendracht* and bought the *St. Jan*; he also had an interest in the *Orangieboom*.[147] The English Council of Trade announced, in October of that year, that three direct voyages from Amsterdam to New York would be permitted annually; in February 1668, Jan Baptist, Abel de Wolff, Gillis van Hoornbeeck, Jacob Venturin, and Cornelis Jacobsz Mooij founded a shipping company to sail with one or more ships to New York and neighboring places in America.[148] In 1669, however, the English king withdrew this seven-year freedom to trade with New York and the surrounding areas – and, as a result, the company was dissolved.[149]

The agents in New York then took advantage their new 'denizen' status to maintain a brisk trade with the Dutch Republic. By taking an oath of allegiance, Dennis Maika has written, the inhabitants of Manhattan could become free denizens of the British empire. Dutch cargoes could then be shipped to New York on vessels owned by New Netherland denizens who, as subjects of the king of England, paid the normal duties in English ports.[150] Once Jeremias van Rensselaer and the Van Cortlandts became denizens of the British empire, the commercial enterprises of the Van Rensselaers were protected by the same English navigation laws that had troubled them in the past.[151] Jan Baptist invested in the *Hartogh van Yorck* in 1670, and in the *Gratie* in 1672. When New York was renamed New Netherland again in 1673, he had interests in the *Croon* and the *Beurs van Amsterdam*. He also would continue in the New York trade after the second English takeover in 1674. In 1676, for example, he invested ƒ23,000 in one ship to 'trade with English Northern Virginia, called lately by us New Netherland.'[152] Van Rensselaer's territorial holdings guaranteed a continuing concern for the colony's future. After the second conquest of New York, when the Van Rensselaers obtained a warrant from the Duke of York, their claim to Rensselaerswijck would be legitimized – thus securing their place within the developing English mercantile system.[153]

Maintaining the trade in New Netherland during Jan Baptist's directorship

Many of the problems Jan Baptist van Rensselaer encountered after his arrival in Rensselaerswijck concerned the trade. As testimony in January 1651 by Nicolaes Blanche van Aken shows, Van Twiller's efforts to monopolize the trade had been seen as a great obstruction for all traders and inhabitants of the community.[154] On this basis, Jan Baptist would continue or, perhaps, re-establish a good trading situation. As a magistrate, he seems to have gone along with the management of affairs in Rensselaerswijck; but in April 1652, everything changed. The establishment of Beverwijck eliminated the chance to maintain a trade monopoly. Trade became free again – and if the Van Rensselaers and their friends or relatives wanted to participate in it, they would have to compete with other private traders who could now establish themselves freely in the West India Company's village. Not only would the Van Rensselaers have to maintain their network in Amsterdam, but – in order to ensure regular trade for themselves and a guaranteed minimum turnover rate in the upper Hudson settlement – it would be important to re-establish good relations with the company and to confirm their friendly connections with the major traders. After all, while it had given up its monopoly in 1639, the company still controlled the regulation of the trade. By issuing ordinances, it maintained oversight of the currency, importation regulations, and Indian relations.

During his directorship, Jan Baptist van Rensselaer tried to resolve problems with the West India Company such as the arrangement of the tapster's excise, the tenth, and the boundary lines. At the same time, however, he needed to maintain good relations with the most important traders in order to keep up a good trade. Among them were traders like Volckert Jansz Douw, Rutger Jacobsz, or Sander Leendertsz Glen – several of whom had come over without any possession, as farmhands under contract with Van Rensselaer. During the previous years, they had earned enough in Rensselaerswijck to acquire some capital and become the leading inhabitants of the area.

Twice a week, ships would come from Manhattan.[155] Their arrival at Beverwijck created a busy time for the inhabitants; the ships that came from *patria*, especially, which brought the latest news from Europe, must have generated much excitement. Merchandise was inspected aboard ship by the commissary of Fort Orange while the ship was anchored in front of the fort. The merchandise would then be carried off the ship, and cartmen would transport the goods to the houses of people who had ordered them. Jan Baptist's goods were probably brought to the patroon's house, where they may have been stored in the shop that had been built during Van Slichtenhorst's days for use by Gerrit Vastrick (see illustration 44). Sailors and passengers provided extra business for local bakers, tavern and inn keepers; not much later, people would sell the goods they had imported at auctions.[156]

Subsequently, the ships would be loaded with the collected furs, sometimes tobacco, wheat, and lumber. Beaver pelts and wheat were transported by carts or wagons from the inhabitants' homes to the ship; boards were usually gathered at the riverside. Furs were especially easy to transport. They were light in weight and easily packaged. To prevent spoilage, they had to be packed dry and beaten before they were put into a case. To separate the different batches of beaver pelts in a case, papers were sometimes inserted between the layers. Then the cover was nailed down and a few hoops put around the case. Packed in cases marked with trading marks (usually the initials of the addressee), the pelts were loaded onto the ships. From Beverwijck, they were shipped to New Amsterdam, were the cases were opened and inspected in the West India Company's warehouse.[157]

Only after this inspection was done, and the excise tax paid, could the goods be loaded onto ships bound for the Dutch Republic. The twelfth article of the 1629-Freedoms and Exemptions, which regulated patroonships, had stipulated that Manhattan would be the 'staple' market of New Netherland. As such, it was the port of New Netherland, where the West India Company collected all import and export duties, and all goods were to flow through it.[158] Furs and other goods from the upper Hudson area and the 'south river' had to go through Manhattan before they could be sent to Holland. Likewise, European consumer goods went through Manhattan before they could go further into New Netherland. As a staple port, Manhattan served as the exclusive entrepôt for the entire colony.[159] Ships arriving from the fatherland had to anchor in the East River, where merchandise was loaded on sloops and transported to the warehouse. There, the goods were compared with the bills of lading. Goods with the destinations Beverwijck and Rensselaerswijck then could be loaded onto the same ship or another vessel – and continue on their way upriver.[160]

This process required much work at New Amsterdam, as well as in Beverwijck; traders from the upper Hudson frequently traveled downriver to take care of business at Manhattan. To get their trading business organized, Jeremias stayed at Manhattan during the summers of 1655, 1656, and 1657, while Jan Baptist managed affairs at Rensselaerswijck. These were good years for the fur trade. In 1656, for example, there had been a great trade in the spring, when at least 36,000 beaver pelts were shipped from Beverwijck through New Amsterdam to Holland. A year later, the trade was even better: Between June 20 and September 27, 1657, more than 37,640 beavers and 300 otters were sent from Fort Orange to New Amsterdam.[161] Dennis Maika found that, between 1657 and 1664, at least six transatlantic ships arrived annually at Manhattan; in 1663, ten ships came directly from Holland, and in 1664 eleven ocean-going vessels came and went before August.[162] Jeremias was kept busy declaring merchandise and colonial wares to West India Company customs, finding ships to transport it to the fatherland, and writing the demanded accompanying bills of lading and letters to the receivers of the goods.[163] Insurance was very high in the 1650s, which caused several traders to sometimes abandon its use. Like most traders, Jeremias tried to ship small quantities of beaver pelts and tobacco on various ships. In August 1657, for example, he sent his mother seventy-five beaver pelts on the *Draetvat*, and sixty-three on the *Vogelesangh*. David Becker he sent 147 whole beaver pelts on the *Vogelesangh*, along with nine *drielingen* (inferior pelts; two-third of an entire pelt) and fourteen half-beavers; and on the *Vergulde Meulen* he sent '24 whole and 132 half-beavers, 110

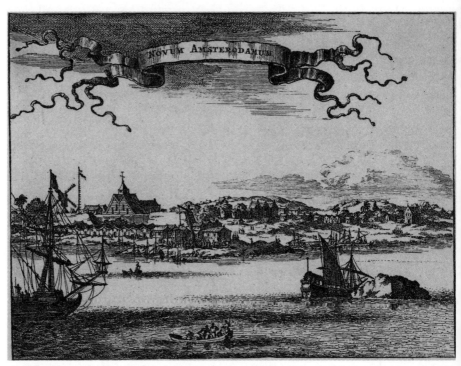

41. *'The Montanus View' of New Amsterdam, ca. 1650.*

ditto pieces and 64 otters' to cousin Jan van Twiller in September. By sending 'little and that by several ships,' he wrote to Anna, 'I shall stand the risk myself.'[164]

At Manhattan, Jeremias certainly was in the right place to discuss the latest news about the trade, and to be busy establishing and maintaining business contacts. He boarded with Oloff Stevensz van Cortlandt, a longtime family contact, and one of a group of successful Manhattan traders.[165] Several of these men had been sent as agent (*factor*) for an Amsterdam merchant firm to prepare cargoes for the return voyage to Amsterdam; after their contracts had ended, they started to trade on their own. Maintaining their connections with Amsterdam, they developed in New Amsterdam into a powerful group of merchants with much influence in the colony's government. Olof Stevensz van Cortlandt, Govert Loockermans, Cornelis Steenwijck, and Johan de Peijster were men who belonged to this group, and they frequently occupied such functions as *burgomaster*, *schepen*, orphan master, or elder or deacon in the church's consistory.[166] By spending much time with these people, Jeremias was able to establish a good network in New Amsterdam; and in the years following Jan Baptist's departure, he could frequently rely on cooperation with his host, Olof Stevensz van Cortlandt.

When Jan Baptist entrusted the direction of Rensselaerswijck to his brother and left for *patria*, in September 1658, he had reason to be confident about the family's trade between Amsterdam and New Netherland. Despite growing unrest at the Esopus, relations between the Indians and the Dutch in the upper Hudson area had been fairly stable. Problems between the West India Company and the patroonship needed to be resolved in Holland, but he and his brother had been able to confirm and establish good relations with several inhabitants of Beverwijck and Manhattan. These relationships were of such a nature that he trusted that they had a good network of friends in New Netherland – friends who would buy his merchandise and provisions, while selling him their furs and tobacco. It would be a trade in which he dared to invest. In the first years after his return to Europe, Jan Baptist's trust in the friends would certainly seem justified; even in 1661, when circumstances had already changed considerably in the upper Hudson, Jeremias could still write to his brother that, as 'far as the friends in the colony are concerned they are well inclined toward you.'[167]

Maintaining the trade in New Netherland during Jeremias's directorship

Soon after Jan Baptist's departure, events at the upper Hudson took a dramatic turn – and after 1657, the trade declined continuously.[168] Relations between the Maquaes and the other Iroquois nations had already become so bad that, in June of that year, the Maquaes asked the Dutch to help them repair their stockades and to host their women and children in case of emergency.[169] In February 1658, against the wishes of the other Iroquois nations, the Maquaes re-opened their war with the French – which may have caused the low supply of beavers that year.[170] As late as August, there was very little fur trade with the Indians, and one beaver sometimes cost 12 to 13 guilders in *sewant*.[171] The following year offered better prospects. In May 1659, everything was still the same as when Jan Baptist had left, according to Jeremias, who thought that the beaver trade could turn out very well, 'for almost all of the river Indians are out hunting.'[172] It seems that the trade was indeed somewhat better that year. Martha Shattuck found that, as a result, more people were able to pay their debts.[173] In August, Jeremias was able to send 290 whole and eight half-beaver pelts to his brother in Amsterdam.[174] The temporary recovery may have helped people whose financial problems were not too deep; but the number of people provided with poor relief had increased from ten in 1658, to seventeen in 1659. Jeremias still had a hard time collecting Jan van Twiller's debts. 'Where there is nothing, one can get nothing,' he wrote Maria Momma, who had asked him to help get payment for the many unpaid bills left by her brother-in-law in 1657.[175]

The situation did not improve; outstanding debts could not be collected, as there were no beavers to be had; and, due to the poor trade, Jeremias would be unable to send anything over to Amsterdam.[176] Thus, prospects for the trade were changing rapidly; and according to Jeremias, they were getting worse every year. In 1660, the deacons of the church supported twenty-six people.[177] La Montagne wrote Stuyvesant that the trade in that year had barely amounted to 30,000 pelts, while Stuyvesant estimated an even lower number of beavers on which recognition was paid, at about 25,000 to 30,000.[178] The Esopus war, as well as the late beaver trade, was creating a bad situation in the upper Hudson. The trade, which had only begun in June, was so poor that Jeremias was even preparing to go into farming, as there was 'no profit in trading here, owing to the underselling.'[179]

Although Jeremias would be able to send over a case with 404 beaver pelts in June 1661, the situation in the colony had only worsened. Taking legal action to collect outstanding debts did not make sense, he wrote, because 'where there is nothing, even the emperor loses his right.'[180] He hardly dared to order any new goods, as he was far behind in his account and did not foresee an opportunity to pay. The *St. Jan Baptista*, which had been hired by the Mommaes after they sold the *Gelderse Blom*, arrived in August with wine and brandy, among others items; but on her return voyage to the fatherland on October 18, 1661, Jeremias would ship no more than about 170 beaver pelts.[181] The situation was so bad that it was almost impossible to dunn people, he wrote to Jan Baptist, and 'Sr. Pieter Hartgers and Jan Bastiaensz, when please God, they safely arrive at your house, will tell you how hard it is to get beavers from the traders.'[182] Jan Bastiaensz van Gutsenhoven, who had been hired as an agent by Guilliaem and Maria Momma, would leave with many unpaid bills that concerned more than 80 people. He gave Jeremias, who had already assisted him for a few years, a power-of-attorney to collect the remaining outstanding debts owed to him, the amounts of which varied between ƒ2 for Marten Cornelisz and ƒ9,753-12 8 for a promissory note for Sander Leendertsz Glen.[183] Bastiaensz was only one of several merchants who would leave the colony that year with unpaid bills, giving friends a power-of-attorney to collect their debts.[184] By September 1661, Jeremias had had 'enough of having solicited so much in vain'; he asked Guilliaem Momma to send someone else over to collect the debts, in the event Jan Bastiaensz did not return to his service; each day, when he made the round to collect those debts, he could not raise even a single beaver.[185]

1662 would bring Beverwijck a better beaver trade and, in August, Jeremias was able to send a case with 464 whole and forty-three half-beaver pelts. Unfortunately, the price of beavers was down again at Amsterdam – so he sent along some tobacco.[186] He also sent forty-five pelts to Oloff Stevensz in payment for a gray mare and two cows; and on August 7, he delivered to Jan Bastiaensz the list of 'obligations, accounts, *sewant*, remainders of goods, together with full satisfaction and payment of whatever his honor had received.'[187] But the situation would not remain so promising. The fur trade would turn out badly again in 1663, as the conflict at the Esopus between settlers and Indians led to another outbreak. There was unrest, as well, among several other groups of Indians. In August, Jeremias explained why he still could not reimburse his brother: 'The trade ceases so suddenly, that one hardly sees a single Indian and this because the path is not safe for the Indians, for one says the French Indians are coming and another that the English are coming with Indians, so that the Maquas are quite in a pinch.'[188]

The bad situation of the upriver community contrasted sharply with the booming tobacco trade at Manhattan. There was a high demand in Amsterdam and tobacco prices were low in Virginia, while the supply was strong. Altogether, the trade would produce a 'tobacco *frenzie*' that drove merchants to pursue this commodity aggressively. The decline in prices stimulated production and maintained a tobacco 'boom' that would last until the 1680s.[189] With so few beavers to offer as payment for merchandise, Jeremias decided in 1661 to pay his relatives in tobacco. Well aware of Manhattan's successful tobacco business, he suggested having someone there each year who could trade a good quantity of the product.[190] In May 1662, he sent over two 650-pound casks of tobacco; and in August, he sent Maria Momma three casks of tobacco that weighed 1,170 pounds.[191] In November 1663, the Van Rensselaers, who on occasion had worked together with Oloff Stevensz van Cortlandt, began working together with this family (which by then had become Jeremias's inlaws), especially with Stevensz's son Stephanus. Their partnership concerned trade regarding some duffels, blankets, and brandy in return for tobacco. Jan Baptist would send over a stock of merchandise annually, while Stephanus attended to the business at Manhattan, and Jeremias in Rensselaerswijck. That way, they could do business together and divide the profits.[192]

The Van Rensselaers were also well aware that, in the second half of the seventeenth century, the size of the wheat trade in Holland was decreasing. A supply of more than 100,000 lasts, common in the first part of the century, would be reached only on rare occasions after the 1640s, when these amounts were imported for several consecutive years. In 1680, when reportedly 80 percent of the warehouses in Amsterdam had been designed for the grain trade, that trade had declined to only 60 percent of its average in the 1640s.[193] While the beaver trade was declining in 1663 and 1664, the Van Rensselaers transported wheat from Rensselaerswijck to the fatherland.[194]

Perhaps with an eye to the diminishing fur trade and a decline in imports of Scandinavian wood in Holland, Jan Baptist suggested in October 1659 that they try to develop a trade in boards:[195]

> If you could make an agreement with Barent or with Spitsbergen to have them saw planks 25 feet in length without or with few knots (on which much depends), and 2 inches thick, I would be willing to pay ƒ2 in *sewant* for them. But they must be sawed evenly and be at least a foot or 5/4 foot wide, namely, only pine planks... I should like to have at least two hundred of them as an experiment, which you must ship in the most convenient way.

Jeremias found out that only these two men were able to saw planks of this length; but as they could not come to an agreement – Teunis Spitsbergen and Barent Pietersz Coeymans wanted 30 stivers in beavers apiece – the brothers gave up on this idea, and only occasionally traded in some lumber.[196]

In 1664, the *Gekruyste Hart* returned from Manhattan to Holland; aboard were, among other things, Jeremias's beavers, wheat, and twenty oaken logs for wainscoting, 14 feet long and a foot thick.[197] The ship may have sailed just in time to escape the English fleet, which had assembled on the 29th of July at Nantucket Island and proceeded west into Long Island Sound. A delegation of ninety-three citizens signed a document calling for the immediate surrender of the colony; and in a meeting at Stuyvesant's *bouwery* (farm), the director general agreed to terms for the surrender of New Netherland on August 27, 1664 (old style).[198] After the English takeover, the Van Rensselaers also were able to continue their trade. Once Jeremias van Rensselaer and the Van Cortlandts became denizens of the British

empire, their commercial enterprises would be protected by the English navigation statutes.[199] Jeremias, together with relatives such as Andries Teller and Philip
Schuyler, was thus able to purchase an interest in vessels that would sail to Holland by way of England.[200]

Altogether, Kiliaen van Rensselaer would probably have been disappointed in
the outcome of the trade: The yield of beavers, especially during the 1650s, had
greatly surpassed his expectations of 1633; but then, after 1657, the decline of the
trade seemed more or less permanent, and would not reach high levels again in the
Dutch period.[201] Rensselaerswijck would never become the great provider of
wheat for Brazil he had dreamt of, either, although by 1664 his sons had sent some
wheat to the Dutch Republic. The tobacco trade in which his sons participated
was centered more around Manhattan, and did not generate much revenue for the
patroonship. The relationship that developed between the Van Rensselaers and
the Van Cortlandts may have benefitted the Van Rensselaers' trade in this commodity.

The Van Rensselaers were responsible for only a fraction of the New Netherland trade – a share that, according to Jaap Jacobs, was not very important to the
total Atlantic trade. In the first twenty years of the seventeenth century, Jacobs
has calculated, the Atlantic trade already represented a total value of 4 to 7.5 million guilders. At its peak in the late 1650s, the fur trade only amounted to 300,000
to 350,000 guilders; exports of New Netherland tobacco accounted for about
400,000 guilders in 1664, and thus had become more important than the peltry
trade. Imports into New Netherland during the 1650s may have fluctuated between 500,000 and 800,000 guilders, according to Jacobs.[202]

The business of the Van Rensselaers was one of the many family firms in Amsterdam. Until corporations became important in the nineteenth century, these
family firms would remain the most important entity for conducting trade. Jeremias and Jan Baptist may not have been able to bring home the great profits their
father and they had hoped for; but despite all the unforeseen difficulties and misfortunes, they were able to continue the family's business, which was always a
trader's first priority.[203] During their lifetime, they would remain among the most
important, if not the most important, traders in the upper Hudson area. In addition to their position as representatives of the patroon, their role as traders ensured the Van Rensselaers an important place in the community – a position in
which they were seen by others and which, as in *patria*, required a life-style in accordance with their status.

Place in the community: life-style

The patroon's property in Beverwijck

According to Beverwijck's court, it was only by its sufferance that Van Rensselaer
could stay in the patroon's house after April 10, 1652. The property was now was
located in the middle of the area between the boundary posts – and was thus in Be-

verwijck.[204] *Schout* Swart and his wife Antonia van Rijswijck had arrived in the colony on July 22, and moved into the house. In the fall of that year, despite attempts by the newly established court of Fort Orange to prevent it, Swart and Jan Baptist van Rensselaer enlarged the rear part of the house that served as the church, by building a middle wall.[205] In September 1654, they were joined in the house for about a year by Jan Baptist's twenty-two-year-old brother Jeremias, who a good year later returned to *patria* for about eight months. Knowing that his brother would come back soon, Jan Baptist wrote to the patroon and co-directors, in November 1655, that he had hired another dwelling for Swart, 'for the freedom of the church and the sessions of the council... The house in which I dwell and which belongs to you does not have one free room,' he explained, 'because in the chamber [*kamer*] or front part of the house [*voorhuys*] the council has to have its sessions, and in the rear house [*achterhuys*] is the church; in the attic grain has to be stored, so that it is very unfree and impossible to be inhabited by two families.'[206] (see illustration 42-44.) When Jeremias returned to Rensselaerswijck in September, there would soon be more space for him, for which board he paid ƒ8 a week until he was appointed director himself.[207] Since the first of May 1655, Swart had lived in a dwelling belonging to Teunis Dircksz; and at the beginning of June 1656, the first stone for a new church was laid. Once the building was ready, the community would attend church services there. The newly available space in the rear house [*achterhuys*] was probably used for storage again; in April 1666, for example, the rear house was full of oats.[208]

The 1656 crisis over Rensselaerswijck's payment of the tapster's exise to the West India Company shows that Swart had been able to live in the patroon's house, since the property had its own jurisdiction within Beverwijck. During that dispute, one tavern keeper who had refused to pay the tax was taken prisoner by Fort Orange's commissary De Deckere. After the tax protester escaped and fled to Van Rensselaer's house, De Deckere failed to compel the tavern keeper to come with him, and had to leave him behind – so close to the fort, yet unable to arrest the man. It was 'in the highest degree absurd,' the commissary complained, 'that there should be an asylum in the midst of our jurisdiction for fugitives, and a free place for other abuses and usurpations, ... not so much through the impulses of the people themselves as indeed through the inducements and persuasions of certain bullies and boasters who have the management of the colony.'[209]

Free manors also existed in the fatherland, where they had their own lords, legislators, and high jurisdiction; they behaved, as much as possible, as if they were independent states. Localities such as Buren, Leerdam, IJsselstein, Vianen, and Culemborg were known as 'free places' for bankrupts, delinquents, and abducted minors.[210] This situation allowed Jan Baptist to provide Swart with housing in the patroon's house – even when he feared that the West India Company would not tolerate the *schout's* living in 'their jurisdiction, as they call it' – and there was nothing the company could do to prevent it.[211] It also enabled Johanna de Laet, daughter of one of the patroonship's co-directors, to hold a public sale in the church or the rear part of the patroon's house, disregarding De Deckere's right in Beverwijck to collect auction fees.[212]

42. *Henk Zantkuijl made reconstructions of the patroon's house [see also illustrations 27, 28, 43-50]. For this important house he assumed a length of about 85 feet. Many houses were 60, 80, and 90 feet long; many were 20, 21, and also 16 feet wide. The width of the patroon's house Zantkuijl assumed to be 18 feet, because the house is one of the earliest wooden skeleton houses in Rensselaerswijck. The measures are not so very important; more important are the impression made by the reconstruction and the arrangement and design. The side aisle is, according to Van Slichtenhorst's descriptions, 15 feet along the warehouse part of the rear house. In the middle house the old situation was brought back, and between C and D a middle wall was built again. This reconstruction of the situation before 1659 shows the cross section of the front house.*

43. *Henk Zantkuijl, patroon's house, frontal view. The situation from before 1648 until 1659. See also comments illustration 42.*

Once the frictions regarding the tapster's excise were resolved (the Van Rensselaers lost the case), the Van Rensselaers appear to have become inhabitants of Beverwijck. On March 25, 1658, Jeremias was granted a patent by the West India Company for a lot, house and garden. By accepting this patent, the Van Rensselaers apparently acknowledged that the patroon's house, and the lot upon which it stood, belonged under Beverwijck's jurisdiction, although there is no evidence that Jeremias ever paid 'chimney money' (chimney tax) for his house. By the early 1660s, the Van Rensselaers would have acquired several pieces of property within Beverwijck. For *f*1,812, Jan Baptist was able to buy a riverside lot from Jan Verbeeck at a public sale in 1657. On the lot was a house two planks long with a 16-square-foot kitchen attached, along with two gardens, a well, and a hogsty.[213] A year later, he and Goosen Gerritsz together purchased a house and lot of six by four rods from Reyer Elbertsz, also located in Beverwijck near the third kill, or *Vossenkil*. In 1661, Jeremias bought a house, barn, and lot of eleven by four rods and two feet on the riverside in Beverwijck from Evert Pels, south of Sander Leen-

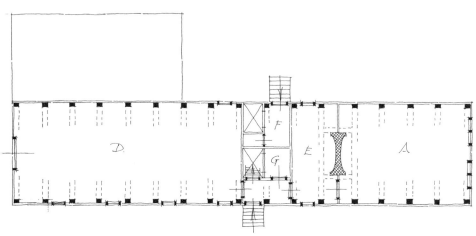

44. *Henk Zantkuijl, patroon's house, ground level. Reconstruction of the situation after 1648 (change in the middle house) and after 1652 (enlargement of the 'church' by taking away a middle wall). A = front house, 'chamber' (meeting room); E = goot-kamertje (kitchen); F -= winckeltgen met een koy (a small shop with a bedstead); G = gijselkamertje (prison); D = warehouse, now enlarged church. See comments ill. 42.*

dertsz's garden. He leased out the existing house, and built another small house of twenty feet long and twenty-two feet wide on the lot.[214] Eventually, the Van Rensselaers would become important property owners in Beverwijck, where they owned some valuable lots conveniently located along, or close to, the riverside (see Appendix 8, II, no. 20, near 33; I, no. 5).

The patent Jeremias received in 1658 was for 'a lot, house and garden located near Fort Orange in the village of Beverwijck; bordering Casper Jacobsz on the west it is in length 34 rods; and on the east side 35 rods; in breadth on the south 22 rods; and on the south of the plain 14 rods...'[215] It was the largest lot in Beverwijck, and the patent concerned the lot on which the patroon's house had been built (Appendix 8, section III, number 3). A year after Jan Baptist's departure, Jeremias was busy repairing the house, as he 'could not stand this way any longer.'[216] The chamber and cellar were torn to the ground. He had the roof shored-up, so that it would remain standing as it always had; he had the cellar completely walled all around with stone, so that it could be used as a kitchen cellar, and another cellar created toward the rear to serve as a vegetable cellar. The fore part – the cellar kitchen, as well as the chamber – became twenty-four feet long, and was built of masonry all around; for this project, Jeremias had *moppen* (Vecht or Utrecht bricks, measuring about 8½ by 4¼ by 1¾ inches) burned. The rear part, which had been used as a kitchen, was repaired and provided with another partition wall.[217] The first stone for the cellar was laid in the summer, on which occasion ƒ40 was spent for the laborers.[218] Andries Herbertsz, who owned a tile and brick kiln north of the *Vossenkil*, provided 18,825 *moppen* at ƒ18 per 1,000. Herbertsz also delivered 4,000 tiles, at ƒ50 per 1,000, to cover the roof. Reyer Elbertsz van

Breuckelen, who owned a brickyard near the third kill, was paid for diverse qualities of brick as well.[219] The building may have been finished sometime in June 1661. In his account book, Jeremias listed on the 18th of that month an expenditure of more than *f*360 for wine, beer, bread and other food for a great celebration (called *de kroegh*), a meal attended by all who had contributed to the building of the house.[220] Jeremias was content with the end result. In the front wall in the cellar was a door, and beside it a half-cross window with three panes, or 'lights.' On the south side there also was a window with three lights. In the chamber, in the front wall were four cloister windows, on the south side three, and on the north side one – so that, according to Jeremias, it was an airy room, at least five feet above the ground. The bottom of the cellar was level with the ground, and in his opinion the structure looked very good[221] (see illustrations 45-50).

The patroon's house on the inside

Once the house had been rebuilt, Jeremias decided that some redecorating needed to be done as well, so that he would be able to receive guests in an appropriate way. In the summer of 1659, when General Stuyvesant was up in the area, he would have liked to have stayed at the patroon's house; but Jeremias had no accommodation to offer. In order to prevent this from happening again, he ordered a bed with curtains and a valance for the new chamber.[222] Such a bed and accessories could be very luxurious, and often cost a goodly sum; at the sale of some furniture of trader Dirck Jansz Croon, a bed was valued at *f*140.[223] Appurtenances for any bed included at least a few pillows, one or two long round cushions (*peluws*), sometimes a spread (*beddekleet*) for on the straw under the 'bed,' some blankets, and possibly a bedspread.[224] Many colonists seem to have had a built-in 'boxstead'; the very few (and nearly always incomplete) surviving inventories and several auction rosters often

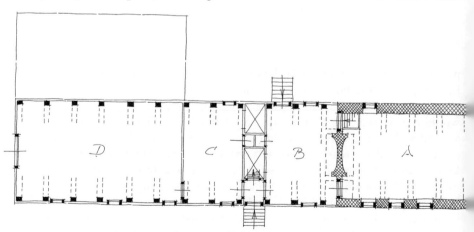

45. Henk Zantkuijl, patroon's house, ground level. Reconstruction of the situation after 1659. A = voorhuys (front house) or 'chamber' (meeting room); B = room in middle house; kitchen-living room C = room in achterhuys *(rear house); D = former church/warehouse, now warehouse with 15-ft. side aisle. See comments ill. 42.*

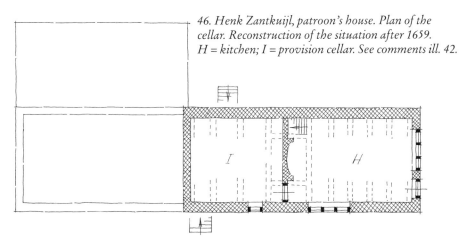

46. Henk Zantkuijl, patroon's house. Plan of the cellar. Reconstruction of the situation after 1659. H = kitchen; I = provision cellar. See comments ill. 42.

list curtains and valances, which were hung in front of the entrance. Built into the wall, a boxstead took up little space and provided a warm sleeping place, while protecting against drafts and the cold climate.[225] While the new bed offered sleeping space in the front room for important guests, or perhaps for Jeremias himself, there were also built-in boxsteads in the patroon's house that may have been used by guests or boarders like Jan Bastiaensz, or Jeremias's servant Marten Gerritsz (see illustration 45). As it was not uncommon for several people to share a bed, more than one person probably slept there.[226] With the presence of so many guests in the summer, day beds (*slaapbanken*) also may have been used; these were simple, inexpensive benches upon which one could lay and sleep. Steven Jansz *timmerman*,

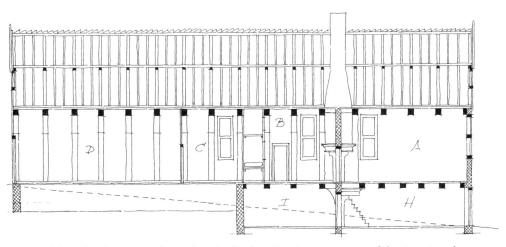

47. Henk Zantkuijl, patroon's house, longitudinal section. Reconstruction of the situation after 1659. A = the versteende (brick/stone) voorhuys or camer (chamber); B = room in the middle house; kitchen, living room (brought back in the situation of 1648); C = room in the achterhuys. The middle wall has been put in again; D = warehouse, because of the middle wall back in the same measure. H = kitchen; I = provision cellar. See comments ill. 42.

48. Henk Zantkuijl, patroon's house.
Cross section of the voorhuys *(entrance*
hall). Reconstruction of the situation
after 1659. See comments ill. 42.

49. Henk Zantkuijl, frontal view of the
patroon's house. Reconstruction of the situation
after 1659. See comments ill. 42.

50. Henk Zantkuijl, left side wall of the patroon's house.
Reconstruction of the situation after 1659. See comments ill. 42.

whose wife had run a tavern, sold one in 1655 for the price of 4 guilders.[227] If there was no boxstead, one probably slept on a 'bed' – a fitted sheet (*hoes*) filled with feathers or straw. It is unknown where, and on what kinds of beds, Jeremias's servants slept. They may have had to use *slaapbanken* or bolsters; others, perhaps slaves, may have only had the use of a simple bolster, and perhaps slept on some straw in the garret in the rear part of the house. In general, the situation in Beverwijck may have been similar to the way people slept in the Dutch Republic. Thera Wijsenbeek, in her study of possessions and the existence of wealthy and poor in Delft between 1700 and 1800, wrote that if space was limited, people most likely slept in the most unexpected places.[228]

In addition to the bed, Jeremias asked Jan Baptist to send eight Spanish chairs (chairs with straight backs and leather upholstery, and higher legs than benches) to be put in the front room for 'the gentlemen, to be used when we hold council, for at present we only use pine benches.'[229] The rush-bottom chairs, which belonged to Jan Baptist, Jeremias may have kept and used in the kitchen or in the two smaller rooms between the front room and the rear house. He may have used the patroon's wooden chairs there, as well. Undoubtedly, like some other wealthier traders, Jeremias had cushions to make sitting more comfortable. Dirck Jansz Croon, for instance, owned chair cushions, and Rutger Jacobsz owned at least three sitting cushions worth about *f*6 apiece. The few listings of sales and inventories indicate that many people, including the less wealthy, owned at least some chairs or a bench and a table, which they sometimes covered with a tablecloth.[230]

For decoration, Jeremias asked that a large mirror of one *ell* wide be sent over, and a six-yard-long valance for the mantelpiece. He may also have used the hearth rug that had been left by Jan Baptist.[231] At Pieter Claerbout's auction in July 1659, Jeremias bought a painting for *f*8:05; but he undoubtedly had more (and probably more expensive) paintings on the walls.[232] In auction or inventory records, paintings appear frequently, in small or large sizes, at various prices between *f*1 and *f*100. In the fatherland, the sale of pictures had become a major business; there was great demand and a growing market for artwork, which demanded specialization and division of the work. New painting techniques had been developed that made greater production possible; after 1640, less time was required to produce paintings of the same size and subject matter (compared to 1610). These advances, in turn, led to lower prices, making artwork available to many people. The historian Ad van der Woude has calculated that, in the Dutch Republic between 1500 and 1800, between 5 and 10 million paintings were produced, including paintings on wood, prints, and drawings.[233] Willem Frijhoff and Marijke Spies have estimated that, in 1650, between 650 and 750 painters were working in the Netherlands; these artisans produced 63,000 to 70,000 paintings, the value of which may have been equivalent to more than half the so important Dutch cheese production.[234] Some evidence of their work was brought to the upper Hudson area. At least seventy-two small and large paintings were traded or mentioned in records of the fourteen auctions and eleven (partial) inventories in Beverwijck studied for this chapter.

Although his brother had left, Jeremias by no means lived alone in the house; on the contrary, it provided space for several people. As one of the area's most important and wealthy inhabitants, Jeremias had several servants. From February 1660 (or perhaps earlier) through 1663, Marten Gerritsz served him as a house servant to look after things, dun the farmers, hand out things to laborers, deliver materials and other such tasks, for which he received four beavers a month and board at *f*1 per night. In July 1664, Gerritsz was referred to as 'former' servant.[235] In September 1663, the carpenter Jacob Meesz had also lived with Jeremias 'for a year or two'; and the merchant Jan Bastiaensz, during the time he worked as an agent for the Mommaes in the upper Hudson, boarded in the patroon's house as well. When he went back to *patria* in 1661, Bastiaensz would leave his servant Jacob Sandersz, who had lived with him for a year, with Jeremias. Bastiaensz paid

Jacob's wages and Jeremias paid for his board, for which Jacob in return would do some writing. In August 1662, Jeremias also mentioned his servant Cornelis Mulder; this man does not appear in his accounts elsewhere, and it is not known where he lived.[236] The maid probably lived in the house as well, while the boy Teunis would be sent away three months after Jan Baptist had left. Jeremias kept his brother's negro, Andries, and later would have two more slaves. Typically, the house was occupied by at least four people; but it is more likely that six, or perhaps seven or eight, people had lived there before Jeremias married Maria van Cortlandt in the summer of 1662.

After the marriage, the patroon's house would also become a home for other people. Immediately after the birth of their first son, Kiliaen, Maria had physical problems and could not manage the household; her twelve-year-old sister Catherine stayed with them during the winter to help.[237] The assistance of a maid and slave was undoubtedly always available. Carpenter Jacob Meesz, servant Marten Gerritsz, and perhaps Cornelis Mulder were still boarding at the house at that time, while the slaves also lived in the patroon's house.

Outer appearance: Clothing

Having a large, nicely furnished house, several servants, and (as we saw in the second chapter) a few slaves – these were signs of status, and greatly contributed to one's reputation. That Jeremias found outer appearances important is also suggested by his attention to clothing. Like every other man in the community, he wore linen shirts. These shirts were fairly long, and were worn directly on the body. In a time when people were not accustomed to washing themselves every day, they had a cleansing function, as they absorbed bodily filth and fluids. At the same time the shirt separated the outer clothing (which was rarely washed) from the skin.[238] As people tried to keep their bodies clean by changing their underwear often, they usually had several shirts. The one complete inventory that seems to remain from Beverwijck lists only eight men's and women's shirts – a small number compared to a place like Maassluis in the Dutch Republic, for example, where the average person owned ten shirts.[239] Most likely, Jeremias was one of the few who had other underwear, as well. According to Le Francq van Berkhey, people in Dutch towns generally did not wear underpants, unlike those living in the countryside. In Beverwijck, at least some people, among whom were Jeremias, seem to have used underpants, although they were not cheap.[240] The fact that underpants (unlike shirts) were not provided to the poor may be an indication that they were not commonly used. It is also possible that they were not used in the modern meaning of 'underwear.'[241] Jeremias, however, seems to have worn underpants regularly, as various tailor accounts in the Van Rensselaer Manor Papers reveal that they had been either made, repaired, or turned inside-out.[242]

Shirts were also worn as outer clothes in combination with the standard outfit, which for a man in the first half of the seventeenth century consisted of a jerkin (*wambuis* or *roxken*) and a pair of pants; at that time, shirts could be quite expensive. Cornelis Bogardus had a shirt with a value of *f*29-10. Sometimes this standard outfit was briefly called a 'suit of clothes' (*pack kleeren*).[243] The knee-length pants were of the same color and cloth as the mantel and jerkin, usually kersey or cloth. In general, the jerkin was worn over the shirt, which could be adorned with beautiful lace, collars, and other decorations. Jeremias owned several jerkins, mostly made of cloth, but he also had one made of leather. On occasion, the tailor decorated them with cuffs (*opslaegen*) and fashionable silver buttons. 'Innocents' - very small jerkins that revealed a large part of the white shirt – became fashionable in the 1650s, and Jeremias surely had the tailor make those for him. The so-called Rhingrave pants ran out so wide to the knee that they resembled skirts; as much as fifteen meters of textile was sometimes used to make them.[244] Over the jerkin or 'innocent,' men often wore a jabot (*bef*), a flat, laying-on-the-shoulders collar that was made in four different models, which varied remarkably in price. In Cornelis Bogardus's wardrobe were two jabots with lace worth *f*22-10, while two others without lace were valued at only *f*2-10. Some of Jeremias's tailor accounts mention these collars, and sometimes list the hooks and eyes and whalebone used to make them.[245] These flat collars had replaced the high 'millstone' collar (*molensteenkraag*) in the 1620s, and hair styles had changed along with this fashion development. In the 1650s, men were growing their hair to about shoulder length, or used a wig, while the great moustaches of the past had given way to a thin moustache and a small goatee; Jeremias probably followed this style.[246]

Jeremias wore his outfit with white or black silk or woollen stockings, which (considering the length of the pants) were an important part of the outfit and could cost as much as 25 guilders. Jeremias owned stockings both with and without feet; those with feet he would frequently have resoled by the tailors. He may have worn understockings to protect the outer pair from sweat and foot odors; in the 1650s, overstockings or 'canons,' which were widened and decorated at the top, better fitted the wider boots worn by men at this time.[247] Overstockings replaced the large, colorful, and eye-catching garters (*kousebanden*) that had previously been very popular, and which protected the expensive stockings from the rough boot. When clothes became more ornate in the 1650s, the footwear changed with the fashion: Shoes were tied with shoe ribbons and bows, and the often colorful garters were then sewn at the knee band of the breeches.[248]

A hat accompanied the whole outfit – and Jeremias owned several of them. He had, for example, a black castor hat and a black hat made of camel's hair, which had a sweatband and a ribbon. Anna van Rensselaer, knowing that her son liked to keep up with the latest trends, sent him a black hat in 1659, instead of a gray one, 'such as are now worn a great deal.'[249]

Jeremias valued good quality cloth and considered it important to keep up with the latest styles. In September 1658, he ordered a coat from the fatherland that was to be made of good, fine cloth and have a little skirt, 'somewhat according to the fashion.' Two years later, he would request a gray suit and a cloak of the same cloth, 'of the latest color and fashion.'[250] When he was the best man at David Pietersz Schuyler's wedding in Manhattan, in 1657, he wore gray clothes with white 'sayette (sagathy)' stockings with silver ribbons, which were attached to black breeches, and a pair of Spanish leather shoes.[251]

French fashion was followed in the Dutch Republic at that time, and people in New Netherland tried to keep up with it as well. The fashion prescribed, among other things, dark colors for men – often black, and many variations of gray for formal occasions; for more informal situations, men wore more colorful clothes.[252] In the second half of the century, the style would become more daring: Men dressed somewhat quasi-sloppily, and had their clothes decorated with ribbons, silver buttons, bows, plumes and lace. It was so important to Jeremias that he follow the fashion that it did not seem to bother him much when, in 1661, he received breeches that were too wide and a jerkin that was too tight; he just took it to be 'on account of the style.' Subsequently, he ordered a serge cloth suit, 'somewhat stylish, to be worn every day.' He also ordered a half dozen bands, of which at least two were to be with lace, and red cloth and silver braid to make a waistcoat (*hemtrock*).[253] Clearly, it was a sign of luxury in New Netherland if one could afford to buy good cloth and follow the latest fashion; it also provided opportunities to show that one could afford to buy new clothes.

Jeremias was not the only person in New Netherland who liked to dress according to the fashion. Lace, silver buttons, and gold and silver braid were among the popular items that were sent over to be traded.[254] Evidence that other, and less wealthy, people in the village also were aware of fashion changes emerges from a hat sale by Jan Claesz Backer in July 1659. According to the style at that time, the hats were all black, and varied in price from ƒ7-18 to ƒ11-16. They probably were tall, and had a wide brim with a ribbon ending in two flapping tail ends.[255]

That wealthier settlers tried to keep up with the latest European fashions does not mean that they could not adjust to their new environment. When Jeremias asked his mother to send him six new shirts in 1658, for example, he explained that the sleeves of three shirts should be somewhat finer than the body and somewhat wider than usual, for he was to wear them daily as half-shirts for the sake of coolness – for in the summer, 'one always goes about here with open sleeves.'[256]

In the Dutch Republic – especially after 1650 when the fashion trend became more daring and had more decorative elements – the position of tailors improved remarkably; they had more business, which gave them more status than when fashions had been less ornate.[257] In the upper Hudson, their situation may have been somewhat similar. In 1651, Jan Michielsz and Evert Wendel were granted the exclusive right to perform the trade of tailoring in Rensselaerswijck; the number of tailors in Beverwijck and the patroonship would increase rapidly during the 1650s. Almost twenty men in the area tried to make their living by tailoring at some time between 1652 and 1664 (see Appendix 6).

Between 1654 and 1662, Jeremias ordered much of his clothing from the fatherland, and thus was provided with clothes that followed the latest trends there. Local tailors made clothes for him on occasion, but much of their work consisted of changing or repairing clothes he already had, or decorating them with buttons and ribbons. Tailor Hendrick Rooseboom, for example, put braids around the pocket holes of Jeremias's cloak, 'innocent,' and pants in 1659, and Jan Vinhaegen decorated Jeremias's pants with ribbons and buttons on various occasions in 1658, 1660, and 1661.[258]

51. *Middle of the seventeenth century fashion for men and women in the Dutch Republic.
In J.H. der Kinderen-Besier,* Spelevaart der mode. De kledij onzer voorouders in de
zeventiende eeuw.*(Amsterdam: Querido's Uitgeversmaatschappij, 1950), 134, 150, 170.*

During the 1660s Jeremias's tailor accounts changed, more often mentioning the making of clothes. After Jeremias married in 1662, various clothing items for women were added to the bills, including standard women clothes like bodices, little mantels, aprons, bay or silk skirts, jackets, aprons, undervests, scarves, and night scarves (*nachthalsdoecken*). The style for women throughout the century did not change much in the fatherland, and certainly the excessive decorations that appeared in men's fashions were not used on women's outfits. Hoops made skirts stand out wide and broadened a woman's hips, while a bodice accentuated the narrow upper body. A woman's figure may almost have looked artificial. Ladies of standing sometimes dressed in a variation of the so-called *vlieger* costume, which usually consisted of a black over-garment that was worn over a bodice and skirt of different colors. It was accompanied by an eye-catching pleated or fan-like collar.[259] The neck line became deeper and broader, and was covered by older women with a collar (*bef*, *rabat*, or *neerstick*), while younger women left it bare and wore a scarf around the shoulders.[260] A *huik* – a cloak, dating from the sixteenth century, which appeared almost exclusively in Netherlands – protected women outside against the cold; it was put on the head with a sort of flat hat with a handle.[261] Maria van Cortlandt's clothes were not ordered from the fatherland, but were made by local tailors.

Not much later, various children's outfits are mentioned as well, such as different kinds of aprons, waistcoats, coats, suits of clothes, small collars (jabots), a small robe, and children's outfits of which the top and bottom parts were made out of one piece. Accounts of Frans Jansz Pruyn for 1668 through 1671 suggest that, when there was a great deal of work to be done, tailors worked at people's houses. Pruyn sometimes boarded for twelve or fifteen days at the house of the Van Rensselaers when he was making and repairing clothes for Jeremias, Maria, the children, Andries *de neger*, the negress and an Indian boy.[262] That tailors increasingly made inhabitants' clothes may be a sign that a style of clothing was developing that was more independent of trends followed in the Dutch Republic.

Wearing jewelry was, of course, a good way to show off one's wealth and position in society. The sale of items from the estate of Rutger Jacobsz, in 1665, was a good opportunity for Jeremias to buy some jewelry for Maria. Of all the bidders he bought most, such as a diamond ring (which were trendy in Amsterdam) for *f*17, a double hoop for *f*26, and a gold chain for *f*80. His purchase of a gold hairpin for *f*29 is interesting, as it indicates that Maria wore a headdress.[263] Originally, this was a simple brace with the purpose of keeping in place several small caps that women would sometimes wear at the same time. They could be very simple silver braces over the head, but they also could be decorated with pearls or other jewelry, a gold hairpin, and sometimes a pendant.[264] Headdresses were commonly worn in the Dutch Republic during the 1650s, and several women in Beverwijck owned them as well. Jan Labatie's wife Jilletje Claes wore one that had cost *f*12, and Jan Gerritsz van Marcken's inventory listed a silver headdress. Van Slichtenhorst's daughter Margaretha, who had married a successful trader, ordered a golden headdress for the value of about six beavers; and as Maria van Cortlandt was one of the most important women in the village, hers was likely made of gold as well.[265]

Maria also had to maintain her appearance so that others could always see that they where of good means. Outer appearance was an important way to demonstrate one's status and ability to allow himself the expense of luxury items. It was an important part of one's social life and role, and contributed a good deal to one's reputation.[266] The Van Rensselaers certainly made an effort to live according to their means, as the number one family in the upper Hudson area. They did this by having a large house, by having servants and slaves, and by following the French fashion. But even more important than outer appearances were the people whom they had to impress, and for whom they had to keep up their high reputation – those with whom the Van Rensselaers wanted to do business. They had to ensure that they maintained and expanded their contacts with these people. In April 1652, it may have seemed to Jan Baptist that they had to start all over again.

Social life: The importance of friends

In June 1651, when twenty-two-year-old Jan Baptist van Rensselaer stepped off the ship, stayed in Van Slichtenhorst's house, and began working on the patroonship in cooperation with Captain Slyter, people in the community must have had mixed expectations. They probably considered him – a 'real' Van Rensselaer – as one of the clicque of Van Slichtenhorst, Van Twiller, and Vastrick, and thus had negative feelings toward him in advance. Some may have thought that the situation would only become worse for them, while others may have hoped Jan Baptist would be able to change the situation somewhat. In any case, Jan Baptist's letter of September 1651 (only part of which survived the 1911 Capitol fire) mentions none of this. As a matter of fact, an impression almost of boyishness emerges as one reads his report of how well his falcon had come over, and how the bird was now 'king of all New Netherland.' What remains of the letter does not even mention Van Slichtenhorst, who by that time may have been back in the colony following his escape from jail in Manhattan.[267] The developing situation after Van Slichtenhorst's return also must have created tense moments for Jan Baptist. Stuyvesant's establishment of the village of Beverwijck, with its own court, must have been a threatening and humiliating experience for the young man.

As director of the patroonship, Jan Baptist understood that he was obligated to maintain contacts with colonists in Rensselaerswijck; but in order to make his family trading business work, he needed to confirm and solidify, and perhaps re-establish, contacts with inhabitants of Beverwijck as well. He had to make sure that he had the trust of the settlers in the upper Hudson. In the new situation, with a West India Company village as the center, he needed to make sure there was a solid, steady basis – consisting of a network of friends upon whom the Van Rensselaers could count – who would buy their merchandise and sell them their peltry.

In the fatherland, these friendships were often established among relatives, who often trusted each other the most; and in the upper Hudson, the Van Rensselaers followed this pattern.[268] They made sure to maintain family contacts in the New World such as cousin Arent van Curler, for example, and 'cousin Phlip' (Philip Pietersz Schuyler), who had become a cousin through his marriage to Margaretha van Slichtenhorst. In his study of friendship and the art of surviving in the seventeenth and eighteenth century, Luuc Kooijmans has described these relationships as friendships among relatives in pursuit of solidarity, in order to guarantee their property, good name, and social status despite all the risks.[269] Although care of the poor and needy, orphans, and the elderly by deaconry and other poor-relief institutions in the Dutch Republic was widely known and praised, anyone living in that time had to safeguard himself and his family against unexpected misfortunes; and he could insure himself and his family, more or less, by establishing a network of friends upon whom he could fall back in bad times. Only from those with whom one maintained obliging relationships – often relatives – could one expect help and support during periods of bad luck. These people were called 'the friends,' and one could turn to them in order to solve problems; in case of illness or decease, for example, they would help with the care of children.[270] Kiliaen van Rensselaer provides us with a good example: When his father died, his mother had been able to send him to his uncle Wolphert van Bijler in Amsterdam, where he learned the jewelry trade – and which would pave his way to success. When Wouter van Twiller was director of New Netherland, he helped his uncle Kiliaen by allowing him to transport animals from Manhattan to Rensselaerswijck. When Van Rensselaer died, the family could also turn to Van Twiller and, together with Anna van Rensselaer's brother Jan van Wely, he became guardian of the children in order to protect their rights to the estate. As we have seen, Wouter van Twiller maintained his involvement in the colony; and after his death, his widow Maria Momma and her brother Guilliam remained involved in the trade with Rensselaerswijck. When they discovered how disorderly Jan van Twiller had kept the accounts, and how much damage he had caused them by leaving Rensselaerswijck in 1657 with many large bills unpaid, the Mommas did not hesitate to ask Jeremias for assistance. He tried to help collect their outstanding debts and boarded their agent Jan Bastiaensz van Gutsenhoven, on whose work and conduct he reported to Guilliam Momma. This friendly exchange of services and favors between relatives had a long-lasting effect, and was carried over from one generation to the next.[271]

   To establish good relationships, Kooijmans found that one had to demonstrate that he or she was worthy of support and solidarity, and that one intended to give something in return. One had to build up credit for the times when it was needed, and make sure that others would feel obligated to support it. It was, in the first instance, important to show that one had something to offer, which usually happened through outward appearances of well-being, power, descent, and upbringing. In order to convince others that one was capable and willing to help, one first had to build up a good reputation – of which honorable and decent social behavior, combined with a sense of duty – were important ingredients. One should take care to be known as a reliable person who fulfilled his duties, such as the specific Christian obligations of going to church, leading a Christian life, and performing acts of charity.[272] To cultivate a friendship it was important to create good will, to which one's good social position and capabilities contributed greatly. One could create good will through various forms of 'politenesses': give compliments or small gifts to an individual, and invite him to get-togethers or dinner parties. Once the relationship was more or less established, it was important to maintain it; or to 'maintain correspondence,' as it was called, which happened through the exchange of letters or various politenesses. The relationship could be confirmed, for example, by asking friends to be godparents of the children or witnesses at a wedding.

Exchanging services with each other enabled people to maintain friendships. These services could vary: They might consist of small errands, or an offer to put up security in a financial transaction, help out with financing, or provide a loan. Reciprocity was the underlying principle of these exchanges of politenesses, services, and favors: A person who had accepted a service or gift considered himself obligated to return the service, although this was not specified or time-bound.[273] Guilliam Momma, for instance, repeatedly mentioned that Jeremias had obligated him by providing help; and when Jeremias suggested to Van Twiller's cousin Robert Vastrick that he send over a half-dozen hogsheads of good French wine, 'in order that the friendship may not entirely die out,' Vastrick replied that he would not fail to reciprocate the old relationship.[274] Although there were no legal sanctions for not fulfilling such expectations, it was considered a matter of honor and conscience – and noncompliance with moral obligations was usually punished by feelings of guilt and an injured reputation.[275] For the granting of credit, it was especially important for a merchant to have steady and reliable relationships, as it could be a long time before he would be paid for his goods. If a debtor failed to pay on time, his credit would usually be extended. Sometimes, this actually created a situation favorable to the creditor, as the debtor was then greatly obligated – and would probably not buy merchandise from anyone else until he had paid off his debt. Thus, extending a debt could guarantee the creditor a certain amount of business.[276]

Maintaining a friendship often required no more than an obligation; but 'true' friendship, based on affection and mutual sympathy, also existed. After his return to Amsterdam, Jan Baptist van Rensselaer wrote to Jeremias, advising his brother to deal only with reliable people. Among the 'friends' mentioned by Jan Baptist were Volckert Jansz Douw and Jan Thomasz, for whom he seems to have felt sympathy.[277] When he did not hear from his friends how they liked the goods he had sent them, he was surprised, especially about Volckert Jansz, 'my special friend, whom for that reason I call a rascal, since otherwise he is so quick with the pen and now, so soon after my departure so slow in writing.'[278] Unrelated individuals such as Pieter Hartgers and Abraham Staets also became close family friends.[279]

Jan Baptist and Jeremias van Rensselaer were closely connected, not only as brothers, but also as trading partners. They seem to have had a good relationship, and Jeremias may have taken mother Anna's advice to heart: '[R]espect your brother as the eldest and always maintain toward each other feelings of brotherly love.' She wrote, in March 1655,

> I am pleased to hear that you get along well with your brother. Continue therein, for it is very fine and lovely if brothers dwell together in harmony, as written in Psalm 133. Always respect him as the eldest brother...[280]

Jeremias always seems to have felt affection toward his brother; in 1663 he wrote that, although he had not written often, 'brotherly love has not died out,' and that he was 'always longing to be with you.'[281]

If we look at the social life of the Van Rensselaers and others in Beverwijck, we should keep in mind this seventeenth-century concept of friendship as a way to guarantee security in life. The establishment of Beverwijck and its court was a major change for the Van Rensselaers, as well as for the inhabitants of the settlement on the upper Hudson. The patroon was no longer in a position to make up the rules for the community; and if the Van Rensselaers wanted to continue a successful trade, they would have to compete; they would need to maintain relations with the most successful inhabitants of the settlement, and cooperate with other traders. They would need to confirm, strengthen, and maintain a network in the New World; they would have to look for reliable trading partners, including family relations as much as possible. Often this was done in the usual Dutch way, by drinking a glass of wine together or sharing a meal. Not only did they need a network in Amsterdam, but now the New World demanded it as well. Although they worked much of the time with their relatives, other inhabitants also became part of the network, in Beverwijck as well as in Manhattan.

Social life: Maintaining friendships in the New World

In the small, young community that was in the process of being built up, where every inhabitant had to work hard to survive, the life-style of the Van Rensselaers undoubtedly represented something of the traditional order as it existed in the fatherland. The brothers, despite their young age, represented the patroon; they managed and were part-owners of a large manor, lived in the largest house in the village, dressed according to the fashion, and had several servants and slaves. They were unique in the sense that, as 22-year-olds, they had arrived with more capital behind them than any of the other colonists. When Claes Gerritsz nicknamed several houses in the community, in 1655, he undoubtedly had this difference in mind when he dubbed the patroon's house '*Vroegh Bedorven*' – 'Spoiled Early.'[282]

Jeremias van Rensselaer certainly participated in social events. In New Amsterdam, he established and strengthened contacts for the trade. Tavern accounts of Abraham de la Noy testify that he spent time at his establishment having a drink, which he occasionally combined with a game at the pool table (*trocktaefel*).[283] Jeremias boarded with Oloff Stevensz van Cortlandt, who had known Kiliaen van Rensselaer in earlier years; and, in 1661, he would make the relationship between the two families even stronger by marrying Stevensz's daughter Maria. In Beverwijck and Rensselaerswijck, Jeremias maintained his relations as well, for example, by going with friends on a pleasure ride with the horses or, during the cold winters, making sure to participate in the popular sleigh races.[284]

It seems that Jeremias got along well with people, and was open to a sense of humor. A month before Jeremias became director of Rensselaerswijck, Evert Nolden was not afraid to joke with him about his future position. Nolden made out an account of *f*15 for wine and beer, which Jeremias used with Sander [Leendertsz] and Stuyvesant, to '*Joncker* Jeremyas van Rensselaer, hereditary commander of Krelo, co-director and burgomaster of the colony of Rensselaerswijck in New Netherland, Captain'; he signed it as 'Evert Nolden, *vijant der funnen*' (enemy of the rascals).[285] After Jan Baptist had left, Jeremias maintained this life-style, as it was of great importance to keep up good relations with their friends. The Van Rensselaer Manor Papers provide us with a glimpse into his social life; an account presented by Anthony Jansz, for example, indicates that Jeremias made sure to entertain the friends in an appropriate way, thus creating and maintaining bonds of friendship and social cohesion. He drank wine in the tavern with his cousins Arent van Curler and 'Phlip' Schuyler, with Andries Teller (who later would become his brother-in-law), and with such inhabitants as the merchant Jan Bastiaensz, tavern keeper and glazier Jurriaen Theunisz, the surgeon *Meester* Jacob, Volckert Jansz Douw, and Hendrick van Bael. With Jan Bastiaensz and Harmen Vedder, in particular, Jeremias seems to have enjoyed combining the tavern visit with *trocken*. All kinds of events offered the opportunity to share drinks – such as, for instance, the sale of some horses, an event 'with the deputees,' the time that 'the English came,' or 'the purchase of the grist mill.' At other occasions he sent out his negro Andries, the maid, or the boy to obtain beer or wine, while entertaining the friends at home in the patroon's house.[286]

After Jeremias's marriage, the patroon's house apparently remained a frequent host to visitors. In August 1662, for example, a month after the wedding, director general Stuyvesant stayed with the Van Rensselaers for ten or twelve days. Jeremias occupied a position in which he was expected to maintain good relationships with important people like Fort Orange's commissary Johannes La Montagne, or other West India Company officials, and this was commonly done by sharing a drink or meal. Most likely, the patroon occasionally provided dinners to entertain important people, such as members of the two courts.[287] Trading relationships remained important; in 1663, at Jan Baptist's request, Jeremias hosted and entertained his brother's business partner Arent Jansz Moesman. In September, he would write that he had fulfilled the request regarding Sr. Arent Jansz Moesman to the extent that he could, 'for according to [our] old custom we lustily drank to one another,' and he had invited him to stay at the house again in a few weeks.[288] Accounts for obtaining wine at the local taverns testify to such events.[289]

Only on a rare occasion is it mentioned that Indians visited the patroon's house while Jan Baptist and Jeremias occupied it. Natives certainly do not seem to have come as frequently, nor in such great numbers, as during Van Slichtenhorst's directorship. After the *bijeenwoninge* was built, they distributed their visits more among the various inhabitants, who then sometimes built special 'Indian houses' to accommodate them. But, when uncertainties arose regarding earlier Indian deeds, Jeremias needed their testimony to prove that the land had been bought for the patroon. In May 1664, for example, the Mahican Queskimiet, (son of Pacies), Wickepe, and *Kleyn Davidtie* (Little David) were at the patroon's house for that reason, together with two interpreters, Jan Dareth and Marten Gerritsz.[290] The note made about the visit is short, and does not mention any kind of entertainment.

The trading season was the time for entertaining to promote the business; the winter offered plenty of opportunities to maintain social contacts within the community, as snow and ice usually isolated it from the rest of New Netherland for several months. The thick ice made it easy to visit people on the other side of the river, while the snow made it possible to take sleigh rides to visit the farmers. After having indulged in sleigh races in earlier years, Jeremias later seems to have readjusted to other activities, such as 'the old winter custom, namely of one neighbor visiting the other.'[291] Altogether, the patroon's house hosted many people during the time the Van Rensselaers occupied it. Contrary to Robert Wheeler's idea that there was hardly any active social life in the director's house, there is certainly no lack of evidence that the Dutch habit of drinking wine and entertaining friends was well maintained there.[292]

Church membership

At the end of 1658, twenty-six-year-old Jeremias was the one in the colony representing the patroon. Not only did he have to maintain the community's respect for himself, but he was also responsible for the reputation of his family. Honorable and decent behavior were key ingredients of the good reputation to which Anna van Rensselaer sometimes referred when she warned Jeremias, for example, to 'shun the company of light [women] of whom New Netherland is full, and guard yourself against drinking, which is the root of all evil.'[293] Entertainment of friends was a requirement for the development and maintenance of a trading network, and outer appearance such as clothing, a large and well-decorated house, and possession of servants (and in New Netherland, slaves) were important ways to show the outside world that one was reliable.

Mother Anna, however, referred several times to something she seems to have considered more important. When her son reported, in June 1658, that he had had bad luck with animals and merchandise, she took the opportunity to speak out about some of her serious concerns. Like many people, she may have thought disasters and bad luck were signs of God's punishing hand; therefore, she suggested that the cause of the trouble could be the fact that he did not serve God as he should. Anna wrote:

> I understand from your brother that he has urged you several times to become a member of God's church, but that he has not been able to induce you to do so, because you wish to have a freer rein and to indulge in greater dissipation in this corrupt world, which grieves me exceedingly. It is namely clearly written that God can be found only by those who seek Him and that one must first of all seek the kingdom of God and His justice and that then all other things will be bestowed upon us. Therefore, let the fear of the Lord be planted in your heart, for that is the beginning of all wisdom, and as you now occupy the place of the patroon, you have the utmost need of wisdom and good judgment. Therefore, see to it that you conduct yourself honorably among the people and not indulge in excessive eating and drinking, in order that you may earn praise and a good reputation...[294]

Anna may have been influenced by the spiritual movement of certain Calvinist ministers that was called the *Nadere Reformatie* (Further Reformation). During the 1650s, this movement sought much publicity and, in several writings, ministers reacted to the moral decay they saw in the world. As a church-goer, Anna probably was familiar with the ideas of Amsterdam ministers like Petrus Wittewrongel about Christian marital, educational, and moral doctrine. She also may have practiced Wittewrongel's extensive instructions on devotion at home, such as reading the Bible, singing psalms, praying, and maintaining edifying conversations and exercises in catechism.[295]

By June 1660, Jeremias seems to have adjusted himself to the task of being the colony's director. At the age of 28, he finally wrote his mother that he had joined the church the year before and had made his confession of faith, so that 'I now also take communion at the Lord's table, in remembrance of Him.' He had already taught himself several psalms; during the long winter evenings, he intended to sing more of them as pleasant entertainment, as did many people in the fatherland.[296] Could his mother make sure that Cornelis de Key made him another psalter to fit his golden clasps, Jeremias asked, 'one of the thinnest and most oblong kind, to carry in the pocket?' In addition, he requested a rhymed psalter, like his uncle Van Wely's.[297]

His increased involvement with religion may also have encouraged Jeremias to read more about the subject. Perhaps (if they had not yet been sold) he would read through the books he had brought when he first came to New Netherland: French and Dutch versions of the Testament, the Mark of Salvation (*Mercktecken der Salicheyt*), Vondel's *Joseph* (*In Dotan* or *In Egypten*, Amsterdam, 1640), or another book he had brought along, a treatment of faith.[298] Literature of a religious nature generally was most popular; and, keeping in mind the further developments in Jeremias's life, it seems likely that he would have intended to develop his interest in religious matters at this point in his life. He would eventually become a loyal church member; he was an occupant of the consistory bench in church from 1667 to 1669, when he served as a deacon, and again in 1673, probably until his death in 1674, when he was elder.[299]

Marriage

Jeremias's interest in religion, and his involvement in church rituals such as the Holy Communion, may have had something to do with his developing relationship with Maria van Cortlandt, a daughter of Oloff Stevensz van Cortlandt, with whom he stayed in Manhattan. She was very religious and, like the majority of women, had joined the church at an early age, a few months before she turned sixteen.[300] Jeremias married Maria on the twelfth of July, 1662. An important step had been taken earlier, when they promised to marry each other. According to Dutch law, a promise of marriage could only be dissolved with the agreement of both parties – it was impossible to end the commitment unilaterally. If one party broke the promise, the other party would usually just agree; but sometimes a woman would insist that the man marry her anyway. This often happened when there had been sexual relations between the two. If she were pregnant, most women would demand marriage in order to regain their 'lost honor.'[301] In Beverwijck, as we saw before, the consistory brought Claes Ripsz before the court in 1654, and Ripsz was put in irons until he promised to marry the woman with whom he often slept, and whose child he admitted fathering. He had refused marriage, claiming that he awaited word from his father about the matter.[302] The disadvantaged party could also demand payment of a sum of money to compensate for the damage, as the woman would have 'lost her honor.' Another Beverwijck inhabitant, the merchant Dirck Jansz Croon, nearly found himself in this circumstance when Maria Wessels, a spinster (*jonge dochter*) at New Amsterdam, intended to sue him over a broken promise to marry her – 'and now on the contrary he has married someone else.' While the document was drawn up by notary public Dirck van Schelluyne, it was never signed, and thus the case does not seem to have been pursued.[303]

In the case of Jeremias and Maria, if one of them had wanted to cancel the marriage promise, it could only have been done by mutual agreement. Maria could still have escaped if her parents had objected, claiming she had given her promise without their permission; until she reached age twenty, Maria still was a minor and needed parental consent. But there were no objections – and the next step was taken on April 27, when the banns were registered in the Dutch Reformed church at New Amsterdam. When they announced their intended marriage, the couple declared their willingness to wed in the presence of a minister or the magistrates; after the announcement, their marriage was considered to be firm commitment. The event started the wedding process, which would be completed by a wedding ceremony in church or at the magistracy. The agreement to marry could no longer be broken, except through the magistracy. It was the rule, in Holland, that the marriage had to be publicly announced three times – so that before the wedding date, interested parties such as family members, friends, or previous fiancees could express objections to the marriage in writing. According to church rules, money, social inequality, or difference in age was not supposed to play a role.[304] The time between the announcement and the wedding usually was a period of various festivities. If the marriage were accompanied by a prenuptial agreement, a great dinner party (*huwelijck-sluitmaal*) would often be organized on the day of the announcement, attended by close relatives such as parents, brothers, sisters, brothers- and sisters-in-law, uncles, and aunts. The three successive public announcements were often occasions for other dinners (*gebodenmalen*) or a pre-wedding (*voorbruiloft*) party, while the wedding party itself sometimes lasted for several days.[305] David Pietersz Schuyler's intended marriage, for example, was entered on October 13, 1657; and on the September 6, Jeremias wrote that they could begin partying almost any day.[306]

Unfortunately, no information about Jeremias van Rensselaer's wedding seems to have survived; but most likely there were several days of celebration between April 27 and July 12. In the Dutch Republic, celebrations could be so exuberant that strict Calvinists protested against some people's extravagant life-style. It is not known whether the so-called luxury law, which had been introduced in Amsterdam in 1655, had any influence on wedding parties in New Netherland. This law was a reaction against the pursuit of luxury and pleasure in some circles in Amsterdam, and had been introduced by the mayor and medical doctor Nicolaes Tulp; the luxury law was directed against the excesses of wedding parties, among others things. It prescribed that a wedding party not last longer than two days, that the number of guests be limited to fifty, and that any one meal should not have more than two courses, in which no sugar dishes were to be included. No more than six musicians were allowed to provide entertainment.[307] In the last weeks of May, Jeremias was still in Rensselaerswijck; but by the end of June, he would be in Manhattan, where at some point they may very well have begun celebrating.[308]

Soon after the wedding, Jeremias wrote to his brother about it, but did not go into any detail about the celebration and festivities. He asked Jan Baptist to announce the marriage to his mother, and to tell Anna van Rensselaer that he would not have ventured to marry without his mother's knowledge if they had not been so far apart.[309] In Holland, parental consent would not have been required for Jeremias, as he was already thirty-one years of age; nevertheless, it usually was strongly desired, even if one was no longer a minor. Men who were eager to marry needed parental consent until they reached their majority at the age of twenty-five. If minor newlyweds had not gotten their parents' permission, the marriage was not valid.[310] Parental consent was considered so important that – even when the newlyweds had both reached their majority, but did not have parental consent – a minister would sometimes punish them for this 'shameful indecency' by excluding the couple from the Holy Communion until they had shown more respect for their parents.[311]

Jeremias would not write to his mother about the marriage until five-and-a-half weeks after the wedding. He tried to assure her that the marriage had not been a foolish or impulsive step; he had already been thinking about Maria for a year or two, when he would occasionally go to the Manhattans on business. That he had not informed his mother of his plans earlier 'was rather due to his timidity,' he explained; and to 'put her mind at ease,' Jeremias thanked the good Lord for His mercy in granting him 'such a good partner':

> [...] To live together so calmly and peacefully with a wife who has always led a good moral life and feared the Lord God is the best thing I could wish for here on earth. You may think perhaps that she is still a little young and therefore not well able to take care of a household. She is only entering her eighteenth year [Maria had turned seventeen on July 20], but nevertheless we get along together very well in the household...[312]

Despite his explanation, Anna may have found it hard to accept; to his disappointment, she would not write back until after the birth of their first son.[313]

Anna van Rensselaer might not have been unhappy with her son's choice, however, if she had been included in the preparations. Indeed, Maria van Cortlandt was a well-selected partner. She led a good Christian life, as Jeremias had informed his mother, having become a member of the church when she was fifteen. She would be a good addition to the family in other ways, as she brought along money and –

especially in New Netherland circles – respect. Oloff Stevensz had been a long-time business contact of the Van Rensselaers, and it was not unusual for a merchant to marry the daughter of a business partner.[314] When Jeremias wrote that he had already considered Maria for a while, he certainly had weighed issues other than love and affection. He could look to his own father's example to see how important the choice of a marriage partner could be. Undoubtedly, the f12,000 dowry of Hillegond van Bijler had encouraged Kiliaen to buy the two lots along the Keizersgracht upon which he built their new home, *Het Gekruijste Hart*.[315] And when Hillegond died in 1627, within a year Kiliaen would marry Anna van Wely, daughter of his former business partner Jan van Wely, one of Amsterdam's wealthiest and most successful jewelers. As soon as a woman married, she lost the right to dispose of her capital; but that did not mean that she was totally at the mercy of her husband, or that he could waste her family fortune. Most likely, lengthy negotiations in the presence of several family members had taken place before Kiliaen and Anna were able to marry. Their prenuptial agreement stated that her personal fortune could be used by Van Rensselaer during his lifetime; but for all legal purposes, chattel and real property would remain forever in her name.[316] The addition of Anna's capital to his own fortune not only contributed to Kiliaen's reclamation project in Het Gooi and the purchase of Crailo, a country home (*lusthoeve*) near the towns of Bussum and Huizen, but also to the establishment and development of Rensselaerswijck.[317] A seventeenth-century marriage was considered a partnership in many respects, and Kiliaen's marriages were good examples of this arrangement.

Maria's father, Olof Stevensz van Cortlandt, had profited of his wife's wealth and influence as well. Stevensz had come to New Amsterdam in 1637 as a soldier for the West India Company; director-general Kieft appointed him as commissary, or superintendent of cargoes at the port. In 1642, he married Anneke Loockermans, a sister of the leading merchant and Indian trader at Manhattan, Govert Loockermans. Shortly after the wedding, Stevensz was appointed keeper of the public store – and thenceforth, his advancement in wealth and influence would be quite rapid. In addition to his appointments under the company, he was the agent for Wouter van Twiller, who upon his return to the fatherland had retained extensive landed interests in New Netherland. Stevensz also took an active part in church affairs as deacon and, between 1655 and 1664, was frequently orphan master and mayor of New Amsterdam.[318] He had long maintained relations with the Van Rensselaers. Anthonie de Hooges, Rensselaerswijck's secretary, had stayed with the Van Cortlandts after his arrival at Manhattan in 1643, and during the 1650s Jeremias was always a welcome guest.[319]

The marriage between Jeremias and Maria meant the addition of important family connections to both Jeremias and the Van Cortlandts; and as a consequence, possibilities for the trade expanded for both families. The establishment of close relations with a leading Manhattan family benefited the interests of the upper Hudson region in general, as well. Anna van Rensselaer, however, may have realized that this marriage also was the beginning of a division in her family, and that ownership of the patroonship and a good part of the family fortune would now be divided between two worlds. As Maria had been born in New Nether-

52. *Evert Duyckinck, stained-glass window from Beverwijck's church with the coat of arms of Jan Baptist van Rensselaer, 1656. Beverwijck's magistrates also had their coat of arms in the windows of the church. Those of Rutger Jacobsz, Philip Pietersz Schuyler, Evert Jansz Wendel and Andries Herbertsz can still be seen in the Albany Institute of History and Art.*
The Metropolitan Museum of Art, bequest of Mrs. J. Insley Blair, 1952.

land, her frame of reference would always be the New World; Holland would be a faraway place, perhaps to be visited some time, but never more than that. As a mother, Anna understood that Maria in later years would fight for the future of her children; she could not have known for sure, but she may have sensed what could happen. The marriage would eventually lead to a situation where, toward the end of the century, Rensselaerswijck was completely in the possession of the family's American branch.[320]

But, in the summer of 1662, the patroon's house was being prepared for Maria van Cortlandt's arrival: Annie *de waster* and Jannetie Pouwels were each paid ƒ11-10 in June for cleaning the house; and in July, Pieter Adriaensz finished the gate. For ƒ16, Manhattan glazier Evert Duyckinck made a stain glass window in the church with Jeremias's coat of arms. The new window would be added to those already there, and which displayed the coats of arms of Jan Baptist and some magistrates of Beverwijck.[321] Thus, Maria was sure to notice the Van Rensselaers' position in the community, and would receive the inhabitants' respect.

Family life: Illness, children, and friends

Despite all preparations, Maria van Cortlandt would not have much opportunity to enjoy living in the patroon's house. In the fall of 1662, she was taken with that most feared of childhood illnesses – smallpox – which raged so severely as to be 'indescribable.'[322] Smallpox was certainly not uncommon at that time, and nearly everyone had it at some time in his or her life. The general notion in the early years of the Dutch Republic, according to Benjamin Roberts (in his study on Dutch childrearing practices in the seventeenth and eighteenth centuries), was that children who survived smallpox would be healthier and stronger because they had built resistance against other illnesses.[323] Jeremias let his mother know that Maria had had her share of the disease, 'so that one can still notice it by looking at her, but it does not amount to much, for, thank God, she came through it all right.'[324] He felt relieved, since many children endured side effects of smallpox that left them disfigured, crippled, or even blind. Although the word *kinderpocken* suggests that only children contracted the disease, adults sometimes fell victim as well. Children, in fact, had the greatest risk of infection; in the Dutch Republic, 90 percent of the victims of smallpox between 1710 and 1810 were younger than ten years old.[325] In Beverwijck, the church buried at least eighteen adults and eighteen children that year, of whom many were probably victims of the epidemic.[326]

After the birth of their son Kiliaen in August 1663, Maria was 'reasonably strong and well,' according to Jeremias; but 'her right leg still hurts her at the hip, so that she cannot use it very well.' The pains lasted at least until April 1664, when she had improved to such an extent that she could move the leg again and 'also began to walk with a crutch under one arm and a cane in the other hand.' Maria could go no farther than the floor of the cellar kitchen, and 'it was not until the second of this month that she was churched' – which means that she did not make her first trek out of the house until then.[327] Usually this church visit, described by Joyce Goodfriend as a religious ritual signifying the end of a woman's confinement, would be performed about six weeks after the delivery of a baby.[328] In the summer of 1664, Jeremias and his family were able to visit Maria's parents.[329] In the following years the ailment would persevere, and various methods were applied to cure it: another childbirth, red salve or balm of Joost de Coge of Haerlem, two or three bottles of oil or sulphur, surgery whereby Jacob de Hinsse cut a hole into the thick of the leg. Nevertheless, the pain and fevers came back repeatedly, and Maria would have a problem with her leg for the rest of her life.[330] In fact, Peter Christoph has suggested, Maria suffered from septic arthritis accompanied by osteomyelitis of the femur, and periods of relative remission concealed the course of the disease raging in her body. Her condition could have been caused by a bacterial infection, which may have entered Maria's hip from a secondary infection of a smallpox lesion.[331] In spite of her pains, Maria was not a person to sit still; and by April 1665 Jeremias had taken up brewing for her sake, since she had always managed this activity in her father's house.[332]

Kiliaen was the first of seven children born to the young couple, of which six would survive.[333] At his birth in 1663, several women and a midwife were probably at the house. As soon as a woman had labor pains, usually another next of kin, neighbors, and friends would be informed.[334] Jeremias's letters do not provide information about the event; but ten years later, when another son Johannes was born, he would write that the little boy had been delivered quickly, 'without our having any other women with us than the midwife and Maria Loockermans (who wetnursed the child), whom an hour or two before we had sent for with the sleigh. Yes, the little fellow came so speedily, that we did not have time to call our nearest neighbor's wife.'[335] Most likely Jeremias was in the immediate area at the time of birth, which seems to have been common. The fact that innkeeper Hendrick Jochemsz's wife was in childbirth, for example, was noted as a valid excuse for his having failed to list a half barrel of beer for the excise.[336] After the delivery of a child, the midwife would check the sex and congratulate the parents. The baby was wrapped in warm diapers and laid in the arms of the grandmother or the next of kin. Afterward, the infant would be lightly swaddled and offered to its father – a symbolic gesture. By accepting the child into his hands, according to Roberts, the father acknowledged the child legally as his own.[337] For Kiliaen's birth, everything seems to have been well organized. Jeremias wrote to Oloff Stevensz that he had a healthy son and, more important, that his wife had survived the delivery:

> ... last Friday, being the 24th August, 1663 at 8.00 in the morning my wife, (your honor's daughter) after she had [document damaged] two or three days, was delivered of a fine young son, who was baptized yesterday, and whom we have had named Kiliaen... My wife is, thank God, still well and strong considering the circumstances, as is also our son, who is a beloved child to his mother and a welcome son to his father. May the good Lord let him grow up in virtue, in order that he may be the same to his grandfather and grandmothers.[338]

That the baby was named after Jeremias's father, Kiliaen, was according to Dutch custom. The second child, a daughter, would be named Anna after her grand-mother (Maria's mother), and the third child Hendrick after Jeremias's grandfather and his eldest brother, 'as the Hendricks had quite died out in the family.'[339]

The old Catholic custom of naming 'godparents' for a child was maintained by the Reformed church as they, or 'baptism witnesses' (*doopgetuygen*) had a very important function. In particular, they were expected to ensure the Christian upbringing of the child in case one of the parents died. The child's father usually announced who would be witnesses at the baptism, and the minister decided whether those individuals were acceptable.[340] Oloff Stevensz and Jeremias's brother Jan Baptist were chosen as godfathers (*compeer*) for little Kiliaen; but because they were not personally present, *Pieteroom* (Pieter Claerbout, who at that time was reader and precentor of the church) acted as sponsor for Oloff Stevensz, and Abraham Staets for Jan Baptist. The mothers of Jeremias and Maria were chosen as godmothers and, due to their absence, Philip Schuyler's wife Margaretha presented the child for baptism in Anna's place, while the *schout*'s wife, Anthonia van Rijswijck, carried it to church in the place of Maria's mother Anna.[341] Jeremias wrote nothing about the christening dinner that undoubtedly took place, as this festivity was very popular in the fatherland.

At the baptism, the witnesses – who were, according to Dutch custom, usually all godparents – promised a christening gift (*pillegift*) for the child. These gifts were significant, and could consist of valuable items such as memorial coins or spoons (*geboortepenning* or *geboortelepel*), a silver bell or beaker, or a baby-linen basket with appurtenances. Money or interest vouchers (*rentebrieven*) could be found among the gifts, as well. In the Dutch Republic, the custom of appointing baptism witnesses sometimes got out of hand; such expensive gifts would be given and so many witnesses chosen that, in various places, limits were imposed on the value of the gift and the number of witnesses.[342] In April 1664, half a year after Kiliaen's birth, Jeremias and Maria received two silver salt cellars from Anna van Rensselaer as a christening gift to Kiliaen, and Jan Baptist sent a present as well.[343] Usually these *pillegifts* were promised at the time of birth, but would be given only after the child had survived the critical phase of the first months or years. Richard van Rensselaer, as the godfather of daughter Anna (born in 1665), promised a piece of gold worth 28 guilders as a christening gift. He may have forgotten his promise, as Maria would remind him about it in 1678.[344] Jeremias and Maria usually asked family members to be godparents; according to Groenhuis, parents in the Dutch Republic often tried to find socially important people for the occasion, so that these witnesses became something of a status symbol. Thus, the witnesses' social status was often the same as or higher than the parents' position. Names of witnesses at a christening often reveal something of a family's social environment, as these individuals were always friends or family members.[345]

The seventeenth century was not a time when people publicly expressed their emotions very much. 'Personal documents were not common outlets for displaying grief, and correspondence had a more informative character than overt display of emotion,' Benjamin Roberts has written, and 'too much expression of sadness in general on the death of a family member was considered un-Christian like.' God had predestined the moment of death, and nobody should resist God's will.[346] Jeremias's communications nevertheless suggest that he was often worried about Maria's health, and that he was happy with his son; he seems to have enjoyed being a father. On September 12, 1663, for example, he wrote to Anna van Rensselaer:

> Young Kiliaen, it seems, will abide with us, for he has already had the jaundice and the rash and is fond of suckling. I hope that the Good Lord will let him grow up in virtue, so that you will still have the joy of seeing your children's children...[347]

It is not so strange that Jeremias referred to the possible death of a child. In the Dutch Republic, 50 percent of children died before reaching age twenty-five; Beverwijck's church buried nine children in 1657, twelve in 1658, fourteen in 1659, seven in 1660, eleven in 1661, eighteen in 1662, and three in 1663.[348] Between 1654 and 1664, the church's small pall was rented for more than a hundred children. Maria and Jeremias had to deal with this sad event when, in 1670, Maria was delivered of a little boy who died in the agony of childbirth. They buried the baby three days later in the patroon's garden.[349] Here and there in Jeremias's letters we can find more information about Kiliaen and, later, the other children. In March 1664, Jeremias would write to grandfather Oloff that the boy was growing bravely, and a month later he let grandmother Anna van Rensselaer know that 'our Kiliaen is a healthy and big, fat [boy].' In October, he was strong and well and ran around everywhere; and in April 1665, the child was growing 'lustily and begins to talk a little in broken language. He is a sweet boy.' Soon he started to recognize people and, according to father Jeremias, he seems to have liked his relatives. In 1665, 'Kiliaen kept calling for a long time for his grandmother and for his uncle and aunt Cornelia, so that even now, when he is asked about them, he answers with a sad voice "Ah", and points to the yachts on the river, although it is now [damaged document] since mother left.'[350]

Jeremias and his family stayed in the patroon's house, where they conducted their family life, had a daughter in the winter of 1665, received people from the village or business partners from *patria*, and where Jeremias administered the patroonship and wrote many letters and accounts. All this would end abruptly in 1666 when, on April 7, the ice in the river began to move. 'Counted roughly,' Jeremias wrote, 'fully forty houses and barns have been carried away, among which our house in which we lived, the barn and the brewery, the new as well as the old are lost also, so that hardly any traces can be found of where they have stood.' A large piece of ice had begun to move – and just carried his house away.[351] The house that had been built by Arent van Curler in the early 1640s, and which had hosted so many Mahicans during various land conveyances in the 1640s and so many Maquaes during their passages and trading visits, the house that for more than eight years had served as a church for all inhabitants, and which had been totally repaired by Jeremias in 1660 to serve as his family dwelling and the patroonship's main quarters – it was simply carried away by a piece of ice.[352]

After the disaster, their relatives and friends helped out. Jeremias's family, which by then perhaps also included his younger brother Richard van Rensselaer, who had arrived in the colony in July 1664, first fled to Philip Schuyler's home, were they found shelter for several days. Subsequently, they moved into the rear chamber of Jan Bastiaensz van Gutsenhoven's house, which probably was the house with the stone gable that Bastiaensz had bought from Sander Leendertsz Glen in 1661, and which stood on the east side of present-day Broadway, a little to the south of the *Ruttenkil*.[353] Van Gutsenhoven died sometime in 1666-67, and the Van Rensselaers stayed in the house for as long as one-and-a-half years, although it seems to have been confiscated by the English in 1667.[354] As this house was also exposed to the danger of ice drifts and freshets, the family moved around June 1668 into the house of Willem Teller, who had become related to them through the marriage of his son Andries to Sophia van Cortlandt (Appendix 8, I, no. 8; III, no. 10). This house was located farther away from the river, at the southwest corner of present-day State Street and Broadway, just north of the *Ruttenkil*. By that time, Jeremias was busy building a dwelling at the fifth creek, at a location where he had already planted an orchard and erected his brewery, and where 'with the help of God, no danger of ice drifts is to be expected.'[355] Having a network of friends certainly proved to be important. In their emergency, Jeremias and his family were able to rely on their friends in Beverwijck for more than two years.

One can only wonder about the bond the Van Rensselaers felt with the land on such a distant continent, far away from patria. When Jan Baptist was back in Holland, after having spent eight years in New Netherland, he would write: 'Being here, I did not like it and was very sorry that I had not remained in New Netherland, but I am getting better used to it.'[356] Surely he would have thought of the Indian summer, which Van Slichtenhorst described as 'the most beautiful he had ever seen in his life.' Not only would he have remembered his friends – when, in

1664, he sent Abraham Staets a pennant to fly on his ship along with the flag of Pieter Hartgers – but also the great Hudson River, its beautiful scenery, and the enormous space of the New World.[357] Later, Jan Baptist would repeatedly consider opportunities to return to Rensselaerswijck; but he never did. In February 1666, he married his cousin Susanna van Wely, who would die less than a year later during the birth of their son Kiliaen. Almost thirteen years later, Jan Baptist would die in Holland at the age of fifty, without ever seeing the New World again. His son would be in Rensselaerswijck from 1689 to 1696.[358]

Like his older brother, Jeremias would never cross the ocean again. He did not mention going back to the Dutch Republic until October 1664, when they planned to justify accounts.[359] As the situation in the upper Hudson became worse, he would occasionally suggest selling farms, and even the whole colony, in order to bring some relief to the situation. He always expressed the wish to keep the family's possessions in Het Gooi, in *patria*. While this may suggest that he did not like Rensselaerswijck, it is hard to estimate his feelings for the country. Jeremias rarely spoke of Rensselaerswijck in negative terms, and only during the hard times of 1660 would he describe his surroundings '*wilde lant*,' which was translated as 'this heathenish land,' but could also mean this 'Indian country'; in 1669, he spoke of it as 'this distant and strange country.' When Maria was ill and needed medical help, he missed the presence of a good doctor and 'wished we were in *patria*,' so that they could determine whether her leg could be cured.[360] His correspondence, however, does not suggest that he ever seriously considered going back to Holland to live; plans to visit with his family in Holland were postponed repeatedly for various reasons: no chance to bring with him any returns from the colony, or too many infringements being made on the patroonship's rights, or Maria's confinement. In the end, Jeremias would never return to *patria*.[361] One could ask whether Jeremias and his relatives, in 1655, had planned that he would always stay in Rensselaerswijck, or whether they might have arranged for their domain to be managed in some other way – for instance, by rotating its direction among the brothers. In any case, Jeremias (perhaps unknowingly) made a decision in 1662 that would have a profound impact on the rest of his own, and the colony's, life: Without his relatives' knowledge, he married a woman who had been born in New Netherland. The marriage fitted-in perfectly within the rules and customs of maintaining friendships and establishing relations as they were followed in the Dutch Republic. The only difference was the setting – the New World. In New Netherland, the marriage enlarged trading possibilities and enhanced Jeremias's prestige, while also causing interests in Rensselaerswijck and the family fortune, from that point on, to be divided between two worlds, the old and the new.

Following his marriage, Jeremias repeated his suggestion that the patroonship be sold. One could ask what he would have done if the patroon and co-directors had followed his advice. Would he have taken Maria and the children back to the Dutch Republic? Or would he have established himself as one of several merchants in the New World, perhaps at Manhattan? Rensselaerswijck had to deal with many hardships. At the same time, the domain provided Jeremias with a position that he probably never would have occupied in the fatherland: As one of the wealthiest and most respected members of society, he lived in the largest house, dressed well, had several servants and even slaves, and dealt with the most important people. Evert Nolden may have seen it clearly in 1658, after all, when he addressed Jeremias as '*joncker.*' Even though Van Rensselaer did not use the title, Rensselaerswijck may have given him the opportunity to feel like a 'nobleman.'[362] His marriage offered the prospect of acquiring more wealth and respect in the New World. Did he really want to go back – or was his desire really to keep the family's country home in Het Gooi as something of an 'emigrant's dream?' Did the family's holdings provide him with some security in the fatherland, to which he could always return, while permitting him to enjoy all the advantages of the New World? Lived in New Netherland since 1654 had made Jeremias more rooted there, and perhaps he felt increasingly responsible for his duties concerning the patroonship – which, then, would often become a reason not to make a planned trip to the fatherland. A voyage to Amsterdam would have brought him back to the security of his childhood; at the same time, it also would have demanded a discussion of accounts, ownership, and other business-related topics about the colony – problems that, in Rensselaerswijck, he could so conveniently refer to the patroon and co-directors. His relatives may even have considered whether it would be wise to appoint someone else as director. Jeremias lived in two worlds: He maintained frequent contacts with his relatives in Amsterdam and always considered their ownership of the patroonship; at the same time, he was becoming ever more rooted in New Netherland due to his personal life. In both worlds, he had strong ties and responsibilities, of which Crailo in Het Gooi perhaps gave him the sense of childhood security.

Jeremias van Rensselaer was forty-two years old when he died on the 12th of October 1674, leaving twenty-nine-year-old Maria with five children and a sixth to come, which would be named Jeremias. He was buried in the patroon's garden, where their stillborn baby also lay; four years later, his brother Nicolaes would be laid to rest there, too.[363] The garden was probably the last resting place for Maria and the other children, as well: Their son Kiliaen, in September 1719, would make clear in his will that he wished to be interred in the old burying place to the north of the old fort at Albany, by which he probably meant the family plot in the patroon's garden.[364]

Conclusion

Trade determined life in Beverwijck. Especially during the spring, summer, and early fall, people adjusted their activities to it. They looked forward to the arrival of Indians with peltries, and regulations were made and continuously changed regarding the way the trade was performed. Rules were made to regulate the trade in various items, specifically weapons and alcoholic drink. The fur trade drew many to the upper Hudson; but when, in the late 1650s, the number of inhabitants increased as the supply of beavers diminished, the changes divided the village. In the end, the rulers were unable to resolve the problems once and for all.

Various people had profited from the trade, among them the Van Rensselaers.

After Stuyvesant established Beverwijck with its own court in 1652, the family not only had to recover and adjust the patroonship to the new situation, but they also had to adapt their ways of trading. While Jan Baptist was director, Jeremias joined him in New Netherland; together, they were able to continue their trading system by re-establishing and maintaining a network of friends in Manhattan and in Beverwijck. Jan Baptist may have left Rensselaerswijck in the fall of 1658 with the idea that the trade was going well. From Amsterdam, he then directed the trade, investing in ships and cargoes and advising Jeremias, who had taken over his position in the patroonship, on issues concerning the domain and the trade. After Johannes van Rensselaer died in 1662, Jan Baptist became guardian of Johannes's son Kiliaen, who at the time was no more than six years old, and who would become the third patroon. Jeremias, as director of the patroonship, was able to refer his problems to a guardian of the patroon who had physically spent a number of years in the upper Hudson, and knew the situation and the people.

After 1657, however, the situation in the settlement changed dramatically. The fur trade never again flourished in the time before the English takeover, and the change influenced all aspects of life in the community. As the beaver supply decreased, the Van Rensselaer brothers attempted to trade more in lumber, tobacco, and wheat. The situation nevertheless remained gloomy, while damaging floods and ice jams occasionally made the situation worse. Three months before the English took over New Netherland, Jeremias was very pessimistic about the future: Problems with the Esopus Indians were causing farmers to flee, the English of New England were threatening Rensselaerswijck's borders, and the West India Company was giving away land inside the boundaries of the patroonship. The challenges often made life so hard for Jeremias that he frequently suggested selling farms, and even the entire patroonship.

Jeremias was not alone in those hard times; while others had to struggle to survive, he was still one of the leading burghers in the community. Other settlers may have regarded him as the wealthiest and most respected inhabitant, a status made visible by his attention to such matters as a large, well-furnished house, good and modern clothing, keeping several servants and even slaves, maintaining his network of friends by sharing a drink or a meal, and by belonging to the church – not only as a member, but by serving in the consistory as well.

Jeremias van Rensselaer was only one of several people for whom life at the upper Hudson has provided a unique opportunity to lead a life very different from the one they would have led in the fatherland. The Van Rensselaers may have set an example for others in the village, especially those who profited greatly from the trade in New Netherland and rapidly climbed the social ladder. Once these settlers became wealthy inhabitants, they may have tried to develop life styles similar to those of the Van Rensselaers. We will meet these successful burghers in the fifth chapter.

IV: Successful burghers

The two petitions discussed in the previous chapter reveal how deeply the community was divided about the trade. Some twenty-five men felt that they were successful enough to afford the expense of Indian brokers, while the majority of the inhabitants preferred to trade with Christian as well as Indian brokers. That it was an altogether difficult issue is clear, when we see that two of the three men who presented the second petition (June 7, 1660) had also been among the twenty-five who signed the first petition (May 25, 1660), and that one shoemaker signed both petitions. Their recently acquired financial position was by no means stable; of the twenty-five, one person who signed the petition would be dependent on poor relief four years later. And although the petitions were signed by seven men who had been magistrates, and three who would occupy the bench after 1660, three former magistrates the six sitting magistrates did not sign either petition. There clearly were more successful inhabitants who not only considered their own, but also the community's interest. If we add them to the twenty-five who signed the first petition, we find that, around 1660, a group of some forty men may have considered themselves successful inhabitants of Beverwijck.[1]

Success in the trade had prepared the way for various men to function in the courts of Rensselaerswijck and, later, Fort Orange; as in *patria*, these positions were usually filled by the community's wealthiest burghers.[2]

A look at the course of life of some of the twenty-two men who had, by 1664, been magistrates in Beverwijck one or more times reveals several features that influenced a person's path to success in the village. Nearly half of these twenty-two had come to the patroonship between 1635 and 1645; six had come in the late 1640s and 1650; of the remaining six, it is not clear exactly when they came to New Netherland, but they first appeared in the Fort Orange records in 1652 or later.[3] It is clear that those who came to the area early had certain advantages. By 1660, some were well familiar with the Indian languages; over time, they had established their own working relationships with the Indians, and were now trying to protect these business relationships.[4] They also had become more familiar with other early settlers over the years, and frequently cooperated in joint projects such as running a mill or a farm. Frequently, their wives were involved in the business as well; not only did they contribute their labor, but through marriage they also added their own family connections to their spouses' network of friends – which expanded their social networks and business possibilities remarkably. Having lived in the area for a number of years, people had become well acquainted with the landscape, the climate, and the Indians' travel patterns; some men knew exactly where to purchase lots in the *bijeenwoninge* or where the land was good, and also well located for farming and perhaps some trading.

Some settlers also were well aware that, in the early settlement, certain trades (e.g., gunstock making) were more lucrative than others for the Indian trade, and became involved in those businesses.

In addition to acquiring some wealth, it was important that one lived a good Christian life; by 1664, eighteen successful inhabitants not only were members of the church, but also had worked in its consistory. While magistrates were directly involved in the laying out of the village, for example, or the making of ordinances, members of the consistory took care of the poor and guarded the community's moral standards by exercising ecclesiastical discipline. Some men would alternate in the work of court and consistory: They served for two years as magistrates, then became members of the consistory for three years, and thereafter magistrates again. By working in these two institutions, some twenty-four successful burghers guided the direction in which the village would develop between 1652 and 1664 in many ways[5] (see Appendix 6).

Although it was important to be a member of the Reformed church, at least two of Beverwijck's magistrates were not. But certainly, one should always live an honorable life. The positions on the court were, as was the case in the Dutch Republic, occupied not only by the wealthiest, but also the 'most honorable, most prominent, most moderate and most peaceable burghers' of the community.[6] And losing one's honor was not difficult, as slander about sexual matters, for instance, would quickly find its way among the people. In addition, the fur trade caused many to risk bankruptcy by risking more than the value of their possessions in buying merchandise. People often gambled that the coming trading season would be good, and would buy merchandise with the promise to pay for it with profits from the next season's trade. After 1657, however, when the beaver trade dwindled (as no beavers were brought to the village) these traders ended up selling investments they had previously made – real estate in the village, land in other areas, a farm, a brewery, or a ship – to pay off their debts.

Some merchants had worked in New Netherland as agents for firms in the Dutch Republic, in order to bring profits back to patria. After spending a number of years in the upriver community, sometimes having crossed the ocean several times, they would return to the fatherland for good. Back in the Republic, they would invest their earnings, and usually maintained their connections and trade with New Netherland. Combining records of the Amsterdam and Albany municipal archives presents an interesting picture of these men, who lived their lives in two worlds for a number of years.

Many merchants would stay in the upper Hudson area after their contracts had ended. Some men, who had come as low-wage farm servants for the patroon, soon collected the profits they had made in the fur trade, and did what merchants in the fatherland did: They invested in real estate and such projects as a farm, mill, brewery, brickyard, and the development of more land. By buying jewelry, fashionable clothing, sometimes even a slave, and decorating their houses, they made their wealth visible. In the New World, wealth was able to bring about change in the traditional Dutch order and values; but as soon as the group of newly prosperous men had reached the stage of wielding power, they closed their privileged circle to protect its existence, creating their own oligarchy – just as in the fatherland. To some on the lower steps of the social ladder in the fatherland, the upper Hudson area offered the possibility of reaching the highest step of that ladder in the New World within a short period, and then to continue the existing social patterns of life in the fatherland. By doing so, they laid the groundwork for their children's future.

In this chapter, we will look at some of these men and the ways they became successful. We also will see what they did with their earnings during the 1650s and early half of the 1660s, and how they contributed to the establishment of Beverwijck.

Dirck Jansz Croon

Active in two worlds

Dirck Jansz Croon was one of the twenty-five men who signed the petition of May, 1660. He worked for the company of Seth and Gillis Verbrugge, and seems to have been in New Netherland as early as 1647, and perhaps earlier.[7] If he was the same individual as the man sometimes just called Dirck Jansz, he was a carpenter by trade, and had a house built in Rensselaerswijck in 1650. On April 27, 1652, he was given a patent for a lot of eight by five rods in Beverwijck south of *Jonckerstraet*, which had 'to the north the common highway, to south the *Fuycken kil*, to the west Goosen Gerritsz, and to east Cornelis Cornelisz Voss.' He also received a patent for a garden 'to the north of Cornelis Voss and to the west of Marten Herbertsz, long seven rods and breadth three rods'[8] (see Appendix 8, XI, DJC). Most likely he was not, as suggested by Donna Merwick, the Derreck Jansz *Smijt* who sold his sloop *De Swarte Arent* on November 7, 1661. While Dirck Jansz Croon lived in Amsterdam in 1662, Derck Yansz *Smit* was in Beverwijck in August of that year, and promised to pay 38 *schepels* of wheat to Anthonie Jansz. The signatures of the (probably two different) men are noticeably distinct from each other: While Derck Yansz *Smijt/Smit* consistently signed Yansz with an initial Y, Croon used a J.[9] Notarial archives at Amsterdam's municipal archives mention a certain Dirck Jansz van der Gouw who, when he was in Amsterdam in February 1651, hired a certain Michiel Rijckertsz to serve in his gunstock maker's shop for two years. In the books of marriage intentions (*ondertrouwboeken*) and the book of burghers (*poorterboek*), he appears as Dirck Croon van der Gouw and Dirck Jansz Croon, from Gouda.[10]

Croon was an active member of the community. In April 1652 (if he was the person called 'Dirrick Jansz'), he was one of the surveyors who worked on the layout of the village, and in May 1653 he was ensign (*vaendrigh*) of the burgher guard.[11] In August 1655, he was chosen as extraordinary magistrate, from which post he retired on May 1, 1657. A year later he was chosen magistrate again, and in September and October 1659 he participated in the meetings with the Maquaes. With the problems at the Esopus and the growing threat of an Indian attack, the commissary and all former and current magistrates gathered at his house on November 4 to discuss the building of a defense, and Croon (along with Abraham Staets, Adriaen Gerritsz, and Françoys Boon) was appointed overseer.[12]

Croon was also an active merchant and, despite the fact that he was involved in building up Beverwijck, he went back and forth between Holland and the upper Hudson at least four times between 1650 and 1661. While in Amsterdam, he would look after the goods he had shipped to the fatherland from New Netherland. This certainly was necessary, as many things could go wrong during the transport. In November 1656, for example, when he asked Gillis and Seth Verbrugge to inspect a parcel of 1,200 beavers stored at the cloth wholesaler Jan Sijbingh's, at the Nieuwendijk, it appears that one-third of the pelts was worthless: On the *Bontecoe*, the beaver skins had been lying next to ox skins, and had been damaged by worms.[13] Croon probably spent quite some time in Amsterdam's business center meeting with his trading contacts, arranging cargoes of trade goods and provisions to go to the New World, and trying to hire men to work in his service as gunstock makers. In 1657, he even did some business with his successful Beverwijck neighbor Goosen Gerritsz, who was also in Amsterdam. At that time, Gerritsz had established a company with Gillis and Seth Verbrugge to trade with New Netherland for at least four years. Gillis Verbrugge provided ƒ12,000 in wares and merchandise, and Gerritsz contributed ƒ4,000 in wares and beavers. Gerritsz would go back to New Netherland and trade with the Indians and other inhabitants, for which he would receive ƒ100 a year and, for each merchantable beaver pelt, one carolus guilder commission. He was only to buy peltries for the company, and none for himself.[14] With Croon, he signed a bottomry bond for ƒ1,000 on the merchandise aboard the ship the *Vogelesangh*, and the insurance (*assurantiepolis*) that he had assigned for this voyage.[15] Serving as a magistrate in Beverwijck did not prevent Croon from making another trip to Amsterdam in the fall of 1658, when he appeared, together with Gillis van Hoornbeeck and Jacob Hay, as an interested party with respect to the cargo of the *Draetvat*.[16]

Before leaving Amsterdam, Croon would often give his friend Jan Hendricksz Sijbingh, who had been in the upper Hudson in 1648 and the early 1650s, a power of attorney to take care of his business.[17] As a tailor, Sijbingh had owned one of the houses in Fort Orange in partnership with Gerrit Jansz Cuyper, who at that time also worked for the Verbrugges. He was able to sell rapidly the cloth, duffels and blankets he had taken along. Once back in Amsterdam, Sijbingh had started a wholesaler's business in cloth, *De Gulden Fortuyn*, which was mostly oriented toward New Netherland; he probably obtained duffels from the textile centers Kampen and Leiden. He did business with, among others, the trading company of Gillis and Seth Verbrugge, which had an intensive trade with New Netherland, and later with company of Dirck and Abel de Wolff. Jan's brother Jacob also was in the business, and was in Beverwijck in October 1653, where he received a patent for a lot with a house; he seems still to have been there in September 1658[18] (see Appendix 8, VIII, 11: 'Nota Bene').

Croon did business with many people in Beverwijck. The mason Marten Herpertsz owed him ƒ27 in beavers in 1654; Daniel Rinckhout, a baker, bought brandy from him with a value of fifty beavers in 1658; and in the same year,

Christoffel Davidsz owed him four beavers for fourteen napkins and twelve pewter plates.[19] The trader Sander Leendertsz Glen had invested much more in Croon's merchandise and, in 1659, owed him seventy-five beavers and thirty beavers in interest. He pledged a house and lot at the hill for the payment of his debt, which he ended up selling in 1664 to Croon's attorney, Adriaen Gerritsz van Papendorp.[20]

Although there is little information about Croon's personal life, Claes Gerritsz may have expressed the feelings of other village inhabitants when, in 1654, he nicknamed Croon's house (in which some of his relatives may have lived, as well) 'The Savings Bank' (*De Spaerpot*).[21] Croon was in the village to make profits in the trade, and to bring those profits back to Holland. Like everyone else, he sued people who were indebted to him; and when the trade started to decline, he would be one of the principal traders who requested, in 1660, that the trade be performed only with the use of Indian brokers. Undoubtedly, he foresaw his profits diminishing if he could not use Indian brokers and the common people were allowed to broker. The effort to limit the trade to major traders would fail, however, and the resolution of the problem may have disappointed Croon. On August 31, 1660, he settled accounts with Jan Nack, whom he had hired as a gunstock maker in 1657; he seems to have decided by then to return permanently to the fatherland.[22] Croon may have left New Netherland together with his brother Adriaen, who planned to depart in August 1660. He was in the fatherland before July 30, 1661 at the latest, when 40-year old 'Dirck Croon van der Gouw, merchant' and Amsterdam widow Lijntje Pieters announced their marriage; they married on August 14, 1661 at Nieuwendam.[23] On October 12 of that year, Dirck was said to have 'been many years inhabitant of New Netherland.'[24]

Back in Amsterdam

Croon probably also realized how much worse the position of the Verbrugge Company had become. The English Navigation Acts of 1651 and the first Anglo-Dutch war (1652-1654) had driven up the costs of the trade, and during the 1650s they were forced to seek partnerships of longer duration and to reassess the risks of direct Amsterdam-Virginia trade. Unlike the De Wolffs, who did not have the majority of their enterprises concentrated in New Netherland, but who also invested in Baltic grain, French wine, and West African slaves, the Verbrugges had the bulk of their capital concentrated in New Netherland, and suffered much during the Anglo-Dutch war. The De Wolffs' total investment in New Netherland remained more liquid, going primarily into the salaries of their agents in the colony and the rental of space aboard ships belonging to others; they invested an average of 80 percent in ships, cargoes and warehouses. At the end of the 1650s, the Verbrugges had financial problems, and Gerrit Zuyck offered a way out by buying out more than half of the company's shares. This financial situation may have prompted Croon to go back to the fatherland and continue the trade from there. Perhaps his return to *patria* was the reason that Gillis Verbrugge hired Storm Albertsz vander Zee in April 1661 to take care of his business in New

Netherland for four years. However, with the rumors of another war with England in 1662, the Verbrugges, whose enterprises were concentrated in New Netherland and tied up in land, ships (sitting idle) and warehouse space, were forced to sell most of their New Netherland assets to meet their creditors' demands for cash.[25]

So when Maria Wessels, a spinster at New Amsterdam, intended to sue Croon in September 1663 over a broken promise to marry her, when he had married someone else, his attorney and brother-in-law Adriaen Gerritsz would have had to resolve the problems. The document was never signed, however, and the case thus does not seem to have been pursued. By then, Dirck had already been married to Lijntje for two years and was living in Amsterdam, perhaps in the house on the Palmgracht that he had bought in March 1662.[26]

Croon may have stayed in Amsterdam because Lijntje had no interest in going to New Netherland; but it could also have been that the Croon family had established a sufficient network in New Netherland, and that Dirck had returned to direct the trade from the Republic. That scenario is similar to what 'Gerrit Janszn Cuyper van Wij Cuyper' (from Wijhe, a village near Zwolle) did. The 34-year old Cuyper married Geertruyt de Wolff from Haerlem in the summer of 1655, and in February of the next year was listed as burgher (*poorter*) of Amsterdam.[27] He then started working with the company of Dirck and Abel de Wolff (his wife's father and brother) who, through Cuyper, in turn became more involved in the New Netherland trade. Together, they organized a company to trade with the colony, for which Dirck de Wolff provided the capital and connections in the Amsterdam merchant community. Abel and Gerrit handled the management of the company in Amsterdam, while the agents Gerrit Bancker and Harmen Vedder took care of business in Beverwijck.[28] The extent to which Cuyper's brother Jurriaen Jansz Groenewout was involved is unclear.[29] In 1684, however, Geertruyt de Wolff, widow of 'Gerrit Jansz Groenwouw alias Kuyper,' appointed the De Wolffs' long-time agent in Beverwijck, Gerrit Bancker, and his wife to collect a payment of f1,039:18 from the estate of 'Jurriaen Jansz Groenewouwt,' her brother-in-law, to which she claimed to be entitled.[30] But most of Jurriaen's property and jewelry had come from his wife, who died after three years of marriage, leaving him with one daughter from her previous marriage. Jurriaen's stepson-in-law declared that Groenewout had excluded his blood relations from his inheritance, '... his own brother's son and all his relatives in Holland...'[31] Gerrit Bancker was the only one who protested by presenting a petition, which mentioned that 'the deceased confessed several times to the petitioner that he still had in Holland brother's and sister's children and poor orphans,' to which the court answered that it would maintain the rights of those relatives in Holland, to the extent that the law and justice permitted.[32]

A family trading network

The Cuyper brothers may have been divided between two worlds, but when Croon returned to Amsterdam for good, he left behind a network that included mainly relatives. He may have departed shortly after August 1660, together with his brother Adriaen Jansz Croon, who was in Beverwijck in January 1659 and was most likely a carpenter as well.[33] Sometime between 1663 and 1668, Adriaen strengthened the family ties with the Sijbinghs by marrying Jacob Sijbingh's widow. Jacob had, in his lifetime, been quite familiar with other members of the Croon family in Beverwijck. He had received a patent for a house and lot in Beverwijck jointly with the carpenter Stoffel Jansz Abeel, who was married to Croon's sister Neeltie.[34] Both Stoffel and Neeltie were very involved in the trading business; Neeltie seems to have known much about textiles, as she was sometimes asked to appraise the value of clothes. Stoffel was in Amsterdam in 1660 when he, Pieter Hartgers, and Jan and Jacob Sijbingh started a company to trade with New Netherland for a period of two years. They had contributed ƒ5,600, for which they bought merchandise to be traded by Abeel in New Netherland. Abeel, who would receive half of the profit, then went back to Beverwijck at their joint expense, while the returning goods would be sold by Hartgers and/or Jan Sijbingh. Apparently, business went well, as it was not until 1668 that the accounts were checked and the partnership was dissolved.[35] If Abeel had been in Beverwijck in 1660, he would, like his brothers-in-law, most likely have signed the petition requesting the use of Indian brokers. Abeel belonged to the group of successful inhabitants of the community. From 1663 through 1665, he served the church as deacon, and in 1664 he was a magistrate in Beverwijck's court.[36]

Another sister of Croon, Catharina, was married to Theunis Cornelisz van der Poel (also known as Spitsenbergh), who for several years ran the saw mills in Rensselaerswijck on the fifth kill, and who frequently served as member of the court of Rensselaerswijck. Probably he was the same person as the Theunis Cornelisz who was a member of the consistory in later years.[37] A third sister who remained in Beverwijck, Jannetie Croon, had married Adriaen Gerritsz Papendorp, who succeeded Croon as extraordinary magistrate in 1657, and who would serve as magistrate in 1658 and 1662, as well. He also was repeatedly a member of the consistory. In 1663, Gerritsz was appointed administrator of the goods and effects of Dirck Jansz Croon, who by then had settled permanently in Amsterdam.[38]

In Amsterdam Croon, like Jan Baptist van Rensselaer and Gerrit Jansz Cuyper, continued to participate in the New Netherland trade; in April 1664, he held a one-eighth share in a company for trade with New Netherland. Johan van Brugge and his brother Reynier had a three-eighth share, Gerrit Zuyck a one-quarter share. Jac. van Noortgau and Abraham Jansz, like Dirck, each had a one-eighth share.[39] In March 1665, Croon, Zuyck and Abel de Wolff jointly chartered *De Eendracht* with insurance that would have covered their losses if the ship had been taken by the English.[40] In 1669, Croon settled his accounts with Adriaen Gerritsz Papendorp. In that same year, Croon, the smith Barent Reyndersz, and Papendorp had three houses built in Amsterdam on the north side of the Leidse Gracht.[41] While Croon and twenty others held an interest in the cargo of the *Faam* in 1670, it is unclear whether he continued the trade after that date.[42] Papendorp did continue, and as late as 1682 would send peltries to Sijbingh's son Hendrick, which were sold for ƒ470.[43]

In May 1664, as Croon's attorney, Adriaen Gerritsz sold some 150 items of his brother-in-law's furniture and household goods at public sale, as well as to family members. Goosen Gerritsz, Philip Pietersz, Gerrit Slichtenhorst, *Meester* Jacob and *Meester* Jan, Volckert Jansz Douw, and Jan Koster van Aecken were among the many prominent inhabitants of the village who came to buy or bid on some of the twenty-six pewter or earthenware saucers that were for sale. Apart from such household items as spoons, plates, cups, pans, salt cellars, pepper mills, a mustard jar, and a sugar tin, they also bought candles, sconces, lanterns, and a powder box. There was a choice of forty-four pictures, varying in price between three for ƒ1-5 and four for ƒ31; a mirror was sold for ƒ10, and a big chest for ƒ11. Three chairs went for ƒ4, and two chair cushions for ƒ14. Adriaen Gerritsz himself bought two bed sheets for ƒ14; he may also have kept the bed, which was valued at ƒ140. Furthermore, there were curtains and valances. All told, the sale brought ƒ427-05; in November of that year, Adriaen Gerritsz also sold to Jan Clute the house and lot that Croon, in partial payment of an existing mortgage, had acquired from Sander Leendertsz Glen.[44]

Croon was remarkable because he contributed much to the shaping of Beverwijck. Through his surveyorship, he contributed to the layout and the construction of the village; and as a magistrate, he took part in some important decisions. It seems that he played an active role in community life. He was probably an ensign (*vaandrigh*) in the burgher guard; and unless the goods offered at the public sale were only merchandise to be traded, they could indicate that Croon had a house in which he received and entertained many visitors. He went back to Amsterdam, and from there, continued the trade with his relatives and other connections in New Netherland, while investing the family's earnings in *patria*.[45] He had decided to stay in Holland; and when Croon died in 1680, his will would mention his interest in houses in the Palmstraat, the Leidse gracht, the Keizersgracht, and in the Kerkstraat. Also mentioned, as heirs, were his relatives in New Netherland, Adriaen Gerritsz van Papendorp, Stoffel Jansz Abeel, and Theunis Cornelisz van der Poel.[46] It is unclear whether Croon stayed in Amsterdam because of his wife or to direct his business. But marriage could greatly influence a man's choice of residence, as demonstrated perhaps by the case of Pieter Hartgers, who most likely stayed in Beverwijck because of his wife – but who, after she died, would soon return to *patria*.

Pieter Hartgers

Family ties

After living for some sixteen years in the upper Hudson community, Pieter Hartgers was back in the Dutch Republic again by 1660. As a 23-year old, he had come over to Rensselaerswijck in 1643 with ƒ260 borrowed from his brother Joost, which he promised to pay back with his wages or with the proceeds of tobacco planting.[47] Some five years after his arrival, Pieter married Sijtje Roelofs, the third daughter of the early settlers Anneke Jans and Roelof Jansz van Masterlant (a corruption of Marstrant). Sijtje had been born sometime after 1632 in Rensselaerswijck and spent her earliest childhood years there, until the family moved to Manhattan in 1636.[48] In 1649, Pieter and Sijtje had a daughter Janneken, who was baptized in the church at New Amsterdam on September 5; Hartgers's brother Joost and Sijtje's sister Sara Roelofs are recorded as having been witnesses – but likely someone else substituted for Joost. In 1652 the couple had another daughter, Rachel.[49] With Joost, an important bookseller in Amsterdam, Pieter seems to have maintained good contact throughout his life. He probably contributed to Joost's publication of the *Beschrijvinghe van Virginia, Nieuw Nederlandt, Nieu Engelandt en d' eylanden Bermudes, Barbados en St. Christopher*, which was a compilation of previously printed texts. This description of Virginia and other settled areas of the New World was published in 1651, and could be purchased at Joost's bookstore on De Dam, at the corner of the *Kalverstraet*. The brothers remained in touch with each other; in 1655, Joost arranged for Pieter to bring Pieter Stevensz to New Netherland to work for his brother for three years.[50]

Undoubtedly, the new family ties brought more contacts and responsibilities; for example, Hartgers seems to have taken care of the property of Sijtje's mother, Anneke, who lived just across the street; he also had good contacts with Sijtje's brother, the carpenter Jan Roelofsz. In 1656, for example, when Roelofsz, by public bid agreed to build the blockhouse church, together with Stoffel Jansz, Pieter offered to provide surety for the performance and fulfillment of all conditions.[51] He maintained good relations as well with Johannes van Brugh, the third husband of Sijtje's sister Trijntje, who lived at Manhattan; and Cornelis Bogardus, Sijtje's step brother, rented one of Hartgers's houses in 1661.[52] The nicknames given by Claes Gerritsz to various houses in Beverwijck suggest that there was quite a different atmosphere in Hartgers's home, which he dubbed 'The Little House Sparrow' (*Het Huysmusgen*, which could also mean the homebody), and that of the Bogardus family, which in Gerritsz's eyes deserved the name 'Vulture World' (*De Gierswerelt*)[54] (see Appendix 8, VII, no. 17 and, XI, PH).

An active community member

Although Hartgers may have expected to grow tobacco when he contracted with Van Rensselaer in 1643, there is no information as to whether he did this in reality. In 1646, he had a brewery. From May 1, 1653 until 1658, he rented a farm on Papscanee Island together with Volckert Jansz Douw and Jan Thomasz, but there is no evidence they grew tobacco there.[54] With the same men, in 1655, he bought a corner of the lot of Femmetje Albertse, the widow of baker Hendrick Jansz Westerkamp, where they ran a successful brewery.[55] (Appendix 8, II, no. 13).

In the 1640s, Hartgers already had the right to trade, and he seems to have done this very successfully. It allowed him to build up good contacts with the natives, which may have made him expert in recognizing the value of *sewant* – and which, in turn, may have enhanced his trading options.[56] There is no information about the extent of his trade; but he certainly did well, frequently using Indian brokers. Had Hartgers been in Beverwijck in the spring of 1660, he probably would have signed the petition along with the other principal traders; but, sometime in 1659, he left New Netherland. In December 1660, he was described as dwelling at Leiderdorp, near Leiden in the province of South Holland.[57]

Due to his success in the trade, Pieter Hartgers frequently held positions in the court and the consistory. During the time of Van Curler's absence from Rensselaerswijck, he assisted Anthonie de Hooges in administering the patroonship; and he was active in Beverwijck's court as a magistrate in 1654 and 1655, and again in 1658-59.[58] This would have required him to be in the fort at least every Tuesday morning at ten o'clock for the weekly court sessions, and at irregular times for extraordinary sessions. The magistracy brought with it various duties 'on the side': Sometimes he would be appointed as a referee to resolve conflicts, or to help stake out proper lines of the lots of some inhabitants; at other times, he would make a trip to Manhattan to meet with the director general and council. In 1655, Hartgers and Jan Verbeeck were chosen and appointed as treasurers of the court to receive the excise moneys (usually in *sewant*) of the impost master, as well as the money promised and due for the lots that had been granted.[59] In May 1658, he was chosen as magistrate again; but although he would be thanked for his services in the court session of May 1, 1660, he may not have been present at that time. It appears that Hartgers did not stay in Beverwijck until the end of the term; the last court session he is listed as having attended is dated July 15, 1659. That he was the only magistrate not present at important meetings with the Maquaes, in September of that year, strongly suggests that by then he had left the colony.[60]

While he lived in Beverwijck, Pieter Hartgers was concerned with affairs related to the well-being of the community; in 1656, for instance, he contributed to the repairs of Willem Jurriaensz's house.[61] By then, he was well aware of the importance of the inhabitants' well-being to the good of the village in general; as deacon of the church, in 1652, he was involved with the care of the poor and shared responsibility for building a poorhouse in the community. From 1655 to 1657, Hartgers served as an elder of the church and, as such, was responsible for supervising the ecclesiastical discipline.[62] Together with *dominee* Schaets and the other elders, he probably made house visits to church members before the celebration of the Holy Communion. Through his involvement in this work, Hartgers may well have become an expert in marital affairs. In 1655, he had to deal with the village's only case of marital separation, the case of Maria Goosens and the carpenter Steven Jansz, which would lead to an official divorce in 1663.[63] A year later, he dealt with an even more complicated case concerning annulment of the marriage of Femmetje Alberts (baker Hendrick Jansz Westerkamp's widow) and Michiel Anthonisz. After learning from a neighbor that his wife Grietge Jacobs had died in Amsterdam, Anthonisz had married Femmetge Alberts in New Netherland. But some time after their wedding, first wife Grietge arrived in Beverwijck – and revealed herself. The consistory then requested the court to give Femmetge a 'letter of freedom,' thus allowing Michiel and Grietge to remain husband and wife.[64]

As an elder, Hartgers also had to deal with another important case involving al-

leged slander against Goosen Gerritsz and Annetje Lievens, who planned to marry in 1657.[65] While Goosen was in Holland on business in the spring of that year,
Jurriaen Jansz Groenewout had boasted (and spread the rumor) that he was 'engaged' to Annetje. Matters of honor – especially when sexuality was involved –
were considered very serious, as they could greatly injure one's reputation. Although Jurriaen had confessed before the consistory that he was not engaged to
Annetje, he still maintained his story in Goosen's presence; thus, Goosen requested in court that Jansz be required prove his statement, or else be ordered to make
honest reparation 'for defamation of his neighbor's character.' The matter was
eventually resolved, whereupon Gerritsz was granted a 'certificate of satisfaction.'
Two days later, on July 30, 1657, Goosen and Annetje signed the contract for their
future marriage; they would have their first daughter, Gerretie, in that same year.[66]
Jansz's statement was indeed an important matter, as sexual relations were usually
permitted once marriage promises had been made between partners. Thus, Jansz's
false claim carried the suggestion that Annetje had slept with more than one man,
in which case she would have 'lost her honor' – the worst thing that could happen
to a woman.[67]

Apart from his involvement in these moral issues, Hartgers's work for the
church was good for his business as well. In November 1657, for example, he was
paid *f*258 for merchandise delivered to the deaconry for the use of the poor.[68]

A farewell to Beverwijck

Sijtje must have died sometime in, or perhaps prior to, 1659. Following his wife's
death, Pieter Hartgers decided to go back to the fatherland, taking his eight- and
ten-year-old daughters with him. But he would remain involved with New
Netherland. In December 1659 and in later years (as noted in chapter 3), he contracted with Jan Baptist van Rensselaer; and in March 1660, he entered into the
trading contract with the Sijbinghs and Stoffel Jansz Abeel.[69] In December 1660,
he planned a final journey to New Netherland. Having remarried, Pieter gave his
second wife Eva van Rijswijck a power of attorney to take care of his business; and
before departing on *De Trouw*, he promised his new brother-in-law Pieter van
Rijswijck, a merchant at Amsterdam, that he would collect a debt for him in New
Netherland.[70]

Hartgers had been one of the successful inhabitants of Beverwijck. In addition
to his trading business, he had to take care of several pieces of property. As a successful burgher married to a woman born in New Netherland, probably with no
plans to go back to *patria*, he had invested his money in various enterprises (like
several other successful burghers). Now that he planned to go back to the fatherland permanently, he had to change his investments; between his arrival at Beverwijck sometime in the spring, and his departure in September 1661, he arranged
many of his affairs. He probably sold his share of the brewery to Douw and
Thomasz. Earlier, in September 1658, he had sold to the trader Johannes Withart
a house he had built on the lot for which he had obtained a patent in 1652.[71] He
would not sell the house on the riverside, south of the third kill, which his brother-

in-law Jan Roelofsz had sold him in 1659.[72] (Appendix 8, II, no. 25). Other houses he rented out: His stepbrother-in-law, the gunstock maker Cornelis Bogardus, occupied one of Hartgers's houses and a lot in the *Berghstraet* (present-day Lodge Street, which would have been just outside the 1659 palisades) while baker Wouter Albertsz van den Uythoff lived in another of his houses in Beverwijck (no location mentioned). Shortly before leaving New Netherland for good, Hartgers renewed a lease to the carpenter Geurt Hendricksz for two years.[73] On September 25, he gave a power of attorney to Gerrit Swart and Abraham Staets, who in the coming years would take care of his business in Beverwijck; in August 1662, they were probably the ones who rented out three of his houses and sold the garden south of Beverwijck.[74]

Like other successful burghers in 1652, Hartgers also owned property in Manhattan; it was located on the *Brouwersstraet*, next to Olof Stevensz van Cortlandt. It is uncertain whether he stayed there irregularly or used it only as a storehouse, or whether he rented it to different tenants. In June 1654 he donated 12½ beavers, the fourth largest of Beverwijck's contributions toward the defense of Manhattan.[75] After Hartgers left, his brother-in-law Johannes van Brugh seems to have had a power of attorney to deal with his property in Manhattan.[76]

Analyzing some of Hartgers' property could lead to interesting conclusions about the value of location. The lot Hartgers sold to Withart for ƒ2,700 was located between the *Jonckerstraet* and the first kill; on the street it was two rods, nine feet broad and in the rear on the kill the breadth was two rods, seven feet. From street to kill it was seven rods long. The house may have been about sixteen feet long; the lot behind it measured five rods, nine feet and six inches. On both sides it had six inches free for drainage.[77] (Appendix 8, XI, PH.)The lot with a house on the river, south of the third kill, was quite a bit larger: Along the wagon road it was nine rods long, on the end of Jan Martensz's lot it was thirteen rods wide, and along the riverbank it was seven rods. On this property, which in 1659 was bought for ƒ1910, Hartgers did not gain much profit. In 1666 this house, along with some forty other houses and barns, would be destroyed by the ice, and Geurt Hendricksz bought it afterwards for ƒ160, on condition that he would look himself for the iron work and the lumber, which might have drifted away.[78] The documents provide no dimensions for the house and lot on the east side of Pearl Street sold to Hendrick Cuyler in 1664. It included a garden south of Fort Orange and was sold for the sum of ƒ850.[79] (Appendix 8, VII, no. 3). The location may have been one reason that the lot was so much cheaper. Comparing the differences in price between these three lots, which Hartgers owned at some time, could lead to the conclusion that lots north of the *bijeenwoninge* were more expensive than those east of present-day Pearl Street, but cheaper than those in the center of the *bijeenwoninge* between the first kill and *Jonckerstraet*, which at that time seem to have been prime property.

In October 1661, Hartgers went back to the fatherland for good. His marriage with Eva van Rijswijck, however, would not last long. In April 1663, when he was back in Leiden, he wrote Jeremias van Rensselaer that his wife had recently died in childbirth after delivering a stillborn child.[80] Eva was probably a sister of *schout*

Gerrit Swart's wife, Anthonia van Rijswijck. Not only do their names indicate this, but when Hartgers left Beverwijck for the last time at the end of 1661 or early in 1662, he not only gave his good friend Abraham Staets a power of attorney to manage his affairs, but Swart as well. A service like this was usually performed by relatives or very good friends.[81]

In January 1664, Hartgers married Maria Pels, with whom he would have three children.[82] English authorities, in 1667, confiscated properties in Albany belonging to men in Holland, most likely including Hartgers's possessions.[83] He moved to Alkmaer, where he seems to have become a brewer at the sign of *De Drie Ruiters.* When Pieter Hartgers died in 1670, Abel de Wolff – who in the same year had married Hartgers's daughter Johanna – became the guardian of his three youngest children. In 1698, some people in Albany may have taken a few minutes to remember the two girls who, together with their father, had sailed away from Beverwijck in 1659 to live in the fatherland. Nearly at the end of the seventeenth century, Ryseck Swart (as Anthonia van Rijswijck, Gerrit Swart's widow, was called in the community) pawned a silver beaker with the inscription *Rachel Hartgers* to the deaconry in return for care, board and drink. It probably was the beaker that Rachel had inherited from her grandmother Anneke Jans in 1663, when the girl was already back in the Republic.[84] By the time Ryseck was in need of care, Rachel had married Barent Holthuyzen van Hocxbergen, the widower of Trijntje de Wolff, and thus also became related to the de Wolffs. At the announcement of the banns on December 31, 1676, 'Rachel Hartgers from Oranje living at the Princegracht' was assisted by her uncle and guardian, Joost Hartgers.[85] It seems that in making the choice to go back to the fatherland, to a country considered by some to be more civilized than the Indian territory across the ocean, Pieter Hartgers definitely had the future of his daughters in mind. But, undoubtedly, he would often remember those years that he had lived on the frontier with Sijtje, the children, his in-laws, and his friends – the people with whom he used to work together.

Volckert Jansz

Early arrival and trade

One of Hartgers's friends was Volckert Jansz Douw, who had come over from Frederickstadt or Stapelholm in the former dutchy of Schleswig. He came to Rensselaerswijck in 1641 on the *Coninck David* and, after 1649 would be charged ƒ32 for his place at the hill on which he built a house, and for which (along with a garden near the river) he received a patent in April 1652. His property was located on the south side of the first kill, just across the stream from Rut Jacobsz and his wife Trijntje Janse van Breestede – whose sister, Dorothee van Breestede, Douw married in April 1650 (see Appendix 8, XI, VJD and RJ). Undoubtedly the families visited with each other regularly, and they helped each other out in hard times.[86] Douw remained in possession of this lot until the 1680s, when he granted parts of it to Gerrit Bancker and Harmen Rutgersz. In 1685, his widow Dorothee granted a part of the lot to the deacons of the Dutch Reformed church.[87]

Douw frequently worked with Jan Thomasz and, together, they were involved in large beaver shipments to the Dutch Republic. In 1654, for example, Jurriaen Tysz of Amsterdam owed them ƒ4,000 for good peltries.[88] In the 1640s, they were already allowed to trade; they probably had to pay ƒ1 over each beaver they sold, but it is open to question whether or not they always declared all of them. Even the surgeon Abraham Staets, who was considered one of the most reliable persons in Rensselaerswijck, did not always keep count. Staets' 1642 contract with the patroon had allowed him to buy cargoes in Amsterdam for a value of ƒ800 and to trade about two hundred beavers per year, of which he had to pay ƒ1 apiece to the patroon, but when he canceled his contract in 1648 he was 'with a good conscience,' not able to say how many beavers exactly he had traded during the time of his contract. Therefore he was, 'in good faith,' to pay ƒ375 to Johan van Wely and Wouter van Twiller on account of the patroon, in addition to his previously paid accounts.[89] Each inhabitant tried to profit as much as possible from the trade, and Douw certainly was no exception. In 1649, his license was even revoked because of his illegitimate trading.[90] Douw, Thomasz, and others who had arrived early in the area were able to understand the Indian languages for the most part, which was certainly to their benefit in the trade. They had established good friendships with the Indians over the course of time, which may have been expressed on May 6, 1665, when the Mahican Indian Wattawit gave Douw, 'as a token of his friendship and in satisfaction of an old debt for maize,' a parcel of land behind Kinderhook.[91]

In Beverwijck, Douw also frequently did business with the Van Rensselaers. In 1659, for example, he ordered a hundred beavers' worth of merchandise, such as serge, a brocade waist, gros-grain with the band for an apron, English damast for an apron, various kinds of stockings, lace, spices, a silver *vignet* and fifty pieces of *hansjoos cord* for the Indian trade from Jan Baptist; and, in 1663, he ensured Jeremias van Rensselaer that, if he needed anything, he would give Jan Baptist the business.[92] Douw traded in goods both in the community and with the Indians. It is not surprising then, that he was willing to represent the community in meetings with the Maquaes in 1659 to answer to their propositions, and to bring them presents. In June 1660, when the community was so divided about the trade, he and Jan Thomasz both signed the petition requesting the use of Indian brokers only, and they both were sued by the officer for having sent brokers in the woods; they both asserted under oath that they had not done so.[93]

Cooperation and investment in land

Douw and Jan Thomasz may have known each other even before they sailed to New Netherland, as Thomasz came from Ostenfeld in Schleswig, a village a few miles east of Husum, and not very far from Stapelholm or Frederickstadt.[94] He is first mentioned in the records in 1644, and from 1647 to 1649 the two men were jointly charged by the patroon for land rent and the right to trade. In 1653, together with Pieter Hartgers, they rented the farm on Papscanee Island that Douw and Thomasz would buy in 1658 from the Van Rensselaers, for 950 beavers or ƒ7,600.[95]

While in Rensselaerswijck, Douw and Thomasz participated with Pieter Hartgers in the rental of a farm; these three men also cooperated on a brewery in Beverwijck. The brewery was situated at a good location on the riverside, just north of the first kill, on part of the lot granted in 1652 to baker Hendrick Jansz Westerkamp, most likely near the good broad road that the patroon had originally planned (see appendix 8, II, no. 13). Various accounts testify that they did good business with local tavern owners and other inhabitants.[96]

Douw and Thomasz continued working and trading together; and when Jan Baptist van Rensselaer left the colony in 1658, he was convinced that they were successful and reliable.[97] Well aware of the value of land, Douw and Thomasz together bought the farm on Papscanee Island, which since 1653 they had been renting, jointly with Pieter Hartgers, from the Van Rensselaers (see illustration 53). During the 1660s, they were able to expand their property by purchasing several tracts of land from the Indians, which turned them into competitors of the Van Rensselaers.[98] In 1661, they acquired land east on the *Binnenkil*, in front of their farm, from Syme, Capachick and Nachonan, together with a little island called the *Cleyne Cuypers eylantie* (little cooper's island), which gave them the use of the entire island.[99] In June 1663, Douw acquired half of *Constapel* Island, located obliquely opposite Bethlehem, from the administrators of the estate of Andries Herbertsz *constapel*. Originally named Pachonackelick, the Dutch also called it Long or Mahicander island.[100] The other half of the island belonged to his brother-in-law Rutger Jacobsz who, together with Herbertsz, had bought it in February 1661 for 'a certain sum of goods.' Together, Jacobsz and Herbertsz had built a house, barn and two hay-ricks; in 1662, they grew winter grain, some rye, and wheat on the island.[101] In October 1663, Douw and Thomasz bought land on the *Goyers kil* on Aepjens Island (Schotack, in the Indian language) from the Mahicans Wattawit and Pepewitsie. Douw's portion of the island was on the river side, Thomasz's portion was on the kill side, and a pasture called the *Calverwey* was to remain undivided as common property. In January 1664, two Mahicander Indians, Panasit and Wapto, sold them the land on the east side of Aepjens Island, starting at the riverbank and running into the woods.[102]

Well aware of the tobacco boom at Manhattan, Douw, like Van Rensselaer and Arent van Curler, was involved in growing tobacco. In May 1661, he hired a servant for his farm to help him plant tobacco and all that appertained thereto, for ƒ24 a month and free board and drink.[103] Exactly where exactly he grew the plants is not clear. It could have been on Aepjens Island, where he and Thomasz started a farm in 1662-63, and where they grew oats and other crops, and kept some livestock. The tobacco was probably not planted on the farm in which they had invested at the Esopus, and which they leased to Gerrit Focken and Jan Gerritsz van Oldenburg. From the beginning of May 1662 until May 1663, these men were to 'enter upon, use and cultivate the land without paying any rent.' They probably mostly grew oats, since Douw and Thomasz would deliver as many

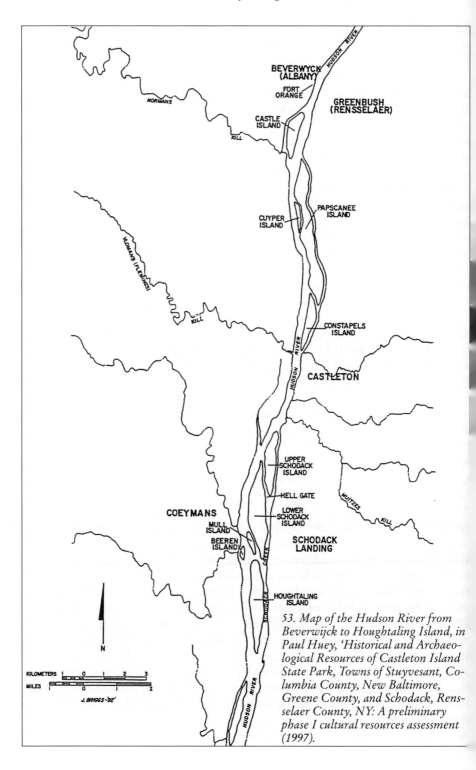

53. Map of the Hudson River from Beverwijck to Houghtaling Island, in Paul Huey, 'Historical and Archaeological Resources of Castleton Island State Park, Towns of Stuyvesant, Columbia County, New Baltimore, Greene County, and Schodack, Rensselaer County, NY: A preliminary phase I cultural resources assessment (1997).

schepels of oats as they could properly sow on the land, on condition that the lessees returned the same quantity at the end of the lease. The lessees also were to build a proper dwelling, barn, rick and fence, as well as a bridge over a kill that bordered their land, for which the lessors would loan them 100 boards; at the end of the lease, all of these structures were to belong to the lessors. Furthermore, Douw and Thomasz delivered three mares, a gelding and two stallions, two cows, two heifers, two sows with pigs, two barrow pigs, six hens and a rooster, which the lessees kept on half shares as to the increase, 'according to the custom of the country.' And finally, they took care that Focken and Van Oldenburg received a plow and a wagon with their appurtenances, except for the chain for the plow, which they were supposed to return in good order at the end of the four-year lease. Each lessee promised to pay the sum of ƒ450 as rent during each of the four years, either in beavers at ƒ8, in grain at market price, or in *sewant* at ƒ16 to the beaver. In February 1663, Douw and Thomasz invested in another farm in the same area, on lot number five, which they leased on similar conditions to Jan Gerritsz van Oldenburg for four years at ƒ325 annually, plus half the increase of the livestock.[104] These agreements were similar to those of the Van Rensselaers, and to one that Abraham Staets had made almost ten years earlier with Barent Gerritsz for a farm at Claverack. For ƒ330, free washing, two pairs of stockings and a pair of shoes, Staets had hired Gerritsz to perform all the farm labor there for one year, except for sowing one particular part.[105] Gerritsz may later have had help from the negro who was bought by Staets at a public auction in 1659, and who may have been put to work on the farm.[106]

A German Lutheran in a Dutch Reformed village

Farming and working together from such an early date was undoubtedly profitable for Thomasz and Douw, as it enabled them to invest in land jointly and acquire some wealth. It may have helped them to attain a position in the court, and to become actively involved in the establishment of the community in the upper Hudson. Although Douw openly displayed his Lutheran faith, this was not considered relevant enough to prevent his selection as magistrate in 1652; he was even allowed to take a different oath than the other court members, omitting the commitment to the Reformed religion prescribed by the Synod of Dordt.[107] As a member of Beverwijck's first court, he helped with the design and construction of the village, which may have been based on the patroon's plans. He was closely involved with laying out the village, and participated in the committee to look after the surveying of lots and gardens. In May 1655, Douw again committed himself to attending court sessions in the fort by replacing Jacob Jansz Schermerhoorn (who had gone to Holland) as magistrate. His contributions to the court must have been appreciated as, notwithstanding the strict ordinance against conventicles published in February 1656, he remained a member of the court and attended all meetings until the official end of the term in May. Thereafter, like other retiring magistrates, Douw was relieved of the obligation to attend the usual burgher watch for one year, except in case of need. In 1659, he was renominated as magistrate.[108]

How other villagers judged Douw is unclear. Although he was Lutheran and had signed the request for a Lutheran minister, he seems to have thought of the Reformed church in its function as a public church and not so much in terms of confession, which may have been why he gave alms to the church on various occasions. In October 1654, he gave as much as ƒ62-5, while promising to give up to ƒ100.[109] He may have been considered a good human being and a capable magistrate. It seems unlikely that Claes Gerritsz, when he nicknamed Douw's house the 'Bird Song' (*De Vogelesanck*) in 1655, thought of Douw as a loose and frivolous person, one of the meanings associated with the name. He may have thought of the nickname in connection with the idea of freedom.[110]

Although they had come over in the 1640s as servants, by 1652 both Douw and Thomasz were considered among 'the wealthiest, most honorable, most prominent, most moderate, and most peaceable' burghers of the community.[111] They would both die before their wives. Douw died in 1683 and left four sons, Jonas, Hendrick, Volckert, and Andries.[112] His wife Dorothee was left in a good financial situation; when she and Jan Thomasz' widow (as did so many other widows in the fatherland) requested a reduction of their assessments in January 1685, 'as they were widows,' the court was 'unable' to do anything.[113] Douw and Thomasz never saw the need to go back to Europe. Clearly, the New World had given them and their wives a better life than they could have had in their homeland of Schleswig, and offered good prospects for their children.

There were different paths to prosperity. Philip Pietersz Schuyler did not come as early as had Douw and Thomasz; he also did not cooperate as much with one other person as they did, nor did he concentrate as much on farming. But through a combination of factors, Schuyler – to an even greater extent than Douw and Thomasz – was able to move up quickly to the one of the highest steps on the social ladder.

Philip Pietersz Schuyler

Gunstocks, marriage, and trade

Philip Pietersz Schuyler was the son of Geertruy Philips van Schuyler and Pieter Diercksz, a baker from the free city of Emden – where many Dutch families had fled in the second half of the sixteenth century from the religious persecutions of the Duke of Alva. His parents had moved to Amsterdam, and around 1650 Pieter came to Rensselaerswijck as a gunstock maker. While guns, by then, were being regularly traded with the Indians, firearms were shipped from *patria* without stocks. Thus, the young Schuyler's trade immediately provided him with good business, as well as great benefits in the fur trade. He was about twenty-two at that time, and would soon marry Margaretha van Slichtenhorst, the daughter of Rensselaerswijck's director, which undoubtedly gave him even more advantages in the trade with the Indians.[114] The marriage also made him a relative of the Van Rensselaers, thereby bringing him into their network of friends.

Marriage probably worked for Schuyler in the same way it had worked for Goosen Gerritsz van Schaick, who had come to Rensselaerswijck in 1637 at wages of only ƒ50 anually for the first three years – but who, after marrying the early settler Brant Peelen's daughter Geertie Brantse, soon became one of the most successful inhabitants of the settlement.[115] When Geertie died in 1655, she left Goosen with four children for whom, two years later, he was able to set aside ƒ6,000.[116] That was considerably more than another successful inhabitant, Evert Jansz Wendel, was able to do. After his wife died, Wendel could only reserve ƒ1,000 for his six children; and Willem Teller was able to distribute ƒ3,500 among his seven children with Margareta Donckesen after her death.[117]

When Claes Gerritsz nicknamed Schuyler's house 'Flying Wind' (*Vliegende Wint*) in 1655, he may have observed that Schuyler knew to make profits quickly.[118] Schuyler was very involved in the trade and had trading contacts in the village, New Amsterdam, Amsterdam, and perhaps New England. In 1652, for example, he owed ƒ99-6 to another gunstock maker in Amsterdam, and in 1654 he paid ƒ2562-10 to Jurriaen Tysz of Amsterdam for goods purchased there.[119] He frequently did business with the Van Rensselaers. In 1661, for example, 'cousin Phlip' (as he was called) bought nine *aams* (1,382.4 liters, or 364.6 gallons) of brandy from Jeremias van Rensselaer. This was important business, as brandy sometimes could go for ƒ160 the half-*aam* – meaning that this deal had a value of about ƒ2,880. Schuyler seems to have sold part of the brandy to local taverns such as Anthony Jansz's, as recorded in December 1662, when Jansz acknowledged a debt of ƒ1,980 to Schuyler for brandy delivered.[120] In 1663, he bought two casks and three hogsheads of brandy (together, 2,534.4 liters, 668.1 gallons, or 66 *ankers*) at 4¾ beavers an *anker* (or 313.5 beavers).[121] Schuyler was interested in other kinds of trade, as well. In 1661, he bought 300 *schepels* (229.2 bushels) of wheat from Van Rensselaer; in the same year, he was also well aware that profits could be made in the trade in *sewant*.[122] After the small beaver trade in the winter of 1660-61, Schuyler noticed that the beads were more in demand, whereas in the summer (according to Van Rensselaer) the *sewant* 'remains in our hands.' In January 1661, through Van Rensselaer, Schuyler asked Olof Stevensz van Cortlandt to do business with him for about two or three thousand guilders' worth, mostly of the white beads, for an assortment of beavers. Evidently it was a successful trade, as Van Cortlandt, in 1665, offered to give Schuyler ƒ2,000 more than he offered in black *sewant*, which would be sent by the next vessel. Schuyler also traded in *sewant* with others; in September 1664, for example, was in debt ninety-one beavers for *sewant* received from Jan Harmensz Weendorp.[123] He may have had some connections with New England traders as well. In 1663, John Willett – a free trader who formerly lived in New England, and who seems to have cooperated with Andries Teller and also dealt with Goosen Gerritsz – owed him about ƒ745 (298 Peruvian/Mexican pieces of eight, at 48 *stivers* apiece) for good beavers. In 1669, Thomas Willet owed him 400 ells of the best English cloth.[124]

As he had such a great stake in the trade, it is not surprising to find Schuyler's signature on the May 1660 petition of the twenty-five traders.[125] As a matter of fact, a year earlier he had been taken to court by officer La Montagne, who accused him of giving a coat to an Indian as an inducement to bring him five natives with beavers from the woods. Through his response to the charge, Schuyler has provided us with a good picture of the situation of the trade at that time: He acknowledged that he had given the coat to the Indian, but said that it had not been for the purpose La Montagne claimed. He had given a present to the Indians, he admitted; but 'if he did wrong in that, [he says that] not a single beaver is bartered in the *Fuyck*, but it is done contrary to the ordinance.'[126] In September 1659, Schuyler made sure that he was among the delegates who went to the Maquaes with presents in order to respond to their proposals. It should not be surprising that he was one of the individuals sued by La Montagne, in 1660, for sending his servant into the woods.[127]

Property and the value of location

It seems that Schuyler carefully thought out where he wanted to acquire property; he organized it in such a way that he could benefit from the location for his work and trading purposes. On the lot on the north side of *Jonckerstraet* that he was granted in 1652, he was allowed to make additions in 1654 and 1656, extending the lot's dimensions about nine and a half rod length by five and a half to six rods width. The lot was bounded on the east side by Marten Herpertsz *metselaer* (see Appendix 8, VII, no. 19/VIII, no. 1). It was thus close to Michiel Rijckertsz and Annetje Bogardus' son Cornelis, two other gunstock makers, and was not far from the lots of several blacksmiths, so that it was easy to cooperate not only with work, but also with personal services. In 1658, for example, he was surety for Jan Dareth, also a gunstock maker, who then bought a house; and when his neighbor-gunstock maker Cornelis Bogardus died in 1664, Schuyler and notary Van Schelluyne administered his estate.[128] The location near the hill on the *Jonckerstraet*, which was sometimes called the *bospad* or the *Maquaes pad*, provided a good opportunity to be first visited by the Indians who would enter the village near his house.[129] But Schuyler saw advantages in other places as well. In 1655, he bought a large parcel of woodland and a house of one board long on the *Beverkil* from Jochem Wesselsz *backer* for ƒ468; it was not far from the Norman's kill, another route where Indians coming from the west sometimes passed through; they could be met there before they passed the fort and entered the village.[130] (Appendix 8, X, no. 13). In 1656, he received a patent for a lot for a garden and a lot for an orchard next to Jeremias van Rensselaer; and in 1659 he acquired another garden next to Annetje Bogardus and *dominee* Schaets, which in the past had been granted to Anthony de Hooges.[131] In 1659 he also owned half of a house and lot on the east side of Pearl Street (Appendix 8, VIII, no. 9), which in 1664 he sold to Goosen Gerritsz, who owned the other half. In September 1661, he bought Pieter Adriaensz's house and lot for ƒ1,306. He sold the lot in 1667 to Jan *de Noorman*, while he had the house removed.[132] He may have moved it to the lot west of Rutger Jacobsz, which he acquired in September 1664, and which seems to have suited him best. This was a part of the large lot of Abraham Staets, and it was located on the south side of *Jonckerstraet*, adjoining the hill and the first kill (Appendix 8, XI, AS). Schuyler sold part of the lot with a house on it on the same day to Gysbert Jansz, but he himself settled on the remaining part of the lot. He seems to have preferred its location close to the hill over the situation of the lot he had owned earlier on the north side, which went to Jan Thomasz; and he may have had his eye on it for a while, as in 1659 he was granted eight feet of ground westward by the commissaries, where later his Indian house would stand.[133] Although Staets himself kept a part of the lot, he may have settled at the east end of *Jonckerstraet*, where in July 1661 he acquired from the innkeeper Hendrick Jochemsz the house and lot that previously had been owned by the baker Hendrick Jansz Westerkamp and his wife Femmetje. From Schuyler, he also bought an adjacent lot there (Appendix 8, II, no. 13). Considering that Staets now owned important pieces of property at both the very western and the very eastern ends of *Jonckerstraet*, and that years later the little alley at the side would be called 'Staets' Alley': Could this have been a possible origin for the name 'State Street,' which is presently used – 'Staets' street?' After all, the *Ruttenkil* and the *Vossenkil* derived their names from Rut Jacobsz and Andries de Vos, who lived next to these creeks; and the first farms (for example, the *De Laetsburch*) may have set the trend when they were named after people in *patria*. Why not apply the same principle to one of the main streets?[134]

Like Staets, Douw and Thomasz, and other successful burghers, Schuyler invested in newly developed areas outside of the village. In September 1662, he owned two lots of land among the allotments of the newly projected village at the Esopus, for which he hired Barent Harmensz on similar conditions as Douw and Thomasz had hired their lessees. Barent was to sow oats, build a dwelling house, barn, rick, and a bridge over the kill, for which Schuyler would deliver a hundred boards. From September 1, 1663, Barent had to pay ƒ450 a year in beavers, grain or *sewant*, while Schuyler delivered horses, cows, sows, on half share according to the custom, and a plow and a wagon with their appurtenances. As in the patroon's contracts, where a lessor had to pay a *toepacht*, Barent had deliver a barrow pig annually for three years.[135]

In following years, Schuyler would expand his possessions. While he sold some land at the Esopus, he acquired more land from the Indians at Half Moon in 1664, together with Goosen Gerritsz. This was done initially to prevent the English in Connecticut from moving in; but, at the same time, it was again a well-chosen location to do some private trading: With the Hudson River as the eastern boundary and the Mohawk as its southern boundary, it was a perfect location to meet the Indians before reached Beverwijck.[136] In 1672, he bought the farm north of Albany, *De Vlackte*, from the Van Rensselaers.

Being a part of the community

After his father-in-law Brant van Slichtenhorst had left New Netherland, Philip Schuyler would become active in Beverwijck's court; and by serving as a magistrate from May 1656 to 1658, and again from 1661 to 1662, he would help make important decisions regarding Beverwijck's future existence.[137] As magistrate, he sometimes arbitrated disagreements, and frequently had to deal with regulation of the liquor trade and Indian relations. His work on the court would be eternalized by Evert Duyckinck, who set the coats of arms of all magistrates that year in stained glass windows for the new church that was built in 1656.[138]

His place in the church seems justified, as Schuyler was a loyal church supporter. Not only did he occasionally do business by selling his merchandise to the deaconry, such as blankets and *dosijnties* (a kind of woolen cloth or kersey) for use by the poor and wine for the communion ritual, but he also frequently gave alms and offered himself as surety for the costs of the building of the 'block house' church in April 1656.[139] From 1658 to 1660, Schuyler was deacon of the church, in which capacity he was called upon to help design a strategy for dealing with the increased number of needy people. Together with such men as Adriaen Gerritsz, Abraham Staets, Evert Jansz Wendel, Gerrit Slichtenhorst, Rutger Jacobsz, La Montagne, and Frans Barentsz, he developed plans for the church. Schuyler was well aware that taking care of the poor was becoming an ever greater task; during the time he kept the deacons' accounts in 1660, the number of people receiving alms rose to twenty-six, the highest number in Albany's Dutch period. The trade had declined since 1658; several inhabitants had fallen victim to the Indian troubles at the Esopus and needed help; and, as a result of the war between the Maquaes and the French, several Frenchmen were ransomed from the Indians, sometimes for a good price. One decision that year was to enlarge the poorhouse by building an extension; but the human aspect was not forgotten: The last expenditure for the poor recorded by Schuyler in the deacons' account book was the only entry between 1652 and 1674 that suggests any kind of compassion for the needy: On December 31, *Meester* Abraham was paid ƒ15-12 for wine and sugar enjoyed by the poor.[140] Schuyler remained active in the church at various times in his life. From 1664 through 1666, and from 1681 through 1683, he was on the consistory again; by that time his family had acquired four hereditary pews in the church.[141]

Signs of success

Schuyler would become one of the wealthiest inhabitants of the area. In 1675, he took an oath that his assets in the New World did not exceed ƒ24,000 in beavers.[142] He had his own network of friends that probably included his brother David, his brother-in-law Gerrit Van Slichtenhorst, and Goosen Gerritsz, as well as the Van Rensselaers – all the more remarkable, in the light of the animosities that took place in *patria* between the Van Rensselaers and Schuyler's father-in-law in the latter's court case, which dragged on from 1656 to 1662. Each party may have seen the benefit to his own business of keeping the other in the network. The families frequently visited with each other, and Margaretha presented two sons of Jeremias and Maria van Rensselaer for baptism (although with the first child, in 1663, she was a substitute for Anna van Rensselaer). At the baptism of Johannes van Rens-

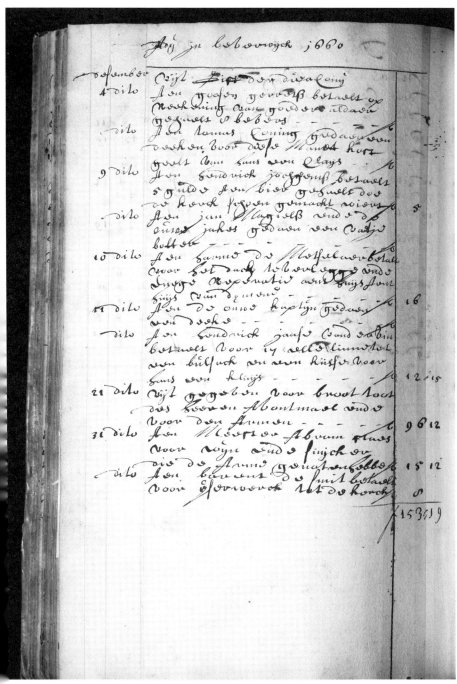

54. *Disbursements of the deaconry in December, 1660. Philip Pietersz Schuyler kept the books in that year.*

selaer in 1671, Philip substituted for godfather Olof Stevensz.[143]

As they were among the wealthiest inhabitants, the success of the Schuylers was probably most visible to others. Here and there, the documents shed light on some of their material possessions. The gold headdress valued at about six black beavers, which Margaretha ordered through Van Rensselaer in 1660, and the purchase of a *f*18 *roosjensring* (rose-cut diamond ring), suggest that their clothing was fashionable and of good quality. The ring by itself cost more than the *f*12 Jan Labatie had paid for his wife's headdress.[144] Margaretha's wardrobe may have been similar to Gerritie Brants,' Goosen Gerritsz's deceased wife, which in 1664 was appraised at 61 beavers at *f*8 apiece – substantially more than the clothes left behind by the needy tailor's wife Trijntie Janssen, which were worth only *f*228 in *sewant*.[145] Gerritie's wardrobe included two scarlet skirts of six beavers each, a silk skirt of nine beavers and an armozine skirt with a green lining, which was worth seven beavers. Also among her goods were eight shirts valued at five beavers, ten aprons worth four beavers, eleven night neckerchiefs worth three beavers, four round handkerchiefs (*neusdoecken*) valued at four beavers, and six regular handkerchiefs worth one beaver.[146] While silk was generally a more costly fabric than wool, there also were very fine woolen textiles; Gerretie's scarlet skirts may have been made of a good quality cloth (*laken*) or baize, rather than the cheaper and more common serge. The undervest (*borstrock*) that was also among her clothes was probably made of warm cloth, and the three small cloaks (*mantelties*) of a heavier sort of cloth. Bodices, which were not mentioned among Gerritie's clothes, but which were a common women's outfit for the upper body, were often made of silk. Her ten aprons may have served various purposes: They may have been used for work, and protected the skirt against dirt. Gerritie may also have worn them for decoration; when a beautiful apron was worn on a simple skirt, it could give it a luxurious accent.[147]

The sale of goods of Rutger Jacobsz's estate, where Schuyler bought the *roosjensring*, provides us with a glimpse of the sorts of jewelry that were in circulation, and Schuyler probably had similar jewelry at home. Nine people bought sixteen pieces of silverware or jewelry, among which were sets of four silver spoons, a silver beaker, a silver salt cellar, bows, golden rings, a diamond ring, a double hoop ring, a gold hair pin, and six silver *mannetiens* (figures of little men, sometimes standing on a plate). These were items affluent Beverwijckers bought: Jeremias van Rensselaer and his brother Richard bought the most, while Arent van Curler and Abraham Staets also were willing buyers.[148] Jewelry is mentioned in some other sales and inventories. Johan de Hulter, for example, sold several rings in 1655: The most expensive ring was bought for *f*92 by Cornelis Theunisz; Cornelis Vos purchased one for *f*61-10, and Arent van Curler bought one for *f*39, while Rutger Jacobsz picked up the cheapest ring for *f*31-10. De Hulter also sold some half moons (*halve maenen*) for *f*24, and many *ricxdaelders* and other pieces of money. In 1659, Pieter Claerbout had a silver girdle (*riem*) and two golden rings, which he sold for *f*20, *f*20, and *f*16; and Jan Gerritsz van Marcken had a silver headdress in his house. Among the goods sold at the auction of Cornelis Bogardus's estate were silver breeches buttons, silver spoons and a little silver beaker.[149]

Although little is known about decorations of Schuyler's house, his 1654 purchase of an inlaid oaken cabinet for twenty-two beavers and *f*10 in beavers, and the 1664 purchase of a *f*100 painting, suggest that he was willing to spend some money on items of luxury, and that his house was well decorated and furnished with good quality furniture.[150] Auctions provide us with an idea of what else Schuyler may have had in his house. At the sale of Rutger Jacobsz's goods, for example, a small victuals box was sold for *f*7, one table for *f*2-5, and another brought eight guilders more; a chair was sold for *f*12-10, three sitting cushions for *f*18, and a chimney valance for *f*9. Gabriel Thomasz paid *f*43-10 for a mirror. Undoubtedly, Schuyler also had various common household items, such as pewter and earthenware plates, saucers and spoons, copper kettles, silver spoons, and *roemers* (rummers), similar to those sold of Jacobsz's goods. Earthenware was generally cheaper than pewter. Twenty-two earthenware objects among Jacobsz's goods brought *f*66, and eighteen pewter items *f*71-10; of the goods of Cornelis Bogardus's estate, twenty-one earthenware items were sold for *f*104-10, and twenty-five pewter items (including six pewter spoons counted as one item) for *f*225:10. At the auction of Dirck Jansz Croon's goods in 1665, sixteen earthenware items brought *f*11-15, and forty pewter items *f*90-10. Prices thus varied according to material, size, decoration and quality. The two pewter saucers Volckert Jansz bought from Jacobsz's goods, for instance, cost *f*25; Jan Bijvanck bought two for *f*10, while at the sale of Croon's goods one could buy two for *f*7.[151] Other items Schuyler may have had in his house perhaps included a tapestry, and a table cover, which on a rare occasion appear in some auctions.[152] The sales of some mirrors indicate that these luxurious items had also found their way to the upper Hudson. The three-dimensional effect of especially large mirrors, and the way they facilitated self-presentation, gave interiors a certain substance, and Schuyler may very well have had one or more in his house.[153]

Among Jacobsz's goods were several well-priced items, of which some paintings were most outstanding; six of the paintings together brought *f*273. The *f*100 painting Schuyler bought was the most expensive, while he also bought a small one for *f*35; Arent van Curler bought a painting for *f*85, while other pictures went for *f*36 and *f*35 to Robert Sandersz and Leendert Philipsz; Johannes Provoost bought the two cheapest 'little paintings' (*schilderijtiens*) for *f*17-10. That price was still high compared to prices of paintings at other auctions, where they went for prices as low as one guilder. Like the paintings bought by Provoost, these were mostly called *schilderijtiens*, and some may have been prints glued to a hard board (*bortjes*), while Schuyler's painting was called a 'painting' (*schilderije*). At the auction of Dirck Jansz Croon's goods, thirty-eight little paintings and six paintings were sold for *f*83, of which six together cost *f*4-15. The addition of the diminutive to the word '*schilderij*' thus does not really explain anything about the type or quality of the picture.[154]

One could find books in Schuyler's house. As he seems to have been a very religious man, he probably had books with religious content, a few bibles, and psalm books. In addition, he may have had an almanac, as these were popular among most people. At a 1654 auction of Gabriel Leendertsz, he bought three books for ƒ16, of which one cost ƒ6 – most likely the popular translation of the Heidelberg Catechism after J. Ursinus, by Festus Hommius, a well-known Reformed Orthodox minister who had been president of the Synod of Dordt. In 1657, Robert Vastrick sent Schuyler a number of books, but no information about them was provided. Unfortunately, titles of books were usually not mentioned; prices were listed, and occasionally sizes, or whether they contained maps.[155]

Reading this information, but having little to compare it with, raises numerous questions: How many other people in the village possessed similar paintings and jewelry? What did it mean that the curators of Jacobsz's estate sold, and that Schuyler bought, a ƒ100 painting? Were Jacobsz and Schuyler exceptions? Did he have more pictures, and were those of similar value? While Jeremias van Rensselaer spent only ƒ8-15 on a painting, did he have other, more expensive, paintings in his house? Why was Schuyler willing to pay ƒ100 for it? Did it have a biblical theme? Or was it perhaps a landscape or a portrait? These genres were popular in the fatherland, and a real collector there would sometimes pay as much as ƒ1,500 for a small, finely painted scene by Gerrit Dou.[156] And the jewelry: Prior to his death, did Jacobsz have more jewelry, which he perhaps sold to friends? Was it meant to be sold, or did these items belong to his and his wife Trijntje's personal belongings; and had their intent been to keep the items in the family? Due to the lack of comparative source materials in Beverwijck, we can only look at Jacobsz's estate for an indication of the types of luxury items that had reached Beverwijck; and we may suspect that other successful burghers such as Schuyler, Abraham Staets, Goosen Gerritsz, Sander Leendertsz, Evert Wendel, Jan Verbeeck, and Arent van Curler may have acquired similar possessions during the 1650s and '60s.

As Schuyler's wealth increased, so did his family. In July 1652, his first boy Gisbert was born; he would be followed by eleven brothers and sisters between 1654 and 1672, of whom eight survived.[157] Philip and Margaretha would provide them all with a good education and legacy; in 1683, each of the youngest four children would be promised the sum of ƒ1,250 in beavers if they had not received an outfit by the time one of their parents died. The orphan masters were excluded from the equal division of the entire estate among the eight children.[158]

Although he had come in 1650 as a baker's son, at the end of his life Philip Schuyler was able to leave behind a good legacy for his fifty-five year-old widow and his children. He was ill in 1682, and when he died in 1683 he was buried in the church.[159] His trade of gunstock maker and his marriage to Van Slichtenhorst's daughter undoubtedly were of great importance to his rapid rise. His keen eye and awareness of the profitability of certain locations, his ability to trade and negotiate while maintaining his connections with important trading partners, and his way of investing in land – all added to his prosperity. Like Abraham Staets, Schuyler was never sued for not having paid his debts, even when the fur trade declined. The same cannot be said of Rutger Jacobsz and Sander Leendertsz Glen, who had invested heavily in the trade. Jacobsz would die at an early age and, as noted above, many of his belongings were sold to pay debts after his death, leaving his widow with little. Sander Leendertsz lived longer, and would become one of Schenectady's leading inhabitants.

Sander Leendertsz Glen

Living and sailing on the Noortrivier: A Scottish family

In October 1638, a thirty-two-year-old sailor from Fifeshire, Scotland, Sander Leendertsz Glen van Dysart, married the eighteen-year old Catelijn Donckes, also from Scotland (Alloa, in Clacmannanshire). Sander had earlier been in New Netherland for several years, 'sailing from one place to another.'[160] Half a year after their wedding, the couple would sign a contract with Kiliaen van Rensselaer and go to Rensselaerswijck for four years as free colonists. As a freeman, Leendertsz was allowed to bring merchandise with him from the Dutch Republic to trade in the colony for peltry, on condition that the pelts be sold to the patroon's agent. During the term of his contract, he was not to settle in other areas of New Netherland.[161] After 1641, Sander and Catelijn sailed two of the patroon's yachts for three years, 'but not while they tapped liquor.' From 1647 to 1652, the patroon charged Leendertsz *f*32 a year for land rent and the right to trade with the Indians.[162]

In 1652, Leendertsz obtained a patent for a lot in Beverwijck that was located south of the first kill, on the riverside (Appendix 8, I, no. 9; III, no. 8). Although he was caught in 1654 for having enclosed too much land on his own authority, Leendertsz's lot must have been large; over time, he would build several houses and various other structures on it. By 1662, he had at least three houses, two small houses, a barn, and two gardens there.[163] They lived close to Catelijn's sister Margareth Donckes and her husband Willem Teller from Hetland (in the Shetland Islands), who was sometimes called Willem *de Hit* (or Willem *Scot*); Teller had come to the area in 1639 as a corporal for the West India Company. In 1652, Teller had a patent for a lot just north of the first kill, on the southwest corner of *Jonckerstraet* and present-day Broadway, on which probably stood the house he had bought in 1649 from Abraham Staets[164] (see Appendix 8, III, no. 10). Baker Thomas Poulusz, who was married to Jannetie Donckes (another of Catelijn's sisters), bought Leendertsz's house and lot on the west side of the street, next to *dominee* Schaets (who lived in the poor house) in October 1662; it was diagonally from Leendertsz' large house with the stone gable[165] (see Appendix 8, III, no. 8).

Leendertsz owned property elsewhere in the *bijeenwoninge*, as well. In 1652, he also received a patent for a lot adjoining the hill; and in 1655 he was given lot number one at the hill, on the west side of Philip Pietersz, which was one of five lots distributed among the magistrates.[166] At some point, he had acquired a lot that had previously belonged to Marten Herpertsz, a mason (Appendix 8, VII, no. 18). He leased a house on this lot in 1656, and perhaps earlier, to master tailor Jacob Tysz; in 1659 and 1660, master tailor Jan Vinhaegen may have lived in the same house, which was located on the north side of *Jonckerstraet* between Jan Thomasz and

Annetje Bogardus. In May 1662, Jurriaen Jansz Groenewout rented the house, and Leendertsz sold it in October 1663 to Jan Clute.[167]

Leendertsz also owned property in other parts of New Netherland. At New Amsterdam, he owned land at the *Smith's Vly* (Valley) in 1646, and in 1656 he and his brother-in-law Willem Teller both owned a lot at the South River (Delaware). When Leendertsz brought his clapboards to build a house, the construction was forcibly prevented by Swedish officers. Eventually, however, he would build his house; in 1657, he obtained a patent for a house and garden located near Fort Casimier on the South River, where at various times he brought bricks from Fort Orange.[168]

Together with his wife Catelijn, Leendertsz remained actively involved in trading and shipping. Jan Baptist van Rensselaer, for example, frequently sent goods to New Amsterdam with his yacht.[169] Sailing to various areas may have enhanced Leendertsz's trading opportunities. Because of his and Catelijn's Scottish background, and their experience at the South River, it is hard to imagine that they would not have had contacts with people in New England and Virginia, especially when sailing their yacht on the South River. As trade was commonly conducted in family firms, Leendertsz may occasionally have worked together with Willem Teller, who also was one of Beverwijck's principal traders; through Teller, he may also have become more involved in trade with the English. Both men seem to have been interested in affairs of England and Scotland, and Teller was well aquainted with the New England trader Paulus Schrick, who lived at Hartford. After his wife Margareth died in 1662, Teller would marry Schrick's widow Maria Varleth in 1664.[170] In later years, after the English had taken over New Netherland, Teller's son Andries would live in Boston and maintain trade relations with Beverwijck from there.

Taking risks

After several years of a successful fur trade, Sander and Catelijn were not afraid to invest in trading goods. Sometime in the late 1640s or early 1650s, for example, they had bought a large quantity of merchandise from the Van Twillers; but Jan van Twiller, who was to collect payment, never transferred any organized accounts to his relatives and trading partners once he was back in the fatherland. By 1659, Wouter van Twiller had died, and his widow Maria Momma and her brother Guilliaem sent Jan Bastiaensz van Gutsenhoven as agent to collect these neglected debts. Of the more than eighty people on Bastiaensz's list, Leendertsz was indebted the most, with a promissory note of ƒ9,753-12-8.[171] The Mommaes were not the only persons to whom Leendertsz owed money. In 1660, he was indebted to trader Dirck Jansz Croon for ƒ576 or seventy-five beavers, and thirty beavers interest on this sum; and in 1661, Catrina (Catelijn) signed a bond, stating that she was indebted for the sum of ƒ535-18 in good whole beavers to New Amsterdam trader Nicolaes de Meyer.[172]

Leendertsz was by no means an exception: Even the successful burgher Rutger Jacobsz was in trouble. Jacobsz had been an 'honorable' magistrate in 1652, 1655-

56, and in 1660-61, a member of the consistory between 1652 and 1654, and from 1657 to 1659, and had even laid the first stone for the blockhouse church. This Jacobsz was also heavily indebted to various traders from whom he had bought merchandise.[173] He owed Johannes Withart *f*1,528 by August 1656, and he was indebted for thirty-eight and thirty-two beavers to Dirck Dirksz Keyser in August 1659. And like Leendertsz's wife Catelijn, Jacobsz's wife Trijntie Janse van Breestede was involved in business as well; in 1658, she acknowledged that she owed the New Amsterdam trader Cornelis Steenwijck *f*5,482-2. According to Jan Bastiaensz van Gutsenhoven's list of August 1661, the Jacobsens owed him *f*835-12; and in September of that year, Jacobsz promised Pieter Simonsz that he would pay him *f*1,032 in July 1662 for received goods, for which he mortgaged his yacht.[174] In August 1661, he owed Teunis Cornelisz van der Poel *f*352, in addition to two *toebevers* and two otters; and in March 1662, he was indebted to Jacob Gevick for *f*1,200 at 12 percent interest, which he promised to pay in wheat.[175] To pay his debts, Jacobsz sold pieces of his property in Beverwijck; and in 1660 he sold his land, house and lot at Manhattan, which he had bought in 1649; in Beverwijck, he sold a large part of his property on the south side of *Jonckerstraet* on which he had built a house, and his garden.[176] (Appendix 8, XI, RJ; I, 2). In 1661, when Jacobsz was not able to pay off all his debts, Volkert Jansz Douw helped out and promised to pay to Jan Hendricksz van Bael 'as his own debt for Rutger Jacobsz, his brother-in-law,' *f*302-8-7 at 10 percent, for which Rutger pledged some jewelry and silverware.[177] The items he pledged for this debt were sold at a public sale in December 1665, along with some furniture, goods, household items, and other silverware and jewelry. They were sold with the express stipulation that no one 'shall pay by deducting moneys due to him from Rutger Jacobsz, but that the buyer shall deliver the money into the hands of the vendue master and wait for a pro rata division.' Prominent traders (but not Sander Leendertsz) were present at the sale and bought some valuable items. In addition to *f*983-10 for various household items, the sale brought *f*512-14 for the gold jewels and silverware, and the whole yield was paid to Jan Hendricksz van Bael and Richard van Rensselaer. The sloop that he commanded, and which he had mortgaged in 1661, was sold a week later; a good year later, another garden was sold as well.[178]

Leendertsz sold parts of his property as well. In August 1660, he gave Captain Thomas Willet a power of attorney to sell his house and lot in the *Smits Vly* at Manhattan, where a certain Laurens Cornelis van (de) Well dwelled, not for less than *f*2,000, 'the more the better.' It was, however, only in the fall of 1675 that the eastern portion of this lot was sold, as well as the original larger part.[179] In 1662, as partial payment for his debt, he sold to Jan Bastiaensz 'his house with the stone gable in which he at present lives, along with the lot and garden, and a small house which is standing behind the large house.' There was also a barn, lot and a garden behind the barn, all located on the west side of the street, opposite the large house. Leendertsz kept for himself the little house opposite the large house, and a small house north of the large house. Included in this *f*3,200 sale were two gardens behind Fort Orange.[180] He sold a house and lot at the hill to Jan Clute in 1663 (see Appendix 8, I, no. 9; III, no. 8; VII, no. 18). In the same year, a garden east of Je-

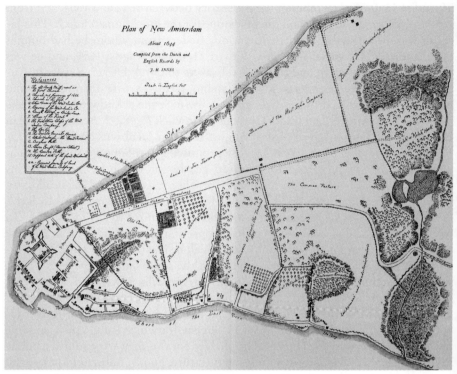

55. Several inhabitants of Beverwijck owned property in New Amsterdam. Sander Leendertsz owned a house and lot in the Smits Vlij.

remias van Rensselaer, for which Leendertsz had received a patent in 1658, went to Caspar Jacobsz; and two gardens behind the patroon's house, on the second street next to the hill, were sold to Jurriaen Theunisz. In 1664, he sold a lot at the hill to Croon's attorney Adriaen Gerritsz, as a 'deduction from his existing mortgage of ƒ526 and interest from the third of January at 10 percent, together with ƒ100 in *sewant* received in cash.'[181] He sold to Jan Hendricksz van Bael another house and lot adjoining Jan Thomasz to the north, and Hendrick Cuyler to the south.[182] In 1671, Leendertsz sold 'his certain lot with a well right over against the king's house, formerly belonging to Jan Bastiaensz van Gutsenhoven, deceased' to Jurriaen Theunisz.[183]

That Leendertsz – like Jacobsz, and many others – had played a dangerous game becomes clear when we look at Willem Brouwer, a master shoemaker who does not appear in the records until January 1657, and who considered himself a principal trader in 1660. By 1664, however, Brouwer was receiving poor relief; and after his death, Brouwer's widow asked permission to renounce the estate so that she could 'receive the same favor as other oppressed persons.'[184] How Jacobsz would have handled his affairs more to his advantage we will never know: He would die in 1664, indebted to various people, and having sold much of his property in Beverwijck, as well as in New Amsterdam. At the time of his death, his entire fortune seems to have been at risk. In the spring of 1667, Jacobsz's widow Trijntje Jans turned over at a court session 'the few remaining goods which were not believed to be of any consequence (except some necessities of life of which your honors could not entirely deprive her).'[185] This case shows how the death of a husband could also mean a great financial loss for a woman. Lysbeth Brouwer abandoned and renounced her estate. Trijntje Jans seems to have lost many of her possessions; and more than a quarter-century would elapse before she remarried in 1695, with a prenuptial agreement. Catelijn Sanders, however, still had her husband, and would continue to trade at such a level that she very well may have been the woman described by Jasper Danckaerts, in 1680, as 'one of the Dutch female traders, who understand their business so well.'[186]

But even indebtedness as great as Leendertsz's and Jacobsz's did not mean that they had lost people's respect; and until 1662, they remained magistrates in Beverwijck's court.[187] Nor had they lost their creditworthiness as yet. While Brouwer ended up receiving alms and losing his reputation, Jacobsz seems to have died in the midst of his financial crisis, leaving his wife with little more than some necessities of life. It is hard to predict what might have happened if Jacobsz had lived longer: He may have ended up like Sander Leendertsz; but there was also a good possibility that he would have taken Willem Brouwer's route.

Leendertsz probably was prepared to move, once plans had been made to begin a new village at the location of present-day Schenectady. In 1663, he was one of the twenty settlers who owned land there, and most likely he hoped to find more opportunities for the fur trade. But Stuyvesant, by enforcing his 1662 order – namely, that the West India Company did not 'intend to erect one place to ruin thereby another, yes, the entire country' – had strictly prohibited trading with the Indians at this site. At this new village on the frontier, settlers were only granted permission to engage in agriculture.[188] In 1670, Leendertsz acknowledged that he was still indebted to Jeremias van Rensselaer and his own son, Jacob Sandersz Glen, who together administered the estate of Jan Bastiaensz, in the sum of ƒ6,000 in beavers for merchandise received; to satisfy this debt, he mortgaged his *bouwerij* at Schenectady with its land, house, barn, ricks, horses and cattle.[189]

A Scotsman in Beverwijck

Besides being an active trader, Leendertsz was also an active member of Beverwijck's community. How well he got along with his relatives remains a question, as they seem occasionally to have had different opinions on relevant issues. With his brother-in-law Willem Teller, he may have had several discussions about construction of the blockhouse church, which was built in 1656. While Leendertsz declared himself as surety for payment of the work, Teller protested emphatically against construction of the building in front of his house by closing off the public road (opposite Abraham Vosburgh) that went to the river, so that it could not be used (Appendix 8, I, near no. 4). He declared that 'the building of the blockhouse or certain proceedings by the court [of which Leendertsz at that time was a member] concerning it would cry to Heaven for vengeance.'[190] Leendertsz seems to have been somewhat more successful than Teller: He served as a magistrate in Beverwijck for two terms, while Teller got no further than once being nominated for magistrate.[191] They may also have had different opinions in 1660, when the village was so divided about the Indian trade. Teller signed the request of the twenty-five principal traders to allow only Indian brokers and, a few weeks later, was even accused of calling people like Cornelis Theunisz Bos and Jacob Tysz 'rabble.'[192] As a sitting magistrate, Leendertsz advised that neither Indians nor Christians ought to run into the woods as brokers; and in June, when the Maquaes brought many complaints about having been abused in the woods, he advised the natives that the Dutch would be forbidden to roam in the woods.[193] Both Teller and Leendertsz were principal traders and dealt with Indian brokers. Their brother-in-law Thomas Poulusz had signed the other petition, requesting that anyone be allowed to do business in order to earn a beaver.[194] As a magistrate, Leendertsz might have had a disagreement with Thomas as well; but he retired from the job in May 1656, just before that could have occurred. In June 1656, the new court fined Poulusz and some other bakers ƒ12 for having baked underweight bread, in order to use the flour for cookies and sweetbreads to sell to the Indians; Jannetie Donckes, Poulusz's wife, was so upset that she called the *schout* and magistrates 'a pack of extortioners and devils,' for which she was fined another ƒ25.[195]

It seems that the live circumstances of the three Donckes sisters, born in Scotland as minister's daughters, had become different as a result of their marriages in Amsterdam, even though they lived close by one another. Catelijn, having married Sander, was financially off best. She was probably even the first, and likely the only woman in Beverwijck, to have had a slave.[196] Thomas Poulusz might have had more chances for prosperity if he had been in New Netherland earlier. While Leendertsz and Teller had been able to build up and maintain contacts with Indians and other settlers, and to establish themselves since 1639, Poulusz first appears in the records only in 1655, after having lived in Brazil since 1641. It is quite possible that, like another baker who had moved from Brazil to Beverwijck, he had been forced to leave investments and possessions behind after the Dutch lost this important colony in 1654.[197] His late start in Beverwijck clearly put Poulusz behind Leendertsz and Teller. Despite their disagreements, they did recognize each other as family, and sometimes were securety or witnesses for each other, or baptism witnesses. When Margareth Teller died in 1662, Leendertsz became guardian of the seven children left behind.[198]

Although it may occasionally have brought him into conflict with his relatives, Leendertsz filled the office of magistrate in 1654-55 and again in 1659-60 and, as such, was involved in various assignments. Through longtime experience, he was quite familiar with the quality of *sewant* beads, which were used as payment; and in 1653, when Leendertsz was 48, he and Abraham Staets (who by then had lived in the upper Hudson for eleven years) were authorized to collect the general tax of ƒ15 assessed on each house for the completion of the bridges. In July 1657, together with Pieter Hartgers, he was authorized to determine the quality of some *sewant*.[199]

Although he declared himself in 1656 as surety for payment of the construction of the blockhouse church, Leendertsz (unlike Willem Teller) was never a member of the consistory.[200] J. H. Innes, who in *New Amsterdam and its People* described Leendertsz as being the same person as Alexander Lindesay of the Glen in Scotland, suggests that he may have had Jacobite (i.e., Catholic) propensities.[201] It is possible that the French prisoner Father Joseph Poncet referred to Catelijn or her sister Margareth when, during his stay in Beverwijck in 1653, he described a 'good Scotch Lady who has shown herself on all occasions very charitable toward the French,' and who took charge of providing him with every conceivable provision for his comfort with much skill and affection.[202]

Leendertsz, like other successful burghers, invested in merchandise, in real estate in the village, and in a farm in a newly developed area. That he kept the respect of the community, despite the fact that he was long indebted for a large sum of money, suggests that this was not considered negatively. Perhaps indebtedness was even seen as part of a trader's life; much as credit, today, is considered the engine of the economy, risk-taking in the seventeenth century created opportunities for new investments, as well. As seems to have been the custom in New Netherland, it seems that he first paid off his most recent debts, so that the old ones remained standing.[203] Dennis Maika found that Manhattan merchants did that, too. Even though most mortgage agreements stipulated that repayment should be made within one year or less, this rarely happened in practice. Some mortgages never brought into court were settled well beyond the time allowed, sometimes being overdue by as long as ten years.[204] Death prevented Jacobsz from ever recovering; but Leendertsz did recover and, in cooperation with Catalijntje, was quite able to manage his affairs. Despite his debts, he served repeatedly as a magistrate in Schenectady, and would also become there one of the new settlement's leading inhabitants.[205]

Conclusion

In the previous chapter, we saw how several factors played a role in the success of a seventeenth-century settler in the upper Hudson area. The clearing of land, and other hard work they had done to get ahead, had tested their flexibility and endurance; by the 1650s, several men knew the different features of nature, the land, and a good part of its inhabitants. By traveling back and forth, several traders maintained continuous contact with the fatherland, while contributing much to the settlement's development as a typical Dutch community.

By 1650, those who had come during the 1630s and 1640s were quite familiar with the Indians, and had developed their own trading practices and personal relationships with the natives. They also had gotten to know their fellow settlers, and had established trading networks. Often, they undertook cooperative projects with other colonists, such as running a farm, a brewery, or a mill, thus increasing their chances of success. Working together helped create a local network of friends upon whom they could count in times of family problems such as illness or decease, and who would help with various services. Like the Van Rensselaers, colonists in this new society usually included relatives in their networks, and people in their neighborhood, or people with whom they worked. After April 1652, some men who had served as members of the court of Rensselaerswijck became Beverwijck's magistrates and leaders.

Some Beverwijck inhabitants returned to the Republic, but intended to remain involved in the trade with New Netherland. By their time of departure, they had established a circle of friends whom they trusted to buy the goods they would send from *patria,* and to pay for them. For those settlers who stayed in the upper Hudson area, it was important to maintain contacts with traders in *patria* to obtain merchandise for themselves and for the Indian trade. Trading relations between the settlement and the fatherland were based on trust and great mobility; several of Beverwijck's inhabitants frequently crossed the ocean.

Generally, anyone's success depended on the supply of beavers and, until about 1657-58, there seem to have been enough pelts for the entire community to share. Being involved in the trade required a knowledge of it, and the willingness to invest and take risks. If this was not done wisely, however, the trade could cause great damage. Risk taking was part of a merchant's life; and traders, even when they were heavily in debt, did not quickly loose people's respect. But going bankrupt meant the loss of one's reputation and honor – and living an honorable life was required in order to earn the community's respect and to hold the position of magistrate.

In addition to leading an honorable life, it was important to lead a good religious life. Several principal traders were not only faithful church members, but also frequently served in the consistory as deacon or elder. By enforcing ecclesiastical discipline and deciding who would or would not receive assistance in times of need, the consistory guided the moral values and social life of the community in specific directions. Yet, the magistrates were not a totally closed circle of believers: Among them were a few non-church members who were valued for their success, age, and long-time experience and insights in the New World. And, most likely, these men lived honorable lives and were married to honorable wives.

Marriage to an economically well-situated partner, and his or her willingness and abilities to be involved in work, were important contributions to success. Important networks of friends could then be combined, and possessions and work forces could be pooled together, thereby creating a solid base for the children and continued business. Successful men who stayed in Beverwijck were usually able to rely on their wives as partners to help them with their work and to raise their children, for whom they could foresee a good future in the new land.

Once colonists had made some profits, they used their earnings as a foundation to develop economic progress further. Sometimes they divided their original patents into smaller lots, which they would sell. They expanded their property by subdividing their lots and by buying more real estate within the village; they often built houses on these lots, which they then sold or leased out. Successful traders also invested in such projects as a brewery, a brick-making business, or a ship – projects of importance to the community. At some point, many settlers bought more land outside of the village, on which they built farms and other buildings.

They provided these farms with animals and farm equipment, and then leased them to others.

To be part of the group of successful burghers, it was important to make one's success visible, and to maintain a certain life-style. As soon as they had acquired some wealth, Beverwijck's inhabitants desired to reach a standard of living and status resembling that of wealthy people in the fatherland. Van Rensselaer – who paid attention to such outer appearances as a large house, fashionable clothing, entertainment of friends, and having servants – may have been the closest example for the settlers. The occasional appearance of an expensive piece of clothing, jewelry, or home decoration in an inventory or at an auction suggests that successful burghers followed the trend of showing their prosperity. That some people in Beverwijck even 'possessed' something a wealthy man in *patria* could not have had – namely, slaves – may indicate the beginning of a process in which an American way of life would eventually replace the Dutch way.

A sixteen-year-old Dutch farmhand could, later in his life, become a magistrate and consistory member in a village on the American frontier, and help shape a new community as he saw fit for himself and his children. In *patria*, he most likely would have stayed a farm hand for the rest of his life or, at most, perhaps have acquired a farm of his own. It is clear, then, that at the upper Hudson these men were better off than in their fatherlands. The area offered people who did not have a wealthy background, but who were willing to work hard, who dared to invest, lived honorable and good Christian lives according to the standards of the fatherland, and who perhaps had a great deal of luck, the chance to climb many steps on the social ladder quickly. This ladder stood in a different continent, in a place on the Indian frontier, where these settlers worked hard in order to establish a society similar the one in patria – the difference being that, now, they had become the wealthiest, most honorable and wisest men leading the community.

In this chapter, we saw that nearly all successful burghers did multiple work, and were involved in several activities such as gunstock making, brewing, farming, or shipping at the same time. In this frontier society, some trades had other prospectives than they had in patria. In the next chapter, we will take a closer look at some of these trades and the reasons one trade in Beverwijck could be more lucrative than another.

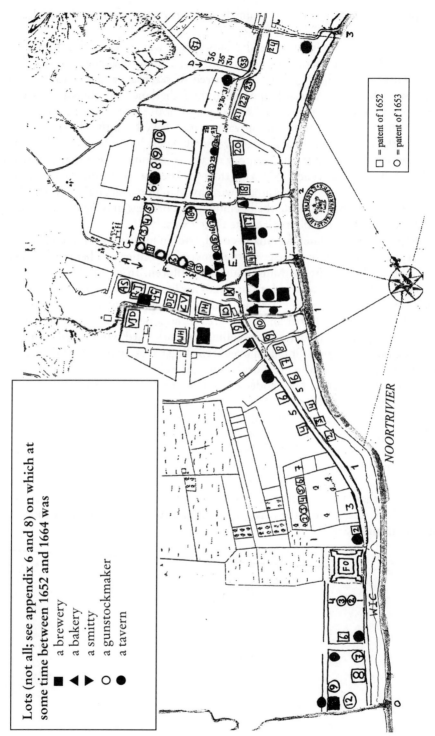

56. *The location of some artisans and tavern keepers in Beverwijck, 1652-1664, filled in on the Römer map. Based on information drawn from* ERA 1-4, Patents, Land Papers, FOCM, DAB.

V. Busy workers

The largest segment of the population was made up of artisans, the people who kept the community going and whose activities filled the village with sounds, smells and images, as they did everywhere else. Beverwijck's lifeline was the trade, as we have seen, which touched the lives of people at all levels of society. After a good trading season there was more to spend; but a bad trading season meant that many people in the village were not able to pay their debts. But more than the trade was required to survive in the wilderness. People needed food and drink, clothing, and shelter against the elements, and many people were engaged in providing for these basic requirements. Counting every appearance of individuals who worked in one or another trade, at some point in Beverwijck's twelve years of existence, leads a researcher to conclude that 'there were at least twenty bakers, thirty people were involved in either ownership or brewing – or both – in the twelve breweries, eleven brick and tile bakers, one distiller, forty-four carpenters (including master-carpenters, ships carpenters, and journeymen), three coopers, one cow herder, four glaziers, seven gunstock makers (two of whom were also carpenters), seven masons, one licensed midwife (who had the right to choose her assistants), five carters, three millers, four sawyers, two private schoolmasters, twenty-three shippers, seven shoemakers, eleven smiths, three surgeons (including Vice Director La Montagne, although it is not known if he practiced), sixteen tailors, twenty-four tavern keepers (four of whom were inn keepers), four wheelwrights, and one tanner.'[1] What immediately draws attention when reading this list is that these numbers are very high. When they are compared with those, for example, of the seventeenth-century village of Graft in North-Holland, or villages in the countryside of the Veluwe, Overijssel, Zeeland or the Noorderkwartier, or various towns in Overijssel, Zeeland or North-Holland, the numbers are indeed impressive and immediately raise the question: Why so many?[2] It is certainly understandable that many carpenters were needed. In a period when a village of about a hundred and twenty houses, along with their related sheds, barns, ricks, stables, and fences was constructed out of the wilderness, there was plenty of work for them. Masons were also needed to build chimneys, ovens and, after some time had passed, to improve the look of the houses by building up gable ends with bricks – or, as we saw at Jeremias van Rensselaer's house, as more bricks were used for general building. Providing shelter also meant work for wood sawyers and woodcutters, millers, brick and tile makers, people transporting those materials, and glaziers. All basic trades were represented in the village, although for some specialties craftsmen from Manhattan were called in. The stained glass windows in the church, for instance, were provided by the New Amsterdam glazier Evert Duyckinck. But even considering the circumstances of a village in the process of being constructed, the number of artisans seems high, and calls for further analysis.

In this chapter, we will take a closer look at these smiths and gunstock makers, bakers, brewers, and tavern keepers.There are several factors to consider when making an enumeration of these workers. First, it should be considered that not all artisans were working simultaneously. Some people came while others left, or for other reasons stopped working in the *bijeenwoninge.* Then, a distinction should be made between the owner of the means of production – for example, the brewery or bakery – and those who actually performed the work.

Sources show that the owner of a business was not always actively involved in that same business, in which case the work was done by hired workers. Furthermore, one person would sometimes buy and sell a business in the course one of a single day, suggesting that this individual was dealing in real estate, rather than practicing that particular trade. Sources often are unclear as to who were the servants and who the masters; this could easily lead a researcher to conclude that an individual was a brewer, for example, while in reality he may have merely assisted at the brewery.

Hundreds of Indian and European visitors created additional summertime activities in Beverwijck, and dramatically changed the consumption pattern in the village itself. The summer trading season stood in sharp contrast to the winter months, during which hardly any contact was possible with the outside world. In an analysis, then, it is necessary to make the distinction between permanent and flexible, seasonal work, and to keep in mind the different consumption patterns.

In analyzing the numbers of people who appear as performing a specific trade we should be aware, as Shattuck has pointed out, that one person frequently worked at more than one job.[3] To interpret work in a twenty-first-century manner, by immediately referring to a person's work activities as a complete job, would be misleading. We should consider that it was common for people to perform multiple tasks in the seventeenth century, and that an individual usually combined a number of part-time jobs.

While, at first sight, the research brings us continually into contact with a world of men, further analysis reveals that women often were involved in the business, thereby making much of work a family affair; women's influence and input is often underestimated, and should be considered in any analysis.

It is understandable that a name such as 'Jan Harmensz *Backer*' could easily lead a researcher to think that this person was a baker; this would certainly need to be researched, as sometimes men named Jan were referred to as 'Jan *de bakker.*' But it is necessary to distinguish between name and occupation. One has to be careful not to take names too literally, and not to treat them too rigidly. Names in the seventeenth century were not fixed, and sometimes an individual could be referred to in five or six different ways, based on factors such as his work, background, or outward appearance.

While researching the activities of blacksmiths, gunstock makers, bakers, brewers, and tavern keepers in greater detail, an overall picture emerges of a flexible, rapidly developing community where interaction appears to be great and change is fast – and where the specialization of work was less definite than has sometimes been suggested. The trade itself was not fixed to as great an extent as the places where the work was executed: Thus, smitties, bakeries, breweries, and some taverns appear to have remained at the same place, while the people working there changed.

Blacksmiths and gunstock makers

Many smiths

For a village of about 120 houses, and perhaps a thousand inhabitants, eleven blacksmiths would seem to be a very high number, especially when compared to various areas in the countryside of the Dutch Republic, where the number of smiths or lock makers varied between 1.4 and 2.0 per thousand. In three urban areas, their numbers varied between 1.5 and 2.6 per thousand.[4] The Van Rensselaer Manor Papers provide us with plenty of evidence that there was work for them to do. Jeremias's accounts list various bills from local smiths for repairing wagons and carts; repairing wheels on the beer wagon; making cow bells, axes, chains, adzes, nails, hinges, and keys; repairing sleighs, plows, and mills; making horseshoes and ironwork for the well; and sharpening scissors.[5] The deacons' account books give an additional glimpse of the daily activities of these smiths. During construction of the church and the poorhouse, for instance, the deacons on various occasions paid for, among others things: door and window hinges, nails and other hardware, or locks for the 'poor boxes.'[6]

It was the trade with the Indians, however, that made the job of smith in Beverwijck especially attractive. As we saw in the previous chapter, arms and ammunition had become the main staples of the beaver trade over the years; in addition, hatchets, axes, knives, adzes, and kettles were usually a part of payments for land or gifts to Indians. Once they possessed these guns and other hardware, the natives would frequently return to Beverwijck for new supplies and necessary repairs. The trade offered plenty of opportunities to do business with the Indians, as suggested by the fact that one smith, Carsten Fredericksz, appeared to have a pack of forty beaver skins and a pack of laps (quarter beavers) in his attic in the winter of 1667.[7] In November 1655, the Indians complained that they had to pay the smiths for their repair work; but the natives were told not to complain again, because the Dutch custom was that 'since one was free, one must earn his own living, and no one was holden to be another's servant for nothing.'[8] Nonetheless, the issue would appear again on a long list of Indian complaints in September 1659; free repairs were again refused, as the smiths 'must earn a living for their wives and children, who would perish otherwise from hunger, and they would depart from our country if they received no *sewant* for their work, and then we and our brothers would be sorely in need of them.'[9]

A closer look at the smiths not only provides us with an impression of who these people were, but (as mentioned above) also reveals that eleven smiths were not pounding their hammers on their anvils at the same time. In reality, over the twelve-year time period, individuals came and left, or stayed. Jan Koster van Aecken worked as a smith in Beverwijck in 1652, and throughout the Dutch period, as did Mijndert and Carsten Fredericksz, two brothers who both were smiths and who were first mentioned in October 1653. These men would stay in Beverwijck for the rest of their lives, and frequently appear in the records for doing smith's work. But Rem Jansz *smit* van Jeveren, who was first mentioned in Rensselaerswijck in 1649, seems to have left the village about 1660, when he relocated to Manhattan.[10] Barent Reyndertsz, whom he had hired as a gunsmith in 1654, remained in Beverwijck, where he died sometime before 1680.[11] Tomas Sandersz – who had come to Rensselaerswijck in 1650, and who acquired a patent for two lots in Beverwijck in 1653 – sold his house and lot in 1654 to Jan Koster and moved back to Manhattan, where he received charity from the Beverwijck deacons on a few occasions in 1655 (see Appendix 8, IV, no. 11). He actually worked only a few years in the village as smith, and apparently did not do well in this trade.[12] In 1660 (or perhaps 1659), however, his son Robert Sandersz lived in Beverwijck and worked as a smith. He bought a house, and seems to have been more successful than his father. In 1672, Robert hired Elias van Ravensteyn to do gunsmith and blacksmith work for him. The younger Sandersz may have worked as a smith until 1682, when he sold his smith tools.[13]

We may question who should be called a 'smith.' Should individuals who occasionally delivered hardware be included in the count? Daniel Vervelen and Jan Bastiaensz van Gutsenhoven, for example, who were primarily traders, sometimes delivered hardware to Jeremias van Rensselaer and in 1655, 1657, and 1659, as well as to the deaconry; but they are never referred to as 'smiths.' Other people, among them the traders Johannes Withart or Jan Hendricksz van Bael, or the house carpenter Pieter de Maecker, also once sold hardware to the deacons. Should these men be considered smiths?[14] Another question mark remains with Pieter Claerbout, the *voorsanger* (precentor) and sexton at the church. Jeremias van Rensselaer once paid him ƒ16-4 for various pieces of hardware and for blacksmith work. However, I have not been able to find any other records indicating that he actually worked as a blacksmith. The deacons' account books frequently list him as doing various chores, and he was probably able (like many other men) to do some blacksmith work, as well.[15] The question remains unanswered even in 1661, when he bought a house from Jan Thomasz that had previously belonged to Rem Jansz *smit*; in 1659, when Thomasz (together with Volckert Jansz and Gerrit Bancker) had bought the house, contained a small smith's shop but no smith's tools, as Jansz had kept those for himself at the sale. In 1664, Claerbout sold part of this lot again to shoemaker Rut Arentsz, who may very well have used the shop for his shoemaking business.[16] Finally, Jan Carstensz, who was a servant of Rem Jansz's in 1643, is mentioned in the court minutes of Fort Orange as having died in 1660. There is no indication that he worked as a smith in Beverwijck, or that he was still a servant to Rem Jansz in the 1650s.[17] Out of the eleven people whom, at first sight, we might have thought were blacksmiths, I could identify with certainty only seven individuals who worked as smiths. At least five of them were work-

ing in the trade in 1653; Barent Reyndertsz was contracted in April 1654, and
Thomas Sandersz left in October of that year. In 1659-60, Robert Sandersz joined
the existing group of five smiths, while Rem Jansz departed from Beverwijck in
1660. A group of five smiths seems to have been employed pretty much throughout the period. The reason for not including people such as Claerbout, Vervelen,
or Carstensz in my count is that I have not found exact references to their having
worked as smiths (see Appendix 6, blacksmiths).

Cooperation with gunstock makers

As mentioned above, arms and ammunition had become a trade of major importance over the years. While the metal parts of a gun were made by a gunsmith
(*roermaker*), a blacksmith was often able to do this as well. Barent Reyndertsz,
who was called 'smith' in Beverwijck, had actually been a *roermaker* in Holland.[18]
The wooden part of the gun was made by a gunstock maker (*lademaker*), and
some carpenters were probably able to do this work as well. Guns were usually
sent over from the fatherland without their wooden stocks, which created a good
work opportunity for gunstock makers in Beverwijck. Thus, it appears that artisans of different trades worked together in the production and repairs of guns.

   As discussed in the previous chapter, the trader and carpenter Dirck Jansz
Croon van der Gouw had a gunstock maker's shop in 1651, and hired Michiel
Rijckertsz to work in it for two years at ƒ130 annually, plus board and laundry.[19]
He did not extend the contract with Rijckertsz, whose life does not seem to have been
among the happiest in Beverwijck. In 1654 Rijckertsz lost a child, was given alms,
and had to undergo treatment by the local surgeon at the cost of the deaconry; he
died in 1656. Even before the end of his contract, Rijckertsz may have been incapable of doing his work; in 1653, Croon was working on gunstock making together with another carpenter, Harmen Bastiaensz.[20] Croon was fully aware of the
great profits gunstock makers could make, so it is not surprising that he contracted with another gunstock maker, Willem Jansz, while he was in Amsterdam in
May 1654. The contract is not dated and signed, however, and Croon probably
left Europe without Jansz.[21] Croon would not give up on the idea, however, and
he made sure to pursue this issue earlier during his next visit to Amsterdam, in
1657. In February, Jan Nack committed himself to go along with Croon and serve
him for three years by making gunstocks for guns and similar weapons at ƒ200 a
year. For each gunstock he produced, Nack would receive six *stivers* above the
ƒ200.[22] Although it is not explicitly mentioned in the records between 1652 and
1664, it is very tempting to suspect that Croon did much business with smith Barent Reyndertsz after 1657, when Reyndertsz's three-year contract with Rem Jansz
smit expired.[23] In 1669, Croon, Adriaen Gerritsz van Papendorp, and Reyndertsz
had three houses built on the Leidse Gracht in Amsterdam, and the men seem to
have worked together long after Croon had returned to the fatherland.[24]

   Blacksmith and principal trader Jan Koster, who was once called Jan Jansz
Koster *Lamaker* at Fort Orange, had the same idea. In April 1658, his brother
Cornelis Koster, a lock and gunstock maker at Utrecht, hired Elias van Raven-

De Smit.

Besteed uw Vlyt,   Ter rechter tydt.

Het Eiser gans door gloeid met Vuur,
Js nu bewercksaam van Natuur;
Dan is het tyd van Fatsoen neere :
ô Mens, bewerckt soo uw Gemoed,
Ter goeder tyd van 's Leevens gloed,
Dat u geen naa berouw turbeere.

De Roeremaaker.

Het Deugd Geweer is goed, voort quaad dat u ontmoet.

Of imand noch soo seeker schiet,
Hy raakt de rechte Vyand niet :
Maar Suchten, die van 't Herte dringen,
Gedreeven door godvruchtigheid,
Syn rechte Waapens in den Stryd,
Om helse Vyandschap te dwingen.

57. Johannes and Caspaares Luiken, 'The Smith' and 'The Gunsmith' in Het menselijk
bedrijf vertoond in 100 verbeeldingen: van ambachten, konsten, hanteeringen en bedrijven;
met versen (Amsterdam, 1694).

steyn (also a lock and gunstock maker) to go to Beverwijck and serve Jan Koster
for three years at a salary of ƒ200 in beavers, plus free board and food.[25] Croon
and Koster may have looked to Philip Pietersz Schuyler who, as we have seen, was
quickly able – like a 'flying wind' (his house was nicknamed *vliegende wint*) – to
make large profits in the trade; his job as gunstock maker certainly contributed to
this ability. Like Croon and Schuyler, Koster also preferred to trade with Indian
brokers; undoubtedly, his gifts to the natives consisted largely of guns and ammunition.

   It was the same for gunstock makers. Some of these men had been there when
the Beverwijck court was erected. Philip Pietersz Schuyler probably worked
throughout the twelve-year period that the village was Dutch, although he may
have involved himself more with the trade than the making of gunstocks. Michiel
Rijckertsz may not have worked as a gunstock maker after his contract with
Croon expired in 1653. Hendrick Andriesz had been in Beverwijck ever since it
had a court; but except for the Amsterdam *poorterboek*, where he is clearly listed

as *ladenmaker*, no references are made to any kind of work he did in Beverwijck, including that of gunstock making. If he worked as a gunstock maker in the village, he probably did so until his death in 1663. Bogardus, who was born in 1640 in New Amsterdam and had moved with his mother and brothers to Rensselaerswijck in 1648, probably worked fairly early in the gunstock trade, as well – perhaps first as an apprentice and then, when he was sixteen or seventeen, probably on his own until his death in 1666. It is not clear when exactly Jan Dareth started working as a gunstock maker. He appears in the court minutes in 1652, when he was indebted to Jan van Aken; it was only in 1657 that he bought a house, and was referred to as working as a gunstock maker.[26] Jan Nack, as we have seen, did not come to Beverwijck until 1657, and Elias van Ravensteyn did not arrive until a year later; they were both active long after their contracts had expired and the English had taken over New Netherland. Both men decided to remain in the colony. In 1663, Nack had a son of Johannes Dijckmans as an apprentice, and taught him the art of gunstock making; Ravensteyn was still working as a gunstockmaker in 1676, when he hired the *voorhuys* (front part or entrance hall) of Hendrick Rooseboom to make gunstocks.[27] Pieter Jansz *lademaker* could not have worked as a gunstock maker before 1656 in the village, since in 1659 – when he was murdered by the Indians while trying to flee to Hartford – he was described as a soldier 'having been in the service of the Company and for a year or two, three set free...'[28] Dirck Jansz Croon and Harmen Bastiaensz, however, who seem to have been involved with making gunstocks, are usually referred to as carpenters and surveyors, and never as being gunstock makers; therefore, I have not listed them in the table. In 1652, then, three or perhaps four gunstock makers were working at the same time, while in 1658 and 1659 this number may have increased to seven. Over the twelve-year Dutch period, I found at least eight gunstock makers who seem to have worked in Beverwijck at some time (see Appendix 6).

Location and success

Most smiths appear to have lived fairly close together, much like in the Dutch Republic, where many old cities had a *Smedenstraat*. In Beverwijck they were located mainly around the northwestern corner of the intersection of *Jonckerstraet* and present-day Broadway. Jan Koster had bought Tomas Sandersz' house and lot there, and Rem Jansz, Carsten, and Mijndert Fredericksz owned here lots as well.[29] (Appendix 8, IV, no. 11). Barent Reyndertsz, who probably lived with Rem Jansz during the three years of his contract, bought a house nearby in 1657, at the south side of *Jonckerstraet* between Rutger Jacobsz and Gerrit Bancker.[30] (illustration 9 and 56). Most likely the smiths cooperated with each other on occasion, as suggested in 1654, for example, when Carsten Fredericksz and Jan Koster together ordered some hardware in Holland.[31] They probably shared the fire they needed for their work, and the location nearly at the end of the *bospadt* made it a convenient place for the Indians to trade when coming to or leaving Fort Orange. For the inhabitants, this location in the center of the *bijeenwoninge* was favorable as well, since they could have their tools or houses repaired without spending a long time traveling. The smiths also worked together with gunstock makers who lived in the same area; in 1657, the gunstock maker Jan Dareth sold Rem Jansz forty-five destroyed gun barrels, which were little more than old iron.[32] That Dirck Jansz Croon and Jan Koster van Aecken hired gunstock makers illustrates the strength of cooperation between the two trades; the people hired probably lived for the first years of their contracts with their employers, indicating that their masters' businesses combined carpentering, gunstock making, and smithing.

Michiel Rijckertsz, also called Michiel de lademaecker, obtained a patent for a lot in the same area between Gerrit Jansz Cuyper and Annetje Bogardus in 1653, which he sold sometime in 1654 and 1656; that the lot was purchased at some point by Hendrick Andriesz, who in Amsterdam had been called a gunstock maker in 1650, may indicate that Andriesz also continued to practice this trade in Beverwijck.[33] (Appendix 8, VII, no. 15). That smitties and gunstock-making shops were concentrated in one area, on the north side of Jonckerstraet, may have been the reason Cornelis Bogardus (who as a twelve-year old in 1652, lived with his mother and brothers just west of these work places) learned the trade of gunstock making.[34] (Appendix 8, VII, no. 17). He may have been apprenticed to one of the nearby artisans, perhaps Philip Pietersz Schuyler, who administered Bogardus's estate after he died in 1666 (Appendix 8, VII, no. 1). It seems that the young Bogardus did well with his business, as some of his furniture, household goods, clothing items and gunstock making tools were sold after his death for ƒ2,015.[35]

As the trade in arms developed, the work of smiths and gunstock makers had become a natural collaboration that frequently proved lucrative for both parties. The Indians' demand for guns had made the smiths' job more profitable than it ever could have been in any other village in the Republic. But there were also differences within the groups of gunstock makers and smiths. During the period when the community was so divided over how to conduct the trade, not all of them signed the same petition, if they signed one at all. Jan Koster van Aecken, Carsten Fredericksz, and Philip Pietersz Schuyler demonstrated – by signing the petition asking to do business with Indian brokers – that they were wealthy enough to afford the costly gifts required.[36] Schuyler, we saw, repeatedly was a magistrate and a member of the consistory; Van Aken was member of the consistory from 1662 to 1664, and was a magistrate in 1664. Barent Reyndertsz was a deacon from 1672 to 1674, and owned three houses in Amsterdam, at the Leidse Gracht, in cooperation with Dirck Jansz Croon and Adriaen Gerritsz van Papendorp. The smiths Rem Jansz and Mijndert Fredericksz (a brother of Carsten), along with gunstock makers Hendrick Andriesz and Cornelis Bogardus, joined the major segment of the population in petitioning to use Dutch and Indian brokers in the trade. The Fredericksens were both members of the consistory of the Lutheran church in later years. The smith Robert Sandersz, who only arrived in 1660, did not sign a petition. Although at first he needed some support from the deacons, he did well in later years, and in 1685 became justice of the peace.[37] Obviously, not all smiths and gunstock makers were equally successful. The unfortunate Rijkertsz – whose contract with Croon was not extended, and who received alms from the deaconry on several occasions after losing a child and undergoing surgery – sold the lots (for which he had obtained a patent in 1653) sometime between 1654 and 1656. After Rijkertsz's death in 1656, the deacons would pay for half a barrel of beer used at the funeral.[38] Pieter Jansz *lademaker* was not faring so well either; he would flee to Hartford after becoming greatly indebted to various individuals.[39] Elias van Ravensteyn seems to have managed by contracting with various employers, often living in their houses. In his old age, however, he was no longer able to take care of himself, and the deaconry of the church provided him with alms, clothing and care between 1693 and 1696. In 1696, they also paid ƒ213 for wine, rum, candles, beer, and tobacco – as well as the coffin – at Ravensteyn's funeral.[40] While life in the New World did not work out so well for some gunstock makers and blacksmiths, for others it brought a fairly successful life; in general, the success of these artisans was not equalled by any trade other than the brewers.

Bakers

A baker's work

As in the Netherlands, bread was the mainstay of the diet in Beverwijck. People normally ate three or four times a day; bread was an important part of all meals, even of the noontime meal, where it was often served as a desert with cheese and/or butter.[41] The work of the person providing the bread required heavy physical exertion. Built with massive bricks (for thick walls, able to retain the heat for a long time), the oven had to be fired with wood, of which the remains were removed when the oven was hot enough. The oven was cleaned with a wet rag on a long stick, after which it could be used for baking. While the oven was being heated, the baker could start preparing the bread. Kneading the dough was done in throughs: white and whole wheat bread by hand, the heavy dark rye bread (*roggebrood*) by foot. Rye breads were put close together in the oven and had to be baked for about twelve hours. Wheat bread had to be kneaded and, after a first rising, it was weighed and shaped; it then needed to rise for a second time; only then could it go into the oven, where it would bake for about an hour. When his bread was ready, the baker could announce this by blowing his baker's horn – often made from the horn of an ox or another bighorned animal.[42] People could buy the bread in the shop, which often was in the room at the front of the bakery. The bakery was sometimes built out somewhat toward the streetside, so that it was easy to bring in supplies. The low roof above that space was good for exhibiting the baked goods, with an awning protecting the goods from the weather. When there was no shop, bread was often sold through a window, while the customers remained outside.[43]

A.Th. van Deursen has written that a family with two children in Holland consumed about five pounds of *roggebrood* per day.[44] If we apply this same estimate to the wheat bread that was eaten in Beverwijck, it seems that week in and week out, the 250 families (who make up the estimated 1,000 inhabitants in 1660) together would have consumed 1,250 pounds of bread per day, or 8,750 pounds per

58. Jan Steen, The Leiden baker Arent Oostwaert and his wife Catharina Keizerswaert, ca. 1658. *37,7x31,5 cm. The little child on the right blows the horn to announce that fresh bread is ready.*

week. This means that each of the twenty bakers in Beverwijck would have baked 62.5 pounds of bread per day, or slightly less than eight 8-pound loaves a day (or 437.5 pounds, or fifty-five 8-pound loaves per week). Van Deursen also wrote that in Durgerdam, in 1740, five bakers worked for a population af about 700. Each baker could take care of about 140 people, or about 35 families. The church wardens of the same village reckoned that selling some hundred pounds of bread a day in a North-Holland village guaranteed an acceptable level of existence.[45] Another North-Holland village, Graft, with 3,000 inhabitants in the seventeenth century, had about twenty bakers, who produced more bread than the required 4,000 pounds needed for the population. Most likely the provisioning of a seagoing vessel (a whaler, for instance) accounted for the production of 5,000 to 7,000 pounds of bread in this village.[46]

Thus, in Beverwijck seven, and certainly eight, active bakers could easily have supplied the inhabitants with bread, if each had taken care of about 140 people, or some thirty-five families. How then, should we interpret the twenty bakers for a village a third of the size of Graft? This seemingly high number certainly deserves further analysis.

First of all, it should be realized that these bakers were counted over a period of twelve years. Did they all work continuously during this entire time period? And was their main trade only baking, or were they (like the traders described in the previous chapter) perhaps involved in other business activities? Who were these men who were willing to get up in the middle of the night in order to provide Beverwijck's inhabitants with fresh bread for breakfast? And who worked in the hot summers in their hot bakeries? In the following section, we will take a closer look at the people who put in such long hours and did this labor-intensive work.

The value of location: Around the first kill

One of the first problems the new court of Fort Orange had to deal with was inherited from the patroonship. Three bakers had a major conflict over land where they lived, just north of the first kill. The seventy-year-old Willem Jurriaensz, who had sailed over as a baker and was paid for baking in 1643 on the farm *De Vlackte*, talked a lot about baking in 1652, but probably did not bake much more than he needed for himself.[47] It took several court sessions to resolve the dispute between Jurriaensz and two other bakers, Jan van Hoesem and Jochem Wesselsz. According to Wesselsz (originally from Jeveren in East Friesland), they had entered into a contract in January 1650 concerning a certain lot north of the first kill, along with Jochem Wesselsz's furniture and baker's business.[48] Apparently they had agreed that Van Hoesem and Jurriaensz would live on the lot already occupied by Jurriaensz, that Van Hoesem would be entitled to a piece of it, and that Jurriaensz would teach Van Hoesem (then about forty-one years old) how to bake bread. But it would not take long before relations between the bakers turned bad, and Jurriaensz accused the magistrates of having drawn-up the contract fraudulently.[49] Although the old man refused to fulfill the contract, Van Hoesem was granted the lot on condition that Jurriaensz be allowed to stay in his house (which was also a bakery) 'as long as he lives or the occasion requires.'[50] This did not suit Jochem Wesselsz, who had also been given permission, in September 1651, to also settle north of the kill and support himself by baking. He had already put a pile of lumber and a hogpen on part of the lot occupied by Van Hoesem and Jurriaensz, but was told by the court to remove them.[51]

The newly established court of Beverwijck maintained this policy, and the tensions among the bakers continued. Even their wives became involved, and the court would be busy dealing with their incidents of slander, as well as other mischief and nastinesses, during 1652 and 1653. On April 23, 1652, thirty-two, possibly forty-two, inhabitants, including Van Hoesem (but not Jochem Wesselsz), were given patents for lots.[52] Thus, in April 1652, the property that Jochem Wesselsz claimed he was prohibited from occupying, according to the contract, was in Jan van Hoesem's possession, while Van Hoesem was providing Willem Jurriaensz with his daily food.[53] (Appendix 8, II, no. 12). Jurriaensz, however, kept refusing to teach Van Hoesem how to bake, and 'by removing the baking utensils made it impossible to do so,' as Van Hoesem complained in October of that year. It was then decided that, 'considering that by the virtue of the contract Van Hoesem had built on part of the lot claimed by Willem Jurriaensz, and that the parties could not live together,' Van Hoesem would pay Jurriaensz 'f125 for improvements made on the lot, while Willem Jurriaensz could, by sufferance, live life-long in the old bake house, have the use of the bake oven and utensils belonging thereto together with his own furniture and household goods.'[54] While Jurriaensz may have done some baking in the early 1650s, it was decided in 1655 that his house was unfit for occupation and could no longer be used as a bakery.[55] Through the joint efforts of neighbors and court, the straw roof was replaced with boards; Jurriaensz was then able to live in the house until January 1660, when he was boarded with Huybert Jansz for f50 per year for house rent and laundry, paid by the deacons of the church.[56]

We may conclude, based on his own words, that Van Hoesem may not have begun baking until the end of 1653. Not much later, however, he must have been in operation as a baker, since in August 1654 the deacons of the church provided a woman in the guardhouse with bread and flour they had obtained from Van Hoesem; in October 1656, he was one of seven bakers who signed a petition in which they proposed to bake year-round.[57] The available source material is too limited to show the full extent of his business: Surviving fragments of the Rensselaer Manor Papers mention wheat deliveries at various times – for example, one in 1660 of 300 *schepels*. Unfortunately, the documents are too heavily damaged to provide a good overview. Once the problems with his neighbors were resolved Van Hoesem would bake until his death in November 1665, after which his wife Volckie continued the business.[58]

Jochem Wesselsz, along with forty-nine others, received a patent for his lot the day after the case between his two neighbors had been put to rest. The property was located between Van Hoesem's lot and the first kill, at the first bridge; he would bake there from 1651 through 1664, and for several years afterward.[59] (Appendix 8, II, no. 11). The relationship with Van Hoesem apparently improved in such an extent, that Geertruyt, Wesselsz's wife, hired Van Hoesem's daughter in her service. But the girl may not have enjoyed her job very much. In April 1657 Geertruyt was fined f30 for 'having kicked the girl from behind when she was stooped over, so that she discharged much blood and for a long time was confined to her bed, suffering great pain, as shown by the report of the surgeon.'[60] Despite the fact that Wesselsz was a Lutheran (as were Van Hoesem, Jurriaensz, and several other bakers), the deacons of the Dutch Reformed church paid him regularly for bread he supplied for the communion ritual, and for several needy inhabitants of the village.[61]

For a while, Wesselsz may have been assisted by his stepson Willem Hoffmeyer, who had been born in the Dutch colony of Brazil. In 1656, Hoffmeyer was about twenty years of age, and one of the seven bakers willing to bake year-round. It is not clear where he worked as a baker – perhaps first in Wesselsz's house, and thereafter in a house that Wesselsz had built on a lot patented to Hoffmeyer.[62] It seems that he was baking on his own in 1658, as he was probably the 'Willem *de backer*' who was sued that year by Albert Gerritsz.[63]

In May 1657, Wesselsz granted a part of his lot to another baker, Wouter Albertsz, who is first mentioned in the records in December 1656, when he was paid *f*80-6 by the deaconry for bread provided for Gerrit Seegersz.[64] In 1663, Albertsz bought a house and lot from David Pietersz Schuyler on the north side of *Jonckerstraet*. On the lot (part of the original patent of Anneke Bogardus) was a small *hansioos* house with a chimney and bake oven inside, where Albertsz would continue his bakery business throughout the Beverwijck period. In 1665, he not only sold bread in his shop, but other goods such as candles and molasses as well.[65] (Appendix 8, VII, no. 17).

Other bakers along present-day Broadway

Hendrick Jansz Westerkamp, who had been given permission in 1648 to seek a living in the colony by day labor or otherwise, also established himself as a baker near the first kill, just to the north of Jan van Hoesem.[66] (Appendix 8, II, no. 13). Although he died in September 1654, his name appears frequently in later records, since his business continued to be managed by his widow Femmetje Albers, also called 'Femmetje *de backster*' (female baker). In 1655 she sold a corner of the lot, which was then used for a brewery. While she may have continued the baking business herself for a while, she rented one of the three houses on the lot to a tavern keeper, and another to baker Jacob Willemsz.[67] In April 1652, Willemsz had left his wife Trijntje Gijsberts in charge of his business in Amsterdam, and by November was living in New Netherland.[68] Sometime after May 1656, when he disappears from the records, Willemsz probably returned to Trijntje in Amsterdam.[69] In 1656, Femmetje was living in Catskil. She rented her corner house to baker Daniel Rinckhout in 1658 (or perhaps earlier, since he was baking at least as early as 1655), who bought it in 1660.[70] When he died sometime in 1668, Rinckhout (who was unmarried) left his property to his brother Jan, who lived in the same house with his family and continued the trade.[71] It was apparently a good location for a bakery: In January 1670, Jan's wife Elisabeth Drinckvelt contracted with another baker, Anthony Lespinard, to use the bakery on shares (they arranged to share profits and the costs of supplies) for one year.[72]

Hendrick Hendricksz, one of seven bakers who signed the 1656 petition to the director general and council, also appears in the records as 'Hendrick *de backer*.'[73]

He may also be the same person as 'Hendrick *de suyckerbacker*,' who was mentioned by Jeremias van Rensselaer in his accounts. Probably he was not a refiner,
as the name indicates, but was perhaps known to bake sweets goods.[74] It is unclear
when Hendricksz came to Rensselaerswijck or Beverwijck; although his baking
business does not appear in the records, he seems to have worked as a baker until
his death in 1661.[75] His widow Geertruyt Barents married brewer Jacob Hevick in
October 1662; she later leased the lot where she had lived with Hendricksz to another baker, Hans Coenraetsz, who is first mentioned in the Beverwijck records
of February 1656[76] (Appendix 8, IV, 15).

Symon Volckertsz Veeder was excused, in May 1653, from fencing in his garden; in September 1654, he was clearly mentioned as baker dwelling in Beverwijck.[77] In 1656, he also signed the petition that he would be willing to bake
throughout the year. After leasing a house (with a bake oven) from Rem Jansz,
Veeder probably located his bakery on the east side of Broadway, where he would
bake until he moved to Schenectady in 1662.[78] (Appendix 8, no. 17). In 1673, after
Albany had been renamed 'Willemstad,' he would rent a house at the hill for three
years; in the house, a bake oven would be built in which a *mudde* of flour (3.056
bushels, or 4 *schepels*) could be baked at one time.[79]

Like Willem Hoffmeyer, baker Thomas Poulusz had been in Brazil, where he
worked in the service of the West India Company. He came from Herrifort, and
had married the Scottish Jannetie Donckes, a sister-in-law of traders Sander Leendertsz and Willem Teller. Poulusz was baking at least as early as 1655, and it seems
that he kept baking in the same house during most of the period; in 1662, he had
fully paid Sander Leendertsz for the lot on which his bakery stood, which was located on the west side of present-day Broadway, opposite the house of Jan Labatie. (Appendix 8, III, no. 8). Poulusz's business seems to have been doing well.
In 1662, when he was about sixty-one years old, he hired Gabriel Thomasz for
two years to assist him in the bread making.[80]

Protecting the home front

The bakers described above more or less set the stage for a long series of interac-
tions between themselves and Beverwijck's court, and eventually the director general and council in Manhattan.

As indicated in Appendix 6, four bakers had signed a petition in 1655 regarding
the sale of sweet bread and cookies, upon which the court responded that they
were not 'to put any sugar, currants, raisins, or prunes in any bread which they
bake and hence to sell the same, on pain of forfeiting fifty guilders.'[81] Two of the
bakers, Daniel Rinckhout and Jacob Willemsz, almost certainly were actively involved in baking at that time; however, they were not among the seven bakers who
petitioned, in October 1656, that all bakers should be allowed to bake year-round,
while others (who baked only during the trading season) should be excluded from
the trade.[82] The two petitions mentioned in Appendix 6 are only a few of many
such actions, but they are the only petitions that identify the bakers. They indicate
that competition was at the heart of the bakers' problem, and that business with

the Indians and competition from outside traders had great impact on their lives. The importance of the trading season to a Beverwijck baker becomes clear when we look at Jochem Wesselsz *backer*'s reaction in May 1657, when he had to appear before the provincial court at New Amsterdam. Wesselsz stood accused of encouraging Pieter, a West India Company negro, to steal powder for him from the company's warehouse. Wesselsz denied the charge and begged to be released, since the principal trading time at Fort Orange had begun; this was extremely important to the baker, and he argued that longer detention would totally ruin him, his wife and his children, which would serve no one's interest.[83]

Throughout much of its history, Beverwijck had to deal with the baker problem. Scarcity of bread had prompted the director general and council to publish an ordinance, in 1649, prohibiting the baking and sale to the Indians of white bread and cake. In February 1653, this ordinance was posted in Beverwijck.[84] Within a month, the village bakers demonstrated the importance of this part of their business: They requested mitigation of the ordinance, and permission to sell some white bread (and especially cake) to the Indians. Their request was not granted; but some of the magistrates, who were going to Manhattan, said they would discuss the matter with the director general.[85] But Jochem Wesselsz could not wait for the outcome. First, he was accused of baking cake and white bread against the ordinance; then, on April 12, he was fined ƒ50 for having publicly blown the horn to announce that his white bread was ready; this was against the ordinance, but Wesselsz claimed to have commissary Dijckman's permission.[86] At the end of May, the director general denied the bakers' request, and even demanded that the courts of Fort Orange and Rensselaerswijck pay stricter attention to previous ordinances regarding the needless baking of bread grain. Two individuals were to be appointed to ascertain how much bread grain each brewer and baker had in store.[87]

In March 1654, the burghers again complained that the bakers 'do not act in good faith in the matter of baking bread for the burghers, but bolt the flour from the meal and sell it greatly to their profit to the Indians for the baking of sweet cake, white bread, cookies and pretzels, so that the burghers must buy and get largely bran for their money, and even then the bread is frequently found to be short of weight, and they ask one guilder, yes, as much as one 24 *stivers* for such poor and short-weight baked bread.' In order to resolve the problem, the court asked the director general and council to set a proper weight and price.[88] Despite the bakers' requests, the old ordinance was renewed; and it would be another two years before the council enacted new regulations.[89]

Beverwijck's bakers felt their livelihood threatened by people who made a profession of baking only during the summer. Since the Indians were anxious to buy sweet breads and baked goods, good business could be done with them. Considering the large profits that could be made in this way, many bakers doubtlessly found it worthwhile to risk the ƒ50 fine, if they could do business that would bring them even greater profit. On March 16, 1655, upon the charge that some freemen were baking without having taken the oath, the court decided to 'issue further resolutions on the subject, as elsewhere no one is allowed to exercise a

trade who has not taken the burgher oath.'[90] The bakers addressed the same issue
two months later, when they again petitioned that the weight of bread be regulated. The court had an immediate answer only to their third request – namely, that
they be allowed to form a guild: For the present time, the court considered it 'for
certain reasons not advisable.'[91]

It was not so unusual for the bakers to have asked for a guild. In Dutch towns,
guilds were the most common form of horizontal association and cooperation
among people; around 1650, there were as many as 1,106 guilds in the area of the
present-day Netherlands. As organizations of a statutory character, approved of
by the local town or city government in order to ensure that trades and small businesses performed in an honest and orderly manner, guild members determined
rules for the performance of a trade, took care of the training of apprentices, took
a craftsman's final examination, and supervised the quality and fixed prices of
products and services. In addition, guilds had important social functions, as they
were obligated to provide for members who were ill, elderly, or handicapped
through collections or gifts in kind, while they also provided assistance to widows
and children of members who had died. Guilds ensured that an honorable funeral was provided for a deceased member.[92] In Beverwijck, some aspects of the work
atmosphere may be detected that were typical of towns in the fatherland; we saw
that the smiths and gunstock makers lived closely together in one area, and that
bakers did the same, especially north of the first kill. Brewers, as we will see,
would settle in an area with moving water. In several Dutch towns today, one can
still find a *Brouwersstraat, -plein, -gracht,* and *kade*; in Amsterdam one can still
walk through the *Bakkerstraat* and the *Smitssteegje* and *-straat*. As a matter of
fact, present-day Broadway was later also called *Brouwerstraet*.[93] Another feature
brought from the fatherland by Beverwijck's artisans was that people within one
a trade would help each other. In May 1657, when Jochem Wesselsz was held prisoner at Manhattan as the trading season was just beginning, two other bakers,
Joost *de backer* and Hendrick *de backer*, offered themselves as sureties for the
sum of f1,200.[94] Other examples of artisans offering security for fellow artisans
or for people in a related branch, suggest that it was certainly not unusual for individuals within a certain trade to support and help each other.[95] These attributes
were similar to the situation in the fatherland; it was only a natural reaction for the
bakers, at a time when they felt threathened, to request the most familiar way of
protecting theselves against *beunhazen* and outsiders.

The court may not have considered it advisable at that time to limit the possibilities for new immigrants to settle; or it may have been afraid of losing control
of the growing community. While, in 1658, the town government of New Amsterdam was in favor of establishing guilds, there is no evidence that they ever proposed it to the director general and council. As Jaap Jacobs has suggested, the directors of the West India Company may not have been in favor of establishing
guilds in such a young colony, preferring instead to have the director general and
council, along with the local courts, oversee tasks such as supervising quality and
determining the number of artisans per trade, which in *patria* were performed by
guilds.[96] Could the fact that, as in Holland, many bakers in Beverwijck wer

Lutheran, and clearly supported the idea of attracting and supporting a Lutheran minister, have been one of the 'certain reasons' that Beverwijck's court opposed establishing a bakers guild?[97]

The issue of baking sweet breads continued to be a problem; in July 1655, as noted above, the magistrates repeated the prohibition against using any sweets in baking. It was perhaps inevitable that this ordinance would be violated. Jochem Wesselsz was caught and fined *f*100 for having sold sugar cookies to Carsten *de Noorman*'s wife and an oblong sugared bun to an Indian. Hendrick Hendricksz *backer* was also fined, and as he openly refused to stop baking; in addition, as an example to others, he was suspended from baking for six weeks.[98] On April 18, 1656, the bakers petitioned once again for regulation of bread prices. They proposed to charge 18 *stivers* for an ordinary wheat loaf of eight pounds, and 5 *stivers* for a white loaf of one pound; only the latter request was granted.[99] Apparently, various people continued to bake sweet bread; on May 30, 1656, some bakers requested that 'they and all other bakers present and future, be prohibited from baking any confections for sale to the Indians.' In this case, the court took a different approach, and 'left it to the petitioners and all other bakers to bake and use the specified confections or not.'[100] Baking light-weight bread continued to be prohibited – as Jochem Wesselsz, Daniel Rinckhout, Willem Hoffmeyer, and Thomas Poulusz soon discovered, when they were caught doing it.[101] Competition remained fierce, and on October 10, 1656, seven bakers took matters into their own hands. This time, they sent a request to the director general and council, in which they complained about competition from other bakers, 'who sell to the Indians and don't serve the burghers, and as soon as the [trading] time is over perform other trades.' They promised to serve the burghers during the whole year, if these seasonal bakers were prohibited from baking; if that did not happen, they would be at too much of a disadvantage to make that promise. Unfortunately, the document is too damaged for us to determine the exact answer to the bakers' request, although they appear to have been given the exclusive right to bake.[102]

Not much later, on October 26, 1656, the director general and council published a new ordinance requiring all bakers to bake both coarse and white bread of the stated weight at least once or twice a week for both Christians and Indians, at the price of 14 *stivers* for the double eight-pound loaf of coarse bread, and 4 *stivers* for the single one-pound white loaf.[103] Now, those baking light-weight or higher-priced bread would be fined 25 pounds Flemish (*f*150) for the first offense, double as much for the second offense, and *f*600 for the third offense, as well as being prohibited from the trade. It was also stipulated that after November 1, 1656, every baker was required to obtain a license for their business, which they would have to renew every quarter-year and pay a fee of one pound Flemish (*f*6).[104] After two years of relative silence, complaints arose again in November 1658 about the scarcity of coarse bread, 'which the bakers, contrary to the October 1656 ordinance, do not bake twice a week, the coarse loaf at 16 *stivers*, the white loaf in proportion, consuming, to the serious prejudice of the community, their flour into baking cookies and white bread for the Indians, without [standard] weight.' Again, all bakers were ordered to bake coarse bread twice a week 'for the accommodation of the community and retail each coarse loaf of 8 pounds for 18 *stivers*, counting 8 white and 4 black *sewanties* to one *stiver* and the white loaf according to the ordinance, and this provisionally on account of the scarcity of grain on penalty of one year suspension of business, have their white bread confiscated and a ƒ50 fine.' The bakers finally had their request of October 10, 1656, satisfied, as it was also ordained that 'the bakers who quit baking after the trading season and before winter, and do not accommodate the public in the winter, shall also not bake in the summer, on pain of ƒ50 and the confiscation of the bread that is found.'[105]

During the following two years, the bakers remained quiet, suggesting that the last measure was effective. Since the records end in 1660, it is not known what happened between 1661 and 1664. In March 1665, however, the bakers petitioned the English governor Richard Nicolls to have itinerant bakers prohibited.[106]

Many bakers

The petitions and ordinances explain the presence of so many more bakers than the seven or eight required to supply the community with its daily bread. Yet, while Appendix 6 lists the names of several other bakers in the village after 1658, we are left with several questions. What should we think of one-time entries such as payments by the deacons to 'Reynier *de backer*,' or '*de backer van Malta*?' Both men were paid once by the deaconry, ƒ3 for bread for the communion ritual and ƒ37 for bread for the poor, respectively.[107] But who were they? Were they more active in the village as bakers than may be concluded from this one entry? Were they full-time bakers, or just individuals who baked in the trading season? The 'Jan (*de*) *backer*' whom we encounter in February 1664 and May 1665, in the deacons' account books, also produces riddles.[108] Who was he? Did the recording deacons in those years mean Jan van Hoesem or Jan Rinckhout? Or was he perhaps the mysterious '*backer van Malta*,' for whom we have no name at all? In attempting to discover the identity of these men, we may be misled by 'Jan Claesz *backer* van Oostsaan' and 'Jan Harmsz *Backer*,' who easily cause confusion due to their family name. However, they appear to be free traders; I have not found evidence that they baked bread, and therefore have excluded them from consideration. Jan van Hoesem and Rinckhout both baked in 1664, and could have been the individuals recorded in these instances.

And then there was another Jan – Jan Barentsz Dullemans – who first appears in the records of April 1661, when the deacons paid him ƒ37 for bread supplied for the poor.[109] In August 1662, he transferred his bakery tools – consisting of eight grain bags, three bolting bags, a bolting chest, a kneading trough, and other implements in the bakery – to Jurriaen Theunisz for 4½ beavers, together with fifty *schepels* of wheat at the house of Laurens van Alen (which Theunisz had rented). At the same time, Dullemans bound himself to serve Theunisz for one year in 'baking coarse and fine bread with whatever belongs thereto, and likewise to chop wood, keep the bakery clean, etc, and both in baking and taking charge of the trading season with the Indians to render his services with all honesty,' for which at the end of the year he would receive 33 merchantable beavers.[110] Dullemans owed Lourens van Alen ƒ70 in July 1663, and owed Barent Reyndertsz 4 beavers for house rent in August 1663.[111] At the end of his 1663 contract, Dullemans proposed to depart for Holland and apparently he did so, as his name does not appear in the records afterward, unless... Was he the person meant by 'Jan *de backer*?[112] Payments to Jurriaen Theunisz for bread are somewhat misleading, as the bread he sold was probably baked by his contractor, Jan Barentsz Dullemans. It seems that the contract with Dullemans was enough of a baking adventure for Theunisz, who is often referred to as 'Jurriaen *de glaesemaecker*' (glazier) or 'Jurriaen Theunisz *herbergier*' (innkeeper), but never as '*Jurriaen de backer*'; he does not seem to have been a baker himself. He was the owner of the lot and the bread, and hired a person to do the baking, who may have been known as the baker. In September 1664, Theunisz was paid for the last time by the deaconry for bread (probably still baked by Dullemans), suggesting that Dullemans indeed had left.[113] Since Jan Barentsz Dullemans was in Beverwijck only briefly, he may have come to Beverwijck with hopes of making a quick fortune.

There also remains a question mark over Helmer Otten. Was he baking only in those years indicated on the list, or was he a permanent baker? In 1661, Otten is twice named '*Helmer Otten baker*,' and in August 1662 the deacons paid ƒ3:10 'to Helmert for bread for the Holy Communion.'[114] Finally, Evert Lucasz and his wife Immetie, who was sometimes called 'Immetie *de baxter*,' are first mentioned in the documents of November 1657. Except for the fact that, until 1670, he was often called 'Evert *de backer*' and the deacons bought lard from his wife (who was still called 'Immetie *backster*' in 1665), no references to their work appear in the records.[115] The scarse material available on the location of their house and lot suggests that Evert and Immetie lived on the north side of *Jonckerstraet*.[116]

In general, it seems that despite the competition, most bakers were doing fairly well. None of them, however, would ever be chosen as magistrate. Only Wouter Albertsz was a deacon of the Reformed church, in 1680 and 1681; and Jochem Wesselsz, Evert Lucasz, and Willem Hoffmeyer were consistory members of the Lutheran church in later years.[117] Of some cases, the wives clearly were actively involved in the bakers' business. Femmetie Alberts and Evert Lucasz's wife Immetie were both called '*baxters*,' suggesting that they did the actual baking; Volckertie Jurriaensen probably did so as well after her husband's death, perhaps with the help of her oldest son, who was then 23 years old. Women often ran the shop, which would be located in the front room of their houses, and where people could sometimes buy other items in addition to bread. Although they are not mentioned in the records, it is likely that wives of other bakers such as Symon Volckertsz, Thomas Poulusz, and Wouter Albertsz were helping in the business as well.

Their regular income as bakers, to which the wives undoubtedly contributed, was enlarged by profits from the Indian trade, which enabled them to lead a decent life and acquire some property. Jochem Wesselsz, for instance, was able to buy several lots in the village. When he died in 1665, Jan van Hoesem owned two houses and a farm at Claverack. Symon Volckertsz later had a farm at Schenectady; Evert Lucasz purchased land in 1665 from the Mahicans in the area of Kinderhook, where he had a farm, and where the widow of Tomas Poulusz also owned land in 1671.[118] Hans Coenraetsz, who originally came from Nüremberg in Bavaria (and, like Poulusz and Hoffmeyer, had lived in Brazil before coming to Fort Orange), did not do so well in the trade. Until about 1659, he was a free baker working in partnership with Jan van Eeckelen.[119] He seems always to have lived on the west side of present-day Broadway, first in a house north of Tjerck Claesz; he subsequently leased the house that Claesz, meanwhile, had sold to Johanna de Laet and Jeronimus Ebbingh in 1660. There, Coenraetsz built a small store in the house and a bake oven in the side aisle, for which he was allowed to make a hole in the wall for the mouth of the oven. According to the contract, at the end of this lease he was to remove whatever he had built for his own use; he then moved to Hendrick Hendricksz's house, which was rented to him by Hendricksz's widow Geertruy Barents. All this would not have been difficult, since the new house was immediately next door, and was probably equipped as a bakery.[120] In 1672, Coenraetsz ended up in need of charity for his family, which was provided until his death in 1674.[121]

Analyzing the number of bakers leads to the conclusion that Beverwijck was not a village where twenty bakers were happily baking together. Indeed, the village inhabitants themselves did not need much more than seven or eight bakers. As soon as more people seized the opportunity to earn extra money by baking sweet breads for the Indians, the permanent bakers had to compete in order to keep their own business with the Indians. On the one hand, not competing meant loss of trade with the Indians. On the other hand, violating the law could result in suspension of business, which would hurt the permanent baker much more than the itinerant baker, as baking was his livelihood. Bakers were the only artisans who used petitions to express their needs. Other artisans did not use this means – certainly not the brewers, whose business (like the bakers') was strictly supervised by the government.

Brewers

The importance of beer

Besides bread, the other mainstay of life was beer. In September 1652, when Jan Baptist van Rensselaer described the damage done by Stuyvesant's action of transferring control of the center of the patroonship to the company, he did not neglect to mention that most of the brewers were in the bijeenwoninge, 'who now also did not give a tun of money anymore to their honors.'[122] In the previous chapter, we met Goosen Gerritsz, Rutger Jacobsz, Jan Thomasz, Pieter Hartgers, and Volkert Jansz Douw, among others. All five men were involved in the brewing business, and followed the tradition of serving as magistrates of Rensselaerswijck and later Beverwijck. As mentioned, they all had been successful in the trade as well and ranked among the more prominent inhabitants of the colony. Losing their contributions to Beverwijck, and those of other brewers, was indeed a great loss for Rensselaerswijck.

59. *Johannes and Caspaares Luiken, 'The Brewer' in* Het menselijk bedrijf vertoond in 100 verbeeldingen: van ambachten, konsten, hanteeringen en bedrijven; met versen *(Amsterdam, 1694).*

De Brouwer.

De haring staat gereed, Waar is het dorstend Leed?

Als Dorst en Dranck malkaar ontmoet,
Js't Bitter d'oorspronch van het Soet:
ô Ziel!, 't Begeeren en het Geeven,
Uw Dorst, en 's Leevens springfontyn,
Sal Eeuwige Verquicking Zyn,
Die Weelden lust, soeck sulck een leeven.

In Holland, brewers were often among the most prosperous inhabitants of a town. Although their incomes varied from town to town, they certainly were well above the average. An annual income of about ƒ1,000 was normal; and when their incomes are compared to those of all households in Amsterdam, they ranked in the top 6 percent. Brewing was among the highest-paid occupations in Holland.[123] Their prosperity opened many doors for the brewers; they played leading roles in town government, which gave them influence over important appointments of individuals who served as the leaders of the town militias, and on boards of the town's hospitals and almshouses, as well as filling patronage jobs such as beer carriers (*bierdragers*).[124]

Carefully estimated, Holland's inhabitants in the first half of the seventeenth century drank 230 liters (69.77 gallons) of beer per head of a household per year (by 1991, this figure had declined to 88 liters, or 23.24 gallons), not including the consumption of 'small beer' (*dun bier* or *scharrebier*).[125] Beer was drunk with just about every meal, and consumption of three glasses a day was not uncommon. This per capita consumption was so high because beer satisfied a basic, everyday need for the entire population, since water was polluted and not reliable to drink. There were only a few substitutes for beer. Tea and coffee were still considered exotic beverages, while distilled liquor was used primarily as a medicine. Wine was the most important substitute, but it was too expensive for most of the popula-

tion. Only in the middle of the seventeenth century would beer consumption begin to decline in Holland, as consumers started to drink 'new' beverages.[126]

Various kinds of beer were drunk at different occasions. 'Small' beer, with
about 2 or 3 percent alcohol, was the cheapest (it was not taxed) and was drunk by
children, in the orphanages, and by laborers at their work and sailors on the ships,
and the poor; those who could afford it drank the more expensive, stronger beers
with their meals and at night. These costlier beers also were drunk at celebratory
occasions such as weddings, funerals, fairs, holidays (especially Christmas or
Easter), or when someone was moving.[127] Beer taken onto ships in Holland or intended for the colonies was most often brewed in the winter, since it lasted longer.
Summer-brewed beer was drunk in the shipyards.[128] Although it is considered a
consumption beverage today, at that time beer was also considered important for
its dietary value. In 1745, for example, pregnant women were encouraged to drink
ale, as it was believed to ensure that they would produce more milk. According to
an eighteenth-century description of beer's dietary value: 'In many areas in the fatherland, especially in Noord-Brabant and Limburg, it is a first necessity of life,
and in many a family it is a substitute for other food, to a certain extent it takes the
place of bread, potatoes, and meat, and can even, as an extract of grains, be compared with meat juices...'[129] Beer certainly was considered beneficial in times of illness or childbirth. In Beverwijck, the deacons of the Reformed church provided
small and good beer to the wife of Gerrit Seegersz when she was in labor; and Ary
de Vries was also provided with half a barrel of small beer when he had surgery.[130]

Kiliaen van Rensselaer had been well aware of the importance of the beverage.
As early as June 1632, he wrote: 'As soon as there is a supply of grain on hand, I
intend to erect a brewery to provide all of New Netherland with beer, for which
purpose there is already a brew kettle there...'[131] In March 1634, he gave his agent
Planck permission to brew at his own risk. In the following years, other people
took up brewing as well – which, according to Van Rensselaer, not only 'hinders
them in the ordinary work, but also exposes the houses of the patroon to danger
of fire and in addition causes the beer to be sold here at very extravagant and high
prices, at f20 a barrel, to the burden of the community.'[132] Nevertheless, not until
June 5, 1642, would he contract with Evert Pels to go to Rensselaerswijck and
work there as a public brewer for six years.[133] By 1650, other colonists like
Goosen Gerritsz, Rutger Jacobsz, Pieter Hartgers, and Teunis Dircksz van Vechten were working as brewers as well.

Bronck's brewery

Basic ingredients for beer were grain, clear water, and hops; it is therefore not surprising that the breweries of the colony and Beverwijck were located at the riverside or alongside a kill, where there was access to plenty of water, and where grain
and hops could be delivered without problems. Efficient distribution from the
brewers to customers and clients – often using hand carts, horse-drawn sleds, and
boats – was also important. Pieter Bronck's brewery was located on the riverside,
between the first and second kills (see Appendix 8, II, no. 16). Bronck was proba-

bly the same man as 'Pieter Jonass Bronck,' a sailor from Jönköping (Juncupping) in Sweden without parents, who had married Hilletje Jans van Quackenbrugge in Amsterdam in October 1645, and who had a brother-in-law named Borchart Jorisz.[134] In May 1649, the couple were described as 'Pieter Jonass Bronck from Sweden and his wife, who three years ago as freeman went to New Netherland.'[135] The couple had a house in Rensselaerswijck before 1650; in 1651, they were allowed to build a house for tapping purposes, where they likely tapped their own beer for the public. Bronck's building lot was approved of by the director general and council in October 1653; on part of it (a parcel of land of about 3 rods, 5 feet wide and 11 rods, 8 feet long) he built a block house with a small house at the side, a dwelling house, a horse stable, a hay house, a mill house, and a brew house.[136] Between the lot with the block house and the lot with the dwelling house and brewery, was an alley 7 feet wide; to the west was one of the main streets, the present-day Broadway.[137]

The brewing process required several different spaces: a place where wheat germs (*gerst*) could soak and sprout in tubs with water; a space (usually an attic) where the sprouts (*groenmout*) could be dried; and a space somewhat elevated with bricks for completion of the drying process, where the sprouts could dry on an *eestkleet* (a sort of mat woven of horse or cow tail hair) above a fire.[138] To grind the roasted *mout*, a mill was required; in Holland, a hand mill was used in small breweries, while wind mills, water mills, or horse mills were used in larger ones. Bronck probably had a horse mill, as did his neighbor Frans Barentsz Pastoor or Pastoor's successor, Philip *de brouwer*.[139] The next phase, the actual brewing, required a tub in which the ground *mout* was mixed with hot water, and then filtered into an underthrough (*onderbak*). This process could be repeated between two and six or seven times, which produced the lighter and cheaper qualities of beer, including small beer, that was often consumed with dinner. What was then left was often fed to the hogs. The *wort*, a byproduct of the first filtering process, was pumped into a beer or brewing kettle. Hop was added, and the mixture was brought to a boil again. This product was filtered again, after which the liquid was brought into a shallow tub to cool. Subsequently, the yeasting processes began in separate tubs, where the sugars of the *wort* were converted into alcohol with carbon dioxide. After about two weeks, the liquid was put into barrels for secondary fermentation and ripening (*rijping op fust*), and where the beverage developed the desired aroma. Top-fermenting beers could be consumed after a week, while bottom-fermenting beers had to settle for about three months before they were ripe (*gerijpt*). The last beer took longer, but was the most long-lasting and clear.[140]

After the tapper's excise had been introduced, Bronck was enjoined in 1655 from tapping strong beer 'for the reason that he brews the same,' which probably caused him considerable damage.[141] In February 1657, he intended to sell his log house, but apparently there was no sale.[142] Two years later, he received permission to build a saw mill at the *Beverkil* with Harmen Bastiaensz 'on condition that Abraham Vosborch shall have the first choice of location, as he was the first applicant.'[143] At that time, he was indebted for ƒ1,895-16-8 to Jeremias van Rensselaer. Bronck tried to sell the brewery in Van Rensselaer's name. But the bidding on the property was held up when the buyer, who offered only ƒ2,000, was unable to furnish surety.[144] How Bronck resolved his financial problems with Van Rensselaer remains unclear. A month later (in August), he acknowledged his ƒ832 debt to skipper Reyndert Pietersz for goods received; and in November 1661, when he owed ƒ2,272 to brewer Jacob Hevick, Bronck mortgaged his brewery and lot in Beverwijck.[145]

Bronck's wife, who was called Hilletje Tyssingh in Beverwijck, probably also tended the bar before 1655, when they were enjoined from tapping good beer; in the meantime, she may have dealt with the management of the brewery, found customers for the beer, and kept track of payments. When they were so deeply in debt, the deacons of the church helped out by paying her for boarding the elderly baker Willem Jurriaensz for several months in 1661; and in August 1661, she leased the front part of her house (consisting of a cellar, front room, and loft) to trader Jan Harmensz Backer, who very well may have worked in the brewery for the next three years.[146] In August 1662, to satisfy his mortgages to Hevick and Pietersz, Bronck sold a part of his 1653 patent to them. In addition to a house and lot lying at the hill, he sold his brewery and dwelling house in the front with the mill house and horse stable, together with the well and the attached lot (see Appendix 8, east of Pearl Street, no. 8; VIII, no. 16). The buyers were to pay ƒ200 in beavers to Bronck.[147] He may not have built the saw mill by then, but he probably lived on the land at present-day Coxsackie, which he had bought from the Indians Sioketas and Sachemoes for ƒ150 in January 1662; at the time of the purchase, he intended to live there by May of that year.[148]

In 1663, Pietersz and Hevick agreed with Jan Harmensz Weendorp (Wintdorp) that he would lease the house that he already occupied, free of rent.[149] Since the mill and the brewery, along with the implements, had fallen into decay, he would repair them at his own expense and use them for his accommodation and convenience until the end of August 1664, or earlier if he returned to Holland before that date. Harmensz committed himself to rebuild the kiln and to provide a new kiln cloth, cooler, vat, tubs, and other items necessary to his convenience; he also was to provide thirty good half-barrels. For any accidental damage to the property that was not his fault, he would not be held responsible. At the end of their agreement, Hevick and Pietersz would pay Harmensz 12 ½ *schepels* of good wheat, while Harmensz would give them half a barrel of good beer. After his contract expired in August 1664, Harmensz returned to Holland.[150] Harmen Harmensz Gansevoort, who previously had worked as a brewer south of Fort Orange in Bethlehem, in Rensselaerswijck, rented the brewery in 1669.[151] Reyndert Pietersz died in 1673; after Hevick had been in possession of the property for another five years, his wife Geertruy Barents sold the brew house and dwelling, together with the mill house, horse stable, well, and the adjacent land to Albert Rijckmans in 1678.[152] With this transaction, Geertruy substituted for Hevick; but when they married in the fall of 1662, the addition of her capital had most likely contributed to the purchase of the brewery, and she probably felt as much an owner as he did.[153]

Organization of the brewing business

In Holland, the organization of the brewing industry varied according to local circumstances. Although brewers were organized as a guild in some towns, and elsewhere as a confraternity, these groups differed remarkably from the typical craft guild. Their regulations did not specify a period of apprenticeship, nor did they require a demonstration to prove the individual's expertise. Thus, the brewers guilds did not seek to ensure the competency of future brewers, or to limit entry into the industry through the usual channels associated with guilds. The brewers also did not have a fund from which they could request financial assistance, which was common practise in other guilds. According to Richard Yntema, brewers generally ranked among the town's wealthier leading citizens; consequently, they did not require such collective security. While a skilled craftsman in Holland might earn several hundred guilders and live in a modest home, a successful brewer earned at least a thousand guilders per year or more, and lived in a finely appointed home, complete with servants. In Amsterdam, most brewers around 1650 were organized in fraternities, of which membership was voluntary and not mandated by city law.[154]

While bakers were the only artisans who ever petitioned to establish a guild in Beverwijck, no guilds would ever be established in the village. Brewers' lives there were regulated by several ordinances drawn up by the director general and council of New Netherland. These ordinances stipulated prices, and ordered brewers to inform the receiver how many *tonnen* (one *tonne* is 155.4 liter) of beer they brewed each time, before it was removed from the premises.[155] An ordinance of November 1649, for example, stipulated that 'brewers were not to deliver any beer they may sell, nor let carters or beer carriers or tapsters take it away, unless a permit therefor be previously exhibited to them on pain of forfeiting the beer and wine and all appurtenances, whether horses, sleighs or any other vehicles.'[156] In June 1651, an ordinance prohibited brewers from selling retail.[157]

When the excise on beer, wine, and distilled liquors was farmed out in 1654, the farmer was allowed to ask a brewer at any time, or have an inquiry made, as to what beer was brewed or imported, without being required to inspect the brewer's houses. Brewers were not allowed to furnish any strong beer to the burghers or tapsters until they had been shown a proper certificate from the farmer or impost master, or his collector.[158] As in Holland, distribution from the brewery to customers at home, or in taverns or inns, became regulated. For example, brewers in Holland could not deliver beer directly to their customers, but were required to use beer carriers or porters (*bierdragers*) to deliver barrels, half-barrels or quarter-barrels of beer to a burgher's house, a tavern, or an inn. These *bierdragers* were officially appointed and were paid a certain amount for each barrel, half-barrel, or quarter barrel they delivered.[159] They were also required to distribute barrels of wine and brandy.

As porters or *bierdragers* in Beverwijck, Teunis Jacobsz and Claes van den Bergh and their helpers had heavy work to do, since one full barrel of beer weighed more than 150 kilos (330 lbs.) and contained 155 liters (in Leiden).[160] A porter had to swear to uphold the law and to deliver only beer on which the excise taxes had been paid. The most important exception to the requirement that a porter's services be used involved the sale of small beer, which was too weak to be taxed and was usually consumed by the poorer members of the community.[161] That Jochem Becker was sued over a pail of good beer, found at some point among the Indians, could mean that (as in Leiden) small beer was collected in buckets without a top in order to prevent cheating.[162] Pieter Bronck's business was probably damaged when he was enjoined from tapping strong beer in May 1655. Clearly, the court had so ruled 'for the reason that he brews the same in whatever manner it may be, and on acting contrary hereto he shall the first time forfeit 25 guilders, the second time forfeit 50 guilders and the third time receive arbitrary correction, provided that he shall be permitted to draw the wines which he has now in his cellar according to the gage.' It would have been too easy for a brewer to escape the excise tax, if he had been allowed to keep a tavern and tap his own beer.[163]

Other ordinances regulated brewers' business over time. When they charged too much money for increasingly poorer and thinner beer, 'making a great, excessive and immoderate profit,' the inhabitants did not refrain from complaining; in November 1655, the brewers were ordered to charge no more than 20 guilders per *tonne* of beer.[164] An ordinance of November 25, 1656, regulated the excise tax on brewers, set fees for brewing and personal consumption, and set penalties for refusing to allow measuring. Everyone had to pay the excise; only the West India Company was excluded.[165] In April 1658, the brewers were again warned not to retail or deliver beer without a permit; and in November 1658, the ordinance was renewed establishing fixed prices for the sale of beer. This time, beer prices were set in silver, beavers, or *sewant*.[166]

Breweries and their success

Of the thirty people who, after a general count, seem to have been involved with Beverwijck's twelve breweries, only a few would acquire wealth and become influential in town and church government.[167] Not all brewers were equally successful; actually, the majority did not reach this level. Why did the brewery trade work out for some, but not for others? A closer look at individual breweries may provide an answer.

Soon after baker Hendrick Jansz Westerkamp's death late in 1654, the active and successful traders Pieter Hartgers, Volckert Jansz Douw, and Jan Thomasz bought a corner of his lot, north of Jan van Hoesem's, from his widow Femmetje Alberts for ƒ300.[168] (Appendix 8, II, no. 13). Intended for their jointly owned brewery, the property was located close to the river and the main roads; it was one of the best locations for the delivery of grain and hops, and for the distribution of the beer. After Hartgers returned to Holland in 1660, Douw and Thomasz would retain possession of this brewery for another fifteen years. In 1675 they sold it to Harmen Rutgersz, who had worked in the brewery for several years, and who then sold it to Goosen Gerritsz and Pieter Lassen.[169] In 1681, Gerritsz's widow

Annetje Lievens sold her half of the brewery to her son Sybrant van Schaick, who then bought Pieter Lassen's half as well.[170] The fact that these important traders stayed with the same business for so many years certainly suggests that they considered the brewery to be profitable.

As described above, the original Bronck brewery also appears to have been successful. Bronck sold it because he was deeply in debt, and it seems that his financial situation had prevented him from making much-needed repairs. After Reyndert Pietersz's death in 1673, brewer Jacob Hevick would retain ownership of the business for five more years until in 1678, when his wife sold it to Albert Rijckmans.[171] Business must have been satisfactory, since he kept the place for sixteen years. That Hevick had been able to buy the brewery in 1662 may have been partially due to the fact that he married Geertruy Barents at the same time.

The history of the original Pastoor brewery also clearly shows the importance of a wife's contribution. (Appendix 8, II, no. 19). In December 1656, Pastoor sold his brewery, together with his house, lot, and garden, for ƒ3,630 to gunstock maker Hendrick Andriesz, who immediately resold the property to Philip Hendricksz *de brouwer* for ƒ4,000.[172] Although he had intended to sell the brewery as early as the beginning of 1662, Hendricksz kept it longer. But in 1663, he accidentally killed Claes Cornelisz Swits on his land at Schenectady; he subsequently sold the brewery on March 29, 1664, to Jan Dircksz van Eps for ƒ1,150. A month later, Van Eps bought the horse mill from Cornelis Theunisz Bos for ƒ112 in beavers.[173] It is not clear how long Van Eps remained the owner. Family ties were probably the reason for the low amount he paid; Hendricksz still owed ƒ3,144 in payments to Hendrick Andriesz in May 1662, for which he then mortgaged his farm on *de Groote Vlackte*, of which he proposed to take possession in the summer of 1662.[174] Jan Dircksz van Eps was the son of Marietje Daemen and her first husband Dirck Evertsz van Eps. Hendrick Andriesz van Doesburgh was Marietje's second husband. On his sickbed, Andriesz declared that most of the estate had come from Marietje, which indicates that she was probably involved in the purchase of the brewery.[175] After Andriesz's death, she married Cornelis van Nes in the spring of 1664. Just before their wedding, Van Nes bought the brewery in Greenbush from Willem Brouwer, together with his son-in-law Jan Oothout.[176]

In contrast to breweries at the riverside, the two breweries west of Broadway, alongside the *Ruttenkil*, don't seem to have lasted very long. Although he sold part of his lot to the brewer Rutger Jacobsz in 1654, Jacob Jansz van Noortstrant (or Jacob *de brouwer*) excluded the mill and brewer's tools from the sale (Appendix 8, XI, JJvN). It is not clear whether the fire that destroyed his house, in May 1657, also destroyed his brewery.[177] The available records don't show any accounts or court cases regarding Van Noortstrant's activities as a brewer, although he was frequently referred to as 'Jacob *de brouwer*' and his wife as 'Jannetie *de brouster*.' In November 1656, however, Van Noortstrant was appointed gauger of the casks; when he was allowed to do that work again in October 1660, La Montagne described Van Noortstrant as 'a cooper by trade and by the people considered an honest man.'[178] Assistance provided on various occasions from the deacons' poor fund, especially in 1662, do not suggest a success story.[179]

The other brewery on the first kill, a little more to the west, belonged to Rutger Jacobsz. This may have been the brewery where he worked in partnership with Goosen Gerritsz until about 1659.[180] (Appendix 8, XI,' VJD/GG). In February 1656, Jacobsz was given permission to build a waterwheel for a small mill in the kill behind his house.[181] About a year later, he sold his house and lot to Harmen Vedder, along with an alley between Goosen Gerritsz and Jacobsz, and 'with a portion of the place where his brewery stands, which brewery will be torn down in the coming month of November 1657, when the place of the brewery will be delivered.'[182] Records after that date don't reveal any brewing business, and this transaction seems to mark the end of brewing along the *Ruttenkil*. In 1663, Jacobsz definitively gave up on brewing when he sold a gelding and a mare, together with two half-barrels, a beer wagon, and a light brew kettle for 57 beavers.[183]

It seems that Marten Hendricksz had an interest in a brewery with Evert Pels in 1651; but it is not clear where this brewery was located. Regarding Pels, no activity related to brewing seems to exist after 1651, and he was probably more involved in his saw mills and shipping.[184] Hendricksz was frequently named Marten *de brouwer* until 1657; after that year, he appears in the records as Marten *de bierkaecker*.[185] Most likely, the malt kiln he had built in 1653 was close to his house, south of the land of Thomas Jansz, near the *Beverkil*.[186] (Appendix 8, X, no. 10).The records make no further mention of this malt kiln, and except for his name, and the permission he was given in January 1652 to support himself by brewing, the available sources offer no insights into Hendricksz's activities as a brewer.[187] The fact that, in August 1657, his wife Susanna would explain her crime of trading alcoholic beverages with the Indians as a result of poverty, suggests that this brewery by that time was no longer a success.[188]

After his six-year contract of May 1649 had ended, Jacob Hevick sold his brew house (also located south of the fort, just north of the house and farm of Thomas Jansz) at public auction. (Appendix 8, X, no. 11). It passed through the hands of Jurriaen Theunisz and Thomas Coningh, and eventually was bought by Adriaen Jansz van Leyden in February 1655.[189] Van Leyden is occasionally referred to with 'tavern keeper' appended to his name – or, when he occupied the position, as farmer of the tapster's excise. Never does he appear in the records as a brewer. In June 1657, Pieter Bronck sued him, demanding payment of *f*180 that 'Van Leyden owed him for two years for beer delivered to him.' Thus, Hevick's original brew house probably did not continue as a brewery after he sold it.[190]

Nothing about Jan Labatie's brewery in Fort Orange appears in the records after 1647, when he was given permission to erect a house in the fort and brew therein.[191] Labatie intended to sell a house in Fort Orange to Adriaen Jansz van Leyden in 1654, but the sale was annulled. In 1661 he sold it to Evert Pels; at that time, Cornelis van Voorhout was indebted to him for *f*425 for the brewery, brew kettle and vat, and appurtenances.[192]

It is not clear where Jeremias van Rensselaer's brewery was located. It could have been on the lot near the patroon's house, or on the original Sander Leendertsz' lot, which in 1661 Van Rensselaer had bought from Evert Pels. (Appendix 8, III, no. 3; II, no. 5). After the 1666 ice flow, Jeremias described how, among the 40 houses carried away, 'our house in which we lived, the barn and the brewery, the new as well as the old, are lost also, so that [not] any traces can be found of where they stood.'[193] Van Rensselaer's accounts show that he was building a house and barn in the *Greene Bos* at that time, which he named Fort Crayloo; it could be that he built the new brewery there. Or he may have been involved in the colony's brewery in the *Greenebos*, which seems to have been in the hands of Cornelis van Nes and Jan Oothout at that time, although it was not entered in the accounts as such.[194] When he was building a house near the fifth kill in June 1668, Van Rensselaer had already erected his brewery in that area near the grist mill that Flodder built on the fifth kill. He had first put it on the other side, in the *Greenebos*, but 'it was very inconvenient for me in the spring and in the fall to get my beer across the river, so that to run a brewery there did not work, for at the most important season we had to sit still.'[195] In 1664, Jeremias hired Jacob Gerritsz van Vorst as a brewer's servant for *f*360 in *sewant*, while he would provide him with reasonable meat and drink and lodging. The contract was repeated for a few years, at least through May 1668.[196]

In conclusion, none of the breweries far from the village center seem to have been successful. In time, the breweries near the *Beverkil* and *Ruttenkil* would disappear. The concentration of the village north of the fort probably put the breweries near the *Beverkil* at a disadvantage, as transportation of inputs and outputs became concentrated between the first and second kills. The kills may not have had a sufficient, constant supply of clear water to make them successful. The three breweries along the river north of the first kill always had ready access to clear water, and were located on sites easily reached for the delivery of ingredients as well as the distribution of beer. Of all the breweries, the one located just behind Hendrick Jochimsz's tavern, next to the village's bakeries, was located on perhaps the best spot in town.

The breweries of the patroonship delivered beer to villagers, as well. One had been located for many years in the *Greenebos*, and was run by individuals such as Teunis Dircksz van Vechten, Willem Brouwer, Cornelis van Nes and Jan Oothout. Another brewery, located in Bethlehem, was owned by Harmen Gansevoort.[197]

With competition among two, or perhaps three operating breweries in Rensselaerswijck, the village does not seem to have been able to support all the breweries. Of the twelve breweries found in a first count, I was not able to find more than eight remaining. Even that number seems too high, as Labatie's brewery in the fort probably was not working anymore. As early as 1657, only the three breweries along the river seem to have been in working order inside the village, while the one owned by Rut Jacobsz at the *Ruttenkil* was torn down in November of that year.

These breweries provided work for a good number of people. All brewers probably had servants at some point; beer carriers had to be hired, and brewer's wives may also have been involved in the business. It is difficult to provide an exact number of people working in the brewing industry, as people were sometimes involved in the buying and selling of a brewery, which does not mean that they had to be brewers themselves. We are left with riddles similar to counting the number of bakers: Who was 'Hendrick *de brouwer*'? Was he, after all, the Hendrick Andriesz who in Amsterdam had been reported to be a *ladenmaker*, and who in Beverwijck owned a brewery for six days before reselling it? And what of names such as 'Barent *de brouwer*' – was he perhaps Barent Pietersz Coeymans, the miller, who was doing a little brewing on the side?[198] And what about Pieter *de brouwer*? Was this Pieter Bronck, or was it perhaps Pieter Hartgers – or was there still another Pieter involved in the business?[199] Counting the people who had to do with the brewing industry throughout the twelve years, a number of thirty does not seem exaggerated; it seems that even more people could have been involved in this important industry, but they were not all working at the same time (see Appendix 6, Brewers). Brewers shared their great dependence on beer with about twenty-four tavern keepers, who were mentioned in our list at the beginning of this chapter. Next, we will take a closer look at this group.

Tavern keepers

Many taverns, many tavern keepers

It is unknown what happened with the *Stadsherberg*, which Nicolaes Coorn was allowed to start in 1648.[200] But there were other places were people could share a drink and socialize. Even before Beverwijck's court had been set up, Gysbert Cornelisz ran a tavern that was located at the south side of the fort.[201] Goosen Gerritsz, who was permitted to engage in the tavern business in 1650, does not seem to have established one himself; but he may have been involved in the tavern that was a little more to the south of Gysbert Cornelisz, toward the land of Thomas Jansz. (Appendix 8, X, no. 5). It was owned by the carpenter Steven Jansz, but was mostly run by Steven's wife Maria Goosens, with whom Gerritsz had a relationship of such a nature that for a long time he took care of her when she needed help.[202] In 1651, Brant van Slichtenhorst asked that in accordance with the instructions from the guardians of the patroon, only two taverns be allowed. He withdrew his request however, when in September the court 'for the convenience of the public' granted Pieter Bronck's request to have a suitable house erected for tapping purposes.[203] As noted above, Bronck's lot was north of Fort Orange at the riverside, east of Broadway. Since the *bijeenwoninge* was being constructed north of Fort Orange, the presence of a tavern at that location was more convenient for the people, who then would not have to go south of the fort to share a drink. As the *bijeenwoninge* (and later the village of Beverwijck) grew, more taverns would rapidly spring up at various locations. Pieter Adriaensz had a tavern in the fort in 1652, and later north of Teunis *de metselaer* at the east side of present-day Broadway.[204] In 1653, Hendrick Jochemsz may have had one just north of Fort Orange. (Appendix 8, III, no. 1 and 2). Adriaen Jansz van Leyden received permission in 1654 to have a lot next to the palisades of Thomas Jansz for a public house, rather than a city tavern. The lot was located south of Fort Orange in Rensselaerswijck, not too far from Jacob Hevick's brew house, which (as we have seen) he would buy a bit later.[205] In the same year, Jurriaen Theunisz *glasemaecker* (at the third kill; Appendix 8, II no. 25), the carpenter Willem Fredericksz Bout (at the west side of *Broadway*; Appendix 8, III, no 7), Roelof Jacobsz (about whom there is no further information), and Ulderic Cleyn (at present-day Columbia Street, Appendix 8, V, no. 32) are mentioned as being tavern keepers. In addition, at that time Marten Hendricksz *de bierkaecker*, who lived close to Steven Jansz, may still have had his house open as a tavern, most likely often run by his wife Susanna, in addition to his brewing business. (see appendix 8, south of Fort Orange, perhaps no. 10). In June 1657, when *dominee* Schaets wrote that the taverns had many visitors, he was referring to at least seven establishments; but nine taverns were probably open during that year.[206] When we consider that, in Amsterdam, there was one tavern per two hundred inhabitants in 1613, this number of taverns seems high; most likely, in some of these establishments the owner merely served beer in a room in their house, rather than a true inn.[207]

Not all taverns, however, were working businesses at the same time. Some tavern keepers, like Maria Dijckman or Evert Nolden, may have worked for only a few years, while we are left to wonder whether some of the others really had a tavern. Jan van Hoesem nor his wife Volckertie are ever referred to as tavern or innkeepers; but in 1654 a group of drunken Indians was at their house, and in 1658 Van Hoesem sued Gysbert van Loenen for a tavern debt amounting to ƒ210. This certainly suggests that the Van Hoesems ran a tavern, in addition to their baking business.[208] Likewise in 1660, Cornelis Cornelisz Vos, who also is never referred to as a tavern keeper, sued Willem Hoffmeyer for ƒ75, and Claes Uylenspiegel for ƒ60 in tavern debts. (Vos had a lot north of Fort Orange, Appendix 8, III, no 2). Does that mean he was a tavern keeper?[209] These small references, which lacked continuous accounts, may indicate that it was easy to have a tavern as a side business, and that these people may have used a small area of their house to entertain guests. Most licensed tavern keepers may have had 'tavern keeper' or 'innkeeper' added to their names, while these other people may never have held a license to keep a tavern.[210]

Some houses may have been better equipped for tavern keeping than others. In May 1655, when Steven Jansz and his wife Maria were separated, he tried to sell the house that had once belonged to Gysbert Cornelisz, who had been a tavern keeper, but who had died sometime in 1653. While it is not clear whether Steven and Maria actually had their tavern there, that may very well have been the case, as the house was probably was well equipped as such.[211] (Appendix 8, X, no. 5). Other tavern keepers bought houses from each other, or used each other's houses: In 1661, Hendrick Jochemsz leased his house, lot, and garden to Anthony Jansz for two years.[212] Jansz, however, bought a house lot and garden in January 1662 from Jurriaen Theunisz on the first kill, behind Jochem Wesselsz *backer*, which he seems to have used as a tavern until he sold it in 1668.[213] (Appendix 8, II, no. 11).

After the blockhouse church had been built, it seems that the area around it became even more popular. Although she resided in Catskill in 1656, Femmetje Westerkamp still owned part of her lot; she leased her houses not only to bakers, but also to people involved in the tavern business. Hendrick Jochemsz bought one of the houses in 1666 – but owned it likely earlier. In 1658 and 1659, Evert Nol-den, possibly in cooperation with Hendrick Bierman, rented a house from Fem-metje for tavern keeping, as well.[214] Maria Dijckmans, who lived with her husband in Hendrick Jochemsz's house from May 1659 until May 1660, first may have run this tavern for a while, perhaps with Evert Nolden's assistance, and afterwards continued in this business.[215] She also may have worked in Jochemsz' tavern just north of the fort (Appendix 8, III, no. 1 or 2). At first, innkeeper and master glazier Jurriaen Theunisz most likely had his tavern at the third kill, where he lived in 1658; but his neighbor, the tavern keeper Jan Martensz *de Wever*, bought a part of his lot in 1660.[216] After 1658, Theunisz maintained his inn business more in the center of the village. For a few years, he seems to have had his business at the lot that he bought from baker Wouter Albertsz in 1660, which was located on the lot originally belonging to Jochem Wesselsz *backer*, until he sold the property to Anthony Jansz in January 1662.[217] (Appendix 8, no. 11).

In Appendix 6, 'Tavern keepers,' the 'x'-marks indicate persons who were clear-ly mentioned as having kept a tavern or as being a tavern keeper; but it seems like-ly that, when there is no such record for one or two particular years, the individ-ual maintained the tavern, but was not linked to the establishment in the records. Ulderic Cleyn's tavern probably was open in 1655, and Willem Fredericksz Bout's in 1656. It seems likely that Jurriaen Theunisz, although he was active in different fields, ran a tavern throughout the years; in the table, a 'pb'-mark indicates that a poor box was located at his place.

In general, the group of tavern keepers was a fairly respectable one, although none of them ever was a magistrate or consistory member. Anthony Jansz was court messenger for the court of Rensselaer; Jurriaen Theunisz was a *glazier*; Hendrick Jochimsz seems to have run a tavern as his major income, and was lieu-tenant of the burgher guard; Pieter Bronck was a brewer; and Willem Fredricksz Bout and Steven Jansz were master carpenters. On many occasions women stood behind the tap, either next to their husbands or on their own. Hilletie Bronck un-doubtedly manned the tap frequently during the period they still were allowed to tap; and Geertruyt Nanningh, Willem Fredericksz Bout's wife, did the same, even when she was not supposed to do so. In November 1655, Geertruyt was fined for serving liquor during the service on the day of prayer.[218] Innkeeper Dirckie Harms and her husband Jan Martensz *de Wever* had their tavern at the third kill. Dirckie seems to have worked with husband Jan, who is also frequently men-tioned in the records as being active in the business.[219]

While a wife sometimes substituted for a husband, it was also possible for a woman to run her own business.[220] It is unclear, for example, whether Egbertie Egbert's husband Teunis Theunisz *de metselaer* was involved at all in the innkeep-ing business she had on their lot in 1656, on the west side of present-day Broad-way.[221] And it seems that Maria Goosens (who was also called '*Lange Marrij*' or 'Tall Mary') did most of the tavern work during the time of her marriage with the carpenter Steven Jansz in their tavern *de Vrouw Maria*. After their separation in 1655 and Maria's subsequent banishment from Beverwijck for a year and six weeks, she would soon run her own place at the other side of the village. Goosen

Gerritsz had bought a house there, near the north gate, together with Jan Baptist van Rensselaer; starting in 1657, he paid for her house rent and some necessities and repairs.[222] (Appendix 8, VI, likely near no. 33). She may not have had a sign there, since Hendrick Jochemsz had bought the one they had at their old place in 1655, at a public sale held by Steven in 1655. When her husband, the former commissary of Fort Orange, became incapacitated, Maria Dijckman's reason for turning to tavern keeping was simple: They needed income, and running a tavern was work that could easily be done by a woman. Maria's husband is never mentioned regarding her business, and Dijckman managed it under her own name. She may have had help from the West India Company – perhaps on the advice of Johannes de Deckere, who in January 1656 asked the director general and council to levy *f*50, *f*60, or *f*100 out of the farmers excise tax to help the Dijckmans, or else inform him what could be done.[224] For a while, tavern keeping would enable Maria to keep her family off the church's list of alms recipients. Maria may have started her job as tavern keeper (*waerdinne*), when the Dijckmans rented a house from Hendrick Jochemsz.[226] Baefje Pietersen also seems to have handled most of the tavern business on her own. While her husband Ulderick Cleyn was imprisoned in September 1654, perhaps for illegal trading, Baefje was the one going after debtors to pay for the beer or wine consumed at her house; and it was she who was sued for debts regarding a brandy delivery or the treatment of important guests. On one occasion, when her husband was sued for payment by Pieter Bronck, Ulderick had no idea of the amount of the bill.[226]

Location undoubtedly influenced the success of an inn. Most taverns had a poor box, and the amounts collected for the poor may indicate a tavern's popularity. Hendrick Jochemsz, Jurriaen Theunisz (after 1658-59), and Anthony Jansz were all located in the center of the village, and poor boxes at their inns frequently had good yields. In 1654, for example, *f*32 was donated in Hendrick Jochimsz's box, while Steven Jansz's contained *f*9-10 and Pieter Bronck's *f*14-11.[227] Unfortunately, the location of poor boxes is not often mentioned. Some deacons listed them simply as 'a box,' while others would add up the money from all the boxes, and write 'collected in [all] poor boxes.'[228] When they were emptied in December 1661, the poor box at Pieter Adriaensz's inn brought *f*16-2 and the one at Jan Martensz's *f*8-3; Marcelis Jansz had *f*8, Antony Jansz *f*11-12, and in Jurriaen Theunisz's tavern *f*24-4.[229] That does not necessarily mean, however, that most people went to Jurriaen Theunisz's place. He also may have collected higher amounts because his tavern was visited by wealthier individuals such as Jeremias van Rensselaer and his friends, who were known to deal with 'Jurrie' Theunisz and visited 'Tony's' tavern. As a good Christian and an important burgher, Jeremias undoubtedly set a good example by frequently putting money in the poor box, as did other important traders.

A risky business

No matter how much a tavern keeper wanted to do business, he may actually have dreaded some customers: those who easily caused trouble, started fights, or caused

damage to his glassware, plates, furniture, or house. In October 1654, word spread
through the village that Herman Jansz van Valckenburgh and some friends had
broken a window, stepped through it into *waert* (tavern keeper) Marcelis Jansz's
house (on the east side of present-day North Pearl Street; Appendix 8, no. 7). They
proceeded to assault and molest Jansz, and started scattered fires on the floor without letting the owner extinguish them. A few months later, tavern keeper Steven
Jansz may not have been pleased to see this particular customer enter his house.
When Van Valckenburgh threatened to beat Steven, he felt compelled to call to the
officer, who took Van Valckenburgh into custody.[230] Likewise Susanna, wife of
Marten Hendricksz *de bierkaecker*, may not have wished to see Jacob van Loosdrecht in her tavern again, after he and a companion had entered the house by kick-
ing in the door 'in such a way that the dowels came out of the posts and casing,' and
slandered her and Marten. Van Loosdrecht finally put out the lamp, desiring 'per
force to get into the woman's bed, and coming near the bed, did not not hesitate to
touch and grab her.'[231]

A tavern keeper always had to be alert. Aside from potential damage to his own
place and belongings, customers could quickly get into trouble. Even when there
were no bad intentions to begin with, alcohol could cause emotions to run high
and set the scene for great damage. On two occasions in Beverwijck, someone was
killed in a tavern fight. At Hendrick Jochemsz's tavern in 1658, Claes Cornelisz
was struck dead with a knife by soldier Daniel Bonvou; another death occurred in
1662, possibly even in the same building, as Anthony Jansz rented the place from
Hendrick Jochemsz between October 1661 and 1663.[232] This time, Seger Cornelisz severely wounded Andries Herbertsz *constapel* by striking him over the
head with a billiard cue, after which Herbertsz stabbed Cornelisz in the belly with
a knife. Cornelisz died later in that night.[233]

Tavern keepers were also protected by, and subject to, many laws and ordinances instituted by the government. These measures were necessary, as the life of
a tavern keeper could be very hard and worrysome. He wanted to be sure that his
customers paid their bill, even though it was sometimes unclear who was responsible. In May 1658, for instance, Hendrick Jochemsz sued Hans Vos for a certain
sum of money for food and drink supplied at his house to Pieter Bronck and
Dirck Bensingh. Hans Vos, however, said he didn't know anything about it, and
Jochemsz was then told by the court that he should recover the money as best as
he could from Bronck and Bensingh, who had spent it at his house.[234] An innkeeper always had to use his head, if he did not want to be cheated. What should he do
when a group of people came in, and at some point one person left? Who would
then be responsible for the payment? Sometimes tavern debts could add up quickly. In July 1654, for example, Lucas Pietersz owed Pieter Bronck ƒ193:2 for tavern
expenses.[235] To protect tavern keepers from individuals who often bought drinks
on credit, an ordinance had been published sometime before July 1658,[236] stating
that the innkeeper was not allowed to give credit for more than ƒ25. Accordingly,
Jan Martensz seems to have lost money when he was unable to collect more than
ƒ25 in his suit against Christoffel Davidsz for payment of a tavern debt.[237]

Regulations and excises

Arguments about prices for drinks were limited, as the cost of various drinks of different sizes was stipulated exactly by ordinance. In November 1658, the price of half a gallon of beer was 6 *stivers* in silver; and as the currency in Beverwijck was often figured in *sewant* or beavers, those prices were added as well: 9 *stivers* in beaver, or 12 *stivers* in *sewant*. A *kan* of French wine (19.2 liters) cost 18 *stivers* in silver, 22 in beaver, and 36 in *sewant*, while a *kan* of Spanish wine cost 24 *stivers* in silver, 36 *stivers* in beaver or 50 *stivers* in *sewant*. A *mutsje* of brandy (0.15 liter) went for 5 *stivers* in silver, 7 *stivers* in beaver, or 10 *stivers* in *sewant*.[238] The tavern keeper himself had to make sure to keep track honestly of the amount his customers consumed. One way to do that was to put marks on a blackboard. In 1650, Maria Goosens was accused of having erased two strokes at the same time, although she had tapped two *roemers* of brandy. Since each stroke apparently represented two *roemers*, by erasing two strokes Maria may have cheated the men who were entitled to the drinks out of a round of brandy. Cases like these could cause great turmoil. This incident ended with four men wrestling on the floor, one person stabbed in the side, and one person confined to the limits of Rensselaerswijck under a *f*300 penalty.[239]

The various measures used in a tavern must have been the same as those in common use in Amsterdam – a *kan*, or a *mutsje*.[240] Burghers could purchase beer in quantities smaller than a quarter-barrel at the tavern, and Jeremias van Rensselaer's accounts frequently mention, besides the many *pinties* (0.6 liter) or *mutsjens* of wine or brandy consumed at the tavern, a *kanne* of beer to take home, often fetched by a servant or slave. So that customers would not be cheated, or complain about such matters as a dent in a can, these standard measures needed to be inspected regularly. Jacob Jansz van Noortstrant was appointed gauger of the casks in 1656; although there is no direct evidence of Van Noortstrant inspecting various measures, the renewal of an existing ordinance in October 1668 suggests that he had also done this work on an earlier date. The ordinance ordered all merchants, brewers, tavern keepers, farmers, and others to have their yard measures, weights, barrels, cans, and *schepel* measures gauged by Jacob *de brouwer*, sealer of weights and measures, in the presence of the officer (*schout*) before January 1, 1669. In some localities in the Dutch Republic, this inspection took place annually; in Deurne, for example, it occurred between Easter and Pentecost, while in some other places it happened between January and April.[241]

Excise taxes levied on beer and other alcoholic beverages accounted for a good part of a city's income; to control this revenue, it was ordered in 1648 that the names and addresses of all tavern keepers in New Amsterdam be registered at the director general and council.[242] When an ordinance regarding the tapsters' excise tax was proposed in Beverwijck in December 1652, magistrates Volckert Jansz Douw and Rutger Jacobsz objected, declaring themselves personally in favor of further communication with the director general.[243] In February 1653, then, the rule in the village was that tapsters were not allowed to charge more than 8 *stivers* for a *mutsje* of brandy and 9 *stivers* for a *canne* of beer. Violating the rule was to be punished with a fine of ƒ100 for the first offense, double the fine for the second offense, and an arbitrary punishment for the third offense. Douw and Jacobsz raised objections to the ordinance, however, which was soon reconsidered. In November 1653, a new ordinance was passed by the court.[244] In order to prevent excise tax fraud as much as possible, all burghers and tapsters had to obtain a proper certificate from the collector, Pieter Ryverdingh, before their purchased heavy beer and wines could be carried into their houses and cellars. At this point they did not have to pay any excise, but only a fee of 2 *stivers* for the certificate of delivery. Commissary Johannes Dijckman was authorized to inspect on occasion, 'as often and repeatedly as it will suit his convenience or circumstances may require it, the houses of all tapsters belonging to this jurisdiction.'[245] In March 1654, however, when fraud was still frequently committed such that 'burghers had to pay the tax put by the tapsters on the liquors,' the magistrates thought to solve the problem by publicly farming out the excise on beer, wine, and distilled liquors in a manner similar to the method used in Holland.[246] In August 1654, Jan Hendricksz Maet (alias *Loserick*) was, when he bid most (ƒ1300) at a public auction, the first to buy the farming of the excise. He would set up regular times in the morning and afternoon when people could obtain their *biljets* from him; and only thereafter could they receive any beer or wine in their cellars, or carry it out of the ships that came up the river. He was to visit the tapsters' cellars, measure the wine and beer, and register the gauging accordingly. If he found that anyone had concealed wine and beer, the officer had to render his assistance. The fines collected for smuggling were given to the farmer, provided that the officer received a one-third share. People caught selling alcoholic beverages to the Indians were to be apprehended and convicted with the support of the officer 'as is fitting,' with their fines handled in the same way as the fines for smuggling. Yachts coming up from Manhattan were to be examined; and after accounting for the wine and beer they brought, the excise farmer was supposed to address himself to the customs house officer.[247]

In September, Maet testified that Maria Jans, Steven Jansz's wife, had sold brandy to an Indian woman.[248] The case does not appear in the records again; but when Maet later came into Steven Jansz's house on February 21, 1655, 'throwing many abusive words' and wounding Jansz with a knife, it probably had everything to do with Maria's deed – and, even more to the point, with Jansz's refusal to pay the excise.[249] Jansz's house was located just outside the limits of Beverwijck; but, as was described in the fourth chapter, the Beverwijck court found that Rensselaerswijck's tappers, like those in Beverwijck, had to pay the excise to the West India Company.[250] In March, the court of Beverwijck fined Maet for ƒ150 for his misbehavior at Steven Jansz's house and for having drawn a knife; but this case would have much greater ramifications.[251] While Jansz had been hurt, and was still in danger of losing his life in May and June, the two courts directly opposed each other; and during 1655 and 1656, the Van Rensselaers would wage their fruitless battle with the company over the tapper's excise.

Beverwijck tavern keepers, too, were occasionally caught for failing to pay the excise tax. Hendrick Jochemsz got away with his explanation that he had been unable to enter a half-barrel of good beer on account of 'the inconvenience of his wife's being in childbed.' He only had to pay the excise, but was warned that he would be fined the next time.[252] Jurriaen Theunisz, who was caught in 1658 for having two half-barrels in his cellar without a certificate of the excise farmer, was not so lucky. He tried to put the blame on Teunis Jacobsz *de bierdraeger* – who, Jurriaen said, he had ordered to fetch a certificate, but who had sent Huybert Jansz in his place. But when the beer carrier denied that he had received orders from Theunisz, the tavern keeper was ordered to 'satisfy the officer or settle with him.'[253]

The excise tax remained a matter of concern. In October 1656, tavern keepers were (like the bakers) required to renew their license quarterly for *f*6, on pain of one pound Flemish (*f*6) and suspension of business.[254] And 'as many open taverns without having applied for it and they refuse to pay the excise,' a new ordinance in January 1657 would again oblige tavern keepers to obtain their licenses and pay the excise.[255] On December 10, 1659, every tapster in Beverwijck had to renew his or her license every three months, on pain of suspension of business.[256]

Other ordinances stipulated the times tavern keepers were allowed to tap liquor. At night, after the ringing of the bell, tapsters were not supposed to serve. Although a 1641 regulation had established a 10:00 p.m. curfew, Stuyvesant changed this in 1647.[257] Not only would any tapster who sold alcoholic beverages after 9:00 p.m. be fined *f*6 for every drinker found in his tavern at the time of his arrest, but he would also loose his license.[258] In Beverwijck, the church bell may have been used after 1656 to remind people of the curfew; before the church was built, they may have rung a bell in the fort, or perhaps the patroon's house had a bell.[259] It seems that, in Beverwijck, punishment was not always imposed exactly according to the ordinance. On December 30, 1660, for example, Marcelis Jansz was caught entertaining guests and serving drinks after the ringing of the bell (Appendix 8, VIII, no. 7). When he declared to the court messenger who fined him that he would serve his guests the entire night in spite of La Montagne, he was fined *f*70 plus an additional *f*50 for his insolent remarks. The same evening, Jurriaen Theunisz, despite his excuse that 'he was not home then and that it happened through his servant,' was found guilty of entertaining and serving guests after the ringing of the bell. He was also fined *f*70, which seems to have been low considering the number of people (twenty) present in his tavern.[260] The frequently renewed ordinance (1648, 1656, 1658) did not prevent violations from happening, while the number of tapsters fined between 1652 and 1660 for serving after the evening bell seems to indicate that these rules were regularly broken, particularly around Christmas, New Year's, and *Shrovetide* (Mardi Gras).[261] Nor was serving liquor allowed during church services; but, as in the fatherland, this rule was frequently neglected despite the *f*25 penalty.[262] Hendrick Jochemsz had to pay *f*12 for entertaining guests in the morning and afternoon on a Sunday in December 1655, and was fined *f*6 for continuing to serve liquor during church services a few weeks later.[263] Herman Jacobsz Bamboes, Jan Martensz, and Willem Fredericksz Bout's wife were among the others fined for violating this rule.[264]

The tavern: A place for business and entertainment

The tavern offered the opportunity to drink, and the Dutch were good drinkers. Drinking was a social ritual: It brought people together, while creating feelings of solidarity, unity, and good fellowship.[265] Some taverns probably offered the opportunity to eat, as well as drink. That, in 1655, the eating house in the village was nicknamed 'Seldom Satisfied' (*Selden Satt*) may indicate that not everyone was excited about the quantity of food served there.[266] It is unknown which place this was, but it seems to have been one of the inns established in the village center, perhaps near the church, at Hendrick Jochemsz's. The colonists in Beverwijck certainly had not lost this piece of their cultural baggage, and they found many occasions for drinking. Public auctions were organized in taverns – in 1654 at Pieter Bronck's, for example, and in 1655 at Marcelis Jansz's. In 1657, Claes Hendricksz bought a house at public sale at Hendrick Jochemsz's and, at the same tavern in April 1655, Marcelis Jansz bought the right to collect the excise for wine and strong beer for ƒ2,030.[267] In February 1655 Cornelis Woutersz held his public sale of goods at Marcelis Jansz's tavern.[268] Many villagers would gather for these events to bid on the items to be sold; or they came solely out of curiosity, or to share in the social aspect of the get-togethers, bringing great business for the innkeepers. Deals were usually sealed by sharing a drink. The magistrates were, on occasion, also to be found in the tavern to discuss certain issues. On December 23, 1653, for example, the entire court was at Pieter Bronck's in order to settle the accounts of some deceased persons; and in August 1657, the magistrates paid ƒ75 for tavern expenses to Willem Fredericksz Bout, when they had made an agreement with Meyndert and Carsten Fredericksz about the place where the house of Jan van Aecken stood.[269] Events like these provided ample opportunity to share a *pintie* or a *kanne*. If they drank like their fellow Dutchmen in the fatherland, the greatest excesses of beer drinking took place at funerals; parties for a wedding, a baptism, or a fair were also excellent occasions for being lifted into higher spheres.[270] In his account books, Jeremias van Rensselaer provides us with many an occasion worth drinking: a joint dinner of the two courts in 1663, an auction, the purchase of a contract for the fourth kill, or talking with business partners like Jan Bastiaensz or Andries Teller.[271]

Drinking while doing business transactions was common; originally, a lawful transaction was considered settled only after it had been drunk to – the drinking ritual, the sharing of a glass as a sign of friendship and loyalty, being an integrated part of the deal.[272] As the tavern was thus a recognized place to do business, transactions and agreements reached there were fully accepted; such deals did have a somewhat provisional character, however, as they could be repealed within twenty-four hours if the other party was informed in a timely manner. It even could happen that a marriage promise would be considered invalid if the prospective groom had been out of his senses when he offered it under influence of drink.[273] In Beverwijck, people were aware of this rule, and on several occasions they tried to make use of it. In one case, the excuse was declared valid. Hendrick Coster, in 1678, backed down from a signed contract to exchange houses with Jan Albertsz

60. Jan Steen, Prince's Day: Celebrating the birthday of Willem III, 14 November 1660. *Oil on panel, 46x62.5 cm.*

Bradt. When even the notary testified that Coster had been drunk and Jan Albertsz sober, the court declared the contract invalid.[274]

Besides taking advantage of the many opportunities to drink and talk, people could also entertain themselves by playing various games. We have seen that Jeremias van Rensselaer, like Seger Cornelisz and Andries Herbertsz, seems to have liked playing billiards with his friends, which they frequently did at Anthony Jansz's place. *Dominee* Schaets mentioned how popular '*tricktrack*' (a board game played with dice and thirty disks) was among the villagers and visitors, when he wrote that the taverns were well visited during the trading season. When Steven Jansz sold his tavern goods in 1655 at a public sale, Baefje Pieters made sure that she bought the *tricktrack* table for her tavern.[275] The court prohibited heavy gambling. In December 1654, for example, the magistrates heard that 'some fellows [*maats*] at the public inns had been playing with *den talingh*, publicly and perniciously, for high sums of money.'[276] Most likely people also gambled by playing other games, cards, and throwing dice.[277] In May 1655, Hendrick Jochemsz was able to get the magistrates' permission to have the burgher guard 'shoot the parrot' (*papegaaischieten*) on the third day after Pentecost.[278] The warning to keep good order was well placed, as in patria this three-day event was usually accompanied by much drinking.[279] Other games, such as 'pulling the goose' (*gans trecken*) around the time of *Shrovetide*, drew people to the tavern as well.[280]

Except for drinking, people also smoked in taverns. Among the items sold by

Steven Jansz in 1655 was thirty-six pounds of tobacco and some pipes. While smoking was still a curiosity in Holland in 1598, this English custom had found its way there by 1640. Although health issues were already subject to debate, tobacco houses were established in the cities. Pipes from this period have been found at several archaeological excavations in Albany, indicating that Beverwijck's taverns were a place where *toeback suyghen*, or smoking tobacco, was not uncommon.[281] The deacons' account books indicate that, in later years, pipes and tobacco were distributed at funerals to the mourners, along with beer, wine, or brandy.[282]

In December 1660, Pieter Bronck, his wife Hilletje, and Jacob *de Looper* declared that Claes Marechael 'one Sunday evening went out of Pieter Bronck's house, befuddled but in a good humor with a big flute in his pocket.'[283] Although it is one of the very few references to musical instruments being used in a Beverwijck tavern, it is hard to imagine that, along with entertainment from games, no music or dancing occasionally accompanied the drinking and smoking in the taverns. In the Dutch Republic, special 'music inns' existed where musical instruments always were available for the guests; some innkeepers even paid musicians to provide music.[284] An ordinance of October 26, 1656, forbade, among other things, 'any lower or unlawful exercise and amusement, drunkenness, frequenting taverns or tippling houses, dancing, playing ball, cards, *tricktrack*, tennis, *balslaen* or ninepins ...' on Sundays; it does not seem too far-fetched to suggest that similar situations appeared in Beverwijck's taverns.[285] The ten wooden flutes found in Jan Gerritsz van Marcken's inventory probably were put to good use; although no musicians are mentioned in the Beverwijck source materials, it is hard to imagine that nobody was around who could play a violin or the rumbling pot, a typical instrument at that time, or beat a drum.[286] That Jeremias van Rensselaer sang psalms at home may indicate that the great culture of singing that existed in the fatherland had continued in the upper Hudson area. In the Dutch Republic, people in all social strata sang – old and young, poor and rich. People believed in the comforting and curative effects of music.[287] Among Dutch settlers, this musical tradition would exist for a long time; as late as 1797, when the consistory would finally decide to have the minister preach only in English, a 'protest song' (*'Nait is van mijn leven'*) was written that could be sung to the well-known melody of an existing psalm.[288]

Taverns at the frontier

Much of tavern life happened as in Holland, and many of the laws and violations were similar. In Beverwijck, however, tavern keepers were also confronted with some typically New World issues. In the winter, when the village was isolated from the rest of New Netherland (and the outside world) for several months, innkeepers were dependent on their local customers. But as soon as the river opened again, ships would be able to go to and from Manhattan, while traders and Indians would be expected for the upcoming trading season. Taverns and inns would be in full swing, providing board, food and drink to the many guests in town. Sullivan had calculated that the majority of fines for violating the tavern laws were imposed in the winter. He put the question clear:

With as many as a thousand people arriving during the trading season, the taverns were surely packed day and night as guilders poured into the pockets of villagers in the form of purchased and sold beavers. In such instances, who to arrest? Was the *schout* about to pester tapsters during the peak of the season when the latter's livelihood and that of the bulk of the community was on the line?[289]

As the success of the trading season depended on the numerous Indians who came to the village, everyone tried to profit by trading with them. Not only was there the possibility of good business for the bakers, but the Indians also desired alcoholic drinks. Past experience had taught that serving alcohol to natives could lead to great damage; since 1643, the director and council had prohibited it, and had prescribed a schedule of fines for violators. Persistent renewals of the ordinance – with penalties ranging from ƒ500 for the first offense to a double fine, arbitrary corporal punishment, banishment, and liability for all damages caused by the sale for the second offense – did little to prevent the liquor traffic.[290] Not only did the use of alcohol help bring about the disintegration of Indian society, but it also resulted in damage to the Dutch when drunken Indians showed disorderly behavior in the village. Despite all the warnings, various people tried to increase their income by participating in this illicit liquor traffic.[291] Although many ordinances were made and renewed, it seems that little was actually done to prevent it. One of the main problems was that Indian testimony was invalid in court. According to Trelease, while the number of drunken Indians in the upper Hudson seems to have been less than elsewhere in New Netherland, the unlawful liquor traffic was never entirely stamped out in Beverwijck.[292]

For a tavern keeper, it must have been very tempting to violate the law; and the court minutes reveal that, indeed, several of them were caught providing Indians with alcoholic beverages. After Willem Fredericksz Bout sold strong beer to the Indians, he was fined ƒ25 in June 1654.[293] In December 1654, Steven Jansz's wife Maria does not seem to have been punished severely for having sold brandy to an Indian woman; but half a year later, when she confessed a second time to selling brandy to the Indians, she would be fined ƒ300 and prohibited from coming into Beverwijck for a year and six weeks, 'and this by way of pardon and intercession in her behalf on the part of the magistrates.'[294] Other women made the same mistake. Egbertjen Egberts and Dirckie Hermense, both innkeepers in Beverwijck who gave beer to the Indians in June 1656 in exchange for some *tapoesjens* (a bag or pouch, likely well-decorated and made of deerskin, used by the Indians to carry tobacco and other small items), were fined 300 guilders, 'taking into consideration their voluntary admission of guilt'; both women had to remain in civil detention until satisfactory security was given.[295] Egbertje does not appear in the records again as a tavern keeper; but Jan Martensz, Dirckie's husband, was sued for selling brandy to the Indians in February 1658 and again in July; he denied the charge on both occasions.[296] In October 1656, the previously published laws regarding the sale of alcohol to the Indians were renewed, this time with a penalty of 500 guilders, in addition to arbitrary corporal punishment and banishment from the colony.[297] In August 1657, the court, 'considering the dangerous consequences of the case and the severe placards and in accordance with the said placards' sentenced Susanna Jansen to pay a fine of an unknown amount for selling a mixture of three pints of beer, brandy, and French and Spanish wine.[298]

With the Maquaes' proposals of September 1659 and the Dutch response, the nature of the problem became clear for both races. The Indians said that their people drank too much brandy, and requested that the Dutch not sell them any more of it. Anticipating conflict with their enemies, the French, the natives acknowledged that 'if we drink ourselves drunk, we cannot fight.' Being fully aware of their own weakness, the Indians added that they would:

> ... [take] some brandy with us and then no more after this time. We shall burn all the kegs, and although we now propose this, it will not stop it. But if the Indians come into the country with brandy, we shall come and tell the Dutch authorities who sold it to them.[299]

Eighteen days later, the Dutch encouraged them not to allow their people to come to the settlers for brandy, so that it would not be sold to them. 'Our leaders are very angry that the Dutch sell brandy to your people and always forbid it to our people,' they added, noting that the Dutch could take the brandy and kegs away from their people if they so directed.[300]

Location may have influenced the sale of alcohol to the Indians. Jan Martensz and his wife Dirckie Harms did not live in the village center but at the north side, close to the third kill. Ulderick Cleyn and his wife Baefje also had their tavern some distance from the center at present-day Columbia Street. It is not clear whether Ulderic was arrested for selling alcohol to the Indians. But when Maria Jans sold brandy to the Indians, the fact that the court decided 'not to enter into any agreement regarding it, until the case against Ulderick Kleyn is taken up also,' could lead a researcher to believe that such had been his crime.[301] 'Lange Maria' and Susanna Jansen both lived south of the fort at the time of their crimes. There is no record that alcohol was sold to the Indians at taverns located in the village center. The awareness that they were not immediately under the schout's eye may have tempted these tavern keepers, along with their desire to make some profit. It is remarkable, too, how often women were involved in providing Indians with alcoholic drinks – illustrating how running a tavern was a job often undertaken by women. Taverns were public spaces, and their purposes were entertainment and relaxation. At the same time, since taverns were usually located in someone's home, in some ways they were places where public and private space came together.

Conclusion

For any type of work discussed in this chapter, it has proven difficult to provide an exact number of people involved in a trade. First of all, to present numbers counted over this twelve-year period changes time into something static, and ignores the possibility of change during years of rapid development and construction. The high number of artisans drawn from the records is the result of counting everyone in the village who, at one point or another, appears to have been involved in a certain trade. But when, in an analysis, we arrange the information chronologically, the outcome represents the tremendous change and development in the village. Determining the number of artisans is complicated by a number of factors.

First, we have to consider that not all workers were simultaneously involved in their specific trade or work; some began their carreers in the village at a time when others stopped their business. Some people were only involved in certain work for a short period of time, and then focused on something else. We also have to keep in mind that the summer village was quite different from the winter village. The numerous traders from New Amsterdam and Holland who gathered in the community in the spring and summer, and the hundreds of Indians who showed up with their furs, provided work for bakers, brewers, tavern keepers and all the other inhabitants of Beverwijck. The atmosphere of activity and energy of all these people at that time must have contrasted sharply with the winters, when outdoor work was probably limited and performed using sleighs, if it was possible at all.[302] As the pace of life slowed, the scope of work was limited to indoor tasks and necessary chores such as baking bread, brewing the necessary beers, processing dried and harvested foods, making brooms and baskets, and preparing for the next trading season.

Thus, much of the work was seasonal. The numerous summer guests created much extra work, especially in the consumption area, for bakers, brewers, tavern and innkeepers, or people who rented-out rooms in their houses. The hundreds of Indians with their love of sweet breads and cookies, for example, were an important source of extra profit for bakers and others who took up preparing just these sweet baked goods. Skippers on the Hudson would sail their yachts to New Amsterdam filled with passengers, furs, and other colonial wares, and return to Beverwijck with provisions and travelers. Those involved in this type of work had to find other ways to earn their living in the winter.

Discovering exactly how many people were involved in a particular trade is not a simple matter. Just as the glazier and tavern keeper Jurriaen Theunisz hired Jan Barentsz Dullemans to bake bread for him, artisans may have attracted people to work for their businesses, while they themselves assumed the role of owner-manager. And when a business was bought and sold within a few days, a researcher could easily be led to conclude that the particular buyer or seller performed that specific trade – whereas, in reality, the person was only dealing in real estate. So, too, it is not always easy to distinguish between master and servant, or between an owner and a lessee.

Something that should be considered in our research, as well, is the fact that an individual in the seventeenth century did not, as is common today, work in just one area; but more typically, a person would be involved in several trades at the same time. Being a cooper did not mean that a person could not also brew beer. Several people are known to have exercised different trades. One person might be a carpenter, surveyor, or trader, and be involved in gunstock making, all at the same time, while someone else could simultaneously be a brewer, trader, farmer, and ship owner.

In searching for artisans, one should also be aware that names can sometimes be misleading, and should not always be taken literally. A person might appear not just under one name, but sometimes under four or five different aliases. Interpretating a name such as Jacob *de brouwer* too literally risks excluding that person from other possible occupations. By fixating on a name such as Jan Harmensz *Backer*, or Jan Martensz *de Wever*, the researcher may be assigning them a trade that, in reality, these men never performed.

When trying to discern the occupation pattern of artisans and tavern keepers in Beverwijck, one should also be aware that, as in *patria*, work was usually a family affair. Much of it was done in the front room of the dwelling, so that all family members were quite aware of the going-ons. When a customer came to the house while the husband was away – in the field, or working elsewhere – a wife (or sometimes, perhaps, even a child) would normally act for the husband, and later discuss it with the household head. Since business was discussed at home, wives naturally participated. Women were often quite capable of taking over the business, and frequently represented their husbands in important business matters.

Thus, a society like Beverwijck was much more flexible, and had less definite specialization, than has often been assumed. It was not so much that the person who did the job was fixed; rather, the place where the work was exercized was constant – the smitty, the brewery, the bakery oven. Over time, different people worked at these places. The focus for certain trades was the place where the work was performed; exactly who worked there was a secondary concern.

Establishing the village center north of the fort seems to have greatly benefitted people who had lots between the *Ruttenkil* and the *Vossenkil*; some of those who lived south of the fort, and who had begun their businesses there, may have suffered considerable damage. As demonstrated by the presence of some breweries and the concentration of bakers, gunstock makers, and blacksmiths in specific areas, certain locations became the focus for particular trades. Stuyvesant's action in 1652 of declaring the 3000-foot area around Fort Orange company grounds would prove to be of major consequence for many artisans. It is perhaps not surprising that of those people who had invested in businesses south of Fort Orange before 1652, some would not be able to recover from these measures. At some point in time, several of these settlers would find themselves among those asking for help. We will meet them again in the following chapter.

VI. Strategies of survival

In June 1657, *dominee* Schaets was seriously thinking of going back to the Netherlands.[1] His contract would expire in July and, because most people were now under the West India Company, Van Rensselaer would not maintain him after the expiration of this term. It was uncertain how the company or the community would then provide for its preacher, and the financial situation was tight.

When Schaets had signed his contract in May 1652 to be a minister in Rensselaerswijck for ƒ800 a year, this salary may have appealed to him. With this income in Holland, he would have belonged to the lower ranks of the 20 percent of the population earning above ƒ600. The *brede burgerij*, who accounted for 12 to 14 percent at the bottom of this group, earned between ƒ600 and ƒ1,000. Only in large cities did ministers receive an annual salary above ƒ1,000, while most village ministers had to survive on about ƒ500.[2] In Beverwijck, however, things were different. After only a year, the ƒ800 salary had appeared to be insufficient to maintain his household of five. In July 1653, it was increased to ƒ1,000, which was still less than the ƒ1,440 suggested in a list of salaries of West India Company employees.[3] In November 1655, Jan Baptist van Rensselaer wrote the patroon and co-directors that he and Schaets had agreed on one more year for ƒ1,300 salary and house rent, 'for which sum the minister at the end of this running year did not intend to continue, as he said he was not able to live there from.' Apparently Van Rensselaer was advised to pay the minister for one additional year, as the contract lasted until July 1657.[4]

In considering whether to return to *patria*, the minister may have somewhat exaggerated the salary of the minister at Manhattan, while elaborating on the dearness of things in the upper Hudson region. He wrote to the Amsterdam *Classis*:

> Victuals are three times more easily procured at the Minades, as the English live in that neighborhood, and they are also on the sea. The salary of the old preacher there who keeps house is two thousand guilders including his house rent; and besides he has free fuel, which here we have not. [In 1650, *dominee* Backerus earned ƒ100 monthly and received ƒ40 for boarding.[5]] Firewood costs us about two hundred guilders, for which the price at the Minades is hardly one hundred and fifty. This is because of the difficulty in hauling it from the woods.

Building a new house in Beverwijck, according to the *dominee*, was also expensive: It cost about four times as much as in the fatherland due to the high carpenters' wages and everything pertaining to building. Renting a house cost around ƒ400 to ƒ450 per year. Schaets was actually lucky, compared to village ministers in the fatherland, who hardly could make ends meet with their salaries of about ƒ500, and whose wives were not supposed to work.[6] He was able to live in the poorhouse, as there were not yet that many poor, and his wife was able to contribute to the household by some trading. He would be able to go back, he figured, if he sold all the household effects he had brought over and immediately started his journey. 'We have never lived luxuriously, and I do not wish to,' the *dominee* wrote. But they had lived 'more simply than any other minister,' and yet 'how different was his situation from the common inhabitants here.'[7]

   In the following pages we will look at those 'common inhabitants' who were not able to survive on their own. By analyzing the ways they were helped, we will see that the Dutch Republic's widely praised system of charity also found its way to the upper Hudson area. It appears that the very first building devoted to the care of the poor in America was built in 1652-53 in Beverwijck. The colonial government gave the patent for it to the deacons of the Dutch Reformed church, illustrating how church and state worked together. While the government made sure the poor could count on free help from notaries and free education, for example, by arranging for various laws and ordinances, the deacons took care of the practical part of the relief. They provided the poor not only with food, clothing, and shelter, but also with the services of a surgeon, care, and education. The basic principle was that those being helped were honest poor, and had exhausted all other means to survive. People in seventeenth-century Beverwijck regarded poverty as a normal aspect of life that easily could happen to themselves or their friends. In church collections and poor boxes, as well as through donations, they frequently contributed money for the benefit of the poor. Thus, we can say that Beverwijck's system of poor relief was based predominantly on voluntary donations.

Living conditions

Prices

How different the situation was between the settlers and their compatriots in Europe will become more clear if we take a look at the basic costs of daily life and the wages of the lowest-paid workers. Daily necessities consisted of the main ingredients of the colonists' menu: bread and beer, and butter and meat. As we saw in the previous chapter, bread prices were often debated; but in 1658, it was stipulated that the cheapest bread (coarse bread that was sold in loaves of eight pounds) at Manhattan was to be sold at 14 *stivers sewant*, while in Beverwijck it would cost 18 *stivers*. In 1659-60, the deacons' poor fund paid ƒ1 for a loaf, and, in 1663, ƒ1-4.[8] That Ysbrant Eldersz's family of four ate ƒ70-15 worth of bread, over three months in 1663, seems to agree with an estimate made by W. P. Blockmans and W. Prevenier.[9] As we saw in the previous chapter, these historians calculated that a family with two children consumed about five pounds a day. In Beverwijck, that would have meant that this family needed 228.12 eight-pound loaves of bread per year, which in 1658 cost them about ƒ273-12 in light money, or ƒ205-6 in beaver value. In 1659-60, these prices were probably about ƒ304 in *sewant*, or ƒ228-12.[10]

The butter with which the bread was consumed – often about a pound per person per week – would have been considered a necessity as well. The deacons paid about ƒ1 for a pound in 1661 or, in 1662-64, ƒ1-5 to ƒ1-10 *sewant* or ƒ1 in *beaver*.[11] A family of four would spend about ƒ4 per week, or about ƒ208 *sewant* per year on butter in 1661.

The price of another mainstay of life – beer – was also established in 1658. The cheapest beer, 'small' beer, was set at ƒ6 *sewant* (or ƒ4-10 beaver and ƒ3 silver) for a *tun* (41.54 gallons, or 155.4 liters).[12] If people drank as much beer in the colony as they did in the fatherland, the same family of four most likely drank between six and twelve *canne* (six to twelve quarts) during a day (or 3,285 *canne* per year), which would bring their annual spending on beer, at a minimum, to between ƒ51 and ƒ102 *sewant*. This is hard to estimate, as it is unknown how much beer women and children drank; it could very well be that, in Beverwijck, people drank more water. According to Adriaen van der Donck, Indians drank water from a fountain or spring, and it is possible that the Dutch followed their example.[13]

In addition, people regularly ate meat (often pork, bacon, or venison). Some poor people received half a deer in November 1660, which cost between ƒ10 and ƒ12 and seems to have lasted them three weeks.[14] This suggests a weekly expense on meat of about 66 *stivers* (ƒ3-6) for these families, or an annual expense of about ƒ172 *sewant*. Added together, a family of four thus would spend at least about ƒ228-12 for bread, ƒ208 on butter, ƒ102 on beer, and ƒ172 for meat, adding up to an annual expense of ƒ845 *sewant* on bread, butter, beer, and meat. Commissary Johannes La Montagne, when he justified his expenses on repairing the fort in 1658 to the director general and council, included a calculation of daily expenses per person that came up with even higher costs. According to him, a day worker used:

> ... about one loaf of bread a week, which cost 18 *stivers* in 1658, and 22 *stivers* in 1659, one pound of fresh meat, which cost 12 *stivers*, and fish much more expensive; so that a laborer needs five pounds of meat per week, or as many pounds of fish or more, which is the usual fare here in the summer. Add to this one *vane* of beer at each of the three meals a day, they have, and furthermore, one pound of butter per week, which also costs a guilder in light money; then one pound of cheese, all at civil price.

Altogether, La Montagne estimated that, in 1658, food alone accounted for 26 *stivers* a day per person. He added that 'it was as incorrect to compare the Manhattans to this place as it would be to compare Holland to New Netherland.'[15] If we would apply La Montagne's calculation for one year, it would mean that one person needed ƒ474-10 *sewant* for food alone. For a family of four, it could bring their annual spending on food for that family to as much as ƒ1,898 in *sewant*. About his own situation, La Montagne (with an annual salary of ƒ900) stated that for bread, small beer, and firewood alone, he needed ƒ800 in light money per year. The excessive dearness of everything had driven him into such neediness and poverty, he wrote, that he had never before felt as constricted in all the sixty-eight years that he had lived. He found himself destitute of all means to provide himself with daily bread and provisions for the winter. Looking at these two calculations, and considering that also Jan Baptist van Rensselaer hardly could get around on his salary of ƒ1,000, and needed to take additional money for his household, suggests that prices indeed were very high. They certainly were higher than in Graft, where annual subsistence costs were between ƒ90 and ƒ100 per person.[16]

Costs for other items, however, were high as well. As we saw, firewood was a major expense that cost the minister ƒ200 a year. Twenty-five pieces of firewood went for ƒ4-10 in April 1660, and two years later about ƒ6.[17] Then there was necessary spending on clothing and blankets. Nothing indicates that cloth was produced in the colony; and although Jan de Wever's name may suggest he was working in this business, there is no evidence that he did. He seems to have made his living by keeping an inn and by farming.[18] Blankets, various types of cloth, and often clothing were imported from the Netherlands. As in the fatherland, local tailors and undoubtedly several women made clothing in the colony.[19] Imported materials, however, were expensive. In addition to the regular price, they carried a portion of the insurance and shipping charges to Manhattan, and of the freightage from there to Beverwijck. On top of that came the commission of the local merchant, which was around 6 percent in the case of Jeremias van Rensselaer, as described in chapter three. And finally, there was the profit each trader needed to make. Prices of imported goods sometimes became so high that, in November 1653, the director general and council stipulated that items should not be sold for more than 120 percent above the original price. A pair of Icelandic stockings was to cost 36 *stivers*, an *ell* of duffel cloth no more than ƒ3-10; and a pair of shoes from size 8 to 12 should cost ƒ3-5.[20] These prices, however, did not remain the same. The deacons' account books list various prices through the years for different items. The price of Icelandic stockings varied from ƒ2 to ƒ6, and while shoes in 1656 went for ƒ5 (one pair cost as much as ƒ15 in 1662); once, in 1664, the deaconry even paid ƒ17 for a pair.[21] Various types of textiles were used to make clothing; prices of duffel varied from ƒ5 to ƒ9, linen ran from ƒ2 to ƒ2-5 the *ell*, *dosijnties* (a kind of woollen cloth or kersey) from ƒ6-10 to ƒ12-10, and cloth cost about ƒ7-8. Shirts could be bought for between ƒ5 and ƒ10, and for a blanket one had to pay between ƒ20 and ƒ30 *sewant*. The sources may show the highest numbers, and people probably found many concrete solutions for their financial problems – and fiddled with money. But nevertheless, we can ask the question: If people with incomes of ƒ1,300, ƒ1,000, and ƒ900 complained about hard times, how did the lowest-paid colonists survive?

Wages and living conditions

The high cost of living mandated that wages paid in Beverwijck had to be high. On average, the lowest pay was earned by day laborers, and Jan Baptist van Rensselaer pointed out that even their wages were high, at ƒ2-10 *sewant* a day. In 1652 he had already urged the patroon and co-directors of Rensselaerswijck to contract ten or twelve farmhands and boys for the colony, as the day workers 'ate up the farmers who were unable to pay their leases. A day worker did not want to work for less than ƒ400 a year,' he wrote. Without his labor, a farmer would otherwise have to let the harvest spoil in the field.[22] In the Republic, the annual income of an unschooled laborer certainly did not exceed ƒ240, and it was usually less; sometimes earnings could be increased by additional income from other family members. Schooled laborers could, during the summer, earn some 25 to 30 *stivers* (ƒ1-5) a day.[23] The records show that, in 1657, a day worker at the upper Hudson on average was paid about ƒ2-10 *sewant* per day, or ƒ2 in Holland's currency, and frequently more in later years.[24] If he worked all days except Sundays and other holidays, such as days of prayer and thanksgiving, or Easter, Christmas, and Pentecost – about 308 work days – he could earn, at best, ƒ616 (or ƒ770 *sewant*) a year. For Van Rensselaer and other employers, it certainly was cheaper to contract for farmhands in the Dutch Republic for varying wages between ƒ40 and ƒ150, and then to provide them with food, board, drink, laundry, and wringing laundry (see appendix 7).

These servants, however, could not always count on being spared from poverty. Thunis Gerritsz, for example, contracted in 1657 to work for Arent van Curler for four years at free passage and ƒ60 per year, with the condition that, 'if he would behave well and loyal, the aforesaid master Curler would improve his wages.'[25] Van Curler does not seem to have approved of his servant's behavior, as in the winter of 1659 Thunis did not have enough warm clothing and was given a coat, two shirts, and cloth trousers by the deacons of the church. The Teunis *van de Vlackte* who, in April and June 1661, was given two shirts and a pair of stockings was likely the same person.[26] Financial problems were also suffered by *Meester* Jacob's maid. She may very well have been the orphan Marritge Jochims, who was hired out in November 1657, at the age of fourteen, by the orphan masters of Amsterdam (*weesmeesters aelmoesseniers*) to serve surgeon Jacob de Hinsse and his wife as a maid for five years. In the fall and winter of 1663, the deaconry gave her a blanket, a shirt, *dosijne*,(a kind of woolen cloth or kersey) and linen; and in March and December of the following year, she was given five and a half *ells* of linen and one and a half *ells* of duffel. Although she still was at *Meester* Jacob's house, Marritge may have been just at the end of her contract, while illness may have contributed to her misfortune.[27]

When Jeremias van Rensselaer wrote his brother in 1661 about how hard it had become to get beavers, even from succesful traders like Goosen Gerritsz, he added: 'You can readily imagine what it is with the poorer people.'[28] The decline of the beaver trade not only brought damage to the successful traders, but affected the lives of poorer people even more directly. To this financial situation we have to add the depreciation of *sewant*, which had earlier caused economical problems for some. *Sewant*, the most common currency for everyday expenses and some wages, had started depreciating in the early 1650s, and caused inflation throughout the 1650s and early 1660s. As we saw in the third chapter, by 1657 it was worth ƒ10-12 per beaver, and by November 1658 it had depreciated to '16 guilders and more' per beaver. The result was that 'a difference of 80, 90, yea 100 percent is made by shopkeepers, tradesmen, brewers, bakers, tapsters and grocers, if they work and sell their wares for beavers or wampum.'[29]

In addition to the monetary crisis, other events could undermine people's security of life. Frequently the community experienced floods and freshets, or other natural disasters that would often have serious consequences. On November 8,

1654, there was no church service because of the high water, which had not only taken away a good part of the fort, but had also destroyed the West India Company's garden 'so that hardly a clapboard remained,' and did much other damage. That workmen were soon contracted to repair the bridges on the third kill, suggests that several individuals suffered great losses at that time, as well.[30] Eleven years later the flooding would be even worse: In April 1666, the river ice took away about forty houses and barns, among which were those of Van Rensselaer, Abraham Staets, Jan Barentsz, and Harmen Bastiaensz. At least they managed to save their lives, 'but not without great peril,' Jeremias wrote to his father-in-law. He had been able to save a few things, 'but the grain and oats we were to send to you, and also that intended for Governor Nicolls, are lost. My garret and also the rear chamber were well filled with oats, but that is gone now.'[31]

When an event like this was followed by a bad harvest, conditions became even worse. In 1655, Jan Baptist van Rensselaer wrote that because of the high water, freezing of the winter wheat and worms in the summer wheat, many farmers had suffered great damage. In 1666, in addition to the damage done by the springtime ice flow, the farmers had such a bad crop that many of them did not have grain for seeding or for making bread.[32]

Indian hostilities and the threat of war did not make life any easier. Settlers repeatedly saw their livestock killed by the natives, and the Esopus wars in 1659-60 and 1663-64 affected the lives of people from the Esopus to Beverwijck. Several individuals were kidnapped or killed, leaving sometimes women and children not only without a husband or father, but also without a main source of income. Harvests were destroyed, soldiers needed to be boarded, and various people fled to Beverwijck and Rensselaerswijck to find safety. Several people were ransomed from the Indians, among them three children of one Waclet, Adriaen van der Donck's widow, and some other children.[33] Some fifteen people needed help due to the hostilities with Indians.

Illness and disease also threatened the security of life. In the fall of 1662, smallpox raged in the village, taking the lives of at least thirteen adults and fifteen children between the end of August and the end of December.[34] Such situations could easily force families with young children into poverty, as the loss of a father meant the loss of most income, while the loss of a mother meant the loss of care for the family. The presence of a barber-surgeon may have provided some security. In 1642, the patroon had hired Abraham Staets as a surgeon to take care of the physical well-being of the colonists. Staets canceled his contract in 1649, and by 1654 Jacob de Hinsse was Beverwijck's surgeon. All inhabitants could count on medical help: Those who could afford it insured themselves and their families against mishaps by making a contract with the surgeon for a certain period of time. It seems that the agreements covered injuries or illnesses that occurred naturally, and not wounds that were inflicted deliberately.[35] Those who were not able to pay the costs themselves were assisted by the deacons of the church. That people could also get help in costly situations was demonstrated in May 1657, for example, when the deacons paid *Myster Jackup* f150 for Willem Albertsz's surgeon's fees when he was unable to take care of the bill himself.[36]

With daily life so expensive, easy access to land was of the greatest importance. Even the poor had access to sufficient land on which they could plant a garden for their own use. Most people were thus able to grow their own vegetables and keep a cow, some hogs, and chickens. The abundance of land certainly was an advantage for the needy.[37] Adriaen van der Donck described how almost everybody had a kitchen garden, in which they grew 'various kinds of salads, cabbages, parsnips, carrots, beets, andive, succory, finckel, sorrel, dill, spinach, radishes, Spanish radishes, parsley, chervil, cresses, onions, leeks and besides whatever is commonly found in a kitchen garden.' In addition, he mentioned various products of the herb garden, and vegetables grown by the Indians, such as squash. Those who were able could hunt, fish, or gather various fruits and vegetables. Van der Donck also wrote that there were plenty of hogs, while deer were easily obtained, sometimes for 5 guilders or often for less. Wild turkeys were heavy and fat, and the Indians sold them for 10 *stivers*. The diet of most people consisted of products made from wheat and corn, such as bread and *sappaan* (a mush made with corn meal).[38] Frequent distributions of venison, pork, and bacon to the poor in times of shortage indicate that meat was a common element of the daily menue, even on the poor man's table, while the rare distributions of vegetables suggest that people grew them on their own. Except for food and shelter, the ability to read and write also were important means to a successful career in Beverwijck.

Literacy as a cultural tool

In a place where people relied so much on the written word, some degree of literacy was demanded. People were encouraged to read the Bible, as it was important to understand the Calvinist religion; but, in practice, it was even a necessity for Beverwijck's inhabitants to be able to handle a variety of legal instruments. Sometimes people signed documents with a mark, yet the papers themselves required reading ability and, particularly for account books, some basic writing ability as well. Whatever the subject of a court case, one could expect that proof would be demanded from the books or accounts, whether it was from Abraham Pietersz Vosburgh (who had to bring his surveyor's book to the court) or a needy female tavern keeper (who demanded that one of her customers pay a tavern debt). Mijndert Fredericksz, a smith, signed a document with a mark in 1668; but, in the same year, was able to present a written account to Jeremias van Rensselaer, listing all the work he had done, varying from making a cow bell to repairing guns, fixing tires on a wagon, or shoeing a horse.[39] We can only wonder whether or not Fredericksz was able to write, or whether his accounts were perhaps written by someone else. The meanings of the sophisticated marks made by some other men are not quite clear: Were they used in order to save time? Was it easier to do it that way? Or, were they not able to write? It is quite possible that several adult people were not able to write when they came over from Europe; but as in Beverwijck they did well economically and they climbed the social ladder, circumstances may have made it desirable for these settlers to learn how to write. The successful traders Jan Koster van Aecken and Goosen Gerritsz, for example, started signing documents with their names after 1662. Prior to that, they signed everything with the same fairly sophisticated mark – Goosen even 'marked' his marriage certificate, while his new wife signed her name. But in 1663 Gerritsz was able to keep the deacons' account book, while Koster did this in 1664.[40] Carpenter and tavern keeper Willem Fredericksz Bout always signed with mark, as well; but as farmer of the excise, he probably kept detailed books on all his transactions for the court. Numerous accounts in the Van Rensselaer Manor Papers in the New York State Library provide us with examples of how tailors, bakers, shoemakers, masons, or carpenters were perfectly capable of presenting the patroon with good, though sometimes less clearly written, accounts.[41] We should not be too quick to conclude that people who used a mark were unable to write; the marks were usually fairly sophisticated, and may have been a more reliable (or just as important) proof of identity than a written signature; in the Dutch Republic, this was especially the case in provinces other than Holland. Although signatures would become increasingly important in the seventeenth century, these house marks remained important, and are found, for instance, on gravestones and coats-of-arms.[42]

Evidence that could provide information about the reading culture of Beverwijck's population is too scarse and incomplete to draw any general conclusions. Reports of only a few inventories and auctions have survived and, of those, only one inventory seems complete. It contained sixteen books, large and small, and two books with maps.[43] In most cases, they cover only part of a person's possessions; for example, an inventory of goods of Gerritie Brants lists only clothing.[44] The completeness of some of the other inventories remains an open question (e.g., the inventory of Cornelis Bogardus, of which everything certainly was not sold).[45] But, while they don't provide a sufficient basis for quantitative conclusions, these incomplete inventories and auctions (of which eleven inventories and fourteen auctions were included in this study) do provide us with names of owners, sellers, buyers, prices, and (on rare occasions) a title of a book.[46] Through the inventory of Gysbert van Imborgh, who lived at the Esopus, we learn that several medical books had found their way to New Netherland. This surgeon had, among others, books on medicine and anatomy by Christophorus Wirtsungh, Ambrosius Paré, and Johannes de Vigo. Van Imborgh also had a book on anatomy by Andreas Vesalius en Valuerda Anatomie, *Een hoochduytsch aertseney ende kunststucke*, two written medicine books, *Medecijnse aenmerkungen* by the famous Amsterdam physician and burgomaster Nicolaes Tulp, *Examen der chirurgie* by Mr. Cornelis Heres, *Een beschreven medecijn en studenteboeck*, and a surgeon's book without a title.[47] The surgeons Abraham Staets and Jacob de Hinsse may very well have brought some of these books to New Netherland, as well; in 1654, De Hinsse bought *Schat der Gesontheyt* (The Treasure of Health) for *f*8 at Gabriel Leendersz's auction.[48] As we saw in the second chapter, Van Imborgh's inventory also contained a great number of educational and religious books, with which *Dominee* Gideon Schaets and school master Adriaen Jansz van Ilpendam most likely were quite familiar.

Jeremias van Rensselaer may have had a collection of books. On his first jour-

61. Prior to 1662 Goosen Gerritsz and Jan Koster van Aecken signed documents with a mark. Thereafter they always wrote their names.

ney to New Netherland in 1654, he took along seven books, of which two were popular works with a worldly subject – namely the life and works of Frederick Hendrick, prince of Orange, which had only recently been published, and a book about Hendrick de Grote. The others had religious themes; there were French and Dutch New Testaments, a book on faith, Vondel's *Joseph*, and one *Merckteecken der salicheyt*.[49] He may still have owned the book his father had sent to Rensselaerswijck in 1632 (*De Huyspostille Schulteti*, a book with sermons by Abraham Scultetus).[50] It is possible that he had one of the eight copies of *De Practijcke der Godtsalicheyt*, although Kiliaen van Rensselaer had sent these for the families in 1638.[51] Especially after he became a church member, Jeremias was interested in religious literature; in 1671, for example, he asked his brother Richard to send a prayer-book or two by Casparus Sibelius; while he already had the first volume of Adrianus Cocquius's *Theologica praxis: De ware practycque der godt-geleerdheit*, he asked his brother to send the second volume, as well.[52] He may have kept the books on law and the administration of justice his father had sent in the past, but these may also have been kept by *schout* Gerrit Swart.[53] Other traders also had books; but a title is not mentioned until 1654, when Philip Pietersz Schuyler bought three books for ƒ16 at Gabriel Leendertsz's auction, of which one was the popular translation of the Heidelberg Catechism after J. Ursinus by Festus Hommius, a well-known Reformed Orthodox minister, who had been president of the Synod of Dordt. In 1657, Robert Vastrick sent Schuyler a number of books.[54] And when Barent Pietersz *molenaer* bought two books and Abraham Staets a 'part of old books' in 1664 from the estate of trader Rutger Jacobsz, it suggests at least that these men could and did read, unless they intended to resell the books.[55] Inhabitants who possessed, sold, or bought books at one time were not limited to the well-to do. Less wealthy people owned books, as well; the estate of a needy tailor's wife contained six books, among which were two Bibles.[56]

If the general population owned just one book, it was a Bible, as the reformatory religions in Europe were stressing individual reading and evaluation of biblical teachings. During the seventeenth century, the quantity of published bibles, sermons, and religious representations in the Dutch language had increased, and would deeply influence the development of individuals from earliest childhood. Considering the education provided by reading and writing, we can understand that far more people could read than write. It explains perhaps why most women had their own Bibles, distinct from the large family Bibles, as well as a '*psalter*' containing the New Testament and the Psalms.[57] Jeremias van Rensselaer asked his mother to send him a *psalter* to carry in the pocket along with a rhymed *psalter*.[58] Besides Bibles and *psalters*, a goodly number of almanacs seems to have circulated in the colony. In auctions and inventories, they appear in various guises, mostly as slate (*bort*) almanacs that cost between 2 and 3 guilders. Jan Jansz Bleecker bought a framed almanac in 1666 from Cornelis Bogardus's estate for ƒ10-15, and Jan Gerritsz van Marcken had a perpetual almanac in his inventory along with a slate almanac.[59] In *patria*, these almanacs were very popular, and one household in four probably had one. With their medical advice and knowledge, historical and religious insights, predictions, satirical, fictional and non-fictional anecdotes and stories, comedies and jokes, they certainly contributed greatly to a common Dutch culture, as well in the upper Hudson area.[60]

Some colonists read European news in newspapers brought over by various visitors. Jan Baptist van Rensselaer sent his brother Jeremias papers on several occasions and, in 1663, Jeremias sent back *De Nieu Nederlanse Marcurius*, in which, along with other events, the Esopus war was described, as well as the situation with the Indians in the upper Hudson area.[61] Unfortunately, no copy of this newsletter has yet come to light; no references to the existence of a printing press in New Netherland have been found until the 1680s, so this may have been a handwritten newsletter.[62] New Netherland news may have been reported along the lines of a paper like *De Hollantse Mercurius*, a newspaper that was published by the Haerlem publisher Pieter Casteleyn between 1650 and 1690. This paper was one of fifteen newspapers that existed until 1665. Considering that the spread of news through pamphlets and newspapers had really taken off in the fatherland, and the frequency with which traders sometimes went back and forth between the Old World and the New, this exchange of newspapers, as well as the establishment of such a paper in New Netherland, should not be surprising. The growth of trade and business had stimulated the success of the printed word in *patria*, and newspapers primarily served the merchants and politicians. The press reported vital information about changes in governments, wars, scarcity and plagues, especially in countries outside the Dutch Republic.[63]

Beverwijck's inhabitants knew where they could go to find structure, focus, and guidance. Many of them found it by going to church and listening to *dominee*, while many also read from the Bible on their own and with their families. People also knew that they could turn to Beverwijck's court when they felt that their rights had been violated, and they were able to bring in the account books demanded as proof in their cases. Many of them were able to sign their name at the bottom of a petition or legal request. Every person who was not able to read or write had the chance to learn to do so in Beverwijck; and when legal documents were required, the notary was required to help the poor for free. In principle, every inhabitant could make use of the written word in a society where this was a requirement. Reading and writing were considered important cultural tools to survive – even also in Beverwijck.

Poverty: Definition and size

In 1652, when there were few poor people as yet, the director general and council granted a lot of eleven by five rods to the deaconry of Beverwijck's church, 'to enter upon, cultivate and employ and use the same for the need of the poor.'[64] That a poor house was built at such an early stage reveals that authorities did not expect everyone to be successful in the New World. This was not so strange, since a world without the poor was unthinkable for people in the seventeenth century, and efforts to make poverty disappear were not made. All that could be done was to make it bearable. Between 1652 and 1664, some eighty-eight individuals and families relied on support of the deaconry to survive, and therefore could be considered poor. The word 'poverty' is used here in the sense of a permanent, as well as temporary, need for material goods, which was provided by poor relief. Some people had too little income to provide basic survival needs such as food, clothing and housing; thus, they would fall within the 'poverty boundary of the biological minimum,' and would be provided with temporary or permanent help.[65] In order to find out where this boundary was, we need to find out more about the costs of a family's basic survival needs. How much income did a family need, in order stay above this poverty line?

As in Holland, bread and beer were the staffs of life in Beverwijck. The settlers ate bread at almost every meal, together with butter and/or cheese. Wheat or ready-baked bread were very basic necessities for the people's existence; and the historians Blockmans and Prevenier calculated that the expenditures for bread should account for no more than 44 percent of family income. Whoever exceeded this percentage fell below the subsistence level, and needed support.[66] As noted above, an eight-pound coarse loaf in Beverwijck cost 18 *stivers sewant* in 1658, while the average daily wages of a day worker were *f*2-10 *sewant* – enough to buy about 2.77 loaves of bread. This differs little from the situation in South-Holland, Utrecht, and the rest of the Republic, where a laborer could buy about 9 to 10 kilograms of rye bread with one day's wages.[67] With this information, if we assume that a family of four in Beverwijck used 1,825 pounds of bread per year (or 228.12 eight-pound loaves), their annual expense on bread would have amounted to 4,106 stivers, or ƒ274. If a day worker could earn 15,400 *stivers* at most, or ƒ770 *sewant* per year, bread purchases would have taken 35.5 percent of this annual income. The poverty line would be reached if these expenses came to about ƒ339 *sewant*. He would not suffer hunger if he worked every day. This number, however, has some restrictions. Blockmans and Prevenier have also estimated that the poorest people, especially, consumed more bread than the average 2,500 grams a day. For those with marginal incomes, they estimated this figure to be 3,200 grams, which seems to be confirmed by expenses on bread for Ysbrant Eldersz's family.[68] Then the weekly need becomes 44.8 pounds of bread, and the weekly expenses rise to a hundred *stivers*. Nor is it correct to assume that a day worker had a steady income. The lowest-paid people, especially, were not always assured of steady work, so their incomes were often less.[69] Finally, as we saw in the previous chapter, prices were exposed to fluctuations. Bread prices rose after 1658: A loaf of bread went for as much as 20 *stivers* (ƒ1, or ƒ1-5 *sewant*) in 1659 and 1660, and for as much as 24 *stivers* in 1663.[70]

Although in August 1659 a 'rattle watch' was charged, among other duties, with watching out for thieves, theft did not appear to be something the poor did as a result of their poverty. That criminality does not seem to have been connected with poverty suggests, not only that basic survival needs – food, clothing, and shelter – were available for everybody, but also that there was plenty of social control in the small community. Many court cases, however, do reveal that the economic situation was tight for most people. Shattuck calculated that debt was a factor in 612 of the 839 court cases between 1652 and 1660. While eighteen cases of debt appeared in the 1652 court minutes, this number had risen to 75 by 1657. By 1658, the first full year of the declining beaver trade, when *sewant* had been devalued to ⅛ beads to the *stiver*, the number of debt cases would jump to 156, but dropped back to 100 and 105 in 1659 and 1660, respectively.[71] For some people, this burden became too heavy. As a result of their many debts, Pieter Jansz *lademaecker* and Jan Bembo secretly left Beverwijck in 1659 for Hartford – only to be killed by Indians on their way.[72]

In reality, the number of alms recipients was more than eighty-eight. Except for five children (including three orphans), two elderly men, five ill men, twelve women (of whom six were with certainty widows), and twenty-five individuals whose background information is unknown, at least thirty-nine families – frequently consisting of more than four members – are included in this count. If we count all members of these families, the number of people who received support from the deaconry is doubled – raising the total to a good 200 individuals. Instead of 8.7 percent, we could then say that about 20 percent were poor – a fifth of the community. In the following table, families have been entered as one unit:

Table 6.1: Number of Beverwijck inhabitants receiving alms, 1653-64*

1653	2
1654	8**
1655	5 (including widows and orphans at Manhattan)
1656	11
1657	10+ 'the poor'
1658	10+ 'the poor'
1659	17
1660	26+ 'the poor'
1661	20+ 'the poor'
1662	21
1663	23+ 'the poor'
1664	25

* Families have been entered as one entity.
** If 'a woman who came from the Manhatan and who asked for alms' was the same person as 'the woman in the guard house,' the number would be 7. See *DAB*, pp. 13, 14, 16.
Source: *DAB*, 1652-1664

Of the eighty-eight needy, twenty-five received alms two to four times, and about thirty only appear on the list once. We should realize, however, that these people were not so far removed from those who were not supported; this larger group belonged to the poor in a broader sense: the potentially poor. These people struggled to survive, and had no financial reserves. Frank van Loo spoke in terms of 'those who don't possess anything but what they daily earn with their hands.'[73] As we saw in the previous chapter, Susanna Jansen was one of several people selling alcoholic drinks to the Indians. While she knew it was a crime, she illegally sold brandy to the Indians on August 12, 1657 to get beavers, in order to support her children.[74] Although she was poor, Susanna's name does not appear in the account books until November 1659, and again in October 1660, on which occasions she was given twenty *ells* of linen, six *ells* of duffels, and four *ells* of *dosijnties*. From then until 1671, her family seems to have been able to survive without the deacons' support. We should be aware not only of the poor mentioned in the deacons' books, who were supported, but also of other inhabitants in the community who, like Susanna Jansen and her family, lived on the edge of poverty. Out of pride, they may not have wanted to take help from the deaconry; or they may have been able to deal with their poverty with the help of family, friends, neighbors, other people of the same religion or nationality, or fellow workers. But only a small mishap was required to put them on the poor list.

Among the eighty-eight alms recipients were many, especially families with small children, who came back to the deaconry for many years. Ary de Vries's family, for example, was given support every year from 1656 to 1668, and also in 1673-74. Ysbrant Eldersz received alms for ten consecutive years, and in later years he occasionally returned on the deacons' list, as well. And although former commissary Dijckman's family was given help only once, in 1660, they were later supported from 1667 until his death in 1672. Of the twenty-five people receiving alms in 1664, thirteen had already received help before; and nine of these thirteen were families with children.

Researching Beverwijck's poverty leaves many questions unanswered. While no other source brings us as close to the daily life of the poor as the deacons' account books, a statistical analysis of these books still provides us with no more than an indication of the extent of poverty, as only those who actually went to the deacons for help are included; what resources they had already exhausted remains unknown. A baker or another food provider may have allowed them to buy on credit for a period of time before they asked for help. Like caretakers of the poor in *patria*, the deacons probably expected those who asked them for help to have tried all possible resources to survive.[75] Another question that remains concerns the standards the deacons used, which remain unknown: Were all people who received alms really incapable of providing for themselves? And were there others who needed support, but who for one reason or another did not receive it? In order to understand how Beverwijck dealt with the existence of poverty, we will first explore the way the village organized its poor relief system.

Organization of poor relief in Beverwijck

Cooperation of state and church

In the Dutch Republic, poor relief was organized locally and was heterogeneous in character. With seven sovereign state boards (*Staten Colleges*) and her numerous city and village boards, a uniform system was impossible. While secular and ecclesiastical charity worked together in towns such as Delft and Zwolle, the opposite was the case in Amsterdam, where the two systems were separated to a great extent. In Beverwijck, care of the poor was organized much like it was in various places in the countryside in the Republic, which again differed from the cities.[76]

With a small population and no church permitted other than the Dutch Reformed, Beverwijck's leaders were active in both the church and the local government. Except for Willem Teller, who was church deacon in 1656-58 but never served as magistrate, all deacons and elders were at some point magistrates, as well. Several persons served a few years as magistrates, and during the time they were off the bench they were members of the church council, after which they would go back into the magistracy – or sometimes they would hold both offices at the same time. Abraham Staets, for example, was magistrate in 1652-53 and 1657-58, and again in 1661-62. In 1659-61 and 1663-65, he signed the deacons' account book as member of the consistory (see Appendix 5). This also happened in some areas in the Dutch Republic – already in the early 1700s, several magistrates in, for example, Amsterdam, Haarlem, Alkmaar, and The Hague were members of the consistory.[77] Although the boundaries between secular and ecclesiastical poor relief in Beverwijck were not very strict, we can distinguish both types.

In the Dutch Republic, the deacons of Dutch Reformed churches who took care of poor relief were supposed to take care of all needy persons; but, in reality, they often limited their care to the poor of their own denomination (*huisgenoten des geloofs*), transients, widows and orphans in the first instance.[78] In Beverwijck, this does not appear to have happened. The Dutch Reformed was the only church in the village; therefore, its organization was the only accepted form of official ecclesiastical charity supported by the state. The deaconry functioned as a public body for poor relief through most of the century, and the deacons were responsible for the practical organization of distributing gifts of charity among those in the community who were in need. The Lutheran church, which was officially recognized in 1666, only seems to have had a charity system toward the end of the century. In January 1695, this church had to provide a third of the alms given to Hendrick Marcelisz and his wife Trijn van den Bergh, as Trijn was 'of that denomination.'[79] By that time, secular authorities also became more involved with the actual providing of alms to the needy, and in the 1690s they contributed money for the care of some indigent persons.[80] This increase of involvement of the town in poor relief also happened in the Dutch Republic, while in Beverwijck it may have been an indication that the English system was implemented to a greater extent. From the 1650s until in the 1690s, however, poor relief provided by the deacons had a public character and was supported by secular authorities.

Care provided by the state

At first sight, it may seem that only the church's deaconry provided help to the needy; but the state was involved, as well. It is interesting to note that the village constructed a poorhouse on a lot granted to the deacons by the director general and council at an earlier date than that it built an official church. At the time the poorhouse was completed, religious services were still being held in the rear part of the patroon's house. The importance of this poorhouse is expressed not only by the early point at which it was built, but also by the location of the building. Situated in the heart of the village that was being constructed, just south of the first kill, close to where the two main roads met and where the church would be built in 1656, it was on the way from the *bijeenwoninge* to church and fort, close to bakeries and breweries (some of which already existed, while others were still to be built) – all of which indicates that support for the poor was an important concern of the authorities. It is possible that the facility – at which people delivered and picked up goods and, as we will see, performed various kinds of work – may also have functioned as community center where many villagers stopped by. Relief for the poor and preventing social problems were central concerns of the whole community, while the building itself may also have been a central point for various activities.

But ensuring that a poorhouse would be built was not the first measure the colonial government had taken to provide for the poor. On April 18, 1641, the director general and council had already stipulated by ordinance that part of the fines imposed by the court would be for the benefit of the poor.[81] The total from fines could amount to a substantial number. In December 1653, for example, the deaconry received ƒ353, which was a sixth part of the fines imposed between October 4, 1656 and December 31, 1657.[82] Baker Jochem Wesselsz contributed a considerable amount to charity in this manner. April 12 1653, for instance, he had not only slandered a magistrate and called him names, but had also threatened to attack him and cut him into pieces. Of the ƒ200 fine he had to pay, one-third went to the court, one-third to the *schout*, and one-third to the poor. Five years later, he was ordered to pay 5 pounds Flemish for beating an Indian. One would suspect that his business was very profitable, since he would donate quite a bit more to the poor in this way in the years that followed. In May 1653, his debt for these fines amounted to ƒ250, and in the following years he would be fined at least another six times, which in fines amounted to ƒ230. Most of his offenses involved slander and assault.[83]

Various ordinances were created to make life somewhat easier for the needy. A 1651 ordinance allowed the poor to lay-in 'small' beer (i.e., beer with a low alcohol percentage) free of excise tax, with the right to sell it retail at a reasonable profit. The poor were also exempt from a weighing fee, and secretaries and notaries were bound by ordinance 'to serve the poor and indigent who ask such as an alms, gratis and *pro Deo.*' Beverwijck's indigent were probably exempt from school fees, as were the poor in New Amsterdam.[84] Another important measure to prevent poverty was the institution of the orphan masters, who oversaw the care of poor and orphaned children. The law in the Dutch Republic prescribed that every person under twenty-five years of age, as well as older persons who were deemed incompetent to manage their own affairs on account of mental or other disability, had to be provided with a guardian. Such guardians, whether designated by will or appointed by the court, performed the office of both tutor and curator. Under the watchful eye of the orphan masters, they had charge of the education and maintenance of minors, as well as of the administration of their estates.[85] While this institution was installed at New Amsterdam in 1656, Jan Verbeeck and Evert Jansz Wendel, both experienced consistory members, were appointed orphan masters in Beverwijck on February 6, 1657. Unlike New Amsterdam, where the orphan masters had their own court, Verbeeck and Wendel communicated directly with the court of Beverwijck. One of their first cases was on February 27, when they reported how badly Christoffel Davidsz administered the estate of his deceased wife, Cornelia Vos, which was left undivided between him and his children. Following, as much as possible, the Dutch custom that grandparents became the guardians of orphans, the court then, at the advise of Wendel and Verbeeck, authorized the father and an uncle of Cornelia to be lawful curators of the estate; and to do all that was fit to benefit the estate and the children.[86]

The first law for support of the poor in New Amsterdam and the rest of New Netherland would not be passed until October 22, 1661, '... to the end that the lazy and vagabond may as much as possible be rebuked, and the really poor the more assisted, and cared for, and from this time onward no assistance shall be given by the deacons of this city [New Amsterdam] to any persons outside of the jurisdiction of this city, unless they bring with them a certificate of their character and poverty...'[87] In Beverwijck, only a woman from Manhattan and *Iersman de Hyer* (probably an Irishman) were noted in the accounts for having asked for alms in the village. Unlike New Amsterdam, Quebec, and probably Montreal, the up-state settlement did not have a need for the mendicant's licenses these cities required, as it did not have a great problem with beggars and the 'undeserving poor.'[88] In the ordinance, the director general and council further mandated collections in each village for the support of the poor. This stipulation was also unnecessary for Beverwijck, where money had been collected for the poor since the 1640s, and where the poorhouse had been operating since the early 1650s.[89]

Care provided by the church

The deaconry of the church was duty-bound to take care of the practical aspects of poor relief. The church was, as noted in chapter two, organized along the principles of the Dutch Reformed church in the fatherland; and like in every church there, Beverwijck's deaconry was required to collect gifts of charity in order to assist the poor materially as well as mentally, and to build up and maintain possession of property and capital so that the poor always could be sure of help. The consistory as a whole selected the people who received assistance, and the deacons were given responsibility for managing the means, and for giving the poor in the community what they needed. In April 1654, for example, they gave Thomas Coningh *f*50 by order of the consistory, and Jan *met de baert* received *f*50 in April 1659.[90] The deacons kept accounts and tried to keep as good a balance between expenditures and income as possible. Besides notes on regular expenses for the church, the communion ritual, building upkeep, and services of the sexton and the *voorsanger*, their account books contain detailed descriptions of expenses on the poor and the yields of church collections and poor boxes, as well as other income. After the selection of persons who needed help, the deacons carefully weighed the form and quantity of assistance offered to each individual; and, by monitoring the person, they usually tried to safeguard their expenses. Help was only provided when the person was genuinely unable to survive on his own income, and was primarily a supplement to the indigent's income and provisions. The amount of relief given was dependent on individual circumstances.

   A needy person most likely went to the poorhouse to obtain alms. The building does not seem to have been used as a place for the needy to find shelter, since poor people who needed personal care were usually boarded out with other villagers – who themselves were often needy. Besides, at least until June 1657 (but probably through 1660), the building functioned as the minister's residence. In September 1652, *dominee* Schaets and his family lived in the house of Arent *de Noorman*, where they remained until the poorhouse was ready. Exactly when that was is unclear, but it seems to have been before November 1653, when Jacob Jansz van Noortstrant paid *f*7 boarding money to the poorhouse.[91] Perhaps the minister had moved into another house by the summer of 1660, when the deacons had work done 'on *dominee*'s house,' but the accounts are not clear about this.[92] While the Schaets family lived in the poorhouse, construction on the building continued for several years (see for the construction of the poorhouse, illustrations 62-68). Bricks and boards were delivered in February, March, May, and November 1654, and later in June and October 1656. In July 1654, a mason installed an oven and hearths, and plastered the hearths. Jurriaen *de glaesemaecker* was paid for puttying the windows in February 1655 and, in May, Jan Roelofsz fenced-off the lot with clapboards. In July 1655, the building was in such shape that Schaets could host Johannes de Deckere, who had come to replace Johannes Dijckman as commissary of Fort Orange.[93] In the following years, various workers who labored on the building boarded- in the poorhouse as well.[94] In January 1656, carpenters were paid for laying the attic; Gysbert van Loene was paid $f7$ in February 1658 for 'carting sods for mother and her bleaching field at the poorhouse'; and the carpenter Willem Bout received $f33-18$ in July 1660 for lathing and other woodwork on the side aisle of the poorhouse.[95] The addition of this extra space to the facility, in the year when the number of poor had increased significantly, indicates that more room was needed; the new space could have been used to expand the work area for processing *sewant*, or to board the *matres* who is frequently mentioned in the account books between June 1658 and April 1661 for stringing *sewant*.[96] In 1657, $f250$ to $f300$ was spent on developing a poorhouse farm; the location is not clear, but it could have been on the same lot, which was five by eleven rods.[97]

The extra space added to the poorhouse by the side aisle may also have been used for storage, or as a place where people obtained their alms. In that case, distribution may have been handled in a way similar to *de Nieuwe Kerk*, in Amsterdam, where the needy could gather at set times to receive alms in two distribution rooms. While one deacon distributed the alms, the deacon-bookkeeper kept his notes, and later copied them into the account book.[98] The records don't reveal how Beverwijck's poor obtained their alms. For example, nothing indicates whether they received notes to exchange for their goods (as did the poor in Delft); and, since there were no more than twenty-six poor people in any one year, it also is unlikely that they had to stand in line. It seems that people could obtain alms every weekday; payments to the providers of some products were even made on Sundays, probably after the church service. Perhaps the *matres* or 'mother' Schaets kept count, and handed the information over to the deacon-bookkeeper.

It seems that the care of Beverwijck's deacons went primarily to the homebound poor (*huiszitten armen*), who were given necessary items such as food, clothing, and money. If necessary, the deacons would provide board to those who could not pay for this themselves. Unlike the *hôpitaux généraux des pauvres* in Montreal, which would be founded around 1698, there are no indications that Beverwijck's poorhouse was occupied by indigents. Not until April and September 1698 would Robert Berris and Jan Kiednie pay rent for use of the deaconry's house; but it is unclear whether or not these individuals were indigent, or exactly which house was meant.[99]

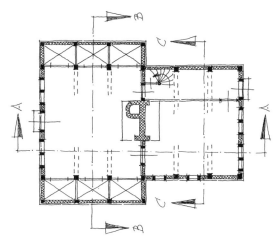

62. *Henk Zantkuijl, reconstruction poor house, ground plan. See also the illustrations 63-67. The basis for these reconstructions are the deacons' accounts for the materials and wages of workers for the building of this house between 1654 and 1657. The accounts themselves are barely a means to draw a reconstruction, but they help make the spatial representation concrete. To create this image one needs to be aware of the functions of this poor house. In the first place it was a storage and distribution possibility for goods, food, and money for* thuiszittende *poor (poor, living at home), which means that there has to be space. The accounts mention the attic and a winding staircase; they make the attic fit for storage. The house also could accommodate people who were unable to board with others. That the minister and his family lived in this house suggests that there were bedsteads. This was not only the most common, but also the most efficient way of taking care in poor houses in the old world. In wooden constructions the side aisle was a much used space for bedsteads. Chosen was in this case for a* driebeuk *(three isles)since that leaves much work space. It offers the possibility for placing large tables, perhaps for stringing sewant. These functions belong to the same group, so that one space is practical. The poor house was a work place where people were busy with, among others, stringing sewant. It could also serve as a meeting place for the deaconry (at least those who took care of poor relief) and the administration of the building. In principle a side aisle was not needed for this; a* eenbeukig *part (one isle) would be sufficient. The functions mentioned are worked into illustration 60. Chosen was (at random) for six beds in two side aisles in order to get a spatial compact part. The middle space could well be used for the types of work mentioned in the account books. Two cross windows and a lower/under and upper door take into account the amount of light (see also ill. 23).*

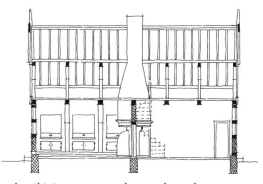

63. *Henk Zantkuijl, reconstruction poorhouse ca. 1656: cross section A-A. The accounts mention more hearths, so there should be more than one mantelpiece. Normally in this type of building hearths are built back-to-back, so that both can use one flue (illustrations 62-68). In the reconstruction the meeting room is, as is common, separated from a* voorhuys *where the entrance and stairway find their place. In the accounts mention is made of an oven. Since there is no indication that this is separate on the poor house lot, a combination with the two hearths is obvious. It saves material and no warmth is lost. Chosen is for the workspace which can be administered from the front space (illustrations 62 and 68).*

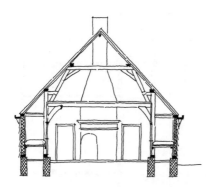

64. Henk Zantkuijl, reconstruction poor house ca. 1656, cross section B-B. As materials are mentioned wood, stone/brick, and iron work. It is possible to find the amount of bricks used from the amounts mentioned and from the price mentioned for an unspecified number of bricks. The total number of bricks is 19000 (at two cents per brick), and 3000 for the hearth. The number of bricks for the in the reconstruction drawn hearth is 3250, which agrees nicely with the 3000 mentioned. Also mentioned is 'bricking up' with half-bricks. This, together with 600 clapboards shows that the thought was to construct a wooden house with filling behind the
clapboards of a half-brick between the posts (stijlen) *as isolation (see picture Jan Maartense Schenck house).*

The foundation under the plate on which the posts are, is in the reconstruction 80 cm. high, because 60 cm below the mowing line is usually assumed for freezing line boundary. The foundation was drawn one and a half brick thick, which means that 240 bricks were needed for strekkende meter foundation. The reconstruction shows a length of 43 m' foundation, for which 10,320 bricks are required. The bricking up of a half-brick requires 2300 bricks for the rear gable, 1800 for the front gable, 1700 for the side walls of the driebeuk and 3300 for the side walls of the front part. Together, this brings it to 19.420 bricks, which number agrees with the 19.000 bricks bought. This could be coincidence and to avoid this as much as possible, the spatial-functional design of a poor house in this surrounding and in this period have been taken as the basis for the reconstruction. See also ill. 62 and 68.

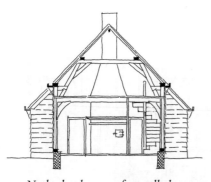

65. Henk Zantkuijl, reconstruction poor house ca. 1656, cros section C-C. As materials are mentioned wood, stone/brick, and iron work. Clapboards, (grenen delen, pine parts), richels, posts (posten) are mentioned for the fence and an attic floor. Also boards were used. Using the Dutch names, a board could be oak, which often is short wood and which can be used very well for roofvoorschotten (top-gevels) and inside panelling (binnenbetimmering). Clapboards were used for gables/walls. They are long parts, which fit over each other and in the
Netherlands were often called getrapte weeg or potdekselen. The accounts do not mention beams and stijlen (posts), which are required for the balkjukken or spanten.Neither is there any mention of kozijnen, windows and doors. These are standard, for example, cross, cloister, and bolcosijnen, which could be delivered ready-made (see ill. 23). Similar to the balkjukken these could have been given as a present, which in this type building is not uncommon. The gutters are large blokgoten, beams from which the gutters are cut. Carsten de boshacker was paid for cutting the gutters (see also ill. 62, 64, 66-68).

66. *Henk Zantkuijl, reconstruction poor house, ca. 1656, voorgevel (front wall). Iron hinges would go per pair, and in total 20 pairs were bought. Each shutter required one pair. The windows drawn for the reconstruction: four* kruiscosijnen *(cross windows), required 8 pairs of hinges; 2 cloister windows, 2 pairs; 2 outside doors (upper and top part), 4 pairs; 3 inside doors, 3 pairs; one closet door under the stairway, one pair; 2 attic shutters in the top gables, 2 pairs; together 2 pairs (see also ill. 62-68).*

67. *Henk Zantkuijl, reconstruction poor house ca. 1656, side wall. From the materials mentioned in the* DAB *one can detemine the construction and the appearance, but of course, it still is a reconstructon without any contemporary images or descriptions. Insecurities remain, such as the roof coverage. No mention is made of it in the accounts, which may mean that it was a gift. In the reconstruction is assumed that tiles were used, which by that time were frequently used (see Jeremias van Rensselaer's accounts, 1658-1674). According to the* DAB *tiles were also used for the roof of the* dominee's *house.*

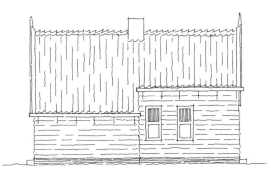

68. *Henk Zantkuijl, reconstruction poor house ca. 1660. Plan after the* uytlaet *(side aisle) has been built in that year. The construction of an* uitlaet *by a mason and his helper is mentioned, and glass in the* afdack *of the 'house of the poor.' This side aisle is drawn here on the north side of the meeting space.*

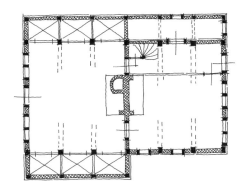

Strategy

Honest poor and efficiency

In the fatherland, only the 'honest poor' received help. Honest poor were those who had become victims, who had become poor through no fault of their own. Despite hard work, these modest people were not able to manage on their own. They often included widows, orphans, the elderly, and the ill, who deserved to be helped, as opposed to those who had caused their own poverty. People who did not want to work, but instead choose to wander around, begging others for food – they were the 'dishonest poor,' or the 'undeserving poor.' Distinguishing the honest poor from the dishonest was a problem everywhere – as much in New Netherland as in the Dutch Republic, or in the other colonies – where provisions were made to help them.[100] What exactly Beverwijck's deacons expected from the poor they assisted, in terms of behavior, is not known; but they certainly expected all needy persons to try to work. Costs of poor relief could be cut substantially if people were put to work, an objective completely in accord with the efficiency principle and humanist ideals of the time.[101]

The deacons assisted the indigent in various ways. They decided how much a person needed, and in what manner the help would be provided, on a case-by-case basis. Despite individual differences for each case, the general rule was that a minimal amount of funds should be used to ensure the highest level of poor relief. The indigent had to be well taken care of, but as cheaply and efficiently as possible. This rule, called the 'efficiency principle' by Herman Gras in his study on poor relief in the province of Drenthe, led to a policy aimed at keeping the number of poor at a minimal level, which in turn led to preventive poor relief. It worked well in a small community with a small number of poor people, and where inhabitants had easy access to a piece of land.[102] The preventive character of this policy worked well; it would be applied throughout most of the seventeenth century, as shown in a 1682 court session. At that time, the deacons noted the 'bad comportment of old Claes Janse *Timmerman*, who daily walks along the streets intoxicated, from which nothing else can be expected but that in a short time he will become a charge upon the deaconry...' The court decided that two guardians would maintain supervision over Claes, collect what he earned and maintain him on it, and keep an account thereof. This plan worked well for ten years; but from 1692 until his death in 1695, the deacons paid for Claes's maintenance, which amounted to more than 2,000 guilders.[103]

The preventive character of the deacons' strategy is illustrated by the fact that many of those helped in the twelve-year period, as we saw, only needed short-term assistance. In those cases, giving alms usually meant the provision of some money, clothing, or food. Robert Sandersz, for instance, who returned to Beverwijck in 1660 after living in New Amsterdam for about five years, was given *f*36, two shirts and three *ells* of linen in the spring of that year, which may have provided him with the help needed at the start of a fairly successful career.[104] Michiel Theunisz from Utrecht, who received *f*25 in 1658, also never appears on the list again.[105] For these two men, short-term assistance was sufficient to improve their situation. The same was true in many cases, and most likely these people relied on their 'social capital': They also received help from family, friends and neighbors, or perhaps from fellow artisans or workmen. People with the same religious or national background may also have helped out.

Help for the longer term

That a person is only mentioned one or two times in the accounts, however, does not necessarily mean that the help provided was small or short-term. Willem Albertsz, for example, appears in the accounts only twice, but the help given to him in 1656 and 1657 was longer lasting. He is first mentioned in December 1656, when the deacons paid ƒ136 for boarding money and 'the trouble that came along with it' to Ulderick Cleyn for seventeen weeks. The second time was in May 1657, when they paid ƒ150 to *Myster* Jacob to cure him, after which he does not appear on the list again.[106] That it is misleading merely to count the number of listings in the accounts is shown even more clearly by the two entries for Ytie and five for Sarte Hendricks, orphan children for whom the deacons paid 'regarding the contract.' These contracts concerned the care of the children for several years, and added up to reimbursement of a good sum of money (ƒ281-19 and ƒ401-5).[107]

More people needed help for a longer period of time, among them orphans, ill people, families with small children, or elderly persons who were no longer able to take care of themselves. One example of an elderly man receiving alms was Willem Jurriaensz, who had been a baker and who was described as being fully seventy years of age in 1650.[108] By 1653, he was considered poor, and, as we saw in the previous chapter, others in the community helped out by replacing the straw roof of his house. Until December 1658, Jurriaensz had been able to provide for himself, as Jan van Hoesem paid him ƒ125 for taking over his lot (see Appendix 8, II, no. 12). According to the contract, Jurriaensz could live on this lot, where he had a garden and kept some chickens, while he could have his meals with Jan van Hoesem if 'he would come in time and behave like a decent old man.' Not until January 1660 does Willem seem to have moved up a few houses to the north, on present-day Broadway. The deacons, by order of the entire consistory, then agreed with Huybert Jansz (who would himself receive some help from the deacons during that year and afterward) on house rent and laundry at 50 guilders a year for 'the Old Captain.' In December 1663, Jansz agreed with the deacons that he would receive ƒ10 every month; in addition, once a year he would receive a barrel of soap, one *schepel* of corn, and two and a half *ell* of linen. Willem's life at Huybert Jansz's does not seem to have been luxurious. During the last eight months of his life, he was given two pounds of butter every three weeks, and occasionally some firewood. Jan Michielsz, a poor tailor, was paid a little for repairing his clothes. The last expenses for Willem were paid in February 1664, when ƒ2-10 was awarded for some beer he drank, and ƒ71 for his funeral shortly thereafter. That he was about 79 years old before receiving the church's charity suggests that the deacons let Willem live as long as possible by his own means, which included the help of neighbors and most likely fellow Lutherans.[109]

Jan Michielsz, the tailor who sometimes repaired Willem's clothes, depended on poor relief for a longer time, as well. In April 1648, he and Jan Verbeeck were granted the trade of tailoring to the exclusion of others, on the condition that they not earn more than 36 *stivers* for a day's work, and their helpers 30 *stivers*.[110] Others would not be excluded from the trade for long, however. Half a year later, Evert Jansz was given permission to set himself up as a tailor in Rensselaerswijck, as well, and by 1660 he would be competing with about eight other tailors in the village.[111] (See Appendix 6).While the forty-six-year-old Verbeeck would be a magistrate and orphan master by November 1660, things did not worked out so well for Michielsz, who was fourteen years older.[112] In that year, Michielsz appears on the poor list for the first time. When his wife died four years later, the proceeds from her estate, valued at ƒ414, went to another tailor, Willem Jansz Schut, who promised to take lifelong care of Jan at ƒ200 per year. During that time, Michielsz had to do all the mending and sewing work for Schut's benefit. Michielsz had to forfeit his own property, and was allowed to keep only practical items such a tailor's scissors, and six books (two of which were Bibles) from his wife's estate. He died at the age of sixty-eight, which was then considered 'old.'[113]

Both Jurriaensz's and Michielsz's examples demonstrate that an individual had to be incapable of surviving on his own in order to receive assistance. A person had to work as long as he or she was able, and was required first to exhaust his own possessions. In later years, the deacons were able to obtain some property in this way. In 1670, the earnings of Andries de Vos were so meager that he was forever exempted from paying the slaughter's excise tax.[114] A few years later, in 1673 and 1674, he made an arrangement with the deacons whereby he was given ƒ25 a month for maintenance; in return, he gave the deacons the house in which he lived, a lot, a piece of land on the *Vossenkil*, and a freshening ('fat with calf') cow[115] (see Appendix 8, VI, no. 37). Hans Eenkluys, in 1683, likewise would turn over his plantation to the poor in Schenectady, in return for support 'in his old age and feebleness.'[116] The arrangements for these two men are very similar to those of elderly people in Holland, who bought a *prove* (a sort of annuity). While they were ensured of care in their old age, the deacons obtained more capital, so that they could guarantee future care of the poor. The number of poor who left anything to the deaconry was small, however; most needy individuals owned little at the time they were placed on the poor list, and elderly people would not leave real estate to the deaconry until the later years.

Families with small children certainly did not bring the deaconry any advantages. Of the ten people who received alms more than twenty times, seven had families with small children; and they accounted for the largest share of the charity budget. When children were old enough, they could sometimes help make ends meet (like Ulderick Cleyn's son, who helped string *sewant*); but when children were too young to contribute to the household, a family on the poor list simply meant more stomachs to fill and bodies to clothe.[117] Several families with small children depended on the deacons for many years. While living in their homes to the extent possible, they were provided with alms such as money, food, clothing, blankets, and sometimes firewood.

Examples of preventive poor relief

Although the following events would occur a few years after Beverwijck became Albany, a look at the family of Carsten *de Noorman* (also called Carsten *de Boshacker* (wood cutter), on occasion) may give an impression of the way the deacons tried to keep poverty from lasting any longer than necessary, even in the case of complications such as the death of one parent in a family with young children. The example also shows some of the costs of bringing up children. In 1663, *De Noorman* had a lot on the plain, behind the fort (see Appendix 8, X, no. 4). He had three children; but his work as woodcutter, for which he was frequently paid *f*2-10 *sewant* by Jeremias van Rensselaer, did not provide enough income to maintain his family.[118] Since 1658, Carsten and his wife had infrequently been given alms up to a value of at least *f*480, as well as additional meat, beaver, linen, cloth, butter, *dosijnties*, and bread, of which no prices were recorded. By September 1665, his daily wages had increased to *f*5 – but the real problems were just beginning. In October of that year, Carsten's wife gave birth to twins and died in childbirth. The deacons took care of her funeral, and immediately arranged for the babies by contracting with two women to serve as wet nurses for a year at *f*35 per month apiece, while an older brother was boarded at Jan Thomasz's. In January 1667, one of the twins was brought to Claes Theunisz (often called 'Uylenspiegel'), who had been a next-door neighbor.[119] The deacons made monthly payments in *sewant* for the twins to their two host families until June 1669, which amounted to *f*384 annually per family. On top of that, on at least thirty occasions, clothing valued at approximately *f*200 (*sewant*) was provided for the two children. Compared to the Dutch Republic, these expenses were high. Wet nurses in Delft received about 24 *stivers* (*f*1-4) a week, and boarding out a healthy child there cost 21.6 *stivers* on average, and a sick child 30 *stivers*; and in Friesland, according to Joke Spaans, boarding out a poor orphan child between birth and age sixteen cost an average of about *f*40 per year.[120]

Uylenspiegel and his wife had at least two small children when they took in one of the twins. Since 1657, they had occasionally received alms such as beer, stockings, peas, *sewant*, cabbages, meat, duffels, shirts and a blanket, as well. The neighbors may have gone together to fetch them since, a few times in 1660, Claes's and Carsten's wives were both given half a deer on the same day.[121] By taking care of one of the twin children, Claes's family was assured of a payment of *f*32 per month by the deaconry. In 1667, a few months after the child had been boarded with his family, Uylenspiegel bought Carsten's lot, even though he probably was living at the Esopus by then, where he had bought a house on a plantation from Goosen Gerritsz. In May 1664, he had contracted to work there for Gerritsz for three years, and was still there in 1679 when he 'released the children of Carsten *de Noorman*, who until this date have lived with him in the Esopus, to wit, a son named Theunis Carstensz, 18 years old, and a daughter named Lysbeth Carstens, now about 14 years old.' Theunis was supposed to stay at Claes's to help in that year's harvest for a normal salary 'like that is paid to others,' which he then had to pay to the consistory at the Esopus, in Kingston. Lysbeth was also supposed to stay during the harvest, for which Claes would give her 'what was reasonable.'[122] It is unknown where the other twin child went after it left Geurt Hendricksz's, whose wife had been one of the wet nurses. The child probably was the same as the 'Hank Carstensz' who, on November 29, 1685, was given his outfit (*uytset*) by Marten Gerritsz, who then 'hired him again for one year at 18 beavers and free laundry...'[123] That this contract is written in the deacons' accounts suggests that part of the wages was paid back to the deacons. It seems that the children were boarded out by the deaconry for payment, which, as they became older, they were supposed to repay by handing over their wages. If Hank indeed was Lysbeth's twin brother, that would mean that he still was indebted to the deaconry at age twenty. That he was required to pay back was not so strange; this also happened in deaconries of other localities in the Dutch Republic like Graft in North-Holland, Delft in South-Holland, or places in the province of Drenthe.[124] In the long run, this preventive policy seems to have worked well. Although old Carsten continued to receive support on various occasions, his children do not often appear on the poor list again. One Roelof Carstensz twice received ƒ20 in September 1685, and Tonis Carstensz and his wife 'in her illness' were given money, beer, and firewood (together valued at ƒ46) in October 1690. The efficiency principle seems to have worked for them. The deacons' strategy seems to have prevented the twins from becoming, like their father, long-term dependents on poor relief. At the same time, Uylenspiegel's additional income for maintaining one of the children may have enabled him to buy the house in the Esopus and enter into a contract with Goosen Gerritsz, which kept him off the poor list.

Not far from *De Noorman*'s and Uylenspiegel's lots lived another family struggling to survive, namely that of Marten Hendricksz *de bierkaecker*. The deacons also applied their preventive policy here, adjusted to this family's needs. Although Hendricksz and his wife Susanna do not appear on the poor list until November 1659, they had, as mentioned before, lived in poverty for some time. In August 1657, Hendricksz had a double hernia and was unable to earn his living while Susanna was burdened with three small children, for whom she could not buy food except with beavers. A week earlier, she had been unable to get beavers for sewant at ƒ12 apiece.[125] Despite their neediness, the family somehow must have been able to make a living, as they would not be given alms on a steady basis until March 1671. Some of the alms they received thereafter illustrate how important the deacons considered it for people to work as much as possible in order to provide their own food. First, Susanna received money (ƒ40 per month in 1671), clothing, and food, and once the deacons paid for repairs to Hendricksz's boat. In 1674, the main gifts consisted of clothing and wheat; but in the following year, the deacons covered the rent of a pigsty, payments for a few pigs in 1675-76, and the rent for a piece of farmland in 1676. Why the family disappears from the poor list thereafter is unclear, as their poverty seems to have continued. On June 21, 1677, Susanna presented a petition to the court, asserting that 'her husband Marten Heyndrix has died, leaving her with eight children, three of whom must be supported as to food and clothing, which she is unable to do, as her husband left her nothing but the children... She, being largely supported by the deacons, requests not to be held to pay the debts which she may owe anybody, nor be troubled about them.'[126] It is unknown what happened to Susanna and her family. She does not appear in the accounts again. Like many widows at that time, she may have married again and improved her economic situation.[127] Like Carsten *de Noorman*, Marten Hendricksz's case reveals that families with children could be very vulnerable. Not only illness or death, but also minor setbacks, could bring long-lasting poverty to a household.

Methods to prevent poverty

Access to land was essential for Beverwijck's inhabitants, as it meant that they could grow much of their basic supplies. That the deacons were very well aware of the value of land is revealed not only by Marten *de Bierkaker*'s example, above, but also by several other occasions on which the needy were given seeds. For instance, Frans Coningh, who had been given alms since 1660, was given peas for sowing in 1667.[128] Sometimes the deacons bought animals for the poor, as they did for *De Bierkaecker's* family; earlier, in 1659, Rut Jacobsz was given ƒ100 to buy a cow for the widow of Abraham *de timmerman*.[129] Possession of land and animals might at first seem to contradict the efficiency principle (i.e., the indigent had not exhausted all their possessions); but in the long run, it helped cut the costs of poor relief and, in some cases, may have eliminated the need for assistance.

Another way to minimize the expense of, or even prevent, poor relief was to provide loans. People in Beverwijck could borrow money from the deaconry at 10 percent interest – which was high compared to interest rates in Holland, where finance charges were no more than 5 percent in 1650, and later even lower.[130] Despite their high rate, such loans allowed people to buy land, start a business, or create a breathing space after an unproductive year. The tailor Jan Michielsz (see above), however, would be unable to repay more than the interest on the money he borrowed. In 1652, he borrowed ƒ300, for which he pledged his house and lot. In 1656, he paid ƒ80 interest, and ƒ30 in 1658. In 1659, Michielsz again paid ƒ30, while still owing the principle of ƒ300. In 1660, he appears on the poor list for the first time. For this individual, the loan does not seem to have helped; on the contrary, it drove him deeper into debt. While loans at a lower interest rate were not provided, occasionally a needy person could borrow money without paying any interest. In December 1661, for example, Mattheus Servaes, was given ƒ28 and Arent Isaacksz ƒ50, 'with the promise to pay it back.'[131] On one occasion in 1663, the deaconry even functioned as a pawn shop when they loaned *Broer* Cornelis's cousin Willem ƒ100 at 10 percent, for which he gave the deaconry two golden rings, two golden hooks, and some pearls as security; in 1664, Willem received ƒ60, 'not at interest, according to his capital, as much as he is able to afford.'[132]

Also in accord with the efficiency principle was the deacons' attention to medical care. Until 1664, the deacons paid surgeon Jacob de Hinsse for each case, which occasionally could add up to large amounts; in 1664, they made a new arrangement with Cornelis van Dijck, who was then hired to serve and cure the poor for an annual salary.[133] In November, Van Dijck was paid ƒ100 as half of his yearly fee for 'serving and curing the poor.'[134] In addition to treatment by a surgeon, the deacons also provided the sick and women in childbirth with good beer, a 'medicine' that was not unusual in the Dutch Republic, either; and elderly persons, in their last weeks of life, were sometimes provided with beer, wine, or distilled liquor.[135]

The deacons' strategy regarding the sick was also in line with the efficiency principle. The faster a sick person recovered, the sooner he could go back to work – and the less money would be needed to support him. That does not mean, however, that Christian charity did not play an important role. Since 1656, Ary de Vries's family had received up to *f*132 in alms, as well as additional alms for which no value is listed, such as meat, two beavers, bacon, 16 *ells* of linen, deerskins for pants, butter, shirts, peas, duffel, shoes, and children's shirts. The deacons were certainly aware that fifty-one year old Ary, who was often called *de malle Vries* (the 'crazy Frysian'), would not be able to pay anything back in the form of work or an estate. Nevertheless, they were willing to pay *f*300 for surgery on his leg in 1662-63, on top of almost *f*650 in alms that year, in addition to items for which the price was not recorded, such as corn, shirts, duffel, linen, two deer skins for pants, shoes for the whole family, and three months' house rent (at *f*35 per month) to Huybert Jansz.[136] In many other cases, however, such as the one concerning Poulus, who lived at Hendrick vanden Bergh's, medical help was the wisest and most logical way to prevent poverty. When Poulus had trouble with his foot in 1656, he was given some money in April; and in June, his foot was treated by the surgeon at the deacons' expense. After that, Poulus appears only once in the deacons' accounts again, when he was paid *f*16-5 for having worked six days at the poorhouse lot.[137]

Education was also thought to be important enough to support, and the deacons made arrangements with those who were willing to learn. The religious motive of Bible reading was important, while basic literacy was completely in accordance with the humanist ideal of bringing up children to economic independence, so that they would not be compelled to beg.[138]

By following the efficiency principle, the deacons exercised a form of preventive care for the poor. At first glance, it might appear that they spent more money than necessary, such as the annual retainer for the surgeon for accidents or illnesses that might not happen, or allowing people some animals and land. In the long run, however, the deacons avoided large expenses with this strategy, and probably prevented even deeper poverty in many cases.

Methods

People living on their own

The deacons followed two main methods to fight poverty: They boarded people out for a certain fee, and they supported those who lived on their own.[139] In addition to expenses for church business, building projects, or loans provided to various colonists, the deacons meticulously noted expenses they made on behalf of the poor. The following table shows these expenses for the poor, which were distilled from their total disbursements. Certainly, in the early years, a good deal of money was spent to build the poorhouse, construction of which had already started in 1652, and a poorhouse farm in 1657. Under the poorhouse, the account includes a few entries for 1660 and 1661 concerning the minister's house.[140] It is not certain which building is meant here.

Table 6.2: Expenditures on the poor

	Individuals	Poorhouse/farm	Totals
1654	ƒ 358-16	ƒ817	ƒ1,175-16
1655	389-04	312-05	701-09
1656	729-13	605-09	1,335-02
1657	1,553-15	751-17	2,305-12
1658	1,566-11	75-08	1,641-19
1659	942-16 + 83 ½ bev.*	190 + 1 ½ bev.	1,132-16 + 85 bev.
1660	1,394-05 +12 bev.	358-02	1,752-0 + 12 bev.**
1661	2,476-04	603-18	3,080-02
1662	4,199-19	157-09	4,357-08
1663	2,657-16	149-17	2,807-13
1664	2,944-15	137-00	3,081-15

* The value of the beaver varied in 1659. Although the established price was ƒ8, the *sewant* price varied due to the depreciation. While it had depreciated to ƒ10-12 per beaver in 1657, a year later it was ƒ15. In 1659, the deacons' accounts list ƒ13 once, and ƒ12-10 another time. For 1660, they received a beaver with a value of ƒ8.[141]
** Includes some work on *dominee*'s house. Although the poorhouse and minister's house are mentioned separately, both are included here, as it is not absolutely certain which building is meant. Entries concern a new window in the house in July 1660, making an *afdack* (lean-to), sand and clay carted to the house, bricks in the oven, removing the roof, and some masonry.[142]
Source: *DAB*

First, we will look at people living on their own. The quantity and nature of the assistance depended on their situation and the extent of their poverty. Some indigent persons owned a house, while for others the deacons occasionally paid rent. It seems that they came to the poorhouse to obtain their goods, which were meticulously administered by one of the deacons so that the consistory had good insight in their individual needs.

The alms often consisted of payments in money or in kind, or a combination of the two. In contrast with the village of Graft in North-Holland, where the deacons hardly ever gave money to the needy (but similar to such towns as Zwolle and Delft), the amounts of money given to Beverwijck's poor could run pretty high.[143] The *Malle Vries*, for example, was given alms eighty-one times between 1656 and 1664; on twenty-two of these occasions he received money valued at nearly ƒ350 overall. And Ysbrant *de steenebacker*, who lived in the *Greenebos* and received alms seventy-eight times between 1659 and 1664, was given money with a total value of more than ƒ590 on thirty-three occasions. In most cases, the deacons did not indicate how the money would be used; but sometimes they specified that it was meant for house rent, for example, or to buy provisions.

In *patria*, the types of donations given to the poor varied. In Delft, the needy were frequently given bread and *stivers*; and in Zwolle, they mainly received money and clothing, peat, and additional gifts such as rent, beer, school money, or education toward a job. In Beverwijck, people could obtain various kinds of alms in different quantities on any weekday. Food, clothing, and money were the main components of the distributions; but occasionally the deacons also gave such items as soap, kettles, or a foot stove. Firewood was expensive, but was not distributed often. The elderly Willem Jurriaensz and two families each received three sleigh-loads of firewood in 1660, and an ill person twice received twenty-five pieces. In April 1662, two families each received fifty pieces of firewood, and in 1664 the old Jan Michielsz and one family were given the same. Other needy may have gathered wood themselves, although the records don't mention that they had (as in the Dutch Republic) acquired the right to do this. The following table lists the alms most frequently distributed and the number of people in need of these items. Individuals listed in the accounts as just being provided with board, or the orphans Ytie and Sartge Hendricks, and Daniel, are not listed under food or clothing, unless specifically noted.

Table 6.3: Number of people receiving various kinds of relief

	Food	Clothing	Money	Board	Medical	Blanket
1652	–	1	–	–	–	–
1653	–	2	–	–	–	–
1654	4	2	3	–	1	–
1655	–	–	3*	–	1	–
1656	3	2	4	2	2	–
1657	4	4	4	1	1	2
1658	3	7	3	1	–	1
1659	5	12	5	2	1	1
1660	17	16	12	2	2	3
1661	10	10	13	2	1	8
1662	10	14	14	4	1	6
1663	8	18	11	1	2	7
1664	17	19	9	3	–	1

* Includes widows and orphans at Manhattan.
Source: *DAB*

Twenty-nine *schepels* of wheat (ƒ106) were distributed between 1652 and 1664, and bread was provided for a value of ƒ870. In addition, fifty-three *schepels* of corn were donated to the poor, and twenty-six *schepels* of peas (ƒ116). While the numbers through 1657 would seem to illustrate the minister's remark in June 1657, indicating that there were not yet many poor (e.g., the need for clothing started in July of that year, and the expenses for food were made after September), the numbers for the following years clearly reflect the bad trade and the Esopus crisis. But it is the sharp rise in the number of people in need of food in 1660 that immediately catches one's attention. Butter, which only three people needed prior to 1660, was in that year given to eleven individuals; in the same year, ten families were provided with bacon and meat, the need for which was especially great between January and April. The reason may have been the bad cattle situation in the year before, when thirty head had died.[144] In general, various kinds of meat were provided such as pork, bacon, and sometimes beef. Usually it came in a barrel, or simply as 'some meat' or 'some bacon.' Venison was also given on occasion. Although Van der Donck stated that a deer could easily be obtained for ƒ5 and often for less, the deacons paid more for it: four and a half *ells* of duffel in 1660, and ƒ20 (or a blanket of that value) in 1662 and 1663.[145] It was often given as 'a deer of which one half/quarter went to … , and the other half/quarter to …'[146]

Beer was not often distributed between 1654 and 1664: altogether, ƒ106-5 in 'small' and ƒ114-10 in 'good' beer. In most cases it went to ill people or women in childbirth. It seems that at least the small beer was available for most people, while it is not likely that people drank regular water.[147]

The need for blankets and clothing items such as shirts, shoes, stockings, coats, waistcoats, hats, or pants also increased after 1657 with the decline of the beaver trade. Pieces of clothing, or various kinds of cloth from which the needy could make clothes themselves, were frequently provided. These textiles were expensive, as they were imported, and (as noted above), merchants tried to make as much profit as possible. Usually the deacons bought a large quantity of cloth from various traders, such as kersey, *dosijnties*, linen, or baize, as well as yarn and buttons from which women sometimes made clothes. Most often, however, this was done by a local tailor, who on occasion provided the material, as well.[148] This tailor later presented his bill to the deacons for textiles and producing the various pieces of clothing. This way, in addition to the needy, the local tailors (as well as bakers, brewers, tailors, shoemakers, and farmers) benefited from the poorhouse, as well, by delivering their products to the deaconry for use by the poor.

In this context, even carpenters are sometimes mentioned as being paid for their work, as the deacons paid bills for coffins, if necessary. On occasion, they would finance a whole funeral, including the services of the undertaker, digging the grave, ringing the bells, transportation, and rent of the pall. Claes *de Wael*'s funeral, in 1660, cost ƒ52-8; and when Ary de Visser was buried in 1676, about ƒ145 was debited.[149] The average funeral noted in the account books of Beverwijk's deacons in the second half of the seventeenth century cost between ƒ100 and ƒ150. Except for the costs already mentioned, a funeral would also include expenses for the visitors, who usually were treated to beer, and sometimes to wine and brandy. Especially in later years, funeral-goers were presented with cookies, as well as pipes and tobacco; at Ary de Visser's funeral, ham, butter, bread, beer, and brandy were distributed among the mourners.[150]

For people who were ill or had other physical problems, the deacons paid the local surgeon for his help. Until 1664, they paid *meester* Jacob de Hinsse case by case.[151] In that year, they made a different arrangement with Cornelis van Dijck, who, after that year, they paid an annual allowance to serve and cure the poor.[152]

In addition to treatment by a surgeon, the deacons also valued the healing and pain-relieving powers of alcoholic beverages and good care. They not only paid two surgeons for tending to *Carwaet*, but also provided the patient with two *ankers* of small beer in 1665; Baefje Pieters, who received alms herself, boarded him from October 1664 until February 1665 for about *f*240.[153] Hans Eenkluys was taken care of in a similar way. From February 20, 1660 until April 1661, he received alms valued at about *f*229, which included a *f*200 surgeon's fee. During his illness, he was not capable of taking care of himself; and between March and June 1660, the deacons paid Jan *met de baert* and his wife Griet (alms recipients themselves since 1659) for thirteen weeks' house rent for Eenkluys, and for attending to his needs during that time, while between July 1660 and May 1661 they also paid *f*16 and *f*20 a month in boarding money for him to Thomas Coningh.[154] Gerrit Seegersz's wife received half a barrel of good beer when she was in childbirth; and the life of Claes Uylenspiegel's wife was eased somewhat on the same occasion, when she was provided with half a barrel of small beer, and half a barrel and an *anker* of good beer.[155] Beer, wine, or distilled liquor was sometimes also provided for people in the last weeks of their lives. The suffering of the 'old Captain,' Willem Jurriaensz, and in later years Teunis Tempel and Elias van Ravensteyn, may have been relieved in this way.[156]

Education was considered important by the deacons, and they paid for the schooling of some children. In 1658 and 1659, for instance, they twice paid about *f*18 to '*mester* Adriaen van Leyden for school going' for Daniel, a fifteen-year-old child who boarded with the needy Marietje Claes at the expense of the deaconry. They also bought a book for 15 guilders for this boy, who was a son of former New Amsterdam school master Adam Roelantsz.[157] Although it is not specifically mentioned, we also can assume that Ytie, an orphan child who was boarded with blacksmith and trader Jan Koster van Aecken, was taught how to read and write. Her signature on a 1667 document certainly suggests that she had a good grasp on the art of writing.[158] In that case, it would seem that her sister Sartge, who was boarded with Frans Barentsz Pastoor (who, like Jan Koster, served as magistrate and member of the consistory in Beverwijck), would have enjoyed a similar education. Education was mentioned in several wills or apprentice contracts, and perhaps not all needy children were provided with education; but it seems that, as in the fatherland, the deacons certainly made such arrangements for everyone who was willing.[159] The deacons, in later years, also made sure that education was included in the contracts of some apprentices, like the sons of the indigent Sacharias Sickels and Poulijn in 1680 and 1686, so that these boys had a better chance of becoming economically independent.[160]

Work

As it was also considered important for poor people to work, to the extent they were able, the deacons made sure this also happened in Beverwijck. There was no need to build workhouses, such as existed in Amsterdam and other localities in the fatherland, as there certainly was no lack of work in Beverwijck. Some of this work the deacons created themselves, such as various jobs at the poorhouse and the poor farm. Besides the regular carpenters, masons, and glaziers, several needy people found work for some time on the building or maintenance of these projects. Carwaet, Jan Roelofsz, Carsten *de Noorman*, and Lambert van Valckenburgh, for instance, were all poor – and were paid repeatedly by the deacons for work on the poorhouse.

The stringing of *sewant* was another task for which the deacons hired at least nine people – both men and women – between 1652 and 1664. *Sewant* beads, fabricated from rough conch shells, needed to be strung lengthwise on hemp strings of about a foot in length. It was exchanged by the fathom, a six-foot length of strung beads. With approximately five beads to the inch, the average fathom consisted of about 360 *sewant* beads.[161] It is not clear whether the beads were produced in Beverwijck, as well; the account books only mention that they were strung. In 1654, for example, Ulderick Cleyn was paid ƒ13-18 for stringing ƒ250 worth of *sewant*, plus yarn thereto, while in 1663 he received ƒ18 for stringing ƒ300 plus yarn. In that same year, he also earned ƒ5 for two days' stringing. This could mean either that Uldrick strung about ƒ46 worth of *sewant* in a day, or that he received the regular day-worker's fee for one day of *sewant* stringing.[162] During the years 1654, and 1662-64, Ulderick and his wife Baefje, sometimes assisted by their son, received more than ƒ240 in wages for this work.

A look at this couple's lives shows that they undertook many other jobs to make ends meet. Ulderick, who came from Staden in the German state of Hessen, had contracted to go to New Netherland in May 1640 as a soldier for the West India Company; and in June 1641, he married Baefje Pieters, from Amsterdam, at New Amsterdam.[163] In 1654, they had a tavern in Beverwijck that seems to have been run mostly by Baefje, but which does not seem to have brought much profit (see Appendix 8, VI, 32). A few court cases suggest that Ulderick was fined in the same year for selling alcoholic beverage to the Indians, which may have marked the beginning of their misery during the years that followed.[164] In December 1656, when they probably had three children, the family is mentioned for the first time in the deacons' account books, when they were paid ƒ136 in boarding money for Willem Alberts, and also ƒ7 in board for 'the little Frenchman.'[165] Their situation in 1657 may have been tight, as Baefje sued various people in September for payment of their tavern debts. She dunned Eldert Gerbertsz in such a way that a dispute arose. Gerbertsz accused Baefje of having been flogged and branded on the scaffold in Amsterdam, asserting that she had 'whored around' with the *malle boer* (crazy farmer) and *hageboom* ('hawthorn') named Jacob Clomp[166] (see also Appendix 8, VI, no. 21, 26, 29).

Despite Baefje's efforts to collect her money, the couple was not able to pay their own debts; and, in August 1659, they sold a house and lot for ƒ709 to Jan Hendricksz van Bael, and a lot for a garden to Jan Thomasz.[167] It is not clear where they lived after that, as the records do not reveal anything about their location after 1659. From the deacons' accounts, we know that they were able to board other people in 1664-65 and in 1669, so perhaps the Cleyns had two houses on the lot by the time they sold it. When Van Bael sold the property to Gerrit Lansing in 1667, the conveyance mentions that this lot was part of a patent for a greater lot dated October 25, 1653.[168] After March 1660, Baefje and her family, which by then had expanded with another girl, regularly received money, food, clothing and blankets; and in July 1666, when they seemed unable to pay for medical expenses themselves, the deacons satisfied a bill of ƒ120 to *meester* Cornelis for curing Uldrick. But that certainly did not mean that they could sit down and enjoy the deacons' alms. From October 1664 until February 1665, the family boarded the sick Carwaet for ƒ15-12 per week; and from 1662 to 1664, as mentioned above, Baefje and Ulderick earned extra money by stringing *sewant*. Baefje also was hired by Evert Nolden to do this work; but when it appeared that, contrary to the contract, he only wanted her to work half time, she took him to court.[169] In addition, Baefje was busy with cleaning and whitewashing the church in the spring of 1662 and 1663, for which she and Tryn van den Bergh were each paid about ƒ4-10 a day. And from January to March 1669, she earned ƒ20 a week for taking care of Claes vanden Bergh.[170] Meanwhile, Ulderick was employed as a cowherd by several burghers of the community. He received ƒ20 for every 'great beast' or for two heifers when he started herding cattle in 1667, which he would to do from the mid-March until mid-November.[171] Although these wages decreased during the following two years, the couple nevertheless would appear less frequently on the poor list, the last time being March 29, 1669. To survive economically remained hard, and in May 1671 Baefje was sentenced by the court to pay ten *schepels* of wheat for the rent of some land.[172] After Ulderick died in the following year, Baefje remarried – to Jan Roelofsz. Although Roelofsz had received alms on two occasions in the past, in 1655, together they would not depend on the deaconry again. Nevertheless, Roelofsz does not appear to have made Baefje's life happier, as she would appear in court, in 1679, asking for a separation. Roelofsz apparently drank heavily and abused her.[173]

Other poor people were put to work as well. Uylenspiegel, as we saw, boarded one of Carsten *de Noorman*'s children at the deacons' cost, and the needy Jan *met de baert*'s wife took care of Carwaet in his illness. Maritie Claes, poor herself, not only boarded Daniel, but also made clothes for him; and Jannitge *Brouwers* was paid for wetnursing Arent Isaacksz's child in January 1664 when his wife Stijntie Laurens, whom he had married in August of the year before, apparently was unable to do so.[174] It seems unlikely that Jannitge's husband Jacob Jansz van Noortstrant, also called Jacob *de Brouwer*, did good business with the brewery: When his house burned down in 1657, he had received ƒ50 in May from the deaconry. As it was for many others, 1662 was a difficult year for Jacob and Jannitge, and they were given money, corn, and butter on a few occasions. Jannitge earned some money that year by stringing *sewant* for the deaconry.[175] Jacob's work as a gager seems to have been sufficient to maintain his family, although in later years they would still receive money for some services (In 1672 he still held the posts of inspector and gager of the casks). In 1667, they received ƒ12 in rent for the *schout*'s maid; and occasionally Jannitge would be paid by the deacons for cleaning the church.[176]

Providing work for the needy certainly was in accordance with the efficiency principle, as the deacons received services in return for their charity. In the fatherland and in other Dutch colonies such as Colombo (later Ceylon/Sri Lanka), Batavia (later Jakarta, Indonesia), and the *Kaap de Goede Hoop* (later Cape Town, South-Africa), deaconries approached poverty in a similar way. Working also enabled people to keep their dignity: It allowed recipients to feel they had done something in return for the alms they were given – that they had earned what they had received.

Boarding

When people were unable to live on their own, Beverwijk's deacons responded in the same way as did deaconries in *patria*: They boarded them out. The decision to board poor people who could not run their own household was in the hands of the deacons, who based their decision on the personal circumstances of the indigent.[177] Between 1652 and 1664, eleven cases of boarding are recorded in the deacons' books, among whom were orphans, the elderly, and people with physical problems. The amount of care these boarders needed, and perhaps the fact that most host families themselves had only meager means, may have influenced the price for boarding.[178] Thomas Coningh, Marietje Claes, Baefje Pieters, and Jan *met de baert* (with the beard) were all provided with alms, just like their boarders. Completely in accordance with the efficiency principle, they were paid for their services to other indigent persons, who were dependent on the care of others for varying periods of time.

People who needed permanent care probably often relied on their family or neighbors. Social services, in the sense that we understand them today, did not exist in the seventeenth century; and parents, once they were no longer capable of earning their own income, most likely relied on their children. This was the case in Delft. But in other towns, like Zwolle, relations between family members were very business-like: Boarding with relatives – even children with parents, and parents with children – was paid for. In such localities, people relied for help more on their neighbors , fellow guild members, or people from the same religious background.[179] In New France the customary procedure was that, in a meeting of all members of the family held before a notary, it was decided who among the children would care for the parents, and how much the others would contribute. An official seal was then affixed to the agreement by the notary, who retained a copy.[180] In Beverwijck, where not everyone had relatives in the village, a combination procedure may have been followed. A 1682 statement in the court by Teunis Slingerlant reinforces the idea that children were expected to take care of their

parents. Teunis complained that 'it is impossible for him to support Albert An-
driesse Bradt alone and that he thinks that it would be fair if the other children
bore the burden with him,' which the court then ordered them to do.[181]

Supervision

Besides collecting alms and distributing them among the poor, it was another task
of the deacons to see to it that their gifts were used in an appropriate manner. They
were thus in a position to influence people's personal lives. In the Dutch city of
Delft, for example, alms recipients were not allowed to enter a tavern, and appropriate moral behavior was demanded. The consistory of Oudewater stipulated in
1622 that alms recipients should live honestly and be God-fearing, and that they
should subject themselves to the consistory's supervision. Drinking, gambling,
fighting or swearing could be a reason to exclude someone from charity for several weeks. Oudewater's consistory also demanded that all poor people completely
disclose their state of affairs. They had to show how much they owned and how
much income they had, while they also had to allow the deacons to conduct regular inspections of their dwellings.[182] Although not mentioned in our sources, some
of these rules were undoubtedly applied in Beverwijck, as well.

As in Oudewater, not all of Beverwijck's alms recipients were church members;
several were not even of the Reformed denomination. Thus, while exclusion from
the communion ritual would have no effect on such individuals, withholding
charity could. The deacons' accounts, however, do not indicate that this happened. Although the conduct of some alms recipients probably did not always
meet with the deacons' approval, it seems that these people were given support
anyway. Willem Jurriaensz, for example, had been banished from the colony three
times due to his bad behavior; in addition, he was a Lutheran who had even allowed other Lutherans to hold secret religious services in his house – despite the
ordinances against it.[183] Ary de Vries and his wife Jannitge Jans, who were steady
recipients of alms from December 1656 at least to 1674, likewise could not brag
about their impeccable past. As noted above, Ary had been imprisoned in 1651 for
refusing to fulfill his contract with Thomas Chambers; and Jannitge had sold
brandy to the Indians in 1655, for which she was publicly displayed at the whip-
ping post and banned from the community.[184] In later years, however, the deacons
would limit their efforts to help the poor. When, for example, they discovered in
1684 that Poulijn Jansz's children could not get enough to eat at their parents,' the
family was asked to board out the children 'to some good people who can support
them and bring them up decently.' But Poulijn and his wife Wijntie refused; and
although they kept receiving alms for two years, in April 1686 Wijntie would receive ƒ148 in food, money, and clothing on the condition that 'she departed to
never come at the expense of the deacons again.' Only for their son were the deacons willing to arrange a contract with Sijmon Schermerhoorn, who would teach
the boy the shoemaker's trade.[185]

The deacons did not restrict their almsgiving to Dutch people; but the group of
indigent who received assistance reflects the ethnic diversity of the population

One of the people receiving alms, for example, was a Croatian (*Carwaet*); and Marten *de Bierkaecker's* wife Susanna Jansen had been born in New England. Carsten *de Noorman* originally came from Norway, Michiel Rijckertsz came from Rouen (France), Claes *de Wael* was a Wallonian, Jacob Jansz *de brouwer* came from Noortstrant in Schleswig-Holstein, and Sacharias Sickels had been born in Vienna. The deacons provided all of these individuals with support when they were in need. In the 1650s and '60s, there is no mention of support for slaves; but in January 1671, Bassie *de neger*, who may have been a freed slave of Arent van Curler's widow Antonia Slaghboom, was provided with board at Poulijn's at ƒ100 *sewant* a month; perhaps Bassie was ill, as a month later the deacons would pay ƒ18-6 for his coffin and ƒ8-8 for brandy and beer at his funeral.[186] He may have made his confession of faith, and in that manner was entitled to alms from the church. Later, this may also have happened with some natives, as suggested by an entry for December 27, 1693, when Rooseboom was paid ƒ12 for burying a Christian Indian.[187]

That the deacons adjusted to the circumstances and the environment is illustrated by several entries unique to the Hudson Valley. On various occasions they supported or helped Catholic victims of wars with the Indians, ransomed prisoners, or people who had fled from the Indians. In November 1657, they gave commissary La Montagne a bunch of *sewant* valued at ƒ60 in order to ransom a child in the Esopus; and in 1659 they helped a boy from 'Kaskyel' by providing him with shoes, stockings, ƒ60 in surgeon's fees for Mr. Gysbert, and ƒ82-6 in boarding money. As mentioned above, Jan Koster and Frans Barentsz Pastoor took care of two sisters, perhaps partially at the deacons' expense, who most likely had become orphans as a result of the Peach War with the Indians in 1655. The girls had been taken prisoner by the Indians and were ransomed, their parents having died in the meantime. In a country of what some Dutch called 'heathens,' the deacons felt it was their responsibility to help fellow Christians. Occasionally, they even helped Catholics. In 1654, for example, they paid fares to transport one ransomed Frenchman, while in 1657 they gave another Frenchman a bolster. They paid 7 guilders for the 'little Frenchman's' board in 1656, and the account books record that two shirts and a pair of shoes were given to a Frenchman who had come walking out of Maquaes country in April 1660. In that year, they also gave duffels to another ransomed Frenchman.[188] The deacons may have helped these people with the idea that it was a public service – a duty of the public church. They may also have had in their minds the thought that, while Calvinists might rank higher than Lutherans or Catholics, in a strange and new country their fellow Christians – in this case, Catholics – were above the heathens. In a colonial environment, it was not so exceptional for help to extend beyond the Dutch Reformed population. As in other Dutch colonies such as *Kaap de Goede Hoop* and Batavia, poor relief was not limited to Reformed inhabitants.[189]

The deacons' strategy and methods of poor relief, as depicted in the previous pages, reveal that the deacons not only provided poor relief in the strict sense of the word, by giving some money, clothing, or food to those in need. Rather, their field was much broader, touching such areas as education, medical care, and financial loans. They gave the community a number of social services that may have gone beyond their primary duty. In many localities in the Republic – while they sometimes supported others as well – deaconries seem to have preferred to support their own poor and some passing transients. Beverwijck's deacons not only brought more security into lives of church members, but also to others; nor did they limit their care to Dutch people, but Germans, Scandinavians, French, English, as well as members of other religious sects such as the Lutherans and French Catholics were provided with relief – sometimes for long periods of time.[190] That people who perhaps did not live exactly according to church standards were helped as well, likewise suggests that the deacons performed their task in a broad-minded manner. It seems that every member of the community could count on relief in bad times.

The poor in the community

Appearance of the poor in the records

Finally, we should take a look at the place of the poor in Beverwijck's society Where did they live? What kind of work did they do? Where did they meet people? How were they looked at? In analyzing the deacons' accounts, one encounters several people who don't appear in any other source. The only reason that we know that they lived in Beverwijck was that they were poor, and that they were given relief by the church. Of some people, like Jobgen, Magyl, or *Bijl de timmerman* (Ax, the carpenter) and his wife, we know only the kind of alms they were given; but Bijl's nickname suggests the kind of work in which he was involved. But often, not even their last names or their places of residence can be traced. Of Gerrit Seegersz, for example, we know that in 1654 he twice asked for a building lot in Beverwijck, and that it was postponed both times. Any other references to a residence seem to be missing, although Seegersz was provided with help on several occasions between 1654 and 1657.[191] Ysbrant Eldersz asked for a building lot near the third kill in 1655, but he does not seem to have received it; in the deacons' accounts he is called Ysbrant in the *Grinnebos* (pine bush) in 1659 while in April 1660 he is also identified as Ysbrant *de steenebacker* (brick baker) in which function he also appeared on a few occasions in an unpublished account of Jeremias van Rensselaer.[192]

In the case of some needy individuals, we can discover more about where they resided. Several lived in Rensselaerswijck; Ary de Vries, for example, was at Bethlehem in January 1662, while Ysbrant Eldersz and Thomas Coningh were both in the *greenebos* in 1663. People were given alms who lived as far away as Catskil and the Esopus. Others lived in places scattered throughout Beverwijck. Michiel Rijckertsz, who was hired to work in Dirck Jansz Croon's gunstock making shop in 1651, lived on the north side of *Jonckerstraet*; Jacob *de Brouwer* lived just west of the poorhouse, south of the first kill; and Ulderick Cleyn had his residence on the north side of Beverwijck (see Appendix 8, VII, no. 15; XI, JJvN; VI, no 32). Th variation in their location suggests that, for most of the poor, the decline of the beaver trade and personal circumstances were the causes of their neediness. Although there generally does not seem to have been a pattern connecting people's poverty with their location, it could be that the situation at the center of the *bijeenwoninge*, to the north of the fort, influenced the economic development of the settlers who lived more to the south. Of the people who lived south of the fort, at least four needed the deacons' assistance. The needy Carsten *de Noorman*, Claes Uylenspiegel, Lambert van Valckenburgh and Marten Hendricksz all had lots south of the fort (see Appendix 8, X, no. 2, 4, 10).

Information on the location of the residence of Lambert van Valckenburgh and his family remains vague: He seems to have lived in Fort Orange, and when he requested a lot in Beverwijck in October 1654, his application was postponed; there is no indication that he ever received a patent. In 1657, he may still have lived in the fort; by that year, according to La Montagne, the old courthouse had 'sagged at the north end at such a way as to crush almost completely the house of Lambert van Valckenburgh.' When the new courthouse was built, the West India Company bought half of Van Valckenburgh's lot for *f*400 and Lambert may have moved to his lot behind the fort, perhaps to the place where he had a garden.[193] Although he did not receive assistance from the deaconry until 1660, the fact that he had been unable to furnish securities when he bought grain for *f*700 at an auction suggests that his financial situation was not strong. In September, Lambert was ordered to pay *f*130 for the difference in bids, *f*3 for commissions, and *f*35 for the auction fees, while he also had to settle his balance with the tavern keeper of *f*12 for brandy consumed and *f*18 for beer.[194] This was a lot of money for which he received nothing in return, and the situation may have contributed to Van Valckenburgh's problems during the hard times brought on by the declining trade. Although Lambert, together with Pieter Winnen, was appointed to the 'rattle watch,' which gave him a steady income (together, the two men earned *f*1,100 in *sewant* and *f*100 in beavers), this salary was not enough for him to provide for his wife Annetie Jacobs van Tonningen, and their two sons of eight and fourteen years old; thus, from January 1660 through 1664, the family was frequently given additional support by the deacons.[195]

Few other needy individuals can be found in the records on account of having bought something at an auction. Van Valckenburg had tried to buy the grain several years before he needed support. When we do find a needy person among buyers at an auction, the sale nearly always was an auction attended by colonists of relatively equal social status; furthermore, the event took place long before, or long after, these persons were given relief. Poor people certainly were not buyers at the public sale of large traders like Dirck Jansz Croon, or at the auction of Rutger Jacobsz's estate in 1664-65. The only alms recipient who bought something at that sale was Robert Sandersz, who by then was doing much better than when he came to Albany in 1660. The help he had been given that year may have provided Sandersz with a needed push on the way to his success.[196] Various needy people appear in the records because they were suing for debt, or they were themselves being sued for the same reason; some were arrested for having provided liquor to

the Indians, while others requested a building lot or sold their house, lot or garden – actions that added their names to the public record. Court records do not
show that they often appeared in taverns. Poor people had no more than the basic
means for survival, while the deacons probably made clear their expectation that
any contributions they made toward a better situation for these individuals
should not be used for things like alcoholic drink.

Poverty in the eyes of fellow villagers

The more successful inhabitants seem to have regarded the existence of poverty as
a natural thing that occurred in society. After all, it was a given that society consisted of wealthy and poor people, and that falling into poverty could happen to
anyone – including oneself and others in the immediate environment. A clear example is provided by Frans Pietersz Clauw, who was described by Jasper Danckaerts in 1680 as a man who lived on a creek near the river, 'whom they usually
called the Child of Luxury, because he had formerly been such a one, but who
now was not far from being the Child of Poverty, for he was situated poorly
enough.'[197] People tried to arm themselves against misfortune; those who could
afford it, for example, insured themselves against medical expenses. Widows and
widowers often remarried within a short time. To avoid situations like Van Valckenburgh's, they maintained personal networks with friends who could help out
in hard times. We saw that in the case of Rutger Jacobsz, who could count on his
brother-in-law Volckert Jansz Douw in difficult times.[198]

   As we noted earlier, even servants of the village's more prominent inhabitants,
like the surgeon's maid and Arent van Curler's servant Thunis Gerretsz, appeared
on the poor list. Apparently this was not unusual, as the deacons helped out servants of other settlers as well. They gave Pieter Meesz's maid a pair of shoes in
1661, and they helped the *schout*'s maid Anna in 1667 by giving her butter and
cash, while in March, they paid for her house rent.[199] These occasions, however,
create an impression of a hard and selfish society, and one wonders for how long,
to what extent, and why these people – who worked so close to those who were
better off – remained in need. Jaap Jacobs has stated that servants in New Netherland were better off than servants in the English colonies, for example: A servant
in the Dutch colony was in charge of his own capacity for work, and he could not
be sold off to another employer. In addition, a servant's complaints about bad
treatment by a master could lead to dissolution of a contract through the court.[200]
But then, the question immediately arises: Why did these servants not go to the
court to complain? Were they too young? Had their contracts expired? Did those
in Rensselaerswijck perhaps go to that colony's court, from which no minutes
survive? Or were the deacons very quick to provide alms to whomever they
thought was needy? Complaints by these servants in court could have revealed
more about their treatment and the attitudes of their masters; but I have found no
more than two occasions on which servants complained about bad treatment by
their masters.[201]

Voluntary poor relief

In his description of the community of Graft, in North-Holland, Dutch historian A.Th. van Deursen wrote: 'Care of the poor and needy is the purest touchstone of the quality and solidarity of a community, certainly when such attention for others is needed permanently.'[203] As we have seen, Beverwijck also knew the burden of poverty. Since the authorities took measures to organize the care of the needy, we can now ask the question: How much were the inhabitants of Beverwijck (and Rensselaerswijck) willing to sacrifice, when it came to the well-being and solidarity of their community?

Once again, the church accounts are an important source that may shed some light on this. Not only did the deacons list their expenses, but they also kept precise track of their income, which came from various sources. Loans with a 10 percent interest rate accounted for a large part of the deacons' income. At the end of 1661, for example, account bookkeeper Gerrit van Slichtenhorst handed over f10318-17 to his successor François Boon. Of that amount, however, f4735-10 was outstanding in eighteen financial bonds.[203]

Other money came from pall rentals. A pall was a piece of black cloth that was put on the coffin at a funeral. Because a pall was very expensive, most people did not own one, but instead rented it from the deacons for f2-10 in 1654 (f10 in 1664) for the large pall, while the children's pall cost half of the rent. Between 1654 and 1664, the large pall was rented at least sixty-six times, and the small one 102 times.

Working with *sewant* was another source of income. After 1650, it was mandated that only strung *sewant* be used as a means of payment; except for 1656, the deacons hired people every year to string the *sewant* beads. The deacons either sold or loaned this *sewant* to colonists, and gave it to the needy.[204] In 1654, for example, they sold loose *sewant* at f11½ and strung *sewant* at f10 a beaver; in 1656, it sold for f12 and f10-07, respectively; there also was inferior *sewant*, which cost f15-10 a beaver.[205]

An important sum of money was obtained in a voluntary way, however, and a closer look at the yield of those contributions reveals more about the willingness of village inhabitants to ameliorate the harsh fate of the poor. Collections during church services yielded most of these voluntary contributions. Every Sunday morning during church, and again during the afternoon service, worshippers dropped their donations into a black cloth bag attached at the end of a pole. One or two deacons would pass the bag in front of churchgoers by reaching with the pole through the rows of people; the little bell attached to the bottom of the bag might wake up those who had dozed off during the sermon. After the service, the proceeds from the collection would be counted and placed in the poor chest, and the amount later recorded in the account book. Most of the donations were made in *sewant*, but on various occasions pieces of silver money, quarters, and pieces of eight (worth 48 *stivers)* were put in the bag, as well. These collections were held not only during Sunday services, but also during services on holidays such as New Year's, Good Friday, Easter, Ascension day, Pentecost, and Christmas; the Easter, Pentecost and Christmas holidays, which lasted two days, usually brought higher

yields. Extra services were held on days of prayer, which often were on Wednesdays, and penitential sermons on Fridays. While almost all inhabitants attended
the Sunday morning services held between nine and ten o'clock, and most likely
the afternoon services on that day, fewer people probably attended these extra services; the collections on those days, as a rule, did not bring in as much money as
those on Sundays.[206] The only exception to this were those days of prayer that
were officially proclaimed as 'general prayer days' by the colonial government. In
general, the most money was collected when the Holy Communion ritual was
held, which happened four times a year. Perhaps moral pressure to give was
somewhat stronger at that time, as the gifts were then collected in *de kom*, an open
pewter bowl, so that everyone could see how much his or her neighbor gave. A remarkable occasion could enhance people's generosity as well. The peace of the
first Anglo-Dutch war was considered so important that on Wednesday, August
12, 1654 the congregation out of gratitude donated ƒ64 at the service held to com-
memorate the peace – an amount that surpassed the yield of all regular Sunday
collections in that year. And before 1700, people never donated so much as during
the fall of 1662, when smallpox raged in the village; more than ƒ400 was gathered
during the December services – more than usually collected in one whole month.
Poor boxes, which were spread throughout the village, yielded another ƒ61-10 in
that month; and during the fall, when the epidemic was at its peak, another ƒ46
was given as individual alms.[207]

In addition to putting money in the collection bag or in the bowl, individuals
frequently made extra donations in the form of alms. These contributions were
entered by the deacons as being specifically for alms, and the name of the donor
was usually mentioned. Seeger Cornelisz's widow bequeathed ƒ100 to the poor in
July 1662 out of generosity, and perhaps with the idea of reconciliation, after her
husband had died of stab wounds inflicted by Andries Herbertsz *constapel* in a
tavern brawl; and when Goosen Gerritsz's wife Gerretie Brant died in 1656, she
left ƒ25 to the poor. One interesting donation was made by Volckert Jansz Douw
who, despite the fact that he was Lutheran, donated ƒ62-5 to the poor in 1654
(when he was a magistrate), with the promise that he would give up to ƒ100.[208]
Most of these entries resemble the following: 'March 20, 1662 – received from
Teunis Spitsenbergh out of generosity for the poor ƒ24-2.' In 1662, nine people
donated alms with a total value of ƒ188, in addition to their contributions in
church. The smallpox epidemic in the fall caused many inhabitants, like Spitsenbergh, to give more than they normally did in regular church collections. In addition to their own feelings of generosity, some may have felt compelled to be more
liberal than at other times, because they believed that the sins of the inhabitants
had brought on God's wrath, which had released itself in the epidemic.

The public status of the Reformed deaconry as a poor relief institution also
meant that collections could be held at locations other than the church. There is
no mention of door-to-door collections in the records; but, as in the fatherland,
the deacons did create opportunities to donate to the poor at places other than the
church by installing poor boxes at strategic sites in the community. Among these
places were several taverns, the court, vice-director's La Montagne's house, or the

house of the farmer of the excise on beer, wine and distilled spirits. Usually, all boxes were emptied once a year at the same time; but just one box might also be opened, which could happen at any time in the year. The yield of these donations varied from box to box. In 1661, for example, they brought in a total of *f*134-10: In the box at Jan Bastiaensz's (an important trader) there was *f*33-7; the box at Pieter Adriaensz's tavern contained *f*16-2; the one at Jan Martensz's tavern *f*8-3 and some silver money; at the farmer of the excise Marcelis Jansz's *f*8 was collected; in the box at Anthony's (Anthony Jansz) tavern was *f*11-12, and at Jurriaen Theunisz's tavern was *f*24-4; the box at La Montagne's house contained *f*25-9, and the box at the house of Rensselaerswijck's court messenger Hendrick Jansz Reur yielded *f*7-13.[209] After the deacons had counted the money, they recorded the amounts in the account books. First mentioned in 1654, these poor boxes appear in the account books until 1690 (see Appendix 8, I, no. 9; II, no. 25; VIII, no. 7; III, no. 1 or 2, or II, 13; II, no. 11).

According to Calvinist doctrine, every person had the Christian duty to give alms. In order to find out what the community was able and willing to sacrifice for the poor, we can separate the income acquired on a voluntary basis from the revenue collected from of promissory notes, pall rentals, and other non-voluntary sources. Distilling the charity gifts out of the deacons' income in this way results in the following overview:

Table 6.4: Voluntary contributions toward poor relief in *sewant* guilders

Year	Church collection	Poor boxes*	Alms**	Total
1654	1,802-8	56-1	160-05	2,018-14
1655	1,846-2	–	15-18	1,862
1656	2,018-14	154-14	100-02	2,273-12
1657	2,130-9	110-06	59	2,299-15
1658	2,820-3	330-10	160?	3,310-13
1659	2,536-14	148-05	3 bev?	2,684-19
1660	2,586-4	103-05	82	2,771-9
1661	2,724-2	135	65-11	2,924-13
1662	2,761-13	76-16	188	3,026-9
1663	2,876-5	107-08	139-18	3,113-11
1664	2,707-13	97-17	46-4+1½ b.	2,804-10

* In 1655, no yield from the poor boxes was noted, as they were not emptied until January 1656. The yield was then *f*102-05, which money in reality was given in 1655. Other boxes were emptied in February (*f*12-11) and July (*f*39-18) 1656. In 1657, the boxes were opened again in January and brought *f*57-02. In May, one brought *f*6-10 and July, *f*28-14. In 1658, they brought *f*151-10 in January, and in August one contained *f*13-09, while in December all boxes were emptied again, bringing *f*165-11. The fact that all boxes were opened twice that year explains the large yield for that year. Thereafter, most boxes were emptied at the end of the year, although on occasion one or two were opened before that time. In 1659, for example, one box was opened in July (*f*19-16), another in August (*f*12-12), and another in September (*f*30), while the boxes were emptied in December, bringing *f*85-12 and *f*4-05.

** Income has been included in this count only if it is specifically indicated as concerning alms.

How should we interpret these voluntary contributions toward poor relief in this New World society? The first thing that catches the eye is that, with the exception of 1655, 1659, and 1664, the total yield seems to have grown, which undoubtedly can be attributed partially to the growth of the population. The year 1658 shows a remarkable high yield of both collections and poor boxes. In alms, about ƒ160 may have come in. The reason these items are marked with a question mark in the table is that Willem Teller, who kept the books that year, did not specify a number of entries for incoming money.[210] Likewise, Adriaen Gerritsz did not include any explanatory information when he noted that two beaver pelts were received out of Hermen *de brouwer*'s hands in July 1659, and one-and-a-half beavers came in from *Jonge* Jan in November. Nor did Jan Koster van Aecken specify this income in 1664.[211] This high yield of contributions in 1658 suggests that the inhabitants had high expectations of the trade that year. Just as remarkable, however, is the decline for the year thereafter; to some extent, the numbers seem to reflect Jeremias van Rensselaer's notes.[212] Despite the tight times described by Van Rensselaer, the community was able to keep the numbers growing, except for 1664. In 1663, total voluntary contributions were only 200 guilders less than in 1658. Once again, the disappointments and insecurities brought on by the failing trade, as well as the English takeover on September 24, seem to be reflected in the collections of 1664.

But what do these numbers reveal about the general community? What was it willing to sacrifice? In June 1657, the minister wrote that he had 300, and sometimes 400, people in church.[213] If we estimate that an average of 350 people attended church services in that year, who together donated ƒ2,130-9 in the collection bag, one could estimate that the average churchgoer gave about 121.74 *stivers* (or ƒ6) per year to the poor, or 2½ *stivers* a week.[214] For each family of four, that would mean a donation of 10 *stivers* (or half a guilder) per week – a fifth of a day laborer's daily wages. Considering that there may have been 600 people in church, as Schaets indicated in the same letter, and that voluntary contributions totaled about ƒ2,300 (34,500 *stivers sewant*) in the same year, one is led to the conclusion that each person donated about 57.5 *stivers* per year, or a little more than one *stiver* per week. For a family of four, that would have come to 4.4 *stivers* per week. If Schaets failed to include the seventy to eighty Lutheran families in his estimate of 600 churchgoers, the average would have been lower, about 0.66 *stiver* per person per week; for a family of four, that would have meant a little more than 2½ *stivers* a week. In 1660, the approximately 1,050 inhabitants made nearly ƒ2,772 (41,580 *stivers sewant*) in voluntary donations, which means that each person gave 0.76 *stiver*, and a family of four 3.04 *stivers*, per week.[215] In June of that year, Jeremias van Rensselaer remarked that 'people are very thrifty and must work hard if they want to eat.'[216] It is hard to imagine that, in a time when even the most successful traders were unable to pay their debts, people would have been able to make great contributions toward poor relief. Before giving to charity, one had to make sure one's own family could survive. Altogether, we can conclude that, in 1657, a family of four gave somewhere between 2.6 and 4.4 *stivers* to the poor per week, or an average of 3.5 *stivers*, while in 1660 this amount was 3.4 *stivers*. With the dramatic changes in the economic situation between 1657 and 1660, it is probable that people gave less in those years than before 1657. That the total yield of voluntary contributions was higher in 1660 than in 1657 supports the idea that the overall population increased in those years.[217]

Of course, not every person spent the same amount and, undoubtedly, those who prospered in the trade gave more than those who barely could make ends meet. But if these numbers have any value, they favor the sense of community in the village: As a community, Beverwijck's inhabitants did provide for their poor fellow villagers. That help may not have been excessive, and was no more than what was needed, but it did help people to survive. On some occasions, it helped people out in an emergency situation, or gave them the necessary push toward a better future; and, in several cases, it prevented poverty in later years.

Was this so remarkable? Compared with the Dutch Republic, the village inhabitants were no exception. In the village of Graft, for example, Van Deursen has estimated that a family put about 4 *stivers* aside for the poor each week – over the year, a family donated about *f*11-4, nearly the amount earned by a good artisan in two weeks.[218] Inhabitants of Delft gave about 3½ *stivers* on average.[219] In the fatherland, this was not unusual; giving was considered a Christian duty, and the fact that money was sometimes collected in an open bowl probably put some pressure on people to give as much as they could – or at least no less than the person sitting next to him or her in church, as everyone could see what they put in the bowl.[220] But compared to other colonies, such as New England, this was remarkable. In Boston, the church deacons were already worrying more about church property and maintenance of the ministry in the 1640s; as a result, they left the problem of the poor (which continued to plague the community), to be a charge on the town.[221] Beverwijk was different from New France, as well. Within the social and economic framework of the seigneurial system of land tenure in the French colony, the settlers, once established (after a three year period of working for a previously established settler), were expected to provide for themselves, and to care for members of their own family who needed help. The only recourse the deserving poor had in these years was the charity of more fortunate members of their society. They were required to obtain a mendicant's license attesting to their need from their local cure or judge.[222]

If we compare the list of income from voluntary sources with the list of expenditures on the poor, we find that in seven of the eleven years the income exceeded the expenses.

Like in the fatherland, for example in Delft, the inhabitants themselves in a direct way financed poor relief in their village.[223] In the bad years the deacons did not hesitate to rely on the extra reserve they had from other sources and remainders of past years in order to give the indigent what they needed. In 1661, on the one hand, when the income from voluntary sources was a little less than the expenditures on the needy, they even gave wine and sugar to the poor at the end of the year. In 1662, with the economic effects of bad trade and the sadness of the smallpox epidemic, they were willing to spend more than ƒ1,300 more than what was brought in from voluntary sources. The list of contributions shows that, in Beverwijck, people voluntarily donated money to the poor; perhaps they gave a little more in better times, and somewhat less in harder times, but at least they were willing to try to the best of their ability, with as much common sense as possible so that nothing would be wasted, to bear the fate of their needy fellow villagers.

Conclusion

Life in Beverwijck was expensive. Salaries at first sight may have seemed high, but the price of food, and especially clothing and other imported goods, quickly made people realize that those salaries were hardly sufficient to survive. The easy access to land somewhat made up for the high prices of goods, as every inhabitant could thereby grow some crops and keep a few animals. Indian threats, illness and disease, floods and failed harvests, severe winters, the depreciation of *sewant* in the 1650s, and especially the decline of the fur trade after 1657, caused life at the upper Hudson to become unstable for many. Only a little bad luck was needed to drive a family or individual into misery.

Orphans, the elderly, or those who were ill or had physical problems became easy victims of the misfortunes mentioned above, especially after the trade declined and poverty increased. In the late 1650s, many people became greatly indebted – and from that point onward, the road to poverty was short. The number of people who asked the deacons for assistance increased dramatically between 1652 and 1664.

Together, church and government worked to organize support for the poor. Through several ordinances, the government granted the needy some free services and education, provided monetary contributions out of the revenue from fines, instituted the office of orphan masters and, in 1652, granted to the deacons a lot for a poorhouse. The government supported the deacons in implementing poor relief in a practical way. The strategy and methods the deacons applied in Beverwijck were very similar to ways the poor were taken care of in the Dutch countryside. They supported the poor as efficiently as possible, so that nothing would be wasted, and future poverty would be prevented as much as possible. This could happen by providing help on a short- or long-term basis. Aid recipients were supposed to have used up all of their own means, and exhausted their credit and 'social capital,' which consisted of the help of friends, family, neighbors, fellow workmen, or fellow countrymen. If possible, they were expected to work as much as they could, sometimes on jobs provided by the deaconry itself. The needy were helped not only by direct gifts in the form of money or in-kind, but also through medical care and education. If they were unable to live on their own, they were boarded out.

Fellow villagers seem to have considered poverty to be a common issue in society. It could easily enter anyone's household; a woman, for example, could lose her husband at any time, and with him all security, as her main source of income disappeared along with her spouse. The ways people dealt with poverty are hard to understand for a person in the twenty-first century; servants of some fairly well-established inhabitants were poor, and asked the deaconry for assistance – while, at the same time, their employers were donating money for the poor. Beverwijck's poor-care system was supported mainly with funds acquired through voluntary contributions.

This way of taking care of the needy was in accord with practices familiar to most first-generation deacons and elders of Beverwijck's church, almost all of whom had been born in the Dutch Republic. In addition, *dominee* Gideon Schaets, who remained minister until 1694, was trained in the Dutch Republic and had worked there as a schoolteacher before coming to the New World. As permanent president of the consistory, he undoubtedly had much influence over decisions made by the consistory. Together these settlers brought along Dutch traditions such as the public service of a poor relief system with strong humanist features. Certainly during the 1650s and '60s, the similarities with the fatherland regarding the deacons' bookkeeping and poor relief are very clear. Therefore, we can say that the first form of poor relief in Beverwijck, New Netherland, and probably in America was performed in a typical Dutch tradition, which lasted throughout the century.

Initially, the deaconry supported all needy inhabitants – transients such as Frenchmen who had fled or been ransomed from the Indians, an Irishman who had been begging, a woman from Manhattan who asked for alms, and others from whom they did not want to withold aid – including those who they knew were not true supporters of the Reformed religion. Encouraged by the Peace of Münster in 1648 and the Grand Assembly in 1651, which had confirmed the Reformed identity of the Dutch Republic, deaconries in the Republic considered themselves public institutions – which weakened the Calvinist element. In a newly established society like Beverwijck, the West India Company strengthened the church's position even more. Not until the 1690s would the church appear to limit its support somewhat to its own members. By that time, the Lutherans would have their own poor fund while, at the same time, government would become somewhat more involved in helping the needy. In 1691, the mayor contributed ƒ64 for the care of *dicke* Jan Cornelisz and, in 1700, ƒ1,585 for the care of Ryseck Swart, widow of *schout* Gerrit Swart. Greater involvement by the town in supporting the poor did not seem strange, as this was happening in the Dutch Republic, as well.[224] At the end of the seventeenth-century, however, this change may also indicate that the English poor relief system (where the local government provided poor relief through a system of taxes) was being applied more extensively in Albany.

In the 1650s and '60s, the Dutch village was still in the process of being constructed – and all available manpower was needed. The deacons had to consider the case of every needy person according to his or her individual situation, so that nothing would be wasted. As a substantial reserve of money was not yet available at all times for the needy, the deacons had no choice but to work pragmatically.

The healthy economics of the efficiency principle, which was applied so extensively in the fatherland, could easily be adapted to the situation in the colony. It certainly proved to be useful in the New World.

Conclusion

On September 8, 1664, former Fort Orange commissary Johannes de Deckere sailed up the Hudson to Beverwijck with powder and negroes; two days before leaving New Amsterdam, he had signed the articles of surrender of New Netherland to Richard Nicolls, commander of an English force of 300 soldiers. In Beverwijck, he found that people had lived in unrest and fear for the last few months. Indians had killed livestock and even burned down Abraham Staets's farm at Claverack; these events occurred, the rumors went, at the instigation and order of the English, who were about to conquer New Netherland.[1] De Deckere had sailed with the intent to arouse the inhabitants to resist the English. On September 10, Colonel Cartwright sailed upriver, as well, with part of the English militia. He bore a letter to the magistrates and inhabitants of 'ffort Aurania, ordering a peaceful surrender,' as they now were 'under the protection and obedience of His Majesty of Great Britaine.' On September 24, La Montagne surrendered Fort Orange and the settlement to Cartwright. After almost twelve and a half years, the inhabitants once again had to take an oath of allegiance – now to the English king, Charles II. De Deckere was exiled from New England on the September 30.[2]

The English, in taking New Netherland, gained control of an area within an important waterway system. With the Hudson River, Delaware Bay, and the Connecticut River as the territory's respective north, south, and east boundaries, New Netherland had access to a large hinterland. Furthermore, sixteen settlements had inferior courts of justice similar to Beverwijck's, and were well organized according to Dutch customs (especially the laws of Holland). At the upper Hudson, the conquerers found a village with urban features, as the area around Fort Orange was inhabited by well over a thousand people. Over the course of some thirty-three years, the settlement had grown into a community with its own identity, and was well enough organized so that no great changes would be made until after a second takeover by the English, in November 1674, which followed upon the Dutch re-conquest of August 9, 1673.

The shaping of a community at the upper Hudson had already begun with the arrival of the first colonists in 1630. A group of people of various backgrounds then started a process in which they had to adjust to each other, and to a new land with its long-time inhabitants. While he found no experienced people with whom to share his ideas (New Netherland being the Dutch Republic's first successful settlement colony), Kiliaen van Rensselaer tried to organize, from Amsterdam, a well-regulated Christian society some 5,000 kilometers away. To make sure that Dutch Reformed religion would be the inhabitants' moral guide, he ordered the colonists to come together on Sundays and usual holidays, when one man would read aloud some chapters from the scriptures. In 1642, Van Rensselaer sent the first minister to give religious and moral guidance to the colonists, whose number by then had grown to about a hundred.[3] At court meetings, the magistrates were to invoke the name of the Lord. But the silver-plated rapier with baldric, a hat with a plume for his colony's *schout*, and silver-banded black hats for the *schepenen* of Rensselaerswijck's first court, the books, and the various officials whom Van Rensselaer sent over – none of these could prevent differences of interest between the patroon and his colonists from soon becoming evident.[4] At such a distance, the local government often worked as an institution for local self-government. While Van Rensselaer's concept was that his colonists would seek to further his advantage, the cohesive and identical interests of the farmers – especially those concerning preemption and prices of grain, payment of the tenth, and the fur trade – remained opposed to his ideas.[5] The colonists banded together and, on or before 1640, even called themselves a *'gemeynte'* (commonalty).[6] Until his death, Van Rensselaer tried to keep control over his colony and, thereafter, this was continued by Van Twiller and Van Wely. Their decision to locate the patroonship's center around Fort Orange, however, would be fatal to the settlement. Stuyvesant's establishment of Beverwijck marked the beginning of a process of loosening ties: Not only was the West India Company's decision intended as a measure to ensure the trade at Fort Orange, but it was also an answer to requests from several colonists that they be liberated from the patroon and live under the company. Now, people received patents for property for themselves, without the obligation to pay rent, and from which they could trade with the natives. They paid one guilder excise tax per beaver to the company, instead of sharing the profit with the patroon. People could now invest earned money in more real estate within Beverwijck and in land outside of the village, as well.

Between 1652 and 1664, under the leadership of the new court (but following the trend set by Van Slichtenhorst), Beverwijck's inhabitants developed the village by separating their private properties from public spaces by fences, and by occupying them with houses, barns, sheds, stables, gardens, bleaching fields, and small Indian houses for trading purposes. They often subdivided the lots they received in 1652 and 1653 and, during the following years, they built houses on these smaller lots, which they then sold. The resulting density created an urban atmosphere. Public spaces were developed for communal use: Cows could graze in common pastures, roads were laid out, bridges built, while a poorhouse and a blockhouse church were established in the center. In a short time, the minimal requirements of a Dutch settlement were met for safety, religion, education, poor relief, and communal service. Until palisades were built toward the end of 1659 to protect against enemies, the village was open: It was more or less part of the landscape, and was easily accessed by whoever wished to enter. The palisades marked a distinct, visible change: Fear of enemies had replaced trust in native neighbors, while at the same time emphasizing the village's increasingly European and urban features.

While it took about twenty years to attract between 200 and 250 settlers to the area, once they could settle freely in the space around the fort and trade independently from their homes, more than 800 people came to Beverwijck over the next eight years. Being of various backgrounds, the settlers together formed a mixed population, in which all men (except slaves) could buy burgher rights and were expected to serve in the local burgher guard – just like towns in the fatherland. Streamlined by the laws and regulations of the West India Company government, and by the church's religious and moral values requiring them to lead honorable Christian lives, a certain community culture developed. But, while certainly comparable with places in the Dutch Republic, which always was the frame of reference, the European culture in Beverwijck simultaneously interacted almost daily with the native culture. Indeed, cultural borders were easily changed and remained fluid. Meetings and negotiations with natives took place with gift exchanges. Beavers and shell beads, sometimes wheat and boards, replaced money, even among the colonists themselves. In addition, the company introduced slavery – and people in the community could own slaves. Life at the frontier was similar to, but at the same time different from, life in *patria*.

Trade determined much of Beverwijck's appearance. Trade had been the reason for the construction of Fort Orange in 1624, and it determined the community's rythmn and arrangement of time. All inhabitants, including women, were involved in trading European items for the valuable pelts, of whatever proportion this exchange might be. Pelts were needed to pay debts or to buy common household goods. They were also used to buy *sewant*, which was also used as payment. Trade was so important for individuals that differences of opinion divided the community over how beavers should be obtained from the Indians. The Van Rensselaers, among the village's major traders, collected beavers from their tenants and customers, and then sent them to Holland. A typical family firm handling trans-Atlantic trade, they worked and organized their business in Beverwijck, New Amsterdam, and Amsterdam, arranging cargoes, hiring ships and crews, arranging to sell the beavers to Russia, and creating trade networks. They informed the outside world of their success by making it visible through their clothing, a well-decorated house, possession of real estate at well-situated locations and, unlike in *patria*, the possession of slaves. Much like people in *patria*, they expanded their trade network (which included relatives and other successful burghers) by marriage and by maintaining friendship relationships, frequently sealing those ties with a drink or dinner.

Their trade was only a small part of the West India Company's trade, and just a fraction of the entire Dutch merchants' fleet which, around 1650, consisted of about 2,000 seaworthy ships, and which was larger than the Spanish, French, and English fleets combined.[7] Some successful burghers had come over as agents for trading firms and, by traveling back and forth, they greatly strengthened the community's Dutch character. When they went back to *patria* for good, they took their earnings with them and invested there. They maintained trade with people who decided to remain in New Netherland, and who invested their earnings in the New World. Some of these men had come over early as farmhands or artisans and, in time, had familiarized themselves well with the land and its inhabitants. They also got to know other colonists, with some of whom they cooperated and established local networks. Well aware of the importance of leading an honorable and

Christian life, most (but not all) successful burghers were members of the Dutch Reformed church, and sometimes served in its consistory. Their early arrival contributed to their profits in the trade, and helped them quickly to climb the social ladder, sometimes as high as the position of magistrate in the court. Once they had 'arrived,' they created their own oligarchies, similar to the way this was done in Holland. For some men, marriage not only increased the work force, but also extended networks and increased trading possibilities, thus contributing to their success. Trade always required taking some risks, and some inhabitants ended up with great problems by not trading wisely, especially after the beaver trade declined. Most successful burghers invested their earnings in land and in real estate at good locations in the village; by 1664, a small group of men owned many of the best-located lots in the *bijeenwoninge*, on which they often started businesses.

As in *patria*, there was little specialization, and people were usually involved in multiple jobs. Sometimes one man owned a business, while hired servants helped him with the work; or, the owner himself worked elsewhere, while others did the work in his business. Usually work was done at home, a family affair in which a wife was usually involved, as well. Not only was this the case in *patria*, but in this new society (where life was more expensive), a wife's cooperation also was necessary; also, women frequently worked on their own. During the trading season, everyone's business increased, as the many visitors completely changed the village's consumption patterns. Location also determined much of the success of a business: A brewery close to the river, and north of the fort, lasted considerably longer than one located elsewhere, while taverns near the church and poorhouse did better business than others. As in *patria*, several trades were concentrated in one area: Smiths and gunstock makers, whose products and services were in great demand by the Indians, were located at the southwest corner of present-day State Street and Broadway, originally the junction of two Indian trails to the fort. Although such business concentrations generally encouraged cooperation, the bakers (of whom several lived just north of the first kill) were never permitted to establish guilds, despite the fact that such guilds florished in *patria* at that time. Seventeenth-century work patterns differed from today's, and illustrate the great flexibility and change. A workplace was frequently used by various people, as one worker left for whatever reason and another came.

Nevertheless, early arrival in the colony, and leading an honorable and Christian life, were no guarantees of success. Life in a seventeenth-century town was vulnerable, and anything could happen. Nature disasters, illness, death in the family, and – in Beverwijck, especially – the decline of the fur trade, were unforeseeable events that could damage everyone's life. With building the *bijeenwoning* north of Fort Orange, people whose businesses were located south of the fort seem to have suffered remarkable damage; and, while there was no residential segregation, several poor people lived south of the fort. To take care of the needy the government created various laws and cooperated with the church, whose deaconry, as in *patria*, developed a system in which people voluntarily contributed to the care of the needy in their society. Trying as much as possible to prevent poverty the deacons not only provided for alms, but paid attention to a much broader field, providing medical care and education, as well. Typical for the area, they took care of ransom payments and the care of prisoners released from the Indians, even if they were French and Catholic. In this new community, everyone's labor was needed; and by paying poor people to work, the deaconry allowed these settlers to keep their honor and the respect of others. The building of a poorhouse in the village center at an early date (most likely the first in America) may have symbolized their intent to establish a society after the Dutch model, under which everyone would have the possibility of and obligation to live his or her life in an honorable way.

Carsten *de Noorman* and Goosen Gerritsz were two men, out of more than a million people of various nationalities, who at one time or another left the harbors of the Dutch Republic for the West Indies, Africa, or Asia; they were two of the 7,000 or 8,000 people who, by 1664, had settled in New Netherland.[8] They had come over on the same ship in 1637, and subsequently spent their lives in the same community in the Dutch Republic's first settlement colony. Some twenty years after their arrival, they found themselves at opposite ends of Beverwijck's social ladder. It is unknown how old they were when they had left their homelands, what they said to their relatives or friends, or what they expected of this new world. We don't know whether they had similar opportunities while aboard ship, but in a new world they both helped in their own way to build a community that was similar to towns in the Dutch Republic. After living spread-out along the river, by 1652 the settlers had developed a certain level of adjustment to each other, their surroundings, the native people, and the religious precepts of the Dutch Reformed church; and they started living closer together. Over the next twelve years, the village grew into an urban-like community with its own identity, along with a willingness to defend itself against competition, including that from other Dutch settlements. From an early date, Goosen was able to accumulate capital from the fur trade and take full advantage of his new surroundings, while Carsten does not seem to have been able to do so. They ended-up on opposite sides of the new social structure. But, whether one was at the top or the bottom, Beverwijck was a community in which both of them could live, marry, become old, and offer their children a better future than they once had.

On the 17th of November, 1684 'Old Carsten' received a pair of shoes from the deaconry. Goosen Gerritsz was already deceased for nine years, and had left his ten children a good inheritance. Three of his sons had acquired hereditary seats in the new gallery of the church in 1682. Three of Carsten's five children were involved with the consistory as well: Roelof twice received ƒ20 from the deacons in 1685, and Hank, at the age of twenty, worked to pay back to the deaconry for the help provided in his childhood. In 1690 Thonis Carstensz received ƒ46 in money, beer and firewood when his wife was ill. But unlike their father, who received alms for many years, none of these three sons appeared on the deacons' poor list again.[9]

Abbreviations

CCS	Court Case Brant Aertsz van Slichtenhorst against Jan van Rensselaer (in Rijksarchief Arnhem).
CJVR	A.J.F. van Laer (trans. and ed.), *Correspondence of Jeremias van Rensselaer 1652-1674* (Albany, 1932).
CMARS	A.J.F. van Laer, (trans. and ed.), *Minutes of the Court of Albany, Rensselaerswijck and Schenectady 1686-1685* (3 vols. Albany, 1926-32).
CMVR	A.J.F. van Laer (trans. and ed.), *Correspondence of Maria van Rensselaer 1669-1689* (Albany, 1935).
Council Minutes, 1552-1654	C.T. Gehring (trans. and ed.), *Council Minutes, 1652-1654* (Baltimore, 1983).
Council Minutes 1655-1656	C.T. Gehring (trans. and ed.), *Council Minutes, 1655-1656,* (Syracuse, 1995).
DAB	Deacons' account books after 1674.
DAB	J.Venema (trans. and ed.), *Deacons' Accounts 1652-1674, First Dutch Reformed Church of Beverwyck/Albany, New York* (Maine/ Michigan, 1998).
Delaware Papers	C.T. Gehring (trans. and ed.), *Delaware Papers (Dutch Period). A Collection of documents pertaining to the regulation of Affairs on the South River of New Netherland, 1648-1664* (Baltimore, 1981).
DHM	*De Halve Maen. Journal of the Holland Society of New York*
DRCHNY	E.B. O' Callaghan, E. B. (trans. and ed.), *Documents Relative to the Colonial History of the State of New York.* 15 vols. (Albany 1853-1883).
DRNN	A.J.F. van Laer (trans. and ed.), *Documents Relating to New Netherland, 1624-1626, in the Henry E. Huntington Library* (San Marino, CA, 1924).
DSSYB	*Dutch Settlers Society of Albany Year Book.*
ERA	J. Pearson and A.J.F. van Laer (trans. and ed.), *Early Records of the City and County of Albany, and Colony of Rensselaerswijck (1656-1657).* 4 volumes, vols. 2-4 revised by A. J. F. van Laer (Albany, 1869).
ER	E.T. Corwin (trans. and ed.), *Ecclesiastical Records. State of New York.* 7 vols. (Albany, 1901-1916).
FOCM	C.T. Gehring (trans. and ed.), *Fort Orange Court Minutes, 1652-1660* (Syracuse, 1990).
FOR	C.T. Gehring, (trans. and ed.) *Fort Orange Records, 1656-1678* (Syracuse, 2000).
GAA	Gemeentearchief Amsterdam.

HNN	E.B. O'Callaghan, *The History of New Netherland; or, New York under the Dutch*. 2 vols. (New York, 1845-48).
LP	C.T. Gehring (trans. and ed.), *Land Papers* (Baltimore, 1980).
LO	E.B. O'Callaghan (trans. and ed.), *Laws and Ordinances of New Netherland, 1638-1674* (Albany, 1868).
LWA	C.T. Gehring (trans. and ed.), *Laws and Writs of Appeal 1647-1663* (Syracuse 1991).
MCR	A.J.F. van Laer (trans. and ed.), *Minutes of the Court of Rensselaerswijck, 1648-1652* (Albany, 1922).
NA	Notarieel Archief.
NNN	Jameson, J.F. *Narratives of New Netherland, 1609-1664* (New York, 1909).
NNP	New Netherland Project.
NYCM	New York Colonial Manuscripts (at NYSA).
NYG&BR	New York Genealogical and Biographical Record.
NYG&B	New York Genealogical and Biographical Society.
NYH	*New York History. Quarterly Journal of the New York Historical Association.*
NYHS	New York Historical Society.
NYSA	New York State Archives.
NYSL	New York State Library.
Patents	The New York Colonial Patents Books, Albany 1664-1690 (in NYSA).
RNA	B. Fernow (trans. and ed.), *The Records of New Amsterdam from 1653 to 1674 anno Domini* (New York 1897, 2nd printing Baltimore 1976).
VRBM	A.J.F. van Laer (trans. and ed.), *Van Rensselaer Bowier Manuscripts, being the letters of Kiliaen van Rensselaer, 1630-1643, and other documents relating to the colony of Rensselaerswijck* (Albany, 1908).
VRMP	Van Rensselaer Manor Papers.
WMQ	*William and Mary Quarterly. A Magazine of early American History and Culture.*
WNT	*Woordenboek der Nederlandse Taal.*

Notes

Introduction

1. *VRBM*, 334, 355-89, 810, 811; *ERA* 1, pp. 47, 200, 240, 342, 361, 362, 363, 386, 423; *ERA* 2, p. 131; *ERA* 3, pp. 193, 269, 306; *MCR*, 40, 43, 134, 137, 157, 205; Patents vol. 2, pt. 2, no. 13; *Patents* 3, pt. 1, no. 65; *GAA*, NA 1307/49 (February 15, 1657); *GAA*, NA 1355/42, 43 (April 1, 1657); *FOCM*, 118, 192, 236, 361; *DAB*, 92, 108, 118, 122, 141-43, 154, 155-206; *ERA* 4, p. 500; *CJVR*, 227.
2. Willem Frijhoff and Marijke Spies, *1650: Bevochten eendracht* (The Hague: Sdu Uitgevers, 1999), 155. For Scandinavian immigration in Amsterdam, see S. Hart, 'Een bijdrage tot de geschiedenis van de houthandel,' 76, 85; 'Geschrift en getal. Onderzoek naar de samenstelling van de bevolking van Amsterdam in de 17e en 18e eeuw, op grond van gegevens over migratie, huwelijk, beroep en alfabetisme,' 127, 170; and 'Zeelieden te Amsterdam in de zeventiende eeuw. een historisch-demografisch onderzoek,' 199, 201, 202 (S. Hart, *Geschrift en getal. Een keuze uit de demografisch-, economisch- en sociaal-historische studiën op grond van Amsterdamse en Zaanse archivalia, 1600-1800* [Dordrecht: Hollandse Studiën 9, 1976]).
3. De Vries and Van der Woude, *Nederland 1500-1815: De eerste ronde van moderne economische groei* (Amsterdam: Uitgeverij Balans, 1995), 98-99; and Henk den Hijer, *Geschiedenis van de WIC* (Zutphen: Walburg Pers, 1994), 31, 77.
4. Rink, *Holland on the Hudson: An Economic and Social History of Dutch New York* (Ithaca. N.Y.: Cornell University Press, 1986), 166-67.
5. *VRBM*, 79, 652.
6. Ibid., 292, 433-37, 459-63, 549, 557; GAA, NA 1659/102 (July 23, 1641).
7. *MCR*, 14; *VRBM*, 838; CCS, 129ᵛ-130, 178ᵛ-180, 112ᵛ-114ᵛ; see also Samuel Nissenson, *The Patroon's Domain* (New York: Columbia University Press, 1937), 355-62; Van Slichtenhorst later claimed that there were about a hundred houses built before Stuyvesant's action. CCS, 67.
8. *FOCM*, xxi-xxv; CCS, 46ᵛ-47.
9. For after 1664, see Robert C. Ritchie, *The Duke's Province: A Study of New York Politics and Society* (Chapel Hill: University of North Carolina Press, 1977).
10. Frijhoff, *Wegen van Evert Willemsz: Een Hollands weeskind op zoek naar zichzelf, 1607-1647* (Nijmegen: SUN, 1995), 625.
11. CCS, 109; *ER* 1, p. 383.
12. Frijhoff, 'Inleiding: Historische Antropologie,' in Peter te Boekhorst, et al., *Cultuur en Maatschappij in Nederland, 1500-1850* (Meppel/Amsterdam: Boom/Open Universiteit, 1992), 25-31, 34; Peter Purke, *Popular Culture in Early Modern Europe* (London/New York: Harper and Row, 1978), xi.
13. G. Rooijakkers, *Rituele repertoires. Volkscultuur in oostelijk Noord-Brabant, 1559-1853* (Nijmegen: SUN, 1994), 78; see also Frijhoff, 'Volkskunde en cultuurwetenschap: De ups en downs van een dialoog' (Mededelingen van de Afdeling Letterkunde, Nieuwe Reeks 60 [3, 1997]: 95); and Frijhoff and Spies, *1650*, 52-55.
14. For Appendix 1, I have counted the men listed in the *VRBM*; through 1644, these names appeared in passenger lists for some fifteen voyages between 1630 and 1644. Thereafter the lists are incomplete, and are based on first appearances of an individual in Rensselaerswijck. For sixty-four men, backgrounds were not given. *VRBM*, 805-45.
15. See also Rink, *Holland on the Hudson*, 144-55; according to David Cohen, the proportion of

foreigners in New Netherland was perhaps as much as 50 percent of the population ('How Dutch were the Dutch of New Netherland?' in *New York History* 62 [1981]: 43-60, 51).

16. Isaac Jogues, 'Novum Belgium and an Account of René Coupil, 1644' (Dean R. Snow, et al. [eds.], *In Mohawk Country: Early Narratives About a Native People* [Syracuse, N.Y.: Syracuse University Press, 1996], 32).

17. *VRBM*, 454.

18. Ibid., 235; in the 1630s, eighty ships annually brought sugar from Brazil to the Dutch Republic (Van Goor, *De Nederlandse koloniën: Geschiedenis van de Nederlandse expansie 1600-1975* [The Hague: Sdu uitgevers, 1997]), 61; see also De Vries and Van der Woude, *Nederland 1500-1815*, 466-67.

19. Raben, 'Batavia en Colombo: The Ethnic and Spatial Order of Two Colonial Cities, 1600-1800' (Ph.D. dissertation; Leiden: Rijks Universiteit, 1996), 33.

20. NYSA, NYCM 13: 138 (August 7, 1653).

21. Dunn, *The Mohicans and Their Land 1609-1730* (Fleischmanns, N.Y.: Purple Mountain Press, 1994), 279-87.

22. For an extensive historiography of New Netherland, I refer to Joyce Goodfriend, 'Writing/Righting Dutch Colonial History' (*NYH* 80: 5-28), in which she also mentions the studies about Beverwijck. I refer to Jaap Jacob's introduction to his *Een zegenrijk gewest*, as well; unlike Goodfriend, he also includes Dutch-language studies (Jaap Jacobs, *Een zegenrijk gewest: Nieuw Nederland in de zeventiende eeuw* [Amsterdam: Prometheus-Bert Bakker, 1999], 14-22).

23. Donna Merwick, *Possessing Albany, 1630-1710: The Dutch and English Experiences* (Cambridge: Cambridge University Press, 1990), pp. 4-5, 286-93.

24. Sung Bok Kim, *Landlord and Tenant in Colonial New York, Manorial Society, 1664-1775* (Chapel Hill: University of North Carolina Press, 1978), 4-5; Martha Dickinson Shattuck, 'A Civil Society: Court and Community in Beverwijck, New Netherland, 1652-1664' (Ph.D. dissertation; Boston: Boston University, 1993), 11.

25. Jan Folkerts, 'De pachters van Rensselaerswijck, 1630-1664: Nederlandse boeren in de wildernis van Noord-Amerika. Een onderzoek naar landbouw en pacht in Nieuw-Nederland' (doctoraal thesis; Groningen: Rijksuniversiteit, 1984).

26. Thomas J. Condon, *New York Beginnings: The Commercial Origins of New Netherland* (New York and London: New York University Press, 1968), viii, 119-20; Dennis Sullivan, *The Punishment of Crime in Colonial New York: The Dutch Experience in Albany During the Seventeenth Century* (New York: Peter Lang, 1997); Shattuck, 'A Civil Society.'

27. Janny Venema, '"For the Benefit of the Poor": Poor Relief in Albany/Beverwijck, 1652-1700' (master's thesis; Albany: State University of New York at Albany, 1990). See also Venema, *Kinderen van weelde en armoede. Armoede en liefdadigheid in Beverwijck/Albany* (Hilversum: Verloren, 1993); Venema, 'Poverty and Charity in Seventeenth-Century Beverwijck/Albany, 1652-1700' (*NYH* 80 [4; October 1999]: 369-90).

28. Richter, *The Ordeal of the Longhouse: The Peoples of the Iroquois League in the Era of European Colonization* (Chapel Hill and London: University of North Carolina Press, 1992); José António Brandão studied the Iroquois in New France in *Your Fyre shall burn no more: Iroquois Policy Toward New France and its Native Allies to 1701* (Lincoln, Nebr., and London: University of Nebraska Press, 1997).

29. Richter, *The Ordeal of the Longhouse*, 106; Matthew Dennis, *Cultivating a Landscape of Peace. Iroquois-European Encounters in Seventeenth-Century America* (Ithaca, N.Y., and London: Cornell University Press, 1993), 143.

30. Paul R. Huey, 'Aspects of Continuity and Change in Colonial Dutch Material Culture at Fort Orange, 1624-1664' (Ph.D. dissertation; Philadelphia: University of Pennsylvania, 1988); see also Huey, 'The Archaeology of Fort Orange and Beverwijck' (N.A. McClure Zeller, ed., *A Beautiful and Fruitful Place: Selected Rensselaerswijck Seminar Papers* [Albany, N.Y.: New Netherland, 1991], 327-49); James Bradley, *The Evolution of the Onondaga Iroquois: Accommodating Change, 1500-1655* (Syracuse, N.Y.: Syracuse University Press, 1987).

31. Jaap Jacobs, *Een zegenrijk gewest.*

32. See Willem Frijhoff, 'Reinventing an Old Fatherland. The Management of Dutch Identity in

Early Modern America' (R. Bendix and H. Roodenburg [eds.], *Managing Ethnicity: Perspectives from Folklore Studies, History and Anthropology* [Amsterdam: Het Spinhuis, 2000], 137).

33. Frijhoff, *Wegen van Evert Willemsz*; see also Frijhoff, 'Identity Achievement, Education, and Social Legitimation in Early Modern Dutch Society: The Case of Evert Willemsz' (paper presented at 'Two Faces of the Early Modern World: The Netherlands and Japan in the 17th and 18th Centuries,' International Symposium in Europe, Netherlands, 1999 [Kyoto, Japan: International Research Center for Japanese Studies, 2001]), 157-58.

34. Jonathan Pearson, (transl. and ed.), *Early Records of the City and County of Albany, and Colony of Rensselaerswijck (1656-1657)* (4 vols.; vols. 2-4 revised by A.J.F. van Laer [Albany, N.Y.: University of the State of New York, 1869]).

35. J. Munsell, *Collections on the History of Albany from Its Discovery to the Present Time with Notices of Its Public Institutions, and Biographical Sketches of Citizens Deceased* (Albany, N.Y.: J. Munsell, 1965), vol. 4, pp. 184-224.

36. Ibid., 184.

37. A.J.F. van Laer, 'The Dutch Grants Along the South Side of State Street: A Contribution Toward the Early Topography of the City of Albany' (*DSSYB* 2 [1926-27]: 11-23).

38. Ibid.; Van Laer, revision of Pearson, *Early Record*, vols. 2-4; Van Laer, *Van Rensselaer Bowier Manuscripts, Being the Letters of Kiliaen van Rensselaer, 1630-1643, and Other Documents Relating to the Colony of Rensselaerswijck* (Albany, N.Y.: University of the State of New York, 1908); Van Laer, *Minutes of the Court of Fort Orange and Beverwijck, 1652-1660* (2 vols.) (Albany, N.Y.: University of the State of New York, 1920-23); Van Laer, *Minutes of the Court of Rensselaerswijck, 1648-1652* (Albany, N.Y.: University of the State of New York, 1922).

39. Van Laer, 'The Dutch Grants,' 12.

40. J. Munsell, *Men and Things in Albany Two Centuries Ago* (Albany, N.Y.: J. Munsell, 1876), 6. The manuscript map is in volume 1 of the 'Land Papers,' as described in *Calendar of Land Papers, 1643-1803* (Albany, N.Y., 1864), 6. The sketch originally was undated, but was placed between two items dated October 20, 1674 and March 1, 1675. The Colonial Albany Project dates the map as 1676, as an after-the-fact notation on the parchment is 'French Map 1676.'

41. John Miller, 'A Description of the Province and City of New York, with Plans of the City and Several Forts as They Existed in the Year 1695' (*Historic Chronicles of New Amsterdam, Colonial New York and Early Long Island* [Port Washington, N.Y.: Friedman]), 9-10, 13, 95.

42. Römer plan, 1698. From the *Crown Collection of Photographs of American Maps*, series 3, plates 237-38. The original is in the National Archives, London.

43. Van Laer, 'The Dutch Grants,' 11-12.

44. Ibid., 12; Simeon de Witt plan, 1794 (J. Munsell [trans. and ed.], *The Annals of Albany*, vol. 3 [Albany, N.Y.: J. Munsell, 1853-59]). The second edition is in the Albany Institute of History and Art.

45. According to Paul Huey, a comparison with a detailed map of Fort Albany, 1710, illustrates the extreme accuracy of Römer's cartography. Römer drew his map with a scale of 175 feet to the inch (Huey, 'Aspects of Continuity,' 122-23).

46. A.J.F. van Laer (transl. and ed.), *Minutes of the Court of Albany, Rensselaerswijck and Schenectady 1686-1685* (3 vols.) [Albany, N.Y.: University of the State of New York, 1926-32]; *Correspondence of Jeremias van Rensselaer 1651-1674* (Albany, N.Y.: University of the State of New York, 1932); *Correspondence of Maria van Rensselaer 1669-1689* (Albany, N.Y., 1935). See also Charles T. Gehring (trans. and ed.), *Fort Orange Court Minutes, 1652-1660* (Syracuse, N.Y.: Syracuse University Press, 1990); *Fort Orange Records, 1656-1678* (Syracuse, N.Y.: Syracuse University Press, 2000); *Council Minutes, 1652-1654* (Baltimore, Md.: Genealogical, 1983); *Council Minutes, 1655-1656* (Syracuse, N.Y.: Syracuse University Press, 1995); *Correspondence 1647-1653* (Syracuse, N.Y.: Syracuse University Press, 2000); *Laws and Writs of Appeal 1647-1663* (Syracuse, N.Y.: Syracuse University Press, 1991); *Land Papers* (Baltimore, Md.:, 1980).

47. Janny Venema (trans. and ed.), *Deacons' Accounts 1652-1674: First Dutch Reformed Church of Beverwyck/Albany, New York* (Maine: Picton Press; Michigan: Wm Eerdman's, 1998); Court Case of Brant Aertsz van Slichtenhorst against Johan van Rensselaer, 1656-1663 (Rijksarchief Gelderland at Arnhem, Oud Rechterlijk Archief kwartier van Veluwe inventaris nummer 438,

dossier 7); see also Venema, 'The Court Case of Brant Aertsz van Slichtenhorst against Jan van Rensselaer,' in *DHM* 74 (1; spring 2001): 3-8; transcriptions of documents at the Gemeente Archief Amsterdam, gathered at the New Netherland Project, Albany, N.Y.

48. A.Th. van Deursen and S. Groenveld, *Cultuurgeschiedenis van de Republiek in de zeventiende eeuw* ('s-Gravenhage, 1990).

49. For example, the patent to Hendrick Marcelisz for a lot which 'abuts to south on Claes Gerritsz, to north on Jacob Tysz, to west on land belonging to Andries de Vos, east on the highway' (Patents, vol. 2, pt, 2, no. 35). When Marcelisz sold half of this lot to Robert Sandersz, it was described as 'leggende ten suyden van Claes Gerritsz ten noorden Jacob Tysz ten westen 't landt toebehorende Ands. de Vos en ten oosten van 's-Heeren wegh [lying to the south of Claes Gerritsz, to the north Jacob Tysz to the west the land belonging to Andries de Vos and to the east of the public highway]' (*ERA* 1, p. 171 [doc. 406]).

50. For example, a 1652 patent to Annetie Bogardus describes her lot as having 'to the north a lot lying in common, to west Marten Herpertsz, to south the wagonway, to east a common pathway.' The original text of Annetje Bogardus's grant to David Pietersz Schuyler, however, puts the street to the north of this lot: 'belendende ten westen den transportant, ten suyden en ten oosten Sander Leendersz, ten noorden de straet; t voorsz erff is lanck ten westen den transportant ses roeden ende drie voeten, voor aen de straet breedt een roede ses voeten acht duym, ten oosten *van* Sander Leendersz ses roeden drie voeten, ten westen breedt een roedt seven voeten en acht duym,' which Pearson translated as: 'adjoining to the west, the grantor, to the south and to the east, Sander Leendersz, to the north, the street; the aforesaid lot is six rods and three feet long to the west on the grantor, in front on the street one rod six feet and eight inches broad, to the east *on* Sander Leendersz six rods three feet to the west one rod seven feet and eight inches broad. [...]' The word 'van' means 'of,' which would place Leendersz west of Bogardus. (Leendersz acquired Herpertsz's lot.) (*ERA* 1, p. 289 [doc. 271]); see also *ERA* 1, p. 277 (doc. 243), where Leendersz's lot is described as 'adjoining to the east Jan Thomasz, to west Anneke Bogardus [belendende ten oosten Jan Thomasz ten westen Annetien Bogardus]'; and *ERA* 1, p. 392. For another example, see *ERA* 1, pp. 382, 383 (docs. 571, 574).

51. GAA, Poorterboek B+J, p. 59, January 12, 1650; Paul Huey, 'Aspects of Continuity,' 573; for more information on archaeologcal excavations, see also Huey, 'The Archaeology of Fort Orange and Beverwijck' (Zeller, *A Beautiful and Fruitful Place*, 327-49).

Chapter 1

1.   *MCR*, 105.
2.   Ibid., 189-90.
3.   CCS, 112-14^v; see also Nissenson, *The Patroon's Domain*, 355-61.
4.   CCS, 112^v-14, 129^v-30, 178^v-80; see also Nissenson, *The Patroon's Domain*, 362-64.
5.   CCS, 112^v.
6.   Ibid., 120.
7.   Ibid., 14-14^v.
8.   *DRCHNY* 14, p. 92.
9.   See also C.T. Gehring, 'The Founding of Beverwijck, a Dutch Village on the Upper Hudson' (*DSSYB* 51 [1989-93]: 4-11).
10. *MCR*, 40, 54.
11. *DRCHNY* 14, pp. 92-93, 101, 102, 149; Beernink, *De geschiedschrijver en rechtsgeleerde Arend van Slichtenhorst en zijn vader Brant van Slichtenhorst, stichter van Albany, hoofdstad van de staat New York* (Arnhem: S. Gouda Quint, 1916), 186-92.
12. CCS 100-1, 108, 142^v.
13. *DRCHNY* 14, pp. 101-2. See also Beernink, *De geschiedschrijver en rechtsgeleerde*, 191.
14. *DRCHNY*, 14: 92, 120.
15. Ibid., 14: 120.

16. Ibid., 14: 135, 120, 133.
17. GAA, NA 1300/1; January 6, 1651. For ownership, rights and privileges of the director and co-directors of Rensselaerswijck, see *VRBM*, 109, 164-65, 516, 528-34, 539-44, 725-30. See also Jacobs, 'Johannes de Laet en de Nieuwe Wereld,' 113-15.
18. GAA, NA 1300/1; January 6, 1651.
19. CCS, 42ᵛ, 46.
20. The story of a siege of Fort Orange in 1633 appears in Aernout van Buchell, *Notae Quotidianae* (Utrecht, 1940), 52-53. See also John H. van Schaick, 'Showdown at Fort Orange' (*DHM* 65 [3; 1992]: 37-45), and Frijhoff, *Wegen*, 669.
21. About the Maquaes see, for example, Brandão, *Your Fyre shall burn no more*; and Richter, *The Ordeal of the Longhouse*.
22. Richter, *The Ordeal of the Longhouse*, 86-87.
23. C.T. Gehring and R.S. Grumet, 'Observations of the Indians from Jasper Danckaerts's Journal, 1679-1680' (*WMQ*, 3rd series, no. 1 [January 1987], 107-8); see also D.R. Snow, 'Mohawk Demography and the Effects of Exogenous Epidemics on American Indian Populations' (*Journal of Anthropological Archaeology* 15 [1996], 160-80); William A. Starna, 'Seventeenth Century Dutch-Indian Trade: A Perspective from Iroquoia' (*DHM* 59 [1986]); and Starna, 'Indian Dutch Frontiers' (*DHM* 64 [1991]: 21-25).
24. *VRBM*, 166-69, 181-83; *LP*, 4. Shirley Dunn, in *The Mohicans and Their Land*, lists the recorded land transactions of the Mahicans, 279-309.
25. CCS, 16, 69ᵛ.
26. Ibid., 16, 69ᵛ.
27. Ibid., 16.
28. Ibid., 16ᵛ.
29. Ibid., 19-20.
30. Ibid., 16, 16ᵛ-20, 70-71, 102ᵛ-4. See also Venema, 'The Court Case of Brant Aertsz van Slichtenhorst,' 5-6.
31. See also the reaction of the XIX to Van Twiller's efforts to monopolize the trade, when they wrote that it could be clearly proven that the West India Company had 'bought vast tracks of land on the South River, the Fresh River, Long Island and many other places in the neighborhood.' The directors thus made clear that New Netherland was not a conquered territory. Only land bought by the company itself was considered its property; Rensselaerswijck, and all land not purchased, was not part of it (*DRCHNY* 14, pp. 135, 120, 133).
32. See William Cronon, *Changes in the Land. Indians, Colonists, and the Ecology of New England* (New York: Hill and Wang, 1983), 65-70. See also Richter, *The Ordeal of the Longhouse*, 21, 24. William Starna thinks that the larger social units (clans, groups of clans, or 'tribes') exercised more deliberate control over the land they used. They actively worked to prevent others from using their lands (personal communication, October 12, 2001). See also Starna, 'Assessing American Indian Studies: Missed and Missing Opportunities,' paper in author's possession.
33. Dunn, *The Mohicans and Their Land*, 133; see also *CJVR*, 225.
34. CCS, 70-70ᵛ. See also A.E. Van Zwieten, '"A Little Land . . . To Sow Some Seeds": Real Property, Custom, and Law in the Community of New Amsterdam' (Ph.D. thesis; Philadelphia: Temple University), 16-18.
35. CCS, 19ᵛ.
36. Ibid., 71-72ᵛ. This was translated and published by C.T. Gehring in the 'Totidem Verbis' (*Nieunederlanse Marcurius*, no. 4 [September 1988] [Albany]), 2-3; see also Johannes Megapolensis, Jr., 'A Short Account of the Mohawk Indians, 1644' (Snow, *In Mohawk Country*, 41).
37. CCS, 71ᵛ.
38. Dunn, *The Mohicans and their Land*, 116-17, 122-23.
39. CCS, 71-71ᵛ.
40. Ibid., 71ᵛ.
41. Ibid., 22, 72.
42. Ibid., 72ᵛ. It is not clear which 'great lake' is meant; Gehring suggests Lake Erie ('Totidem Verbis,' 3).

43. A.J.F. van Laer, 'Arent van Curler and His Historic Letter to the Patroon' (*DSSYB* 17 [1941-42]): 27-28.
44. *MCR*, 127-30.
45. Ibid., 131.
46. Ibid., 129.
47. Ibid., 131-32.
48. *VRBM*, 33-34; K. Zandvliet, *Mapping for Money: Maps, Plans and Topographic Paintings and Their Role in Dutch Overseas Expansion During the 16th and 17th Centuries* (Amsterdam: Batavian Lion International, 1998), 210-11.
49. *VRBM*, 454-55.
50. Ibid., 611-12. As a reaction to Kieft's Indian taxes in 1639, the Raritans had attacked David Pietersz de Vries's farm on Staten Island, killing four of his tenant farmers and burning the house and barn.
51. Ibid., 619.
52. Ibid., 663.
53. Ibid., 200.
54. Ibid., 69, 79, 199, 275, 294.
55. Ibid., 613, 621, 624, 627.
56. Ibid., 474.
57. Nissenson wrote that Van Rensselaer's primary object was the capture of the coveted fur trade (Nissenson, *The Patroon's Domain*, 81). See also Folkerts, 'De pachters van Rensselaerswijck,' 27-28.
58. *VRBM*, 578.
59. Ibid., 487, 497.
60. Ibid., 474.
61. Van Laer, 'Arent van Curler and His Historic Letter,' 11-29. See also Charles Gehring, 'The Founding of Beverwijck,' 8.
62. *DRCHNY* 14, pp. 50-51, 55-56, 57-59; see also Nissenson, *The Patrioon's Domain*, 198-200.
63. CCS, 178ᵛ-79ᵛ.
64. *VRBM*, 454.
65. Ibid., 553, 578.
66. See Gehring, *FOCM*, xxi-xxv; Shattuck, 'A Civil Society,' 49, 51; Jacobs, *Een zegenrijk gewest*, 127-28.
67. *DRCHNY*, 14: 97.
68. Scheepvaart museum Amsterdam, Handschriften van de Van Rensselaer familie, folder 53414; mss. 25-40, IN: B III 828 II, 67, third page; see also Nissenson, *The Patroon's Domain*, 366.
69. *MCR*, 181.
70. CCS, 122; Beernink, *De geschiedschrijver en rechtsgeleerde*, 175; *DRCHNY* 14, p. 92.
71. *DRCHNY* 14, pp. 89-90.
72. For information on Fort Amsterdam at Curaçao, see Ron van Oers, *Dutch Town Planning Overseas During VOC and WIC Rule, 1600-1800* (Zutphen: Walburg Pers, 2000), 44.
73. Ibid., 117-19.
74. *DRCHNY* 14, p. 92.
75. Ibid., 89, 93-95; *MCR*, 72, 211.
76. *DRCHNY* 14, p. 93.
77. Ibid., 96.
78. *MCR*, 40.
79. *DRCHNY* 14, p. 102.
80. Ibid., 93, 95, 97, 153; CCS, 56.
81. *MCR*, 54.
82. *DRCHNY* 14, pp. 92, 95, 96.
83. CCS, 23.
84. *VRBM*, 829; see also *ER* 1, p. 158.
85. CCS 21ᵛ, 22, 23ᵛ; see also *MCR*, 207; C.W. Fock, et al. (eds.), *Het Nederlandse Interieur in*

beeld 1600-1900 (Zwolle: Waanders, 2001), 97. House marks are still used among burghers and farmers in large parts of the Netherlands. W. Frijhoff, personal communication.

86. *MCR*, 74-75; CCS, 21ᵛ; 74.
87. *VRBM*, 551, 646.
88. *MCR*, 174.
89. Ibid., 181.
90. Ibid., 141; CCS, 26.
91. Raben, 'Batavia and Colombo,' 33.
92. *MCR*, 27; Gisbert Cornelisz, Goosen Gerritsz, Steven Jansz, and Pieter Bronck also had permission to tap (ibid., 48, 123, 132, 143, 162).
93. Beernink, *De geschiedschrijver en rechtsgeleerde*, 197.
94. *DRCHNY* 14, pp. 152-54.
95. *HNN* 2, 176; *MCR*, 173.
96. *MCR*, 188.
97. Gehring, *Council Minutes, 1652-1654*, 18-19. See also *DRCHNY* 14, p. 162.
98. *MCR*, 14; *DRCHNY* 14, pp. 191.
99. *MCR*, 199; CCS, 23, 73-75, 90; *DRCHNY* 14, pp. 91-92.
100. *DRCHNY* 14, pp. 171, 187.
101. CCS, 44.
102. Ibid., 46ᵛ, 47.
103. Ibid., 46ᵛ-47.
104. *FOCM*, xxii, xxiii. The 600 paces were five feet each, or together 250 Rhineland rods (Gehring, *Council Minutes, 1652-1654*: 18-19).
105. CCS, 65.
106. The 418-page volume of this court case is deposited in the Rijksarchief of the province of Gelderland, at Arnhem, and is marked 'N 15.3.3 Rensselaer Ca V. Slichtenhorst.' Transcription by Janny Venema at the NNP. See also Beernink (*De geschiedschrijver en rechtsgeleerde*, 245), who discusses a large part of this court case.
107. Beernink, *De geschiedschrijver en rechtsgeleerde*, 216, 260; GAA, NA 3218/342-342v (April 2, 1674); GAA, NA 3218/340 (April 2, 1674).
108. CCS, 67. For the fifty-two to fifty-four people, information was drawn from *VRBM*, *MCR*, CCS, and the Van Rensselaer Manor Papers in the New York State Library. See Appendix 2.
109. The original reads: 'In corten seer is toegenomen ende rechtevoort wel 38 huysen sijn staende en 4 a 5 noch half gemaeckt leggen' (CCS, 109).
110. Ibid., 56.
111. *MCR*, 151; in 1684, Jeremias van Rensselaer's son Kiliaen still referred to the area by this name (*CMVR*, 153).
112. *FOCM*, 3.
113. CCS, 109.
114. *FOCM*, 3.
115. Ibid., 4.
116. Ibid., 3.
117. The information is drawn from patents, *ERA*, *FOCM*, *LP*, *VRBM*, and CCS.
118. *FOCM*, 67.
119. Scheepvaartmuseum Amsterdam, Handschriften van de Van Rensselaer familie, folder 53414; mss. 25-40 IN: B III 828 II, p. 69; see also C.T. Gehring, 'An Undiscovered Van Rensselaer Letter' (*DHM* 54 [3; fall/winter, 1979]: 28).
120. *ERA* 1, p. 209.
121. The number is drawn from patents, and information in *ERA* 1-4, *FOCM*, *LP*.
122. CCS, 109-109ᵛ.
123. Donna Merwick wrote that, in 1664, ninety-one patents had been distributed to seventy-four inhabitants; seventy-five were patented before 1655, and fifty-four went to forty-three inhabitants who were Rensselaerswijck colonists before 1652 ('Dutch Townsmen and Land Use: A

Spatial Perspective on Seventeenth-Century Albany, New York' [*WMQ*, 3rd ser., January 1980]), 60; *Possessing Albany*, 73.

124. CCS, 109; *FOCM*, 41.

125. I.N.P. Stokes, *The Iconography of Manhattan Island, 1498-1909* (New York: R.H. Dodd, 1915-28), vol. 4, pp. 115, 184.

126. *LO*, 105; see also 325-27; *RNA* 7, p. 148.

127. *FOCM*, 53, 55, 70.

128. Henk Zantkuijl, 'Bouwen in de Hollandse stad' (Ed Taverne and Irmin Visser, *Stedebouw. De geschiedenis van de stad in de Nederlanden van 1500 tot heden* [Nijmegen: SUN, 1993]), 69.

129. *FOCM*, 33, 70, 80, see also pp. 94, 97.

130. CCS, 109-109ᵛ.

131. D. Merwick, 'Dutch Townsmen and Land Use,' 62.

132. *FOCM*, 3, 4, 67; perhaps Dirck Jansz left this office; his name is not mentioned in this function again.

133. Van Oers, *Dutch Town Planning*, 119.

134. E. Taverne, *In 't land van belofte: in de nieue stadt. Ideaal en werkelijkheid van de stadsuitleg in de Republiek, 1580-1680* (Maarssen: Gary Schwartz, 1978), 77-78.

135. CCS, 21ᵛ; *FOCM*, 119, 128, 184; *CMARS* 1, pp. 52.

136. Taverne, *In 't land van belofte*, 77-78.

137. C.L. Temminck Groll, 'Nieuw Amsterdam in Noord-Amerika, vergeleken met andere Nederlandse 17de-eeuwse stedestichtingen' (*Leids Kunsthistorisch Jaarboek*, 1984).

138. Peter Kalm, *Peter Kalm's Travels in North America: The English Version of 1770* (New York: Dover, 1964); revised (from the original Swedish) by Adolph B. Benson, ed. (New York: Dover, 1987), 342.

139. Huey, personal communication, January 30, 2002.

140. NYSL, VRMP, box 29 (the date is eligible, because of damage to document; the entries before this one, however, are dated April and May 1650).

141. *FOCM*, 126.

142. *LO*, 74; Stokes, *Iconography*, vol. 1, p. 129.

143. *FOCM*, 41, 44.

144. Ibid., 8-9.

145. Ibid., 37, 39, 40, 43, 51.

146. Ibid., 97, 129.

147. Van Oers, *Dutch Town Planning Overseas*, 119.

148. *FOCM*, 96.

149. For the whole Vosburgh surveying business, see *FOCM*, 96, 101, 125, 133, 135-38, 141, 148, 184, 189.

150. Ibid., 161-62.

151. Ibid., 148-49.

152. Ibid., 125-26, 137.

153. Ibid., 189.

154. Ibid., 234-35.

155. Ibid., 36; Patents, vol. 2, pt. 2, no. 66; *ERA* 4, p. 160; *ERA* 2, pp. 50, 92.

156. *LO*, 442.

157. *CJVR*, 358.

158. Kalm, *Peter Kalm's Travels in North America*, 342; *ERA* 1, pp. 308, 150; *ERA* 2, pp. 285, 384.

159. Stokes, *Iconography*, vol. 1, 129, 160, 185.

160. *CMARS* 2, pp. 376, 446.

161. Kalm, *Peter Kalm's Travels in North America*, 342.

162. *FOCM*, 57; Stokes, *Iconography*, vol. 1, pp. 120-21; *CMARS* 2, p. 395.

163. Rooijakkers, *Rituele repertoires*, 342-56; Stokes, *Iconography*, vol. 1, p. 177.

164. *FOCM*, 133.

165. Kalm, *Peter Kalm's Travels*, 342; *ERA* I: 150, *ERA* II: 285.

166. *FOCM*, 473-74.

167. *CMARS* 1, pp. 148.
168. *ERA* 4, p. 86.
169. *ERA* 1, p. 213; author's translation.
170. *FOCM*, 106, 119, 128, 153.
171. *MCR*, 141.
172. NYSL, VRMP, box 39 (November 11/21, 1667).
173. Raben, 'Batavia and Colombo,' 33.
174. Hannadea van Nederveen Meerkerk, *Recife: The Rise of a 17th-Century Trade City from a Cultural-Historical Perspective* (Delft: Van Gorcum, 1989), 95.
175. Zandvliet, *Mapping for Money*, 78-79.
176. Van Oers, *Dutch Town Planning*, 121-22.
177. D.B. Rutman, *Winthrop's Boston: A Portrait of a Puritan Town, 1630-1649* (Chapel Hill and London: University of North Carolina Press, 1965), 68-69.
178. *FOCM*, 469; for fences, see Adriaen Van der Donck, *A Description of the New Netherlands* (J. Johnson [trans.], T.F. O'Donnell [ed.]; Syracuse, N.Y.: Syracuse University Press, 1968), 29-30; see also D.S. Cohen, *The Dutch-American Farm* (New York and London: New York University Press, 1992), 76-80.
179. R.H. Blackburn and R. Piwonka, *Remembrance of Patria: Dutch Arts and Culture in Colonial America 1609-1776* (Albany, N.Y.: Albany Institute of History and Art, 1988), 108-12.
180. *FOCM*, 492; *ERA* 3, p. 212.
181. See, for instance, many property transfers in *ERA* 1.
182. Blackburn and Piwonka, *Remembrance of Patria*, 105-6.
183. Merwick, referring to Gerald L. Burke's book on the making of Dutch towns, mentions that the houses were not remarkably smaller than houses of common folk in the Netherlands ('Dutch Townsmen,' 62-63); Gerald L. Burke, however, mentions that it was not unusual for the frontage of houses in Leiden, Haarlem, Gouda, Groningen, and Dordrecht to be fifteen feet, but he adds that the depth of these houses generally was three times the length of its frontage (*The Making of Dutch Towns. A Study in Urban Development from the Tenth to the Seventeenth Centuries* [London: Cleaver/Hume Press, 1956], 138).
184. Frijhoff and Spies, *1650*, 158-59.
185. Van Nederveen Meerkerk, *Recife*, 134. See also J.A.G. de Mello, *Nederlanders in Brazilië (1624-1654). De invloed van de Hollandse bezetting op het leven en de cultuur in Noord-Brazilië* [Rio de Janeiro, 2001; trans. Zutphen: Walburg Pers]), 65.
186. Henk Zantkuijl, 'Hollandse huizen, gebouwd in de 17de eeuw in Amerika, II' (*Amsterdamse Monumenten* 3 [5de jaargang no. 3, October 1987], 52-55.
187. *VRBM*, 837; *ERA* 1, p. 12.
188. For more examples, see *ERA* 1, pp. 31, 52, 215, 249, 269, 274, 304, 370.
189. *ERA* 4, p. 21; see also *ERA* 1, pp. 219, 271, 290-91, and Huey, 'Aspects of Continuity,' 728.
190. J. Schipper, 'Rural Architecture: The Zaan region of the Province of North Holland' (R.A. Blackburn and N.A. Kelley [eds.], *New World Dutch Studies: Dutch Arts and Culture in Colonial America, 1609-1776* [Albany, N.Y.: Albany Institute of History and Art, 1987]), 173, 175; see also Gonsalves de Mello, *Nederlanders in Brazilië*, 68.
191. *ERA* 1, p. 285; *FOCM*, 6; for Dutch barns, see also John Fitchen, *The New World Dutch Barn* (Syracuse, N.Y.: Syracuse University Press, 1968). In Albany, the Dutch Barn Society does ongoing research about Dutch barns in the Hudson and Mohawk valleys.
192. *DAB*, 73.
193. *ERA* 1, p. 465.
194. Zantkuijl, 'Bouwen in de Hollandse stad,' 63-64.
195. Fock, *Het Nederlandse interieur in beeld*, 21, 25; see also Zantkuyl, 'The Netherlands Town House: How and Why It Works' (Blackburn and Kelley, *New World Dutch Studies*, 143-60); Schipper, 'Rural Architecture,' 171-84; H.A. Zantkuijl, et al., *De ontwikkeling van het woonhuis tot 1940 in Hoorn* (Hoorn: Publicatiestichting Bas Baltus, 2001), 24-43.
196. *ERA* 1, p. 31; *ERA* 4, p. 68.
197. *ERA* 3, pp. 91, 353.

198. Zantkuyl, 'The Netherlands Town House,' 150.

199. *ERA* 1, pp. 323, 372.

200. Ibid., p. 12.

201. Ibid., p. 43.

202. *CMARS* 2, p. 136.

203. Stokes, *Iconography*, vol. 4, p. 129.

204. *FOCM*, 105-6; *ERA* 1, p. 22.

205. Zantkuijl, personal communication, October 31, 2001; *DAB*, 32; *ERA* 4, p. 110.

206. *ERA* 4, p. 110; *ERA* 1, p. 370.

207. *ERA* 4, p. 27; *ERA* 1, p. 314.

208. *ERA* 1, p. 314; *CMARS* 2, p. 136.

209. Kalm, *Peter Kalm's Travels*, 121.

210. Blackburn and Piwonka, *Remembrance of Patria*, 109.

211. Stokes, *Iconography*, vol. 4, p. 163; *RNA* 1, p. 20; *RNA* 2, pp. 18, 19; *LO*, 207-8; see also *FOCM*, 259.

212. CCS, 108; *FOCM*, 224.

213. *FOCM*, 259, 416; *ERA* 4, p. 27.

214. Kalm, *Peter Kalm's Travels*, 341.

215. *ERA* 1, p. 269; *DAB*, 38.

216. *FOCM*, 465.

217. *ERA* 1, p. 53; *FOCM*, 176.

218. G.D.J. Schotel, *Het maatschappelijk leven onzer vaderen in de zeventiende eeuw* (Amsterdam and Arnhem: J.G. Strengholt's Uitgeversmaatschappij N.V en Gijsbers en Van Loon; reprint ed 1905), 189. For signs, see Jan ter Gouw, *De volksvermaken* (Haarlem: Bohn, 1871; reprinted Arnhem, 1969).

219. *ERA* 1, pp. 43, 53, 269.

220. *ERA* 4, pp. 40, 52; *ERA* 1, p. 223.

221. *ERA* 1, pp. 18-19. See also Merwick, 'Dutch Townsmen,' 63.

222. An average density of five dwellings per acre then seems too high (Merwick, 'Dutch Townsmen,' 63-64).

223. *ERA* 1, pp. 17, 18, 22, 43, 323; *ERA* 3, p. 170; *ERA* 4, pp. 8, 36.

224. *ERA* 1, pp. 249, 304, 314, 323; *ERA* 4, p. 7; see Frijhoff, *Wegen van Evert Willemsz*, 633.

225. *ERA* 1, pp. 319, 323.

226. *FOCM*, 268; *ERA* 1, p. 43; *ERA* 3, p. 204; *DAB*, 47.

227. *FOCM*, 274; *ERA* 1, p. 43.

228. *ERA* 3, p. 170; *ERA* 1, p. 492.

229. *ERA* 1, p. 12; NYSL, VRMP, box 39 (1666; further date unreadable due to fire damage).

230. *CMARS* 3, p. 249.

231. A.J.F. van Laer, 'Albany Notarial Papers 1667-1687' (*DSSYB* 14 [1938-39]), 2.

232. *ERA* 4, p. 59; *FOCM*, 520.

233. *CMARS* 2, p. 446.

234. *FOCM*, 123.

235. In the patents, some dimensions of gardens in Beverwijck were: 7 by 5.5; 7 by 5; 16.5 by 3r, 8.5 ft.; 15 by 7; 6r 8 ft. by 8; 6.5 by 9.3; 5 by 7; 5.2 by 9r 8 and 5.9; 5 rods square; 7 by 3; 6.5 by 8; See also Van Oers, *Dutch Town Planning*, 121.

236. *ERA* 1, p. 213, author's translation.

237. Van der Donck, *A Description of the New Netherlands*, 24-25, 61-71.

238. Anne Grant, *Memoires of an American Lady. With Sketches of Manners and Scenery in America, as They Existed Previous to the Revolution* (2 vols.; London, 1818; New York: Dodd, Mead, 1970), 30.

239. *FOCM*, 65, 96.

240. For Fort Orange, see Paul R. Huey, 'Aspects of Continuity and Change.'

241. *FOCM*, 184.

242. Lotte van de Pol, *Het Amsterdams hoerdom. Prostitutie in de zeventiende en achttiende eeuw* (Amsterdam: Wereldbibliotheek, 1996), 185.

243. *DAB*, 14, 16.
244. A.W. Trelease, *Indian Affairs in Colonial New York: The Seventeenth Century* (Lincoln and London: University of Nebraska Press, 1997), 138-48; *ERA* 1, p. 425; *DAB*, 42, 93.
245. *DAB*, 11, 36, 38, 71, 74, 77, 94, 101.
246. *ERA* 1, p. 239.
247. CCS, 107.
248. R.S. Alexander, *Albany's First Church and Its Role in the City* (Delmar, N.Y.: Newsgraphic, 1988), 38.
249. Van Nederveen Meerkerk, *Recife*, 57, 59.
250. *MCR*, 241.
251. *ER* 1, p. 158; CCS, 21^v.
252. C.A. van Swigchem, et al., *Een huis voor het woord. Het Protestantse kerkinterieur in Nederland tot 1900* ('s-Gravenhage: Staatsuitgeverij, 1984), 222-23.
253. CCS, 109^v.
254. *FOCM*, 29, 30.
255. CCS, 108.
256. H.E. Niemeijer, 'Calvinisme en koloniale stadscultuur. Batavia 1619-1725' (Ph.D. thesis; Amsterdam: Vrije Universiteit, 1996), 104-5.
257. *FOCM*, 231-32.
258. *ERA* 1, p. 239.
259. Stokes, *Iconography*, vol. 4, p. 169.
260. Van Nederveen Meerkerk, *Recife*, 144-50; Raben, 'Batavia en Colombo,' 38; Gonsalves de Mello, *Nederlanders in Brazilië*, 84.
261. *ERA* 1, pp. 344, 383 (author's translation); *HNN*, vol. 2, p. 307.
262. Alexander, *Albany's First Church*, 37-38. The rooster can still be seen in Albany's First Dutch Reformed Church.
263. Ibid., 44, 49, 50.
264. Ibid., 38, 57, 133.
265. *Ibid..*, 51, 59, 72, 85, 90, 98, 178, 190; *ERA* 1, p. 344.
266. *DAB*, 38, 57.
267. *ERA* 1, p. 70; Van Swigchem, *Een huis voor het woord*, 71, 93, 159, 219.
268. *FOCM*, 380.
269. *CMVR*, 57; *MCR*, 74-75; J. Pearson, *Genealogies*, 98; NYSL, *DAB*, February 28, 1694; see also A. Eekhof, *De Hervormde Kerk in Noord-Amerika* ('s-Gravenhage: Martinus Nijhoff, 1913), vol. 1, p. 165.
270. The patent, signed by Petrus Stuyvesant, is in Albany's First Church.
271. Stokes, *Iconography*, vol. 1, p. 132; *LP*, 71.
272. *DAB*, 2, 6-9, 11, 13.
273. *Ibid.*, 32.
274. Stokes, *Iconography*, vol. 4, p. 157; *DAB*, 39-41, 43, 51.
275. *Ibid.*, 47, 73, 74, 204.
276. Work on the minister's house, *DAB*: 73-76, 78, 85, 207, 260; Schaets only received a patent for a house lot in 1668, while he had a grant for a garden lot in 1653.
277. Stokes, *Iconography*, vol. 1, pp. 122, 125.
278. Steven Innes, *Labor in a New Land* (Princeton, N.J.: Princeton University Press, 1983), 34-36.
279. *VRBM*, 406, 497, 505.
280. Ibid., 816.
281. Gehring, 'An Undiscovered Van Rensselaer Letter,' 28.
282. *VRBM*, 811; NYSL, VRMP, box 16 (January 31, 1646).
283. *VRBM*, 828.
284. *FOCM*, 39, 41.
285. Ibid., 41, 97.
286. *ERA* 3, pp. 46, 197, 198; *ERA* 1, pp. 292-93, 216, 404, 422.
287. *FOCM*, 223.

288. Ibid., 429.
289. NYSL, VRMP, box 33 (1655, 1661); CCS, 108.
290. NYSL, VRMP, box 29 (likely April or May 1650).
291. *FOCM*, 183, 196; *DAB*, 21, 90, 260.
292. Stokes *Iconography*, vol. 4, p. 137.
293. *FOCM*, 267; NYSA, NYCM 9: 432.
294. *CMARS* 1, pp. 31, 300.
295. Pat Barbanell has done extensive research on brick and tile yards in the upper Hudson area. Her dissertation, 'A Ceramic History of Colonial Albany, New York: A Curricular Model Integrating Art and Local History in Education' (New York: Columbia University, 1987) was helpful and confirmed research done on the following information.
296. *VRBM*, 160, 207, 283; *MCR*, 194.
297. *VRBM*, 283, 606, 658.
298. *MCR*, 181, 194.
299. *ERA* 2, p. 207.
300. Barbanell, 'A Ceramic History,' 97-109.
301. NYSL, VRMP, box 37 (January 10, 1660).
302. Barbanell, 'A Ceramic History,' 110; see also *FOCM*, 297; and *ERA* 4, p. 23; Munsell, *Annals of Albany*, vol. 4, p. 85.
303. *ERA* 1, p. 57; *VRBM*, 829.
304. *ERA* 1, p. 316.
305. *ERA* 2, p. 38; see also the reports of the archaeological excavation in 2001 by Hartgen Archaeologists (Albany, N.Y.).
306. *ERA* 1, p. 56.
307. *FOCM*, 297.
308. NYSL, VRMP, box 37 (December 1658; June, December 1659; June 1660; July 1661).
309. *ERA* 1, p. 446.
310. *DAB*, 71, 75, 88, 89; *ERA* 3, p. 29.
311. NYSL, VRMP, box 37 (January, July, August 1660; February, July 1661).
312. Venema, 'For the Benefit of the Poor,' 156.
313. NYSL, VRMP, box 37 (January 10, 1660).
314. NYSL, VRMP, box 37 (December 16, 1658; June 24, November 30, 1659; December 16, 1660; July 9, 1661; April 7, 1662).
315. *LO*, 207-8.
316. C.T. Gehring, *Delaware Papers (Dutch Period). A Collection of Documents Pertaining to the Regulation of Affairs on the South River of New Netherland, 1648-1664* (New York Historical Manuscripts: Dutch, vols. 18-19 [Baltimore Md.: Genealogical, 1981]), 111, 112, 114, 128, 139, 342.
317. Gehring, 'An Undiscovered Van Rensselaer Letter,' 28.
318. *FOCM*, 76, 304, 306, 453-55, 463, 503.
319. Ibid., 45, 46, 242-43, 416; *LO*, 112-13; 361-62.
320. *ERA* 1, p. 236. The settlers may not have been as alarmed as is suggested by the translation, which says that a vessel had set sail and the watch had doubled, while the original text reads .' . . midlertijt hebben een ooch int zeyl ende de wacht verdubbelt,' meaning that the Dutch kept 'an eye in the sail,' an expression meaning that they would pay extra attention.
321. *FOCM*, 123.
322. Ibid., 10.
323. *ERA* 1, pp. 43, 304, 314; *ERA* 4, p. 7; *ERA* 1, pp. 249, 323, 319.
324. Stokes, *Iconography*, vol. 4, p. 161.
325. *FOCM*, 288.
326. Ibid., 354.
327. *ERA* 3, p. 109.
328. *CJVR*, 381.
329. Ibid., 381.

330. A.J.F. van Laer, 'Albany Notarial Papers, 1666-1693' (*DSSYB* 13 [1934-44]), 1-2.

331. *CMARS* 1, pp. 303.

332. Ibid., pp. 306.

333. *FOCM*, 465.

334. Ibid., 469.

335. *LO*, 385.

336. The manuscript map is in volume 1 of the 'Land Papers,' as described in *Calendar of Land Papers, 1643-1803* (Albany, 1864), 6. The sketch originally was undated but was placed between two items dated October 20, 1674 and March 1, 1675. The Colonial Albany Project dates the map as 1676, since an after-the-fact notation on the parchment is 'French Map 1676.'

337. Joel Munsell, *Men and Things in Albany*, 7.

338. Megapolensis, ' A Short Account ,' 41, 43.

339. *FOCM*, 514.

340. *CJVR*, 232.

341. The words *wreede barbaren* may also mean 'strange people whom they did not understand'; NYSA, NYCM 9: 55-56, 67 (February 9, 1660).

342. NYSA, NYCM 9: 55-56, 67 (February 10, 1660); Frijhoff and Spies, *1650*, 127, 172; Arend van Slichtenhorst, *XIV boeken van de Geldersse geschiedenissen* (Arnhem, 1653); Johannes Smetius, *Nijmegen, Stad der Bataven* (Nijmegen, 1644; revised Nijmegen: SUN, 1999).

343. *FOCM*, 492.

344. Ibid., 514; *ERA* 1, p. 492.

345. *FOCM*, 497. The footnote in *FOCM* does not seem to be correct. See chapter 5 for the location of *Lange Maria*.

346. The translation says 'on the hill'; but, unfortunately, the document with the original text is illegible at this place on account of fire damage. In the *ERA*, the original text for this translation was 'aen het gebergte or aen de bergh,' meaning 'at the hill.'

347. *LO*, 425-26; NYSA, NYCM 10: 186 (August 5, 1662).

348. *LO*, 426-27. NYSA, NYCM 10: 195 (August 12, 1662).

349. *LO*, 442.

350. *CJVR*, 332, 358.

Chapter 2

1. Only 36 percent of the men and women who gave notice of their intended marriage between 1646 and 1650 was born in Amsterdam; 23 percent came from other Dutch provinces, and 41 percent from other countries (Frijhoff and Spies, *1650*, 160). See also Hart, 'Geschrift en Getal,' 136-81.

2. Sung Bok Kim states that only 200 inhabitants had come solely for the trade (*Landlord and Tenant*, 4-5); Martha Shattuck found, based on Beverwijck's court minutes, that the population was 1,051 in 1660 ('A Civil Society,' 11).

3. Condon (*New York Beginnings*, 116-72) and Ritchie (*The Duke's Province*, 31) both found that institutional life in New Netherland had been weakly rooted. See also Merwick, 'Dutch Townsmen,' 66; and Nissenson, *The Patroon's Domain*, 153.

4. See David Cohen, 'How Dutch Were the Dutch of New Netherland,' 51; and Oliver Rink, *Holland on the Hudson*, 155.

5. Frijhoff and Spies (*1650*, 50) cite De Laet.

6. Rink, *Holland on the Hudson*, 20, 146-48, 165-69.

7. Ibid., 146-48, 165-69; Frijhoff, *1650*, 190-92; and Shattuck, 'A Civil Society,' 140-90.

8. *ER* I, 483. The original reads: .' . . alsoo der wel tusschen de 3 en somtijts 4 hondert te kercken gaen en soo sij alle liefhebbers waren souden wel 600 sterck sijn behalven den koopluyden die hier soomers veel koomen. . . .' (New Brunswick Theological School, GASL, AC box 1, no. 9 [26 juni 1657]). See also Eekhof, *De Hervormde Kerk* 1, p. 147.

9. The Lutherans in Amsterdam had established a full-fledged congregation in 1588 (Rooden-burg, *Onder Censuur. De kerkelijke tucht in de gereformeerde gemeente van Amsterdam, 1578-1700* [Hilversum: Verloren, 1990], 175-76). For religious toleration in the Republic see Willem Frijhoff, 'Religious Toleration in the United Provinces: From "Case" to "Model" (R. Po-Chia Hsia and H. van Nierop [eds.], *Calvinism and Religious Toleration in the Dutch Golden Age* [Cambridge: Cambridge University Press, 2002], 27-52).

10. A.J.F. van Laer, *The Lutheran Church in New York, 1649-1772. Records in the Lutheran Church Archives at Amsterdam, Holland* (New York: New York Public Library, 1946), 14, 13, 40, 130-17.

11. Ibid., 39; and *FOCM*, 4, 6, 39, 40, 120, 188. See also Frijhoff, 'Religious toleration,' 35, 45.

12. *LO*, 211-12. See also *LWA*, 55-56.

13. *FOCM*, 216, 220.

14. *ERA* 1, p. 239.

15. *FOCM*, 236.

16. *ER* 1, p. 409.

17. Van Laer, *The Lutheran Church*, 24-45.

18. *ER*: 482-83.

19. *FOCM*, 425.

20. Roodenburg, *Onder Censuur*, 150.

21. François-Joseph le Mercier and Joseph-Antoine Poncet de la Rivière, 'Of the Capture and De-liverance of Father Joseph Poncet' (Snow, *In Mohawk Country*, 99, 100).

22. *FOCM*, 144.

23. *ER* 1, 432-33; and Eekhof, *De Hervormde Kerk* 2, appendix 7.

24. Frijhoff and Spies, *1650*, 180, 185-88.

25. Ibid., 185. See also Frijhoff's chapter on the excommunication of Lubbert Dincklage by *dominee* Everhardus Bogardus in 1635 (*Wegen van Evert Willemsz*, 676-83).

26. Shattuck, 'A Civil Society,' 219.

27. Frijhoff and Spies, *1650*, 185. See also Rooijakkers, 'Vieren en markeren,' in Ton Dekker, et al. (eds.), *Volkscultuur: Een inleiding in de Nederlandse etnologie* (Nijmegen: SUN, 2000), 197-200.

28. Frijhoff, 'Reinventing an Old Fatherland,' 134.

29. Frijhoff and Spies, *1650*, 183, 185.

30. Ibid., 182-83. For burghership, see also J.Ph. de Monté ver Loren and J.E. Spruit, *Hoofdlijnen uit de ontwikkeling der rechterlijke organisatie in de Noordelijke Nederlanden tot de Bataafse omwenteling* (Deventer: Kluwer, 1982), 163-66; Maarten Prak, *Republikeinse veelheid, democratisch enkelvoud. Sociale verandering in het revolutietijdvak, 's-Hertogenbosch 1770-1820* (Nijmegen : Sun, 1999), 35-43.

31. Knevel, *Burgers in het geweer. De schutterijen in Holland, 1550-1700* (Hilversum : Verloren, 1994), 45-47.

32. Frijhoff and Spies, *1650*, 182-83.

33. Jacobs, *Een zegenrijk gewest*, 304.

34. *HNN* 2, p. 176; and *MCR*, 173.

35. *MCR*, 28, 35.

36. CCS, 47; and *FOCM*, 5.

37. Ibid., 4-5.

38. Ibid., 183, 190. See also chapter 5, 19-22.

39. Jacobs, *Een zegenrijk gewest*, 307, n. 95.

40. NYSA, NYCM 8: 429-63 (January-February, 1657).

41. NYSA, NYCM 10-3: 193-94 (April 22, 1664).

42. See Jacobs (*Een zegenrijk gewest*, 303-10) regarding New Amsterdam's burgher right.

43. NYSA, NYCM 10-3: 187-89, 189-90, 191-92, 193-94 (March 13 and 20, April 22, 1664); *LO* 462.

44. Frijhoff and Spies, *1650*, 183-84.

45. Knevel, *Burgers in het geweer*, 238.

46. *HNN* 2, p. 176; and *MCR*, 173.
47. *LO*, 35. See also *RNA* 1, p. 65; *RNA* 5, p. 23.
48. Gehring, 'An Undiscovered Van Rensselaer Letter,' 28.
49. *CJVR*, 222.
50. A 1653 ordinance on the burgher guard of Beverwijck, mss. 12802; incomplete; not translated; New York State Library (C.T. Gehring, *A Guide to Dutch Manuscripts Relating to New Netherland* [Albany: State University of New York, 1978], 164).
51. *FOCM*, 88-90, 93.
52. *HNN* 2, p. 569. See also Jacobs, *Een zegenrijk gewest*, 310-15; and Ottomar H. van Norden, 'New Amsterdam's Burgher Guard' (*DHM* 32 [4]).
53. *HNN* 2, p. 540; *ER* 1, p. 383. See also Shattuck, 'A Civil Society,' 11; and Jacobs, *Een zegenrijk gewest*, 252-54.
54. *FOCM*, 237; and Jacobs, *Een zegenrijk gewest*, 312.
55. *FOCM*, 300; Knevel, *Burgers in het geweer*, 126, 130.
56. *FOCM*, 192, 300.
57. Ibid., 220, 299.
58. Ibid., 299; *DAB*, 67, 71, 77, 85, 86, 89, 90, 119; *CMARS* 2, p. 50; see also Appendix 5.
59. *FOCM*, 54, 89; Knevel, *Burgers in het geweer*, 143, 145, 147; *ERA* 3, p. 251.
60. Knevel, *Burgers in het geweer*, 233-38.
61. Ibid., 291; refers to 'Ordonnantie voor de Schutterye t' Alckmaer' (Handvesten . . . der stadt Enchuysen, 70-75, art. 38).
62. Knevel, *Burgers in het geweer*, 135, 292, 295, 301-5, 312.
63. *FOCM*, 88-90, 299.
64. Ibid., 192.
65. Knevel, *Burgers in het geweer*, 292, 295. For 'shooting the parrot,' see also G. Rooijakkers, *Rituele repertoires*, 501-9, 518-19, 527-31.
66. *FOCM*, 451; September 3, 1659; Knevel, *Burgers in het geweer*, 225. See also Lotte van de Pol, *Het Amsterdams hoerdom*, 183, 184, 246.
67. Eekhof, *De Hervormde Kerk* 1, pp. 166-67; *FOCM*, 470; *RNA* 7, p. 198.
68. *CJVR*, 295; *ERA* 3, p. 165; *ER* 1, p. 383.
69. Author's translation. The original reads either 'marresighten' or 'narresighten' (*ERA* 1, p. 219).
70. Rooijakkers, *Rituele repertoires*, 406-7.
71. *ERA* 1, pp. 219, 245; *FOCM*, 101. See also Frijhoff, *Wegen van Evert Willemsz*, 722-23, 774-75.
72. *FOCM*, 180; NYSA, NYCM 5, pp. 217-21 (25-26 February, 1654); NYSA, NYCM 8, p. 742 (26 February, 1658).
73. NYSL, VRMP, box 45 (March 1675).
74. Roodenburg, *Onder Censuur*, 333.
75. See Frijhoff, 'Reinventing an Old Fatherland,' 135. See also Rooijakkers, 'Vieren en markeren,' 212-17.
76. *ERA* 3, p. 116.
77. *CJVR*, 441.
78. Frijhoff and Spies, *1650*, 214-15.
79. *FOCM*, 123, 520.
80. Ibid., 172, 183, 208, 223.
81. Frijhoff and Spies, *1650*, 210-13. See also G. Dorren, *Eenheid en verscheidenheid. De burgers van Haarlem in de Gouden Eeuw* (Amsterdam: Prometheus en Bakker, 2001), 73-78; and Rooijakkers, 'Vieren en markeren,' 197-200.
82. *FOCM*, 190.
83. NYSA, NYCM 9, pp. 224, 225, 226; NYSL, VRMP, box 37 (June 18, 1661).
84. *HNN* 1, pp. 320, 441; *VRBM*, 835-36. For hangmen, see Pieter Spierenburg, *The Spectacle of Suffering. Executions and the evolution of Repression: From a Preindustrial Metropolis to the European Experience* (Cambridge: Cambridge University Press, 1984) 13-42. See also Frijhoff, *Wegen van Evert Willemsz*, 769; NYSL, VRMP box 29 (date unknown because document is damaged), 37; *MCR*, 143, 195; *FOCM*, 8, 12, 13, 16.

85. Eekhof, *De Hervormde Kerk* 1, p. 38; 2, p. 148.
86. *VRBM*, 152-53.
87. Frijhoff, *Wegen van Evert Willemsz*, 501, 766; refers to ds. Godfried Udemans, *'t Geestelyck Roer van 't Coopmans Schip* (2nd printing 1640).
88. Joyce Goodfriend, 'Burghers and Blacks: The Evolution of a Slave Society at New Amsterdam' (*NYH* 59), 128; Frijhoff, *Wegen van Evert Willemsz*, 768; Gehring, *Correspondence 1647-1653*, 5.
89. Gehring, *Correspondence*, 134-35, 145, 160, 172; Goodfriend, 'Burghers and Blacks,' 134.
90. Goodfriend, 'Burghers and Blacks,' 133-34, 138, 142, 144.
91. *MCR*, 143, 195; *FOCM*, 8, 12, 13, 16.
92. *CJVR*, 59, 60.
93. Ibid., 167.
94. NYSA, NYCM 10, p. 228 (May 29, 1664).
95. NYSA, NYCM 14, p. 19; Frijhoff, *Wegen van Evert Willemsz*, 768.
96. *CJVR*, 167.
97. *ERA* 4, p. 112.
98. NYSA, NYCM 9, p. 760 (September 2, 1661). See also ibid., 882.
99. A. Blakely, *Blacks in the Dutch World: The evolution of Racial Imagery in a Modern Society* (Bloomington and Indianapolis: Indiana University Press, 1993), 25.
100. *CJVR*, 364-65.
101. *ERA* 1, pp. 241-42; *FOCM*, 458.
102. *ERA* 1, p. 241; *FOCM*, 458; NYSA, NYCM 9, p. 915 (November 7, 1661).
103. *ERA* 3, p. 294; *CMARS* 2, pp. 401, 405, 414, 417.
104. NYSL, VRMP box 43 (May 16, 1662; dates are hard to read due to fire damage); *CJVR*, 152.
105. *CJVR*, 167-68, 353; NYSL, VRMP box 43 (October 7, 1667).
106. *CJVR*, 255.
107. NYSA, NYCM 9, pp. 915-17 (November 7, 1661).
108. GAA, NA 2442/408 (January 4, 1657). For freed negroes, see Peter R. Christoph, 'The Freedmen of New Amsterdam,' in N.A. McClure Zeller, ed., *A Beautiful and Fruitful Place*, 157-69; and Jacobs, *Een zegenrijk gewest*, 321-24.
109. *CMARS* 1, pp. 94, 102. See also Tomas E. Burke, *Mohawk Frontier: The Dutch Community of Schenectady, New York, 1661-1710* (Ithaca, N.Y.: Cornell University Press, 1991), 134; *DAB*, 223.
110. *FOCM*, 13, 458; *ERA* 4, p. 112; *ERA* 3, p. 249.
111. *CMARS* 2, pp. 431-44; *ERA* 1, p. 149.
112. *DRCHNY* 1, pp. 689-90; 3, p. 905; Burke, *Mohawk Frontier*, 137.
113. Christoph, 'The Freedmen,' 157; Jacobs, *Een zegenrijk gewest*, 324.
114. Much of this part was derived from Martha Dickinson Shattuck, 'A Civil Society,' 20-72.
115. *FOCM*, 3.
116. *RNA* 1, pp. 48-49.
117. Jacobs (*Een zegenrijk gewest*, 147) lists Heemstede, (1644), Vlissingen (1645), 's-Gravesande (1645), Breuckelen (1646), Beverwijck (1652), Middelburgh (1652), Amersfoort and Midwout, (1654), Oostdorp and Rustdorp (1656), Haerlem (1660), Boswijck, Wiltwijck, Bergen, New Utrecht (1661), and Staten Island (1664).
118. *DRCHNY* 1, p. 120.
119. Jacobs, *Een zegenrijk gewest*, 155-56.
120. *LO*, 147.
121. *DRCHNY* 1, p. 123.
122. *LO*, 329-33.
123. *LO*, 351-56.
124. See Wiltwijck's and Bergen's charters (*LO*, 395-410, 403-8).
125. Shattuck, 'A Civil Society,' 20-66.
126. Gerard Rooseboom, *Recueil van verscheyde Keuren en Costumen. Midtsgaders Maniere van Procederen, binnen de Stadt Amsterdam* (Amsterdam, 1656), 18, 20. See also Frijhoff and Spies, *1650*, 195.

127. *FOCM*, 30.

128. Van Deursen, *Mensen van klein vermogen. Het kopergeld van de Gouden Eeuw* (Amsterdam: Bert Bakker, 1991), 185-86; Monté ver Loren and Spruit, *Hoofdlijnen*, 117.

129. *MCR*, 40, 43.

130. Blackburn and Piwonka, *Remembrance of Patria*, 53.

131. Shattuck, 'A Civil Society,' 51.

132. *VRBM* 805-46; *LIR*, 144; Patents, vol. 2, pt. 2, # 25; GAA, ondertrouwboeken # 482, p. 197.

133. Sullivan, *The Punishment of Crime*, 90.

134. *VRBM*, 294.

135. *MCR*, 202.

136. Shattuck, 'A Civil Society,' 55-56.

137. *DRNN*, 97-98. For the office of *schout* in Amsterdam, see Rooseboom, *Recueil*, 9-15; see also Lotte van der Pol, *Het Amsterdams hoerdom*, 184-85.

138. GAA, NA: 1099/509-10 (April 24, 1652); see also *HNN* 2, pp. 564-65.

139. *MCR*, 19; *MCARS* 1, pp. 7, 196, 197, n. 2.

140. *FOCM*, 275, 277.

141. NYSA, NYCM 9, pp. 216, 235 (May 13, 1660).

142. *FOCM*, 355.

143. *FOCM*, 389-90, 392, 418.

144. *ERA* 1, p. 241; *FOCM*, 458.

145. GAA, NA 2442/408 (January 4, 1657); NYSA, NYCM 8, p. 571 (May 8, 1657).

146. *VRBM*, 642; *CJVR*, 365.

147. J.A. Schiltkamp, *De geschiedenis van het notariaat in het octrooigebied van de West-Indische Compagnie* ('s-Gravenhage: N.V. de Nederlandse Boek-en Steendrukkerij v/h H.L. Smits, 1964), 61; Van Laer, *Council Minutes 1638-1649*, pp. 16, 73; *LO*, 17, 24.

148. *LO*, 59, 108; NYSA, NYCM 8, p. 681; 16, p. 130 (January 25, 1658).

149. *LO*, 329-33.

150. For Van Schelluyne's commission and career in New Amsterdam, see Van Laer's introduction to *ERA* 3, pp. 9-13.

151. Ibid., p. 7.

152. For the history and performance in New Netherland of the function of notary, see ibid., 1-23; and Schiltkamp, *De geschiedenis van het notariaat*.

153. *FOCM*, 5.

154. *LO*, 351-56.

155. NYSA, NYCM 8, pp. 134, 135 (August, 7 1656); *FOCM*, 281.

156. GAA, NA 1300/233v-234 (November 20, 1651).

157. *NYSA, NYCM* 8, p. 228 (September 20, 1656).

158. NYSA, NYCM 8, pp. 228-29 (20 September, 1656).

159. NYSA, NYCM 5, p. 25 (March 5, 1652).

160. Shattuck, 'A Civil Society,' 66.

161. Ibid., 68; *DRCHNY* 14, p. 259; *FOCM*, 67, 161-62.

162. Shattuck, 'A Civil Society,' 69-70.

163. *FOCM*, 278.

164. For the description that follows, information was derived from the following articles: A.J.F. van Laer, 'The Orphan Chamber of Amsterdam'(*DSSYB* 11 [1935-36]), 1-9; Adriana E. Van Zwieten, 'The Orphan Chamber of New Amsterdam' (*WMQ* 53 [1996]), 319-40; Simon Groenveld, 'De Republiek der Verenigde Nederlanden en haar wezen, ca. 1572-1795' (Groenveld, et al. [eds.], *Wezen en Boefjes: Zes eeuwenzorg in wees-en kinderhuizen* [Hilversum: Verloren]), 13-245.

165. *FOCM*, 273, 278.

166. Stokes, *Iconography* 4, pp. 158, 159, 165; Van Zwieten, 'The Orphan Chamber,' 323-24; *DAB*, 25.

167. *RNA* 1, pp. 56, 380.

168. *FOCM*, 280.

169. See Rooseboom (*Recueil*, 103-19) for fifty-one articles about orphans and minor persons (*weesen ende onmondige kinderen*) in Amsterdam.
170. Ibid., 104. See also Van Zwieten, 'The Orphan Chamber,' 331.
171. Van Zwieten, 'The Orphan Chamber,' 331.
172. *ERA* 1, p. 25.
173. *ERA* 3, pp. 269-70.
174. Van Zwieten, 'The Orphan Chamber,' 332.
175. B. Fernow, *Minutes of the Orphanmasters, Court of New Amsterdam 1655-1663* (New York: Francis P. Harper, 1902), 245; Van Zwieten, 'The Orphan Chamber,' 328.
176. *ERA* 1, p. 321. For some other examples see ibid., 50, 311, 327, 346, 390.
177. Groenveld, 'De Republiek,' 32, 119.
178. A.J.F. van Laer, 'Albany Wills and Other Documents' (*DSSYB* 6 [1930-31]) 15-16.
179. *MCARS* 2, pp. 13-16, 75.
180. David Narrett, *Inheritance and Family Life in Colonial New York City* (Ithaca, NY: Cornell University Press, 1992), 59-60; Jaap Jacobs, personal communication, May 2001.
181. GAA, Arch. no. 366: 254, leerjongensboeck van het chirurgijnsgilde, p. 41 (August 14, 1635).
182. Van Deursen, *Een dorp in de polder. Graft in de zeventiende eeuw* ((Amsterdam: Bert Bakker, 1994), 114-15; D.J.B. Ringoir, *Plattelandschirurgijns in de 17e en 18e eeuw. De rekeningboeken van de 18e-eeuwse Durgerdamse chirurgijn Anthonij Egberts* (Bunnik: Lebo, 1977), 82.
183. Eekhof, *De Hervormde Kerk* 2, pp. 162-64; *Kingston Papers* 2, pp. 567-69.
184. *FOCM*, 128, 165; *ERA* 1, p. 326; *DAB*, 18, 29, 31, 41, 73, 76, 83, 100, 111, 117-19, 124, 132, 199.
185. *FOCM*, 63.
186. New York Public Library, Bontemantel Collection, New Netherland Papers, box 1, folder 'Official list of New Netherland' (undated, about 1650).
187. For a discussion of salaries of West India Company servants, see Jaap Jacobs, *Een zegenrijk gewest*, 293-94.
188. *RNA* 1, p. 34.
189. *FOCM*, 257.
190. Ibid., 522.
191. NYSL, VRMP, box 37 (August 1, 1660).
192. *CJVR*, 328-29, 343, 348-49, 358b, 367, 372, 377, 384-87, 392, 388, 392, 402, 414. See also P. Christoph, 'Worthy, Virtuous Juffrouw Maria van Rensselaer,' 26-29.
193. Eekhof, *De Hervormde Kerk* 2, p. 166.
194. *ERA* 3, p. 74.
195. Van Laer, 'Albany Wills and Other Documents,' 14. Part of the manuscript is damaged.
196. Eekhof, *De Hervormde Kerk* 2, p. 162.
197. Munsell, *The Annals of Albany* 4, p. 16; *CMARS* 2, p. 182.
198. NYSA, NYCM 9, p. 207 (May 11, 1660). See also Frijhoff, *Wegen van Evert Willemsz*, 608-10.
199. Frijhoff and Spies, *1650*, 354. See also Frijhoff, 'Religious Toleration,' 33.
200. Van Lieburg, *Profeten en hun vaderland. De geographische herkomst van de gereformeerde predikanten in Nederland van 1572-1816* (Boekencentrum: 1996), 25-26.
201. *ER* 1, p. 383.
202. E. Kloek, *Wie hij zij, man of wijf. Vrouwengeschiedenis en de vroegmoderne tijd* (Hilversum: Verloren, 1990), 91; for Delft and Delfland, see Wouters, *Nieuw en ongezien. Kerk en samenleving in de classis Delft en Delfland, 1572-1621* 1 (Delft: Eburon), pp. 261-66; *ER* 1, p. 383.
203. Niemeyer, *Calvinisme en koloniale stadscultuur*, 214; Goodfriend, 'The Social Dimensions of Congregational Life in Colonial New York City,' 55; Jacobs, *Een zegenrijk gewest*, 251.
204. Jacobs (*Een zegenrijk gewest*, 251) quotes Rothchild ('The Social Distance Between Dutch Settlers and Native Americans,' in A. van Dongen [ed.], *One Man's Trash is Another Man's Treasure* [Catalogue Museum Boymans van Beuningen, Rotterdam, 1995-96/Jamestown Settlement Museum, Williamsburg, Va., 1996], 190-91).
205. *CJVR*, 131.
206. Frijhoff and Spies, *1650*, 364-69.
207. Eekhof, *De Hervormde Kerk* 2, p. 64; *Kingston Papers* 2, pp. 569, 574.

208. *CJVR*, 231.
209. *ER* 1, pp. 383, 483.
210. Frijhoff and Spies, *1650*, 355-56.
211. Ibid., 357.
212. Groenvelt, *Huisgenoten des geloofs. Was de samenleving in de Republiek der Verenigde Nederlanden verzuild?* (Hilversum: Verloren, 1995), 20; Van Deursen, 'De dominee,' in H.M. Beliën, et al., *Gestalten van de Gouden Eeuw.Een Hollands groepsportret* (Amsterdam: Bert Bakker, 1995), 132, 138; Frijhoff, 'Religious Toleration,' 31-35.
213. Frijhoff, *Wegen van Evert Willemsz*, 581.
214. G. Groenhuis, *De Predikanten. De sociale positie van de gereformeerde predikanten in de Republiek der Verenigde Nederlanden voor 1700* (Groningen: Wolters-Noordhoff, 1977), 13.
215. J. Schiltkamp, 'On Common Ground.'
216. Frijhoff, *Wegen van Evert Willemsz*, 545-46; 'The West India Company and the Reformed Church,' 59-68. See also A. Eekhof, *Bastiaen Jansz*, 22-23.
217. Jacobs, *Een zegenrijk gewest*, 159.
218. Van Deursen, *Bavianen en Slijkgeuzen. Kerk en kerkvolk ten tijde van Maurits en Oldenbarnevelt* (Franeker: van Wijnen, 1991), 30-31.
219. *FOCM*, 84-85, 105-7.
220. Van Deursen, *Bavianen en Slijkgeuzen*, 36, 42-44; quotes from *Kerkelijk Handboekje* (p. 70, Not. Oudewater, *Jaerlicxsche Ordonnantien, 1611*, and Not. Edam, November 19, 1595; 168-69), 44. For religious service at Flatbush, see E. Nooter, 'Between Heaven and Earth: Church and Society in Pre-Revolutionary Flatbush, Long Island' (Ph.D. thesis; Amsterdam: Vrije Universiteit, 1994), 96.
221. GAA, NA 1711/521 (March 6, 1659).
222. *CMR*, 30.
223. Van Laer, *Council Minutes 1638-1649*, p. 579; Gehring, *Council Minutes 1652-1654*, pp. 159-60.
224. Stokes, *Iconography,* 4, p. 138.
225. Van Deursen, *Bavianen en Slijkgeuzen*, 27.
226. *DAB*, 37-46.
227. *LO*, 25, 61, 93, 95, 311, 342, 416, 426, 451.
228. For observance of the Sabbath in the Dutch Republic, see Frijhoff, *Wegen van Evert Willemsz*, 303-6; Roodenburg, *Onder Censuur*, 321-44; Van Deursen, *Bavianen en Slijkgeuzen*, 26-30; Van Dorren, *Eenheid en verscheidenheid*, 78-79.
229. *FOCM*, 211, 228-29.
230. *LO*, 99, 258-59; *LWA*, 71.
231. *FOCM*, 284.
232. Van Deursen, *Bavianen en Slijkgeuzen*, 21.
233. For this so-called *beschavingsoffensief*, see Frijhoff, *Wegen van Evert Willemsz*, 358-59; *FOCM*, 84-85.
234. *LO*, 448-49.
235. Nooter, 'Between Heaven and Earth,' 98.
236. Ibid., 101-2; *DAB*, 228.
237. Frijhoff and Spies, *1650*, 185; Van Wijngaarden, *Zorg voor de kost, Armenzorg, arbeid en onderlinge hulp in Zwolle* (Amsterdam: Prometheus/Bert Bakker, 2000) 223, 226.
238. Groenhuis, *De predikanten*, 30. See also Rooijakkers, 'Vieren en markeren,' 197-200.
239. *DAB*, 147; Venema, '"For the Benefit of the Poor",' 179.
240. *RNA* 1, p. 172. See also Roodenburg (*Onder Censuur*, 330), who cites Petrus Wittewrongel, *Oeconomia christiana. Ofte christelicke huys-houdinge. Vervat in twee boecken. Tot bevoordeninge van de oeffeninge der ware godtsalicheydt in de bysondere huys-gesinnen. Naer den reghel van het suyvere woort Godts te samen-gestelt*, 2 vols. [Amsterdam, 1661], 1066); *ERA* 1, pp. 219, 245; *FOCM*, 101.
241. *ER* 1, p. 483.
242. H. Dosker, *Levensschets van Rev. A. C. Van Raalte, DD* (Nijkerk, 1893), 69-70.
243. *ER* 1, pp. 249, 252.

244. Nooter, 'Between Heaven and Earth,' 18.

245. Van Deursen (*Bavianen en Slijkgeuzen*, 35-36) quotes the *Kerkelijk handboekje*, 193.

246. Van Deursen, 'De dominee,' 143-46.

247. Van Deursen, *Bavianen en Slijkgeuzen*, 55-57.

248. Ibid., 70, 77. See also Nooter, 'Between Heaven and Earth,' 18-19.

249. *ER* 1, p. 290.

250. CCS, 10.

251. Alexander, *Albany's First Church*, 27-29. For Grasmeer, see also Eekhof, *De Hervormde Kerk* 1, pp. 122, 126-39. See also *VRBM*, 841; *ER* 1, pp. 271-77, 283-84, 285, 301.

252. Eekhof, *De Hervormde Kerk* 1, pp. 140-41; *ER* 1, p. 304.

253. Ibid., p. 142.

254. Ibid., 143; *ER* 1, p. 253.

255. Ibid., pp. 143-44; *ER* 1, p. 309.

256. Van Deursen, *Bavianen en Slijkgeuzen*, 35; Frijhoff, *Wegen van Evert Willemsz*, 156-57, 549-53, 557; Van Lieburg, *Profeten en hun vaderland*, 65.

257. GAA, NA 1100/23v, p. 26 (8 May, 1652). See *ER* 1, pp. 309-10; *HNN* 2, p. 567.

258. Eekhof, *De Hervormde Kerk* 1, p. 155. See also his signature at the end of each year in the *DAB*, 19, 27, 37, 46.

259. *VRBM*, 844; Nissenson, *The Patroon's Domain*, 157; Alexander, *Albany's First Church*, 42.

260. *ER* 1, p. 434.

261. Eekhof, *De Hervormde Kerk* 1, pp. 164-65; Venema, '"For the Benefit of the Poor",' 234.

262. *ER* 1, pp. 398-99. See also E.B. O'Callaghan, *Documentary History of the State of New York*, vol. 3 (Albany, N.Y.: Weed, Parsons, 1849-51), 69-72.

263. Pierre Esprit Radisson, 'Voyages of Pierre Esprit Radisson, 1651-1654' (Snow, *In Mohawk Country*, 92).

264. Jasper Danckaerts, 'Journal of a Voyage to New York and a Tour in Several of the American Colonies in 1679-1680' (Snow, *In Mohawk Country*, 193-220).

265. Danckaerts, 'Journal,' 196-97; *ERA* 2, pp. 300-1; J. Munsell, *Collections on the History of Albany* 4, p. 170.

266. Danckaerts, 'Journal,' 204.

267. J. Pearson, *Genealogies of First Settlers of Schenectady*, 229.

268. *GAA*, notes from the *Classis* no. 379, Buitenlandse Kerk, 2nd book, 425.

269. *FOCM*, 285.

270. *ER* 1, p. 384. See also Eekhof, *De Hervormde kerk* 1, p. 148; *CMARS* 2, 193.

271. *NYSA*, *NYCM* 15, pp. 49, 56 (August 30, 1663; September 10, 1663). See also *ER* 1, pp. 534, 542-43; Eekhof, *De Hervormde Kerk* 1, p. 158; and *DAB*, 103, 106, 111, 113-14, 116.

272. Van Deursen, *Bavianen en Slijkgeuzen*, 77.

273. The oldest consistory minutes date back to the 1680s and only contain fragments of notes. These are in Albany's First Dutch Reformed Church and are at present being translated by C. T. Gehring.

274. Danckaerts, 'Journal,' 215.

275. Van Deursen, 'De dominee,' 138.

276. Van Deursen, *Bavianen en Slijkgeuzen*, 93-94; A.Ph.F. Wouters, *Nieuw en ongezien*, 335. See also J. Venema, '"For the Benefit of the Poor",' 231-35.

277. Van Deursen, *Bavianen en Slijkgeuzen*, 48-49; 200-217; for Delft and Delfland, see Wouters, *Nieuw en Ongezien* 1, 315-22; Roodenburg, *Onder censuur*, 126-27, 37.

278. Frijhoff and Spies, *1650*, 363-64.

279. Abels, *Nieuw en ongezien* 2, pp. 38-41.

280. The case was not only of personal interest, but also showed the struggle between church and state for leadership of the people. See Frijhoff, *Wegen van Evert Willemsz*, 676-97, especially 684.

281. *ER* 1, pp. 383, 386.

282. *FOCM*, 162-64, 171.

283. Ibid., 248-49; author's translation. For the strict standards regarding bigamy, see Manon van

der Heijden, *Huwelijk in Holland Stedelijke rechtspraak en kerkelijke tucht, 1550-1700* (Amsterdam: Bert Bakker, 1998)., 160-63, 246-48.

284. *DAB*, 122.

285. *FOCM*, 273.

286. Van Deursen, *Bavianen en Slijkgeuzen*, 94-95.

287. *FOCM*, 214; *DAB*, 27.

288. See appendix 4 in Venema, '"For the Benefit of the Poor",' 231-35. For list of magistrates and consistory members, see Appendix 5.

289. Groenhuis, *De predikanten*, 26.

290. *ER* 1, p. 386; *CCS*, 10; *VRBM*, 825.

291. *DAB*, 76, 124, 126, 127, 133. See also NYSA, NYCM 9: 206-7 (May 11, 1660).

292. Van Swigchem, *Een huis voor het Woord*, 192-93.

293. Van Deursen, *Bavianen en Slijkgeuzen*, 176.

294. Ibid., 174-79.

295. *DAB*, 93.

296. *DAB* 45, 49, 52, 53, 112, etc.; Van Swigchem, *Een huis voor het Woord*, 301.

297. *DAB*, 44, 53, 75; NYSL, VRMP, box 37 (January 23, 1659; January 10, 1660); *ERA* 3, p. 113.

298. *DAB*, 124, 127, 133, 154, 205.

299. Rudolf Dekker, *Uit de schaduw in 't grote licht. Kinderen in egodocumenten van de Gouden Eeuw tot de Romantiek* (Amsterdam: Wereldbibliotheek, 1995), 18.

300. *ER* 1, p. 402.

301. Dekker, *Uit de schaduw*, 167-69; *LO* 9, pp. 199, 240, 461, 478.

302. In the Dutch Republic, these amounts would be 4 stivers per month for reading, 6 stivers for writing, and 8 to 12 stivers for calculating. Frijhoff and Spies, *1650*, 241; For Pietersz in Nieuw Amsterdam, see *ER* 1, pp. 563, 575, 577; Eekhof, *De Hervormde Kerk* 2, pp. 124-25.

303. Groenvelt, *Huisgenoten des geloofs*, 24, 25.

304. Eekhof, *De Hervormde Kerk* 2, p. 64.

305. E.P. De Booy, *Kweekhoven der Wijsheid: Basis-en vervolgonderwijs in de steden van de provincie Utrecht van 1580 tot het begin der 19e eeuw* (Zutphen: De Walburg Pers, 1977), 42-52.

306. Translated titles: *Short Understanding, Spirited Wills, Hour of Death, Glorious Proofs of People's Misery, History of Joseph, Epistle and Gospel Books, Short Manner*. See Eekhof, *De Hervormde Kerk* 1, pp. 166-69; 2, p. 164. See also Frijhoff, *Wegen van Evert Willemsz*, 600-1; *Kingston Papers* 2, p. 569; and W.H. Kilpatrick, *The Dutch Schools of New Netherland and Colonial New York* (Washington, D.C.: U.S. Government Printing Office, 1912), 19-38.

307. De Booy, *Kweekhoven der Wijsheid*, 48-49. See also E.P. De Booy, *De Weldaet der scholen: Het plattelandsonderwijs in de provincie Utrecht van 1580 tot het begin der 19e eeuw* (Zutphen: De Walburg Pers, 1977), 43-45, Kilpatrick, *The Dutch Schools*, 223-24; Frijhoff and Spies, *1650*, 369-70.

308. *LO*, 461.

309. Ron Howard, 'Apprenticeship and Economic Education in New Netherland,' in McClure-Zeller, *A Beautiful and Fruitful Land*, 205-18.

310. *CJVR*, 49.

311. Howard, 'Apprenticeship,' 209; *ERA* 3, pp. 422, 485, 524, 530, 532, 544, 547, 561, 585.

312. Frijhoff and Spies, *1650*, 243; Howard, 'Apprenticeship,' 207. See also Van Deursen, *Mensen van klein vermogen*, 147-49.

313. Howard, 'Apprenticeship,' 207, 209; Edmund S. Morgan, *The Puritan Family*, 68-77.

314. Howard, 'Apprenticeship,' 209; Frijhoff and Spies, *1650*, 243.

315. Howard, 'Apprenticeship,' 207.

316. Eekhof, *Hervormde kerk*, 2, pp. 124-25.

317. P.A. de Planque, *Valcooch's regel der Duytsche schoolmeesters. Bijdrage tot de kennis van het schoolwezen in de zestiende eeuw* (Groningen: P. Noordhoff, 1926), 180, 221; D. Haks, *Huwelijk en gezin in Holland in de 17de en 18de eeuw. Processtukken en moralisten over aspecten van het laat 17de- en 18de-eeuwse gezinsleven* (Utrecht: Hes uitgevers, 1985), 161.

318. R. Dekker, *Uit de schaduw*, 19, 139.

319. *MCR*, 29, 172.

320. GAA, NA 1100/23v, p. 26 (May 8, 1652); *HNN* 2, p. 567. See also Kilpatrick (*The Dutch Schools*, 121), who used O'Callaghan's translation.

321. Van Deursen, *Bavianen en Slijkgeuzen*, 161-63.

322. *VRBM*, 843; GAA, NA 2279 III/18 (December 8, 1651).

323. *FOCM*, 526; Frijhoff and Spies, *1650*, 241.

324. NYSA, NYCM 8, p. 134 (August 7, 1656); *FOCM*, 281.

325. *DAB*, 50, 56, 60, 63, 66, 71, 72, 76, 82, 83; Frijhoff and Spies, *1650*, 241.

326. Van Deursen, *Bavianen en Slijkgeuzen*, 164.

327. *ERA* 3, pp. 16, 20-21.

328. Stokes, *Iconography* 4, pp. 156, 163; *ER* 1, p. 386; Shattuck, 'A Civil Society,' 11.

329. Much of the information is derived from J. Venema, '"For the Benefit of the Poor",' and *Kinderen van weelde*. See also Venema, 'Poverty and Charity,' 369-90.

330. Wouters, *Nieuw en ongezien* 1, p. 323.

331. *LO*, 122.

332. Ibid., 122, 331.

333. Eekhof, *De Hervormde Kerk* 2, 125.

334. *LO*, 411-12.

335. Venema, *Kinderen van weelde*, 55; 'Poverty and Charity,' 385; S. Groenveld, 'Geef van uw haaf/een milde gaaf/Ons arme WEESEN." De zorg voor wezen tot 1800, als onderdeel van de armenzorg' (S. Groenveld [ed.], *Daer de orangie appel in de gevel staat. In en om het weeshuis der doopsgezinde collegianten 1675-1975* [Amsterdam, 1975], 17); C. Ligtenberg, *Armezorg te Leiden tot het einde van de zestiende eeuw* ('s-Gravenhage: M. Nijhoff, 1908), 15-16.

336. Roodenburg, *Onder censuur*, 140.

337. Lynn Ceci, 'The First Fiscal Crisis in New York' (*Economic Development and Cultural Change* 4), 847.

338. *LWA*, 69-70, 87-89.

339. *LO*, 433-34.

340. G.R. Hamell, 'The Iroquois and the World's Rim: Speculations on Color, Culture, and Contact' (*American Quarterly* 16 [4]), 46.

341. *DRNN*, 220-23, 227, 228.

342. Bradley, *Evolution of the Onondaga Iroquois*, 161, 179.

343. Bradley, *Evolution of the Onondaga Iroquois*, 179-80. The English used the Algonquian word *wampum*. Beads consistent in form and size go back 4,000 years, and were made with stone tools, as was the earliest *wampum*. See George Hamell, 'Wampum: Light, White and Bright Are Good to Think' (Van Dongen, '*One Man's Trash*), 45.

344. D.K. Richter, *The Ordeal of the Longhouse*, 84-85. See also Bradley, *Evolution*, 67-69, 91, 179-80; Fenton, *The Great Law*, 226-28; *DRNN*, 212.

345. *LO*, 115-17. George Hamell, personal communication, March 25, 2002.

346. *LO*, 358.

347. *LO*, 115-117.

348. Ceci, 'The First Fiscal Crisis in New York,' 846.

349. *FOCM*, 328; *LO*, 289; *LWA*, 88.

350. *LO*, 359.

351. *LO*, 357-60, 434; *FOCM*, 328.

352. *DRCHNY* 14, p. 559.

353. Shattuck, 'A Civil Society,' 104-5.

354. Hamell, 'Wampum,' 45.

355. For the idea of reciprocity as an underlying principle governing social interaction, whereby obligations are incurred and met, see Richter, *The Ordeal*, 8-11, 23. About reciprocity, see also Aafje Komter, *The Gift*; Luuc Kooijmans, *Vriendschap en de kunst van het overleven in de zeventiende en achttiende eeuw* (Amsterdam: Bert Bakker, 1997). Irma Thoen is preparing a dissertation, 'The Gift in Seventeenth-Century Holland' (Florence: European University).

356. Bradley, *Evolution*, 170-80. See also Hamell, 'Wampum,' 41-51.
357. Gehring and Grumet, 'Observations of the Indians,' 108.
358. W.N. Fenton, *The Great Law and the Longhouse: A Political History of the Iroquois Confederacy* (Norman: University of Oklahoma Press, 1998), 254-55. For conferences between Europeans and Indians in the mid-eighteenth century, see Nancy L. Hagedorn, '"A Friend To Go Between Them": The Interpreter as Cultural Broker During Anglo-Iroquois Councils, 1740-70' (*Ethnohistory* 35 [1]), 63.
359. Van der Donck, 'A Description of New Netherland' (Snow, *In Mohawk Country*, 125).
360. Gehring and Grumet, 'Observations,' 109.
361. *FOCM*, 457.
362. *ERA* 1, p. 237; Van der Donck, 'A Description,' 125.
363. *ERA* 1, pp. 29, 237; partially author's translation.
364. Frijhoff and Spies, *1650*, 37.
365. Ibid., 127.
366. Ibid., 129.
367. Van der Donck, 'A Description,' 107.
368. *CJVR*, 358.
369. Richter, *The Ordeal*, 47-49; also 87, 95.
370. *FOCM*, 146-47.
371. Ibid., 150, 518; *ERA* 1, pp. 237, 453, 456.
372. *FOCM*, 304, 453, 463, 503, 515-17. See also Van der Donck, 'A Description,' 125.
373. Richter, *The Ordeal*, 86-87; George Hamell, personal communication, March 25, 2002.
374. Van Laer, 'Arent van Curler and His Historic Letter,' 27-28.
375. George R. Hamell, 'Strawberries, Floating Islands, and Rabbit Captains: Mythical Realities and European Contact in the Northeast During the Sixteenth and Seventeenth Centuries' (*Journal of Canadian Studies* 21 [4]), 78; see also Hagedorn, 'A Friend To Go Between Them,' 63.
376. J. Megapolensis, 'A Short Account,' 41, 43.
377. *CCS*, 71, 20.
378. *FOCM*, 457.
379. Ibid., 454.
380. Ibid., 453-54, 463, 503, 515-18; *ERA* 1, pp. 236-37.
381. F. Jennings, *The Ambiguous Iroquois Empire* (New York: W.W. Norton, 1984), 57.
382. *ERA* 1, p. 237; *FOCM*, 146-47, 456.
383. NYSA, NYCM 9, p. 112 (March 1, 1660).
384. *FOCM*, 255.
385. Ibid., 456; *DRCHNY* 13, p. 309.
386. Lois Feister, 'Linguistic Communication between the Dutch and Indians in New Netherland, 1609-1664' (Campisi and Hauptmann, *Mercury Series* 39 [Ottawa, 1978], reprinted *Ethnohistory* 20), 192.
387. See W.J. Eccles, *The Canadian Frontier, 1534-1760* (Albuquerque: University of New Mexico Press, 1983), 51-52, for attempts by the French, who had similar problems to understand the Huron.
388. Matthew Dennis, *Cultivating a Landscape of Peace*, 143, 155, 167, 179.
389. Megapolensis, 'A Short Account,' 41, 45. About *dominée* Bogardus and the Indians, see also Frijhoff in his *Wegen van Evert Willemsz*, 779-91.
390. Guarnier is quoted by Eccles (*The Canadian Frontier*, 51-52).
391. Richter, *The Ordeal*, 106, 328, n. 2.
392. Dennis, *Cultivating a Landscape of Peace*, 143, 166-67.
393. Van der Donck, 'A Description,' 106.
394. *MCR*, 129; *ERA* 3, p. 51; *CCS*, 19, 24, 25; *ERA* 1, pp. 72, 74, 173, 353, 449; NYSA, NYCM 13, pp. 95, 98.
395. Frijhoff, *Wegen van Evert Willemsz*, 627-28; *DRCHNY* 13, pp. 375-77.
396. *DRCHNY* 12, p. 89 (August 13, 1658).

397. NYSA, NYCM 8, p. 571 (May 8, 1657).
398. For example, *FOCM*, 122-23, 128, 141, 154, 197, 200, 201, 252, 254, 255, 263, 323-24, 352, 354.
399. Frijhoff, 'New Views,' 24.
400. *FOCM*, 141.
401. Ibid., 263.
402. Ibid., 211, 345, 347, 354.
403. *DRCHNY* 13, pp. 119-21, 127, 136, 182.
404. *FOCM*, 453.
405. Ibid., 354.
406. *ERA* 1, p. 74. For other examples, see also *ERA* 1, pp. 2, 151, 199-200; *ERA* 3, p. 556.
407. Megapolensis, 'A Short Account,' 43.
408. *FOCM*, 454.
409. GAA, NA 1711/521 (March 6, 1659).
410. Jacobs, *Een zegenrijk gewest*, 325, 334.
411. *LWA*, 19-20; *DRCHNY* 13, pp. 46, 119-21; *FOCM*, 459; *CMVR*, 44; Dunn, *The Mohicans and Their Land*, 141; DAB (September 2 and October 5, 1689).
412. For the matrilinear character of their lineage, see Van der Donck, 'A Description,' 114; Fenton, *The Great Law*, 28, 32; Richter, *The Ordeal*, 20.
413. *VRBM*, 817; *CMARS* 2, p. 86.
414. Danckaerts, 'Journal,' 195-98.
415. *FOCM*, 78.
416. Ibid., 78; *DRCHNY* 13, pp. 261, 278; Feister, 'Linguistic Communication,' 193. See also Fenton, *The Great Law*, 273; Richter, *The Ordeal*, 103-4, 120.
417. L.H. Leder (ed.), *The Livingston Indian Records 1666-1723* (Gettysburg: Pennsylvania Historical Association, 1956), 29, 31, 34; *ERA* 3, p. 200. The term 'cultural brokers' was first used by Nancy Hagedorn in '"A Friend to Go Between Them",' 61, 63, 65.
418. Gehring and Grumet, 'Observations of the Indians,' 107.
419. W.A. Starna, 'Seventeenth-Century Dutch-Indian Trade,' 7; and 'The Biological Encounter.' See also Bruce Trigger, 'Early Iroquoian Contacts with Europeans' (Trigger [ed.], *Handbook of North American Indians: Northeast*, vol. 15 [Washington, D.C.: Smithsonian Institution, 1978]), 352; D.R. Snow, 'Mohawk Demography,' 174; D.R. Snow and W.A. Starn, 'Sixteenth-Century Depopulation,' 144-47.
420. Richter, *The Ordeal*, 32-33. For experiences of captives among the Maquaes, see Radisson, 'Voyages of Pierre Esprit Radisson,' 62-92; and Le Mercier, et al., 'On the Capture and Deliverance of Father Joseph Poncet,' 93-103 (Snow, *In Mohawk Country*).
421. J.A. Brandão, *Your Fyre Shall Burn No More*, 41, 42, 72, 76-77.
422. Fenton, *The Great Law*, 245.
423. Frijhoff, 'New Views,' 15, 17; 'Reinventing an Old Fatherland,' 136-37; Frijhoff and Spies, *1650*, 138-41; *DRCHNY* 13:2, p. 114.

Chapter 3

1. De Vries and Van der Woude, *Nederland 1500-1815*, 470, 472.
2. Groenhuis, *De predikanten*, 47, refers to Deductie Cap. 6, 42 en tweede deel, Cap. 1, 58.
3. *VRBM*, 654-55.
4. W. de Vries, 'De Van Rensselaer's in Nederland,' in *De Nederlandsche Leeuw* 66 (1949): 203-4.
5. *CJVR*, 5. See also Luuc Kooijmans, 'De koopman,' in Beliën, *Gestalten van de Gouden Eeuw*, 87.
6. GAA, NA, 1072/218 (November 14, 1644); GAA, NA, 1075/1089 (November 18, 1645); GAA, NA, 1079/180v (June 16, 1646).
7. *FOCM*, 476.
8. NYSA, NYCM 13:138 (August 7, 1653).

9. A.J.F. van Laer, 'Letters to Evert Jansen Wendel,' in *Dutch Settlers Society Yearbook* 4 (1928-29), 7.
10. *CJVR*, 111; the document is damaged so that not everything is readable.
11. Ibid., 333.
12. See also Merwick, *Possessing Albany*, 84-88; B.H.D. Hermesdorf, *De herberg in de Nederlanden. Een blik in de beschavingsgeschiedenis* (Assen: Van Gorcum, 1957), 172-78.
13. Van Laer, 'Letters to Evert Jansen Wendel,' 7.
14. Frijhoff, *Wegen van Evert Willemsz*, 647; Patents, vol. 2, part 2, no. 66 (October 12, 1661).
15. *ERA* 3, pp. 235, 239, 256.
16. Patents, vol. 2, part 2, no. 36.
17. *ERA* 1, p. 244; *CJVR*, 53-57, 62-63; *DRCHNY* 1, pp. 119-23.
18. *ERA* 4, p. 39; *ERA* 1, pp. 375, 383; *ERA* 3, pp. 84, 92.
19. See, for example, *ERA* 1, pp. 297, 308, 362, 371, 358-59; *ERA* 3, pp. 67, 191.
20. Van Laer, 'Arent van Curler and His Historic Letter,' 20; *CJVR*, 307.
21. Richter, *The Ordeal*, 76.
22. The meaning of the word *hansioos* or *hansjoos* is unknown, but definitely has to do with the Indians. The word is often used to indicate these houses, but one auction lists *hanjoos* jewelry, which the translator has translated with 'trade jewels' (C.T. Gehring [transl. and ed.], *Fort Orange Records*, 145). It most likely is an Indian word taken over by the Dutch.
23. *CJVR*, 381, 390.
24. Merwick, *Possessing Albany*, 110.
25. C. Wilcoxen, 'Dutch Trade with New England' (*DHM* 60, no. 2 [October 1987]: 1-5).
26. *CJVR*, 416.
27. Ibid., 56, 112.
28. *ERA* 1, p. 258.
29. NYSA, NYCM 13: 314 (September 4, 1659).
30. *ERA* 3, pp. 235, 239, 256.
31. D.J. Maika, 'Commerce and Community: Manhattan Merchants in the Seventeenth Century' (Ph.D. dissertation; New York: New York University), 113-20; NYHS, Stuyvesant-Rutherford Papers (1648; May 11, 1649).
32. NYSA, NYCM 8: 136 (August 11, 1656).
33. *CJVR*, 12, 14, 24.
34. Van der Donck, 'A Description of New Netherland,' 78.
35. Letter of De Rasières, September 23, 1626, in *DRNN*, 231; *CJVR*, 63.
36. Margriet de Roever, 'Koopmanschappen voor Nieuw Nederland/Merchandises for New Netherland' (Van Dongen (ed.), *One Man's Trash*, 71-93).
37. Bradley, *Evolution*, 130-65; Charles F. Wray, 'The Volume of Dutch Tradegoods Received by the Seneca Iroquois, 1600-1687 A.D.,' in *New Netherland Studies: An Inventory of Current Research and Approaches. Bulletin KNOB*, Tijdschrift van de Koninklijke Nederlandse Oudheidkundige Bond 84, no. 2-3 (1985), 100-12.
38. *FOCM*, 59, 75, 91, 127, 387-88.
39. Ibid., 453-54.
40. Ibid., 154, 194, 252, 254, 328.
41. Ibid., 456; CCS, 16v, 17v, 19-20; Dunn, *The Mohicans and Their Land*, 279-87.
42. Nicolaes van Wassenaer, 'Historisch Verhael,' in *NNN*, 73; Trelease, *Indian Affairs*, 95.
43. Trelease, *Indian Affairs*, 97-98; *DRCHNY* 1, pp. 312, 337; 14, p. 89.
44. 'Answer to the Representation of New Netherland by Cornelis van Tienhoven, 1650,' in *NNN*, 368-69; *DRCHNY* 1, pp. 335, 337, 342, 345, 373-74, 501.
45. Trelease, *Indian Affairs*, 100; *DRCHNY* 1, pp. 388-89, 392.
46. *LO*, 128; see also ordinances in 1656, 1658, renewing the old ordinances and establishing inspection; *LO*, 236-37, 346; *DRCHNY* 1, pp. 501, 524; *DRCHNY* 14, pp. 166, 176; see also Trelease, *Indian Affairs*, 101.
47. *DRCHNY* 13, pp. 35-36; Trelease, *Indian Affairs*, 101-2.
48. *FOCM*, 150.

49. *Ibid.*, 456.
50. Trelease, *Indian Affairs*, 135-36; *DRCHNY* 2, p. 496.
51. Frijhoff and Spies, *1650*, 18; NYSA, NYCM 8: 136 (August 11, 1656).
52. *FOCM*, 10; *ERA* 3, p. 109; *ER* 1, p. 383.
53. *CJVR*, 104, 107, 114-15, 326.
54. Van Laer, 'Arent van Curler and his Historic Letter,' 29.
55. Martha Shattuck, 'A Civil Society,' 237-92. Much of the following text is derived from her description.
56. *VRBM*, 626-27.
57. Ibid., 722-23.
58. *MCR*, 70-71; *VRBM*, 814.
59. *LO*, 137.
60. *DRCHNY* 13, p. 175; *FOCM*, 492.
61. Gehring, *Council Minutes, 1655-1656*, 61.
62. *FOCM*, 195, 197, 200, 203; Shattuck, 'A Civil Society,' 259, 270-71.
63. *FOCM*, 195, 197.
64. Ibid., 434-37.
65. Ibid., 444-45, 465.
66. *DRCHNY* 14, p. 444.
67. *DRCHNY* 13, p. 175.
68. *FOCM*, 492, 502.
69. Ibid., 453-54, 463-64; *DRCHNY* 13, p. 114.
70. *FOCM*, 503-4.
71. Ibid., 511-14.
72. Ibid., 513-14; for a discussion of the trade problem, see also Merwick, *Possessing Albany*, 88-99; Burke, *Mohawk Frontier*, 9-13; Sullivan, *The Punishment of Crime*, 145-60.
73. See also Shattuck, 'A Civil Society,' 140-90; and Martha Shattuck, 'Women and Trade in New Netherland,' in *Itinerario, European Journal of Overseas History* 2, vol. 18 (1994): 40-47.
74. Frijhoff and Spies, *1650*, 191-92.
75. Shattuck, 'A Civil Society,' 155, 162-64.
76. Van Deursen, *Een dorp in de polder*, 119-29; Frijhoff and Spies, *1650*, 191.
77. De Vries and Van der Woude, *Nederland 1500-1815*, 472; Frijhoff and Spies, *1650*, 191-92; see also Els Kloek, 'De vrouw' (Beliën, *Gestalten van de Gouden Eeuw*, 261-62).
78. NYSL, VRMP, box 39 (likely 1661 or June 1662; the dates are hardly readable due to fire damage; GAA, NA1206/159 (November 27, 1657).
79. Schmidt, *Overleven na de dood*, 134; see also Van Deursen, *Dorp in de polder*, 127.
80. The connection between Gerritsz and Marij Goosens (or *Lange Marij*) is intriguing: She is not mentioned as one of Geerties's children; and yet, Goosen took care of a house for her. NYSL, VRMP box 39 (1657; 1659; February 4, 1660; August 10, 1661? Various dates are missing or hardly readable due to fire damage); an incomplete and canceled document suggests that in 1655 Gerritsz thought about being surety for Steven Jansz for a ƒ300 fine in 1655, which was the money for which Maria was fined because she sold brandy to an Indian. *ERA* 4, p. 107. Why did Gerritsz support her? Was she a child of a previous marriage, perhaps in Holland? Was she a sister, perhaps? She was too old to be the seven-year-old girl who was molested by Frans Gabriels in 1652, as she came over from the Republic with Steven Jansz in 1649, and in the same year had a daughter. GAA, NA 1089/12-12v (May 5, 1649); VRBM, 839. She probably differed no more than thirteen years in age with Goosen, so that it also is unlikely that she was his natural daughter. To the extent that the documents mention Goosen's and Maria's names together, they leave their relationship a mystery. *FOCM*, 25; Gehring, *Council Minutes 1652-1654*, 40.
81. *ERA* 1, p. 248; *ERA* 3, p. 183; Venema, 'For the Benefit of the Poor,' 154.
82. For women paid for work by the deacons, see Venema, 'For the Benefit of the Poor,' 217-27, especially 223.
83. For Amsterdam, see Rooseboom, *Receuil*, 215.

84. NYSL, VRMP, box 45 (1669, May 19, 1670). The same happened in Graft; see Van Deursen, *Een dorp in de polder*, 126.
85. *ER* 1, p. 385.
86. *ERA* 1, pp. 206, 221, 226, 273; *ERA* 4, pp. 53, 78, 79, 80; Ariadne Schmidt, *Overleven na de dood*, 136-37.
87. Frijhoff, *Wegen van Evert Willemsz*, 631-32.
88. Danckaerts, 'Journal,' 204.
89. *ERA* 3, p. 271; *ERA* 1, p. 442; GAA, NA, 1520/245 (October 20, 1668); ibid., 2297/II/19 (September 27, 1668); ibid., 2297 III/19-23, 28-29 (December 28, 1668).
90. Frijhoff and Spies, *1650*, 192.
91. *ERA* 3, p. 116; *ERA* 1, pp. 61, 345.
92. Narrett, *Inheritance and Family Life*; see also Shattuck, 'A Civil Society,' 155-57.
93. *ERA* 3, p. 38; Beernink, *De geschiedschrijver en rechtsgeleerde*, 260.
94. GAA, poorterboek B and J, 59; Shattuck, 'A Civil Society,' 158.
95. *ERA* 3, p. 271.
96. Frijhoff and Spies, *1650*, 191.
97. *ERA* 3, pp. 273-74; Laurel Thatcher Ulrich, *Goodwives: Images and Reality in the Lives of Women in Northern New England 1650-1750* (New York and Toronto: Oxford University Press, 1980), 7; see also Shattuck, 'A Civil Society,' 155-58.
98. *ERA* 3, pp. 273-74.
99. *VRBM*, 578.
100. GAA, NA 1067/189-190v (July 20, 1643).
101. GAA, NA 1081/197-197v (August 9, 1647); NA 1088/61, 61v (January 18, 1649).
102. Maika, 'Commerce and Community,' 89-90.
103. GAA, NA 1300/1 (January 6, 1651).
104. Maika, 'Commerce and Community,' 92, 101; Luuc Kooijmans, 'De Koopman,' 72.
105. GAA, NA 1096/338, 338v (March 30, 1651).
106. *CJVR*, 75, 77; Jacobs, *Een zegenrijk gewest*, 226.
107. W. de Vries, 'De Van Rensselaer's in Nederland,' 203-4.
108. *CJVR*, 5.
109. H. Klompmaker, *Handel in de Gouden Eeuw* (Bussum, 1966), 109-10; Frijhoff and Spies, *1650*, 238; see also Kooijmans, 'De koopman,' 87.
110. J.I. Israel, *Dutch Primacy in World Trade, 1585-1740* (Oxford: Clarendon Press, 1989), translated as *Nederland als centrum van de wereldhandel 1585-1740* (Franeker: Uitgeverij Van Wijnen, 1991), 77-78.
111. De Vries and Van der Woude, *Nederland 1500-1815*, 165-66.
112. Frijhoff and Spies, *1650*, 19-22; see also Maika, 'Commerce and Community,' 84-85.
113. Israel, *Dutch Primacy*, 76-77.
114. Ibid., 78-79.
115. Frijhoff and Spies, *1650*, 20.
116. In the Dutch Republic, a widow often used her maiden name or a combination of this and her married name. Anna van Wely, after her husband's death, signed her letters with 'Anna van Rensselaer'; Jeremias also addressed her this way in his letters.
117. *CJVR*, 12-14, 27-28, 36, 38, 39, 41, 46.
118. According to Jacobs, the average trip lasted about 93 days. The fastest journey, Jacobs found, lasted 51 days, while the return journey took 55 days. Jacobs, personal communication, August-September 2001.
119. *VRBM*, 355-89.
120. Ibid., 580-603.
121. *CJVR*, 12-14.
122. NYHS, Stuyvesant-Rutherford Papers, 2:6 (November 1, 1647).
123. De Vries and Van der Woude, *Nederland 1500-1815*, 171.
124. Maika, 'Commerce and Community,' 84.
125. *CJVR*, 30, 45.

126. Ibid., 73, 106, 114; J. Parker, *The World for a Market Place: Episodes in the History of European Expansion* (Minneapolis, Minn: Associates of James Ford Bell Library, 1978), 79.

127. *CJVR*, 90.

128. Ibid., 22, 29.

129. Israel, *Dutch Primacy*, 74-75.

130. De Vries and Van der Woude, *Nederland 1500-1815*, 184.

131. Klompmaker, *Handel in de Gouden Eeuw*, 109; Kooijmans, 'De koopman,' 86.

132. *CJVR*, 207.

133. Rink, *Holland on the Hudson*, 196, 197; *VRBM*, 323; GAA, NA 1045/120-121, 121v (August 8, 1636).

134. Rink, *Holland on the Hudson*, 198-99; see also *VRBM*, 399-401, 403, 405, 670.

135. *CJVR*, 133-34, 137-39, 150, 153.

136. Ibid., 246.

137. Rink, *Holland on the Hudson*, 200.

138. GAA, NA 2793/515-17 (April 9, 1661); *CJVR*, 260, 266.

139. *LWA*, 65-66; Rink, *Holland on the Hudson*, 207.

140. *CJVR*, 276, 292, 296, 320, 345.

141. Ibid., 405.

142. Cuyper was also involved in other Van Rensselaer undertakings. In November 1661, he, Van Rensselaer, Gerrit Arentsz Zuyck, and Abel de Wolff jointly chartered *De Rode Roseboom* and *De Bonte Coe*. GAA, NA 1143/150 (November 9, 1662); in March 1663, they chartered together another journey of *De Bonte Coe*. GAA, NA 1368/43 (March 21, 1663); in December 1663, Cuyper and Van Rensselaer bought the flute (*fluytschip*) *Eendracht*, and in 1664 sent it for a journey to New Netherland and back. After it returned a profit for the investors, they sold the ship to Johan Philip Silvercroon. Rink, *Holland on the Hudson*, 185; GAA, NA 2224/32, 33 (May 5, 1667); ibid., 2223/913 (April 27, 1667); in 1667, Cuyper and Abel de Wolff outfitted and supervised the successful enterprise of *De Orangeboom*, in which Verbrugge, Van Rensselaer, Zuyck, and Van Hoornbeeck also participated. Through Abel de Wolff, Cuyper may have been involved in the trading company that was founded by De Wolff, Jan Baptist van Rensselaer, Gillis van Hoornbeeck, Jacob Venturin, and Cornelis Jacobsz Mooij in February 1668, but which was dissolved in 1669 when the English king withdrew the seven-year freedom to trade with New York and the surrounding areas. Maika, 'Commerce and Community,' 141.

143. Rink, *Holland on the Hudson*, 176-77.

144. Maika, 'Commerce and Community,' 131.

145. *CJVR*, 342, 345, 346.

146. Carel H. Jansen, 'A Dutch Family's Ties with Colonial America: II,' in *DHM* 40, no. 3 (October 1965), 13. Den Heijer writes that the name *Greinkust* is derived from a kind of pepper, *grein* (*Goud, ivoor en slaven*, 71). With thanks to Jaap Jacobs.

147. GAA, NA 2223/913 (April 27, 1667); NA 2225/39-40 (September 3, 1667); NA 2845/.. (February 3, 1667).

148. Maika, 'Commerce and Community,' 141.

149. GAA NA, 2790/663, 664 (August 20, 1669).

150. Maika, 'Commerce and Community,' 148.

151. Rink, *Holland on the Hudson*, 200.

152. *VRBM*, 790, 795; GAA NA: 4058/227 (October 18, 1672); NA 2243/309-311 (January 31, 1674); NA 3777/279-81 (June 14, 1674); NA 2629/... (June 12, 1676).

153. Rink, *Holland on the Hudson*, 200.

154. GAA, NA 1300/1 (January 6, 1651).

155. NYSA, NYCM 13: 138 (August 7, 1653).

156. NYSA, NYCM 9: 213 (May 11, 1660); CCS, 21ᵛ.

157. *CJVR*, 256-57.

158. *VRBM*, 142-43, art. 12.

159. Maika, 'Commerce and Community,' 107; see also Jacobs, *Een zegenrijk gewest*, 223-24, 462.

160. *LWA*, 63, 65-66.
161. *CJVR*, 29; *ERA* 1, p. 244. Adding the numbers gives a different outcome, as the one of 40,940 provided between brackets by Prof. Pearson.
162. Maika, 'Commerce and Community,' 223.
163. *CJVR*, 29.
164. Ibid., 53-57, 62-63; see also ibid., 345, and Kooijmans, 'De koopman,' 75.
165. *CJVR*, 29, 55; NYSL, VRMP box 43 (September, October, April through August 1655).
166. Dennis Maika's dissertation ('Commerce and Community') discusses these merchants; see also Jacobs, *Een zegenrijk gewest*, 483-85.
167. *CJVR*, 273.
168. Ibid., 104, 106, 107.
169. *FOCM*, 304.
170. *CJVR*, 104, 106, 107; Trelease, *Indian Affairs*, 124; Jennings, *The Ambiguous Iroquois Empire*, 108.
171. *CJVR*, 104, 106, 115.
172. Ibid., 160, 173.
173. Shattuck, 'A Civil Society,' 252.
174. *CJVR*, 168.
175. Ibid., 168, 170, 175; *DAB*, 46-66; *VRBM*, 840.
176. Ibid., 237, 240.
177. *DAB*, 67-78.
178. NYSA, NYCM 13: 123 (September 13, 1660); ibid., 131, 6 (October 6, 1660).
179. *CJVR*, 218, 227, 229, 232.
180. Ibid., 255.
181. Ibid., 261-62.
182. Ibid., 268.
183. *ERA* 3, pp. 110-14.
184. Ibid., pp. 109-16.
185. *CJVR*, 261, 269, 263-64.
186. Ibid., 296, 298-99.
187. Ibid., 304-5; *ERA* 3, p. 115.
188. *CJVR*, 326, 329, 332.
189. Maika, 'Commerce and Community,' 118-23.
190. *CJVR*, 254-56, 271, 273.
191. Ibid., 293, 299.
192. Ibid., 317, 333, 337.
193. De Vries and Van der Woude, *Nederland 1500-1815*, 482-83; *CJVR*, 413.
194. *CJVR*, 321, 325, 333-34, 342, 350, 355, 357-58a, 363, 364, 367-68, 368.
195. Simon Hart, 'Een bijdrage tot de geschiedenis van de houthandel,' (Hart, *Geschrift en Getal*), 85; *CJVR*, 184-85, 217-18.
196. *CJVR*, 184-85, 217-18, 235.
197. Ibid., 357, 358, 358a, 359, 363.
198. R.C. Ritchie, *The Duke's Province*, 22. See also Rink, *Holland on the Hudson*, 263. The English used the Julian calendar, where the first day of the year was March 25 (old style). It lagged ten days behind the modern Gregorian calendar, which had already been adopted by the Dutch (new style). The 11th of January was now reckoned as the first.
199. Rink, *Holland on the Hudson*, 200; Maika, 'Commerce and Community,' 148.
200. *CJVR*, 424.
201. *VRBM*, 244.
202. Jacobs, *Een zegenrijk gewest*, 227-28.
203. Kooijmans, 'De koopman,' 78.
204. *FOCM*, 30.
205. Ibid., 29; CCS, 109v.
206. CCS, 108.

207. *CJVR*, 29, 242.
208. Ibid., 387.
209. *ERA* 1, pp. 241-42 (doc. 131: 'door indusie en pesuasie van eenige smoeshanen ende groot-sprekers die bestier over de colony sijn hebbende').
210. Frijhoff and Spies, *1650*, 86.
211. CCS, 45 (September 7, 1652); see also Venema, 'A 1652 Letter by Jan Baptist van Rensselaer,' in *DHM* 75 (1), 12.
212. *ERA* 1, pp. 241-42.
213. Ibid., pp. 12-13, 38; Patents, vol. 2, part 2, no. 34: The lot was on the east side 4 rods, 8 feet broad, on the west side 6.5 rods; in length it was on the south side 19 rods, and on the north side 16 rods, 10 feet.
214. *ERA* 1, pp. 292, 361; *ERA* 4, p. 13; *CJVR*, 268-69, 270.
215. NYSA, The New York Colonial Patents Books, Albany 1664-1690. (Patents). The translation in Patents, vol.2, pt. 2, 35 describes the property as follows: 'lot, house and garden in Beverwijck. West of Caspar Jacobsz, length 34 rods, to east 35 rods; breadth to south, 22 rods, to south of the plain 14 rods.' The original text for the *LP* reads .' . . een erff tot huys en tuyn gelegen aende fortresse Orangie inden durpe Beverwijck, ten westen Casper Jacobsz, lanck vier en dertich roeden, ten suyden breet, twee en twintich roeden, ten oosten lanck vijffendertich roeden ten suyden het pleyn breet veertien roeden,' which literally translates as 'to the west Caspar Jacobsz' and 'to the south the plain' (*LP*, 94). The translation of the patent clearly reveals the problem one faces if one attempts to locate the properties of Beverwijck inhabitants: How can one trust the existing patents, of which only the translation remains?
216. *CJVR*, 176.
217. Ibid., 176-77.
218. NYSL, VRMP box 37 (August 23, 1659).
219. Ibid. (June 24, 1659; January 30, 1660; January 10, 1660).
220. NYSL, VRMP box 37 (June 18, 1661); see also NYSA, NYCM 9: 225 (September 4, 1660).
221. *CJVR*, 223-24.
222. Ibid., 238, 266. The original reads 'leedekant met behansel.' See Johan A. Kamermans, *Materiële cultuur in de Krimpenerwaard in de zeventiende en achttiende eeuw. Ontwikkeling en diversiteit* (Wageningen: A.A.G. Bijdragen, 1999), 82-83; see also Hester Dibbits, *Vertrouwd bezit. Materiële cultuur in Doesburg en Maassluis, 1650-1800* (Nijmegen: SUN, 2001), 90-91. With thanks to Hester Dibbits.
223. *ERA* 1, p. 350.
224. H. Dibbits, *Vertrouwd bezit*, 89.
225. Fock, *Het Nederlandse Interieur*, 23, 104.
226. Dibbits, *Vertrouwd bezit*, 89-91.
227. *ERA* 1, p. 255; Dibbits, *Vertrouwd bezit*, 88. Kamermans, *Materiële cultuur*, 83.
228. Thera F. Wijsenbeek-Olthuis, *Achter de gevels van Delft. Bezit en bestaan van rijk en arm in een periode van achteruitgang (1700-1800)* (Hilversum: Verloren, 1987), 192; see, for example, *FOCM*, 257.
229. *CJVR*, 238; Thera Wijsenbeek-Olthuis, 'Vreemd en eigen: ontwikkelingen in de woon- en leefcultuur binnen de Hollandse steden van de zestiende tot de negentiende eeuw,' (Te Boekhorst, *Cultuur en Maatschappij*), 97.
230. *CJVR*, 136; *ERA* 1, p. 83.
231. *CJVR*, 238 (author's translation; the original reads 'een valletie voor de schoorsteen'), 136, 387. For mirrors and mantlepieces, see Fock, *Het Nederlands Interieur*, 31, 44-45, 94, 109-10.
232. *ERA* 1, p. 249.
233. Ad van der Woude, 'The Volume and Value of Paintings in Holland at the Time of the Dutch Republic,' in David Freedberg and Jan de Vries (eds.), *Art in History: History in Art. Studies in Seventeenth-Century Dutch Culture* (Santa Monica, Calif.: University of Chicago Press, 1992), 297, 303, 309; see also Ad van der Woude, 'De schilderijenproductie in Holland tijdens de Republiek. Een poging to kwantificatie,' in A. Schuurman, et al., *Aards geluk. De Neder-*

landers en hun spullen, 1550-1850 (Amsterdam: Balans, 1997), 239-43; Fock, *Het Nederlands interieur*, 44-45, 109-10.

234. Van der Woude, 'The Volume and Value of Paintings in Holland,' 302; Frijhoff and Spies, *1650*, 496.
235. NYSL, VRMP box 37 (November 2, 1662); *CJVR*, 316, 357-58.
236. *CJVR*, 123, 263, 298, 316, 329.
237. Ibid., 372.
238. Kamermans, *Materiële cultuur*, 211; Bibi Panhuysen, *Maatwerk. Kleermakers, naaisters, oud-kleerkopers en de gilden (1500-1800)* (Amsterdam: Stichting beheer IISG, 2000), 92.
239. *ERA* 1, pp. 340, 343-44; Dibbits, *Vertrouwd bezit*, 195.
240. Dibbits, *Vertrouwd bezit*, 194-95, quotes Le Francq van Berkhey, *Natuurlyke Historie* 3 (2): 799; Kamermans, *Materiële cultuur*, 211-12; *ERA* 1, pp. 89, 87-90.
241. Kamermans,, *Materiële cultuur*, 211-12.
242. NYSL, VRMP box 43 (1659; 1659; July 8, 1661?), box 29, (July 29, 1658).
243. Panhuysen, *Maatwerk*, 92; *ERA* 1, pp. 88-89; M. Conrads and G. Zwartjes, *Tirions Kostuum-gids. Westerse kledingstijlen van de vroege middeleeuwen tot heden* (Baarn: Tirion, 1993), 48.
244. J.H. der Kinderen-Besier, *Spelevaart der mode. De kledij onzer voorouders in de zeventiende eeuw* (Amsterdam: N.V.EM. Querido's Uitgeversmaatschappij, 1950), 135, 170-74; Panhuysen, *Maatwerk*, 94. With thanks to Hester Dibbits.
245. *ERA* 1, p. 89; NYSL, VRMP, box 43 (December 14, 1660); Der Kinderen-Besier, *Spelevaart der mode*, 135-36.
246. Der Kinderen-Besier, *Spelevaart der mode*, 136-37.
247. *ERA* 1, p. 88; NYSL, VRMP, box 43 (November 26, 1659; 1660); Panhuysen, *Maatwerk*, 94.
248. Der Kinderen-Besier, *Spelevaart der mode*, 138-41; Conrads and Zwartjes, *Tirions Kostuum-gids*, 61.
249. *CJVR*, 16, 132; see also Der Kinderen-Besier, *Spelevaart der mode*, 137-38.
250. *CJVR*, 110, 241; the original for coat reads 'keelt,' which may be the same as 'kiel,' a wide and short outer garment.
251. *CJVR*, 60; the word 'breeches' is not readable due to damage to the document.
252. Der Kinderen-Besier, *Spelevaart der mode*, 174.
253. *CJVR*, 266, 271-72.
254. Ibid., 63.
255. *ERA* 4, p. 112; Der Kinderen-Besier, *Spelevaart der mode*, 153.
256. *CJVR*, 104.
257. Groenhuis, *De predikanten*, 55.
258. NYSL, VRMP, box 43 (July 29, 1658; 1659, 1660, 1661; the documents are badly damaged by the 1911 fire, so that it is not possible to see the precise dates).
259. Der Kinderen-Besier, *Spelevaart der mode*, 144-45.
260. Ibid., 147.
261. Ibid., 152; Panhuysen, *Maatwerk*, 93-94.
262. NYSL, VRMP box 45 (tailor accounts 1668-71); the women's clothes were named in the original 'rijghlijfjes, mantelties, voorschote, borsrockies, halsdoecken, nachthalsdoecken,' and for children were mentioned 'overtrecsels, borsrockies, rock, pak, leybande, schort, befjes, tabbertien, aperockjens.'
263. *ERA* 3, p. 117; *ERA* 1, p. 85.
264. Dibbits, *Vertrouwd bezit*, 200-2.
265. *CJVR*, 232; GAA NA 604/265 (May 8, 1652).
266. Kooijmans, 'De koopman,' 88.
267. *CJVR*, 9.
268. Kooijmans, *Vriendschap*, 328.
269. Ibid., 326.
270. Frijhoff and Spies, *1650*, 213-16; Kooijmans, 'De koopman,' 80-81.
271. *CJVR*, 145-46, 170, 173, 191-92, 192-95, 212-13.

272. Kooijmans, 'De koopman,' 79, 80; about friendship, see also the forthcoming dissertation by Irma Thoen, 'The Gift in Seventeenth-Century Holland.'

273. Kooijmans, *Vriendschap*, 326-27.

274. *CJVR*, 147, 178, 191, 247.

275. Kooijmans, *Vriendschap*, 327-28.

276. Kooijmans, 'De Koopman,' 77.

277. *CJVR*, 214.

278. Ibid., 181, 214.

279. Ibid., 319, 334, 343.

280. Ibid., 15, 17.

281. Ibid., 332.

282. *FOCM*, 173, 174.

283. NYSL, VRMP box 43 (April-August and September-October 1655). In Van Rensselaer's accounts, it is also named 'trocken'; the line in his accounts: 'op den trock verdient ... f ...' suggests that he won money playing the game. The *trokspel* was a precursor of the *biljart* game. *WNT*, 3085.

284. *CJVR*, 148, 159, 229, 307.

285. A.J.F. van Laer, 'Evert Nolden, the First Schoolmaster of Rensselaerswijck,' in *DSSYB* 17 (1941-42), 13.

286. NYSL, VRMP box 43 (due to fire damage, the dates of this account are hard to read, and seem to mention 1660 and May 16, 1662, but these dates could also be 1664 and 1667).

287. *CJVR*, 297, 333; NYSL, VRMP box 37 (January 22, 1663); *CMVR*, 37.

288. *CJVR*, 317, 333.

289. NYSL, VRMP box 43 (October 4 and 17, 1663).

290. *ERA* 1, p. 353.

291. *CMVR*, 51; *CJVR*, 370.

292. Robert G. Wheeler, 'The House of Jeremias van Rensselaer, 1658-1666,' in *New York Historical Society Quarterly* (January 1961), 86.

293. *CJVR*, 37; see also 78, 131.

294. Ibid., 99, 131.

295. Frijhoff and Spies (*1650*, 369-70) mention P. Wittewrongel, *Oeconomia christiana*; Groenhuis, *De predikanten*, 46-47; Frijhoff (*Wegen van Evert Willemsz*, 355-61) mentions, for further literature on the Nadere Reformatie, L.F. Groenendijk, *De Nadere Reformatie van het gezin. De visie van Petrus Wittewrongel op de christelijke huishouding* (Dordrecht, 1984), especially pp. 18-34; F.A. van Lieburg, *De Nadere Reformatie in Utrecht ten tijde van Voetius* (Rotterdam: Boek en muziek, 1989), and *Levens van vromen. Gereformeerd pietisme in de achttiende eeuw* (Kampen, 1991), 175-99; G.J. Schutte, 'Nederland: Een calvinistische natie?' in *Bijdragen en mededelingen betreffende de geschiedenis der Nederlanden* 107 (1992), 690-702); J.P. Heering and F. Hoppenbrouwers, *Katholieke en protestantse spiritualiteit rond 1650* ('s-Gravenhage, 1995).

296. Frijhoff and Spies, *1650*, 591; David Beck, *Spiegel van mijn leven; een Haags dagboek uit 1624* (ed. Sv.E. Veldhuizen; Hilversum: Verloren, 1993), 52, 62, 117, 121, 138.

297. *CJVR*, 231.

298. Ibid., 13.

299. *DAB*, 184, 200, 210, 252.

300. *CJVR*, 300, 322; Joyce Goodfriend, 'Recovering the Religious History of Dutch Reformed Women in Colonial New York,' *DHM* 64, no. 4 (winter 1991): 55.

301. Van der Heijden, *Huwelijk in Holland.*, 61-63.

302. Haks, *Huwelijk en gezin in Holland*, 119, 121, 122; Van der Heijden, *Huwelijk in Holland*, 15; Roodenburg, *Onder Censuur*, 236-44. For Claes Ripsz, see *FOCM*, 162-63, 171.

303. *ERA* 3, p. 251.

304. Haks, *Huwelijk en gezin*, 65, 115; Van der Heijden, *Huwelijk in Holland*, 65.

305. Haks, *Huwelijk en gezin*, 65.

306. *CJVR*, 60.

307. Frijhoff and Spies, *1650*, 30.

308. *CJVR*, 292-94, 295.
309. Ibid., 296-97.
310. Haks, *Huwelijk en gezin*, 117; Van der Heijden, *Huwelijk in Holland*, 67.
311. Van der Heijden, *Huwelijk in Holland*, 193.
312. *CJVR*, 300-1.
313. Ibid., 328-29, 349, 367.
314. Haks, *Huwelijk en gezin*, 106, 138, 151.
315. De Roever, 'Kiliaen van Rensselaer en zijne kolonie Rensselaerswijck,' in *Oud Holland* 8 (Amsterdam, 1890), 34.
316. Kooijmans, 'De koopman,' 86; N. de Roever, 'Kilaen van Rensselaer,' 37; Rink, *Holland on the Hudson*, 195.
317. For Crailo, see A.P. Kooyman-van Rossum and D.F. Winnen, *Crailo. De geschiedenis van een landgoed* (Bussum: Spieghelprint, 1986).
318. J.H. Innes, *New Amsterdam and its People. Studies, Social and Topographical of the Town under Dutch and Early English Rule* (Port Washington, N.Y.: Ira J. Friedman, 1902/1969), 75-79; for his position as deacon, see also Frijhoff, *Wegen van Evert Willemsz*, 756-59.
319. *VRBM*, 433, 621, 655.
320. Nissenson, *The Patroon's Domain*, 343-50.
321. NYSL, VRMP box 37 (June 1 and 21, 1662); see also Blackburn and Piwonka, *Remembrance of Patria*, 53.
322. *CJVR*, 328; the translation says 'chickenpox,' but Jeremias wrote 'kinderpockjens,' which means 'smallpox.'
323. Benjamin Roberts, *Through the Keyhole: Dutch Child-Rearing Practises in the 17th and 18th Century. Three Urban Elite Families* (Hilversum: Verloren, 1998), 93.
324. *CJVR*, 328.
325. Roberts, *Through the Keyhole*, 92, 93.
326. *DAB*, 94-107.
327. *CJVR*, 328-29, 348, 349.
328. J. Goodfriend, 'Recovering the Religious History,' 57; see also Roberts, *Through the Keyhole*, 72.
329. *CJVR*, 368.
330. Ibid., 367, 384-85. For a detailed description of Maria's disease, see Christoph, 'Worthy, Virtuous Juffrouw Maria van Rensselaer.'
331. Christoph, 'Worthy, Virtuous Juffrouw Maria van Rensselaer,' 26-27.
332. *CJVR*, 377-78.
333. Ibid., 326, 380, 394, 417, 432, 472; *CMVR*, 14n.
334. Roberts, *Through the Keyhole*, 78.
335. *CJVR*, 432.
336. *FOCM*, 71.
337. Roberts, *Through the Keyhole*, 78.
338. *CJVR*, 326-27.
339. Ibid., 326, 328, 380, 394; children were named after close family members, usually first after the grandfather from the father's side, then grandmother from the mother's side, the grandfather from mother's side, and the grandmother from father's side. After that came uncles and aunts, and sometimes other relatives or 'friends.' Frijhoff, *Wegen van Evert Willemsz*, 134-35.
340. G. Groenhuis, *De predikanten*, 59-60.
341. *CJVR*, 326-27.
342. Groenhuis, *De predikanten*, 60.
343. *CJVR*, 358b, 364, 367.
344. *CMVR*, 23.
345. Groenhuis, *De predikanten*, 61.
346. Roberts, *Through the Keyhole*, 148; Rudolf Dekker, *Uit de schaduw*, 207, 211.
347. *CJVR*, 329.
348. Dirk Damsma, *Het Hollandse huisgezin 1560-heden* (Utrecht/Antwerpen: Kosmos-Z&K Uitgevers, 1993), 39; *DAB*, 37-120.

349. *CJVR*, 417; *CMVR*, 57.
350. *CJVR*, 348, 364, 377, 382.
351. Ibid., 386.
352. *VRBM*, 551, 563, 646.
353. *CJVR*, 387, 399-400; see also NYSL, VRMP box 39 (1666 in Memorandum book, 1658-67).
354. *CJVR*, 400.
355. Ibid., 358b, 399, 400, 403.
356. Ibid., 133.
357. CCS, 43; *CJVR*, 343.
358. *CJVR*, 133, 204, 215, 234, 300, 301, 350; Nissenson, *The Patroon's Domain*, 343-45.
359. *CJVR*, 364.
360. Ibid., 225, 241, 392, 416. By 'wilde lant,' he likely meant a land of uncultivated non-Europeans.
361. Ibid., 378, 443, 472.
362. Van Laer, 'Evert Nolden, the First Schoolmaster,' 13.
363. *CMVR*, 57.
364. 'Abstract of Wills,' in *Collections of the New York Historical Society* (New York, 1893), 216.

Chapter 4

1. Although they certainly were principal traders, the six sitting magistrates at that time did not sign either one of the petitions: Sander Leendertsz Glen, Andries Herbertsz, and Evert Jansz Wendel expressed their opinion in court that neither Indians nor Christians ought to run into the woods as brokers; Jan Verbeeck and Frans Barentsz Pastoor found that the matter should be regulated according to the vote of the majority of the community. Goosen Gerritsz, Jan Labatie, Pieter Hartgers, and François Boon, Stoffel Jansz Abeel, Cornelis Theunisz Bos, and Jan Hendricksz van Bael, who had been or would become magistrates, as well as Jeremias van Rensselaer, surgeon Jacob de Hinsse, and the agents Gerrit Bancker and Harmen Albertsz Vedder did not sign either, although they can be considered to have been principal traders with an interest in using Indian brokers (*FOCM*, 491-92).
2. Seven of the twenty-five petitioners who requested the use of Indian brokers at some time had occupied the office of magistrate; three others would occupy the bench in 1664, and one in 1673. See Appendix 5.
3. Abraham Staets, Volckert Jansz Douw, Cornelis Theunisz van Westbroeck, Jan Labatie, Pieter Hartgers, Rutger Jacobsz, Sander Leendertsz Glen, Jan Verbeeck, Jan Thomasz, and Goosen Gerritsz van Schaick came to Rensselaerswijck between 1635 and 1645; Dirck Jansz Croon, Jacob Jansz Schermerhoorn, Evert Jansz Wendel, Gerrit van Slichtenhorst, and Andries Herbertsz came in the late 1640s; Philip Pietersz Schuyler came in 1650; the magistrates Adriaen Gerritsz Papendorp, François Boon and Frans Barentsz Pastoor, Jan Hendricksz van Bael, Jan Koster van Aecken and Stoffel Jansz Abeel are not mentioned in Beverwijck's records until 1653.
4. See also Shattuck, 'A Civil Society,' 275, 277-280, 291.
5. Jacobs, *Een zegenrijk gewest*, 485-86; Venema, 'For the Benefit of the Poor,' 231-32; see also Appendix 5.
6. Gerard Rooseboom, *Recueil*, 18, 20. See also Frijhoff and Spies, *1650*, 195.
7. NYHS, Stuyvesant-Rutherford Papers: Letter by Govert Loockermans to Gillis and Seth Verbrugge, likely of date April 27, 1647.
8. *VRBM*, 840; *MCR*, 208; Patents vol. 2, part 2, no. 24; see also *ERA* 1, pp. 269, 330; *ERA* 4, pp. 7, 47, 106.
9. Merwick, *Possessing Albany*, 111; GAA, NA 1366/39 (March 4, 1662); *ERA* 3, pp. 133, 134, 171.
10. GAA, NA 1575/II 35 (February 27, 1651); GAA, NA 3941/202-211 (January 27, 1680); GAA, ondertrouwboeken, no. 482, p. 197; GAA, poorterboeck, part 2, p. 123 (July 18, 1662). Rijc-

kertsz received a patent in 1653 for a lot, garden, house and yard north of *Jonckerstraet.* NYSA, Patents, vol. 2, part 2, no. 16.

11. *FOCM*, 3, 54.
12. Ibid., 206, 294, 463, 466.
13. GAA, NA 1579/428 (November 7, 1656).
14. GAA, NA 1307/49v (February 15, 1657).
15. GAA, NA 1355/43 (April 1, 1657).
16. GAA, NA 1127/181-181v (November 19, 1658).
17. For example, GAA, NA 1108/171, 172v (May 20, 1654), and GAA, NA 1307/67 (March 15, 1657).
18. Patents, vol. 2, part 2, no 43; De Roever, 'Merchandises,' 79, 82.
19. *FOCM*, 122, 358, 390.
20. Ibid., 466, 509; *ERA* 1, pp. 270, 277, 391.
21. *FOCM*, 173.
22. GAA, NA 2686/... (February 27, 1657).
23. GAA, Ondertrouwboecken, no. 482, 197. This record does not mention any previous wife for Croon, which suggests that he was not the Dirck Jansz who married Jannetie Teunis in December 1641. This Dirck Jansz married Geertie Jans van St Marten in North Holland after Jannetie's death in October 1659. Samuel S. Purple, 'Records of the Reformed Dutch church in New Amsterdam and New York. Marriages from 11 December 1639 to 26 August 1801,' in *Collections of the New York Genealogical and Biographical Society* 1 (New York, 1890; reprinted in 1961), 11, 24; Shattuck, 'A Civil Society,' 144, 146.
24. GAA, NA 1364/132 (October 12, 1661).
25. GAA, NA 1363/73v-74 (April 27, 1661); see also *ERA* 3, pp. 83, and NYSA, NYCM 9: 711-13; Rink, *Holland on the Hudson*, 178, 180-191, 202; see also NYSA, NYCM 10: 287, 293.
26. *ERA* 1, pp. 350; GAA, Ondertrouwboeken no. 482, 197 (30 July, 1661); GAA NA 1366/39 (4 March, 1662).
27. GAA, Ondertrouwboek no. 474, p. 411 (June 10, 1655); Poorterboek, no. 1, p. 178 (February 15, 1656).
28. GAA, NA 1346/12v (March 9, 1651); NA 2297III/25-27 (December 28, 1668). See also *FOCM*, 200; Rink mentions that Cuyper stayed in New Netherland. Rink, *Holland on the Hudson*, 191.
29. *FOCM*, 195; *RNA* 1, p. 125. A document of the April, 1658 council minutes could provide a clue as to whether he was involved in his brother's company at all, but unfortunately the document is damaged and partially unreadable; the text reads '[consigned?] by Gerrit Jansz Kuyper to Jeuriaen Jansz 3 small chests ...' NYSA, NYCM 8, p. 848.
30. GAA, NA 2323/129-31 (February 5, 1684).
31. During the following years, Wijntie's husband Pieter Bogardus repeatedly bothered Groenwout and accused him in court of fraud regarding the estate of Wijntie's mother, *CMARS* 1, pp. 116, 119, 128, 135, 153, 165, 175, 230, 244, 244; *CMARS* 3, pp. 352, 355.
32. *CMARS* 3, p. 353.
33. *ERA* 1, pp. 277-78; *DAB*, 57.
34. GAA, NA 2787/776, 777 (December 31, 1668); Patents 2, part 2, no. 43 (October 23, 1653).
35. *ERA* 3, pp. 270; GAA, NA 2459/121-122 (March 16, 1660); GAA, NA 1369/78 (July 27, 1663); GAA, NA 2787/776-777, (31 December, 1668).
36. See Appendix 6; *FOCM*, 491; *DAB*, 122, 134, 159.
37. *VRBM*, 846; *DAB*, 200, 210, 221.
38. A.J.F. van Laer, 'Letters to Adriaen Gerritsen van Papendorp,' in *DSSYB* 16, pp. 1, 3-6; Appendix 6; *FOCM*, 491; *DAB*, 46, 56, 66, 68, 108, 122, 134; *ERA* 1, pp. 350, 391; *ERA* 3, pp. 251.
39. GAA, NA 1371/61v-62v, 63 (April 17, 1664).
40. GAA, NA 2218/497, 498 (March 7, 1665).
41. GAA, NA 1606/3A-46 (July 18, 1669); see also NA, 1606/3H33, 313v (February 20, 1671), and Van Laer, 'Letters to Adriaen Gerritsen Papendorp,' 2-3.
42. GAA, NA 3205/311-13 (November 28, 1670).

43. Van Laer, 'Letters to Adriaen Gerritsen van Papendorp,' 3-6.
44. *ERA* 1, pp. 270, 277, 350-52, 391; *ERA* 2, pp. 46; *FOCM*: 509.
45. GAA, NA 3941/202-211 (January 27, 1680); see also Van Laer, 'Letters to Adriaen Gerritsen van Papendorp,' 8-9.
46. GAA, NA3941/2002-211 (January 27, 1680).
47. GAA, NA 491/357 (August 24, 1643).
48. Frijhoff, *Wegen van Evert Willemsz*, 624.
49. Thomas Grier Evans (ed.), Records of the Reformed Church in New Amsterdam and New York. Baptisms from 25 December 1639 to 27 December, 1730 (N.Y. 1901; reprint 1968), 26.
50. Frijhoff, *Wegen van Evert Willemsz*, 648; GAA, NA 2035/545 (April 27, 1655).
51. NYSL, VRMP, box 29, Van Slichtenhorst book, 45v (1649, 1650) *Patents* 2, part 2, no. 66; *VRBM*, 834; *FOCM*, 70, 231; *ERA* 1, pp. 267, 269-70; *ERA* 4, pp. 10.
52. *ERA* 3, p. 212.
53. *FOCM*, 173.
54. *VRBM*, 834.
55. *ERA* 1, p. 219.
56. *VRBM*, 834; *FOCM*, 319; *DAB*, 14.
57. *FOCM*, 445; GAA, NA 2659/.. (December 18, 1660).
58. *VRBM*, 834; Appendix 5.
59. *FOCM*, 16, 79, 129, 187, 213.
60. Ibid., 446, 453, 456-60, 486.
61. Ibid., 224.
62. *DAB*, 1, 19, 27, 37, 46.
63. *ERA* 3, p. 263.
64. *FOCM*, 248-49. According to the translation, Femmetge was granted letters of divorce, but the original text says that she was given '*een brieff van vrijheijt*,' meaning a letter of freedom.
65. *ERA* 1, p. 47.
66. GAA, NA 1307/49 (February 15, 1657); *FOCM*, 319, 322-23, 327; *ERA* 1, p. 47; J. Pearson, *Contributions for the Genealogies of the First Settlers of the Ancient County of Albany, from 1630 to 1800* (Albany, N.Y.: J. Munsell), 131.
67. Haks, *Huwelijk en gezin*, 70-73, 78-82.
68. *DAB*, 45.
69. *CJVR*, 196, 201, 206, 208, 221, 244, 288; GAA, NA 2459/121-122 (March 16, 1660); GAA, NA 1369/78 (July 27, 1663). *CJVR*, 313, 315, 324-25, 331, 352, 358a, 362, 376, 390, 405.
70. *CJVR*, 196, 201, 206, 208, 221, 244, 246; GAA, NA 2659/... (December 18, 1660); GAA, NA 2479/324 (December 11, 1660).
71. *ERA* 4, p. 40; *ERA* 2, p. 286.
72. *ERA* 1, pp. 267, 269, 270; *ERA* 4, pp. 10, 100.
73. *ERA* 3, pp. 212, 213, 120.
74. *ERA* 1, p. 306; *ERA* 3, pp. 174, 120, 212; *ERA* 1, p. 421; *ERA* 2, pp. 367; *ERA* 3, p. 266.
75. *FOCM*, 140; Innes, *New Amsterdam and Its People*, 79-80.
76. Handwritten comment by the translator and editor, A.J.F. van Laer, in the copy of *ERA* 3 at the NNP, 60.
77. *ERA* 4, p. 40; *ERA* 2, p. 286.
78. *CJVR*, 386; *ERA* 1, pp. 86, 269, 270; *ERA* 4, p. 10.
79. *ERA* 1, p. 421; *ERA* 2, p. 367; *ERA* 3, p. 266.
80. *CJVR*, 319-20.
81. *ERA* 3, p. 174; *ERA* 1, p. 421.
82. GAA, NA 2738/38, 39, 43, 45 (January 11, 1664).
83. *CJVR*, 400; refers to State Historian, *Second Annual Report*, 1896 (Colonial Series 1), 187.
84. Peter Christoph (ed.), *Administrative Papers of Governors Richard Nicolls and Francis Lovelace, 1664-1673* (Baltimore, Md.: Genealogical, 1980), 38, 40; Carel H. Jansen, 'A Dutch Family's Ties with Colonial America: II,' in *DHM* 40, no. 3 (October 1965), 14; *DAB*, 1698; see also Venema, 'For the Benefit of the Poor,' 179, 182-83; *ERA* 3, p. 205.

85. GAA, Ondertrouwboek, no. 503, p. 453 (December 31, 1676).
86. *ERA* 3, p. 116.
87. *VRBM*, 826; Patents, vol. 2, part 2, no. 33; see also CCS, 49v (August 24, 1648); *ERA* 3, pp. 382, 383; *ERA* 2, pp. 91, 126; *ERA* 1, pp. 91, 127, 331, 332.
88. *ERA* 3, p. 483; *ERA* 1, p. 197; for more trading commitments, see *FOCM*, 115, 116.
89. GAA, Archive number 366: 254 in the leerjongensboek of the chirurgijnsboek; GAA, NA 1054/67- (February 1, 1642); CCS, 24-24v, 27 (July 11, 1648).
90. *MCR*, 70; *VRBM*, 814.
91. *FOCM*, 255; *ERA* 1, p. 74.
92. *CJVR*, 138-39, 256, 315.
93. *FOCM*, 456, 491, 498, 500.
94. *ERA* 3, p. 483.
95. *VRBM*, 826, 834; *MCR*, 70-71; *CJVR*, 232, 237; *ERA* 3, p. 483.
96. *FOCM*, 429, 434; NYSL, VRMP, box 29 (1650).
97. *CJVR*, 214.
98. *ERA* 1, p. 354; *CJVR*, 353; *CMARS* 1, pp. 157, 167; *CMARS* 3, p. 108.
99. *ERA* 3, p. 50.
100. *ERA* 1, pp. 325, 397.
101. Ibid., pp. 291, 318, 324, 325, 355; *LP*, 101.
102. *ERA* 1, pp. 334, 342, 353, 354; *CMARS* 3, pp. 455, 467.
103. *ERA* 3, p. 66.
104. Ibid., pp. 154, 208.
105. *ERA* 1, p. 213.
106. *ERA* 4, pp. 112-13.
107. *FOCM*, 119-20, 188, 236-37; Van Laer, *The Lutheran Church*, 28, 40.
108. *FOCM*, 4, 32, 36, 39, 137, 188, 425; *LO*, 211-12.
109. *DAB*, 18.
110. *WNT*, 598-99.
111. Rooseboom, *Recueil*, 18, 20; Frijhoff and Spies, *1650*, 195.
112. *CMVR*, 125; *CMARS* 3, p. 242.
113. *CMARS* 3, p. 506; Ariadne Schmidt, *Overleven in de Gouden Eeuw*, 172.
114. Florence Christoph, *Schuyler Genealogy: A Compendium of Sources Pertaining to the Schuyler Families in America Prior to 1800* (Albany, N.Y.: Friends of Schuyler Mansion, 1987), 3.
115. *VRBM*, 806, 811; Van Slichtenhorst spoke of 'Brant Pelen swaeger Goossen Gerritsen.' CCS, 43.
116. *DAB*, 25; the children were Geertie (7), Gerrit (5), and Sybrant (probably named after Brant Peelen, 3), and the newborn Antony. For naming system, see Frijhoff, *Wegen van Evert Willemsz*, 134-35.
117. *ERA* 1, pp. 327, 345.
118. *FOCM*, 173.
119. GAA, NA 2279/16-17 (May 10, 1652); *ERA* 1, p. 196.
120. *CJVR*, 158, 232, 298; *ERA* 3, p. 200.
121. *CJVR*, 331, 334, 352.
122. Ibid., 267, 268, 298.
123. Ibid., 307, 372; *ERA* 3, p. 291.
124. *ERA* 3, pp. 235, 256; *ERA* 1, p. 461; *ERA* 2, p. 36. In August 1663, Willet and Teller, at that time merchants at Fort Orange, owed Gerritsz 606 good pieces of eight at 48 *stivers* each (at ƒ1,454).
125. *FOCM*, 491.
126. Ibid., 435-36.
127. Ibid., 456, 513.
128. *ERA* 4, p. 73; *ERA* 1, pp. 87-90, 422; see also Frijhoff, 'Dominee Bogardus als Nieu-Nederlander,' in *Jaarboek van het Centraal Bureau voor Genealogie* 50 (The Hague: CBG, 1996), 66.
129. *FOCM*, 21, 33, 112, 242.
130. *ERA* 1, p. 217.
131. *LP*, 81, 95; *ERA* 1, p. 271.

132. *ERA* 1, pp. 363, 371, 417.

133. Ibid., pp. 363, 364, 415;*LP*, 101; in October 1653, Staets had a patent for a house and lot at the hill on the south side of *Jonckerstraet*. With its breadth of eight and six rods, and a length of eighteen and twenty-five rods, it was one of the largest lots in the community. Patents, vol. 2, part 2, nos. 7 and 12.

134. *ERA* 1, pp. 372, 449, 457; *ERA* 2, pp. 137, 145.

135. NYSA, NYCM 10:3, doc. 263; *ERA* 3, p. 189.

136. *ERA* 1, pp. 462, 463, 464; NYSA, NYCM 10:3: 263. See also *CMARS* 1, p. 310.

137. Appendix 5. 138. *FOCM*, 213, 323.

139. *DAB*, 15, 36, 86, 88, 101, 110; *FOCM*, 232.

140. *DAB*, 71, 73-77, 78.

141. Ibid., 134, 160, 171; *CMARS* 3, p. 280.

142. *CMARS* 2, p. 48.

143. Ibid., p. 75; *CJVR*, 267, 326, 432.

144. *CJVR*, 232; GAA, NA 604/265 (May 8, 1652); *ERA* 4, p. 85; *FOR*, 136.

145. *ERA* 3, p. 270; *ERA* 1, pp. 69-70.

146. *ERA* 3, p. 270; author's translation.

147. Dibbits, *Vertrouwd bezit*, 184; see also Panhuysen, *Maatwerk*, 104-5, and Kamermans, *Materiële Cultuur*, 219-20, 222.

148. *ERA* 1, p. 83; see also *FOR*, 136.

149. *ERA* 1, pp. 89, 222-23, 250, 344, 460; GA, NAA 604/265 (May 8, 1652); for the auction of Bogardus's estate, see also Frijhoff, 'Dominee Bogardus als Nieu-Nederlander,' 64-66.

150. *ERA* 1, pp. 83, 194.

151. Ibid., pp. 83-84, 87-90, 350-52.

152. Ibid., p. 25; p. 69 mentions a *tappeyt*, which likely was a hanging tapestry, as textile floor carpets were very rare in the seventeenth century; when they appeared, it was always near a bed. Tapestries from the east were often displayed on the wall or on a table. Fock, *Het Nederlandse Interieur*, 107.

153. Dibbits, *Vertrouwd bezit*, 117; see also Fock, *Het Nederlandse Interieur*, 36, 101, 107.

154. *ERA* 1, pp. 83-85, 351-52; for value and quality of paintings, see Van der Woude, 'The Volume and Value of Paintings,' 285-329; and John Michael Montias, 'Works of Art in Seventeenth-Century Amsterdam,' in Freedberg and De Vries, *Art in History*, 370.

155. *ERA* 1, p. 206, author's translation. Pearson read the name of the seller as Gerrit Teunisz, while I think Gabriel Leendertsz is intended; *CJVR*, 81.

156. Frijhoff and Spies, *1650*, 496.

157. Christoph, *Schuyler Genealogy*, 3-4.

158. *CMARS* 3, pp. 280, 426-27.

159. *DAB*, May 29, 1683; ibid., May 16, 1711.

160. GAA, NA 731/22 (January 12, 1639) says he is thirty-five years old.

161. GAA, NA 1054/60-65 (March 28, 1639) says he is about thirty-four years old and his wife Cathalina Jacobs is about twenty years old; GAA, ondertrouwboek no., p. 214 (October 16, 1638) says he is thirty-two years old and she is eighteen. See also Gordon L. Remington, 'The Duncanson Wives of Four New Netherland Settlers: Glen, Teller, Powell, and Loockermans,' in *NYG&BR* 128, no. 1 (January 1997): 1, 5.

162. *VRBM*, 821; *MCR*, 68.

163. A patent for the lot has not been found, and the information regarding his lot has been derived from various sources, of which none, however, mentions the actual size. *FOCM*, 97; *ERA* 1, pp. 293, 313-14; *ERA* 4, p. 98.

164. Patents, vol. 2, part 2, no. 65;*LP*, 90; NYSL, VRMP, box 29 (September 1650); Remington, 'The Duncanson Wives,' 5, n.15; CCS, 79.

165. *ERA* 1, pp. 313, 314.

166. Ibid., p. 300; *FOCM*, 184.

167. *FOCM*, 296; *ERA* 1, pp. 270, 277, 336; *ERA* 3, p. 210.

168. *LP*, 90.

169. *MCR*, 88; *LP*, 43; *CJVR*, 59.
170. *CJVR*, 214, 273, 372; *DAB*, 106; Van Laer, 'Albany Notarial Papers, 1666-1693,' 3; *ERA* 4, p. 26l; *LP*, 90; *ERA* 1, p. 345.
171. *ERA* 3, p. 111. For Leendertsz's account with Van Twiller/Mommaes, see also *CJVR*, 174, 191-92, 194-95.
172. *FOCM*, 509; *ERA* 3, pp. 86-87.
173. Appendix 5; *DAB* 19, 46, 56, 67, viii.
174. *ERA* 1, pp. 2, 257, 279, 384; *ERA* 3, pp. 100, 112.
175. *ERA* 1, p. 300.
176. *ERA* 3, p. 32; Innes, *New Amsterdam and Its People*, 173-74; *ERA* 1, pp. 19, 21, 22, 30, 35, 202, 305 382, 383; *ERA* 4, p. 75.
177. *ERA* 3, p. 117.
178. *ERA* 1, pp. 83, 86, 90, 384.
179. *ERA* 3, p. 33; Innes, *New Amsterdam and Its People*, 305; for skipper Laurens Cornelisz, see Frijhoff, *Wegen van Evert Willemsz*, 699, 742, 751, 776.
180. *ERA* 1, p. 313, author's translation; *ERA* 2, p. 111; see also *CJVR*, 191, 194-95.
181. *ERA* 1, p. 270; *FOCM*, 509; *ERA* 1, p. 391.
182. *ERA* 1, pp. 336, 341, 358.
183. Ibid., p. 492.
184. *FOCM*, 272; *DAB*, 125-28, 133, 146-52, 154, 194, 196; *CMARS* 1, pp. 47, 54.
185. *ERA* 1, p. 86; A.J.F. van Laer, 'Albany Notarial papers, 1667-1687,' in *DSSYB* 14, pp. 1-2.
186. Ariadne Schmidt wrote about how widows in the seventeenth century tried to find new ways to survive honorably. Schmidt, *Overleven na de dood*, 204.
187 See Appendix 5.
188. *CMARS* 3, pp. 494-96.
189. *ERA* 1, pp. 369, 313, 505; *ERA* 2, p. 111; *CJVR*, 191, 194-95.
190. *FOCM*, 231, 234-35; *ERA* 1, p. 239.
191. *FOCM*, 359.
192. Ibid., 495.
193. Ibid., 491, 504.
194. Ibid., 502.
195. Ibid., 246.
196. Remington, 'The Duncanson Wives,' 5-6; *MCR*, 191; *FOCM*, 4, 13, 16; Antonia Slaghboom, Arent van Curler's widow, may in the 1660s have set her slaves free. *CMARS* 1, pp. 94, 102; *CMARS* 2, p. 231.
197. *ERA* 3, p. 246.
198. *ERA* 1, pp. 61, 345; *ERA* 3, p. 34; *DAB*, 106.
199. *FOCM*, 65, 96, 250, 319.
200. Ibid., 232.
201. Innes, *New Amsterdam and Its People*, 302, 304. Remington, however, did not find any results in finding the name 'Lindsay' in the Scottish Church database. Remington, 'The Duncanson Wives,' 3.
202. Joseph-Antoine Poncet de la Riviére, 'Of the Capture and Deliverance of Father Joseph Poncet, 1653' (Snow, *In Mohawk Country*), 100.
203. *CJVR*, 101.
204. Maika, 'Commerce and Community,' 274.
205. *CMARS* 1, pp. 54, 267, 319.

Chapter 5

. Shattuck, 'A Civil Society,' 92-94; see also J. Venema, *Kinderen van weelde*, 14; Sullivan (*The Punishment of Crime*, 12) has different numbers, but refers to Shattuck.

2. Van Deursen, *Een dorp in de polder*; De Vries, and Van der Woude, *Nederland 1500-1815*, 593-600.
3. Shattuck, 'A Civil Society,' 94, 99-100.
4. De Vries and Van der Woude, *Nederland 1500-1815*, 593, 594.
5. NYSL, VRMP, probably box 43-44 (accounts for 1665, 1667-68, 1672-1674). Among the Van Rensselaer Manor Papers (VRMP) are several accounts for blacksmith work, among others of Barent, Mijndert, and Carsten *de smit*. These are not translated, and were in the process of being reorganized at the time I transcribed them.
6. *DAB*, 36, 46, 49, 58, 59, 78, 79, 119, 152, 179.
7. Van Laer, 'Albany Notarial Papers, 1667-1687,' 3.
8. *ERA* 1, p. 237.
9. *FOCM*, 454, 457-58.
10. *VRBM*, 841; *MCR*, 59.
11. Van Laer, 'Letters to Adriaen Gerritsen van Papendorp,' 2.
12. *MCR*, 118; Patents, vol. 2, part 2, no. 51; *FOCM*, 158; *ERA* 1, p. 203; *DAB*, 22, 24.
13. *ERA* 1, pp. 308, 410; *ERA* 3, pp. 42, 399, 536.
14. Vervelen and Van Gutsenhoven, NYSL, VRMP, box 37 (July 26, 1659; May 18, 1660; August 26, 1661); *DAB*, 26, 42, 58, 59, 62; Withard and Van Bael, *DAB*, 51, 114; De Maecker, 52.
15. NYSL, VRMP, box 37 (June 21, 1661); *DAB*, 76.
16. *ERA* 3, p. 102; *ERA* 1, pp. 64, 66.
17. *FOCM*, 485.
18. GAA, NA 2697/435 (11 April, 1662); GAA, NA 1801/220 (23 April, 1654).
19. GAA, NA 1575/II, 35 (February 27, 1651).
20. *FOCM*, 42, 45.
21. GAA, NA 228/III, 57 (May 1654).
22. GAA, NA 2686/... (February 27, 1657).
23. GAA, NA 1801/220 (April 23, 1654).
24. Van Laer, 'Letters to Adriaen Gerritsen van Papendorp,' 2-5; GAA, NA 4492/183 (April 20, 1676); GAA, NA 3941/206 (January 27, 1680).
25. GAA, NA 2697/435 (April 11, 1662); GAA, NA 2801/759 (April 25, 1658).
26. *FOCM*, 16, 17, 21, 201, 316; *ERA* 1, p. 39.
27. *ERA* 3, pp. 211, 353.
28. NYSA, NYCM 13:31[4] (September 17, 1659).
29. *ERA* 1, pp. 203, 406; *ERA* 4, pp. 92, 73, 105.
30. GAA, NA 1801/220 (April 23, 1654); *ERA* 1, pp. 31, 250.
31. *FOCM*, 169.
32. Ibid., 169; *ERA* 4, p. 67.
33. Patents, vol. 2, pt. 2, no. 16; *FOCM*, 29; *ERA* 3, p. 271; GAA, Poorterboek B + J, 59 (January 12, 1650).
34. Patents, vol. 2, pt. 2, no. 66.
35. *ERA* 1, pp. 87-90; see also Frijhoff, 'Dominee Bogardus als Nieuw-Nederlander,' 64-66.
36. *FOCM*, 491, 502.
37. *DAB*, 68, 70; *CMARS* 3, p. 553; *ERA* 2, p. 73.
38. *DAB*, 15, 17, 18, 23, 27-29, 33; Patents, vol. 2, pt. 2, no. 16; *FOCM*, 29.
39. NYSL, NYCM 13: 31[4] (September 17, 1659).
40. Venema, 'For the Benefit of the Poor,' 182-83.
41. Jozien Jobse-van Putten, *Eenvoudig maar voedzaam: Cultuurgeschiedenis van de dagelijkse maaltijd in Nederland* (Nijmegen: SUN, 1995), 156-80. See also Museum Boymans-van Beuningen, *Brood: De geschiedenis van het brood en het broodgebruik in Nederland* (Rotterdam: Museum Boymans-van Beuningen, 1983), 65.
42. Museum Boymans-van Beuningen, *Brood*, 32, 34, 36.
43. Ibid., 45.
44. Van Deursen, *Een dorp in de polder*, 108; and *Mensen van klein vermogen*, 16-17; See also W.P. Blockmans and W. Prevenier, 'Armoede in de Nederlanden van de 14de tot het midden van de 16de eeuw: bronnen en problemen,' in *Tijdschrift voor Geschiedenis* 88 (1975), 502.

45. Van Deursen, *Een dorp in de polder*, 108.
46. Ibid., 105, 108.
47. NYSL, VRMP, box 26 (July 18, 1641).
48. *FOCM*, 35.
49. *MCR*, 119.
50. Ibid., 181.
51. Ibid., 164, 182.
52. Patents, vol. 2, pt. 1, no. 17; *FOCM*, 35.
53. *FOCM*, 51.
54. Ibid., 66-67.
55. Ibid., 183.
56. *FOCM*, 172, 208, 224; *DAB*, 67.
57. *DAB*, 16; NYSA, NYCM, 8: 244 (October 10, 1656).
58. *DAB*, 126, 133, 156, 160, 209.
59. Patents, vol. 4, pt. 1, no. 27.
60. *FOCM*, 278, 293.
61. *DAB*, 'Holy Communion': 110, 113, 133, 152, 158, 164, 167, 183, 197, 199, 202; 'needy': 118, 130-31, 188, 197. As in Amsterdam, several bakers were immigrants from Germany. For German immigrant bakers in Amsterdam, see J.L. van Zanden and A. Knotter, 'Immigration and the Labour Market in Amsterdam in the Seventeenth Century,' in Van Zanden, *The Rise and Decline of Holland's Economy: Merchant Capitalism and the Labour Market* (Manchester, U.K.: Manchester University Press, 1993), 44-66.
62. *FOCM*, 297; *ERA* 4, p. 18.
63. *FOCM*, 297; 365, 386, 396.
64. *DAB*, 36.
65. Ibid., 147, 155, 236.
66. *MCR*, 25; *VRBM*, 839; *ERA* 1, p. 417; Patents, vol. 2, pt. 1, no. 17.
67. *DAB*, 17; *FOCM*, 186.
68. GAA, NA 2158/825 (April 18, 1652); GAA, NA 561/224 (November 27, 1652).
69. *FOCM*, 241.
70. *ERA* 4, p. 63; *ERA* 3, p. 60.
71. *FOCM*, 467, 479-80; *ERA* 3, p. 181.
72. *ERA* 3, p. 366.
73. NYSA, NYCM 8:244 (October 10, 1656); *FOCM*, 250.
74. NYSL, VRMP, box 37.
75. *DAB*, 87.
76. *CMARS* 1, p. 109; *ERA* 2, p. 18.
77. *FOCM*, 55; *ERA* 1, p. 202.
78. *FOCM*, 306; see also *ERA* 1, p. 43, 76, 408.
79. *ERA* 3, p. 410.
80. *ERA* 3, p. 246; *FOCM*, 197; *ERA* 1, p. 314; *ERA* 2, p. 61.
81. *FOCM*, 199.
82. NYSA, NYCM 8:244 (October 10, 1656).
83. Ibid., 571-73, 575-76, 582-83 (May 8, 11, 1657).
84. *FOCM*, 41; *LO*, 111-13.
85. *FOCM*, 41.
86. Ibid., 43, 49.
87. *FOCM*, 45, 46; C.T. Gehring (trans. and ed.), *Council Minutes, 1652-1654*, 72; see also *LO*, 146.
88. *FOCM*, 109-110. In the Netherlands inspection on the use of flour for white bread and cake was also made in times of scarsity. Van Deursen, *Mensen van klein vermogen*, 215-16.
89. Gehring, *Council Minutes, 1652-1654*, 136.
90. *FOCM*, 183. See Chapter 3.
91. *FOCM*, 190.

92. Frijhoff and Spies, *1650*, 204-7; see also Monté ver Loren and Spruit, *Hoofdlijnen*, 173-79; Catharina Lis and Hugo Soly, 'Ambachtsgilden in vergelijkend perspectief: De Noordelijke en Zuidelijke Nederlanden, 15de-18de eeuw,' in C. Lis and H. Soly (eds.), *Werelden van verschil: Ambachtsgilden in de Lage Landen* (Brussels: VUB Press, 1997), 15-16; Piet Lourens and Jan Lucassen, 'De oprichting en ontwikkeling van ambachtsgilden in Nederland (13de-19de eeuw),' in Lis and Soly, *Werelden van verschil*, 43-44, 54.

93. *ERA* 2, p. 323; *ERA* 3, p. 582; see also R. Dekker, 'Handwerkslieden en arbeiders in Holland,' (Te Boekhorst, *Cultuur en Maatschappij in Nederland*), 119-22.

94. NYSA, NYCM 8:573 (May 11, 1657).

95. See, for example, for bakers: *ERA* 1, p. 64; carpenters: *ERA* 1, pp. 28, 63, and *ERA* 4, p. 10; brick-makers: *ERA* 1, pp. 57, 59, and *ERA* 4, pp. 23, 28; brewers: *ERA* 1, p. 194, and *ERA* 4, p. 82.

96. Jacobs, *Een zegenrijk gewest*, 209-10.

97. J.L. van Zanden, *Arbeid tijdens het handelskapitalisme: Opkomst en neergang van Hollands economie 1350-1850* (Bergen: Octavo, 1991), 64, 71; see also De Vries and Van der Woude, *Nederland 1500-1850*, 401. About the guilds, see also I.H. van Eeghen, *De gilden: Theorie en practijk* (Bussum: C.A.J. van Dishoeck, 1965), 35-36. For an example of the founding of a guild, see L. Appel, 'Bakkers en brood in Monnickendam,' in Jaarverslag, *Het menselyk bedryf: De backer* (Monnikendam: Vereniging 'Oud Monnickendam,' 1984), 25-82.

98. *FOCM*, 211, 217, 250.

99. Ibid., 231.

100. Ibid., 243.

101. Ibid., 243.

102. NYSA, NYCM, 8:244-45: .' . . *en tot merckelijcke populatie* [. . .] *backers geadmitteert w*[. . .] *bij niemant eenich broot, om te* [. . .] *aen christenen of wilden gebac*[ken . . .] *ofte vercocht worde, als bij de supplianten* [. . .] *sijn gedaene belofte presteere en naercomen*' ([. . .]: and to con-siderable population [. . .] bakers admitted w[. . .]by nobody any bread to [. . .] to Christians or Indians bak[ed . . .] or will be sold as by the petitioners [. . .] the promise he made, will fulfil and observe [. . .]).

103. *LO*, 261, the single coarse four-pound loaf would cost 7 *stivers*; the half two-pound loaf, 3 ½ *stivers*; the double white two-pound loaf, 8 *stivers*; the single one-pound loaf 4 *stivers*; and the half ½-pound loaf 2 *stivers*.

104. *LO*, 261-62.

105. *FOCM*, 415-16.

106. Peter R. Christoph and Florence A. Christoph (eds.), *Books of General Entries of the Colony of New York, 1664-1673: Orders, Warrants, Letters, Commissions, Passes and Licenses Issued by Governors Richard Nicolls and Francis Lovelace*, vol. 1 (Baltimore: Genealogical, 1982), 86.

107. *DAB*, 97, 86.

108. Ibid., 124, 150.

109. Ibid., 83; 93.

110. *ERA* 3, p. 179.

111. Ibid., pp. 230, 237.

112. Ibid., p. 241.

113. *DAB*, 130; for other payments to Theunisz for bread, *DAB*, 109, 110, 112, 115.

114. *ERA* 3, pp. 66, 78; *DAB*, 101.

115. *DAB*, 146.

116. *ERA* 1, p. 503.

117. Venema, 'For the Benefit of the Poor,' 233; *CMARS* 2, p. 50; *ERA* 3, p. 307.

118. *ERA* 1, pp. 74, 161.

119. GAA, NA, 1359/106 (August 16, 1659); *FOCM*, 465, 482; see also *FOCM*, 432, 521.

120. *ERA* 1, p. 322; Van Laer, 'Notarial Papers 1666-1693,' 4-5; *CMARS* 1, p. 109.

121. *DAB*, 234, 237, 241.

122. *CCS*, 199.

123. Richard Yntema, 'The Welfare of the Brewers. Guilds and Confraternities in the Brewing In-dustry,' in R.E. Kistemaker and V.T. van Vilsteren (eds.), *Bier! Geschiedenis van een volks-*

drank (Beer! The story of Holland's favourite drink) (Amsterdam: De Bataafse Leeuw, 1994), 127-29.

124. Ibid., 126.
125. Wim de Bel, 'Het kooksel van Dees: Bier in Amsterdam, 1600-1800' (*Ons Amsterdam* 6 [1994]), 145, 170; the estimate is between 250 and 400 liters. Yntema also wrote that in the early seventeenth century, the per capita beer consumption stood at 300 liters, excluding small beer ('A Capital Industry: Brewing in Holland, 1500-1800,' in Kistemaker and Van Vilsteren, *Bier!/Beer!*, 79).
126. Yntema, 'A Capital Industry,' 79.
127. H. Schippers, 'Bier: Volksdrank en genotmiddel' (*Ons Amsterdam* 6 [1994]), 170.
128. J. Gawronski, 'Bier voor de VOC. De produktie en inkoop in Amsterdam in het midden van de 18de eeuw' (in Kistemaker and Van Vilsteren, *Bier!*), 143.
129. Schippers, 'Bier,' 173.
130. *DAB*, 39, 41, 97.
131. *VRBM*, 200.
132. Ibid., 253, 679.
133. *VRBM*, 638; GAA, NA, 1062/110 (June 5, 1642).
134. GAA, NA Reg. DTB 462/321 (October 7, 1645); GAA, NA, 1861/328 (August 19, 1644).
135. GAA, NA 1947/129 (May 11, 1649).
136. *ERA* 1, p. 305; *ERA* 2, p. 240.
137. *ERA* 1, pp. 22, 170, 266, 304, 305; *ERA* 2, p. 240.
138. Vincent van Vilsteren, 'Looking Over the Brewer's Shoulder. Life in a 16th-Century Brewery' (in Kistemaker and Van Vilsteren, *Bier!/Beer!*), 62. See also Schippers, 'Bier,' 175.
139. *ERA* 1, p. 349.
140. Schippers, 'Bier,' 175-76.
141. *FOCM*, 190.
142. *ERA* 1, p. 22.
143. *FOCM*, 429.
144. Ibid., 439-40; *CJVR*, 237; *ERA* 1, p. 266.
145. Ibid., pp. 276, 297.
146. *DAB*, 84, 89; *ERA* 3, p. 91.
147. *ERA* 1, pp. 276, 304, 305; *ERA* 3, p. 170.
148. *ERA* 1, pp. 178-79, 298, 471; *CMARS* 3, p. 467.
149. Although Jan Harmensz has here a different surname, it seems likely that he was the same person as the Jan Harmensz Backer who leased the front room from Hilleken Bronck. Their signatures are not the same, but do show some similarities in the handwriting; *ERA* 3, pp. 255, 389-90, 391.
150. *ERA* 3, pp. 255, 289 (documents 389-90).
151. *CMARS* 2, pp. 467, 473.
152. *ERA* 2, p. 17.
153. *ERA* 1, p. 311. In February 1680, Hevick's wife Geertruy Barents, according to the bond of March 25, 1669, demanded payment of the rent for the brewery 'belonging to her and Reyndert Pietersz jointly' (*CMARS* 2, pp. 467, 473).
154. Yntema, 'The Welfare of the Brewers,' 119, 122-23.
155. *LO*, 41.
156. Ibid., 110-11.
157. Ibid., 121-22.
158. *FOCM*, 151; see also *ERA* 1, pp. 199, 193, 194, 200.
159. Yntema, 'A Capital Industry,' 88.
160. *FOCM*, 422, 541; R.J. Yntema, 'Beer in Abundance: Distribution and Consumption in Early Modern Holland' (in Kistemaker and Van Vilsteren, *Bier!/Beer!*), 88-92.
161. Yntema, 'Beer in Abundance,' 88, 90.
162. *FOCM*, 185. In Leiden, people were required to collect small beer in buckets or jugs without a top, so as to prevent cheating (R.J. Yntema, 'Beer in Abundance,' 92).

163. *FOCM*, 190; see also Cora Laan, 'Bruisend in het glas: De rol van het pasglas in de 16de en 17de eeuw' (Kistemaker and Van Vilsteren, *Bier!*), 97).

164. *LO*, 204.

165. Ibid., 264-65.

166. Ibid., 343-44, 359.

167. Shattuck, 'A Civil Society,' 92; Venema, *Kinderen van weelde*, 14; Jacobs, *Een zegenrijk gewest*, 212.

168. *ERA* 1, p. 219.

169. *ERA* 1, p. 114; *ERA* 3, p. 391. Harmen Rutgersz may have been a son of Rutger Jacobsz, who was born after 1647; but it could also be the Harmen Rutgersz from Daerper, near Münster, who was hired March 7, 1651, by Oloff Stevensz for three years as a *brouwersknecht*. In May 1661, a certain Harmen Rutgersz signed as a witness, indicating that the man hired by Stevensz very well may have come up-river after the end of the contract. Rutger Jacobsz's son could not have been older than thirteen or fourteen at that time (GAA, NA 1346/12 [March 7, 1651]).

170. *ERA* 2, pp. 145, 146.

171. Ibid., p. 17.

172. *ERA* 1, p. 12.

173. *ERA* 1, p. 300 (in the original, it is doc. 311, which was not translated by Pearson); *ERA* 3, p. 267; *ERA* 1, pp. 346, 349.

174. Ibid., p. 301.

175. *ERA* 3, p. 271.

176. Ibid., p. 278.

177. *ERA* 1, p. 202; *DAB*, 41.

178. *ERA* 1, pp. 23, 272, 397; *FOCM*, 267; NYSA, NYCM 9:432-33 (October 20, 1660).

179. *DAB*, 86, 88, 96, 102, 104, 105, 126, 146, 177, 215.

180. *FOCM*, 424.

181. Ibid., 223.

182. *ERA* 1, p. 21, author's translation; the original document reads: '*met een stuck daer sijn brou-werij op staet, welcke brouwerij sal gebroocken worden toecoomende november 1657 ende de plaets van het brouhuys sal dan gelevert worden*' (doc. 50), which Pearson translated as: 'which brewery shall be worked [by the seller] until next November of the year 1657, and the lot of the said brewhouse shall then be delivered. . . .'

183. *ERA* 3, p. 168.

184. *VRBM*, 821; *MCR*, 162, 163; *ERA* 3, pp. 20, 244.

185. *FOCM*, 42, 52, 145, 246, 295, 298, 323, 324.

186. *FOCM*, 52; Patents, vol. 3, pt. 1, no. 78 (April 23, 1652, and March 24, 1654).

187. *MCR*, 183.

188. *FOCM*, 328.

189. *MCR*, 74; *VRBM*, 835, 839.

190. *FOCM*, 305.

191. *VRBM*, 813.

192. *ERA* 1, pp. 212, 290, 291; *ERA* 3, p. 65 ; *ERA* 4, p. 21. By then, Labatie had long moved out of the fort. Labatie was, from 1654 to May 1655, charged for ƒ150 in rent and, thereafter, for ƒ300 for the farm on Castle Island, and does not seem to have lived in the fort anymore (*VRBM* 814).

193. *CJVR*, 377-78, 386, 387; *ERA* 1, pp. 292-93 ; *ERA* 4, pp. 98-99.

194. NYSL, VRMP, box 37 (October 1662-February 1666).

195. *CJVR*, 399.

196. NYSL, VRMP, box 39 (1664; 9/19 March 1667; April 1667).

197. *ERA* 1, pp. 41-42.

198. *FOCM*, 368.

199. Ibid., 375, 385, 392.

200. *MCR*, 27.

201. Ibid., 181; *FOCM*, 48.

202. *MCR*, 123, 132, 133; NYSL, VRMP, box 39 (for example: 1659; February 4, 1660; August 1661).
203. *MCR*, 162.
204. *FOCM*, 32; *ERA* 1, p. 370.
205. *ERA* 1, pp. 248, 372; *ERA* 4, p. 17 ; see also Appendix 8, III, no. 1 and 2; *FOCM*, 137.
206. *ER* 1, p. 385.
207. Van Deursen, *Mensen van klein vermogen*, 124.
208. *FOCM*, 122, 354.
209. Ibid., 244, 247, 310.
210. Ibid., 473-74; *LO*, 367.
211. *FOCM*, 230.
212. *ERA* 3, p. 87.
213. Ibid., p. 140; *ERA* 1, pp. 393, 403, 442. It is confusing where Jansz kept his tavern: In 1665, he lived in the house that he had bought from Jurriaen Theunisz; but in 1666 and 1668, Jurriaen Theunisz lived in it.
214. *FOCM*, 248, 424, 465.
215. *ERA* 1, p. 248; *ERA* 3, p. 183. Nolden may have worked as servant in Dijckman's tavern in September 1662.
216. *ERA* 4, p. 9; *ERA* 1, pp. 18, 21-22, 263.
217. Ibid., pp. 262, 393, 403.
218. *FOCM*, 207, 209.
219. Ibid., 254, 355, 382.
220. Van Deursen, *Een dorp in de polder*, 127; Schmidt, *Overleven na de dood*, 134-36.
221. *FOCM*, 252.
222. Ibid., 166, 194; VRMP, box 39 (1659; February 14, 1660; 1661). The dates are unclaer because of damage to the documents. The gate meant by Jan Harmensz was probably not south, but north of the fort. Gerritsz's role in this is unclear; he paid for the expenses for Maria, whose last name clearly was Goosens, which also suggests that he may have been her father. This seems impossible, however, as they differed in age by no more than thirteen years (*ERA* 3, p. 263; *FOCM*, fn. p. 497).
223. *ERA* 1, p. 225.
224. Ibid., p. 238.
225. *ERA* 1, pp. 238, 248; *ERA* 3, p. 184. The document reads: '*waerdinne*' (doc. 260), which Van Laer read as '*weduwe*,' and thus translated as 'widow.'
226. *FOCM*, 157, 161, 164, 289, 297.
227. *DAB*, 14, 17. The poor boxes at Bronck and Steven were emptied in May; but the one at Jochimsz's was emptied in September, which may also explain the difference.
228. *DAB*, 29, 37, 40, 47.
229. Ibid., 91.
230. *FOCM*, 179, 180.
231. Ibid., 145.
232. *ERA* 3, p. 73.
233. NYSA, NYCM 10, pt. 1:174-176 (July 11, 1662); *ERA* 3, pp. 87, 166.
234. *FOCM*, 363.
235. Ibid., 171, 178.
236. Ibid., 382.
237. Ibid., 382.
238. *LO*, 359-60; NYSA, NYCM 8:1023 (November 11, 1654).
239. *MCR*, 132.
240. *LO*, 25, 359-60. See also NYCM 8: 1023. An Amsterdam *kan* is 19.2 liters for wine and 19.4 liters for beer (J.M. Verhoeff, *De oude Nederlandse maten en gewichten* [Publicaties van het P.J. Meertens-Instituut voor Dialectologie, Volkskunde, en Naamkunde van de Koninklijke Nederlandse Akademie van Wetenschappen 3; Amsterdam: 2de druk, 1983]), 5; a gallon is 3.78533 liters.

241. *CMARS* 1, p. 31; Hermesdorf, *De herberg in de Nederlanden*, 137; J. Baart, 'In kannen en kruiken. Drinkgerei voor bier tot in de 17de eeuw' (in Kistemaker and Van Vilsteren, *Bier!/Beer!*), 60.
242. *LO*, 96.
243. *FOCM*, 32; *LO*, 110.
244. *FOCM*, 31, 41-42, 422.
245. Ibid., 68.
246. Ibid., 109.
247. *FOCM*, 152; *ERA* 1, pp. 193-94, 199, 200.
248. *FOCM*, 154.
249. *ERA* 1, pp. 223, 224; see doc. 86 for the missing text.
250. *FOCM*, 109.
251. Ibid., 183.
252. Ibid., 71.
253. Ibid., 371-72.
254. *LO*, 262-63.
255. Ibid., 296-97.
256. *FOCM*, 473-74; *LO*, 367.
257. Ibid., 25.
258. Ibid., 61.
259. *FOCM*, 251.
260. Ibid., 542.
261. *LO*, 25, 61, 95, 259, 342; see also Sullivan, *The Punishment of Crime*, 91-92; for other violations see, for example, *FOCM*, 211, 267, 284, 355.
262. *LO*, 25, 61, 99, 259, 311, 342; Cornelis Daniel van Strien, 'British Travellers in Holland during the Stuart Period' (Ph.D. dissertation; Amsterdam: Vrije Universiteit, 1989), 103-4, 107-9, 147-48.
263. *FOCM*, 211, 216-17.
264. *Ibid.*, 209, 228, 355.
265. For various anthropologist perspectives on drinking, see Mary Douglas (ed.), *Constructive Drinking: Perspectives on Drink from Anthropolgy* (Cambridge: Cambridge University Press, 1987).
266. *FOCM*, 174 (*satt* in the meaning of 'stuffed with food').
267. *ERA* 1, p. 61.
268. Ibid., pp. 220-21.
269. *FOCM*, 73, 341; for the history of the inn being residence of court and police, see Hermesdorf, *De herberg in de Nederlanden*, 20-28.
270. Cora Laan, 'Bruisend in het glas,' 98.
271. VRMP, box 43-44 (1660, probably1662; dates are not readable due to fire damage).
272. Hermesdorf, *De herberg in de Nederlanden*, 167-78; see also Jansen, *De eeuwige kroeg. Hoofdstukken uit de geschiedenis van het openbaar lokaal*, 60.
273. Van Deursen, *Mensen van klein vermogen*, 122.
274. *CMARS* 2, p. 302.
275. *ER* 1, p. 385; *ERA* 1, p. 225.
276. Ibid., p. 216; author's translation; Pearson translated '*maats*' with the person of 'Jan Hendrickse Maat.'
277. *CMARS* 3, p. 182.
278. *FOCM*, 192.
279. *Ibid.*, 192; see also Gerard Rooijakkers, *Rituele repertoires*, 501-3.
280. *FOCM*, 180; for games, see also Ter Gouw, *De volksvermaken*.
281. Van Deursen, *Mensen van klein vermogen*, 125-26; see also Margriet de Roever, 'The Fort Orange "EB" Pipe Bowls: An Investigation of the Origin of American Objects in Dutch 17th Century Documents' (*New World Dutch Studies: Arts and Culture in Colonial America, 1609-1776* [Albany, N.Y.: Albany Institute of History and Art, 1987]), 51-61; Paul Huey, 'Archaeo-

logical excavations in the Site of Fort Orange, A Dutch West India Company Trading Fort built in 1634' (*Bulletin KNOB* 84, nos. 2 and 3 [Amsterdam: Bohn, Scheltema and Holkema, 1985]), 76-77.

282. For instance, in the deacons' account books for 1696, at Elias van Ravensteyn's funeral; or in 1700, at the funeral of the widow of *schout* Swart, Ryseck Swart; and at Hans Christiaan's funeral in 1697.

283. *ERA* 3, p. 49.

284. Frijhoff and Spies, *1650*, 592.

285. *LWA*, 71.

286. *ERA* 1, p. 344.

287. Matthias Beck, *Spiegel van mijn leven*, 117, 121, 128; Frijhoff and Spies, *1650*, 591; L.P. Grijp, 'Zingen in een kleine taal: De muzikale taalkeuze van Nederland,' in *Zingen in een kleine taal: De positie van het Nederlands in de muziek* (*Volkskundig Bulletin* 212 [October 1995]), 169-73.

288. The original for this is in Albany's First Dutch Reformed Church.

289. Sullivan, *The Punishment of Crime*, 92.

290. *LO*, 34, 52, 100, 259-60.

291. Trelease, *Indian Affairs*, 93; see for example, *FOCM*, 141, 255, 263, 357-58, 388.

292. Trelease, *Indian Affairs*, 93-94.

293. *FOCM*, 128.

294. Ibid., 166, 194.

295. Ibid., 252, 254.

296. Ibid., 354, 392.

297. *LO*, 259-60.

298. *FOCM*, 328.

299. Ibid., 453-54. See also Trelease, *Indian Affairs*, 125.

300. *FOCM*, 458.

301. Ibid., 161.

302. Brian Fagan, *The Little Ice Age: How Climate Made History, 1300-1850* (New York: Basic Books, 2000).

Chapter 6

1. Letter, Gideon Schaets to *dominee* Laurentius (June 27, 1657), *ER* 1, pp. 382-86.

2. GAA, NA 1100/23v, 26 (May 8, 1652); see also *ER* 1, pp. 309-10, 384; *HNN* 2, pp. 184, 565, 567; De Vries and Van der Woude, *Nederland 1500-1850*, 650; Frijhoff and Spies, *1650*, 23; Frijhoff, *Wegen*, 635.

3. ARA, SG 12564.30A, 'Rapport ende advijs over de gelegentheijt van Nieu nederlant' (December 15, 1644); see also Frijhoff, *Wegen*, 634-35.

4. CCS, 107v (November 29, 1655), for salary, see Schaets, 1655; *VRBM*, 844.

5. Frijhoff, *Wegen*, 634.

6. Frijhoff and Spies, *1650*, 23; Ariadne Schmidt, *Overleven na de dood*, 196-97.

7. *ER* 1, p. 385.

8. *LO*, 359-60; *FOCM*, 415; *DAB*, 61, 71, 109.

9. *DAB*, 109, 115; Eldersz was married and, at this time, had two daughters ages nine and three, and possibly a baby. See Barbara A. Barth, 'The Family of Ysbrant Eldersz of Rensselaerswyck,' *NYG&B R* 128, nos. 3 and 4 (1997), 157. If we interpolate the figures for the three months into those for a year, it would mean that this family ate bread valued at ƒ283 in one year. This amount would pay for 235.83 loaves (or 1,886.6 pounds) of bread per year; and this, in turn, would indicate a daily use of bread of about 5.16 pounds.

10. Blockmans and Prevenier, 'Armoede in de Nederlanden,' 502.

11. *DAB*, 83-85, 94-97. The 'Old Captain,' in 1663, was for a while given two pounds of butter

for different periods of time: 21, 25, 32, 26, 30, 27, and 20 days. He then boarded with Huybert Jansz, who likely provided him with food, as well.

12. Verhoeff, *De oude Nederlandse maten en gewichten*, 5.
13. Van der Donck, 'A Description of New Netherland,' 107.
14. *DAB*, 76, 104.
15. NYSA, NYCM 9: 227 (September 4, 1660).
16. NYSA, NYCM, 14:71 (1) (August 18, 1662); *CMVR*, 33; Van Deursen, *Een dorp in de polder*, 214.
17. *DAB*, 71, 97.
18. *FOCM*, 354, 355, 382; *ERA* 3, p. 184; *ERA* 1, pp. 320, 349, 353.
19. Panhuysen, *Maatwerk*, 107.
20. *LO*, 150-51.
21. *DAB*, 38, 43, 53, 94; 36, 103, 131.
22. CCS, 48.
23. Frijhoff and Spies, *1650*, 23; De Vries and Van der Woude, *Nederland 1500-1815*, 651, 703-7.
24. *DAB*, 40, 41, 43, 45, 46, 85, 105, 157; NYSL, VRMP, box 37 (November 29, 1658; August 1659; September 20, 1660; April 1661). Jeremias van Rensselaer, who frequently paid Carsten *de Noorman* ƒ2-10 *sewant* per day, paid him ƒ5 per day in 1664. The deacons also paid more: In 1661, they paid church cleaners ƒ4 a day; they paid Lambert van Valckenburgh ƒ5 for one day's work in 1662, and Carsten *de Noorman* received ƒ8-15 for one and a quarter day's cutting and digging at the church yard fence in 1665.
25. GAA, NA 2442/478-79 (March 28, 1657).
26. Ibid.; *DAB*, 66, 83, 85. I think that Thunis was the same person as the Theunis *van de Vlackte*, who is mentioned in 1661. Arent van Curler had leased the farm on *De Vlackte* (the Flatts) since 1647.
27. GAA, NA 1206/159 (November 24, 1657); *DAB*, 117, 118, 119, 124, 132.
28. *CJVR*, 268-69.
29. *FOCM*, 328; *LO*, 357.
30. *DAB*, 18; *ERA* 1, p. 213, author's translation.
31. NYSL, VRMP, box 39; *CJVR*, 386.
32. CCS, 106; *CJVR*, 388.
33. *CJVR*, 179, 220, 326; *Kingston Papers*, introduction; CCS, 107v.
34. *CJVR*, 303, 328; *DAB*, 102-6.
35. *FOCM*, 282.
36. *DAB*, 41.
37. Ibid., 67.
38. Van der Donck, *A Description of the New Netherlands*, 45, 50, 75.
39. *ERA* 1, pp. 321, 441; NYSL, VRMP, box [43, 44]; among various accounts, badly damaged by the 1911 Capitol fire, not encapsulated and not labeled.
40. *DAB*, 108, 122. See also the efforts made by Anneke Jans, at the time *dominee* Everhardus Bogardus's wife, to write her name. Frijhoff, 'New Views,' 27-28.
41. NYSL, VRMP, box 37, 39, 43, 44, and 45, for example, which contain accounts of the tailors Hendrick Rooseboom, Jan Vinhaegen, the smith Mijndert Fredericksz, Andries Herbertsz for bricks and tiles, the baker Jochem *backer*, and Teunis *de metselaer*.
42. W. Frijhoff, personal communication, February 18, 2001.
43. *ERA* 1, pp. 340, 343-44.
44. *ERA* 3, p. 270.
45. W. Frijhoff, '*Dominee* Bogardus als Nieu-Nederlander,' 64-66.
46. *ERA* 1, pp. 24-25, 68-69, 69-70, 77, 83-85, 86, 87-90, 90, 91, 190-92, 192-93, 206-7, 220-25, 249-50, 273, 340, 343-44, 351-52; *ERA* 3, pp. 117, 270; *ERA* 4, pp. 53-55, 78-80, 112, 137-38.
47. Eekhof, *De Hervormde Kerk* 2, pp. 162-64; *Kingston Papers* 2, pp. 567-69. These books may have been a translation by Johannes Burgundus of Christopher Wirsung, *Medicyn-boeck daerinne alle gebreken des menschelijcken lichaems, mitsgaders de remedien der selven, claerlijck aenge-wesen wort.* (Amsterdam: Jan Evertsen Cloppenburg, 1627); a translation by D

Carolum Battum of *De chirurgie, ende opera van alle de wercken van Mr. Ambrosius Paré* (Rotterdam: de Weduwe van Matthijs Bastiaensz, 1636); a translation by Jan Haghens of *Medecyn boec, ende chyrurgie D. Johannis de Vigo . . . Welck een principael fondament van alle chyrurgijen is, beyde in de theorijcke ende practijcke . . . Noch is hier achter bygevoeght een grondigh ende ervaren medecijnboeck inhoudende veel schoone ende versochte remedien* (Dordrecht: Peter Verhaghen, 1614); Juan Valverde de Amusco, *A. Vesalii en Valverda Anatomie, ofte af-beeldinghe van de deelen des menschelijcken lichaems, en derselver verklaringhe. Met een aenwijsinghe om het selve te ontleden, volgens de leeringe Galleni, Vesalii, Fallopii en Arantii* (Amsterdam: C. Danckertsz, 1647); Nicolaes Tulp, *De drie boecken der medicijnsche aenmerkingen, in 't Latijn beschreven.* (Amsterdam, Jacob Benjamyn, 1650).

48. *ERA* 1, p. 206, author's transcription. Pearson read the name of the seller as 'Gerrit Teunisz,' while I think 'Gabriel Leendertsz' is intended; Jan van Beverwijck, *Schat der gesontheyt* (Dordrecht: Hendrick van Esch, 1637); the 1643 sixth edition was improved and entitled *Johan van Beverwyck schat der gesontheyt: verçiert met historyen, kopere platen, als oock met verssen van Heer Jacob Cats, ridder, raedtpensionaris van Hollandts* (Amsterdam: voor de weduwe van Everhard Cloppenburgh).

49. *CJVR*, 13; Isaac Commelin, *Frederick Hendrick van Nassauw Prince van Orangien, zijn leven en bedrijf* (2 vols.; Utrecht, 1652); P.C. Hooft, *Henrik de Grote, zijn leven en bedrijf* (Amsterdam, 1626). A revised edition of this life of King Henri IV, of France, was published in 1638; it is unknown whether Vondel's *Joseph in Egypten*, or *Joseph in Dothan* (both written in 1640, and published in Amsterdam in 1644) is meant; the *Merckteecken* may have been a translation by Josua Sanders of *The righteous man's evidence for heaven* by Timothy Rogers: *Klare ende onwederleggelicke merckteeckenen der salicheyt van den mensche die door het geloove voor Godt gerechtveerdight is* (...). This was published for the fifth time in Dordrecht in 1658. With thanks to Fred van Lieburg.

50. *VRBM*, 208.

51. Ibid., 418; these may have been *De practijcke ofte oeffeninghe der godtsalicheydt* (Amsterdam: Jan Marcus, 1620), a translation by ds. Everhardus Schuttenius of Lewis Bayly's *Practise of piety* which was very popular. A translation with an introduction by ds. Gisbertus Voetius appeared in 1642.

52. *CJVR*, 430, 435, 442; Casparus Sibelius, *Christianae precationes et gratiarum actiones* (Deventer, 1658), translated as *Christelijcke gebeden en danckseggingen* (Amsterdam, 1667); Adrianus Cocquius, *Theologia praxis, de ware practycke der godt-geleerdheit* (...), Utrecht, 1658. With thanks to Fred van Lieburg.

53. *VRBM*, 294, 564; CCS, 74v (Hugo de Groot, *Inleydinge tot de Hollandtsche regts-geleertheyt* ('s-Gravenhage, 1631).

54. *ERA* 1, p. 206; *CJVR*, 81.

55. Ibid., pp. 83-85.

56. Ibid., p. 70.

57. Joyce Goodfriend, 'Incorporating Women into the History of the Colonial Dutch Reformed Church: Problems and Proposals,' in: R. House and J. Coakley (eds.), *Patterns and Portraits* (Grand Rapids, Mich.: Wm.B. Eerdmans), 21.

58. *CJVR*, 231.

59. *ERA* 1, pp. 88, 340; Frijhoff, '*Dominee* Bogardus als Nieu-Nederlander,' 65.

60. Frijhoff and Spies, *1650*, 262-63.

61. *CJVR*, 329, 332.

62. David Voorhees found references to the existence of a printer in the 1680s, and forms saying 'printed in New York.' Personal communication with David Voorhees, August 21, 2001.

63. Frijhoff and Spies, *1650*, 261-62.

64. '[. . .] omme t' voorsz erff te mogen aenvaerden, bebouwen ende tot alle nootsaeckelijckheyt der armen vervorderen ende gebruycken.' The original is in Albany's First Dutch Reformed Church.

65. Seebohm Rowntree, 'Poverty: A Study of Town Life,' 451. Quoted in Frank van Loo, 'De Armenzorg in de noordelijke Nederlanden 1770-1854,' in X.D.B. Block, W. Prevenier, D.J. Roor-

da, J.A. van Houtte, H.F.J.M. van Erenbeemt (eds.), *Algemene geschiedenis der Nederlanden* (Haarlem: H. Balthazar, 1981), 10.

66. Blockmans and Prevenier, 'Armoede in de Nederlanden,' 502.
67. *FOCM*, 415-16. J.L. van Zanden, 'Lonen en de kosten van levensonderhoud, 1600-1850' (Van Zanden, *Arbeid tijdens het handelskapitalisme*, 141).
68. Blockmans and Prevenier, 'Armoede in de Nederlanden,' 503.
69. J.L. van Zanden has estimated that the number of 'true' work days, due to Sundays, holidays and unemployment, was 264. This would make the actual earned wages the 264/365th part of the average day wages. Van Zanden, 'Lonen en de kosten van levensonderhoud,' 144.
70. *DAB*, 61, 71, 109.
71. Shattuck, 'A Civil Society,' 105-6.
72. NYSA, NYCM 13: 31v (September 4, 1659).
73. F. van Loo, *Den arme gegeven. . . . Een beschrijving van armoede, armenzorg en sociale zekerheid in Nederland, 1784-1995* (Meppel: Boom, 1981), 10. Source of the quote unknown.
74. FOCM, 324-25.
75. I. Van der Vlis, *Leven in armoede: Delftse bedeelden in de zeventiende eeuw* (Amsterdam; Prometheus/Bert Bakker, 2001), 215, 217, 277.
76. Van der Vlis, *Leven in armoede*, 37-40; Van Wijngaarden, *Zorg voor de kost*, 54; Groenveld, 'De Republiek der Verenigde Nederlanden en haar wezen, ca.1572-1795,' 58.
77. Van Deursen, *Bavianen en slijkgeuzen*, 83-84.
78. Groenveld, 'De Republiek der Verenigde Nederlanden en haar wezen,' 63. Edam, Monnikendam, and Purmerend considered the care of their own poor most important, but found some space to help passing transients. In Edam, the deaconry was willing to help poor non-members. Liesbeth Geudeke, 'Bedelen of bedélen. Kerkelijke en burgerlijke armenzorg op kleinstedelijk niveau: Edam, Monnickendam en Purmerend (1572-1650),' in *Mensen van de Nieuwe Tijd. Een Liber Amicorum voor A.Th. van Deursen* (Amsterdam: Uitgeverij Bert Bakker, 1996), 124-27; see also A.Th. van Deursen, *Bavianen en slijkgeuzen*, 102, 116, 117-127.
79. DAB, January 24, 1695.
80. Ibid., May-June 1691; March 1700. See also Venema, *Kinderen van weelde*, 40.
81. *LO*, 26.
82. *FOCM*, 343.
83. Ibid., 50, 352.
84. *LO*, 122, 331; Eekhof, *De Hervormde Kerk* 1, p. 125.
85. Groenveld, 'De Republiek der Verenigde Nederlanden en haar wezen,' 31-32; Van Laer, 'The Orphan Chamber of Amsterdam,' 1-9; A.E. van Zwieten, 'The Orphan Chamber of New Amsterdam,' 319-40.
86. *FOCM*, 278.
87. *LO*, 411-12.
88. For Montreal and Quebec, see W.J. Eccles, 'Social Welfare Measures and Policies in New France,' in *Essays on New France* (Toronto: Oxford University Press, 1987), 41-42.
89. *LO*, 411-12.
90. *DAB*, 13, 59.
91. CCS, 45-45v; *DAB*, 7.
92. Ibid., 73-76, 78.
93. *ERA* 1, p. 234.
94. *DAB*, 28, 34, 48, 61.
95. Ibid., 27-28, 47, 73.
96. The identity of the matres is never given; could she be the same as 'mother' from the bleach field, or 'mother' Schaets? *DAB*, 47, 51, 84, 249. She is only mentioned as being paid for stringing *sewant*, and therefore may also have been the same person as Greete *de sewant reesters* (the female *sewant* stringer). Greete, *DAB*, 42, 43; the matres stringing *sewant*, *DAB*, 50, 60, 63, 66, 71, 72, 76, 82, 83; see also the section on education in chapter II.
97. *DAB*, 39-41, 43, 51.
98. J. Wagenaar, *Amsterdam en zijne opkomst, aanwas, geschiedenissen, voorrechten, koophandel,*

gebouwen, kerkenstaat, schoolen, schutterije, gilden en regeeringe, vol. 3 (Amsterdam: 1760-67), p. 158.

99. For Montreal, see Eccles, 'Social Welfare Measures and Policies in New France,' 46-47; 'The Role of the Church in New France,' in *Essays on New France* (Toronto: Oxford University Press, 1987), 53; Robert Berris paid rent, DAB (April 27, 1698); Jan Kiednie, September 5, 1698.

100. Van Deursen, *Mensen van klein vermogen*, 58-59, 82; A. Biewenga, *De Kaap de Goede Hoop: Een Nederlandse vestigingskolonie, 1680-1730* (Amsterdam: Prometheus-Bert Bakker, 1999), 152; Raben, 'Batavia en Colombo,' 274; Eccles, 'Social Welfare,' 43.

101. J. Spaans, *Armenzorg in Friesland, 1500-1800. Publieke zorg en particuliere liefdadigheid in zes Friese Steden Leeuwarden, Bolsward, Franeker, Sneek, Dokkum en Harlingen* (Hilversum: Verloren, 1997), 40.

102. Gras, *Op de grens van het bestaan*, 85-128.

103. *MCARS* 3, p. 303.

104. *DAB*, 53, 68, 70. Sandersz's father was Thomas Sandersz, a blacksmith who had left Beverwijck for Manhattan, where he was twice sent money (together, ƒ51-10) by Beverwijck's deaconry in June and October of 1655. In the Dutch Republic, the rule was that someone who moved to another locality would not receive any poor relief from that town, but had to be supported by his town of origin for a year after his departure. This rule, an important feature of Vives's humanism, was intended to prevent beggary, and was strongly emphasized in the Republic. Spaans, *Armenzorg in Friesland*, 42-43.

105. After the settlement with Femmetje Alberts concerning the anullment of their marriage, Michiel Theunisz was released from all debts contracted during their partnership. *FOCM*, 248-49, 332-33.

106. *DAB*, 35-36, 41.

107. Ibid., 42-44, 46; 57, 93.

108. *VRBM*, 820.

109. *FOCM*, 183, 223-24, 5; *DAB*, 67, 72, 74, 76, 119.

110. *MCR*, 28.

111. Ibid., 35. See appendix 6.

112. *FOCM*, 90; GAA, NA 1054/67 (July 11, 1641).

113. *ERA* 1, pp. 69; Van Deursen, *Mensen van klein vermogen*, 267.

114. *MCARS* 1, pp. 174, 196.

115. *DAB*, 241-49, 253-62; March 20, 1675; see also *ERA* 1, p. 109.

116. *CMARS* 3, p. 347.

117. *DAB*, 132.

118. In 1659, Carsten worked at least 44½ days for Van Rensselaer, and in 1660 he was paid for 63 days' digging, cutting and loading. By September 1665, his wages had increased to ƒ5 a day. NYSL, VRMP, box 37.

119. *DAB*, 141-42, 169, 170-71.

120. Van der Vlis, *Leven in armoede*, 120; Spaans, *Armenzorg in Friesland, 1500-1800*, 22.

121. *DAB*, 76.

122. *ERA* 1, pp. 423, 462; *ERA* 3, pp. 294, 477.

123. DAB, November 29, 1685.

124. Van Deursen, *Een dorp in de polder*, 221; Van der Vlis, *Leven in armoede*, 170; Gras, *Op de grens van het bestaan*, 122-24.

125. *FOCM*, 328.

126. Ibid., 323-24, 328; *MCARS* 2, p.249; *DAB*, 224 and passim.

127. Van der Vlis, *Leven in armoede*, 162; Schmidt, *Overleven na de dood*, 211-40.

128. *DAB*, 177.

129. Ibid., 64.

130. Frijhoff and Spies, *1650*, 20.

131. *DAB*, 90; see also 83, 104.

132. Ibid., 138; 124, 211. For loans from the church, see also 1-7, 135-44.

133. Ibid., 111, 114, 119, 132, 140; *ERA* 3, p. 74.

134. *DAB*, 132, 140.

135. Ibid., 41, 39, 131-33, 146, 148; DAB, 1687-88; January 1696.

136. GAA, NA, 1096/286-287v (March 20, 1651). He was then forty years old. '*Malle*' can mean someone who makes jokes, but in the seventeenth century it more often meant 'crazy.' *DAB*, 100, 111.

137. Ibid., 29, 31, 41.

138. Spaans, *Armenzorg in Friesland*, 42.

139. In analyzing the methods of poor relief, I followed the example of Herman Gras, who wrote about poverty in eighteenth-century Drenthe. It is not surprising to find many similarities with Drenthe and other areas in the Dutch countryside. These regions, like the upriver colony, were sparsely populated, had relatively few poor, and offered easy access to land, while they practiced the same religion. In Drenthe, just about the whole population was Reformed, and its deaconry also was the general provider for the poor. Gras, *Op de grens van het bestaan*.

140. *DAB*, 73, 76, 78.

141. Ibid., 42, 53, 54, 59, 73, 75.

142. Ibid., 73-76, 78, 84-85.

143. Van Deursen, *Een dorp in de polder*, 218; Van der Vlis, *Leven in armoede*, 111, 113; Van Wijngaarden, *Zorg voor de kost*, 109.

144. *CJVR*, 226.

145. *DAB*, 76, 89, 109; Van der Donck, *A Description of the New Netherlands*, 45.

146. *DAB*, 16, 49, 65, 67, 76, 71.

147. Van der Donck, 'A Description of New Netherland,' 107.

148. Venema, 'For the Benefit of the Poor,' 218-19.

149. *DAB*, 81, 105; DAB, April 26 and May 1, 1676.

150. Ibid., April 26 and May 1, 1676.

151. *DAB*, 111, 114, 119.

152. *DAB*, 132, 140.

153. Ibid., 131-33, 146, 148.

154. Ibid., 70, 72, 73, 75-77, 81, 83, 84.

155. Ibid., 41, 39.

156. DAB, 1687-88; January 1696.

157. *DAB*, 51, 58, 59.

158. *ERA* 1, p. 425.

159. Groenveld, 'De Republiek der Verenigde Nederlanden en haar wezen,' 194-202; P.Th.F.M. Boekholt and E.P. de Booy, *Geschiedenis van de school in Nederland vanaf de middeleeuwen tot aan de huidige tijd* (Assen and Maastricht: Van Gorcum, 1987), 42-44.

160. *ERA* 3, pp. 465, 585; DAB, July 1, 1686.

161. Elizabeth S. Peña, 'Wampum Production in New Netherland and Colonial New York: The Historical and Archaeological Context' (Ph.D. dissertation; Boston: Boston University, 1990), 23.

162. For more wages for stringing *sewant*, see *DAB*, 11, 14, 16, 23, 26, 42-44, 50,56, 60, 71, 72, 76, 82, 83, 88, 93, 95, 96, 98-102, 110-11, 115, 117, 119, 126, 129, 132.

163. GAA, NA 1314/191v (May 22, 1640); S. Purple, *Marriages from 1639 to 1801 in the Reformed Dutch Church, New York*, Collections of the NYG&BS, vol. 1, 1890, repr. as vol. 9, 1940, p.10. For more information on the Kleyns, see also Henry B. Hoff, 'The Family of Ulderick Kleyn and Baefje Pieters,' in *NYG&BR* 129:3 (July 1997).

164. *FOCM*, 157, 161; there is no complete information about the reasons for Ulderick's confinement.

165. *DAB*, 35-36.

166. *FOCM*, 332, 336-37, 349, 351.

167. *DAB*, 35-36; *ERA* 1, p. 268; *ERA* 4, p. 51.

168. *ERA* 1, p. 413.

169. *FOCM*, 240.

170. *DAB*, 98, 112, 202-4.

171. *ERA* 1, pp. 430-31.

172. *MCARS* 1, p. 244.

173. *CMARS* 2, pp. 399, 419.

174. Purple, *Marriages in the Dutch Church in New York*, August 9, 1663.

175. *FOCM*, 267; *DAB*, 41, 96, 102, 104, 105, 122, 126, 127.

176. *CMARS* 1, pp. 31, 295, 300; *DAB*, 177, 175, 215; DAB, May 22, 1677.

177. Gras, *Op de grens van het bestaan*; Van der Vlis, *Leven in armoede*, 119-20; Van Wijngaarden, *Zorg voor de kost*, 115-17; Biewenga, *De Kaap de Goede Hoop*, 150.

178. In addition to the people mentioned earlier, the orphans Ytie and Sartge Hendricks were boarded out; in February 1659, blacksmith Jan van Aken was paid ƒ200 for three years' boarding money for the child kept by him (*DAB*, 57); Daniel, Adam Roelantsz's fourteen-year-old son, was boarded with the needy Marietie Claes for ƒ25 per week in 1658-1662, and for ƒ30 in 1662 and 1663. The elderly Willem Jurriaensz stayed with the needy Huybert Jansz. Five people were boarded because of their physical problems. Hans Eenkluys first stayed at Jan *met de Baert*'s house in 1660, and for another five months in 1661 at Thomas Coningh's, for ƒ20 per week. A boy from Catskil needed surgeon Gysbert's (van Imbroch, at the Esopus) help, and boarded at Philip *de [brouwer*'s?] in 1659; and when the *henckman* (hangman) was ill in 1664, the deacons paid ƒ7 for seven days at Trygen aen de Bergh's (the regular fare for boarding paid by Jeremias van Rensselaer, as well). *DAB*, 129; NYSL, VRMP box 37; Ary de Vries was taken care of by Huybert Jansz when he had a ƒ300 surgery on his leg in 1662. *DAB*, 41, 35-36, 100, 129, 133, 146.

179. Van Wijngaarden, *Zorg voor de kost*, 209-14.

180. W.J. Eccles, 'Social Welfare and Politics in New France,' 41.

181. *CMARS* 3, pp. 261-62.

182. Van Deursen, *Bavianen en Slijkgeuzen*, 114-15.

183. *FOCM*, 220.

184. *MCR*, 163, 165; *FOCM*, 210.

185. *CMARS* 3, p. 432; DAB, April 19 and July 1, 1686.

186. *DAB*, 223-24.

187. According to the DAB, another Indian was paid for clearing in the pasture in September and October 1689; on December 16, 1689, an Indian was given a coat and shirt with a value of ƒ54-04; on December 27, 1697, ƒ108 was paid for Davit the Indian's burial; on March 20, 1701, the magistrates were paid ƒ120 for maintaining Jacob the Indian boy. These native Americans may have become Christians.

188. *DAB*, 11, 36, 38, 71, 77.

189. Biewenga, *De Kaap de Goede Hoop*, 151; Niemeijer, 'Calvinisme en koloniale stadscultuur: Batavia, 1619-1725,' 279.

190. See, for instance, Van Deursen, *Bavianen en Slijkgeuzen*, 102, 116; Geudeke, 'Bedelen of bedélen,' 124-27.

191. *FOCM*, 151, 159; *DAB*, 12,16, 32, 33, 35, 36, 44.

192. *FOCM*, 183; *DAB*, 66, 71; NYSL, VRMP, box 37 (January 9; July 6 and 17, 1660; February 4 and July 1661).

193. NYSA, NYCM 9: 212, 229 (May 11 and September 4, 1660). Hendrick Andriesz, in October 1653 received a patent for a garden lying next to the fort in Beverwijck, which abutted to the south on Lambert van Valckenburgh's land, to the west a path by the vacant lot, to north Gerrit Vastrich and Gisbert Cornelisz; *DRCHNY* 1, p. 525; *FOCM*, xxvii; *ERA* 1, p. 212, mentions clearly that the garden was south of the fort, while at other places (p. 375) it is described as being behind the fort on the *pleyn*; *ERA* 3, p. 376; *ERA* 4, p. 18.

194. *FOCM*, 329.

195. Ibid., 451. *DAB*, 67. For their two sons, see Thomas Grier Evans, *Records of the Reformed Church in New Amsterdam and New York. Baptisms*, November 4, 1646; July 21, 1652.

196. *ERA* 1, pp. 84, 88, 352; *DAB*, 68, 70.

197. Bartlett Burleigh James, and J. Franklin Jameson (eds.), *Journal of Jasper Danckaerts, 1679-1680* (New York: Scribner, 1913), 217-18.

198. *ERA* 3, p. 116.
199. *DAB*, 73; 66, 83, 85, 172, 175.
200. Jacobs, *Een zegenrijk gewest*, 95.
201. *MCR*, 163; *FOCM*, 413-14.
202. Van Deursen, *Een dorp in de polder*, 211.
203. *DAB*, 92.
204. Ibid., 8, 9, 10, 22, 28, 99, 116, and passim.
205. Ibid., 9, 10, 28.
206. GAA, NA 1711/521 (March 6, 1659); *DAB*, 10, 12, 13, 38, 58, 64.
207. *DAB*, 16, 102-6.
208. Ibid., 18, 29, 99; Van Laer, *The Lutheran Church*, 17, 40.
209. *DAB*, 91.
210. Ibid., 46-56.
211. Ibid., 61, 64; 124, 127, 128, 130.
212. *CJVR*, 100, 104, 106.
213. *ER* 1, p. 383.
214. ER, 383.
215. Shattuck, 'A Civil Society,' 11.
216. *CJVR*, 227.
217. Rink, *Holland on the Hudson*, 164-71.
218. Van Deursen, *Een dorp in de polder*, 216.
219. Van der Vlis, *Leven in armoede*, 319-21.
220. Van Wijngaarden, *Zorg voor de kost*, 131.
221. J. Demos, *A Little Commonwealth: Family Life in Plymouth Colony* (London, Oxford, and New York: Oxford University Press, 1970), 111; Rutman, *Winthrop's Boston*, 217-20.
222. Eccles, 'Social Welfare Measures and Policies in New France,' 41-42.
223. Van der Vlis, *Leven in armoede*, 323.
224. Venema, 'For the Benefit of the Poor,' 146, 179; Spaans, *Armenzorg in Friesland*, 217.

Conclusion

1.   *CJVR*, 356, 358.
2.   P. and F. Christoph, *Books of General Entries of the Colony of New York*, 35-38, 47. Cuyler Reynolds (ed.), *Albany Chronicles: A History of the City Arranged Chronologically from the Earliest Settlement to the Present Time* (Albany: J. Lyons, 1906), 59-67.
3.   *VRBM*, 208.
4.   Ibid., 204-5, 208-12. Books he sent over were Jacques Thuys, *Ars notariatus, dat is: konste en stijl van notarischap* (Amsterdam, 1628); Joost de Damhouder, *Practycke in criminele saecken* (Rotterdam, 1628); and Joost de Damhouder, *Practycke in civile saecken* ('s-Gravenhage, 1626). An inventory of the patroon's house in 1652 also turned up Hugo de Groot's *De inleydinge vande Hollantsche rechtsgeleertheyd* (first printing: 's-Gravenhage, 1631). CCS, 74v.
5.   *VRBM*, 430-31, 433-34, 437-38, 439, 496-97, 512, 664, 687.
6.   Ibid., 491, 493.
7.   De Vries and Van der Woude, *Nederland 1500-1815*, 351, 469-71.
8.   J. van Goor, *De Nederlandse Koloniën: Geschiedenis van de Nederlandse expansie 1600-1975* (The Haag: Sdu uitgevers, 1997), 102; Rink, *Holland on the Hudson*, 166-67.
9.   *CMARS* 2, pp. 34, 47; *CMARS* 3, p. 280; NYSL, *DAB*, November 17, 1684; September 22 and 26, 1685; November 29, 1685; October 24, 1690. See also J. Venema, *Kinderen van weelde*, 46 and 'For the Benefit of the Poor,' 166.

Appendices

Appendix 1: Population size

Population of Rensselaerswijck/Beverwijck*

going to Rw:	people	men**	leaving	specifics
1630	13	9		
1631	8	6		
1632			1	
1633	5	5	1	
1634	11	6	9	
1635			1	
1636			1	
1637	37	27	3	
1638	27	19	1	
1639	10	9	2	
1640	15	12	0	
1641	4	4	1	
1642	38	27	2	100 in church
1643	4		3	@100 (14-15 farms)
1644	21	18	3	
1645	2	2	0	
1646	10	10	1	
1647	5	5	1	
1648	19	14	2	40 households
1649	17	15	3	
1650	17	13	2	
1651	17	17	1	45 take oath Rw
1652	11	6	0	
1653				230 men bear arms
1654				
1655				
1656				
1657				120+ houses Bw; 14-15 farms Rw; 300-400 in church, if all *liefhebber*, 600 people could be in church; 70-80 Lutheran families. 130 church members
1658				
1659				
1660				200 church members
1661				
1662				
1663				
1664				

* The numbers of people coming and leaving are based on Van Laer, *VRBM*, 334, 805-845. The specifics are drawn from *VRBM*, *MCR*, *FOCM*, *ERA* 1-4, *ER*, CCS.
** Men: The numbers under "people" include men, and if mentioned, women and children. The numbers under "men" only refer to men, single or married.

Additional information regarding the population size:

1642   158 persons had arrived and 30 had left. Megapolensis wrote that about a hundred people attended his first sermon. [*VRBM*, 652]

1643   According to the Jesuit Isaac Jogues there were about a hundred people in Rensselaerswijck who resided in about 25 or 30 houses built along the river, as each found most convenient. ["Novum Belgium, by Father Isaac Jogues, 1646" in *NNN*, 262]

1648   24 August; Van Slichtenhorst lists forty (forty-one with the minister) lots occupied [CCS, 48ᵛ-50ᵛ: *Opcomste vanden jaere 1648*].
       If four-person families, then population size would be about 160; if family size of five, 200. Likely population between 160 and 200. Also servants.

1651   45 people take the oath of loyalty to the patroon; at four-person family: 180; five-person family, 225 inhabitants. So likely between 180 and 225 inhabitants.

1652   Although Brant van Slichtenhorst claimed that a hundred houses had been built, Jan Baptist van Rensselaer wrote in September that thirty-eight houses were standing and four or five half finished. [CCS, 67, 109]

1653   Jan Baptist van Rensselaer: there are 230 men capable of bearing arms in Beverwijck and Rensselaerswijck [Scheepvaart museum Amsterdam, Handschriften van de Van Rensselaer familie, folder 53414, mss. 25-40 In: BIII 828 II, p. 69; see also CT. Gehring, 'An Undiscovered Van Rensselaer Letter,' in *DHM*, fall/winter 1974, LIV, no. 3, p. 28].

1657   Schaets: there are more than 120 houses in Beverwijck if not more, and others are springing up daily; no more than fourteen or fifteen farms in Rensselaerswijck. Usually between 300 and 400 people come to church and if they were all *liefhebbers* there could be as many as 600 [*ER* I: 383]. There are seventy to eighty Lutheran families [Van Laer, *The Lutheran Church in New York*, 39].

1660   200 church members [*ER* I: 483]
       1,051 inhabitants according to Shattuck ['A Civil Society,' 11]

Appendix 2: People who may have had a lot on the river's west side before april, 1652: 53 or 55 people likely had property in the area of the *Fuyck* before April, 1652.*

Adriaensz, Jacob (*wagenmaecker*) 1652, possibly 1653
Andriesz, Arent 1652, possibly 53
Barentsz, Jan [Wemp] possibly 1653
Bastiaensz, Harmen 1652
Bogardus, Annetje 1652, possibly 1653
Bronck, Pieter possibly 1652; 1653
Cornelisz, Cornelis [Vos] 1652
Cornelisz, Gysbert [*de waert*] 1653
Cornelisz, Teunis 1652
Deaconry, for poorhouse
De snijder, Rut (Adriaensz) 1652, 1653
De Hooges, Anthonie 1652
De *metselaer*, Marten [Herpertsz] 1652, possibly 1653
Elbertsz, Reyer possibly 1652; 1653
Fransz, Jan [Van Hoesem], 1652, 1653
Fredericksz, Willem [Bout] 52, possibly 1653
Gerritsz, Albert 1652, 1653
Gerritsz, Goosen 1652, 1653
Harmensz, Marten
Hartgers, Pieter 1652, possibly 1653
Hendricksz, Marten 1652
Jacobsz, Casper 1652, possibly 1653
Jacobsz, Rut 1652, 1653
Jacobsz, Teunis 1652
Jansz, Jacob [Hap] 1653
Jansz, Jacob [van Noortstrant] 1652, 1653
Jansz, Willem [Stoll] 1653
Jansz, Rem 1653
Jansz, Lourens 1653
Jansz, Dirck [Croon] 1652
Jansz, Hendrick [Reur]
Jansz, Adriaen [schoolmaster/ van Ilpendam] 1652; 1653
Jansz, Thomasz 1653
Jansz, Steven
Jansz, Hendrick [Westerkamp] 1652, possibly 1653
Jansz, Evert [*kleermaecker*; Wendel] possibly 1652; 1653
Jansz, Volckert [Douw] 1652
Jurriaensz, Willem
Labatie, Jan 1653
Lambertsz, Jacob
Leendertsz, Sander 1652
Michielsz, Jan 1652
Pietersz, Abraham [Vosburgh] 1652
Pietersz, Adriaen [van Alckmaar]
Sandersz, Tomas 1653

Staets, Abraham 1653
Symonsz, Jacob [Clomp] 1653
Theunisz, Jurriaen 1653
Theunisz, Cornelis (van Westbroeck) 1652
Thomasz, Harmen
Thomasz, Jan 1652
Verbeeck, Jan 1653
Wesselsz, Jochem [*Backer*] 1653

---

total **53 people**, including the deaconry

Somewhat uncertain:
Ariaensz, Jacob [*ramaecker*]
De backer, Hendrick ?

Of these 53 people,
26 received a patent in 1652
25 received a patent in 1653
6 received a patent in 1652 and 1653.
I did not see a patent in 1652 or 1653: Marten Harmensz
                                        Hendrick Jansz Reur
                                        Steven Jansz
                                        Jacob Lambertsz
                                        Adriaen Pietersz v. Alckmaer
                                        Harmen Thomasz

---

* The findings are based on information from the *VRBM*, pp. 811-845, the VRMP, the CCS, and the *MCR*. The addition of 1652 or 1653 behind a name indicates that this person received a patent in that year. See also appendix 3 for patents between 1652 and 1661.

Appendix 3: Lots in Beverwijck, 1652-1664

Hardly any original patents of lots in Beverwijck have been preserved, so that there is a gap in the records of the Dutch patents between 1651 and 1654, when most of the grants were made. Our knowledge about these grants must be derived from rare Dutch deeds and English confirmatory patents of later date.

The latter can be found in the New York Colonial Patents Books, Albany 1664-1690, in the New York State Archives. References to early patents or ground briefs can also be found in later deeds, of which many are translated by Jonathan Pearson in the *Early Records of the City and County of Albany and Colony of Rensselaerswijck,* in 1869 (indicated as ERA I); the volumes 2-4, revised by A.J.F. van Laer, were published in 1916-1919 (indicated as ERA I-IV). Charles Gehring translated and edited *Land Papers* (indicated as LP), which also contain several translations of original patents. Information regarding the original inhabitants and their lots can also be derived from Charles Gehring, transl. and ed., *Fort Orange Court Minutes* (indicated as FOCM), although this material does not contain original patents.

In 1652, at least thirty-two patents were distributed. The following information is drawn from the source materials mentioned above, and is not a complete. list. When using the *ERA* info, only those documents, making mention of the specific year of the patent are noted. The *FOCM* provide more information regarding the use of lots, although it is hardly ever mentioned that a person received a patent. Not considering it in the count of patents, I still include this information in the following overview, as it provides an insight in the use of land in the area of Beverwijck in the respective years.

Filling out the lots on a map is no easy task, as frequently existing translations are incorrect, while of the remaining translated patents no original texts remain (see also appendix 8). The question then remains how much we can trust the information provided by the translated patents. In addition, the Dutch text itself is not always clear: a description of a specific lot as *belendt ten suyden Jan Hendricksz* is sometimes used in the meaning of *belendt ten suyden aen Jan Hendricksz* (the south side of the lot abuts to Jan Hendricksz), while at other times it is used in the meaning of it *belendt ten suyden van* (the lot abuts to the south side of Jan Hendricksz' lot). Another problem is caused by the fact that payments were made in various terms, so that it is often unclear, when a particular lot changed owner. A person also seems to have had the use of a lot before he received a patent. Thomas Chambers, for example, received, according to the *FOCM,* a lot in 1656, but the Patent books, *LP,* and *ERA* show that he only received a patent in 1658. More complications are added when the spouse of a person deceased, and the survivor remarried. Property thus often became in the ownership of a second or third husband, f.e., Harmen Thomasz frequently completed or continued a transaction, begun by Dirck Bensingh, his wife's first (deceased) husband. François Boon did that with transactions started by Gysbert Cornelisz *de weert,* and Cornelis van Nes, the third husband of Maritie Damen, had to deal with property that first belonged to his predecessors.

Considering these obstacles, the following documentation by no means pretends to be complete. It is the intention to provide other researchers with a starting point, to which he/she can add his/her own information, leading to his/her conclusion.

Abbreviations:

ERA = Pearson, Jonathan, transl. and ed. *Early Records of the City and County of Albany, and Colony of Rensselaerswijck (1656-1657)*. (Albany, 1869). 4 volumes, vols. 2-4 revised by A.J.F. van Laer.

FOCM = Gehring, Charles T., *Fort Orange Court Minutes, 1652-1660*. (Syracuse, 1990)

LP = Gehring, Charles T., *Land Papers* (Baltimore, 1980)

pat. = New York Colonial Patent Books, Albany 1664-1690 in the NYS Archives (v = volume, pt. = part, # = number)

L = lot; **H** = house; **G** = garden

patent indicates that the person received a patent (also named ground brief) in this year.

PATENTS 1652

Adriaensz, Rut *patent* for L: pat. v.2 pt.2 # 72; H+L, sold to Hendrick Gerritsz, tailor, who, in March, 1655 sold it [H+L] to Rem Jansz [FOCM: 183], who in Sept., 1660 sold part of it [H+L] to Cornelis Theunisz Bos and part [H+L] to Jan Thomasz [ERA I: 283-84]

Adriaensz, Jacob *patent* for L: pat. v. 2, pt. 2 # 42

Aertsz, Wouter l: FOCM: 7, given use of land

Andriesz, Hendrick g: FOCM: 8, enlarged garden

Andriesz, Arent *patent* for L: pat. v 2, pt. 2, # 47

Arentsz, Rut: *see* Adriaensz, Rut

Bastiaensz, Herman *patent*: ERA I:306, sells part, H+L, to Carsten Claesz in Aug., 1662; FOCM: 4, allowed to erect house.

Bensingh, Dirck G: FOCM: 8, granted garden on condition

Bogardus, Annetje *patent* for L, G pat. v.2, pt. 2, # 66; ERA I: 289, sells part of lot to David Pietersz Schuyler, Dec, 1660; ERA I:324, 424, in 1663, heirs sell h+l to Dirck Wesselsz; 392, David Pietersz Schuyler sells part, l. with h. and barn, to Wouter Albertsz vanden Uythoff, 1 sept. 1665.

Cassersz, Hendrick (v. Oldenburgh) l; FOCM: 33, granted L for plantation and hop yard on condition.

Cornelisz, Teunis *patent* for H+L: ERA I: 404 sells part of lot to Willem Fredericksz Bout, Sept. 1666; 66-7, 405 WFBout sells H+L to Jan Cloet, Sept., 1666/Jan. 1665; ERA I: 76/7, Teunis Cornelisz sells H+L+G to Jan Evertsz, July, 1665; 404 [Slingerlandt?]

De Lademaecker, **Michiel (Rijckertsz)** L: FOCM: 29, granted.

De Hooges, Antonie *patent* for L+H: pat. v. 2, pt.2, # 36; ERA I: 231, sells west part of L. to Volckert Jansz, 5 May, 1655; ERA II: 53, widow Storm vander Zee grants L to Cornelis van Dijck, 18 June, 1679; 246, Roelof Swartwout made patent over to Storm Albertse, 1 May, 1662; widow's second husband, Willem Ketelheyn granted H+L to Sybrant van Schayck, 1 Nov., 1684.

Deaconry *patent* for L for poorhouse: is in 1st church

Elbertsz, Reyer land: @ 3rd kill; FOCM: 7, he is granted the use

Fransz, Jan van Hoesem *patent* for L: pat. v. 2, pt. 1,# 17; ERA II: 163, Gerrit Visbeeck sells H+L to Thomas Davitsz Kikebell, Aug, 1682; FOCM: 6, lot Willem Jurriaensz assigned to JFvH.

Fredericksz, Willem *patent* for H+L G: pat. v. 3, pt. 2, # 53; ERA II: 203, Teunis Dircksz van Vechten sells H+L to Marcelis Jansz, Nov. 1683.

Gerritsz, Albert *patent* H+L; pat v. 2, pt. 2,# 41; pat. for H+L, in the keeping of A van Ilpendam: ERA I: 407, Jan Koster sells part (H+L) to Gerrit Bancker, April, 1667; 418, GA sells
H+L to Jan van Eeckelen, April, 1667.

Gerritsz, Goosen *patent* for L-G-G: pat. v. 2, pt. 2, # 13.

Hartgers, Pieter *patent* for L; ERA IV: 40 and ERA II: 172, 286, sells H on part of the L to
J. Withart, 4 July, 1658.

Hendricksz, Marten Verbeeck *patent* for L; pat. v. 3, pt. 1, # 78, 87; FOCM: 5, inhabitant

Herbertsz, Andries *patent* for L; pat. v. 2, pt. 2, # 22, Hendrick Hendricksz grants part
patent, L+H, to Stoffel Jansz, 15 Aug., 1659; ERA I: 36-7, 263, sells part, H, L and G, to
Leendert Philipsz, 10 July, 1657; 272, L. Philipsz grants H+L to Hendrick Hendricksz, 15
Aug., 1659; 332, L. Philipsz grants G to Nicolaes Meyer, 27 Aug., 1663.

Herpertsz, Marten (*de metselaer*) *patent* for L, ERA I: 390, 392, commissaries sell H+L to
Sander Leendertsz Glen, 22 nov. 1664; 358, Sander Leendertsz grants H+L to Jan Hendricksz van Bael, 18 Aug. 1664; FOCM, 26, inhabitant Bw; 33, granted L beh. his place.

Jacobsz, Rutger *patent* for L; ERA I: 305, sells part, H+L, to Cornelis Steenwijck, 7 Aug.
1662; 382, sells part L to Gerrit Bancker, 2 Sept. 1661; 383, sells part L to Barent Reyndertsz, 9 Sept. 1661.

Jacobsz, Caspar FOCM: 6, granted lot

Jacobsz, Teunis *patent* for L; pat. v. 2, pt. 2, # 70

Jansz, Hendrick Westerkamp *patent* for L; ERA I: 417-18, Femmetie Alberts sells part,
H+L, to Daniel Rinckhout, 19/29 April, 1667; 399, widow Femmetje sold part of lot to
Hendrick Jochemsz, who sold it to Philip Pietersz Schuyler, 19 June, 1666, and [ERA I:
457] to Abraham Staets, 12 July, 1669. ERA II: 137, Femmetje sold part lot to Hendrick
Jochemsz, who sold it to Abraham Staets, 22 Aug., 1688.

Jansz, Dirck *patent* for L, G; pat. v. 2, pt. 2, # 24 ERA I: 491, Marten Cregier grants two
houses *aen malcanderen* to Jurriaen Theunisz Tappen, 13 Sept., 1672; ERA II: 180, Jurriaen Theunisz sells them to Harmen Rutgersz; (waarsch.) ERA IV: DJC proposes to sell
H+L, ?, 1658

Jansz, Jacob van Noortstrant *patent* for L; pat. v. 3, pt 2, # 153; FOCM: 6, granted addi-
tion to house; likely, ERA I: 202, sells H and G to Rutger Jacobsz, 3 September, 1654; 272,
Teunis Cornelisz Slingerlant grants part of patent, H+L, to Jan Dareth, 15 Aug., 1659;
ERA II: 68, sells L with 2 houses and l to Hendrick Gerritsz vander Meulen, 16 Jan, 1679;
ERA IV: 43, JJvN sells lot to Hendrick Gerritsz, who sells part, H+L, to Teunis Slinger-
lant, 12 Sept. 1658 (**NB, check: poorhouse has part of patent in 1654 of his house**)

Jansz, Jacob Schermerhoorn *patent* for L+G; pat. v. 2, pt. 2, # 27

Jansz, Volckert *patent* for L,G; pat. v. 2, pt. 2, # 33; ERA II: 91, grants part of L to Gerrit
Bancker, 11 Feb. 1680; 126, sells part of L. to Harmen Rutgersz, 20 June, 1681. **Perhaps**
ERA II: 331-32, widow sells part of L. and H. to deacons Lutheran Church, 4 Dec. 1685.
ERA III: 331, idem.

Kleermaker, **Evert** (Jansz; Wendel), FOCM: 32, committee to lay out lot and road for him,
3 Dec., 1652

Leendertsz, Sander *patent* for G+L+H; ERA I: 293, Evert Pels grants part of patent, G., to
"Messieurs," 14 maart, 1661; 300, SLG grants part of patent, a L., to Jan Thomasz, 17
April, 1662; 314, SLG grants part of patent, H+L, to Tomas Poulusz, 26 Oct., 1662; ERA
IV: 99, SLG grants L to Willem Fredericksz Bout, 17 March, 1659.

Luyersz, Jacob FOCM: 14, request for place for H. granted on place where his present H
stands, 18 June, 1652; ERA I: 313

Michielsz, Jan, *patent* for L, 1650; pat. v. 2, pt. 2, # 2

Pietersz, **Abraham Vosburgh** *patent* for L; pat. v. 4, pt. 2, # 1; FOCM: 3, granted permission to proceed with erection of his house

Pietersz, **Philip Schuyler** FOCM: 21, granted lot; 33, lot definitely granted to him

Steenwijck, **Cornelis** *patent* for L, G; pat. v. 2, pt. 2, # 36

Teller, **Willem** *patent* for L, G; pat. v. 2, pt. 2, # 65

Theunisz, **Cornelis Bos** *patent* for L, G; ERA I: 288, grants part patent to commissaries, 12 Oct. 1660; 399-400, Jurriaen Jansz Groenewout grants part of L, with H., to Paulus Martensz, 6/26 June, 1666; 408, widow and Jurriaen Jansz Groenewout sell part L, with H., to Symon Volkertsz, 19 April, 1667; 409, widow and Jurriaen Jansz Groenewout sell part of patent, L and G, to Huybert Jansz, 9 April, 1667. NB: **Jansz, Jurriaen Groenewout** *patent* for l; pat. v. 2, pt. 2 # 37. [NB: I think this was patent to Cornelis Theunisz Bos, whose widow married JJG)

Thomasz, **Jan** *patent* for H+L '52; ERA I: 30, 33, JT grants H+L and G to Claes Hendricksz, 1 May, 1657, 23 June, 1657; 77-8, Claes Jansz *Timmerman* grants part of patent, H+L, to Andries Jochemsz, 3 Aug. 1665; 293, Willem Jansz Stoll grants part of patent, H+L, to Jan Verbeeck, 15 March, 1661

Verbeeck, **Jan**; FOCM: 4, inhab; took burgher oath, 17 April, 1652

Vosch, **Cornelis (Cornelisz)** *patent* L, G; ERA I: 301, sells garden to Abraham Staets, 5 May, 1662; 416, sells part, L, and H built by JTG, to Jurriaen Theunisz *Glaesemaecker*, 12 April, 1667; 372, 375, likely references to patent

According to the translated patents and *ERA*, thirty-two people received a patent in 1652. From information in the *FOCM*, for example, it is clear, however, that many more used land at that time. More than fifty people may have been at the west side of the river before 1652. Several of these, only received a patent in 1653. In the patents and grants to the people in the above list, ten people are mentioned as neighbors of some of the above, but are not referred to as getting land granted:

Cornelisz, Cornelis; Cornelisz, Gysbert [v. Weesp]; De Cuyper, Gerrit; Jacobsz, Pieter; Jansz, Jacob; Jansz, Lauris ; Jansz, Thomas; Slichtenhorst, Gerrit

PATENTS 1653

Adriaensz, **Rut** *patent, L+G*; pat. v. 2, pt. 2, # 72

Aertsz, **Wouter** *patent, L/G* [parcel] – pat. v. 2, pt. 2, # 41

Andriesz, **Arent** [burgher oath] FOCM: 37

Andriesz, **Hendrick,** *patent, L+G* – pat. v. 2, pt. 2, # 17

Barentsz, **Frans** *patent, L+H+Y* – pat. v. 2, pt. 2, # 18

Barentsz, **Jan (Wemp)** shows his patent, FOCM: 95

Bensingh, **Dirck** *patent, H+L+G*; ERA I: 394

Bronck, **Pieter** *patent, H+L+Br+Millh+H+well* [not blt], ERA I: 305

Bruynsz, **Hage** *patent, H+L* – pat. v. 2, pt. 2, # 41

Claesz, **Jan (Brant)** l – FOCM: 35-36, 39

Cornelisz, **Gysbert** (Lysbeth; m. François Boon) *patent, L+H*; FOCM: 41, ERA I: 38 (L), 365, 413 (L)

Cornelisz, **Cornelis** *patent, H+L*; pat. v. 2, pt. 2, # 45

De Vos, **Andries,** *patent,* woodland L+H+stable-; pat. v. 2. pt. 2, # 75; FOCM: 75/6

Dijckman, **Johannes** L; FOCM: 49

Elbertsz, **Reyer** *patent, H+L+G*; pat. v. 2, pt 2, # 10; ERA I:361; ERA II:207

Fransz, Jan (van Hoesem) *patent*, L+G; pat. v. 2, pt. 1, # 17; FOCM:37; ERA II:163 (H+L)

Fredericksz, Carsten *patent*, L; pat. v. 2, pt. 2, # 30; ERA I: 406

Fredericksz, Willem, allowed to build horsemill on his lot if he keeps with street line, FOCM: 41

Gerritsz, Goosen *patent*, H+L [not blt]; ERA I: 261, 362; ERA IV: 57

Gerritsz, Albert *patent*, G/H+L [not built]; ERA I: 356 (G)

Hendricksz, Jacob (Sijbingh) & Stoffel Jansz *patent*, H+L – pat.v. 2, pt. 2., # 44

Hendricksz, Ruyter (?)

Herbertsz, Andries *patent*, ERA I: 397 (G)

Hofmeyer, Willem *patent*, L ; ERA IV: 18, 22

Jacobsz, Caspar *patent*, L+G+H; pat. v. 2, pt. 2, # 21

Jacobsz, Rut, *patent*, L to West of H; ERA I: 30

Jansz, Adriaen (van Ilpendam) *patent*, L+G// L+H+Y; pat. v. 2, pt. 2, # 9

Jansz, Adriaen (v Leyden) *patent*, [not blt] H+Y+L+G; pat. v. 2, pt. 2, # 49; FOCM 49 (L); ERA II: 193

Jansz, Arent ?

Jansz, Carsten, *patent*, H+L, ERA I: 263

Jansz, Evert (v Embden; Wendel) *patent*, (L where his H stood)/L+G; pat. v. 2, pt. 2, # 25

Jansz, Gerret mentioned in other patents

Jansz, Jacob (Hap) *patent*, L+G; pat. v. 2, pt. 2, # 21

Jansz, Jacob (Schermerhoorn) *patent*, L+G; H+L+Y, pat. v. 2, pt. 2, # 27

Jansz, Jacob (v. Noortstrant) *patent*, L, ERA II: 370

Jansz, Jan (Cuyper) mentioned as neighbor in patent of Jacob Symonsz Clomp

Jansz, Lourens *patent*, L where H stood l+g; pat. v. 2, pt. 2, # 29

Jansz, Rem *patent*, G/H+L+smithy [not built]; ERA I: 6 (H)

Jansz, Stoffel *patent*, H+L; ERA I: 272 (see also Jacob Hendricksz Sijbingh)

Jansz, Thomas *patent*, L+H+G; pat. v. 2, pt. 2, # 74; ERA II: 61

Jansz, Willem (Stoll/Hap) *patent*, ERA IV: 30

Jochemsz, Hendrick G (formerly D Bensingh's); FOCM: 52

Ketelheyn, Jochem *patent*, H+L [not blt]; pat. v. 2, pt. 2, # 26? H+L, pat. v. 2, pt. 2, #38; FOCM: 39

Kleyn, Ulderick *patent*, H+L+G; ERA I: 268, 413

Labatie, Jan *patent*, H+L/new H; pat. v. 2, pt. 2, # 28; FOCM: 36, 44, 49 (l); ERA I: 308

Leendertsz, Gabriel -G- [not blt on lot]; mentioned as neighbor on Andries de Vos's patent

Lodt, Pieter – not blt in '54; '53 neighbor lot Hage Bruynsen

Loockermans, Pieter *patent*, L+G; pat. v. 2, pt. 2, # 40

Loockermans, Pieter (*de oude*) *patent*, H+L; ERA I: 275

Lourensz, Lourens *patent*, H+L; pat. v. 2, pt. 2, # 10; ERA I: 362, 363; ERA II: 38 (Y); ERA IV: 91-92

Luyersz, Jacob *patent*, H+L; ERA I: 313

Martensz, Jan, garden given to Labatie. FOCM, 36

Pietersz, Gillis *patent*, L+H+Y; pat. v. 2, pt. 1, # 17

Pietersz, Lucas, G borders EJWendel's; not blt in '54, FOCM, 125, 149

Pietersz, Philip (Schuyler) may enlarge lot, FOCM, 112

Rijckertsz, Michiel (*de Laedemaecker*) *patent*, L+G+H+Y; pat. v. 2, pt. 2, # 16

Rinckhout, Daniel *patent*, H+L; ERA I: 278, 322

Roelofsz, Jan mentioned as neighbor in Goosen Gerritsz's patent (had patent in '54)

Ryverdinck, Pieter L; FOCM: 49

Sandersz, Thomas *patent,* L+G; pat. v. 2, pt. 2, # 51 (G); v 2, pt. 2, # 52
Schaets, Gideon *patent,* L+G; FOCM: 49, 52 (G); ERA I: 416 (G)
Staets, Abraham *patent,* H+L; G; L-G; pat. v. 2, pt. 2, # 7; v. 2, pt. 2, # 12; v. 2, pt. 2, # 24;
    FOCM: 36, 49; ERA I: 363, 415
Symonsz, Jacob (Clomp) *patent,* H+L, G [not blt]; pat. v. 2, pt. 2, # 46; ERA II: 356
Theunisz, Jurriaen *patent,* H+L; ERA I: 37, 270
Tysz, Jacob, mentioned in Gb AdV, N of 3d kil
Tysz, Jacques (?) Jan Labatie has lot 'past Tijssen's' FOCM, 58
Van Valckenburgh, Lambert (?) in FO; has garden; mentioned in patent Hendrick An-
    driesz as neighbor
Verbeeck, Jan *patent,* L+H+Y; pat. v. 2, pt. 2, # 18; v 2., pt. 2, # 34
Wesselsz, Jochem *patent,* H+L+bake shop; pat. v. 3/4, pt. 2, # 27; ERA IV: 45

In 1653 various people were mentioned because they had not fenced in their gardens or
lots. An extension for not having fenced in the garden was given to A. Jansz van Ilpen-
dam, Tomas Sandersz, Symon Volckertsz Veeder. Fined ƒ25 for not having fenced in garden were in December Rem Jansz, Adriaen Jansz van Leyden, Machiel *de lademaecker*
(Rijckertsz), Pieter Bronck, Goosen Gerritsz, Pieter Hartgers, Pieter Hartgers for Annetje
Bogardus, Merten *Metselaer* (Herpertsz). Excused were: Adriaen Jansz van Ilpendam and
Gabriel Leendertsz; default: Albert *de timmerman* en Jochem Keteleyn.
At least forty-nine people received a patent in 1653, of whom six had received one in
1652 as well. The *FOCM* suggest that another eleven people received lots, of whom two
had received a patent in 1652. Before the end of 1653, then, at least seventy-four, but possibly ninety-three people had received one or more patents. During the years following
patents were distributed, but never again this many.

PATENTS 1654

Bensingh, Dirck, FOCM: 112, 135 (g); ERA 215 (is burgher)
Bogardus, Annetje, FOCM: 92 (possession of – Jacob Jansz Schermerhoorn)
Company's house, FOCM: 135
Cornelis, Lysbeth, FOCM: 87 (in FO, buys it from Gerrit Jansz)]
Cornelisz, Pieter, wife: FOCM: 158
Gerritsz, Claes, FOCM: 83, 87 (G)
Gerritsz, Wijnant, *patent,* L, pat. v. 2, pt. 2, # 53
Hendricksz, Jan (Sijbingh) FOCM: 114 (G laid out), 125
Hendricksz, Marten, *patent,* Land, pat. v. 3, pt. 1, # 79; v. 2, pt. 2 # 87
Herbertsz, Andries, FOCM: 82 (G); ERA I: 214 (has residence + small H)
Jacobsz, Caspar, *patent,* Land, L+G, Parcel; pat. v. 2, pt. 2, # 11
Jacobsz, Rut G (will build house next to dwelling house) FOCM: 120
Jansz, Adriaen (v Leyden) *patent,* L+H+G, pat. v. 2, pt. 2, # 50; ERA II: 369
Jansz, Adriaen (v Leyden), FOCM: 137 (publ. house)
Marcelisz, Hendrick, *patent,* H+L+L, pat. v. 2, pt. 2, # 35; FOCM: 93 ; ERA I: 411
Megapolensis, Johannes, FOCM: 159
Philipsz, Leendert, *patent,* L, pat. v. 2, pt. 2, # 52
Pietersz, Gillis, *patent,* L+H+G, pat. v. 2, pt. 1, # 17; ERA I: 323
Pietersz, Lucas, FOCM: 136 (G enclosed)
Roelofsz, Jan, *patent,* G, ERA I: 251

Asking for lots in 1654:

Adriaensz, Jacob	25 nov. FOCM, 162
Albertsz, Barent	20 oct. FOCM, 159
Andriesz, Albert	20 oct. FOCM, 159
Bastiaensz, Harmen	17 febr. FOCM, 98
Carstensz, Carsten	20 oct. FOCM, 159
Claesz, Adriaen	25 nov. FOCM, 162
Cornelisz, Teunis (Slingerlant)	20 oct. FOCM, 159
Gerritsz, Hendrick	20 oct. FOCM, 159
Hendricksz, Claes (*Timmerman*)	25 nov. FOCM, 162
Jacobsz, Claes	20 oct. FOCM, 159
Jansz, Willem (Stoll/Hap)	25 nov. FOCM, 162
Labatie, Jan	25 nov. FOCM, 162
Lammersz, Jan (*soldaet*)	idem
Segertsz, Gerrit	20 oct. FOCM, 159
Van Loosdrecht, Jacob	21 oct. FOCM, 160
Van Valckenburgh, Lambert	20 oct. FOCM, 159

Not built upon lots:

Brijnsz, Ancker	FOCM, 114
Bronck, Pieter	114
Gerbertsz, Eldert not enclosed lot in time	FOCM, 128
Gerritsz Hendrick	125
Gerritsz, Wijnant	125
Groot, Simon	124
Hendricksz (Sibbinck), Jan	
Jansz (Flodder), Jacob	128
Jansz, Lourens not fenced in his garden	
Leendertsz, Gabriel	125
Lodt, Pieter	125
Lourensz, Lourens	114
Philipsz, Leendert	127
Pietersz, Lucas	125
Roelofsz, Jan	132 (not blt)

1654: gardens to be laid out, FOCM, 125

PATENTS 1655

Barentsz, Frans, FOCM, 184

De Karreman, **Michiel,** FOCM, 183. (requested by Rem Jansz *Smit*)

Eating house *Selden Satt,* FOCM, 174 (this already exists; whose tavern is it? H. Jochimsz?)

Gauw, Jan, FOCM, 192 (requests the lot heretofore granted to Carsten living in the *Grenenbos,* granted upon condition that he will pay Carsten

Hartgers, Pieter, FOCM, 184

Jansz, Rein, H+L Before '55; had patent in 1653

Leendertsz, Sander, FOCM, 184

Thijsz, Jaques, FOCM, 171

Thomasz, Jan, FOCM, 184

N.B.: FOCM, 184 Lots at the hill granted to magistrates: no. 1 to Sander Leendertsz (west of Philip Pietersz); 2 to Frans Barentsz; 3 to Pieter Hertgers; 4 to Jan Thomasz, on the west side of the guard house; 5. on the west side, adjoining it.

Asking for lots:
De Vlamingh, Pieter, FOCM, 191 req. L 5, inspection will be made.
Gerbertsz, Eldert, FOCM, 174 (G, postponed until river is open).

PATENTS 1656

Abrahamsz, Mattheus, *patent* L+H, pat. v. 2, pt. 2, # 33
Albertsz, Barent, G, FOCM, 239
Blockhouse church, FOCM, 231
Chambers, Thomas, L for H, 2 G's; FOCM, 214
Jacobsz, Rut -permission to build waterwheel in kill behind his dwelling, FOCM, 223
Jansz, Volckert (Douw), Jan Thomasz, and Pieter Hertgers, FOCM, 223 (5 or 6 feet of ground of the public road included within the enclosure of the lot on which their brewery stands; granted.
Pietersz, Philip (Schuyler), *patent* L; L+G, *LP:* 81, 100-101, L; L+G
Van Hoesem, Jan, L for H, FOCM, 239
Not built on lots:
Bruynsz, Ancker, FOCM, 232
Jansz, Arien (van Leyden), FOCM, 232
Jochem Keteluyn, FOCM, 232
Jan Verbeeck, FOCM, 232
Requesting lots:
Gysbertsz, Albert: lot for G; court will inspect place so as to accommodate AG according to its location.
Jansz, Thomasz (Mingael) Cornelis Theunisz requests for Thomas Jansz Mingael a lot for a H between Pieter Loockermans and Pieter Meesz; under advisement.

PATENTS 1657

Hendricksz, Claes, *patent*, L+H+G; G; *LP*, 93; ERA I: 294
Jansz, Willem (Stoll), *patent* L; ERA I: 294
Requesting:
Meesz, Pieter G; FOCM, 273 (after inspection will be accommodated)

PATENTS 1658

Chambers, Thomas, *patent*, L+H+G; pat. v. 2, pt. 2, # 8; *LP,* 95; ERA IV: 97; ERA II: 215
Jacobsz, Pieter, *patent*, L+H+G; *LP*, 96
Jansz, Jurriaen (Groenewout), *patent*, L+H; pat. vol. 2, pt. 2, # 23; is likely patent to Cornelis Theunisz Bos
Jansz, Volckert & Jan Thomasz, *patent*, pasture land, *LP*, 96
Leendertsz, Sander, *patent*, L; *LP:* 94; ERA I: 58
Meesz, Pieter, *patent*, L+H+G; ERA I: 414; *LP*, 95
Pietersz, Philip (Schuyler), *patent*, L+O+G; pat. v. 2, pt. 2, # 11; *LP,* 95
Van Curler, Arent, *patent*, land, *LP*, 96
Van Rensselaer, Jeremias, *patent*, L+H+G; pat. v. 2, pt. 2, # 35; *LP,* 94

PATENTS 1659

Andriesz, Jan, *patent,* L, *LP,* 96

Hartgers, Pieter, *patent,* L+H; L+H+G; vol. 2, pt. 2, # 67/8; *LP,* 97, 98

Jansz, Volckert & Jan Thomasz, *patent,* pasture; v. 2. pt.2, # 31/2; *LP,* 96

Pietersz, Philip (Schuyler) *patent,* L; vol. 2, pt. 2, # 7

Theunisz, Claes L; G; FOCM, 428

Van Curler, Arent *patent,* L; pat. v. 2, pt. 2, # 33; v. 4, pt. 2, # 97; ERA II: 114, 115, 125; *LP,* 96

PATENTS 1660

Dareth, Jan, *patent,* L+H+G; pat. v. 2, pt. 2, # 6; ERA I: 290; ERA II: 209; *LP,* 98

Hartgers, Pieter, *patent,* L for H; *LP,* 98

Jacobsz, Pieter *patent,* L; pat. v. 4, pt. 1, # 25; ERA I:380

Meesz, Pieter (Vrooman) *patent,* L; L+G; ERA I: 282 (H+L+G); *LP,* 98

Theunisz, Jurriaen land; ERA I:393

PATENTS 1661

Thomasz, Jan, *patent,* L; L+G; *LP,* 100, 101

Van Aecken, Jan, *patent,* H+G; *LP,* 100

PATENTS 1662

PATENTS 1663

Symonsz, Symon (Groot), *patent,* pat., v. 2, pt. 2, # 25

PATENTS 1664

Thomasz, Jan, *patent,* L+ G; pat. v. 2. pt. 2, # 19 (This is the same as *LP,* 100 (1661)

Pietersz, Gillis, *patent,* piece of ground; pat. v. 2, pt. 2, # 20 (I think that this was 1654)

Appendix 4: measurements of some houses

Owner	ft. length	ft. width	otherinfo
Jan van Hoesem	24	19	with 5-feet side aisle, room, attic, lot 10x4 rods
Jacob Joosten, '57	16	?	'new bedstead; trap door; ƒ570; lot is 30 wood-feet x 28 feet in rear'
Cornelis de Vos, '57?	25	21 and half	'has sign; old house; lot width 25 and half ft.'
Cornelis de Vos, '61	25	18	'lean-to with chimney and oven; with alley except for lean-to.' length lot 9 rods, width 17 and half rear, 18 ft. front
Cornelis de Vos, '58	25	18-4/18	lot: 19 ft 4 inch, rear 14 ft
Dirck Bensingh, '54	16	?	pantry, 3 girders, brackets, garret
Jochem Wesselsz	16	?	
Evert Pels	39-40	?	in Fort Orange
Pieter Bronck, '59?	16	?	'rental; Indian house nearby; except little shed'
Pieter de Maecker	25	18?	'gutter; proper drip when C. de Vos' house torn down'
Symon Symonsz Groot	20 woodft.	20 ft square	'except horse stable; lot 4x7 and a half rods'
Tjerck Claesz, '60	20	30	width includes side-aisle
Teunis Cornelisz Slingerlant	30 woodft	22 woodft	with lot on side of house
Teunis Cornelisz Slingerlant	15	15 ft. square	small house
Ulderick Cleijn, '58	16	20	ƒ709 with lot of 4x8 rods
Jan Harmensen, '58	15/18?	18	with hog pen, oven, third interest in well, lot
Jan Lambertsz, '59?	20	20	'built up all around with half-brick; lot 6x3 rods'
Jacob Loockermans, '59?	15	24	'with kitchen, cellar, small chamber built up with brick; stairs to attic and cellar; bedstead in chamber, gable of matched boards; lot 30 ft. wide; l. to AH's fence'
Pieter Adriaensz	37 and half	26	'fitly built up w. stone; ƒ1306; lot 10x4 rods'
Gysbert Jansz, '62	30	22	lot length 11 rods, 22 rhineland ft.
Symon Volckertsz, '73	15-20	15 wft.	'with bake oven which can bake one mudde flour in 1x; cellar 10 feet square.'
Hans Hendricksz, '79	15/18	22	'2 door frames, 2 window frames with crossing transom and mullion, stairs; window with 2 lights in garret, roof overlapping boards; common mantelpiece'
William Loveridge, '82	55	24/8? 40-3/30?	small house large house
Hendrick Rooseboom, '83	18	10	'balcken inne te laeten in the large house; standing gable, garret, back door;' chimney mantle, window.

Sources: ERAI: 31, 39, 53, 215, 304, 306, 360, 370, 372; ERA III: 410, 471; ERA IV: 21, 36, 44, 51, 68, 110, 111.
Henk Zantkuijl's illustrations are based on the above information.

Appendix 5: magistrates and consistory members, 1652-1664

	1652	1653	1654	1655	1656	1657	1658	1659	1660	1661	1662	1663	1664
Barentsz, Frans (Pastoor)			d, m	fd, m					m	m			
Boon, Francois									d	d, m	d, m	m	
De Hooges, Anthony	d												
Gerritsz, Adriaen (van Papendorp)						d, em	d, m			d, m	c, m	c	c
Gerritsz, Goosen					em	m				d, m	c, m	d, m	
Hargers, Pieter	m		m	e, m	em	e	m						
Hendricksz, Jan (van Bael)						e	m						c, m
Herbertsz, Andries	m	m		e, m	e, m	e	e	m	m				
Jacobsz, Rutger	m	m		m	m		e	fe					
Jansz, Dirck (Croon)	m			m	em		em	m	m	m			
Jansz, Evert (Wendel)				em	d								
Jansz, Jacob (Schermerhoorn)		m	m					c	e, em	fe, m			c, m
Jansz, Stoffel	m		m			m							
Jansz, Volckert (Douw)	m	m		m							c, m	c, m	c, m
Koster, Jan (van Aecken)	m										c	c	d, m
Labatie, Jan	m	em											
La Montagne, Johannes									e	e	c		
Leendertsz, Sander (Glen)			m	m		m		m	m	m			c
Pietersz, Philip (Schuyler)					m	m	e, m	c	d	m	m	c	c
Staets, Abraham	m					m	d		d				
Teller, Willem					d	d	d						
Theunisz, Cornelis (van Westbroeck)	m				fd	m	m						
Thomasz, Jan (Witbeck)		m		d		m			m	m	m	m	m
Van Nes, Cornelis										e	c	c	
Van Slichtenhorst, Gerrit								c	d	d			
Verbeeck, Jan		m	m	e	e	fe		em	m			m	m

e = elder   fe = former elder
d = deacon   fd = former deacon
c = consistory member em = extraordinary magistrate
m = magistrate

Appendix 6: Jobs in Beverwijck, 1652-1664

At first sight many artisans worked in Beverwijck. Further analysis of their number makes clear that they were not all working at the same time. The following lists are based on counting the appearance of an individual in various records (especially *FOCM*, *ERA* vols. 1-4, *DAB*, *VRBM*, *CMR*, *CJVR*, *CMARS* vols. 1-3). I have listed the brewers in the first section in a descriptive way, so that some of the problems faced with counting these individuals are illustrated. The results of the count of other artisans and workers I have listed in tables. When specific mention is made in a document referring to an individual's trade, I have listed this in the table with 'x.' When it is clear that the individual was in the village, but no reference was made to their trade, I have marked that with a '?.' In this situation I think that the person was performing his trade.

Brewers

Frans Barentsz Pastoor	12 Nov. '57, grants his h+l+brewery to Hendrick Andriesz [inv.] for ƒ3630. '56, HA surrenders his claim to the same to Philip Hendricksz, for ƒ4000. 29 april '64, PH sells the same to Jan Dircksz van Eps for ƒ1150.
Hendrick Andriesz	11 dec. 57 buys brewery Frans Barentsz Pastoor (ƒ3630). Sells it 17 Dec. '56 to Philips Hendricksz; he is listed as gunstock-maker in GAA, NA; **I don't think he is a brewer.**
Philip Hendricksz	Philip *de Brouwer;* 17 dec, 56, HA surrenders claim on brewery FBP to PH;1660 he purchases brewery, indebted to HA, pledges brewery and bouwery @ Schenectady. Sept. '63, kills Claes Cornelisz Swits accidentally. 29 April, '64, he sells brewery to Jan Dircksz van Eps (son Maritie Damen); sells bouwery to Cornelis van Nes, stepfather Jan Dircksz van Eps); Cornelis Theunisz Bos has bought horse mill, sells that to Jan Dircksz van Eps May 1, 1664.
Jan Dircksz van Eps	29 April, 1664 buys the house, brewery and mill house of Philip Hendricksz; also kettle, 2 tubs and cooler, with mill house reserving the mill. ƒ1150, C van Nes and Pieter van Alen sureties. Buys horse mill from CTBos, which he bought at public sale of estate of Philip Hendriksz, ƒ112 in beavers.
Pieter Bronck	1645 to Rw; tavern in '51; 9 May '55 enjoined from tapping strong beer as he brews the same; 1660? brewery for sale [invent]; indebted to Reyndert Pietersz ƒ832, pledges brewery. Frans Barentsz Pastoor attorney. '61, lease front part house to Jan Harmensz; indebted ƒ2272 to Jacob Hevick and pledges brewhouse, mill house; aug. '62, sells brewery, house, mill house, horse stable, hay barn, well (or pond?) and lot to Reyndert Pietersz and Jacob Hevick.
Reyndert Pietersz	with Jacob Hevick, buys brewery, dwelling house w. mill house and horse stable, well and lot; also h+l; 5 aug. 62. RP owns ƒ1456 in it, and to Jacob Hevick is coming ƒ2256. In July, 1678 sold to Albert Rijckman. In 1663 they have contract with Jan Harmensz Weendorp, trader.

Jacob Hevick

1. May 3, 1649, leased h+g from director north of Thomas Jansz's house and farm for six years. Owned house and brew house sold at public auction through various hands to Adriaen Jansz van Leyden on Febr. 19, 1655. **2.** In 1662 he buys Pieter Bronck's brewery, together with Reyndert Pietersz. Pietersz owns ƒ1456 in it, and to Hevick is coming ƒ2256. In 1663 they contract with Jan Harmensz Weendorp for a year. Reyndert Pietersz deceased in 1673. Hevick's wife, Geertruy Barents sells in July, 1678 the brew house and dwelling house, mill house and horse stable and land adjacent to Albert Rijckmans.

Jan Harmensz Weendorp

Jurriaen Theunisz owes him 92 bevers for 23 ankers of brandy [7 dec. '61]. Also ƒ736:5 in 1663. 18 aug. '61 he leases front part of Hilleke Bronck's house and 4 Oct. '63 he has a contract with Reyndert Pietersz and Jacob Hevick until end August 1664 regarding living in house and repairing the mill and brewery [ERA III: 255], 19 juli he plans to go to the Republic and is then called a trader. In '74, '75 JH works with Pieter Lassen in brewery.

Jurriaen Theunisz

bought brewery Jac. Hevick [1] 19 Febr. '55. Sold it to Thomas Coningh in 1655. In 1658 he sold hop with Teunis Teunisz *Metselaer* on land of Jan Jansz Otterspoor, dec. **Not a brewer.**

Coningh, Thomas

buys brewery from Jurriaen Theunisz on Febr. 1, 1655. Belonged formerly to Jacob Hevick. Sells it Febr. 19, 1655 to Adriaen Jansz van Leyden. **Probably not a brewer**

Adriaen Jansz v Leyden

19 Febr. '55 buys brewery from Tomas Coningh who bought it from Jurriaen Theunisz on Febr. 1, 1655. Belonged formerly to Jacob Hevick.

Rutger Jacobsz? Excise, '58-60. '73 deacons help him to repair the distilling kettle. **He was likely not a brewer in Beverwijck.**

Jacob Jansz van Noortstrant. Jacob *de Brouwer* and his wife Jannetie *de Brouster*. In May, 1657 received alms when his house burned down. 28 nov. '56, *eyckmeester over de vaeten*. Sold parts of his lot to Rutger Jacobsz [1654], except for mill and brewer's tools; Hendrick Gerritsz (1658). Was called a cooper by La Montagne. I have not noticed anything indicating that he really was brewing, except for his name.

Rutger Jacobsz

1650, brews with Goosen Gerritsz. Is against ordinance tapster's excise being posted. 18 March, '59: Gerritsz and Jacobsz, 'formerly in partnership.' Several beer deliveries. Sells his H+L to Harmen Vedder, with a portion where his brewery stands, which will be torn down in the coming month of November, 1657 [Trans. Pearson incorrect]. Buys H+l+g from JJvN, except for mill and brewer's tools, 9 March, '54. Feb. 56 asks for waterwheel in kill behind dwelling house. Indebted in 1661; in '62 he sells ten half-barrels, a beer wagon, a light beer brew kettle and two horses.

Goosen Gerritsz	'49-50, leases brewery with Rut Jacobsz; '50, allowed to tap. '54, beer deliveries; March, '59: RJ&GG formerly in partnership; 71, surety, '75, buys with Pieter Lassen brewery Harmen Rutgers.
Harmen Vedder	buys house and lot Rut Jacobsz, 31 Jan. '57. Dit is de *brouwerij die gebroocken sal worden.* I think the brewery is gone when he buys the lot. **He was likely not a brewer.**
Pieter Hartgers	Seems to have had a brewery in 1646. In January 1655 buys a corner of the lot of Femmetje Alberts, together with Volckert Jansz Douw and Jan Thomasz. In 1656, five or six ft. of the public road included withing the enclosure of their brewery lot was granted to them. April, 1656, Harmen Jacobsz Bamboes is indebted to them for ƒ1408. April, 1659 Jurriaen Theunisz is indebted for ƒ660 to them, and Jan Martensz ƒ139 (these are tavern keepers).
Volckert Jansz Douw	April, '75, sells his half to Harmen Rutgersz. Hires 6 November, 1656 Livijn Bohner from West Phalia, brewer's servant in Amsterdam for three years at. 350 Carolus guilders a year in beavers plus food, drink, board and passage. No compensation if wounded during work time. (GAA, NA1306/202ᵛ)
Jan Thomasz	April, '75 sells his half to Harmen Rutgersz.
Harmen Rutgersz	owns brewery in June, 1666. Bought 1/2 in March 1675 of Jan Thomasz [ERA I: 111], other half of VJDouw in April, 1675. Nov. 1671 he sold it to Pieter Lassen. 31 mei, '75 sells brewery to Goosen Gerritsz and Pieter Lassen.
Pieter Lassen	Buys with Goosen Gerritsz. Herman Rutgersz' brewery in 1675.
Labatie, Jan	June 15, '47, permission to erect house in Fort Orange and brew therein. Nov. 54 he intends to sell his h in FO to Adriaen Jansz vLeyden @ S-angle of fort; this is canceled. In '61 sells it to Evert Pels. May, '61: Cornelis Cornelisz van Voorhout is indebted ƒ425 to Labatie for purchase and delivery of brewery, brew kettle, vat and appurtenances. This is sold in '67 to Jacob Joosten at Antony Jansen' s.
Cornelis Cornelisz and Jan Witmondt	sell their brewhouse in Greenbush to Willem Brouwer for ƒ1207:–, 19 sept. 1657.
Willem Brouwer	Buys brewery in 1657 from Cornelis Cornelisz and Jan Witmond [invent.], and sells it to Cornelis van Nes and Jan Oothout.
Cornelis van Nes and Jan Oothout	father and son-in-law, both own half of the brewery in Greenebos, bought of Willem Brouwer. Declared March, 21, 1664. They both own half a share.
Evert Pels	contract 5 June '42 for 6 years [1 jan, '43 – '49]; allowed to trade as A Staets; Salary *boven het draff 54 st. vande tonne* of which he can draw 34 for the right to wood and hops of which the patroon will get 20 st. Toestemming AvC nodig om bier op crediet te verkopen. Niet boven ƒ500. Feb. '47 leases farm S Walichsz but in 1649 leases with Willem Fredericksz Bout

farm in Greenbush formerly occupied by Jacob Jansz Flodder until 1658. Jacob Adriaensz works with EP; id. Quirijn Cornelisz. Sept. '51 with Marten Hendricksz promises to make payment for brewery, total is ƒ2501:8. 19 Oct, '51, Gilis Fonda wants to distill liquor in EP's house next to brewery in Greenbush.

Marten *de Brouwer*

(= Marten Hendricksz) Had interest in brewery with Evert Pels in 1651; Feb.'52, lot, shall support himself by brewing. April, '53, had built a malt kiln, used 2000 brick. Likely south of Fort Orange. In 1654 referred to as 'M *de brouwer.*' May, '57 referred to as innkeeper and *bierkaecker*. Poverty, recipient alms.

Harmen Gansevoort

Harmen Harmensz; has brewery in Bethlehem in 1660; buys hops from Claes Bever.

Teunis Dircksz van Vechten

In 1648/9 had half interest in the colony's brewery.

Maria van Rensselaer

1664 Jeremias hires Jacob Gerritsz van Vorst as brewer's servant in the brewery at Rensselaerswijck for ƒ360 in sewant, and no more. Will provide him with reasonable meat and drink and lodging [NYSL, VRMP box 39 (April 1667, 1668].

Jacobus Gerritsz

Hired by Jeremias van Rensselaer in 1664 for ƒ360 in Rensselaerswijck's brewery for ƒ360 annually in sewant, 'and no more.' JvR will provide him with reasonable meat, drink, and lodging.

Nota Bene:

Barent *de brouwer* is ??

Hendrick *de Brouwer* is ??

Jacob *de brouwer* is likely Jacob Jansz van Noortstrant,

Jan *de brouwer* could be Labatie, Oothout, van Eps

Jannetie *de brouster* is Jacob van Noortstrant's wife

Marten *de Brouwer* is Marten Hendricksz (later *de Bierkaecker*)

Philip de Brouwer is Philip Hendricksz

Pieter *de Brouwer* could be Pieter Hartgers, Pieter Lassen, or Pieter Bronck

Appendix 6, jobs: tavern and inn keepers, 1652-1664

	1652	1653	1654	1655	1656	1657	1658	1659	1660	1661	1662	1663	1664
Adriaensz, Pieter	x	x		x	x	?	?	?	?	pb	pb	?	pb
Bierman, Hendrick						e							
Bronck, Pieter		x	pb										
Cleyn, Ulderick & Baefje Pieters			x	?	x	x							
Conincx, Trijntie (J. Luyersz)			x										
Cornelisz, Cornelis (Vos)					x								
Cornelis, Gysbert (*de weert*)	x	died											
Dijckmans, Maria								?	x	?	x	pb	?
Egberts, Egberts													
Fredericksz, Willem (Bout)			x	x	?	xe	e					e	e
Gerritsz, Albert (*de timmerman*)					x	x	?						
Goosens, Maria													
Hendricksz, Jan (Maet)			e	e									
Hendricksz, Marten &Susanna			x	?	?	x							
Jacobsz, Harmen (Bamboes)				x	x	e	died						
Jacobsz, Roelof			x	?	x								
Jansz, Adriaen (van Leyden)			x	xe	xe								
Jansz, Marcelis			x	xe	e	x	?	x	x	pb e	pb e	pb	pb
Jansz, Anthony									x	pb	pb	pb	pb
Jansz, Steven & Maria			pb	x									
Jochimsz, Hendrick		x	pb	x	x	x	x	pb					
Loockermans, Pieter (sr.)									?	pb			?
Martensz, Jan & Dirckie Harms					x	?	x	x	?				
Nolden, Evert						x	x				x		
Teunisz, Jurriaen			x	?	?	?	x	?	x	pb	pb	pb	pb
Van Hoesem, Jan			?										

x = mentioned in documents as tavern/inn keeper
pb = mentioned as having a poor box in the tavern
? = Not mentioned in documents, but likely running a tavern at that time
e = farmer of the excise on alcoholic drinks

Appendix 6, jobs: blacksmiths and gunstockmakers, 1652-1664

	1652	1653	1654	1655	1656	1657	1658	1659	1660	1661	1662	1663	1664
blacksmiths													
Coster, Jan (van Aecken)	x	x	x	x	x	x	x	x	x	x	x	x	x
Fredericksz, Carsten	x	x	x	x	x	x	x	x	x	x	x	x	x
Fredericksz, Mijndert	x	x	x	x	x	x	x	x	x	x	x	x	x
Jansz, Carsten			x										
Jansz, Rem	x	x	x	x	x	x	x	x					
Reyndersz, Barent			x	x	x	x	x	x	x	x	x	x	x
Sandersz, Robert								x	x	x	x	x	x
Sandersz, Thomas	x	x	x										
gunstockmakers													
Andriesz, Hendrick	?	?	?	?	?	?	?	?	?	?	?	died	
Bogardus, Cornelis		?	?		?	?	?	?	?	?	?	?	
Dareth, Jan	?	?	?	?	?	x	x	x	?	?	?	?	?
Jansz, Pieter (*laedemaecker*)					?	?	x	killed					
Nack, Jan						x	x	x	x	x	x	x	x
Pietersz, Philip (Schuyler)x	x	x	x	x	x	x	x	x	x	x	x	x	x
Rijckertsz, Michiel	x	x	?	died									
Van Ravensteyn, Elias							x	x	x	x	x	x	x

? = lives in village but not specifically mentioned as doing smith/gunstockmaker's work
x = worked as smith/gunstockmaker

Appendix 6, jobs: bakers

	1652	1653	1654	1655	1656	1657	1658	1659	1660	1661	1662	1663	1664
Albertsz, Wouter ('56)					p	x	x	?	?	?	?	?	x
Barentsz, Jan (Dullemans; '61)										x	x	x	
Coenraetsz, Hans ('56)							x	x	?	?	?	x	
De Backer, Pieter													
De Backer, Reynier											x		
Hendricksz, Hendrick ('56)					p	?	?	?	?	died			
Hoffmeyer, Willem ('53)	?	?	?	?	p	?	x	?	?	?	?	?	?
Jansz, Hendrick (Westerkamp;'48)	x	x	died										
Jurriaensz, Willem (38)	?												
Lucasz, Evert ('57)						x	?	x	x	?	?	?	?
Otten, Helmer										x	x		
Poulusz, Thomas ('55)				p	p	?	?	?	?	?	x	x	x
Rinckhout, Daniel ('53)	?	?	x	p	?	?	x	x	x		x	?	x
Rinckhout, Jan ('62)											x	?	
Thomasz, Gabriel (Striddles, '62)											x	?	x
Van Hoesem, Jan ('39)	?	?	x	?	p	?	x	?	?	?	x	?	x
Van Malta, de backer										x			
Volckertsz, Symon (Veeder '53)		?	x	x	p	?	?	x	?	?		?	x
Wesselsz, Jochem ('51)	x	x	x	p	p	?	x	x	x	x	x	x	x
Willemsz, Jacob ('52)				p	x								

x = appears in documents as baking

p = signs petition regarding baking

('52) = behind name: year first mentioned in Rensselaerswijck/Beverwijck

? = not specifically mentioned in documents as baker, but possibly performing this trade

Appendix 6, jobs: carpenters

	1652	1653	1654	1655	1656	1657	1658	1659	1660	1661	1662	1663	1664
Abrahamsz, Mattheus					?	x	x	? ?	?	?			?
Barentsz, Fop		x			?	x	?	?					
Barentsz, Jan		?			x		x		x				
Bastiaensz, Harmen (Hoorn??)	x	x	x	?	x	?	?	x	x	?	?	?	
Bensingh, Dirck (van Brevoort)	?	?	x	?	x	?	?	x	died			?	
Chambers, Thomas	?	?		?	Esopus	?	?						
Claesz, Carsten			?			?	x	x	?				
De *maecker*, Pieter					x	?	x	x / in A'dam					?
De *timmerman*, Cornelis					x		x						
De timmerman, Kaerel					x			x					
Fredericksz, Willem (Bout; van Leiden)	x1642	?		?	?	?	?	?	?	?	x	x	?
Gerritsz, Albert	?	x	x		x	x	?	?	?	?	x	x	
Gerritsz, Wijnant (*kistemaecker*)			x			?	died	?	?	mc		?	?
Hendricksz, Claes (van Schoonhoven)			x	x		?	died						
Hendricksz, Geurt				?		?	?	?	?	?	x	?	mc
Hendricksz, Jan			?		x		?						
Jacobsz, Claes (van Rotterdam)		?	x	?		?	?		?	?	x	?	?
Henderiksz, Jacob (Maet/Loosdrecht)			x	?					?				
Jansz, Arent								x	?	in patria	x	x	x
Jansz, Ariaen (Kroon)			x					x		x			
Jansz, Claes (v. Baern or Nijkerck)	x1650	x	x	x		?	?	?	?	in patria		?	x65
Jansz, Dirck (Kroon)	x1642	?	?	?	?	?	?	?	?	?			
Jansz, Jacob (Flodder; v. Kampen)			?	?			x	x	x	?	?	?	x
Jansz, Pieter (Loockermans, *de jonge*)			?	?						?		?	x78
Jansz, Steven (van Nijkerck)	mc48	x	x	x		x	x	x	x	?	?	?	
Jansz, Stoffel		?	x		x	x		?			?	?	mc68
Jurcksz, Paulus						?	?	?	x		?	?	
Meesz, Pieter				?	?	x	?		?	?		?	mc81
Pietersz, Abraham (Vosburgh)	x	x	mc	x	?	x	?	killed	?	x	mc		
Pietersz, Frans (Clouw?)					?				?	x			

Appendix 6, jobs: masons and coopers

Wisselpenningh, Reymer

x = mentioned in the documents as being involved in carpenter's work
? = mentioned in records, but not specifically as carpenter
mc = master carpenter

	1652	1653	1654	1655	1656	1657	1658	1659	1660	1661	1662	1663	1664
masons													
Cornelisz, Jan (Gauw/Vijselaer)		?	x	?	?	?	x	x	?	mm	?		
De *metselaer*, Harmen			x				x	x	x	x		?	?
Gelesz, Pieter (Yelle)					x	x	x	x					
Herpertsz, Marten	?	x	x			x	x						
Teunisz, Teunis			x		?	x	x	x	x				x
coopers													
Abrahamsz, Jacob (van Deusen)													x65
De *cuyper*, Jan (Andriesz??)	?					?		?					?69
Jansz, Jacob (van Noortstrant)	?				?	?			x	x		?	
Jansz, Jan (*de kuyper*)						x							?69
Jansz, Willem (Stoll/Hap)	x	?	?	?	x	?			?	?			

x = appears in document as doing mason or cooper's work
? = appears in documents, but not as specifically doing this work
mm = master mason

Appendix 6, jobs: glaziers, transporting, wheelwrights

	1652	1653	1654	1655	1656	1657	1658	1659	1660	1661	1662	1663	1664
Glaziers													
Bogardus, Pieter	x												
Duyckinck, Evert										x		x	x
Marechael, Claes									x	x			
Teunisz, Jurriaen	?	?	x		x	?	x	?	?	mg	?	?	?
Transporting													
Claesz, Tierck				x	?	?	x		?				
De Kerreman, Claes										x			
De Karreman, Michiel				x									
Wheelwrights													
Adriaensz, Jacob	x	x	x	x	x	?	?	?		x			
Aertsz, Wouter	x			x			x	x		x			mw
De Rademaker, Meus				x									
Gysbertsz, Albert					x	x	x	x	x	x			
Martensz, Poulus					?	?	x	?	?		?		w68

x = mentioned in documents as doing this work
? = mentioned in documents, but not specifically as doing this work
mw = master wheelwright
mg = master glazier
w68 = named wheelwright in 1668

Appendix 6, jobs: tailors

	1652	1653	1654	1655	1656	1657	1658	1659	1660	1661	1662	1663	1664
Adriaensz, Rutger	x	x	died										
Barentsz, Jan (*snijder*)												x	?
Cuyler, Hendrick												?	?
De kleermaecker, Gisbert													x
De snijder, Abraham							x	?	?	?	?	?	?
De snijder, Cobus (Jansz)							x	?	?	?	?	?	?
De snijder, Hendrick (Cordiael)			?	?	x	?	?	?	?	?	?	?	
De snijder, Leendert (Philipsz)			?	?		?	?	x	?	mt	?	?	mt
De stijve snijder, Hendrick					x								
Gerritsz, Hendrick *			?	x	?	?	?	?	?	?	mt	?	?
Jansz, Evert (Wendel)	x		?	?	?	?	?	?	?	?	?	?	
Jansz, Frans (Pruyn)									?	?			
Jansz, Hendrick (Rooseboom)			?	?				x	x			?	
Jansz, Willem (Schut)			?	?		?	?	?	?	?		x	?
Machielsz, Jan	x	?	?	?	?	?	?						
Thijssen, Jacob (van der Heijden)			?	mt/A'd		mt	x						
Van den Berch, Arent													mt65
Verbeeck, Jan	x	?	?	?	?	?	x	x	?	?	?	?	?
Vinhaegen, Jan			?	?	?	?	?	?	?	?	?	?	mt67

x = noted in documents as working as tailor

? = not specifically mentioned as tailor, but likely working as such

mt = master tailor

mt/A'd = master tailor in Amsterdam

mt67 = called master tailor in 1667

* = possibly the same person as Hendrick de snijder or Hendrick de stijve snijder

Appendix 6, jobs: shoemakers

	1652	1653	1654	1655	1656	1657	1658	1659	1660	1661	1662	1663	1664
Arentsz, Rutger	ms	?	?	?	?	?	?	x	x	?	?	x	x
Bries, Hendrick										in Bw	?	ms	x
Brouwer, Willem						x	?	?	?	ms	ms	?	x
Evertsz, Jan													x
Isaacksz, Arent								ms	x	?	x	x	x
Meyndertsz, Barent						?	?	ms	?	x	?	x	x
Teunisz, Cornelis (Bos)	*schoester*	?	?	?	?	?	x	?	x	?	?	?	?
Thomasz, Harmen							?	?	?	?	?	ms	?

ms = first time mentioned as master shoemaker
x = appears in document as shoemaker
? = mentioned in documents, but not especially referred to as shoemaker

Appendix 7: Wages for migratory farmhands

Name	Year	Age	Term	Earnings
CEW	1651	24	3 yrs	ƒ125 + passage, food, drink as that is the custom there.
LBvN		26	3	ƒ120 + id.
GPhvV		34	3	ƒ125 + id
JHvH		21	3	ƒ120 + id.
FGvA		15	6	first 2 yrs ƒ40, next 2 yrs ƒ50, last 2 yrs ƒ60 + id.
EEvN		14	6	first 2 yrs ƒ30, next 2 yrs ƒ40, last 2 yrs ƒ50 + id.
PPvA		15	6	idem
CJvB		16	6	idem
SJvA		19	6	first 2 yrs ƒ52, next 2 yrs ƒ62, last 2 yrs ƒ72 + id.
RCvN		16	4	first 2 yrs ƒ50, last 2 yrs ƒ65
RJvB		19	3	ƒ100 per yr + id.
ADvB		40	3	ƒ125 per yr + id.
TJvH	1656	20	4	ƒ80 + food, drink, board
CLvC	1657		4	ƒ135 Hollands in wares, + food, board, passage
CCV	id		4	idem
TGvC	id		4	ƒ60; free passage. If comportment good and loyal, better wages at Van Curler's decision.
PPL	1659	24	4	ƒ137:10, half in beavers, half in sewant + food, drink, board and passage
JHvG	id	29	4	idem
CTvH	id	28	4	idem
CCvH	id	17	6	first 4 yrs ƒ40, last 2 yrs, ƒ62:10 + food, drink, board and passage
PPCvS	59	6		idem
TWvM	1660	26	4	ƒ150, half in beavers, half in sew.+ board, food and drink
DMvM	id	20	4	first 2 yrs, ƒ100, last 2 yrs. ƒ120, half beaver, half sew. + id.
CSMvL	id	21	6	first 3 yrs ƒ100, last 3 yrs ƒ140 in grain or beavers + board at JvR
CTvW	id	21	4	first 2 yrs ƒ120, last 2 yrs ƒ130 in grain or beavers' price + board at JvR
STvW	id	20	4	first 2 yrs ƒ100, last 2 yrs ƒ120 + board at JBW
JJvK	1662	21	4	ƒ120 in half beaver, half grain + food, drink and board @ Leendert Cornelisz's
GL	1663	18	6	first 2 yrs ƒ60, next 2 yrs ƒ80, last 2 yrs ƒ100 + board at Jan Thysz
JR	id	16	6	board at JvR's and clothing at patroon's discretion + passage

two servant girls:

Name	Year	Age	Term	Earnings
ETvQ	1655	ydr.	3	ƒ60 car. guldens + passage, board, food, drink, laundry, wringing
MJ	1657	14	5	first yr. ƒ50, 2nd yr. ƒ60, last 3 years ƒ70 + passage, food, drink/board

*   Most information is drawn from the Notarial Records in the Amsterdam Gemeentearchief, where Simon Hart counted 175 contracts, of which 28 concerned Rensselaerswijck. The contracts for Rensselaerswijck concerned 65 persons, while the other 147 contracts concerned 165 people. S. Hart, *Geschrift en getal* (Dordrecht, 1976), 329. The farmhands listed in the table were contracted to work in Rensselaerswijck. The two girls were hired by inhabitants of Beverwijck.The people listed in the table are Cornelis Eversz Wijncoop, Lubbert Besselsz van Niekerck, Gysbert Philipsz van Velthuysen, Jan Henrichsz van Horst, Frans Gabriel van Amersfoort, Elbert Elbertsz, Pauwel Pauwelsz van Amersfoort, Cornelis Jansz van Bunschoten, Sweer Jansz van Amersfoort, Rijck Claesz van Niekerck, Roelof Jacobsz van Bunschoten, Adriaen Dircksz van Bil [?], were all contracted to work in Rensselaerswyck in the service of Joan van Rensselaer, and would sail with *De Gelderse Blom*, 20 March, 1651. NA 1096-287; Teunis Jacobsz van Hamersfelt contracted to work for Jeremias van Rensselaer and was to sail with *Den Otter*, 14 June, 1656 NA 1117/181; Coenraet Luycasz van Ceulen, Cornelis Cornelisz Verwey, Teunis Gerritsz van Cuylenburg were hired by Goosen Gerritsz to work for Arent van Curler. NA 2442/470-71, 29 March 1657; NA 2442/476-77, 29 March, 1657; NA 2442/478-79, 28 March 1657; Pieter Pietersz Lassen, Jan Hansz van Grandich in Jutlant, Carsten Thomasz van Huyer, Carsten Carstensz van Huyer, and Pieter Claesz van Suyderstapel were contracted by Jan Baptist van Rensselaer, 18 April, 1659. NA 1129/54v; Teunis Willemsz van Martensdijck and Dirck Martensz van Martensdijk were hired by Jan Baptist van Rensselaer, 9 January, 1660. NA 1132/30v; Cornelis Stevensz van Lambroeck, Gerrit Teunisz van Westbroeck, Sweer Teunisz van Westbroeck, were contracted by Jan Baptist van Rensselaer. NA 1135/338-38v, 8 December 1660; Jan Jansz van Klijn Glebbick contracted with Jan Baptist van Rensselaer, 24 Aug. 1662. NA 1142/187v; Gerrit Lambertsz and Jan Rutgersz contracted with Jan Baptist van Rensselaer, April 12, 1663. *DSSYB* V, 31-32; Elsgen Tierck van Quins in Ost Vrieslant, *jonge dochter,* was hired as servant girl by Jacob Jansz Schermerhoorn, 19 April, 1655. NA 1353/43v; Marritge Jochims was hired out by the *weesmeesters aelmoesseniers* at Amsterdam to serve Jacob de Hinsse and his wife Annitge Hendricx as servant girl, 24 Nov. 1657. NA 1206/159.

Appendix 8: Lots and occupants

The following accompanies the map of Beverwijck, and lists the lots as they were first distributed in the early 1650s. For the map [see ill. 9 and 56] I have used Römer's plan of Albany (1698) as basis. The numbering starts mostly at the fort; north of it they follow the south-to-north direction, south of the fort, north to south. On State Street, they run from east to west. The sizes of the lots are not shown in the map, but they are listed as much as possible in the accompanying comments; Sometimes I have noted size as, for example, 1-2-3, meaning 1 rod, 2 feet, 3 inches. A notation as [5x7] means that the lot was 5 rods wide and 7 rods long. As source materials were used *the Early Records of Albany*, vols. I-IV, *Land Papers, Fort Orange Court Minutes*, in some cases the *Van Rensselaer Bowier Manuscripts*, and the *Minutes of the Court of Albany, Rensselaerswijck and Schenectady,* vol. 1-3. The researcher who wants to research a specific lot, can find a good start here, but is advised to check all original source materials carefully, as they often can be explained in more than one way. In several cases of mis-translation or doubt about the interpretation of the original text, this Dutch text is added in italics. Although several sources are listed, my intent has not been to give a complete overview of all source materials. The researcher will in most cases be able to find additional materials in the material used here, and perhaps in other scattered sources.

Section I (no. 1-10): lists the lots, east of present-day Broadway until the first kill;
Section II (no. 11-25): lists the lots east of Broadway from the first to third kill;
Section III (no. 1-10): lists lots north of Fort Orange, west of Broadway;
Section IV (no. 11-18b): lists lots on West Broadway, between State Street and Maiden Lane;
Section V (no. 19-32): lists the lots west of present-day Broadway, between Maiden Lane and Columbia Street;
Section VI (no. 33-37): is west of Broadway, westward along Columbia Street;
Section VII (no. 11-19): is along the north side of State Street;
Section VIII (no. 1-10): lists the lots on the east side of present-day North Pearl Street;
Section IX (no. 1-7): shows garden lots behind the patroon's house;
Section X (1-12): lists lots distributed south of Fort Orange. These are more difficult to locate, and need more research. Other individuals are referred to as having a lot 'behind the fort.' They are listed in the appendix, but not filled in on the map.
Section XI : The lots on the south side of State Street I have filled in with the initials of the first people who received a patent here. I refer to the research done by A.J.F. van Laer, (1926) 'The Dutch Grants along the South side of State Street. A Contribution Toward the Early Topography of the City of Albany,' in: *DSSYB* 2, pp. 11-23, and especially pp. 24-27 ('Patents and deeds relating to lots 1-33, on map of Dutch grants along the south side of State Street,') and plate 9.

Abbreviations used:
H = House
L = Lot
G = Garden
r = rod ; ft = feet

I: East Broadway, from Fort Orange until the Fuycken Kil

1. Jeremias van Rensselaer

a. patents, vol. 2, pt. 2, # 35 [25 March, 1658]; see also LP, 94. H+L *ten westen Caspar Jacobsz l. 34 roeden, ten suyden breet 22 roeden, ten oosten lanck 35 roeden, ten suyden 't pleyn breet 14 roeden.*

2. Rutger Jacobsz

a. ERA I: 19 [29 Jan. 1657]: RJ sells to Frans Barentsz Pastoor garden acc. to patent except for sage trees and fruit for ƒ286; lying by Hr. van Rensselaer on the riverside and westerly the road. [l. 8 r. 7 ft, along river 8r; bounded on the north on Goosen Gerritsz' lot 6 rods, br. on south side 3 and a half rods.

b. ERA I: 25, 35 [26 Febr. 1657] garden sold to Christoffel Davitsz for ƒ330.[6 June, 1657]; ERA I: 52 [7 sept. 1657] Kit Davitsz sells it to Jan Thomasz for ƒ350. ERA IV: 94 [3 Jan. 1659] public sale of Jan Teunisz' garden next to mr. Rensselaer; ERA IV: 95-96 [4 jan. 1659]: Jan Teunisz sells to Willem Fredericksz Bout garden over against Jeremias van Rensselaer (cancelled).

c. **But see also** Cornelis Steenwijck, patents, vol. 2, pt. 2, # 36 [23 April, 1652]: was transported to CS. G, l. 10 r, br. 4 r, 4ft; east and south the path way, and to north Goosen Gerritsz, west the wagon way from whence striking the river.

3. Goosen Gerritsz

a. patents, vol. 2, pt 2, # 13 [23 April, 1652]: G having on south Rut Jacobsz, on north Willem Teller, extending from wagon way to path by river [6 r 8 ft x 8 r].

4. Willem Teller

a. Patents, vol. 2, pt. 2, # 65 [23 april, 1652]: G adjoining on north to Sander Leendertsz, on south to Goosen Gerritsz; l. wagon way to path that goes to the river; br. 10 rods; See also FOCM, 234: WT closes off path to river opposite Vosburgh.

5. Sander Leendertsz

a. ERA IV: 98-99 [17 March 1659]: SLG grants to Willem Fredericksz Bout lot adjoining northerly the grantee, southerly Willem Teller, extending from street to path at river [10x7]; ERA IV: 99 [14 March, 1659] WFB grants to Evert Pels a H+L+G, the lot has heretofore been used as a garden. Adjoins northerly Volckert Jansz, southerly Sander Leendertsz, west the wagon road, east the path to the river [11x4.2]. ERA I: 292 [14 March, 1661]: Evert Pels grants it to Jeremias van Rensselaer.

6. Willem Fredericksz Bout

a. Patents vol. 3, pt. 2, # 53 [25 Oct. 1652 ('53?)]; G abuts to north on Volckert Jansz, on the south on Sander Leendertsz, on the west the wagon path, on east the path that goes to the river [11x4r 2 ft] Lies on square. Transported to Teunis Dircksz. See also ERA I: 293.

7. Volckert Jansz Douw

a. Patents vol. 2, pt. 2, # 33 [23 April, 1652]: G to north of Harmen Bastiaensz, to south of Willem Bout. From wagon way to path by river [11x4r 2 ft]. **NB:** is reverse!

8. Harmen Bastiaensz

a. ERA I: 306 [12 Aug, 1662]: HB grants to Carsten Claesz H+L adjoining to north the grantor, to south Jan Hendricksz van Bael; part of patent 28 April, 1652.

b. Patents, vol. 2, pt. 2, # 24 [2 jan, 1656]: H+L [5 x 3 and half] stretching in length to the falling of the river; abuts to south on Jan Hendricksz van Bael, north on Sander Leendertsz, and west on the common wagon way.

c. ERA I: 176 [25 febr. 1678]: Attorney JHvBael grants to Paulus Martensz *Ramaecker* lot without the town of Albany where the court house stands, bounding on the north a garden of HB, to the south the common way to the shore, to east of highway, length to river path. By virtue of patent to Van Bael.

d.   ERA II: 25 [1678?]: Hbastiaensz grants to Gerrit van Nes lot or garden to south of lot Paulus Martensz.

9. Sander Leendertsz

a.   ERA I: 217 [1655?]: Not executed: Willem Fredericksz Bout wants to sell lot and timber for H. See also FOCM, 97 [17 Febr. 1654]: lot behind Sander Leendertsz is good for horsemill Rutger Jacobsz and Willem Fredericksz Bout. Sander Leendertsz had fenced it in.

b.   ERA I: 313 [25 Oct., 1662]: SLG grants to Jan Bastiaensz van Gutsenhoven lot with house with stone gable and other buildings, for ƒ3200.

c.   ERA III: 148 [24 March, 1662]: SLG grants to Jan Labatie H+L bounded on south by seller, north by buyer, on west by street, east also by street, strand and river.

10. Jan Labatie

a.   Patents, vol. 2, part 2, # 28 [18 Febr. 1653]: abuts to north on Jochem Wesselsz, to west on street, to south on Jan Labatie, to east the riverside. Part arranged for highways. Transported to Jacob de Hinsse; see also ERA I: 308 [20 Aug, 1662]: JL grants to Jacob de Hinsse H+L See also ERA IV: 65 [12 aug, 1658]: Jan Baptist van Rensselaer for Jan Labatie grants to J de Hinsse H+L adjoining northerly the kill, southerly Sander Leendertsz, for ƒ2350 in beavers and so much scarlet cloth as is required for a waistcoat for Labatie's wife.

II: East Broadway from Fuyckenkil to Vossenkil

11. Jochem Wesselsz *backer*

a.   Patents, vol. 4, pt. 1, # 27 [23 April 1653; Oct. 25?]: L+H by first bridge, kill to south, north the way, west way over the bridge [3r 6 ft x4r 8 ft].

b.   ERA I: 28 [30 May, 1657]: JWB sells to Wouter Albertsz H+L adjoining to the south the kil, to north the alley [*steeghje*], east the river side, west the new house of JWB [4.8 x 7.10]. See also ERA IV: 45 [16 July, 1658] for ƒ1950; according to patent 25 Oct. 1653.

c.   ERA I: 262 [2 Febr. 1660]: Wouter Albertsz grants to Jurriaen Theunisz H+L to south of street 18 r. 6 ft, north of kill 18 r. 7 ft, to west Jochem *de backer* 4 r. 8ft, east br. 5 r.

d.   ERA II: 140 [14 jan. 1662]: Jurriaen Theunisz grants to Antony Jansz H+L+G, bounded north and east by streets, south by kill, west by JWB.

12. Jan Fransz van Hoesem

a.   patents, vol. 2, pt. 1 # 17 [23 April, 1652]: L having to south and west the wagon way, to north Hendrick Jansz Westerkamp, to east a way that goes between G and the L. G is east of his lot. See also FOCM 43, 66, 165: Willem Jurriaensz may live in old bake house and have use of bake oven; he has lived long on this lot and used it as garden. JvH pays W Jurriaensz ƒ125 for it.

b.   ERA II: 163 [1 aug. 1682] : Gerrit Visbeeck who married Van Hoesem's widow Volckje, grants H+L to Thomas Davidsz Kikebel, next to Gideon Schaets' lot, extends northward until Abraham Staets' fence, southward as broad as the H is long. L as patent 1652 mentions. Also a G over the town's palisades.

13. Hendrick Jansz Westerkamp (widow Femmetje Alberts)

a.   ERA III: 60 [8 March, 1660]: Femmetje Alberts (widow HJW) grants to Daniel Rinckhout H+L, l & br according to patent 23 April, 1652. ERA IV: 63, he occupies it in 1658. See also ERA I: 254. See also FOCM, 423.

b.   Patents, vol. 2, pt. 1 # 117 [16 April, 1666]: Femmetje grants to Hendrick Jochimsz H+L, abuts to north on L of Daniel Rinckhout, to east the brewhouse of Volckert Jansz and Jan Thomasz, to south on lot of Jan Fransz van Hoesem. Also garden by the river with space for a door to go from L to G; ERA III: 87 [16 August 1661]: Anthony Jansz leases H+L+G for 2 years.

c.   See also ERA I: 457 [12 july, 1669], ERA II: 137 [22 Aug. 1681]: H Jochimsz grants it to Abraham Staets. ERA I: 218 [17 Jan., 1655]: Femmetje grants to Jan Thomasz, Volckert Jansz Douw and Pieter Hartgers corner of lot [5r 6 ft x 6 r, 8 ft].

d.   ERA I: 399 [19 June, 1666]: Hendrick Jochimsz (through Volckert Jansz Douw) grants to Philip Pietersz Schuyler part of lot granted to Hendrick Jochemsz,. ERA I: 449 [15 Sept. 1668]: PPS grants it to Abraham Staets.

e.   Patents vol. 4, pt. 2, # 2 [24 March, 1668/9]: confirmation to Volckert Jansz and Herman Rutgersz of a lot at Albany whereon stands a brewery, on east side of highway, 6-9-10; length on south 5-11; abuts on passage to Abraham Staets on the west to Capt. Staets 6 r 5 ft; on north by the highway 7 r, 1 ft; also G bounded on west side by highway [6r 9 ft], north by way [4 r 7 ft], east the river 7r 5 ft], and south next to A Staets [5.5]. See also ERA I: 218 [17 jan. 1655]: widow Femmetje sells corner of her lot to Volckert Jansz, Pieter Hartgers and Jan Thomasz [5r 6 ft x 6r 8 ft] for ƒ300].

14. Jan Thomasz

a.   ERA I: 29 30 [1 May, 1657] 33, [23 June, 1657]: JT grants to Claes Hendricksz H+L bounded on north by Andries Herbertsz, on south by common highway, west and east by common road [4x6 and half], with G bounding on south side on Hendrick Jansz Westerkamp, on east, west and north a common path [6.10 x 6.1 r]. Patent was of 23 April 1652.

b.   ERA I: 293 [15 March, 1661]: Willem Jansz Stoll (married Claes Hendricksz' widow) grants H+L to Jan Verbeeck; part of patent JT, 23 April, 1652. south, west and east common street, to north Claes Jansz. See also ERA II: 285 [24 October, 1685] Jan Verbeeck grants it to Reynier Schaets. See also ERA I: 15 [22 January, 1657]: Dirck Bensingh and Harmen Jacobsz sell H where JT at present dwells and the lot for ƒ2019 to Jan Verbeeck. See also ERA I: 374, 378 [July/August 1661], new house, and old house; ERA II: 284, 261 [17 Febr. 1685]; ERA III: 218 [26 May, 1663]: neighbor of Harmen Thomasz and Cathalijn Berck. See also ERA I: 272-73 [15 August, 1659], and ERA I: 78 [3 August, 1665]: Claes Jansz *timmerman* grants to Andries Jochimsz H+L, bound on north by Jan Verbeeck, to south by Stoffel Jansz Abeel, east and west by street by virtue of patent to Jan Tomasz, 23 April, 1652.

15. Andries Herbertsz

a.   ERA I: 36-37 [10 July, 1657]: AH grants to Leendert Philipsz H+L+G for ƒ1800 in beavers. Part of patent AH, 23 April, 1652. See also ERA I: 263 [19 Febr. 1660]: adjoins to north Pieter Bronck and to south Jan Verbeeck.

b.   ERA I: 272: Leendert Philipsz grants to Henderick Hendericksz part patent AH, H+L to south Claes Jansz, to north grantor, to east river bank, to west highway; see also ERA I: 273 and Patents, vol. 2, pt. 2, # 22, [15 August, 1659]: Henderick Hendricksz sells it to Stoffel Jansz Abeel. See also ERA III: 398 [27 July, 1672]: Stoffel Jansz grants it to Claes Jansz Stavast [clear that it was used as shop!].

c.   ERA I: 332 [27 August, 1663]: Leendert Philipsz grants to Nicolaes Meyer a G, to west river bank, east the street, to south Pieter Bronck, to north also street [reverse?].

d.   ERA I: 402-403 [19/29 July, 1666]: Nic. Meyer grants G to Daniel Rinckhout; fully paid.

16. Pieter Bronck

a. ERA I: 304-305 [2/5 August, 1662]: PB grants to Jacob Gevick and Reyndert Pietersz brewery and dwelling house in the front with the mill house and horse stable together with the well and the lot attached [3r 1 ft /3 r, 8ft x 11r 8ft]. Part of patent 23 Oct. 1653. See also ERA I: 22 [Febr. 1657], 310 [13 Sept, 1662], ERA III: 170 [4 Aug, 1662], 91 [18 Aug 1661], ERA II: 240-41 [23 Sept. 1684]: Hilleke Bronck sells to Hendrick Martensz Beeckman the lot on which the log house stood, and where is a new house. 11 June, 1667 Pieter Bronck received patent for lot north of Jurriaen Jansz Groenewout and south of Leendert Philipsz [6 r 11 ft/5 rods, 7 and half ft; l. 13 r. 2 ft] **NB:** directions seem reverse.

17. Cornelis Theunisz Bos

a. Patents vol. 2, pt 2, # 37 [23 April, 1652]: has to north Theunis Cornelisz, to south Pieter Bronck, to east and west the wagon way [13x7r, 5 ft], there lying between H and G a common wagon way. Lot devolved on Jurriaen Jansz Groenewout, who married the widow.

b. ERA I: 288 [10 Dec. 1660]: CTB grants to commissaries lot for public use of street, adj. to south of Jan Teunisz *de paep*, [13x2 rods], part of patent 23 April, 1652.

c. ERA I: 400 [26 july, 1666]: JJGroenewout grants to Paulus Martensz lot on which PM has built a H. Highway was cutt of from this lot. Mary Dijckman has lot to south in use.

d. ERA I: 408 [9 April, 1667]: JJGroenewout grants to Symon Volckertsz Veeder *backer*; l. south along common street, l. 20 r, 9ft, to west a street [4r], to north Teunis Cornelisz [20-9], to east river [br. 9 ft].

e. ERA I: 409 [9 April, 1667]: JJGroenewout grants to Huybert Jansz lot [7 r, 9ft/6r 10 ft x 2r/ 2 r, 6ft] and G. over the highway on the riverside [4 r x 2r, 7ft/3 r]; bounds on south side grantor, east the river, south and west the street. ERA I: 419 [23 April/2 May 1667] Huybert Jansz grants it to Cornelis van Nes.

18. Teunis Cornelisz

a. ERA I: 76 [28 July, 1667]: TC grants to Jan Evertsz a H+L; bounded north by Symon Volckertsz, south by Willem Fredericksz, east the street, G in the rear; being whole patent to TC, about 7 rods broad, l. to fence of G sold to Jacques Tysz. [**NB:** reverse?] See also Patents vol. 2, pt. 2, # 38.

a. ERA I: 404 [8 Sept. 1666]: TC grants to Willem Bout lot, adjoining to north Jacques Tysz, to south and east TC, and west public street [br. 3r, l. as long as lot JTysz]; ERA I: 405 [8 Sept. 1666]: W Bout sells it to Jan Clute; mentions that to the east has stood the mill of Van Rensselaer. NB: ERA III: 198 [18 Nov. 1662]: WFB grants to Jeremias van Rensselaer his horse mill, mill house, etc. bounded north by Jacques Tysz, south by Teunis Cornelisz *alias Jonge Poentie*. Lot consists of free alley and G. See also ERA I: 421 [25 April, 1667]: Jeremias van Rensselaer grants small piece of ground (behind the lot where mill house and horse mill stood) with little garden to Jan Evertsz.

19. Frans Barentsz Pastoor

a. Patents, vol. 2, pt. 2, # 18 [25 Oct. 1653]: pat. for H+L+Y, abutting to north on Jan Verbeeck, to east the river, to south Teunis Jacobsz, to west the highway. Br. west 6.5 r, east 5 r, 6 ft; l. north 19 r, south 21 rods. Purchased by Hendrick Andriesz. **NB:** I am not sure how Teunis Jacobsz. Fits here. Did he buy it at some time from Pastoor? I did not find other references to him being located here.

b. ERA I: 10, 21 [11 Dec. 1657/ 10 Febr. 1657]: FBP sells to Hendrick Andriesz his H+L+Brewery+G for ƒ3630. Also horse stable and hogsty. ERA I: 12 [17 dec. 1656]: Hendrick Andriesz grants the same to Philip Hendricksz for 4000 carolus guilders.

ERA I: 346 [29 April, 1664]: Philip Hendricksz grants H+brewery + mill house to Jan Dircksz van Eps for ƒ1150.

20. Jan Verbeeck

a.   Patents, vol. 2, pt. 2, # 34 [25 Oct. 1653]: L+H+Y, abuts to north Arent Andriesz, to south on ground formerly belonging to Frans Barentsz, east side (of??) river, west side (of??) highway [br. 4 4, 8ft/6.5 r x 19r/16r 10ft]. Transported to Jeremias van Rensselaer.

b.   RA I: 12 [10 Jan. 1657]: JV sells to Claes Hendricksz his H on the riverside with lot with two gardens and well etc. for ƒ1812. ERA I: 38 [18 July 1657]: Jan Verbeeck grants the lot to Jan Baptist van Rensselaer for ƒ1812.

21. Arent Andriesz

a.   patents, vol. 2, pt. 2, # 47 [23 April, 1652]: lot abuts to north on Jacob Adriaensz, and to south on Jan Verbeeck [19x17 rods] before and behind the common highway.

22. Jacob Adriaensz *Neus* (*Rademaecker*)

a.   patents vol. 2, pt. 2, # 42 [23 April, 1652]: lot abuts to north on Caspar Jacobsz, to south on Arent Andriesz, before and behind on highway [15r 5 ft x 11r 6 ft before and behind].

23. Caspar Jacobsz

a.   Patents, vol. 2, pt. 2 # 21 [25 October, 1653]: L+H+Y, to north Teunis Jacobsz, to south Jacob Adriaensz, to west and east the highway [4 r, 4ft x 16 r 7 ft lying on a square], which is confirmation to Barent Pietersz *meulenaer*. See also FOCM, 6 [30 April, 1652]: CJ has consent to have L between J Adriaensz *Rademaecker* and Teunis Jacobsz.

b.   ERA I: 16 [22 jan. 1657]: Caspar Jacobsz sells to Harmen Jacobsz a H+L+G [16 r x 4r 4 ft], except for cherry trees for ƒ810. Sureties are Abraham Pietersz and Adriaen Jansz. ERA I: 41 [21 July, 1657]: Harmen Jacobsz grants it to Claes Hendricksz for 900 carolus guilders.

24. Teunis Jacobsz

a.   Patents vol. 2, pt. 2 # 70 [23 April, 1652]: lot has to north the third kill, to south Caspar Jacobsz, before and behind the common highway [11x18 rods]. See also *DSSYB* 13: 5 [13 March, 1667].

25. Jurriaen Theunisz *glaesemaecker*

a.   ERA I: 18 [29 jan. 1657]: Jurriaen Theunisz grants to Andries Herbertsz H+L, [10x10 rods] with 2 hogsties for ƒ1510. See also ERA I: 37: patent was 25 Oct. 1653. See also ERA I: 263 [24 Febr. 1660]: AH grants it (plus additional piece) to Jan Martensz *de Wever* and, ERA I: 21 [10 Febr. 1657]: for ƒ2300.

b.   ERA I: 270: [14 Aug. 1659]: Jurriaen Theunisz grants to Jan Roelofsz H+L *besuyden de derde kil, beoosten Jan Martensz*, along the street 9 rods long, at the end of Jan Martensz' lot 13 rods, at the river side 7 rods. See also ERA IV: 9 [10 Jan., 1659]: Jurr. Theunisz grants to Jan Roelofsz H+L where he now dwells, save the tools.

a.   ERA IV: 100 [24 March, 1659]: Jan Roelofsz grants to Pieter Hartgers half of his house. See also ERA I: 267 [July, 159?]: Incomplete: Jan Roelofsz and Pieter Hartgers want to sell H on third kill where Jan Roelofsz dwells.

III: Lots north of Fort Orange, west of Broadway

1. Jacob Luyersz.

a.   ERA I: 313, patent 25 Oct. 1653, for H+L [8x4¹/₂ rods]: near FO, bounded on the north by Abraham Staets, on the south by the fort.

b.   ERA I: 40, 18 July, 1657: sells it to Hendrick Jansz van Wytert for ƒ813.

c. ERA I: 313, 12 Oct. 1662: Paulus Martensz sells it to Claes Cornelisz van den Bergh.
    See also FOCM, 489; ERA IV: 73]

2. Cornelis Vos

a. ERA I: 301, patent for G [5x7 rods], 23 April, 1652;
b. 5 May 1662: Vos sells lot to Abraham Staets (has to north Van Slichtenhorst's gate and
    to west Dirck Jansz);
c. Staets sells it to Johannes de Wandelaer, 6 August, 1681 (ERA II: 133). This has to north
    the patroon's orchard and to west lot formerly belonging to Dirck Jansz.

But see also

a. ERA I: 372 [20 July, 1661]: **Hendrick Jochimsz** sells his H+L without Fort Orange to
    Abraham Staets. See also Patents, vol. 2, pt. 2, # 8 [5x7]. It seems that Jochimsz may
    somehow have had possession of the two lots [1, 2] north of Fort Orange. He may have
    had his tavern here until he bought lot Femmetje Albers. A location close to the court
    house in Fort Orange makes sense, and once the *bijeenwoninge* became more estab-
    lished the meeting place may have moved north as well. Jeremias van Rensselaer wrote
    that around 1660 hardly anybody came to the fort anymore.

Hendrick Jochimsz

a. ERA I: 248 [16 July 1659]: sells H+L to Cornelis Cornelisz Sterrevelt (Cornelis Theu-
    nisz Bos and Cornelisz Theunisz van Slijck sureties) for ƒ140. Johannes Dijckman
    dwells in it. Located *ontrent* or north of Fort Orange [5x7 rods].
c. ERA IV: 17 [April, 1658?]: H. Jochimsz wants to sell the H+L wherein Jan Clute
    dwells, lying to S. of the H wherein he dwells, in length to Mr. Rensselaer's fence, br. as
    much as H+L to south of the house; + G.

3. Jeremias van Rensselaer (patroon's lot)

a. LP, 94: Patent 25 March, 1658: Lot for H+G *ten westen* (to west) Casper Jacobsz, l. 34
    r; on east 35 r; in br. on south 22 r; to south of the *pleyn* br. 14 rods.
b. See also patents, vol. 2, pt. 2, # 35. It is enlarged.

4. Abraham Pietersz Vosburgh

b. Patent at AIHA [23 April, 1652]: To south L+G Van Slichtenhorst, North vacant, from
    wagon road to stockade in rear [10 rods square]. See also Patents, vol. 4, pt. 2, # 1: to
    south of a lot and G adjoining Gerrit Slichtenhorst, and north of an unmanured lot,
    striking along wagonway to behind the palisades. Vosburgh is deceased, title devolves
    on his widow Geertruy.
b. ERA I, 18: Jan. 1657? Not executed: APV wants to sell H+L where he dwells from
    Tomas Clapboard's house to south side of house [10x4].

5. Thomas Chambers (Clapboard)

a. patents vol. 2, pt. 2, # 8 [8 November, 1658]; see also LP, 95 [lot for H+G]
b. sold to Abraham Staets 1 april, 1667 (ERA IV: 97). See also FOCM, 214 (18 January,
    1656); lot for two Gs.
c. Staets sells to Johannes Wendell, 21 Feb. 1684 (ERA II: 215), lot between G of Geertruy
    Vosburgh and lot heretofore belonging to Claes Hendricksz.

6. Claes Hendricksz

a. LP, 93 [15 Sept. 1657]: Lot north of T Chambers, south of Willem Fredericksz Bout;
b. idem other lot [5x4$\frac{1}{2}$ rods] behind Abraham *timmerman*. See also ERA III: 397
c. ERA I: 294 [15 March, 1661]; death Claes Hendricksz, Willem Jansz Stol marries wid-
    ow and sells half the lot to Jan Barentsz, and other half to Claes Jacobsz van Rotterdam.
d. ERA I 227: **N. B.:** This lot may first have been used by Johannes Dijckman; he sold lot
    to Claes Hendricksz, adjoining on the south side of Abraham Pietersz Vosburgh and on
    the north side Mr. Jacob. Could this be the original patent to Jan Michielsz?

Jan Michielsz

a. Patents, vol. 2, pt. 2, # 2 [23 April 1650; should probably be 1652]; confirmed to Asser Levy, 11 April, 1667.

b. See also ERA I: 216 [11 Jan 1655]: Willem Fredericksz Bout sells to Teunis Dircksz H+L adjacent on south upon Jan Michielsz.

7. Willem Fredericksz Bout

a. Patents, vol. 3, pt. 2, # 53 [25 Oct. 1653]; confirmed to Teunis Dircksz van Vechten

b. ERA I: 216 [11 January, 1655], WFB sells H+L, occupied by himself, to Teunis Dircksz [12r long by 9 r. 5 ft in rear, 9 r. 10 ft. in front] for ƒ1920.

c. ERA II: 202 [30 nov, 1683]; Teunis Dircksz sells H+L to Marcelis Jansz; Jansz hired Dircksz' H+L+G 6 March, 1662 for two years at 17 beavers a year.

8. Sander Leendertsz

a. [13 July 1658]; granted lot west of Jeremias van Rensselaer's lot, north of Caspar Jacobsz

b. Patents, vol. 2, pt. 2, # 11 [29 Dec., 1663]; Sander Leendertsz grants to Caspar Jacobsz a L+G, to west ground of Jeremias van Rensselaer, to north the lot of Caspar Jacobsz. [16.5 r x 3 r 8.5 ft]. See also ERA I: 341.

c. ERA I: 313 [25 October, 1662]: SL grants to Jan Bastiaensz van Gutsenhoven part of his patent with the large house with the stone gable, west of the street.
    ERA I: 492 [10 Jan., 1671]: SL grants to Jurriaen Theunisz lot with well over against the *koningshuys*, formerly belonging to Jan Bastiaensz van Gutsenhoven, deceased, in front on the street until the *stadtsheyninge toe* and wide in the rear until the last post of the former town fence [*tot aen de achterste post van de gewesene stadtsheyninge]*.

d. ERA I: 314 [26 Oct, 1662]: SL grants to Thomas Poulusz H+L next to *dominee* Schaets, bounded south and west by street, to north Jan Bastiaensz van Gutsenhoven; l. north, 10 r, south, 10 r 8 and a half ft; br. in front on street 2 r 10 ft, to west along fence Jan Bastiaensz 5 r, 3 ft. Part patent 1652.

e. ERA I: 341 [28 Dec. 1663]: SL grant to Juriaen Theunisz 2 Gs behind Jeremias van Rensselaer's house *in de tweede straet naar de bergh toe*, bounded to S. by Jan Bastiaensz van Gutsenhoven, on north to Goosen Gerritsz.

9a. Poor house (deaconry of the church)

a. patent in first church [23 April, 1652], lot is 11 r. long, 5 rods wide. To the west of this lot was

9b. Jacob Jansz van Noortstrant

a. Patents, vol. 4, pt. 1, # 153 [23 April, 1652]: has to south the wagon way, to north the Fuyck kill, west a wagon path, east the hospital (*armenhuys?*) [9 x 8.5 rods]. See also ERA I: 202 [3 Sept 1654]: JJvN sells to Rutger Jacobsz for ƒ830 H+L to west Hendrick Gerritsz, to east the alms house, plus a G behind FO. See also ERA II: 67 [16 Jan. 1679]: JJvN sells to Hendrick Gerritsz Vermeulen L on which the H of Teunis Slingerland and some other small house stand; adjoining southerly and westerly the common road, easterly grantor, northerly the *Fuyckse kil;* south and north 30 ft wide, length 8 rods and a half. Also some ground in rear on the kill. See also ERA II: 102-104 [8 Febr. 1680]: HG grants lot to Pieter Meesz Vrooman; it also goes to Robert Gardiner and the administrators of James Penniman. See also ERA II: 178, ERA III: 595, DAB, 41, CMARS III: 47.

10. Willem Teller

See for information the data collected by A.J.F. van Laer in 1926 regarding the south side of State Street.

IV: West Broadway, State Street to Maiden Lane

11. Thomas Sandersz

a. Patents vol. 2, pt. 2 # 52 [25 Oct. 1653]: lot, there having been before some building. Has to north Lourens Jansz, to south and east the highway. [Br. tow. Rut Arentsz 4r, behind 1r 5ft, l. north 8r, south 10r]. Transported to Carsten Fredericksz and by him to Jan Koster van Aecken [March 16] who conveyed out of it a H+L north of church to Jan Clute. L on east side of Evert Lucasz 6-9-2, on west side of Rut *de schoenmaecker* id. On south side of highway, north side of Jan Dareth. **NB:** this is reverse. See also ERA I: 203 [4 Sept. 1654] Tomas Sandersz grants to Jan van Aecken H+L, adj. to north Carsten and Mijnder Fredericksz, to south, east and west a road.

b. ERA I: 261 [10 dec. 1659]: Carsten and Mijndert Fredericksz grant to magistrates, and they grant to Jan Koster van Aecken l for H to west Rem Jansz, to north Jan Dareth, to east Jan Harmensz, on street. See also ERA I: 406-407 [26 March, 1667]: Jan van Aecken has granted it to Jan Clute. See also FOCM, 406 [13 May, 1656]: magistrates shall have liberty to set church as far on his smithy as the width of a door on conditon that they set up his house acc. to regulation of the *rooyinge van* Rem Jansz *smit* and leave a proper lot for the bakery and remove the great house at their own expense.

12. Lourens Jansz

a. Patents, vol. 2, pt. 2, # 29 [23 October, 1653]: this is a confirmatory patent to Mijndert Fredericksz (pat. 3 May, 1667), and mentions: 'where his house stood in Beverwijck.' Abuts on north to Jan van Ackers, on east to highway, on south to Thomas Sandersz, and south to Rut Adriaensz [l. 6.5 rods, br. before way 8, behind 7 rods]. Patent was transported on July 30, 1655 to Cornelis Steenwijck and Lourens Jansz for Gabriel Leendertsz and on the same day by Steenwijck to Carsten and Mijndert Fredericksz, there being an agreement about the division of the lots.

b. patents, vol. 2, pt. 2, # 30 [25 October, 1653]: transport out of lot in Beverwijck. Lot to belong to Carsten Fredericksz (patent 4 May, 1667)

c. confirmation of lot Evert Luycasz, Patents, vol. 3, pt. 1, # 59. Carsten Fredericksz sells the lot to Jan Harmensz *de oude*, on north side Mijndert Fredericksz, south side the street, on east Carsten Fredericksz and west, Jan van Aecken. Harmensz sells it to Evert Lucasz (patent 26 June, 1668). See also ERA IV: 59, 91, and FOCM, 393 [20 July, and 30 November, 1658].

d. patents, vol. 2, pt. 2, # 44 [30 November,1658]: Carsten Fredericksz sells to Mijndert Fredericksz part of lot, to west of street, to south of Jan Dareth, to west of Jan van Aecken, to north of Carsten Fredericksz. See also ERA IV: 92, it was part of patent Lourens Jansz. ERA I: 260 [10 Dec. 1659]: Mijndert and Carsten Fredericksz grant lot for a house to magistrates, who at the same time grant it to Jan Koster van Aecken, to the west Rem Jansz, to north, Jan Dareth, to the east, Jan Harmensz, and on the street.

13. Albert Gerritsz

a. FOCM, 379, 385, 392 [July, 1658]: house attached and sold. Patent 23 April, 1652 [ERA I: 418].

b. ERA I: 60 [May 10, 1658]: AG proposes to sell H in Beverwijck, bounded on north by Gerrit Bancker's H, south by his own H where Jan van Eeckelen dwells. Br. 20 ft, with lot long 94 ft, wide 20 ft; with a bakery.

c. ERA I: 418 [20 April, 1667/bill of sale 3 March 1660]: Van Ilpendam for AG, who lives in the Esopus, sells to Jan Jansz van Eeckelen H+L, by virtue of patent to AG, 23 April, 1652. **NB**: ERA I: 355 [7 July, 1664]: Jan van Eeckelen pledges his H+L, *belent ten noorden Jan Dareth, besuyden Pieter Loockermans* (transl. reverse).

d.   Part of the above was transferred to Jan van Aecken and went later to Gerrit Bancker: ERA I: 202 [4 september, 1654]: AG sells to Jan van Aecken 45-feet lot in br. on the road, running back to the *royinge* besides H standing thereon. Joining to south Carsten and Mijndert Fredericksz, to north the seller.

e.   ERA I: 407 [8 April, 1667]: Jan van Aecken sells to Gerrit Bancker H+L occupied by Jan Dareth, adj. to north Jan van Eeckelen, to S., Mijndert Fredericksz, br. in front on street 3r, 4 ft, in rear 102 Rhinel. ft. Part of patent AG, 23 April, 1652.

f.   ERA IV: 94 [1659]: AG proposes to sell H+L, adjoining to north Pieter Loockermans, to south Jan van Eeckelen, to east the street, to west the fence of Adriaen Gerritsz.

14. Pieter Loockermans

a.   Patents, vol. 2, pt. 2, # 40 [3 July, 1653]: L of 4x10 rods. Abuts to north on Albert *de timmerman*, to south on Willem Jansz, to east wagonway, to west a void/common lot.

b.   ERA I: 275 [2 August, 1660]: Pieter Loockermans grants to Jan Koster van Aecken H+L adjoining to south Hendrick *de backer*, to north grantor. In front on street 1r 11 ft.
     NB: Could these neighbors be reverse?

15. Willem Jansz Stoll

a.   ERA IV: 30 [4 June, 1658]: WJS grants to Huybert Jansz the south part of his lot, which was granted to him 25 October, 1653. [10x2r]. bounded east and west by common highway, on southside by P Loockermans. Huybert Jansz sells it to Tomas Jansz.

b.   ERA I: 251 [July, 1659?]: Tomas Jansz proposes to sell H+L. Note Van Laer: confirmatory patent to Jacob Hevick, who married Hendrick *de backer*'s widow, Geertruy Barentsz.

c.   What happened to the northern half? I think this went to Tjerck Claesz de Witt. ERA I: 322 [29 April 1656]: somehow Michiel Rijckertsz may have bought this, and sold it to Dirck Bensingh, whose widow married Harmen Thomasz. Thomasz sold it to Tjerck Claesz on 28 May, 1663, who on September 1,1660 sold it to Jeronimus Ebbingh [ERA I: 285]. See also FOCM, 212.
     NB: The dates are confusing, perhaps because of various terms of payments.

16. Dirck Bensingh [widow Catalijn married Harmen Thomasz]

a.   ERA I: 394 [19 Oct. 1665]: Harmen Thomasz, who married Cathalijn Berck (widow of Dirck Bensingh) sold to Cobus Jansz, and Jansz to Jan Verbeeck a H+L+G according to the patent to DB of 25 Oct. 1653, plus a small strip of the lot of Gillis Pietersz, adj. to east highway, to s., Lambert van Neck, to west also highway, to north Jacob Tysz van der Heyden. See also ERA IV: 32: Cobus paid *f*1210. Lot was 15 ft br, 10 r long. Small house next to Bensingh's large H.
     ERA I: 348 [20 Oct. 1665]: Verbeeck grants it to Jacob Tysz vd Heyden. See also ERA IV: 32 [12 July, 1658].

b.   ERA I: 278 [23 Aug. 1660]: commissaries grant to Adriaaen Jansz van Ipendam and Catalijn Berx L in Beverwijck *besuyden* Dirck Bensingh, deceased, *benoorden* AJ van Ilpendam; br. 28 ft 4inch; Catalijn grants to Jacob Tysz van der Heyden: L length to north 10 rods, br. east and west 1 r, 11 ft; part of patent to Daniel Rinckhout, 25 October, 1653, south of A Jansz van Ilpendam, *benoorden den acceptant.*

17. Daniel Rinckhout

a.   ERA I: 24 [23 Febr. 1657]: leases H to Reynier Wisselpenningh @ *f*100 per year. See also FOCM, 355.

b.   ERA I: 278 [23 Aug. 1660): Cathalijn Berck grants to Jacob Tysz H+L *ten suyden van Adriaen van Ilpendam, benoorden den acceptant.* Length north and south 10 rods, east and west br. 1-11-6. Was part of patent to Daniel Rinckhout, 25 October, 1653.

c.   ERA I: 322 [28 May, 1663]: Harmen Thomasz grants to Lambert Albertsz van Neck
     H+L [10r x 25/6 ft] adjoining to north Tjerck Claesz, to south Frans Barentsz Pastoor.
     Part patent Daniel Rinckhout, 25 Oct, 1653.

18. Willem Hoffmeyer

a.   ERA IV: 18 [7 Oct. 1658]: Willem Hoffmeyer sells to Jochem Wesselsz a lot adjoining
     to south and east a road, to west a plain [4x9 rods]; according to patent 25 Oct. 1653.
     ERA IV: 22 [14 March, 1658] and ERA I: 228/9 [28 Febr. 1656]: JW sells it to Adriaen
     Jansz van Ilpendam for *f*1300. See also FOCM, 297. Ilpendam had patent 21 May, 1667,
     on which appears that the lot had an addition [Patents, vol. 2, pt. 2, # 48].

NB: behind Van Ilpendam, to the west was Gillis Pietersz:

18b. Gillis Pietersz

a.   Patent, vol. 2, pt. 1, # 17 [25 Oct. 1653]: Lot for H+Yard by lot # 2. Has to north Jacob
     Hendricksz Sijbingh, to west and south the common highway, being a corner of three
     angles. Br. before highway 6 r, farther along highway 5 rods.
b.   Patents, vol. 2, pt. 1, # 17 [14 April, 1654]: L+H+G. Has to south Evert Jansz, to north
     and west wagon way, to east Dirck Bensingh and Michiel Rijckertsz. Length. S, 9.5 r,
     north 5 rods, br. W. 7.5 r, e: 8 rods.
     ERA I: 322 [28 May, 1663]: GP grants this entire lot to Harmen Thomasz, who grants
     part of it to Maritie Damen on 29 May, 1663 [ERA I: 323], and part to Cobus Jansz on
     19 October, 1665 [ERA I 394]. Cobus Jansz grants a H+L+G to Jan Verbeeck. ERA I:
     322: Thomasz also grants part to Tjerck Cleasz, which is bounded to south by Lambert
     van Neck, north by Hans Coenraetsz, to west by street. Received from Dirck Ben-
     singh, who had obtained it from Machiel Rijckertsz. See also FOCM, 212 about the sale
     of the lot.
c.   **NB:** Jochem Ketelheyn sells a lot to Barent Mijndertsz which is across from Gillis
     Pietersz
d.   Part of the patent [patents, vol. 2, pt. 2, # 44; 10 Oct., 1653] to Jacob Hendricksz Sij-
     bingh and Stoffel Jansz Abeel is sold on 8 August, 1663 to Jochem Wesselsz *backer*
     (through F. Boon), and Wesselsz sells it to David Pietersz Schuyler: a L+H, has to east,
     west, south a highway and north Gillis Pietersz.
     NB: The lot north of Evert Jansz stays in GP's hands; what happens with a and d?

V: West side Broadway, between Maiden Lane and Columbia Street

19. Jochem Ketelheyn

a.   Patents, vol. 2, pt. 2, # 38 [25 October, 1653]: H+L has to west, north and east the high-
     way, to south, Willem Hoffmeyer [4 x 9r].
b.   ERA I: 71 [19 febr. 1665]: JK grants to Barent Mijndertsz L opposite [*tegenover*] H
     Gillis Pietersz. Has to south and west '*s heerenwech*', to south Aernout Cornelisz, to
     east grantor [br. 29 Rhinel. ft, l. 40.5 ft]; see also ERA III: 202 [17 Jan. 1663]: for 21
     beavers @ *f*8 and a pair of women's, child's shoes and a pair of good boots.
c.   ERA I: 72 [19 febr. 1665]: JK grants to Jacob Abrahamsz *cuyper,* adjoins east grantor's
     lot, north grantor's house, west the street, south, Aernout Cornelisz. ERA I: 186 has the
     reverse: [20 June, 1678]: Jacob Abrahamsz sells to Jan Gauw, who sells to Jan Andriesz
     cuyper a H+L to north on Jan Gauw, to south and west upon JK, to east on public street
     [l. 3r.9 ft, br. 1r, 8 ft]. Alley between Jan Gauw and Jan Andriesz *kuyper* shall remain in
     common.

20. Jan Koster van Aecken

a.   LP, 100 [7 March, 1661]: patent lot for H+G, *ten suyden Jochem Ketelheyn (l. 8-6-3), aen de wech br. 2-10; ten noorden Wijnant Gerritsz (6-11), in rear 3-10.*
     NB: LP transl. is reverse.

b.   Pat. Vol. 2, pt. 2, # 43 [17 March, 1663]: JcvA grants to Aernout Cornelisz H+L; l to south of JK 8-6, north of Wijnant Gerritsz 6-11, br. Before highway 2-0. ERA I: 498 [13 aug. 1672]: A. Cornelisz sells it to Jan Cornelisz Vijselaer (= Jan Gauw); see also ERA I: 320 [17 March, 1663], and ERA I: 509 [3 March 1679], when Pieter Loockermans sells to Jan Andriesz *de cuyper.*

21. Adriaen Dircksz de Vries/Wijnant Gerritsz van der Poel

a.   Patents, vol. 2, pt. 2, # 54 [29 Aug. 1654]: lot north of Jan *cuyper* (6-2-10), to south of Aernout Cornelisz (6-9-6); l. to west of highway 9-2-4, to east of highway 7-6-8.

b.   ERA I: 189-90 [21 aug. 1654]: exchange of lots Adriaen Dircksz de Vries and Wijnant Gerritsz. WG will put barn AD on his own lot. ERA I: 303 [22 June, 1662]: occupies his H+L.

22. Rem Jansz [*smit*]

a.   Patents vol. 2, pt. 2, # 37 [25 Oct. 1653]: H+L abuts to south upon Arent Jansz [Dircksz?] de Vries, to north on Hage Bruynsz, to east and west the wagon way [5x7.5 upon square]. Was conveyed to Hendrick Gerritsz and by him transported to Pieter Jansz Loockermans, junior. See also ERA I: 7 [16 Oct. 1656].

b.   ERA I: 509 [3 March, 1679]: PJ Loockermans grants H+L to Jan Andriesz *de kuyper.*

23. Mattheus Abrahamsz

a.   patents, vol. 2, pt. 2, # 33 [1656]: H+L before highway 2 r. br, behind on west 1r, 10.5 ft; on north 6.5 r, south 6r, 5.5 ft.

b.   ERA I: 155 [26 June, 1677]: MA grants to Poulus Martensz H+L, bounded south by Pieter Loockermans, north by H Laurence van Alen and Jan Jansz Bleecker; in rear on west side 1r, 10 ft and a half, north 6r and half; ERA I: 170 [13 Dec. 1677]: Poulus Martensz grants it to Harmen Jansz *lijndraeyer.*

24. Hage Bruynsz

a.   Patents, vol. 2, pt. 2, # 41 [25 Oct. 1653]: H+L, has to south Rein Jansz, to north Pieter Lodt, to west and east common wagon way [br. 4 r; l. as far as to the wagon way]. Is confirmation to Teunis Teunisz.

b.   ERA I: 260 [2 Nov. 1659]: HB grants to Gillis Pietersz, who grants to Thomas Jansz Mingael, who grants to Teunis Teunisz *metselaer* H+L *belendende benoorden Mattheus Abrahamsz, besuyden Wouter de Raemaecker, beoosten en bewesten de straet.*

25. Pieter Lodt

a.   According to patent Hage Bruynsz Lodt lives to north of HB. See also *CJVR,* 151 where is mentioned the house 'in which Haemel and Lodt live,' which is charged to 'the masters.' Did Jan Jansz *de Noorman* obtain it?

26. Jacob Simonsz Clomp/Wouter Aertsz.

a.   Patents, vol. 2, pt. 2, # 46? [25 Oct. 1653], pat to Jacob Simonsz Clomp; has to south Wijnant van der Poel, to west a certain way, to north Jan Jansz *Cuyper,* to east the wagon way [10.3x4 r]; also garden by lot # 27 [7x5]. Transported to Wouter Aertsz on Nov. 9, 1655.

c.   ERA II: 357 [2 nov. 1696]: Wouter Aertsz grants to Johannes Cuyler lot without north gate.

27. Albert Gysbertsz *Raedemaecker*

a.   ERA I: 292 [1 March, 1661] Albert Gysbertsz grants to Arent van Curler a new H +

L+G adjoining to east Jan Barentsz Wemp, on south Wouter *de Ramaecker*, west the highway, on north the defense of Beverwijck; see also ERA II: 115 [10 March, 1681].

28. Jan Barentsz Wemp

a. Perhaps Cornelis de Vos was here first? See ERA IV: 56 [24 July, 1658]: Cornelis Cornelisz and Thomas Poulusz grant to Jan Barentsz Wemp their lots lying next to each other, adjoining easterly and westerly a road, southerly Wouter *de ramaecker*, northerly the grantee and *Rademaecker* together [9 x 4 rods]. **N.B:** I am not sure how Thomas Poulus obtained this lot.

29. Eldert Gerbertsz *de Gooyer*

a. VRBM 845: exchange of H+L with Jan van Bremen for farm at Catskil. See also ERA II: 216 [25 March, 1680]: Reyer Jacobsz Schermerhoorn, married to widow of Elmer Otte grants to Barent Albertsz Bratt certain old H+L without the northgate on the west side between the H of BABratt and the lot of Pieter Bogardus; by virtue of patent of 25 March, 1680 to Elmer Otte; after Jan van Bremen's death the lot was sold at public outcry and bought by Elmer Otte.

b. ERA III: 535 [2 May, 1682]: Barent Albertsz Bratt has two houses there.

30. Pieter Meesz Vrooman

a. LP, 98 [17 August, 1660]: lot *ten suyden Simon Root [l. 7r, 5ft], ten oosten een wech [br. 4 r], ten noorden Eldert de Gooyer [l. 7r, 4 ft, ten westen een wech, [br. 4r].*

b. ERA I: 282 [1 Sept. 1660] PMV sells to Cornelis Cornelsz Sterrevelt H+L *to south Symon Symonsz Groot, ten oosten een wech, ten noorden Eldert de Gooyer ten westen een wech.* Sterrevelt grants the same to Cornelis Theunisz Bos. Is it possible that this lot ended up with Pieter Bogardus? He married the daughter of Cornelis Theunisz Bos, and may have received it through the second husband of the girl's mother, Jurriaen Jansz Groenewout.

31. Symon Symonsz Groot

a. Patent vol. 2, pt. 2, # 25 [11 May, 1663]: lot in Beverwijck south of Jan Hendricksz, to north of Jan [Gauw?], to east and west of highway [7.5 x 4]. See also ERA I: 145 [22 Sept. 1676]: Johannes Withart attorney for SSG grants to Wouter Pietersz Quackenbos H+L bounded south by Jan Bricker, north by Barent Albertsz Bratt, east and west by highway. See also ERA I: 274: H is 20 feet square, and shall be delivered except for horse stable.

b. See also ERA III: 191 [30 Sept. 1662]: SSG appoints J. Withart to sell his H+L, bounded south by Jan Hendricksz, north by Jan Gauw. **NB:** so directions are reverse from a. It seems that a is right.

32. Ulderick Cleyn

a. ERA I: 268 [2 Aug. 1659]: UC grants to Jan Hendricksz van Bael H+L bounding to south on Symon Groot, to north Reyer Elbertsz, east and west the cart road [4X8R]. According to patent 23 Oct, 1653. See also ERA IV: 51 [22 july, 1658]: house is 16 feet long, 20 ft. broad; lot 8x4. For ƒ709.

    See also *DSSYB*, XVI, 17 [0-6-1664?]: UC binds his H between the houses of Pieter Meesz and Wouter Pietersz Quackenbos.

b. ERA I: 413 [25 April, 1667]: Jan Hendricksz grants H+L to Gerrit Lansingh: to north the road where Reyer Elbertsz is *tegenover* [across].

VI: West side Broadway, along Columbia westward

33. Reyer Elbertsz

a. Patents, vol. 2, pt. 2, # 10 [25 Oct. 1653]: H+L+G near Fort Orange in Beverwijck; has to north Jurriaen *de glaesemaecker*, to west the swamp by the third kill, lying four square, to north and east of highway. NB: FOCM, 7: outside limits of Fort Orange.

b. Patents, vol. 2, pt. 2, # 11 [25 April, 1667]: L+H on third kill, sold by RE to Goosen Gerritsz and Jan Baptist van Rensselaer; to south and east it abuts on highway, to north and west ground of RE. See also ERA IV: 12 [17 jan. 1658] ƒ856.

c. ERA I: 32 [1657?] RE proposes to sell H+L except brick ovens and bricks [4x20r].

d. ERA I: 32 [2 Aug., 1658]: Ulderick Cleyn has RE to north, Simon Groot to south, cart road to east and west.

e. ERA II: 114 [10 March, 1681]: Arent van Curler grant for land north of RE along *binnenweg*, westwards into the woods. CMARS II: 442 [an addition after survey]; 125: over against fence Arent Andriesz, later Claes Jansz van Bockhoven. Arent van Curler grants it to RE and Claes Jansz April, 30, 1663.

f. ERA II: 206 [11 Dec. 1683]: Gerrit Reyersz grants to Barent Meyndertsz and Adriaen Gerritsz (admin. Rutger Arentsz) land without north gate west of highway, having to south the third kill.

34. Albert Gysbertsz *de rademaecker*

a. ERA I: 292 [1 March, 1661]: garden lies in between Andries de Vos' land.

35. Pieter Meesz [Vrooman]

a. ERA I: 282 [1 Sept. 1660] patent for garden; grants it through Cornelis Cornelisz Sterrevelt to Cornelis Theunisz Bos.

 NB: LP, 98: original reads: *een thuyn gelegen aen de derde kil, ten oosten Albert de R, lanck 9 roe, ten noorden Andries de Vos, breet 5 roe, 7 voet, 6 duym, ten oosten een leeg erff is lanck 7 roe, ten suyden een wagenwech breet 5 roe, 7 voet, 6 duym.*

36. Hendrick Marcelisz

a. Patents, vol. 2, pt. 2, # 35 [24 March, 1654]: patent for lot, abuts to south on Claes Gerritsz, to north Jacob Tysz, to west on land of Andries de Vos, east on highway [br. 5 r in front, 4r 4ft in rear, l. 20 rods].

b. ERA I: 171 [14 Dec. 1677]: H+L without north gate sold to Robert Sandersz, who sells it to Poulus Martensz [21 Febr. 1678] [10x4] See also ERA I: 410.

c. ERA I: 411 [13/23 april 1667]: HM sells lot to Volckertie van Hoesem.

37. Andries de Vos

a. Patent in first church; see also patents vol. 2, pt. 2, # 75 [25 October, 1653]: L+H north of third kill, east of wagon way, south of plain; 20x6.5 rods upon square. Also a garden *palende beoosten* Gabriel Leendertsz, *besuyden* Daniel Rinckhout, [*bewesten?*] *de wegh, benoorden d'pleyn* [transl.: to west the highway, to north the plain].

b. ERA I: 109 [1 April, 1675]: AdV grants to deaconry H+L+G *belent besuyden de 3e kil, benoorden 's heerenwech, bewesten Poulus Martensz, beoosten erf transportant; en stuckjen hoplant* lying below on kill, bounding to east Reyer Elbertsz, to north and south the kill.

c. see also Pieter Meesz Vrooman's grant to Cornelis Cornelisz Sterrevelt, and to Cornelis Theunisz Bos [LP, 98; 17 Aug., 1660].

VII: North side State Street, from Broadway to Pearl Street

[For XI, south side, see A.J.F. van Laer's research in 1926]

11.Thomas Sandersz

a. Patents vol. 2, pt. 2 # 52 [25 Oct. 1653]: lot, there having been before some building. Has to north Lourens Jansz, to south and east the highway. Br. tow. Rut Arentsz 4 r, behind 1r 5ft, l. north 8 r, south 10 r. Transported to Carsten Fredericksz and by him to Jan Koster van Aecken [March 16] who conveyed out of it a H+L north of church to Jan Clute. L on east side of Evert Lucasz 6-9-2, on west side of Rut *de schoenmaecker* id. On south side of highway, north side of Jan Dareth. **NB:** this is reverse. See also ERA I: 203 [4 Sept. 1654] Tomas Sandersz grants to Jan van Aecken H+L, adj. to north Carsten and Mijndert Fredericksz, to south, east and west a road.

b. ERA I: 261 [10 dec. 1659]: Carsten and Mijndert Fredericksz grant to magistrates, and they grant to Jan Koster van Aecken l for H [to west Rem Jansz [6-4-4], to north Jan Dareth [in rear 2 r], to east Jan Harmensz 6-11-3], on street [2-6-8 which breadth of the lot extends as far as th present H]. See also ERA I: 406-407 [26 March, 1667]: Jan van Aecken has granted it to Jan Clute. See also FOCM, 406 [13 May, 1656]: magistrates shall have liberty to set church as far on his smithy as the width of a door on conditon that they set up his house acc. To regulation of the *rooyinge* van Rem Jansz *smit* and leave a proper lot for the bakery and remove the great house at their own expense.

12. Rut Adriaensz/Arentsz

a. Patents, vol. 2, pt. 2 # 72 [23 April, 1652]: lot has to north Albert Gerritsz, to south the wagon way, to west the plain, to east Lauris Jansz [5x4 rods].

b. FOCM, 183 [16 March, 1655]: Rut Arentsz *kleermaecker* had granted to Hendrick Gerritsz *kleermaecker,* and now Gerritsz grants to Rem Jansz H+L, bounded south by road, west by plain, east by Lourens Jansz or whoever bought his house.

c. ERA I: 283 [3 Sept. 1660]: Rem Jansz grants to Cornelis Theunisz Bos H+L *belendende ten oosten Adriaen Gerritsz, ten westen Jan Thomasz* [l. west and east 6-3; south 2-2, north 2-8]. See also ERA I: 43 [23 July, 1657]: great house, bleach field with bake oven, cow stable and hogsty. Free alley between both houses.

d. ERA I: 283 [3 Aug. 1660]: Rem Jansz grants to Jan Thomasz H+L, *belendende ten westen Jan van Aecken, ten oosten CTBos,* See also ERA IV: 108 [16 June, 1659], and ERA I: 43, Gysbert Jansz dwells in the little house. ERA I: 64 [7 Dec. 1664]: Jan Thomasz (and Gerrit Bancker) grant the same to Pieter Claerbout. ERA I: 66 [17 dec. 1664]: Claerbout grants it to Rut Arentsz [*schoenmaecker*] See also ERA III: 195 [2 Nov. 1662]. **NB:** the descriptions are complicated, also in Dutch. Van Laer in ERA III: 102 puts this in note on south side State Street, which, I think, is incorrect.

13. Adriaen Jansz van Ilpendam [*Meester Adriaen*]

a. Patent vol. 2, pt. 2, # 9 [23 Oct. 1653]: L+H+Y, has to south a common highway, to north a lot of low ground [*leegh erf?*], to west Gerrit Jansz, to east Rut Arentsz [l. east 9-10-5, west 8-8 and half ft; br. 4 rods]. Reserving small space.

b. ERA I: 7 [28 Oct. 1656]: Adriaen Jansz van Ilpendam grants to Adriaen Gerritsz a H+L, bounded on north by Pieter Loockermans, west by Gerrit Jansz, east by Rut Arentsz; excepting small corner for Rem Jansz. See also ERA I: 228, mentions 3 feet on east side for Rem Jansz, whose house then will stand on its own ground.

14. Gerrit Jansz Cuyper

a. see patent Van Ilpendam.

b. see patent Michiel Rijckertsz [see no. 15].

c.   Patents, vol. 3, pt 1, # 81[13 August, 1668]: confirmation to Thomas Willett for H+L tenure of Pieter van Alen on north side of road that goes up to the hills, having Adriaen Gerritsz's H on east side, and Cornelis van Nes to the west. H+L were confiscated on 10 October, 1665. Cuyper was mentioned as agent for Van Alen] See also ERA I: 487 [2 Sept. 1671]: Thomas Willet grants to Philip Pietersz Schuyler, and ERA II: 36 [7 April, 1679]: Schuyler sells it to Maria van Rensselaer. H+L between Adriaen Gerritsz and Marietje Damen (who married Cornelis van Nes).

15. Michiel Rijckertsz [de laedemaecker]

a.   Patents, vol. 2, part 2, # 16 [25 Oct. 1653]: L+H+Y bounded east by Gerrit Jansz, north by plain; br. in front toward street 4 rods, north 3 r 8 ft; length 11 r. 9 ft. This is confirmation to Cornelis van Nes.

16. Evert Jansz Wendel (van Emden)

a.   patents, vol. 2, pt. 2, # 25 [25 October, 1653]: for a lot where his H stood near the fort in Beverwijck: having to east Michiel Rijckertsz, to south and west the common highway, to north the plain [br. in front 3r 6ft, behind 3r; length on east 10r 9ft, west 10r].

b.   See FOCM, 32 [3 Dec. 1652]: committee to lay out lot for Evert *kleermaecker* between the road near Anneke Bogardus and Machiel *de lademaecker*.

c.   ERA I: 324 [21 June, 1661]: heirs Anneke Bogardus sell to Dirck Wesselsz H+L in which Anneke lived before she died, adjoining to east Pieter and Jonas Bogardus, to west Evert Jansz Wendel. **NB:** this seems to be reverse.

17. Anneke Bogardus

a.   Patents, vol. 2, pt. 2, # 66 [25 April, 1652]: has to north lot lying in common, to west Marten Herpertsz, to south the wagon way, to east common path way. Length 6 rods, lying on a square.

b.   ERA I: 289 [22 Dec. 1660]: AB grants to David Pietersz Schuyler part of lot adjoining to west the grantor, to south and east Sander Leendertsz, to north the street. In front on street 1-6-8; [*ten oosten van* Sander Leendertsz, 6-3; *ten westen breet* 1-7-8]. ERA I: 392 [1 Sept. 1665]. DPSchuyler grants the same [L+H+ *vorder getimmer*] to Wouter Albertsz van den Uythof. *Belent ten suyden en ten oosten Sander Leendertsz, ten noorden de straet, ten westen de transportant,*l. 6.3, br. 1-7-8 west, 1-6-8 *aen straet*. Patent was 25 April, 1652. See also ERA III: 210. ERA II: 51 [12 June, 1679]: Wouter Albertsz grants to Antony Lespinard H+L adjoining eastwardly AL's new house, westwardly Jan Jansz Oudekerck, south the street, north Timothee Cooper. Also lot next to the H on which AL's new house stands, provided that mr. Wesselsz' house stay drip free.

c.   ERA II: 50 [6 June, 1679]: Pieter and Jonas Bogardus grant to Wouter Albertsz part of lot between houses of Dirck Wesselsz and Wouter Albertsz, on which new house Anthony Lespinard stands.

d.   ERA III: 204 [29 Jan. 1663] will Anneke Bogardus, leaves to Pieter and Jonas Bogardus H+L on west side of dwelling house, extending in length to rear of bleach field.

e.   ERA I: 324 [21 June, 1663]: heirs of Anneke Bogardus grant to Dirck Wesselsz H+L adjoining east Pieter and Jonas Bogardus, to west Evert Jansz Wendel, mentions *afdack* on east side house, that was rented out. [west the length is 5r 9ft, east 5 rods, 8 feet and a half, south is 2r 7ft. She lived in it until she died.

18. Marten Herpertsz (metselaer)

a.   patents, vol. 2, pt. 2, # 66, Anneke Bogardus mentions MH to west.

b.   ERA I: 392 [22 nov. 1664]: commissaries grant to Sander Leendertsz by virtue of public execution, H+L adjoining to north the street, to south Jan Hendricksz van Bael, to east Jan Thomasz, to west Wouter Albertsz. Sander Leendertsz grants this to Adriaen Gerritsz, attorney for Dirck Jansz Croon. Was part of patent to Marten Herpertsz, 23 April, 1652. **NB:** this should be reverse. See also FOCM, 80, 94, 97 [Jan/Febr. 1654]. ERA I: 336 [17 Oct. 1663]: SLG grants to Jan Clute H+L adjoining to east Wouter Albertsz, and west Jan Thomasz. ERA I: 63 [22/12 Nov. 1664]: Adriaen Gerritsz, grants to Jan Clute H+L bounded north by street, south by Jan Hendricksz van Bael, east by Jan Thomasz Mingael, west by Wouter Albertsz. **NB:** ERA II: 46: Jan Clute sells it to Ludovicus Cobes: this lot was on the north side of State Street – see ERA II: 46-47, deed Jan Thomasz to Cornelis Steenwijck. **NB: descriptions contradict.**

c. ERA I: 358 [18 aug. 1664]: Sander Leendertsz grants to Jan Hendricksz van Bael H+L, adjoining to north Jan Thomasz, south Hendrick Cuyler, east and west the highway, for ƒ876. was bought by commissaris at public sale on excution made on Marten Herpertsz.

19. Philip Pietersz Schuyler

a. FOCM 33 [6 Dec. 52] Philip Pietersz Schuyler is granted lot west of Marten *Metselaer;* FOCM, 242 [30 May, 1656] granted an addition; FOCM, 184 [16 March, 1653]: magistrates granted lots, Sander Leendertsz west of PPS; *LP,* 81 [16 June, 1656] Patent was granted to PPS on 25 October, 1553, but magistrates have allowed him an addition. **NB:** original reads *belent ten suyden de waagewech, ten westen den berch, ten noorden Pieter Hartgers, ende ten oosten Sander Leendertsz,* etc. *LP*, 100-101 [31 May, 1657]: after this, grant was lost and is confirmed to Jan Thomasz. It is in front along the street 4-5-6, on the east along Sander Leendertsz, 6 r 2ft in length, on north 5 rods, 8 inches, on west 6-2. Also lot for G, on east along the road 12-7; on north Jan Hendricksz, 6 r 6 ft in br.; on west 12. 8; on south along Evert Jansz Wendel 8-10 in br.

b. ERA I: 277 [13 aug, 1660]: Sander Leendertsz pledges his H+L adjoining to east Jan Thomasz to west Anneke Bogardus. **NB:** I think the location is reverse.

c. ERA I: 300 [17 april, 1662] Sander Leendertsz grants to Jan Thomasz lot to east the grantee, to west the grantor. This was part of patent to grantor 23 April, 1652 [l. east 6 rods, w 6 r, front on street 1-4-6; north the same].

VIII: East side Pearl Street, northward until Steuben

NB: new count: 19 State Street = 1. on Pearl Street: Philip Pietersz Schuyler.

2. Marten Herpertsz

a. Patents vol. 2, pt. 2, # 27 [23 October, 1653]: Jacob Jansz Schermerhoorn abuts on south to Marten Herpertsz.

b. FOCM, 33 [3 Dec, 1652]: is granted lot behind his place. Has to build. This seems to be on north side State Street.

3. Pieter Hartgers

a. FOCM, 242 [30 May, 1656]: Philip Pietersz Schuyler is granted addition of lot, adjoining to south on wagon road, west the hill, east Sander Leendertsz and north Pieter Hartgers. See also *LP,* 81 [16 June, 1656]. See also *LP*, 100.

b. ERA III: 266-67 [27 Febr. 1664]: administrators Pieter Hartgers grant to Hendrick Cuyler H+L at hill. Bounded on north by Jacob Jansz Schermerhoorn, on east by highway, on south by Sander Leendertsz, on west also by highway. See also ERA I: 421 [2 May, 1667]: for ƒ850. **NB:** Not clear how Hartgers obtained this lot.

4. Jacob Jansz Schermerhoorn

a. Patents vol. 2, pt. 2, # 27 [25 Oct. 1653]: pat for H+L+Y, abuts on west to hills, on south to Marten Herpertsz, on east to highway, on north to void lots [5.5 x 20 rods on a square]. **NB:** MH's lot on State Street?

b. FOCM, 41 [11 Febr. 1653]: sues Adriaen Jansz van Leyden about certain lot next to JJS; it is now given to Lysbeth Cornelis (the widow of Gysbert Cornelisz).

c. ERA I: 144 [22 Sept. 1676]: Jan Hendricksz van Bael grants to Gerrit Hardenberg a H+L bounded westerly by Jacob Jansz Schermerhoorn, to east A. van Tricht, northerly by Captain John Backer. ERA III: 430 [18 Sept. 1675] mentions A. van Tricht as neighbor. **NB:** I think he stays on this lot; perhaps his children move on to it as well.

5. Gysbert Cornelisz *de weert* (widow Lysbeth marries François Boon)

a. FOCM, 41 [1 Febr. 1653]: JJSchermerhoorn sues Adriaen Jansz van Leyden about lot next to JJS, near the hill, no. 4, drawn by him, but afterwards promised to JJS or to Lysbeth Cornelis (Gysbert's widow). Lot now assigned to Lysbet. Lysbeth married François Boon.

b. ERA I: 38 [17 July, 1657]: Andries Herbertsz grants to Willem Jansz Schut lot next to his lot which he received from F. Boon on 22 August, 1654, acc. to patent to Gysbert Cornelisz of 25 October, 1653. Length to the north a road, 10-1; to east a road, br. 2 r; to west the hill, 1 rod, for ƒ200. ERA I 413 [25 April, 1667]: Willem Jansz Schut grants H+L occupied by him, to Jacob Loockermans. H+L stand *beneden de wegh, 2 r 8 and half ft; beoosten de wegh, 3 r; besuyden 1-11; bewesten 2-7*; with the regulation of the *rooyinge* piece taken off at one side and added to the other side on 6 Oct. 1656. ERA I: 333 [11 sept. 1663]: Willem Jansz Schut grants to Pieter Bogardus H+L, bounded on west side by H+L Andries Herbertsz (now Jurriaen Jansz), to north the street, to east Jacob Loockermans, to south the garden of Jurriaen Jansz.

c. ERA I: 316 [16 nov. 1662] Boon to Andries Herbertsz, and Herbertsz' administrators grant to Jurriaen Jansz Groenewout H+L+barn for ƒ1350; see also ERA I: 365 [1 Oct, 1664]: H+L at hill *palende besuyden* Jacob Schermerhoorn, on north and east a road, on west the hill, acc. to patent Gysbert Cornelisz, 23 Oct 1653.

6. Jan Roelofsz

a. ERA I: 1 [16 Oct. 1656]: Thomas Jansz Mingael sells to Jan Roelofsz half of his H+L, bounded south by street, north by Marcelis Jansz, east by cross street, west by hill [besuyt bepalende aen de straet, benoort aent erf van Marcelis Jansz, beoost aen een dwarsstraet, bewest aent geberchte] acc. to patent to Jan Roelofsz of 24 March, 1654. For 110 beavers. ERA I: 32 [June, 1657? not executed]: Jan Roelofsz wants to sell H+L at the hill, br. 7r 5ft, west along hill 4 r 11 ft, to north Marcelis [Jansz?] 17 r. long. Tries to sell lot north of his H, 1 r 11 ft// 2 and a half r; length 5 r. ERA I: 51 [20 August, 1657]: JR sells to Cornelis Segersz L at the hill, l. 20 r, br. 5 r 1 ft, west the hill 7 and a half r. See also ERA I: 60 [10 December, 1657]: for ƒ2021.

b. ERA I: 288 [10 Dec. 1660]: Cornelis Segersz grants to Gerrit Slichtenhorst H+L adjoining to south Marcelis Jansz, north, south, east the street [**NB:** Pearson has northeast; **NB:** location likely reverse]; same dimensions.

7. Goosen Gerritsz

a. ERA I: 200 [2 Sept. 1654]: Goosen Gerritsz grants to Marcelis Jansz a H+L at the hill joining upon north Pieter Bronck, upon south Jan Roelofsz. H will be broken down and set up again and is at present occupied by GG. Cellar is at MJ's expense. See also ERA IV: 57-58 [26 July, 1658]: sells the H+L, except the G.

b. ERA I 362 [15 Sept, 1664]: Marcelis Jansz grants to Asser Levy H+L at hill, adj. to north Gerrit Slichtenhorst, to south the lot of Claes Ripsz, east and west the highway, [21 and a half r x 6, except 30 ft. br taken of for behoof Claes Ripsz] acc. to patent to GG, 25 Oct. 1653. ERA I: 309 [7 Sept. 1662]: Asser Levy sells H+L which he bought from Marcelis Jansz to Robert Sandersz for ƒ1920 in beavers and three beavers for a hat.

c. ERA I: 261 [11 Dec. 1659]: Marcelis Jansz grants to Cornelis Wijncoop H+L, to north Pieter Bronck, to south the grantor, west the hill, east the street. Br. 30 woodft, length according to patent, except what was taken for a street; Patent to Goosen Gerritsz, 25 Oct. 1653. ERA I: 404 [25 Aug. 1666]: Cornelis Wijncoop grants to Claes Ripsz his H+L which he received from Marcelis Jansz; ERA I: 507 [17 Sept. 1672] Claes Ripsz grants the H+L to Gerrit Teunisz.

8. Pieter Bronck

a. ERA I: 305 [5 August, 1662]: Pieter Bronck grants to Jacob Hevick and Reyndert Pietersz a H+L at the hill [5x20, lying in a square]. See also ERA I: 266 [July, 1660]: PB wants to sell H+L at hill [5x20], occupied by Jan van Bremen. Has little house connected. See also ERA I: 249 [July, 1659?]: not executed: PB wants to sell H+L at hill, occupied by Jacob Teunisz. H is one board long, *met een wildenhuys daerbij* [also Indian house nearby except little shed [*een lootsjen*]. See also ERA I: 22, 297, Patents, vol. 2, pt. 2, # 23 ; ERA IV: 12, and FOCM, 114, 377, 383.

b. ERA I: 309 [13 Sept, 1662] Hevick and Pietersz grant it to Rooseboom for ƒ550. See also ERA I: 92 [14 June, 1673]: administrators of Reindert Pietersz grant to H. Rooseboom H+L at hill *palende besuyden Goosen Gerritsz, benoorden* Lourens Lourensz, on west by hill, on east by wagon way [5x20 in square].

9. Lourens Lourensz

a. Patents, vol. 2, pt. 2, # 10 [23 Oct. 1653]: pat. for L+H+Y, bounded to south by Pieter Bronck, to north by lots of low ground [*leegh erf?*], to east the wagon way to west the hills [5x20r]. Transported to Hendrick Coster by Goosen Gerritsz on 15 Sept. 1664.

b. ERA IV: 11 [11 Jan. 1658]: Willem Fredericksz grants H+L at hill [5x20] to Goosen Gerritsz, which he had bought on 6 Oct. 1657 from Lourens Lourensz for ƒ708. Adjoins to north Hendrick Andriesz, to south Pieter Bronck. ERA I: 363 [15 Sept. 1664]: Philip Pietersz grants to Goosen Gerritsz his half of H+L, adjoining to north Hendrick Rooseboom, to south widow of Hendrick Andriesz, east and west the highway [5x20]; ERA I: 362 [same date]: Goosen Gerritsz grants H+L to Hendrick Coster, *belent benoorden* Hendrick Rooseboom, *besuyden* the widow of Hendrick Andriesz, etc. See also ERA IV: 109 [16 June, 1659]: PPS wants to sell his house next to Pieter Bronck.

c. ERA II: 38 [10 April, 1679]: Jan Lansing [married Geertie, widow of Hendrick Coster] grants to Jan Claets H+L+Orchard, adjoining southerly Hendrick Rooseboom, northerly Marte Cregier, east and west the street [5x20].

10. Jan Verbeeck

a. Patents, vol. 2, pt. 2, #34 [25 Oct. 1653]: patent for L+H+Y, abuts to north the low lots [*leeghe erven?*], to south on Lourens Lourensz, on west the hills, to east the wagon way [5x20 r].

b. ERA I: 13 [10 Jan. 1657]: Jan Verbeeck grants to Hendrick Andriesz a H+L at hill *besuyden het huys van Lourens Lourensz, benoorden de gemeene wegh* for ƒ1210.

Nota Bene:

I am not sure where the following patents were located; they must have been somewhere in this same area, near Gillis Pietersz.

Jacob Hendricksz Sijbingh and Stoffel Jansz Abeel

a. patents, vol. 2, pt. 2, # 43 [25 Oct. 1653]: patent to Jacob Hendricksz Sijbingh and Stoffel Jansz Abeel; part was transported by Jochem Wesselsz Backer to David Pietersz Schuyler of H+L. Has to east, west, south the highway, on north the H of Gillis Pietersz. See also ERA IV: 8 [March, 1658?]: canceled: Stoffel Jansz wants to sell H+L east, west, north enclosed by street, to south Gillis Pietersz. See also ERA I: 355 [17 July, 1664]:

François Boon grants to Jochem Wesselsz a H+L *belent oost en west ende besuyden 's heerenwegh ende benoorden Gillis Pietersz*; by virtue of conveyance from Stoffel Jansz Abeel, 15 August, 1659. See also ERA I: 297 [18 Nov. 1661]: Boon grants to Wesselsz H+L+*koockhuys*. Delivery 1 august 1662, Boon will occupy it until 1 November. Deduct 13 beavers from the *f*1502. See also ERA I: 78: [8 August, 1665]: H+L *belent ten oosten, westen, suyden 's heerenwegh, ten noorden het huys van Gillis Pietersz*. ERA I: 319 [20 May, 1662]: Wesselsz to David Pietersz Schuyler for *f*1007. **NB:** ERA IV: 27 [20 May, 1658]: Thomas Jansz Mingael wants to sell H opposite mr. Boon.

b. Patents, vol. 2, pt. 1, # 17 [25 Oct. 1653]: patent Gillis Pietersz for H+L+Y by lot # 2. Has to north JH Sijbingh to west and south the common highway, being a corner of three angles. Br. before highway 6r, farther along highway 5r. See also ERA IV: 8 [canceled]: GP wants to sell H+L lying next to Stoffel Jansz with lot extending from one road to another, br. 35 wood ft, leaving 5-ft. alley on the south side.

Adriaen Jansz van Leyden

a. patents, vol. 2, pt 2, # 49 [25 Oct. 1653]: L+H by lot # 6, has on south side JH Sijbingh, on east, west, north a common highway [9x4, lying on square].

a. ERA I: 360, 370 [11 Sept. 1664]: Pieter Adriaensz *Soogemackelijck* grants to Philip Pietersz Schuyler H+L adjoining to north Adriaen Appel [= Van Leyden], to south Jan Barentsz Wemp, to west the street. ERA I: 417 [28 april, 1667]: Philip Pietersz grants to Jan *de Noorman* lot where his house has stood, *belent ten noorden Adriaen Appel, ten suyden Jan Barentsz Poest*, deceased [4x10].

b. See also FOCM, 41 [1 Febr. 1653], sued by Jacob Jansz Schermerhoorn about lot next to Schermerhoorn.

Carsten Jansz

a. ERA I: 396 [21 Nov. 1665]: administrators of Andries Herbertsz grant to Cornelis van Nes (married Marietje Damen] half of H+L of which other half Marietje Damen is now owner by virtue of conveyance by Teunis *de metselaer* to Andries Herbertsz on 19 Febr. 1660. Adjoins to north Pieter Adriaensz *Soogemackelijck*/ Philip Pietersz, *ten suyden Adriaen Jansz van Leyden, ende oost en west 's heeren straete*.

Jan Barentsz Wemp (Poest)

a. FOCM, 95 17 Febr. 1654]: JBWemp had fenced off lot next to Gysbert Cornelisz, deceased, on the south side. He shows his ground brief [patent].

IX: Behind the patroon's house

1. church yard

a. *MCR*, 75 [15 April, 1649]: Pieter Hartgers and Anthony de Hooges rent a garden for three *years benoorden dicht onder Fort Oranje, besuyden naest aenden hoff vande E: Heer patroon [...] ende beoosten het kerckhof*. Translated as 'to the north of the Fort Orange, to south of and next to the yard of the honorable patroon, and to the east of the churchyard.'

2. Adriaen Jansz van Ilpendam

a. Patent Adriaen Jansz van Ilpendam, patents, vol. 2, pt. 2, # 9 [25 Oct., 1653]; a G by lot # 5, having to east Jan Baptist van Rensselaer, to west common highway, to north Abraham Staets, to south the church yard [5x7]. ERA I: 7, Adriaen Jansz sells G to Adriaen Gerritsz [28 Oct. 1656].

b. ERA I: 440 [3 July, 1667]:Gerritsz sells the G (allotment # 5, adjoining on the east side Jeremias van Rensselaer, on the south side the burial grond) to Carsten Fredericksz.

3. Abraham Staets
a. Patents: vol. 2, pt. 2, # 12 [23 October, 1653]: L+G abuts to north on lot Ruyter Hendricksz, west to way, east to garden Mr. Rensselaer, south Aryaen van Ilpendam [15x7 r].
b. ERA I: 195 [27 October, 1655]: Staets sells the garden plus a H+L in Fort Orange to Jan van Twiller.

4. Rut Adriaensz
a. patents: vol. 2, pt. 2, # 72 [23 April, 1652]. Rut Adriaensz was deceased in the beginning of 1654. Did Staets obtain his lot? In pat. v2, pt. 2, # 12 is mentioned that he bought the G adjoining to south of Adriaen [=Albert meant?], to north Anneke Bogardus, east to mr. Rensselaer, west to way [15x7].

5. Albert Gerritsz
d. ERA IV: 41: Gerritsz received patent for G on 25 October, 1653; sold it on 4 July, 1658 to Jan Roelofsz for ƒ120 in beavers [7x5 rods].
e. ERA I: 356-57 [24 July, 1664]: Jan Roelofsz sells it to Willem Brouwer, who sells it on the same day to Abraham Staets. It adjoins in the rear of Mr van Rensselaer's lot, to the south of the heirs of Anneke Bogardus, to the east of the road, and to the north of the grantee. See also pat. v. 2, pt. 2, # 12, and ERA II: 73.

6. Anneke Bogardus
a. Patents, vol. 2, pt. 2, # 66 [23 April 1652], G [5x7]; on the south side of Dirrick Jansz, on the north side of Albert Gerritsz.
b. ERA II: 73 Abraham Staets has purchased garden, adjoining on the south to Adriaen Gerritsz and on the north to the lot of Anneke Bogardus on the east to Mr. Rensselaers, and on the west to the way.

7. Dirck Jansz
g. ERA I: 301 [5 May, 1662] Cornelis Vos sells to Abraham Staets garden of 5x7, adjoining to the west Dirck Jansz;
h. Abraham Staets sellls it to Johannes de Wandelaer
N.B.: If Cornelis Vos would have been to the north of Jeremias van Rensselaer/Van Slichtenhorst's gate it would fit: Anneke Bogardus had Dirck Jansz to the north and Cornelis Vos had Dirck Jansz to the west side.
But Jacob Luyersz is clearly immediately next to Fort Orange, and has Staets to his north side, so it has to be to the south of Jeremias van Rensselaer.

Other people who may have had a lot in this area:
Jan Verbeeck: Patents, vol. 2, pt. 2, # 76 [April 19, 1667] grants garden on plain behind Abraham Vosburgh to Jan Jansz Bleecker.
Philip Pietersz Schuyler: Patents, vol. 2, pt. 2, # 11 [10 Sept. 1658]: patent for lot, orchard and garden ; in length to south of Jeremias van Rensselaer 33 r, to north of plain 29 r; east of the way 16 r, w. of the hills the like. The directions seem to be reversed.

X: Lots south of the fort: from Beverkil until Fort Orange

N.B.: location is harder to determine as the Römer map does not show the area south of the fort in detail. On the map I have guessed where approximately these lots may have been. It seems that the numbers 7-10 may have been farthest away from the fort, and closer to the boundary line between Beverwijck and Rensselaerswijck.

1. Jan Labatie
a. ERA I: 212-13 [11 Nov. 1654], annulled: Jan Labatie grants to Adriaen Jansz van Leyden H in FO [ ] and a G and hogpen therein to south of the fort, adjoining to west Lam-

bert van Valckenburgh, on south side Pieter Jacobsz, to north a road, to east the Company's garden.

b.   ERA I 290 [4 Febr. 1661]: Jan Labatie grants to Evert Pels a H in FO [...] with a G without the fort, according to patent of 12 April, 1650. See also ERA I: 291 [4 Febr. 1661]: Evert Pels grants the above to Jan Barentsz Wemp, according to patent Jan Labatie, 12 April, 1650. see also ERA IV: 21, grant Evert Pels to Jan Barentsz Wemp.

2. Lambert van Valckenburgh

a.   patent Hendrick Andriesz, vol. 2, pt 2, # 17 [23 Oct. 1653] for L+G abuts to south on LvV's ground, to west a way by void ground, to north Gerrit Vastrick and Gysbert Cornelisz [10x3.4 in middle]. Patent C van Nes, 27 April, 1667.

c.   ERA IV: 18 [7 Oct. 1658]: Willem Hoffmeyer grants to Jochem Wesselsz *Backer* a G behind FO, bounded on east by Pieter Jacobsz, on north by L van Valckenburgh, on south and west by a road, almost triangular [7x3]. ERA IV: 22 [14 March, 1658]: Jochem Wesselsz grants the G to Adriaen Jansz van Ilpendam, who had a patent May 21, 1667. See also patents, vol. 2, pt. 2, # 48.

d.   ERA I: 375-76 [26 nov. 1670] Jac. Louwys grants to rev. Fabritius a H+L and other lot next to same in Albany on the *pleyn*, next to Lambert van Valckenburgh and on the west side some vacant lots. Originally it was Carsten Carstensz' lot.

e.   ERA III: 376 . See Carsten Carstensz *de Noorman's* grant to Claes Teunisz.

f.   ERA II: 67 [12 dec. 1679]: Pieter Jacobsz Borsboom grants to Cornelis van Dijck G behind the old fort, adjoins southerly G of Jan Jansz Bleecker and Jan Bijvanck, northerly Harmen Vedder, westerly Jochem Wesselsz, and easterly the common lane [*gangh*].

3. Hendrick Andriesz

a.   Patent Hendrick Andriesz, vol. 2, pt 2, # 17 [23 Oct. 1653] for L+G abuts to south on LvV's ground, to west a way by void ground, to north Gerrit Vastrick and Gysbert Cornelisz [10x3.4 in middle]. Patent C van Nes, 27 April, 1667.

b.   ERA II: 395 [16 May, 1702]: Wouter Aertsz says that in 1660 or so he sold a G behind FO and south of Beverwijck to Evert Lucasz, west of highway, south of Evert Wendel for ƒ40. See also *CMARS* III: 534 [5 May, 1685].

4. Carsten Carstensz *de Noorman*

a.   Patents, vol. 3, pt. 1, # 65 [27 April, 1667]: confirmation to Claes Teunisz: Carsten Carstensz grants to Claes Teunisz lot behind FO upon plain; to west of Claes Teunisz, 6 r; to east idem; by a lot that lies void having to north the highway where br. is 3 r, id. To south by plain. See also ERA I: 423 [7 May, 1667]: *bewesten Claes Teunisz, oost een leeghe erve.* See also FOCM, 428 [7 May, 1659]: Claes Teunisz is granted lot on plain to west Carsten *de Noorman*, l. 6 r; to north a road, west 6 r; to east vacant lot, br. 6 r; to south the plain, 3 r.

b.   ERA I: 375 [26 nov. 1670] Jac. Louwys grants to rev. Fabritius a H+L and other lot next to same in Albany on the *pleyn*, next to Lambert van Valckenburgh and on the west side some vacant lots. Originally it was Carsten Carstensz lot. **NB:** could this have come from Hendrick Andriesz?

5. Gisbert Cornelisz *de weert*

a.   Patent Hendrick Andriesz, vol. 2, pt. 2, # 17 [25 October, 1653]; L+G abuts to south on Lambert van Valckenburgh's ground, to west way by void ground, to north Gerrit Vastrick and Gisbert Cornelisz.

b.   patents, vol. 2, pt. 2, # 27 [9 nov. 1652]: Jacob Jansz Schermerhoorn has L+G near fort, east of highway, south of Gysbert Cornelisz, to west of Pieter Jacobsz, to north of ground heretofore belonging to WIC.

c.   ERA I: 193 [24 Aug. 1654]: François Boon [married Lysbeth, GC's widow] grants H+L to Steven Jansz . ERA I: 230 [1 May, 1655] Steven Jansz wants to sell H+ *koockhuys* + G + hogpen and lot, formerly owned by Gysbert Cornelisz. Pieter the Fleming rents it.

d.   **NB:** FOCM, 48 [10 April, 1653]: 8 lots past Gysbert Cornelisz laid out. # 1. Dijckman, 2. Schaets, 3. Abraham Staets, 4. Jan Labatie, 5. Adriaen Jansz van Leyden, 6. Pieter Ryverdingh, 7, ?, 8. ?

6. Pieter Jacobsz Borsboom

a.   patents, vol. 2, pt. 2, # 27 [9 Nov., 1652]: patent Jacob Jansz Schermerhoorn for L+G near FO, east of highway, south of Gysbert Cornelisz, west of Pieter Jacobsz, north of garden heretofore belonging to WIC. Br. 6r 8ft, l. 18 r; farther behind more 3 r 2 ft.

b.   ERA IV: 18 [7 Oct. 1658]: Willem Hoffmeyer grants to Jochem Wesselsz *Backer* a G behind FO, bounded on east by Pieter Jacobsz, on north by L van Valckenburgh, on south and west by a road, almost triangular [7x3]. ERA IV: 22 [14 March, 1658]: Jochem Wesselsz grants the G to Adriaen Jansz van Ilpendam, who had a patent May 21, 1667. See also patents, vol. 2, pt. 2, # 48.

c.   ERA II: 67 [12 dec. 1679]: Pieter Jacobsz Borsboom grants to Cornelis van Dijck G behind the old fort, adjoins southerly G of Jan Jansz Bleecker and Jan Bijvanck, northerly Harmen Vedder, westerly Jochem Wesselsz, and easterly the common lane [*gangh*].

g.   ERA I: 212-13 [11 Nov. 1654], annulled: Jan Labatie intends to grant to Adriaen Jansz van Leyden H in FO [ ] and a G and hogpen therein to south of the fort, adjoining to west Lambert van Valckenburgh, on south side Pieter Jacobsz, to north a road, to east the Company's G.

7. Willem Hoffmeyer

a.   ERA IV: 18 [7 Oct. 1658]: Willem Hoffmeyer grants to Jochem Wesselsz *Backer* a G behind FO, bounded on east by Pieter Jacobsz, on north by L van Valckenburgh, on south and west by a road, almost triangular [7x3]. Patent was of 25 Oct, 1653. ERA IV: 22 [14 March, 1658]: Jochem Wesselsz grants the G to Adriaen Jansz van Ilpendam, who had a patent May 21, 1667. See also patents, vol. 2, pt. 2, # 48.

b.   ERA II: 67 [12 dec. 1679]: Pieter Jacobsz Borsboom grants to Cornelis van Dijck G behind the old fort, adjoins southerly G of Jan Jansz Bleecker and Jan Bijvanck, northerly Harmen Vedder, westerly Jochem Wesselsz, and easterly the common lane [*gangh*].

8. Jacob Jansz Schermerhoorn

a.   patents, vol. 2, pt. 2, # 27 [9 Nov., 1652]: patent for L+G near FO, east of highway, south of Gysbert Cornelisz, west of Pieter Jacobsz, north of garden heretofore belonging to WIC. Br. 6r 8ft, l. 18 r; farther behind more 3 r 2 ft.

h.   FOCM, 52 [29 April, 1653]: Dirck Bensingh is granted garden behind FO, with consent Jacob Jansz Schermerhoorn, who gets # 16 in place of it. See also FOCM, 135. **NB:** not clear what happens with Bensingh's garden. Did Hoffmeyer get that and sell it to Jochem Backer, who sold it to Ilpendam? See FOCM, 304, 307; ERA 22 [14 March, 1658].

c.   ERA II: 370 [1 Dec. 1700] : Jacob Jansz van Noortstrant acknowledges that he sold a lot for G to Jacob Tysz van der Heyden witin Albany's limits in the consistory's great pasture, now bounding G of the heirs of Jacob Schermerhoorn and the little pasture of Robert Sandersz and Joh. Beeckman by # 19.

9. Thomas Jansz

a.   Patents, vol. 2, pt. 2, # 72 [25 Oct. 1653]: pat for H+L+G south of Fort Orange, north of *Beverkil.* Bounded to east by common way to river, to south, west with land occupied by Tomas Jansz. Br. before way 14 rods, behind on west 18 r; length north 14 r, south 24 r.

b.   ERA II: 60 [27 August, 1679]: Jacob Salomonsz grants to Pieter Bogardus H+L+G south of Albany, south of old fort where PB now dwells, adjoining east common wagon way on river side, south, west, north pasture of commander of fort Albany. Same dimensions.

10. Marten Hendricksz Verbeeck

b.   patents, vol. 3, pt. 1, # 78 [23 April, 1652]: Lot near fort on north of Tomas Jansz' lot [15x5] before highway to river. Has on south outward limits of the fort, on north land Tomas Jansz. Confirmed 17 March, 1669.

c.   Patents, vol. 3, pt. 1, # 78 and 87 [24 March/24 May 1654]: piece of land, has to north Tomas Jansz, to west the highway, to south the plain, to east place where formerly stood Marten Hendricksz' house [19.5 x 15]. **NB:** # 87 says that both lots were confirmed by Nicolls. MH sold to Steven Jansz [pat. 17 March, 1669].

d.   ERA IV: 93 [1659]: MH wants to sell H+L+land behind the house, adjoining to north Thomas Jansz, to south colony of Rensselaerswijck, to east a road, to west a road. Acc. to two patents, except brewer's tools. Delivery 1 May, 1659.

11. Adriaen Jansz van Leyden

a.   Patents, vol. 2, pt. 2, # 49 [16 dec. 1654]: pat. for L+H+G in Beverwijck, has to south the common highway, reaching Tomas Jansz's fence [5.8x14]. To west of a swamp, north of a void lot, lying in common. See also *DRCHSNY* XIV: 258 [30 April, 1654]: permission to keep inn for travelers close to palisades of Tomas Jansz, as exception upon new houses between its hills which might obstruct FO. See also, FOCM, 137 [17 June, 1654]: AJvL wants lot next to palisades TJ's land, etc; see also*LP*, 78 [16 dec. 1654].

b.   patents, vol. 2. pt. 2, # 49 mentions also another L+G by lot # 9. Abuts to south on Jochem Ketelheyn, to west Pieter Bronck, to north Gerrit Jansz [5x7]. See also ERA II: 192 [19 July, 1683; deed from AjvL to Barentje, widow of Jan Harmsz Backer] which mentions garden without Albany, by lot # 9.

c.   FOCM, 49 [10 April, 1653]: lots beyond Gysbert Cornelisz until palisades of Tomas Jansz: Adriaen Jansz van Leyden has # 5, Jan Labatie # 4, and Pieter Ryverdingh # 6.

d.   FOCM, 269 [5 dec. 1656]: AJvL is a tavern keeper in Rensselaerswijck
     NB: If this lot is south of FO, it is clear that the area south of FO was also called Beverwijck.

12. Wouter Aertsz *Rademaecker*

a.   Patents, vol. 2, pt. 2, # 41 [25 Oct. 1653]: parcel near fort. Abuts to south on limits fort, to west on Marten Hendricksz, to north on Steven *de timmerman* (= Jansz). Br. along way 26 r, tow. woods 25 r. length tow. woods 28 r. Patent 16 May, 1667 to Cornelis Segersz van Voorhout.

b.   ERA III: 442 [14 Sept. 1677] : Jacob Casparsz bought from J Albertsz Bratt land at the Normans kill ; he bought it from Jan Hendricksz van Bael, who bought it from Wouter Aertsz *Raemaecker*

c.   ERA II: 395 [16 May, 1702]: Wouter Aertsz says that in 1660 or so he sold a G behind FO and south of Beverwijck to Evert Lucasz, west of highway, south of Evert Wendel for ƒ40. See also *CMARS* III: 534 [5 May, 1685].

Others who may have had a lot south of the fort:

Gideon Schaets, patents, vol. 3, pt. 2, # 41 [29 May, ?]

Rutger Jacobsz: patents, vol. 2, pt. 2, # 50 [April 'last']; garden behind the fort was transported to Jan Clute

Gilis Pietersz, patents, vol. 2, pt. 1, # 17 [14 April, 1654]; garden behind fort, north of Schaets.

Jochem Wesselsz *backer*: patents, vol. 2, pt. 2, # 39 [17 July, 1656]; grants parcel of wood-land to Philip Pietersz Schuyler, abutting to south on Beaver kill. See also *ERA* I: 217.

Pieter Loockermans: patents, vol. 2, pt. 2, # 40 [July 7, 1653]; patent for garden, which 'has to the west the fort, to south, Abraham Staets, to north Hendrick Driesen, to east common highway.' I think that the directions east and west may have been reversed in the translation.

Pieter Jacobsz Borsboom: may have had another lot behind the fort. *LP* 96, [23 febr. 1658]: patent to PJB, length E, 23 r, W, 17 r; br. N, 5 r, S. 16 r. Kill described as being on the north of the lot. See also Patents, vol. 4, pt. 1, # 25 [29 Aug., 1661]: confirmation to Abraham Staets and Goosen Gerritsz, at Fort Albany, '**by the first kill**'; same dimensions. That would mean that the Beaver kill is referred to as first kill.

XI: South of State Street, Broadway until Pearl Street

For further information I refer to the research done by A.J.F. van Laer, 'The Dutch Grants along the South side of State Street. A Contribution Toward the Early Topography of the City of Albany,' in: *DSSYB* 2, pp. 11-23, and especially pp. 24-27, and plate 9. See also ill. 3.

PH. Pieter Hartgers
CV. Cornelis Vos
DJC. Dirck Jansz Croon
GG. Goosen Gerritsz
RJ. Rutger Jacobsz
AS. Abraham Staets
SOUTH OF THE *FUYCKEN KIL*
JvN. Jacob van Noortstrant
VJD. Volckert Jansz Douw

Unpublished primary sources

Albany
New York State Archives

New York Colonial Manuscripts, volumes 8, 9, 10, 13
Deacons' Account Books 1665-1676
Deacons' Account Books 1680, 1681, 1684, 1686-1715
The New York Colonial Patents Books, Albany 1664-1690.

New York State Library

Van Rensselaer Manor Papers
Ordinance on the burgher guard of Beverwijck, (mss 12802)

Albany County Hall of Records

Fort Orange Court Minutes
Notarial Papers Beverwijck, Albany

First Dutch Reformed Church, Albany

Deacons' Account books 1652-1664
Deacons' Account Books 1682, 1683, 1685

Albany Institute of History and Art

Livingston Indian Records (copy at the NNP)
Letters Adriaen Gerritsz van Papendorp (copies at the NNP)

New Brunswick
New Brunswick Theological Seminary, Gardner A. Sage Library

Amsterdam Correspondence

New York
New York Public Library

Bontemantel Collection (microfilm NNP)

New York Historical Society

Stuyvesant Rutherford Papers (microfilm NNP)

Amsterdam
Gemeentearchief

Baptism, marriage, and funeral records
Notarial Records
Poorterboeken

Nederlands Scheepvaartmuseum Amsterdam

Van Rensselaer Bowier Manuscripts (microfilm at NNP)

Arnhem
Rijksarchief

Court case of Brant Aertsz van Slichtenhorst against Jan van Rensselaer (microfilm at NNP)

Bibliography

Abels, P.H.A.M. 1994. *Nieuw en ongezien. Kerk en samenleving in de classis Delft en Delfland 1572-1621*, vol. 2. Delft: Eburon.

Alexander, R.S. 1988. *Albany's First Church and Its Role in the City*. Delmar, N.Y.: Newsgraphic Printers.

Appel, L. 1984. 'Bakkers en brood in Monnickendam.' In Jaarverslag, *Het menselyk bedryf: De backer*, pp. 25-82. Monnikendam: Vereniging "Oud Monnickendam."

Bachman, Van Claef. 1969. *Peltries or Plantations: The Economic Policies of the Dutch West India Company in New Netherland, 1623-1639*. Baltimore: John Hopkins University Press.

Bakker, B. 1985. 'Nieuw Nederlandse Studiën. Een inventarisatie van recent onderzoek/ New Netherland Studies: An Inventory of Current Research and Approaches.' *Bulletin KNOB. Tijdschrift van de Nederlandse Oudheidkundige Bond*, 84.

Barbanell-Edelstein, P. 1987. 'A Ceramic History of Colonial Albany, New York: A Curricular Model Integrating Art and Local History in Education.' Ph.D. dissertation. New York: Columbia University.

Barth, Barbara A. 1997. 'The Family of Ysbrant Eldersz of Rensselaerswyck.' *NYG&B Record* 128 (3; 4): 153-60; 229-37.

Beck, D. 1993. *Spiegel van mijn leven; een Haags dagboek uit 1624*. Annotated by Sv. E. Veldhuijzen. Hilversum: Verloren.

Beernink, G. 1916. *De geschiedschrijver en rechtsgeleerde Arend van Slichtenhorst en zijn vader Brant van Slichtenhorst, stichter van Albany, hoofdstad van de staat New York*. Arnhem: S. Gouda Quint.

Beliën, H.M., A.Th. Van Deursen, and G.J. Van Setten, eds. 1995. *Gestalten van de Gouden Eeuw. Een Hollands groepsportret*. Amsterdam: Bert Bakker.

Biewenga, A. 1999. *De Kaap de Goede Hoop. Een Nederlandse vestigingskolonie, 1680-1730*. Amsterdam: Prometheus-Bert Bakker.

Blackburn, R.H., and N.A. Kelley [eds]. 1987. *New World Dutch Studies: Dutch Arts and Culture in Colonial America 1609-1776*. Albany, NY.: Albany Institute of History and Art.

Blackburn, R.H., and R. Piwonka. 1988. *Remembrance of Patria: Dutch Arts and Culture in Colonial America 1609-1776*. Albany, N.Y.: Publishing Center for Cultural Resources, Albany Institute of History and Art.

Blakely, A. 1993. *Blacks in the Dutch World: The Evolution of Racial Imagery in a Modern Society*. Bloomington and Indianapolis: Indiana University Press.

Blockmans, W.P., and W. Prevenier. 1975. 'Armoede in de Nederlanden van de 14de tot het midden van de 16de eeuw: bronnen en problemen.' *Tijdschrift voor Geschiedenis* 88: 501-38.

Boekholt, P.Th.F.M., and E.P. de Booy. 1987. *Geschiedenis van de school in Nederland vanaf de middeleeuwen tot aan de huidige tijd*. Assen en Maastricht: Van Gorcum.

Boxer, Ch.R. 1957. *The Dutch in Brazil, 1624-1654*. Oxford: Oxford University Press.

Bradley, J.W. 1987. *Evolution of the Onondaga Iroquois: Accommodating Change, 1500-1655*. Syracuse, N.Y.: Syracuse University Press.

Brandão, J.A. 1997. *Your Fyre shall burn no more: Iroquois Policy Toward New France and Its Native Allies, to 1701*. Lincoln and London: University of Nebraska Press.

Brasser, T.J. 1974. 'Riding the Frontier's Crest: Mahican Indian Culture and Culture Change.' Paper 13, *National Museum of Man Mercury Series, Ethnology Division*.

——. 1978. 'Mahican.' In Bruce G. Trigger (ed.), *Handbook of North American Indians: Northeast*, vol. 15. Washington, D.C.: Smithsonian Institution.

Bressani, F.G. 1996. 'Two Letters of Bressani, 1644.' In D.R. Snow, et al. (eds.), *In Mohawk Country: Early Narratives About a Native People*, pp. 47-55. Syracuse, N.Y.: Syracuse University Press.

Bruggeman, M., ed. 1996. *Mensen van de Nieuwe Tijd. Een liber amicorum voor A.Th. van Deursen*. Amsterdam: Bert Bakker.

Burke, G.L. 1956. *The Making of Dutch Towns: A Study in Urban Development from the Tenth to the Seventeenth Centuries*. London: Cleaver/Hume Press.

Burke, P. 1978. *Popular Culture in Early Modern Europe*. London and New York: Harper and Row.

Burke, T. 1986. 'The New Netherland Fur Trade, 1657-1661: Response to a Crisis.' *DHM* 59: 1-4, 21.

Burke, T.E. 1991. *Mohawk Frontier: The Dutch Community of Schenectady, New York, 1661-1710*. Ithaca, N.Y.: Cornell University Press.

Campisi, J. 1978. 'The Hudson Valley Indians Through Dutch Eyes.' In L.M. Hauptman and J. Campisi, *Neighbors and Intruders: An Ethnohistorical Exploration of the Indians of Hudson's River*. Paper 39, Canadian Ethnological Service.

Ceci, L. 1980. 'The First Fiscal Crisis in New York.' *Economic Development and Cultural Change* 4: 839-47.

Centraal Bureau voor Genealogie. 1996. *Jaarboek van het Centraal Bureau voor Genealogie* 50. The Haag: CBG.

Christoph, P. 1980. *Administrative Papers of Governors Richard Nicolls and Francis Lovelace, 1664-1673*. Baltimore, Md.: Genealogical.

Christoph, F. 1987. *Schuyler Genealogy: A Compendium of Sources Pertaining to the Schuyler Families in America Prior to 1800*. Albany, N.Y.: Friends of Schuyler Mansion.

Christoph, P., and Florence Christoph. 1982. *Books of General Entries of the Colony of New York, 1664-1673: Orders, Warrants, Letters, Commissions, Passes and Licenses Issued by Governors Richard Nicolls and Francis Lovelace*. Baltimore, Md.: Genealogical.

Christoph, P.R. 1991. 'The Freedmen of New Amsterdam.' In N.A. McClure Zeller (ed.), *A Beautiful and Fruitful Place: Selected Rensselaerswijck Seminar Papers*, pp. 157-69. Albany, N.Y.: New Netherland.

——. 1997. 'Worthy, Virtuous Juffrouw Maria van Rensselaer.' *DHM* 70 (2).

Cohen, D. 1981. 'How Dutch Were the Dutch of New Netherland?' *New York History* 62: 43-60.

Cohen, D.S. 1992. *The Dutch-American Farm*. New York and London: New York University Press.

Condon, T.J. 1968. *New York Beginnings: The Commercial Origins of New Netherland*. New York and London: New York University Press.

Conrads, M., and G. Zwartjes. 1993. *Tirions Kostuumgids. Westerse kledingstijlen van de vroege middeleeuwen tot heden*, 7th ed. Baarn: Tirion.

Corwin, E.T., trans. and ed. 1901-16. *Ecclesiastical Records. State of New York.* 7 vols. Albany, N.Y.: James B: Lyon.

Cronon, W. 1983. *Changes in the Land: Indians, Colonists, and the Ecology of New England.* New York: Hill and Wang.

Damsma, D. 1993. *Het Hollandse Huisgezin. 1560-heden.* Utrecht and Antwerp: Kosmos-Z&K Uitgevers.

Danckaerts, J. 1996. 'Journal of a Voyage to New Netherland and a Tour in Several of the American Colonies, 1679-1680.' In D.R. Snow, et al. (eds.), *In Mohawk Country: Early Narratives About a Native People*, pp. 193-220. Syracuse, N.Y.: Syracuse University Press.

De Bell, W. 1994. 'Het kooksel van Dees. Bier in Amsterdam, 1600-1800.' *Ons Amsterdam* 6: 142-46.

De Boer, L.P. 1929-30. 'The Ancestry of Domine Gideon Schaets (1607-1694) in the Netherlands from the Year 1520.' *DSSYB* 5: 4-6.

De Booy, E.P. 1977. *De Weldaet der scholen. Het plattelandsonderwijs in de provintie Utrecht van 1580 tot het begin der 19e eeuw.* Zutphen: De Walburg Pers.

——. 1980. *Kweekhoven der Wijsheid. Basis- en vervolgonderwijs in de steden van de provincie Utrecht van 1580 tot het begin der 19e eeuw.* Zutphen: De Walburg Pers.

Dekker, R. 1992. 'Handwerkslieden en arbeiders in Holland.' In P. te Boekhorst, et al. (eds.), *Cultuur en Maatschappij in Nederland, 1500-1850*, pp. 109-47. Meppel and Amsterdam: Boom and Open Universiteit.

——. 1995. *Uit de schaduw in 't grote licht. Kinderen in egodocumenten van de Gouden Eeuw tot de Romantiek.* Amsterdam: Wereldbibliotheek.

Dekker, T., H. Roodenburg, and G. Rooijakkers, eds. 2000. *Volkscultuur. Een inleiding in de Nederlandse etnologie.* Nijmegen: SUN.

De Laet, Johannes. 1625-40. '"From the New World," by Johan de Laet, 1625, 1630, 1633, 1640.' In J. Franklin Jameson (ed.), *Narratives of New Netherland, 1609-1664.* New York: Charles Scribner's Sons, 1909.

——. 1644. *Iaerlyck verhael van de verrichtinghen der geoctroyeerde West-Indische Compagnie in derthien Boecken*, ed. S.P. L'Honore Naber. 4 vols. 's-Gravenhage: Martinus Nijhoff Leiden, 1931-37.

De Mello, J.A. Gonsalves. 1947. *Nederlanders in Brazilië (1624-1654). De invloed van de Hollandse bezetting of het leven en de cultuur in Noord-Brazilië.* Rio de Janeiro, 2001 (translation published at Zutphen by Walburg Pers).

De Monté ver Loren, J.Ph., and J.E. Spruit. 1982. *Hoofdlijnen uit de ontwikkeling der rechterlijke organisatie in de Nooordelijke Nederlanden tot de Bataafse omwenteling.* Deventer: Kluwer, zesde druk.

Demos, J. 1970. *A Little Commonwealth: Family Life in Plymouth Colony.* London, Oxford, and New York: Oxford University Press.

Den Heijer, H. 1994. *De geschiedenis van de WIC.* Zutphen: Walburg Pers.

——. 1997. *Goud, ivoor en slaven. Scheepvaart en handel van de Tweede Westindische Compagnie op Afrika, 1674-1740.* Zutphen: Uitgeversmaatschappij Walburg Pers.

Dennis, M. 1993. *Cultivating a Landscape of Peace: Iroquois-European Encounters in Seventeenth-century America.* Ithaca, N.Y., and London: Cornell University Press.

De Planque, P.A. 1926. *Valcooch's regel der Duytsche schoolmeesters. Bijdrage tot de kennis van het schoolwezen in de zestiende eeuw.* Groningen: P. Noordhoff.

Der Kinderen-Besier, J.H. 1950. *Spelevaart der mode. De kledij onzer voorouders in de zeventiende eeuw.* Amsterdam: N.V. EM. Querido's Uitgeversmaatschappij.

De Roever, M. 1987. 'The Fort Orange "EB" Pipe Bowls: An Investigation of the Origin of American Objects in Dutch 17th-Century Documents.' In *New World Dutch Studies: Dutch Art and Culture in Colonial America, 1609-1776*. Proceedings of symposium organized by the Albany Institute of History and Art in conjunction with the exhibition, 'Remembrance of *Patria*: Dutch Arts and Culture in Colonial America, 1609-1776' (August 2-3, 1986), pp. 51-61. Albany, N.Y.: Albany Institute of History and Art.

—. 1996. 'Koopmanschappen voor Nieuw Nederland/ Merchandises for New Netherland.' In A. van Dongen, et al. (eds.), *'One Man's Trash Is Another Man's Treasure:' The Metamorphosis of the European Untensil in the New World*. Catalogue Museum Boymans-van Beuningen Rotterdam. Rotterdam: Museum Boymans van Beuningen, 1995; and Williamsburg, Va.: Jamestown Settlement Museum, 1996.

De Roever, N. 1890. 'Kilaen van Rensselaer en zijne kolonie Rensselaerswijck.' *Oud-Holland* 8 (Amsterdam): 29-74, 241-96.

De Vries, D.P. 1911. *Korte Historiael ende Journaels Aenteyckeninge van verscheyden voyagiens in de vier delen des werelts-ronde als Europa, Africa, Asia ende America gedaen*, red. H.T. Colenbrander. Werken Linschoten Vereeniging 3. 's-Gravenhage.

De Vries, J., and A. van der Woude. 1995. *Nederland 1500-1815. De eerste ronde van moderne economische groei*. Amsterdam: Uitgeverij Balans.

De Vries, W. 1949. 'De Van Rensselaer's in Nederland.' *De Nederlandsche Leeuw* 66: 150-72, 194-211.

Dibbits, H. 2001. *Vertrouwd bezit. Materiële cultuur in Doesburg en Maassluis, 1650-1800*. Nijmegen: SUN.

Dorren, G. 2001. *Eenheid en verscheidenheid. De burgers van Haarlem in de Gouden Eeuw*. Amsterdam: Prometheus and Bert Bakker.

Dosker, H. 1893. *Levensschets van Rev. A.C. van Raalte, DD*. Nijkerk: C.C. Callenbach.

Douglas, M., ed. 1987. *Constructive Drinking: Perspectives on Drink from Anthropology*. Cambridge: Cambridge University Press.

Dunn, S. 1997. 'Settlement Patterns in Rensselaerswijck: Farms and Farmers on Castle Island.' *DHM* 70: 7-18.

Dunn, S.W. 1994. *The Mohicans and Their Land 1609-1730*. Fleischmanns, N.Y.: Purple Mountain Press.

Eccles, W.J. 1983. *The Canadian Frontier, 1534-1760*. Albuquerque: University of New Mexico Press.

—. 1983. 'The Fur Trade and Eighteenth-Century Imperialism.' *WMQ*, 3rd ser. (40): 341-62.

—. 1986. 'Review of B.G. Trigger, *Natives and Newcomers*.' *WMQ*, 3rd ser. (42): 480-83.

—. 1987. 'Social Welfare Measures and Policies in New France.' In W.J. Eccles, *Essays on New France*, pp. 38-49. Toronto: Oxford University Press.

—. 1987. 'The Role of the Church in New France.' In W.J. Eccles, *Essays on New France*, pp. 26-37. Toronto: Oxford University Press.

Eekhof, A. 1910. *Bastiaen Jansz. Krol, Krankenbezoeker, Kommies en Kommandeur van Nieuw-Nederland (1595-1645)*. 's-Gravenhage: Martinus Nijhoff.

—. 1913. *De Hervormde Kerk in Noord-Amerika*. 2 vols. 's-Gravenhage: Martinus Nijhoff.

—. 1926. *Jonas Michaëlius, Founder of the Church in New Netherland*. Leyden: Sijthoff's.

Fagan, B. 2000. *The Little Ice Age: How Climate Made History, 1300-1850*. New York: Basic Books.

Feister, L. 1973. 'Linguistic Communication Between the Dutch and Indians in New Netherland, 1609-1664.' In Campisi and Hauptmann, *Mercury Series* 39 (Ottawa, 1978): 192. Reprinted with permission from *Ethnohistory* 20: 25-38.

Fenton, W.F., and E. Tooker. 1978. 'Mohawk.' In B.G. Trigger (ed.), *Handbook of North American Indians: Northeast*, vol. 15, pp. 466-80. Washington, D.C.: Smithsonian Institution.

Fenton, W.N. 1978. 'Northern Iroquoian Culture Patterns.' In B.G. Trigger (ed.), *Handbook of North American Indians: Northeast*, vol. 15, pp. 296-321. Washington, D.C.: Smithsonian Institution.

Fenton, W.N. 1998. *The Great Law and the Longhouse: A Political History of the Iroquois Confederacy*. Norman: University of Oklahoma Press.

Fernow, B., ed. 1897. *The Records of New Amsterdam from 1653 to 1674 anno Domini*. 7 vols. New York; 2nd printing, Baltimore, Md.: Genealogical, 1976.

——. 1902. *Minutes of the Orphanmasters Court of New Amsterdam 1655-1663*. New York: Francis P. Harper.

Fitchen, J. 1968. *The New World Dutch Barn*. Syracuse, N.Y.: Syracuse University Press.

Fock, C.W. 2001. '1600-1650.' In C.W. Fock, et al. (eds.), *Het Nederlandse Interieur in beeld 1600-1900*, pp.16-79. Zwolle: Waanders.

——. 2001. '1650-1700.' In C.W. Fock, et al. (eds.), *Het Nederlandse Interieur in beeld 1600-1900*, pp.81-179. Zwolle: Waanders.

——. 2001. 'Semblance or Reality? The Domestic Interior in Seventeenth-Century Dutch Genre Painting.' In M. Westerman (ed.), *Art and Home: Dutch Interiors in the Age of Rembrandt*, pp. 15-81. Zwolle: Waanders.

Fockema Andreae, S.J. 1969. *De Nederlandse staat onder de Republiek*. 3rd ed. Amsterdam: N.V. Noord-Hollandsche Uitgevers Maatschappij-Amsterdam.

Folkerts, J. 1984. 'De pachters van Rensselaerswijck, 1630-1664. Nederlandse boeren in de wildernis van Noord-Amerika. Een onderzoek naar landbouw en pacht in Nieuw-Nederland.' Doctoraal thesis. Groningen: Rijksuniversiteit.

——. 1991. 'Kiliaen van Rensselaer and Agricultural Productivity in His Domain: A New Look at the First Patroon and Rensselaerswijck Before 1664.' In N.A. McClure Zeller (ed.), *A Beautiful and Fruitful Place: Selected Rensselaerswijck Seminar Papers*, pp. 295-308. Albany, N.Y.: New Netherland.

Freedberg, D., and J. de Vries, eds. 1992. *Art in History. History in Art: Studies in Seventeenth-Century Dutch Culture*. Santa Monica, Calif.: Chicago Press.

Frijhoff, W.Th.M. 1986. 'Vraagtekens bij het vroegmoderne kersteningsoffensief.' In G. Rooijakkers and T. van der Zee, *Religieuze volkscultuur. De spanning tussen de voorgeschreven orde en de geleefde praktijk*, pp. 71-98. Nijmegen: SUN.

——. 1992. 'Inleiding: Historische Antropologie.' In P.te Boekhorst, et al. (eds.), *Cultuur en Maatschappij in Nederland, 1500-1850*, pp. 11-38. Meppel and Amsterdam: Boom and Open Universiteit.

——. 1995. *Wegen van Evert Willemsz. Een Hollands weeskind op zoek naar zichzelf, 1607-1647*. Nijmegen: SUN.

——. 1996. 'Dominee Bogardus als Nieu-Nederlander.' In *Jaarboek van het Centraal Bureau voor Genealogie* 50, pp. 37-68. The Haag: Centraal Bureau voor Genealogie.

——. 1997. 'The West India Company and the Reformed Church: Neglect or Concern?' *DHM* 70: 59-68.

——. 1997. 'Volkskunde en cultuurwetenschap: de ups en downs van een dialoog.' *Mededelingen van de Afdeling Letterkunde, Nieuwe Reeks* 60 (3): 89-143.

——. 1998. 'New Views on the Dutch Period of New York.' *DHM* 71: 23-34.

——. 1999. 'Identity Achievement, Education, and Social Legitimation in Early Modern Dutch Society: The Case of Evert Willemsz.' Paper presented at 'Two Faces of the Early Modern World: The Netherlands and Japan in the 17th and 18th Centuries,' international symposium in Europe (Netherlands). Kyoto, Japan: International Research Center for Japanese Studies.

—. 2000. 'Reinventing an Old Fatherland: The Management of Dutch Identity in Early Modern America.' In R. Bendix and H. Roodenburg (eds.), *Managing Ethnicity: Perspectives from Folklore Studies, History and Anthropology*, pp. 121-41. Amsterdam: Het Spinhuis.

—. 2002. 'Religious Toleration in the United Provinces: From "Case" to "Model".' In R. Po-Chia Hsia and H. van Nierop (eds.), *Calvinism and Religious Toleration in the Dutch Golden Age*, pp. 27-52. Cambridge: Cambridge University Press.

Frijhoff, W., and M. Spies. 1999. *1650. Bevochten eendracht.* The Haag: Cdu Uitgevers.

Gawronski, J. 1994. 'Bier voor de VOC. De produktie en inkoop in Amsterdam in het midden vande 18de eeuw.' In R. Kistemaker and V. van Vilsteren (eds.), *Bier! Geschiedenis van een volksdrank*, pp. 132-45. Amsterdam: De Bataafse Leeuw.

Gehring, C.T. 1978. *A Guide to Dutch Manuscripts Relating to New Netherland.* Albany: State University of New York.

—. trans. and ed. 1979. 'An Undiscovered Van Rensselaer Letter.' *DHM* 3: 13, 28.

—. trans. and ed. 1980. *Land Papers.* New York Historical Manuscripts: Dutch, vols. GG, HH, and II. Baltimore, Md.: Genealogical.

—. trans. and ed. 1981. *Delaware Papers (Dutch Period): A Collection of Documents Pertaining to the Regulation of Affairs on the South River of New Netherland, 1648-1664.* New York Historical Manuscripts: Dutch, vols. 18-19. Baltimore, Md.: Genealogical.

—. trans. and ed. 1983. *Council Minutes, 1652-1654.* Baltimore, Md.: Genealogical.

—. trans. and ed. 1990. *Fort Orange Court Minutes, 1652-1660.* Syracuse, N.Y.: Syracuse University Press.

—. trans. and ed. 1991. *Laws and Writs of Appeal 1647-1663.* Syracuse, N.Y.: Syracuse University Press.

—. trans. and ed. 1995. *Council Minutes, 1655-1656.* Syracuse, N.Y.: Syracuse University Press.

—. trans. and ed. 2000. *Correspondence 1647-1653.* Syracuse, N.Y.: Syracuse University Press.

—. trans. and ed. 2000. *Fort Orange Records, 1656-1678.* Syracuse, N.Y.: Syracuse University Press.

Gehring, C.T., and R.S. Grumet, trans. and eds. 1987. 'Observations of the Indians from Jasper Danckaerts's Journal, 1679-1680.' In *WMQ*, 3rd ser. (1): 104-20.

Gehring, C.T., and W.A. Starna, trans. and eds. 1988. *A Journey into Mohawk and Oneida Country, 1634-1635: The Journal of Harmen Meyndertsz van den Bogaert.* Syracuse, N.Y.: Syracuse University Press.

—. 1992. 'Dutch and Indians in the Hudson Valley: The Early Period.' *Hudson Valley Regional Review: A Journal of Regional Studies* 9-2: 1-25.

Gehring, C.T., W.A. Starna, and W.N. Fenton. 1987. 'The Tawagonshi Treaty of 1613: The Final Chapter.' *New York History* 68: 373-93.

Geudeke, L. 1996. 'Bedelen of Bedélen. Kerkelijke en burgerlijke armenzorg op kleinstedelijk niveau: Edam, Monnickendam en Purmerend (1572-1650).' In *Mensen van de Nieuwe Tijd. Een Liber Amicorum voor A.Th. van Deursen*, pp. 118-46. Amsterdam: Uitgeverij Bert Bakker.

Goodfriend, J.D. 1989. 'Burghers and Blacks: The Evolution of a Slave Society at New Amsterdam.' *New York History* 59: 124-44.

—. 1989. 'The Social Dimensions of Congregational Life in Colonial New York City.' In *WMQ*, 3rd ser. (46): 252-78.

——. 1991. 'Recovering the Religious History of Dutch Reformed Women in Colonial New York.' *DHM* 64: 53-59.

——. 1999. 'Incorporating Women into the History of the Colonial Dutch Reformed Church: Problems and Proposals.' In R. House and J. Coakley (eds.), *Patterns and Portraits*. Grand Rapids, Mich.: Wm.B. Eerdmans.

——. 1999. 'Writing/Righting Dutch Colonial History.' *New York History* 80: 5-28.

Grant, A. 1808. *Memoires of an American Lady: With sketches of Manners and Scenery in America, as They Existed Previous to the Revolution.* 2 vols. London, 1808; New York: Dodd, Mead, 1901.

Gras, H. 1989. *Op de grens van het bestaan. Armen en armenzorg in Drenthe 1700-1800.* Zuidwolde: Stichting Het Drentse Boek.

Grijp, L.P. 1995. 'Zingen in een kleine taal. De muzikale taalkeuze van Nederland.' *Zingen in een kleine taal. De positie van het Nederlands in de muziek. Volkskundig Bulletin* 212: 153-84.

Groenhuis, G. 1977. *De Predikanten. De sociale positie van de gereformeerde predikanten in de Republiek der Verenigde Nederlanden voor 1700.* Groningen: Wolters-Noordhoff.

Groenveld, S. 1975. '"Geef van uw haaf/een milde gaaf/Ons arme WEESEN." De zorg voor wezen tot 1800, als onderdeel van de armenzorg.' In S. Groenveld (ed.), *Daer de orangie-appel in de gevel staat. In en om het weeshuis der doopsgezinde collegianten 1675-1975.* Amsterdam.

——. 1995. *Huisgenoten des geloofs. Was de samenleving in de Republiek der Verenigde Nederlanden verzuild?* Hilversum: Verloren.

——. 1997. 'De Republiek der Verenigde Nederlanden en haar wezen, ca.1572-1795.' In S. Groenveld, et al. (eds.), *Wezen en Boefjes. Zes eeuwen zorg in wees- en kinderhuizen.* Hilversum: Verloren.

Hagedorn, N. 1988. '"A Friend to Go Between Them": The Interpreter as Cultural Broker During Anglo-Iroquois Councils, 1740-70.' *Ethnohistory* 35 (1): 60-80.

Haks, D. 1985. *Huwelijk en gezin in Holland in de 17de en 18de eeuw. Processtukken en moralisten over aspecten van het laat 17de- en 18de-eeuwse gezinsleven.* Utrecht: Hes uitgevers.

Hamell, G. 1995. 'Wampum: Light, White and Bright Are Good to Think.' In Alexandra Van Dongen, et al. (eds.), *'One Man's Trash Is Another Man's Treasure': The Metamorphosis of the European Utensil in the New World*, pp. 41-51. Rotterdam: Museum Boymans-van Beuningen.

Hamell, G.R. 1986-87. 'Strawberries, Floating Islands, and Rabbit Captains: Mythical Realities and European Contact in the Northeast During the Sixteenth and Seventeenth Centuries.' *Journal of Canadian Studies* 21 (4): 72-94.

——. 1992. 'The Iroquois and the World's Rim: Speculations on Color, Culture, and Contact.' *American Quarterly* 16 (4): 451-69.

Hart, S. 1959. *The Prehistory of the New Netherland Company: Amsterdam Notarial Records of the First Dutch Voyages to the Hudson.* Amsterdam: City of Amsterdam Press.

——. 1976. 'Een bijdrage to de geschiedenis van de houthandel.' In S. Hart, *Geschrift en getal. Een keuze uit de demografisch-, economisch- en sociaal-historische studiën op grond van Amsterdamse en Zaanse archivalia, 1600-1800*, pp. 71-92. Dordrecht: Hollandse Studiën 9.

——. 1976. 'Geschrift en getal. Onderzoek naar de samenstelling van de bevolking van Amsterdam in de 17e en 18e eeuw, op grond van gegevens over migratie, huwelijk, beroep en alfabetisme.' In S. Hart, *Geschrift en getal. Een keuze uit de demografisch-, econo-misch- en sociaal-historische studiën op grond van Amsterdamse en Zaanse archivalia, 1600-1800*, pp.115-81. Dordrecht: Hollandse Studiën 9.

——. 1976. 'Nederlanders en Noord-Amerika in de eerste helft van de zeventiende eeuw. Enige aspekten.' In S. Hart, *Geschrift en getal. Een keuze uit de demografisch-, economisch- en sociaal-historische studiën op grond van Amsterdamse en Zaanse archivalia, 1600-1800*, pp. 315-31. Dordrecht: Hollandse Studiën 9.

——. 1976. 'Zeelieden te Amsterdam in de zeventiende eeuw. Een historisch-demografisch onderzoek.' In S. Hart, *Geschrift en getal. Een keuze uit de demografisch-, economisch-en sociaal-historische studiën op grond van Amsterdamse en Zaanse archivalia, 1600-1800*, pp. 193-208. Dordrecht: Hollandse Studiën 9.

Hermesdorf, B.H.D. 1957. *De herberg in de Nederlanden. Een blik in de beschavings-geschiedenis.* Assen: Van Gorcum.

Howard, R.W. 1991. 'Apprenticeship and Economic Education in New Netherland and Seventeenth-Century New York.' In N.A. McClure Zeller, *A Beautiful and Fruitful Place: Selected Rensselaerswijck Seminar Papers*, pp. 205-18. Albany, N.Y.: New Netherland.

Huey, P. 1985. 'Archaeological Excavations in the Site of Fort Orange, A Dutch West India Company Trading Fort Built in 1634.' In B. Bakker (ed.), *Nieuw Nederlandse Studiën. Een inventarisatie van recent onderzoek* (New Netherland studies: An inventory of current research and approaches). *Bulletin KNOB. Tijdschrift van de Nederlandse Oudheidkundige Bond* 84, pp. 68-79. Amsterdam: Bohn, Scheltema and Holkema.

——. 1988. 'Aspects of Continuity and Change in Colonial Dutch Material Culture at Fort Orange, 1624-1664.' Ph.D. dissertation. Philadelphia: University of Pennsylvania.

——. 1991. 'The Archaeology of Fort Orange and Beverwijck.' In N.A. McClure Zeller, *A Beautiful and Fruitful Place: Selected Rensselaerswijck Seminar Papers*, pp. 327-49. Albany, N.Y.: New Netherland.

——. 1997. 'Historical and Archeological Resources of Castleton Island State Park, Towns of Stuyvesant, Columbia County; New Baltimore, Greene County: and Schodack, Rensselaer County, New York: A Preliminary Phase I Cultural Resources Assessment.' Waterford, N.Y.: New York State Office of Parks, Recreation and Historic Preservation, Bureau of Historic Sites.

Innes, J.H. 1902. *New Amsterdam and Its People: Studies, Social and Topographical, of the Town under Dutch and Early English Rule.* Port Washington, N.Y.: Ira J. Friedman, 1969.

Innes, S. 1983. *Labor in a New Land.* Princeton, N.J.: Princeton University Press.

Israel, J.I. 1989. *Dutch Primacy in World Trade, 1585-1740.* Oxford: Clarendon Press. Translated into Dutch as *Nederland als centrum van de wereldhandel 1585-1740.* Franeker: Uitgeverij Van Wijnen, 1991.

Jacobs, J. 1996. 'Johannes de Laet en de Nieuwe Wereld.' In *Jaarboek van het centraal bureau van de genealogie* 50, pp. 108-30. The Haag: Centraal Bureau van de genealogie.

Jacobs, J. 1999. *Een zegenrijk gewest. Nieuw Nederland in de zeventiende eeuw.* Amsterdam: Prometheus-Bert Bakker.

Jameson, J.F. 1909. *Narratives of New Netherland, 1609-1664.* New York: Charles Scribner's Sons.

Jansen, C.H. 1965. 'A Dutch Family's Ties with Colonial America, II.' *DHM* 40: 13-14.

Jansen, G.H. 1976. *De eeuwige kroeg. Hoofdstukken uit de geschiedenis van het openbaar lokaal.* Meppel: Boom, reprinted 1987.

Jennings, F. 1984. *The Ambiguous Iroquois Empire*. New York: W.W. Norton.

Jessurun, J.S.C. 1917. *Kiliaen van Rensselaer van 1623 tot 1636*. The Haag: Martinus Nijhoff.

Jobse-van Putten, J. 1995. *Eenvoudig maar voedzaam. Cultuurgeschiedenis van de dagelijkse maaltijd in Nederland*. Nijmegen: SUN.

Jogues, I. 'Novum Belgium and an Account of René Coupil, 1644.' In D.R. Snow, et al. (eds.), *In Mohawk Country: Early Narratives about a Native People*, p. 29-37. Syracuse: Syracuse University Press, 1996.

Juet, R. 1610. '"From the Third Voyage of Master Henry Hudson" by Robert Juet 1610.' In J. Franklin Jameson (ed.), *Narratives of New Netherland, 1609-1664*. New York: Charles Scribner's Sons, 1909.Kamermans, J.A. 1999. *Materiële cultuur in de Krimpenerwaard in de zeventiende en achttiende eeuw. Ontwikkeling en diversiteit*. Wageningen: A.A.G. Bijdragen 39.

Kalm, P. 1770. *Peter Kalm's Travels in North America: The English Version of 1770*. Revised from the original Swedish by A.B. Benson, ed. (New York: Dover, 1987).

Kilpatrick, W.H. 1912. *The Dutch Schools of New Netherland and Colonial New York*. Washington, D.C: U.S. Government Printing Office.

Kim, S.B. 1978. *Landlord and Tenant in Colonial New York: Manorial Society, 1664-1775*. Chapel Hill: University of North Carolina Press.

Kistemaker, R., and V. van Vilsteren (eds.), 1994. *Bier! Geschiedenis van een volksdrank* (Beer! The story of Holland's favorite drink). Amsterdam: De Bataafse Leeuw.

Kloek, E. 1990. *Wie hij zij, man of wijf. Vrouwengeschiedenis en de vroegmoderne tijd*. Hilversum: Verloren.

—. 1995. 'De vrouw.' In H.M. Beliën, et al. (eds.), *Gestalten van de Gouden Eeuw. Een Hollands groepsportret*, pp. 261-79. Amsterdam: Bert Bakker.

Klompmaker, H. 1966. *Handel in de Gouden Eeuw*. Bussum: C.A.J. van Dishoeck.

Knevel, P. 1994. *Burgers in het geweer. De schutterijen in Holland, 1550-1700*. Hilversum: Verloren.

Komter, A. (ed), 1996. *The Gift: an interdisciplinary perspective*. Amsterdam: Amsterdam University Press.

Kooijmans, L. 1995. 'De koopman.' In H.M. Beliën, et al. (eds.), *Gestalten van de Gouden Eeuw. Een Hollands groepsprortret*, pp. 65-92. Amsterdam: Bert Bakker.

—. 1997. *Vriendschap en de kunst van het overleven in de zeventiende en achttiende eeuw*. Amsterdam: Bert Bakker.

Kooyman-van Rossum, A.P., and D.F. Winnen. 1986. *Crailo. De geschiedenis van een landgoed*. Bussum: Spieghelprint.

Laan, C. 1994. 'Bruisend in het glas. De rol van het pasglas in de 16de en 17de eeuw.' In R. Kistemaker and V. van Vilsteren (eds.), *Bier! Geschiedenis van een volksdrank*, pp. 96-102. Amsterdam: De Bataafse Leeuw.

Lalemant, J. 1646. 'Of the Mission of Martyrs, Begun in the Country of the Iroquois, 1646.' In D.R. Snow, et al. (eds.), *In Mohawk Country: Early Narratives about a Native People*, pp. 56-61. Syracuse, N.Y.: Syracuse University Press, 1996.

Laslett, P., ed. 1972. *Household and Family in Past Time*. Cambridge: Cambridge University Press.

Leder, L.H., ed. 1956. *The Livingston Indian Records 1666-1723*. Gettysburg, Pa.: Pennsylvania Historical Association.

Le Mercier, François-Joseph, and Joseph-Antoine Poncet de la Riviére. 1653. 'Of the Capture and Deliverance of Father Joseph Poncet, 1653.' In D.R. Snow, et al. (eds.), *In Mo-*

hawk Country: Early Narratives about a Native People, pp. 93-103. Syracuse, N.Y.: Syracuse University Press, 1996.

Ligtenberg, C. 1908. *Armezorg te Leiden tot het einde van de zestiende eeuw.* 's-Graven-hage: M. Nijhoff.

Lis, C., and H. Soly. 1997. 'Ambachtsgilden in vergelijkend perspectief: De Noordelijke en Zuidelijke Nederlanden, 15de-18de eeuw.' In C. Lis and H. Soly (eds.), *Werelden van verschil. Ambachtsgilden in de Lage Landen.* Brussel: VUB Press.

Lourens, P., and J. Lucassen. 1997. 'De oprichting en ontwikkeling van ambachtsgilden in Nederland. 13de-19de eeuw.' In C. Lis and H. Soly (eds.), *Werelden van verschil. Ambachtsgilden in de Lage Landen.* Brussel: VUBPress

Maika, D.J. 1995. 'Commerce and Community: Manhattan Merchants in the Seventeenth Century.' Ph.D. dissertation. New York: New York University.

McKew Parr, C. 1969. *The Voyages of David de Vries, Navigator and Adventurer.* New York: Thomas Y. Crowell.

Megapolensis, Johannes Jr. 1644. 'A Short Account of the Mohawk Indians, 1644.' In D.R. Snow, et al. (eds.), *In Mohawk Country: Early Narratives about a Native People*, pp. 38-46. Syracuse, N.Y.: Syracuse University Press, 1996.

Merwick, D. 1980. 'Dutch Townsmen and Land Use: A Spatial Perspective on Seventeenth-Century Albany, New York.' *WMQ*, 3rd ser.: 53-78.

———. 1990. *Possessing Albany, 1630-1710: The Dutch and English Experiences.* Cambridge: Cambridge University Press.

Miller, J. 'A Description of the Province and City of New York, with Plans of the City and Several Forts as They Existed in the Year 1695.' In *Historic Chronicles of New Amsterdam, Colonial New York and Early Long Island.* Port Washington, N.Y.: Ira J. Fried-man.

Monté ver Loren, J.Ph. de, and J.E. Spruit. 1982. *Hoofdlijnen uit de ontwikkeling der rechterlijke organisatie in de Noordelijke Nederlanden tot de Bataafse omwenteling.* 6th ed. Deventer: Kluwer.

Montias, J.M. 1992. 'Works of Art in Seventeenth-Century Amsterdam.' In D. Freedberg and J. de Vries (eds.), *Art in History. History in Art. Studies in Seventeenth-Century Dutch Culture*, pp. 331-372. Santa Monica, Calif.: University of Chicago Press.

Morgan, E.S. 1944. *The Puritan Family: Religion and Domestic Relations in Seventeenth-Century New England.* New York: Harper and Row, reprinted 1966.

Munsell, J., trans. and ed. 1853-59. *The Annals of Albany*, vols. 1-10. Albany, N.Y.: J. Munsell.

———. 1865. *Collections on the History of Albany from Its Discovery to the Present Time, with Notices of Its Public Institutions, and Biographical Sketches of Citizens Deceased.* 4 vols. Albany, N.Y.: J. Munsell.

———. trans. and ed. 1865-70. 'Albany Papers. Reformed Protestant Dutch Church of Albany.' In *Collections on the History of Albany from Its Discovery to the Present Time*, pp. 1-57. Albany, N.Y.: J. Munsell.

———. 1876. *Men and Things in Albany Two Centuries Ago.* Albany, N.Y.: Joel Munsell's Sons.

Museum Boymans-van Beuningen. 1983. *Brood. De geschiedenis van het brood en het broodgebruik in Nederland.* Rotterdam: Museum Boymans-van Beuningen.

Narrett, D.E. 1992. *Inheritance and Family Life in Colonial New York City.* Ithaca, N.Y.: Cornell University Press.

Niemeijer, H.E. 1996. 'Calvinisme en koloniale stadscultuur. Batavia 1619-1725.' Ph.D. thesis. Amsterdam: Vrije Universiteit.

Nissenson, S.G. 1937. *The Patroon's Domain.* New York: Columbia University Press.

Nooter, E. 1994. 'Between Heaven and Earth: Church and Society in Pre-Revolutionary Flatbush, Long Island.' Ph.D. thesis. Amsterdam: Vrije Universiteit.

Nooter, E., and P. Bonomi. 1988. *Colonial Dutch Studies. An Interdisciplinary Approach.* New York and London: New York University Press.

O'Callaghan, E.B. 1845-48. *The History of New Netherland; or, New York Under the Dutch.* 2 vols. New York: D. Appleton.

——. trans. and ed. 1849-51. *Documentary History of the State of New York.* 4 vols. Albany, N.Y.: Weed, Parsons.

——. 1865. *Calendar of Historical Manuscripts in the Office of the Secretary of State, Albany, N.Y., Part I. Dutch Manuscripts, 1630-1664.* Albany, N.Y.: Weed, Parsons; Ridgewood, N.J.: Gregg Press, reprinted 1968.

——. 1865. *Register of New Netherland 1424-1674.* Albany, N.Y.: Weed, Parsons.

——. trans. and ed. 1868. *Laws and Ordinances of New Netherland, 1638-1674.* Albany, N.Y.: Weed, Parsons.

O'Callaghan, E.B., and B. Fernow, trans. and eds. 1853-87. *Documents Relative to the Colonial History of the State of New York.* 15 vols. Albany, N.Y.: Weed, Parsons.

Panhuysen, B. 2000. *Maatwerk. Kleermakers, naaisters, oudkleerkopers en de gilden. 1500-1800.* Amsterdam: Stichting beheer IISG.

Parker, J. 1978. *The World for a Market-Place: Episodes in the History of European Expansion.* Minneapolis, Minn.: Associates of the James Ford Bell Library.

Pearson, J., trans. and ed. 1869. *Early Records of the City and County of Albany, and Colony of Rensselaerswijck, 1656-1765.* 4 vols. Vols. 2-4 revised by A.J.F. van Laer, 1916-19. Albany: University of the State of New York.

——. 1872. *Contributions for the Genealogies of the First Settlers of the Ancient County of Albany, from 1630 to 1800.* Albany, N.Y.: J. Munsell.

——. 1873. *Contributions for the Genealogies of the Descendants of the First Settlers of the Patent and City of Schenectady, from 1662 to 1800.* Albany, N.Y.: J. Munsell.

Phelps-Stokes, I.N. 1915-28. *The Iconography of Manhattan Island: 1498-1909.* 6 vols. New York: R.H. Dodd.

Peña, E.S. 1990. 'Wampum Production in New Netherland and Colonial New York: The Historical and Archaeological Context.' Ph.D. dissertation. Boston: Boston University.

Po-Chia Hsia, R., and H. van Nierop, eds. 2002. *Calvinism and Religious Toleration in the Dutch Golden Age.* Cambridge: Cambridge University Press.

Poncet de la Riviére, J.A. 'Of the Capture and Deliverance of Father Joseph Poncet.' In D.R. Snow, et al. (eds.), *In Mohawk Country: Early Narratives About a Native People*, pp. 93-103. Syracuse, N.Y.: Syracuse University Press, 1996.

Prak, M. 1999. *Republikeinse veelheid, democratisch enkelvoud. Sociale verandering in het revolutietijdvak, 's-Hertogenbosch 1770-1820.* Nijmegen: SUN.

Purple, S.S. 1890. 'Records of the Reformed Church in New Amsterdam and New York. Marriages from 11 December 1639 to 26 August 1801.' In: *Collectons of the New York Geneaological and Biographical Society*, I. New York: Published privately; reprinted in 1997.

Raben, R. 1996. 'Batavia en Colombo: The Ethnic and Spatial Order of Two Colonial Cities, 1600-1800.' Ph.D. dissertation. Leiden: Rijks Universiteit.

Radisson, P.E. 'Voyages of Pierre Esprit Radisson, 1651-1654.' In D.R. Snow, et al. (eds.), 1996. *In Mohawk Country: Early Narratives About a Native People*, pp. 62-92. Syracuse, N.Y.: Syracuse University Press, 1996.

Remington, G.L. 1997. 'The Duncanson Wives of Four New Netherland Settlers: Glen, Teller, Powell, and Loockermans.' *NYG&BR* 128 (1): 1-10.

Reynolds, C., ed. 1906. *Albany Chronicles: A History of the City Arranged Chronologically from the Earliest Settlement to the Present Time.* Albany, N.Y.: J. Lyons.

Richter, D.K., 1982. 'Rediscovered Links in the Covenant Chain: Previously Unpublished Transcripts of New York Indian Treaty Minutes 1677-1691.' In American Antiquarian Society, pp. 50-52.

——. 1992. *The Ordeal of the Longhouse: The Peoples of the Iroquois League in the Era of European Colonization.* Chapel Hill and London: University of North Carolina Press.

——. 1998. 'Brothers, Scoundrels, Metal Makers: Dutch Constructions of Native American Constructions of the Dutch.' *DHM* 71 (3): 59-64.

Ringoir, D.J.B. 1977. *Plattelandschirurgijns in de 17e en 18e eeuw. De rekeningboeken van de 18e-eeuwse Durgerdamse chirurgijn Anthonij Egberts.* Bunnik: Lebo.

Rink, O.A. 1986. *Holland on the Hudson. An Economic and Social History of Dutch New York.* Ithaca, N.Y.: Cornell University Press.

Ritchie, R.C. 1977. *The Duke's Province: A Study of New York Politics and Society.* Chapel Hill: University of North Carolina Press.

Roberts, B. 1998. *Through the Keyhole: Dutch Child-Rearing Practises in the 17th and 18th Centuries. Three Urban Elite Families.* Hilversum: Verloren.

Roodenburg, H. 1990. *Onder Censuur. De kerkelijke tucht in de gereformeerde gemeente van Amsterdam, 1578-1700.* Hilversum: Verloren

Rooijakkers, G. 1986. *Rituele Repertoires. Volkscultuur in oostelijk Noord-Brabant, 1559-1853.* Nijmegen: SUN.

——. 2000. 'Vieren en markeren: feest en ritueel.' In Dekker, et al. (eds.), *Volkscultuur, een inleiding in de Nederlandse etnologie*, pp. 212-17. Nijmegen: SUN.

Rooijakkers, G., and T. van der Zee. 1986. *Religieuze volkscultuur. De spanning tussen de voorgeschreven orde en de geleefde praktijk.* Nijmegen: SUN.

Rooseboom, G. 1656. *Recueil Van verscheyde Keuren, en Costumen. Midtsgaders Maniere van Procederen binnen de Stadt Amsterdam.* 2nd ed. Amsterdam: Jan Hendricks, Boeck-Verkooper op de Roüaensche Kay.

Rutman, D.B. 1965. *Winthrop's Boston: A Portrait of a Puritan Town, 1630-1649.* Chapel Hill and London: University of North Carolina Press.

Schama, S. 1987. *The Embarrassment of Riches: An Interpretation of Dutch Culture in the Golden Age.* London and New York: Fontana Press.

Schiltkamp, J.A. 1964. *De geschiedenis van het notariaat in het octrooigebied van de West-Indische Compagnie (voor Suriname en de Nederlandse Antillen tot het jaar 1964.* 's-Gravenhage: N.V. de Nederlandse Boek-en Steendrukkerij v/h H.L. Smits.

——. 1997. 'On Common Ground. Legislation, Government, Jurisprudence, and Law in the Dutch West Indian Colonies: The Order of Government of 1629.' *DHM* 70 (4): 73-80.

Schipper, J. 1987. 'Rural Architecture: The Zaan Region of the Province of North Holland.' In R.A. Blackburn and N.A. Kelley (eds.), *New World Dutch Studies: Dutch Arts and Culture in Colonial America, 1609-1776*, pp. 171-84. Albany, N.Y.: Albany Institute of History and Art.

Schippers, H. 1994. 'Bier. Volksdrank en genotmiddel.' *Ons Amsterdam* 6: 170-213.

Schipper-van Lottum, M.G.A. 1993. *Advertenties en berichten in de Amsterdamse Courant uitgetrokken op kleding, stoffen, sieraden en accessoires tussen de jaren 1672-1765.* 6 vols. Amsterdam: Published privately.

Schmidt, A. 2001. *Overleven na de dood. Weduwen in Leiden in de Gouden Eeuw.* Amsterdam: Prometheus/Bert Bakker.

Schotel, G.D.J. 1905. *Het maatschappelijk leven onzer vaderen in de zeventiende eeuw.* Amsterdam and Arnhem: J.G. Strengholt's Uitgeversmaatschappij N.V en Gijsbers en Van Loon.

Schuurman, A., J. de Vries, and A. van der Woude. 1997. *Aards geluk. De Nederlanders en hun spullen, 1550-1850.* Amsterdam: Balans.

Shattuck, M.D. 1993. 'A Civil Society: Court and Community in Beverwijck, New Netherland, 1652-1664.' Ph.D. dissertation. Boston: Boston University.

——. 1994. 'Women and Trade in New Netherland.' *Itinerario, European Journal of Overseas History* 2 (18): 40-47.

Smetius, J. 1644. *Nijmegen, stad der Bataven.* Nijmegen: SUN, reprinted 1999.

Snow, D.R. 1980. *The Archaeology of New England.* New York: Academic Press.

——. 1996. 'Mohawk Demography and the Effects of Exogenous Epidemics on American Indian Populations.' *Journal of Anthropological Archaeology* 15: 160-80.

Snow, D.R., C.T. Gehring, and W.A. Starna, eds. 1996. *In Mohawk Country: Early Narratives About a Native People.* Syracuse, N.Y.: Syracuse University Press.

Snow, D.R., and W.A. Starna. 1989. 'Sixteenth-Century Depopulation: A View from the Mohawk Valley.' *American Anthropologist* 91: 142-49.

Spaans, J. 1997. *Armenzorg in Friesland, 1500-1800. Publieke zorg en particuliere liefdadigheid in zes Friese Steden Leeuwarden, Bolsward, Franeker, Sneek, Dokkum en Harlingen.* Hilversum: Verloren.

Spierenburg, P. 1984. *The Spectacle of Suffering. Executions and the Evolution of Repression: From a Preindustrial Metropolis to the European Experience.* Cambridge: Cambridge University Press.

Starna, W.A. 1986. 'Seventeenth-Century Dutch-Indian Trade: A Perspective from Iroquoia.' *DHM* 59: 5-8, 21.

——. 1991. 'Indian Dutch Frontiers.' *DHM* 64: 21-25.

Stokes, I.N.P. 1915-28. *The Iconography of Manhattan Island, 1498-1909.* 6 vols. New York: R.H. Dodd.

Sullivan, D. 1997. *The Punishment of Crime in Colonial New York: The Dutch Experience in Albany During the Seventeenth Century.* New York: Peter Lang.

Tantillo, L.F. 1996. *Visions of New York State: The Historical Paintings of L.F. Tantillo.* Wappingers Falls, N.Y.: Shawangunk Press.

Taverne, E. 1978. *In 't land van belofte: in de nieue stadt: Ideaal en werkelijkheid van de stadsuitleg in de Republiek, 1580-1680.* Maarssen: Gary Schwartz.

Taverne, E., and I. Visser, eds. 1993. *Stedebouw: de geschiedenis van de stad in de Nederlanden van 1500 tot heden.* Nijmegen: SUN.

Te Boekhorst, P., P. Burke, and W. Frijhoff, eds. 1992. *Cultuur en Maatschappij in Nederland, 1500-1850.* Meppel and Amsterdam: Boom/Open Universiteit.

Temminck Groll, C.L. 1984. 'Nieuw Amsterdam in Noord-Amerika, vergeleken met andere Nederlandse 17de-eeuwse stedestichtingen.' In *Leids Kunsthistorisch Jaarboek.* Leiden.

Ter Gouw, J. 1871. *De volksvermaken.* Haarlem: Bohn.

Thoen, I. (forthcoming). 'The Gift in Seventeenth-Century Holland.' Ph.D. dissertation. Florence: European University.

Tooker, E. 1978. 'The League of the Iroquois: Its History, Politics, and Ritual.' In B.G. Trigger (ed.), *Handbook of North American Indians: Northeast,* vol. 15, pp. 418-41. Washington, D.C.: Smithsonian Institution.

Trelease, A.W. 1997. *Indian Affairs in Colonial New York: The Seventeenth Century.* Lincoln and London: University of Nebraska Press.

Trigger, B.G. 1971. 'The Mohawk-Mahican War (1624-1628): The Establishment of a Pattern.' *Canadian Historical Review* 52: 277.

———. 1978. 'Early Iroquoian Contacts with Europeans.' In B.G. Trigger (ed.), *Handbook of North American Indians: Northeast*, vol. 15, pp. 344-56. Washington, D.C.: Smithsonian Institution.

Ulrich, L.T. 1980. *Goodwives: Images and Reality in the Lives of Women in Northern New England 1650-1750*. New York and Toronto: Oxford University Press.

Van de Pol, L. 1996. *Het Amsterdams hoerdom. Prostitutie in de zeventiende en achttiende eeuw*. Amsterdam: Wereldbibliotheek.

Van der Donck, Adriaen. 1655. *A Description of the New Netherlands*, trans. J. Johnson, ed. T.F. O'Donnell. Syracuse, N.Y.: Syracuse University Press, 1968.

———. 1655. 'A Description of New Netherland.' In D.R. Snow, et al. (eds.), *In Mohawk Country: Early Narratives About a Native People*, pp. 104-30. Syracuse, N.Y.: Syracuse University Press, 1996.

Van der Heijden, M. 1998. *Huwelijk in Holland. Stedelijke rechtspraak en kerkelijke tucht, 1550-1700*. Amsterdam: Bert Bakker.

Van der Vlis, I. 2001. *Leven in armoede. Delftse bedeelden in de zeventiende eeuw*. Amsterdam: Prometheus/Bert Bakker.

Van der Woude, A. 1982. 'The Volume and Value of Paintings in Holland at the Time of the Dutch Republic.' In D. Freedberg and J. de Vries (eds.), *Art in History. History in Art: Studies in Seventeenth-Century Dutch Culture*, pp. 285-329. Santa Monica, Calif.: University of Chicago Press.

———. 1997. 'De schilderijenproductie in Holland tijdens de Republiek. Een poging to kwantificatie.' In A. Schuurman, et al., *Aards geluk. De Nederlanders en hun spullen, 1550-1850*. Amsterdam: Uitgeverij Balans.

Van der Woude, A.M. 1972. 'Variations in the Size and Structure of the Household in the United Provinces of the Netherlands in the Seventeenth and Eighteenth Centuries.' In Peter Laslett and Richard Wall (eds.), *Household and Family in Past Time*, pp 299-318. Cambridge: Cambridge University Press.

Van Deursen, A.Th. 1986. 'Volkscultuur in wisselwerking met de elitecultuur in de vroegmoderne tijd.' In G. Rooijakkers and T. van der Zee (eds.), *Religieuze volkscultuur. De spanning tussen de voorgeschreven orde en de geleefde praktijk*. Nijmegen: SUN.

———. 1991. *Bavianen en Slijkgeuzen. Kerk en Kerkvolk ten tijde van Maurits en Oldenbarnevelt*. 2nd ed. Franeker: Van Wijnen.

———. 1991. *Mensen van klein vermogen. Het kopergeld van de Gouden Eeuw*. Amsterdam: Bert Bakker. In translation: *Plain Lives in a Golden Age: Popular Culture, Religion and Society in Seventeenth-Century Holland*. Cambridge, New York, and Melbourne: Cambridge University Press.

———. 1994. *Een dorp in de polder. Graft in de zeventiende eeuw*. Amsterdam: Bert Bakker.

———. 1995. 'De dominee.' In H.M. Beliën, et al. (eds.), *Gestalten van de Gouden Eeuw. Een Hollands groepsportret*, pp. 131-55. Amsterdam: Bert Bakker.

Van Deursen, A.Th., and S. Groenveld. 1990. *Cultuurgeschiedenis van de Republiek in de zeventiende eeuw*. 's-Gravenhage: Stichting voor Historisch Onderzoek.

Van Dongen, A., et al., eds. 1995. *'One Man's Trash Is Another Man's Treasure': The Metamorphosis of the European Utensil in the New World*. Rotterdam: Museum Boymans van Beuningen.

Van Dorren, G. 2001. *Eenheid en verscheidenheid. De burgers van Haarlem in de Gouden Eeuw*. Amsterdam: Prometheus/Bert Bakker.

Van Eeghen, I.H. 1965. *De Gilden. Theorie en Practijk*. Bussum: C.A.J. van Dishoeck.

Van Egmond, F. 1992. 'Onderwerelden: Marginaliteit en misdaad in de Republiek.' In P. te Boekhorst, et al. (eds.), *Cultuur en maatschappij in Nederland 1500-1850*, pp. 149-77. Meppel, Amsterdam, and Heerlen: Boom/Open Universiteit.

Van Goor, J. 1997. *De Nederlandse Koloniën. Geschiedenis van de Nederlandse expansie 1600-1975.* The Haag: Sdu uitgevers.

Van Grol, G.J. 1934-47. *De grondpolitiek in het West-Indisch domein der Generaliteit; een historische studie.* 's-Gravenhage: Algemeene Lantsdrukkerij, reprinted 1980.

Van Laer, A.J.F., trans. and ed. 1908. *Van Rensselaer Bowier Manuscripts, Being the Letters of Kiliaen van Rensselaer, 1630-1643, and Other Documents Relating to the Colony of Rensselaerswijck.* Albany: State University of New York.

——. 1916, 1918, 1919. *Early Records of the City and County of Albany, and Colony of Rensselaerswijck (1656-1657)*, vols. 2-4, rev. Jonathan Pearson, trans. and ed. Albany: State University of New York.

——. trans. and ed. 1920-23. *Minutes of the Court of Fort Orange and Beverwijck.* 2 vols. Albany, N.Y.: University of the State of New York.

——. trans. and ed. 1922. *Minutes of the Court of Rensselaerswijck, 1648-1652.* Albany: State University of New York.

——. trans. and ed. 1924. *Documents Relating to New Netherland, 1624-1626, in the Henry E. Huntington Library.* San Marino, Calif.: Henry Huntington Library and Art Gallery.

——. 1926. 'The Dutch Grants Along the South Side of State Street: A Contribution Toward the Early Topography of the City of Albany.' *DSSYB* 2 (1926-27): 11-23.

——. trans. and ed. 1926-32. *Minutes of the Court of Albany, Rensselaerswijck and Schenectady 1686-1685.* 3 vols. Albany: State University of New York.

——. 1927-28. 'Documents Relating to Arent van Curler's Death.' *DSSYB* 3: 30-34.

——. trans. and ed. 1928-29. 'Letters to Evert Jansen Wendel.' *DSSYB* 4: 1-7.

——. 1929-30. 'Settlers of Rensselaerswijck, 1659-1664.' *DSSYB* 5: 18-34.

——. trans. and ed. 1930-31. 'Albany Wills and Other Documents.' *DSSYB* 6: 13-26.

——. trans. and ed. 1931-32. 'Deacons' Account Book, 1652-1664.' *DSSYB* 7: 1-11.

——. 1932. *Correspondence of Jeremias van Rensselaer 1651-1674.* Albany: State University of New York.

——. 1935. *Correspondence of Maria van Rensselaer 1669-1689.* Albany: State University of New York.

——. 1935-36. 'The Orphan Chamber of Amsterdam.' *DSSYB* 11: 1-9.

——. 1937-38. 'Albany Notarial Papers, 1666-1693.' *DSSYB* 13: 1-18.

——. 1938-39. 'Albany Notarial Papers, 1667-1687.' *DSSYB* 14: 1-18.

——. trans. and ed. 1939-40. 'Letters to Adriaen Gerritsen van Papendorp.' *DSSYB* 15: 1-12.

——. trans. and ed. 1941-42. 'Arent van Curler and His Historic Letter to the Patroon.' *DSSYB* 17: 11-29.

——. 1941-42. 'Evert Nolden, the First Schoolmaster of Rensselaerswijck.' *DSSYB* 17: 13-15.

——. 1946. *The Lutheran Church in New York 1649-1772. Records in the Lutheran Church Archives at Amsterdam, Holland.* New York: New York Public Library.

——. trans. and ed. 1974. *Council Minutes 1638-1649.* Baltimore, Md.: Geneaological.

Van Lieburg, F.A. 1989. *De Nadere Reformatie in Utrecht ten tijde van Voetius. Sporen in de gereformeerde kerkeraadsacta.* Rotterdam: Boek en muziek.

——. 1996. *Profeten en hun vaderland. De geografische herkomst van de gereformeerde predikanten in Nederland van 1572-1816.* Amsterdam: Boekencentrum.

Van Loo, F. 1981. *Den arme gegeven... Een beschrijving van armoede, armenzorg en sociale zekerheid in Nederland, 1784-1965.* Meppel: Boom.

Van Meteren, Emanuel. 1909. 'On Hudson's Voyage, by Emanuel van Meteren.' In J.F. Jameson, ed., *Narratives of New Netherland, 1609-1664.* New York: Charles Scribner's Sons.

Van Nederveen Meerkerk, H. 1989. *Recife: The Rise of a 17th-Century Trade City from a Cultural-Historical Perspective.* Assen: Van Gorcum.

Van Nierop, H. 1984. *Van ridders tot regenten. De Hollandse adel in de zestiende en de eerste helft van de zeventiende eeuw.* Hollandse Historische Reeks. Translation: *From Knights to Regents, 1500-1650.* Cambridge: Cambridge University Press, 1993.

Van Norden, O.H. 1958. 'New Amsterdam's Burgher Guard.' *DHM* 32 (4): 00.

Van Oers, R. 2000. *Dutch Town Planning Overseas During VOC and WIC Rule, 1600-1800.* Zutphen: Walburg Pers.

Van Schaick, J.H. 1992. 'Showdown at Fort Orange.' *DHM* 65: 37-45.

Van Slichtenhorst, Arend. 1653. *XIV boeken van de Geldersse geschiedenissen.* Arnhem.

Van Strien, C.D. 1989. 'British Travellers in Holland During the Stuart Period.' Ph.D. thesis. Amsterdam: Vrije Universiteit.

Van Swigchem, C.A, T. Brouwer, and W. van Os. 1984. *Een huis voor het woord. Het Protestantse kerkinterieur in Nederland tot 1900.* 's-Gravenhage: Staatsuitgeverij.

Van Vilsteren, V.T. 1994. 'Looking Over the Brewer's Shoulder: Life in a 16th-Century Brewery.' In R.E. Kistemaker and V.T. van Vilsteren (eds.), *Beer! The Story of Holland's Favourite Drink.* Amsterdam: De Bataafse Leeuw.

Van Wijngaarden, H. 2000. *Zorg voor de kost. Armenzorg, arbeid en onderlinge hulp in Zwolle, 1650-1700.* Amsterdam: Prometheus/Bert Bakker.

Van Zanden, J.L. 1991. *Arbeid tijdens het handelskapitalisme. Opkomst en neergang van Hollands economie 1350-1850.* Bergen: Octavo. Translation: *The Rise and Decline of Holland's Economy: Merchant Capitalism and the Labour Market.* Manchester: Manchester University Press, 1993.

——. 1991. 'Lonen en de kosten van levensonderhoud, 1600-1850.' In J.L. van Zanden (ed.), *Arbeid tijdens het handelskapitalisme. Opkomst en neergang van de Hollandse economie 1350-1850*, pp. 135-50. Bergen: Octavo.

Van Zanden, J.L., and A. Knotter. 1993. 'Immigration and the Labour Market in Amsterdam in the Seventeenth Century.' In J.L. van Zanden (ed.), *The Rise and Decline of Holland's Economy: Merchant Capitalism and the Labour Market*, pp. 44-66. Manchester: Manchester University Press.

Van Zwieten, A. 1996. 'The Orphan Chamber of New Amsterdam.' *WMQ*, 3rd ser. (53): 319-40.

Van Zwieten, A.E. 2001. '"A Little Land... To Sow Some Seeds": Real Property, Custom, and Law in the Community of New Amsterdam.' Ph.D. thesis. Philadelphia: Temple University.

Venema, J. 1990. '"For the Benefit of the Poor": Poor Relief in Albany/Beverwijck, 1652-1700.' Master's thesis. Albany: State University at New York at Albany.

——. 1993. *Kinderen van weelde en armoede. Armoede en liefdadigheid in Beverwijck/Albany.* Hilversum: Verloren.

——. trans. and ed. 1998. *Deacons' Accounts 1652-1674, First Dutch Reformed Church of Beverwyck/Albany, New York.* Maine: Picton Press; and Michigan: Wm. Eerdman's.

——. 1999. 'Poverty and Charity in Seventeenth-Century Beverwijck/Albany, 1652-1700.' *New York History* 80 (4): 369-90.

——. 2001. 'The Court Case of Brant Aertsz van Slichtenhorst Against Jan van Rensselaer.' *DHM* 74 (1): 3-8.

——. trans. and ed. 2002. 'A 1652 Letter by Jan Baptist van Rensselaer.' *DHM* 75 (1): 9-13.

Verhoeff, J.M. 1983. *De oude Nederlandse maten en gewichten*, 2nd ed. Amsterdam: Publicaties van het P.J. Meertens-Instituut voor Dialectologie, Volkskunde, en Naamkunde van de Koninklijke Nederlandse Akademie van Wetenschappen 3.

Versteeg, D., trans.; P.R. Christoph, K. Scott, and K. Strijcker-Roddha, eds. 1976. *Kingston Papers 1661-1675*. New York Historical Manuscripts: Dutch, 2 vols. Baltimore, Md.: Genealogical.

Vries, J. de, and A.M. van der Woude. 1995. *Nederland 1500-1815. De eerste ronde van moderne economische groei*. Amsterdam: Uitgeverij Balans.

Wagenaar, J. 1760-67. *Amsterdam en zijne opkomst, aanwas, geschiedenissen, voorrechten, koophandel, gebouwen, kerkenstaat, schoolen, schutterije, gilden en regeeringe*. 3 vols. Amsterdam.

Weslager, C.A. 1967. *The English On the Delaware, 1610-1682*. New Brunswick, N.J.

Westerman, M. 2001. '"Costly and Curious, Full of Pleasure and Home Contentment": Making Home in the Dutch Republic.' In M. Westerman (ed.), *Art and Home: Dutch Interiors in the Age of Rembrandt*, pp. 15-81. Zwolle: Waanders.

Wheeler, R.R. 1961. 'The House of Jeremias van Rensselaer, 1658-1666.' In *New York Historical Society Quarterly*: 75-88.

Wijsenbeek-Olthuis, Th.F. 1987. *Achter de gevels van Delft. Bezit en bestaan van rijk en arm in een periode van achteruitgang. 1700-1800*. Hilversum: Verloren.

Wilcoxen, C. 1979. 'Arent van Curler's Children.' *NYG&B* 110: 82-84.

Wouters, A.Ph.F. 1994. *Nieuw en ongezien. Kerk en samenleving in de classis Delft en Delfland 1572-1621, I*. Delft: Eburon.

Wray, C.F. 1985. 'The Volume of Dutch Tradegoods Received by the Seneca Iroquois, 1600-1687 A.D.' In *New Netherland Studies: An Inventory of Current Research and Approaches*. Bulletin Knob, Tijdschrift van de Koninklijke Nederlandse Oudheidkundige Bond 84 (2-3): 100-12.

Yntema, R.J. 1994. 'A Capital Industry: Brewing in Holland, 1500-1800.' In R. Kistemaker and V. van Vilsteren (eds.), *Beer! The Story of Holland's Favourite Drink*, pp. 72-82. Amsterdam: De Bataafse Leeuw.

——. 1994. 'Allerhande soorten bier. Over biersoorten en hun distributie' (Beer in abundance: Distribution and consumption in early modern Holland). In R. Kistemaker and V. van Vilsteren (eds.), *Beer! The Story of Holland's Favourite Drink*, pp. 82-96. Amsterdam: De Bataafse Leeuw.

——. 1994. 'The Welfare of the Brewers: Guilds and Confraternities in the Brewing Industry.' In R. Kistemaker and V. van Vilsteren (eds.), *Beer! The Story of Holland's Favourite Drink*, pp. 118-32. Amsterdam: De Bataafse Leeuw.

Zandvliet, K. 1998. *Mapping for Money: Maps, Plans and Topographic Paintings and Their Role in Dutch Overseas Expansion During the 16th and 17th Centuries*. Amsterdam: Batavian Lion International.

Zantkuijl, H. 1983. 'Bouwen in de Hollandse stad.' In E. Taverne and I. Visser (eds.), *Stedebouw. De geschiedenis van de stad in de Nederlanden van 1500 tot heden*, pp. 63-71. Nijmegen: SUN.

——. 1985. 'Reconstructie van enkele Nederlandse huizen in Nieuw-Nederland uit de 17e eeuw.' In B. Bakker, *Nieuw Nederlandse Studiën. Een inventarisatie van recent onderzoek* (New Netherland studies: An inventory of current research and approaches). *Bulletin KNOB. Tijdschrift van de Nederlandse Oudheidkundige Bond* 84. Amsterdam: Bohn, Scheltema and Holkema.

——. 1987. 'The Netherlands Town House: How and Why It Works.' In *New World Dutch Studies: Dutch Arts and Culture in Colonial America, 1609-1776*, pp. 143-60. Albany, N.Y.: Albany Institute of History and Art.

——. 1987. 'Hollandse huizen, gebouwd in de 17de eeuw in Amerika.' *Amsterdamse Monumenten* 3, 4 (5de jaargang): 47-60, 63-76.

Zantkuijl, H., G. de Galan Boezaard, and C. Roozendaal. 2001. *De ontwikkeling van het woonhuis tot 1940 in Hoorn*. Hoorn: Publicatiestichting Bas Baltus.

Zeller, N.A. McClure. 1991. *A Beautiful and Fruitful Place: Selected Rensselaerswijck Seminar Papers*. Albany, N.Y.: New Netherland.

Samenvatting
Beverwijck.
Een Nederlands dorp aan de Amerikaanse frontier, 1652-1664

In 1636 sloten Carsten Carstensz uit Noorwegen en Goosen Gerritsz van Schaick uit de provincie Utrecht een contract met de Amsterdamse juwelier en koopman Kiliaen van Rensselaer om voor een aantal jaren in diens kolonie Rensselaerswijck in Nieuw Nederland (Noord-Amerika) te gaan werken. Zes jaar daarvoor had Van Rensselaer met toestemming van de West Indische Compagnie, die het bewind over Nieuw Nederland voerde, van de Mahicanen een gebied gekocht aan de bovenloop van de Hudson. Het was ongeveer zo groot als de provincie Gelderland, en het lag aan beide zijden van de Hudson – aan de west-zijde rondom het al in 1624 door de WIC gebouwde Fort Oranje. Carstensz en Gerritsz staan model voor een groter aantal kolonisten dat Van Rensselaer naar zijn patroonschap stuurde, mensen die het gebied moesten bevolken om er landbouw te bedrijven. Beide man-nen reisden tegelijk naar Rensselaerswijck, en beiden werkten daar, trouwden er en kregen kinderen. Toen ze stierven – Gerritsz in 1675 als een van de aanzienlijksten van de gemeen schap, en Carstensz rond 1684 als een van de armsten – had het grootste deel van hun leven bestaan uit een zich steeds opnieuw aanpassen: aan een nieuwe omgeving, een ander klimaat met een andere flora en fauna, en aan inheemse inwoners die bijna dagelijks de gemeenschap bezochten maar een totaal andere cultuur hadden. Nieuwe immigranten voegden zich in steeds groter getale bij de kleine kolonistengemeenschap, zodat ook onder de Europeanen onderling een proces van voortdurende adaptatie plaats vond. Toen Carsten en Goosen in 1637 in Rensselaerswijck arriveerden troffen ze nog geen dertig kolonisten aan, maar in 1642 waren er al honderd. Niet alleen uit Holland kwamen deze mensen, maar ook, zoals Goosen, uit andere provincies en, net als Carsten, zelfs uit andere landen. Met name toen de WIC in 1639 haar monopolie op de lucratieve beverhandel prijs gaf lokte de mogelijkheid om snel winst te maken meer handelaars naar het gebied rond de bovenloop van de Hud-son. Kiliaen van Rensselaer wilde het centrum van zijn kolonie aan de oostkant van de rivier bouwen, tegenover Fort Oranje, maar na zijn dood werd dat plan gewijzigd en in 1648 be-gon men met de aanleg van deze "bijeenwoning" aan de westkant, direct rondom het fort. Dat had tot gevolg dat Petrus Stuyvesant, directeur generaal van Nieuw Nederland, een ge-bied van 3000 voet rondom het fort, waar toen de meeste kolonisten woonden, tot Com-pagniesgrond verklaarde. Hij noemde het Beverwijck. Totdat de Engelsen in 1664 Nieuw Nederland veroverden, bleef de gemeenschap deze naam dragen. Beverwijck gedurende de twaalf jaren van haar bestaan is het onderwerp van deze studie.

De locatie van het plaatsje is niet vreemd. De nabijheid van het fort zal de kolonisten een gevoel van veiligheid hebben geboden, maar ook de natuurlijke omgeving had zijn voorde-len. Diverse killen (riviertjes) maakten de bouw van koren- en houtzaagmolens mogelijk, en vormden tegelijkertijd goede natuurlijke begrenzingen in het noorden en het zuiden. Aan de oostkant stroomde de rivier. Iets verder naar het noorden werd zij onbevaarbaar vanwege de enorme waterval bij Cohoes, en zuidwaarts zorgde ze voor de verbinding met de rest van Nieuw Nederland. Het gebergte aan de westkant scheidde het dorp van het enorme achter-land vanwaar de Indianen met hun pelzen kwamen. Omdat Indianen vroeger al op verschil-lende plaatsen maïs verbouwd hadden was omliggend land redelijk geschikt om landbouw te bedrijven. Maar het belangrijkste was dat de Indianen maar al te graag hun pelzen ver-ruilden voor Europese handelsgoederen. Voor deze handel had zich rond 1650 al een be-paald patroon ontwikkeld waarbij de Indianen Fort Oranje en het daarnaast gelegen pa-troonshuis bezochten. Zoals de ruimtelijke locatie de ligging van de vestiging bepaald had, speelde ze ook een belangrijke rol in het vormgevingsproces van het dorp. Zodra besloten was de bouw van een bijeenwoning ten noorden van het fort te beginnen werd de ontwik-keling ervan door die ligging versneld en kregen afzonderlijke personen bijzondere kansen doordat ze er erven op gunstige locaties verwierven.

De bijna constante in- en externe verandering, beweging en ontwikkeling waaraan de im-migranten zich steeds opnieuw moesten aanpassen moet duidelijk zichtbaar geweest zijn in het dorp dat vanaf april 1652 werd opgebouwd. Onder leiding van een nieuwe schepenbank brachten Beverwijcks inwoners het dorp tot ontwikkeling. Oude Indianenpaden die naar Fort Oranje leidden werden veranderd in wagenwegen, en bruggen werden gebouwd om ook met wagens gemakkelijk de killen te kunnen oversteken. De grond in Beverwijck werd opgedeeld in erven die verdeeld werden onder de inwoners, en omheind. In korte tijd ver-rezen er woonhuizen, schuren, stallen, wildenhuisjes ten behoeve van de Indianen, en ande-re constructies, terwijl er ook erven werden gebruikt als tuinen en bleekvelden. De mensen die in 1652 en 1653 grondbrieven kregen van de Compagnie, vermoedelijk tussen de 73 en 94, splitsten hun erven al gauw op in kleinere erven, en verkochten die weer door. Zo wer-den huizen in de bijeenwoning steeds dichter op elkaar gebouwd, wat de samenleving al snel een stedelijk karakter gaf. In vijf jaar groeide de bijeenwoning van een vestiging van zo'n veertig huizen uit tot een dorp van meer dan 120 huizen. Middenin kwam een armenhuis, en een paar jaar later een blokhuiskerk, die in tijden van dreiging ook als vluchtoord moest fun-geren. Tot het einde van 1659 had het dorp een open karakter: het maakte deel uit van het landschap en was toegankelijk voor ieder die het wilde bezoeken. Daarna kon de omheining die in dat jaar werd gebouwd om het dichtstbebouwde gedeelte te beschermen tegen vijan-delijke invallen dit dorpsgedeelte geheel afsluiten van de omgeving. De bouw van deze pa-lissaden maakt duidelijk dat het vertrouwen dat de kolonisten eens in de inheemse bevol-king hadden, had plaats gemaakt voor angst. In deze beperkte ruimte zullen de stedelijke trekken des te duidelijk uitgekomen zijn, en binnen de palissaden zal het dorp waarschijn-lijk een Nederlandser (of Europeser) karakter hebben gehad.

Had het zo'n twintig jaar geduurd om meer dan tweehonderd kolonisten in Rensselaers-wijck te krijgen, na april 1652 kon men zich vrij vestigen in Beverwijck, en in de volgende acht jaren kwamen er meer dan 800 mensen naar het gebied rondom Fort Oranje. Ze kwa-men van verschillende provincies in de Republiek en zelfs daar buiten; een gemeenschappe-lijk verleden deelden ze dus niet. Een nieuwe gemeenschapscultuur ontwikkelde zich, die werd gestroomlijnd door de wetten en regelingen van het WIC bestuur. Net als in de steden in het vaderland konden alle mannen het burgerrecht kopen en waren ze verplicht in de lo-cale burgerwacht te dienen. De wetten werden gehandhaafd door een naar Hollands model ingericht gerecht van schout en schepenen, dat juridische en bestuurlijke taken had, en dat trouw moest zweren aan de Staten Generaal, de bewindhebbers van de West Indische Com-pagnie en de directeur generaal en raden van de WIC in Nieuw Amsterdam. Het had echter geen aparte vertegenwoordiging bij de directeur generaal en raden. Alle ordonnanties die het maakte moesten afzonderlijk worden goedgekeurd door deze koloniale regering. De ge-reformeerde kerk als publieke kerk voerde zulke diensten als doop, huwelijk en begrafenis uit. Haar kerkdiensten waren toegankelijk voor alle inwoners, ook niet-kerkleden. Ze hield toezicht op de religieuze en morele waarden van de gemeenschap door haar kerkelijke tucht en had een concreet programma voor de armenzorg. De benoeming van dominee Schaets, nog gecontracteerd door de patroon in 1652, was goedgekeurd door de classis Amsterdam, die het toezicht over de koloniale kerken had. Schaets preekte tot 1690 en was voorzitter van de kerkenraad, waarvan de ouderlingen en diakenen werden aangevuld door coöptatie. Zo voldeed de gemeenschap in een mum van tijd aan eisen van veiligheid, religie, onderwijs, onderstand en gemeenschappelijke dienstverlening, de minimale eisen van een Nederlandse bewoningskern. Maar al was Beverwijcks cultuur duidelijk vergelijkbaar met die van plaatsen in de Republiek, die toch steeds het referentiepunt bleef, tegelijk was ze anders. Omdat er bijna dagelijks contact met de inheemse bevolking was, waren de culturele grenzen flexibel. Zo gingen officiële bijeenkomsten en onderhandelingen met de Indianen bijna altijd gepaard met het uitwisselen van geschenken, en omdat er nauwelijks zilvergeld in omloop was, fungeerden bevers en de voor Indianen zeer waardevolle, van schelpen gemaakte kralen als geld, zelfs bij de kolonisten onderling. Onder invloed van de voortdurende aanwezigheid van de oorspronkelijke bewoners en de druk van de fysieke omgeving onderging de cultuur van de kolonisten een aantal veranderingen. Bovendien voerde de WIC slavernij in: in tegenstelling tot het vaderland konden Beverwijcks burgers slaven bezitten. Slaven waren eigendom van de slavenhouders, geen volwaardige inwoners van de gemeenschap; ze konden bijvoorbeeld geen burgerrecht kopen. Ook al leek het leven aan de frontier in veel opzichten op dat in het vaderland, het was tegelijkertijd wel degelijk anders.

De pelshandel was in 1624 de aanleiding tot de bouw van Fort Oranje geweest en zij bepaalde het levensritme en de tijdsindeling van Beverwijcks inwoners. Sneeuw en ijs sloten het plaatsje in de winter af van de rest van Nieuw Nederland en het vaderland, maar zodra de rivier weer bevaarbaar was, vanaf april, kwamen talloze kooplieden naar Beverwijck om handel te drijven met de honderden Indianen die in juni met hun pelzen arriveerden. Alle inwoners, ook vrouwen, waren betrokken bij het verhandelen van Europese goederen als textiel, ketels, bijlen, messen, tabakspijpen, kralen, alcoholische drank, geweren en buskruit, voor de begeerde huiden. Vaak werden de pelzen gebruikt om schulden te betalen, of om kleding, voedsel, en andere huishoudelijke dingen te kopen, voordat ze uiteindelijk naar de Republiek werden vervoerd. De pelshandel was zo belangrijk dat, toen na 1657 de Indianen minder bevers brachten, er een crisis ontstond waarbij de gemeenschap totaal verdeeld raakte over de manier waarop men de huiden van de Indianen moest verkrijgen.

Jan Baptist en Jeremias van Rensselaer, twee zoons van Kiliaen, behoorden tot de belangrijkste handelaars van de gemeenschap. Ze verzamelden de huiden door ze van hun pachters als betaling voor de huur te accepteren, en door Europese waren te verhandelen met de inwoners en de Indianen. Na in Nieuw Amsterdam de vereiste exportheffing aan de Compagnie te hebben betaald zonden ze de pelzen naar Holland. Samen met een aantal "vrienden" (familieleden en andere succesrijke kooplieden) dreven de Van Rensselaers transatlantische handel in een klein familiebedrijf. Terwijl Jan Baptist en Jeremias aanvankelijk de zaken in Beverwijck en Nieuw Amsterdam regelden, deden andere familieleden, met name hun moeder, en na 1658 Jan Baptist, dat in Amsterdam. Ze organiseerden het transport, huurden schepen en bemanningen, regelden het verdere vervoer van de huiden naar Rusland, en onderhielden hun handelsnetwerk. Jeremias, die in de Nieuwe Wereld bleef en er stierf, maakte het succes van de Van Rensselaers zichtbaar door modieuze kleding te dragen en in een groot huis te wonen, dat hij inrichtte met nieuw en modieus meubilair. Het bezit van onroerend goed op gunstige locaties in Beverwijck en van land en slaven was eveneens een teken van rijkdom. Zijn positie in de kerkenraad beklemtoonde nog eens extra dat hij tot de meest eerbare, aanzienlijke en rijke inwoners van de gemeenschap behoorde. Door een goed huwelijk te sluiten en de juiste vriendschappen te onderhouden breidde hij het handelsnetwerk van de Van Rensselaers in de Nieuwe Wereld uit. Zo kon hij gemakkelijker deelnemen aan de bloeiende tabakshandel in Nieuw Amsterdam, die de pelshandel al in 1660 overtrof. Net zoals in patria gebruikelijk was, werden de vriendschappen herhaaldelijk bevestigd door het gezamenlijk drinken van alcoholische drank.

Enkele andere succesrijke Beverwijckers waren vroeg overgekomen als handelsagenten voor familiebedrijven als De Wolff en Verbrugge. Door geregeld heen en weer te reizen brachten deze agenten niet alleen koopwaar over, maar ook de laatste nieuwtjes uit de Republiek. Zo versterkten ze het Nederlandse karakter van de gemeenschap. Sommigen gingen voorgoed naar patria terug en investeerden hun verdiensten daar, terwijl ze handel bleven onderhouden met mensen die in Nieuw Nederland bleven. Onder deze "blijvers" waren er die al vroeg waren overgekomen als boerenknechten of ambachtslieden en die in de loop der tijd het land, de oorspronkelijke inwoners en de andere kolonisten goed hadden leren kennen. Soms werkten ze met elkaar samen en zetten locale netwerken op. Ze hadden al vroeg van de lucratieve bonthandel weten te profiteren, waardoor ze tot de rijksten en aanzienlijksten van deze nieuwe gemeenschap waren gaan behoren en soms zelfs tot magistraat werden gekozen. Evenals in patria was het belangrijk een eerbaar en christelijk leven te leiden. De meeste succesrijke inwoners waren dan ook lid van de gereformeerde kerk, en werden soms in de kerkenraad gekozen. Toch wisten ook enkele niet-kerkleden op de nieuwe sociale ladder omhoog te klimmen en magistraat te worden. Eenmaal in die hoogste contreien van de gemeenschap aangeland, stichtten deze nieuwe aanzienlijken weer hun eigen oligarchie, zoals dat ook gebeurde in de Republiek. Door huwelijken breidden ze niet alleen hun werkkracht uit, maar tevens hun netwerk, zodat hun handelsmogelijkheden toenamen, wat weer bijdroeg aan hun succes. Terwijl handel altijd belangrijk bleef, investeerden veel succesrijke inwoners een gedeelte van hun verdiensten in onroerend goed op strategische punten in de bijeenwoning en in grondbezit elders. Daar begonnen ze dan weer een bedrijf, vaak gezamenlijk.

Zeventiende-eeuwse werkpatronen verschilden van die van vandaag, en waren flexibel en veranderlijk. Er was nog weinig arbeidsspecialisatie; mensen waren actief in verschillende soorten werk tegelijk. Het kwam ook wel voor dat een man een bedrijf bezat en arbeidskrachten inhuurde om hem te helpen met het werk, of dat hij zelf elders werkte en de arbeid in zijn bedrijf geheel door anderen liet verrichten. De werkplaats was meestal onderdeel van de woning; werk was een gezinsaangelegenheid waar de vrouw en soms ook andere gezinsleden bij betrokken waren. In deze nieuwe gemeenschap, waar het leven veel duurder was dan in de Republiek, was de bijdrage van de vrouw zelfs een dringende noodzaak. Niet zelden werkten vrouwen ook zelfstandig. De beste zaken werden gedaan in het handelsseizoen, want dan was de vraag naar producten en diensten het grootst. De vele bezoekers van Beverwijck die het inwonergetal dan soms wel verdubbelden, veranderden het hele consumptiepatroon van het dorp.

Een goede locatie bepaalde veel van iemands succes met een bepaald bedrijf; een brouwerij die dicht bij de rivier was gelegen, en ten noorden van het fort, bestond langer dan een brouwerij elders, en herbergen vlakbij de kerk en het armenhuis deden betere zaken dan andere. Met name op gunstige locaties werd een werkplaats dan ook vaak door meerdere mensen achtereen gebruikt; als iemand zijn huis verkocht of verhuurde was het vaak iemand met hetzelfde werk die het overnam. Net als in patria lagen de bedrijven van mensen met dezelfde ambachten dicht bij elkaar. Smeden en lademakers, wier producten en diensten erg in trek waren bij de Indianen, bijvoorbeeld, woonden op de zuidwestelijke hoek van de tegenwoordige State Street en Broadway. Zo'n concentratie van ambachtslieden bevorderde in het algemeen samenwerking. Toch kregen de bakkers, waarvan verscheidene ten noorden van de eerste kil vlakbij elkaar woonden, geen toestemming om een gilde te vormen, terwijl die in het vaderland in diezelfde tijd juist een bloeitijd doormaakten.

Het leven in de zeventiende eeuw was in het algemeen kwetsbaar, en net als elders kon een natuurramp, ziekte of een sterfgeval veel schade veroorzaken. In Beverwijck maakten vijandelijkheden door de Indianen en het verval van de pelshandel het bestaan nog onzekerder. Zo kon het gebeuren dat iemand die zichzelf in 1660 nog als een belangrijk handelaar zag, in 1664 aangewezen was op armenzorg. Met name gezinnen met kleine kinderen, zieken en ouderen konden gemakkelijk tot armoede vervallen. De vestigingsplaats van een bedrijf kon ook een rol spelen. Zo leden mensen die al voor april 1652 een bedrijf begonnen waren ten zuiden van Fort Oranje, schade toen uiteindelijk de bijeenwoning ten noorden van het fort werd gebouwd. En ook al was er geen duidelijke residentiële segregatie, toch lijkt het alsof de meeste bedeelde inwoners ten zuiden van het fort woonden. In verschillende resoluties en ordonnanties werd rekening gehouden met de armen. De diaconie van de kerk ontwikkelde in samenwerking met het plaatselijke gerecht een systeem dat ook in veel plaatsen van de Republiek bestond, waarin mensen vrijwillig bijdroegen aan de zorg voor de behoeftigen in hun gemeenschap. Door een vorm van preventieve armenzorg te bedrijven hoopten de diakenen armoede op lange termijn te voorkomen. In de vorm van voedsel, kleding, geld of brandstof gaven ze concrete aalmoezen, terwijl ze ook in medische zorg en soms onderwijs voorzagen. Typisch voor Beverwijck was dat ze van de Indianen soms gevangenen vrijkochten, aan wie ze dan enige onderstand gaven – zelfs als het Franse en katholieke krijgsgevangenen betrof. In deze nieuwe gemeenschap was ieders arbeidskracht dringend nodig, en net als in patria betaalden de diakenen armen geregeld voor verricht werk; zo konden ook deze mensen hun eer behouden en het respect van anderen blijven genieten. Dat er een armenhuis verrees (waarschijnlijk het eerste armenhuis in Amerika) nog voordat er veel armen waren, kwam voort uit de zeventiende-eeuwse gedachte dat de wereld altijd uit arme en rijke mensen bestond. In tegenstelling tot wat vroegere historici wel geschreven hebben, zou het wel eens symbolisch kunnen zijn voor de bedoeling van de West Indische Compagnie om een samenleving te stichten naar Nederlands model, waarin iedere inwoner – zowel de succesrijke Goosen Gerritsz als de arme Carsten Carstensz – de mogelijkheid en de plicht had zijn of haar leven een eerbare vorm te geven.

List of maps and illustrations

Personal Name index

Geographical index

Curriculum Vitae
Jansje Venema

Janny Venema was born in 1951 in Nijeveen (Dr.), the Netherlands. After finishing high school in Meppel she studied Dutch and history at Ubbo Emmius, a college in Groningen especially oriented towards teaching. From 1977 to 1984 she taught both topics in Haarlem, the Netherlands. Since 1985 she works in the New York State Library's New Netherland Project in Albany NY, a project responsible for translating the official records of the Dutch colony and promoting awareness of the Dutch role in American history. In addition to transcribing the records, she has published two volumes of high school educational materials, a translation of the deacons' account books of Albany's First Dutch Reformed Church, and various articles about Beverwijck. Her master's thesis from the State University of New York at Albany was published in the Netherlands under the title *Kinderen van weelde en armoede. Armoede en liefdadigheid in Beverwijck/ Albany, c. 1650-1700.* This dissertation is the result of Venema's research for the New Netherland Project in both the Netherlands and the United States.